Children's Literature

Children's Literature

An Invitation to the World

Diana Mitchell

Co-Director, National Writing Project, Michigan State University
Consultant to Public Schools

with

Pamela Waterbury, *Aquinas College*
Rose Casement, *University of Michigan, Flint*

Boston | New York | San Francisco
Mexico City | Montreal | Toronto | London | Madrid | Munich | Paris
Hong Kong | Singapore | Tokyo | Cape Town | Sydney

Series Editor: Aurora Martínez Ramos
Developmental Editor: Alicia Reilly
Editorial Assistant: Beth Slater
Senior Marketing Manager: Elizabeth Fogarty
Editorial-Production Administrator: Annette Joseph
Editorial-Production Service: Lifland et al., Bookmakers
Text Designer: Deborah Schneck/Carol Somberg
Electronic Composition: Monotype Composition
Composition and Prepress Buyer: Linda Cox
Manufacturing Buyer: Megan Cochran
Cover Administrator: Linda Knowles
Cover Designer: Studio Nine

For related titles and support materials, visit our online catalog at *www.ablongman.com*.

Between the time website information is gathered and then published, it is not unusual for some sites to have closed. Also, the transcription of URLs can result in unintended typographical errors. The publisher would appreciate notification where these errors do occur so that they may be corrected in subsequent editions.

Library of Congress Cataloging-in-Publication Data

Mitchell, Diana.
    Children's literature : an invitation to the world/Diana Mitchell with Pamela Waterbury, Rose Casement.
        p. cm.
    Includes bibliographical references and index.
    ISBN 0-321-04915-2
    1. Children's literature—History and criticism. I. Waterbury, Pamela. II. Casement, Rose. III. Title.

PN1009.A1 .M54 2002
809´.89282--dc21   2002067584

Printed in the United States of America

10 9 8 7 6 5 4 3 2 1   VHP   07 06 05 04 03 02

Chapter-opener art by Ted Lewin

Text credits: *Credits appear on page 402, which constitutes a continuation of the copyright page.*

To my mother, Mary Dawson, who read to me

To Leah Graham and Joan Tresize, who reawakened my love for children's literature

To Virginia Blanford, who helped me shape my vision and believed in me

To my husband, Robert, who is my constant support

ℬRIEF ℭONTENTS

CHAPTER 3

The World of Picture Books

CHAPTER 4

Responding to Books Through Talk, Art, Writing, Drama, Movement, and Music

C H A P T E R 5
The Delights of Poetry

140

CHAPTER 8

Traditional or Folk Literature

226

CHAPTER 9

Realistic and Historical Fiction

258

C H A P T E R **10**

Modern Fantasy and Science Fiction

300

C H A P T E R **11**

Nonfiction Books

324

CHAPTER 12
Biography and Autobiography

FEATURES

Favorite Authors and Illustrators...

Criteria for...

Applying the Criteria...

Taking a Look at the Research

Children's Voices...

Response to First Reading of a Book

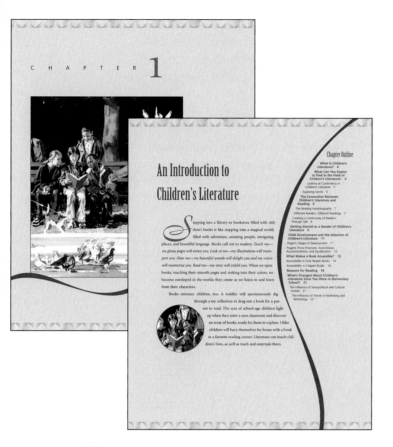

CHAPTER 1

An Introduction to Children's Literature

Stepping into a library or bookstore filled with children's books is like stepping into a magical world, filled with adventure, amazing people, intriguing places, and beautiful language. Books call out to readers: *Touch me—my glossy pages will entice you. Look at me—my illustrations will transport you. Hear me—my beautiful sounds will delight you and my voices will mesmerize you. Read me—my story will enfold you.* When we open books, touching their smooth pages and sinking into their colors, we become enveloped in the worlds they create as we listen to and learn from their characters.

Books entrance children, too. A toddler will spontaneously dig through a toy collection to drag out a book for a parent to read. The eyes of school-age children light up when they enter a new classroom and discover an array of books, ready for them to explore. Older children will bury themselves for hours with a book in a favorite reading corner. Literature can touch children's lives, as well as teach and entertain them.

Children's Literature: An Invitation to the World is designed to help readers appreciate the beauty and depth of children's literature. Unlike any other text, this text asks readers to take a *world view* of literature—discussing what it is, how to recognize one's own, and how to recognize an author's—and encourages readers to see children's literature through a lens that includes people not like themselves. The text tackles tough issues such as gender and racial bias and how they can be insidiously promoted in literature. No other text on the market engages readers to such an extent in its material. By working with and exploring the literature, readers will become confident in their ability to evaluate and select literature for children. Above all, this text's purpose is to encourage readers to delight in children's literature and to discover works that resonate deep within.

This book grew out of my love for children's literature and my desire to invite readers into the literature, instead of simply telling them about it. Rather than just presenting topics, the text asks, "What can we learn from them?" Thus, although this textbook covers all aspects of children's literature, it is accessible and informal in style. In addition, it contains visual aids for readers to facilitate comprehension, such as use of boldface italics within the text to denote titles of recommended books. Attending to the "affective" aspects of literature rather than focusing strictly on a cognitive interpretation of literature, the text asks, "What about the affective?" This question is directly and indirectly answered; along with the information presented is an explanation of why it's important. This thread is woven throughout, as readers are asked to examine as evaluative

PREFACE

criteria the *emotional* and *imaginative* impact of books in each genre. For example, instead of simply telling about poetry, Chapter 5 shows readers what it does for children. And instead of just explaining art terminology, Chapter 2 shows readers how that terminology can help them understand their reactions to the visual in children's literature.

This text is organized in such a way as to encourage immediate immersion in the literature. Although most of the chapters deal with specific genres, several unique chapters are organized around issues:

- Chapter 1 focuses on the close connection between reading and children's literature.

- Chapter 4 presents an expanded view of responses to literature, including talk, art, writing, drama, movement, and music.

- Chapter 6 explores the context of children's literature, taking a critical look at authors' world views, the implicit values contained in literature, and the presence of sexism, racism, and classism.

- Chapter 7, Multicultural and International Literature, offers in-depth coverage of multicultural topics not always found in other texts, as well as an international focus that is truly unique in the marketplace.

Instructors may choose to use the material in any order that they find suitable for their classes.

This book has the following distinctive features.

1. **Favorite Authors and Illustrators.** An annotated list in every genre chapter gives readers the information they need to seek out and select books written by respected authors and illustrated by talented artists.

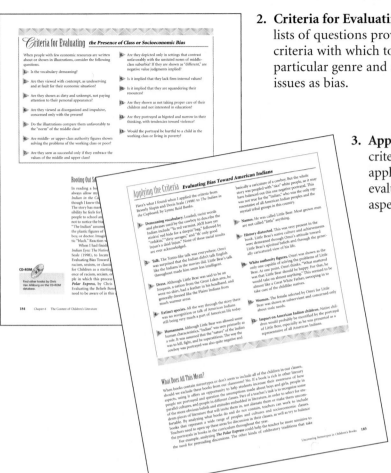

2. Criteria for Evaluating. In seven chapters, lists of questions provide readers with concrete criteria with which to evaluate books in a particular genre and analyze content for such issues as bias.

3. Applying the Criteria. Following the list of criteria for evaluating a genre is often a model application, showing readers how to go about evaluating and analyzing genres and other aspects of a particular book.

4. Taking a Look at the Research. In six chapters, research boxes give in-depth information on reading and other critical issues without interrupting the flow of the text.

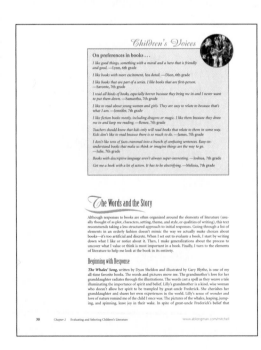

5. Children's Voices. In every chapter, quotations from children talking about real books bring children's perspectives to the text, allowing readers to hear what children have to say about the genre and book selection.

6. **Invitations.** At the end of every chapter, an Invitations section provides readers with opportunities to interact with and respond to the text and children's literature in engaging ways that will further their understanding and interest.

7. **Classroom Teaching Ideas.** In every chapter, readers are provided with concrete examples of how the literature can be used in classrooms.

8. **Internet and Text Resources.** Readers who want more information about the issues raised in the chapter can use this list of URLs and other resources to find author pages, book reviews, and teaching ideas. This list also offers a connection to the role technology plays in children's literature.

9. **Children's Books.** Extensive book lists with publication data appear at the conclusion of all chapters.

10. **Wrapping It Up.** A short section at the end of the book provides end-of-course project ideas to help readers wrap up their thinking about children's literature in concrete and specific ways.

Here are some other highlights of this text:

- A friendly authorial voice.

- Numerous headings and numbered lists, which break information into meaningful chunks so that the reader can easily digest it.

- Organization of the discussion of nonfiction around the Dewey decimal system so that readers get a glimpse of the richness of each classification.

- A focus on using literature across the curriculum. For example, Chapter 9 includes book lists, organized by theme and by historical time period.

- References to multicultural literature throughout the text, in addition to a chapter devoted to the subject.

- A focus on the importance of international literature and its use as a vehicle for looking at cultural values and beliefs. For example, Chapter 8 includes a comparison of several Japanese folk tales.

- Criteria for evaluating common reference materials, such as dictionaries and encyclopedias.

- Original cover art and illustrations by Ted Lewin, who received a Caldecott Honor award for illustrating Elisa Bartone's *Peppe the Lamplighter*. His *I Was a Teenage Wrestler* was selected as a *Booklist* Editors' Choice and a *School Library Journal* Best Book of 1993. His *Market!* was named one of the ten best illustrated children's books of 1996 by the *New York Times Book Review*.

- CD-ROM marginal annotations throughout the text, which provide additional information on how to integrate the use of the CD-ROM with the text.

- Website marginal annotations throughout, which provide URLs of additional sites pertaining to children's literature.

The title, *Children's Literature: An Invitation to the World,* reflects my belief that the rich field of children's literature provides access to the whole vast world. Children's books dazzle the eye with brilliant artwork, helping us see the world in fresh ways. They delight the ear with finely tuned, lilting language that takes us to new places and allows us to feel deeply. Inside of the story or text, we catch glimpses of the world. We learn what the world is like, what's important in it, what's wonderful about it, what's sad about it. We meet people and have experiences not otherwise available to us. We recognize the commonality of the essence of all humans. Through the glorious vastness of children's literature, we learn, we feel, we appreciate, and we recognize our own humanity.

Supplements for Students and Professors

Both students and instructors will find the following supplements invaluable in extending their learning.

- *Children's Literature: An Invitation to the World Database CD-ROM.* Integrated with the text, this CD-ROM allows users to quickly perform key word searches to find information about 250 authors and illustrators and about all the books discussed in the text and included in the index. It also offers key activities and teaching ideas and has the capability to print out a convenient "shopping list" to take along to the bookstore or library. This searchable CD-ROM database includes bibliographic information for over 1,000 books.

- **Professionals in Action: Children's Literature: Meet the Authors Video.** This video is available as a free supplement to instructors who adopt the text. It offers interviews with and readings by several of the children's book authors and illustrators featured in the text: Joseph Bruchac, Alma Flor Ada, Pat Mora, Carmen Lomas Garza, Walter Dean Myers, Patricia Polacco, Robert Sabuda, John Archambault, Barbara Park, and Gerald McDermott.

- **Companion Website.** The website found at www.ablongman.com/mitchell provides additional activities and strategies for teaching children's literature, self-assessments, and links to websites related to children's literature (for example, award, author, and research sites) that will help students delve deeper into text topics. Students will have an opportunity to review learning objectives for each chapter as well as enjoy other interactive features.

- **Instructor's Manual with Test Bank.** For each chapter, the instructor's manual features summaries, a series of learning objectives, an annotated outline, suggested activities, and recommended assessment tools. A comprehensive syllabus, which provides ideas on how to structure the course, is also included. The test bank contains an assortment of multiple-choice, matching, true/false, and short essay questions for each chapter. This supplement was written by Rose Casement and Pamela Waterbury, who worked with the author in the development of the text.

- **TestGen EQ Computerized Test Bank.** The test bank is also available electronically through Allyn & Bacon's computerized testing system, TestGen EQ. The fully networkable test-generating software is available on a multiplatform CD-ROM. The user-friendly interface enables instructors to view, edit, and add questions; transfer questions to tests; and print tests in a variety of fonts.

Search and sort features allow instructors to locate questions quickly and arrange them in any preferred order.

■ **Allyn & Bacon's Children's Books Library.** Featuring titles from Penguin/Putnam, this library, available to adopting instructors, consists of 20 children's books representing a variety of genres and themes. It includes such books as *The Very Hungry Caterpillar,* by Eric Carle; *Revolting Rhymes,* by Roald Dahl; *Roll of Thunder, Hear My Cry,* by Mildred D. Taylor; *Charlie and the Chocolate Factory,* by Roald Dahl; *Tales of Uncle Remus,* by Julius Lester; *Bingo Brown and the Language of Love,* by Betsy Byars; and *The Devil's Arithmetic,* by Jane Yolen. (Contact your sales representative for details.)

In addition, Allyn & Bacon offers an array of student and instructor supplements on the general topic of literacy. All of the following supplements are available with this textbook:

Allyn & Bacon Digital Media Archive for Literacy. This CD-ROM offers still images, video clips, audio clips, web links, and assorted lecture resources that can be incorporated into multimedia presentations in the classroom.

Professionals in Action: Literacy Video. This 90-minute video consists of 10- to 20-minute segments. The first four segments provide narrative and classroom teaching footage on these topics: phonemic awareness, teaching phonics, helping students become strategic readers, and organizing for teaching with literature. The final segments present, in a question-and-answer format, discussions by leading experts on topics such as literacy and brain research.

Allyn & Bacon Literacy Video Library. This library consists of three videos that address core topics covered in the classroom: reading strategies, developing literacy in multiple intelligences classrooms, developing phonemic awareness, and much more. The videos feature renowned reading scholars Richard Allington, Dorothy Strickland, and Evelyn English.

VideoWorkshop Teaching Guide for Reading (with CD-ROM). VideoWorkshop is a total teaching and learning system containing 50 to 60 minutes of video footage illustrating textbook concepts. It presents a multitude of ideas, teaching suggestions, and answers. A correlation guide helps you relate the materials to the text. (Available free when packaged with an Allyn & Bacon textbook. Special package ISBN required from your sales representative.)

VideoWorkshop Student Learning Guide for Reading (with CD-ROM). This combination VideoWorkshop student learning guide and CD-ROM package includes all the materials students need to get started: a CD-ROM containing specially selected video clips and a tear-page workbook

with learning objectives, web links, observation questions, next-step questions, and a multiple-choice quiz. (Not sold separately. Available only when packaged with an Allyn & Bacon textbook. Special package ISBN required from your sales representative.)

Allyn & Bacon PowerPoint Presentation for Elementary Reading Methods. This PowerPoint presentation, available on the web at www.ablongman.com/ppt, consists of approximately 100 slides that cover a range of reading topics, including assessment, building vocabulary, comprehension instruction and theory, developing literacy programs, teaching special needs students, and emergent early literacy.

Allyn & Bacon Transparency Package for Reading Methods. This set includes 100 full-color transparencies.

CourseCompass Content for Elementary Reading Methods. CourseCompass, powered by Blackboard, is the most flexible online course management system on the market today. By using this powerful suite of online tools in conjunction with Allyn & Bacon's preloaded textbook and testing content, you can create an online presentation for your course in under 30 minutes. You will find course objectives, lecture outlines, quizzes, essay activities, tests, and a glossary of key reading terms that you can adapt for your course. In addition, you will find web links that provide access to a wealth of resources in the field of reading. Log on at www.coursecompass.com, and find out how you can get the most out of this dynamic teaching resource.

Research Navigator Database for Education (access code required). Order access to Research Navigator for your students! Available at www.ablongman.com/researchnavigator, this free research database, searchable by key words, provides immediate access to hundreds of scholarly journals and other popular publications. Students will also receive access to the *New York Times* database, in which they will have available articles previously published. Ask your local sales representative for details. (Not sold separately. Available only when packaged with an Allyn & Bacon textbook. Special package ISBN required from your sales representative.)

Research Navigator: A Student's Guide for Education. This guidebook includes information on how to access and use Research Navigator, a research database, as well as tips for conducting searches and citing research materials in a paper. (Valuepack item only.)

iSearch: Education. This resource guide covers the basics of using the Internet, conducting web searches, and critically evaluating and documenting Internet sources. It also contains Internet activities and URLs specific to the discipline of education. (Not sold separately. Available only when packaged with an Allyn & Bacon textbook. Special package ISBN required from your sales representative.)

LiveText. LiveText is a set of online tools for developing, sharing, and evaluating lesson plans, portfolios, and projects. (Not sold separately. Available only when packaged with an Allyn & Bacon textbook. Special package ISBN required from your sales representative.)

Allyn & Bacon LiteracyZone SuperSite with Research Navigator (access code required). Available at www.ablongman.com/literacy, this website contains a wealth of information for pre-service and in-service teachers—whether you want to gain new insights, pick up practical information, or simply connect with one another! It includes state standard correlations, teaching resources, ready-to-use lesson plans and activities for all grade levels, subject-specific web links for further research and discovery, Allyn & Bacon professional titles to help you in your teaching career, up-to-date "In the News" features, a discussion forum, and much more.

Acknowledgments

I would like to thank the following people, who read all or part of the manuscript and provided me with needed feedback: Austin Jackson, Renee Webster, Annie Mitchell, Amy Huntley, Michelle Ellis, and Hannah Furrow. I am grateful to the following teachers, who helped me gather responses for the Children's Voices sections: Katie Bowling, Gayle Boyd, Dennis Clark, Mary Dekker, Michelle Ellis, Deb LaFleur, Ursula Morris, Tabatha Otto, Peggy Pinter, and Renee Webster. Thanks also go to the children's librarians at East Lansing Public Library for their patience and help. I am also deeply indebted to the following reviewers for their comments and careful questions: John D. Beach, University of Nebraska at Omaha; Karen J. Brauer, Crawford Elementary, Aurora Public Schools; Linda Burns, Southeast Missouri State University; Donna Camp, University of Central Florida; Anita P. Davis, Converse College; Carol Fox, Emporia State University; Marilyn Freedlund, Illinois State University; Carol J. Fuhler, Northern Arizona University; John H. Funk, University of Utah; Myrna R. Gifford, Wright State University; Holly Johnson, Texas Tech University; Dottie Kulesza, University of Nevada, Las Vegas; Richard F. Osterberg, California State University, Fresno; Scot Smith, University of Tennessee; Dee Storey, Saginaw Valley State University; Maria Weimer, Medaille College; and Terrell A. Young, Washington State University.

And last but not least, I wish to express my thanks to Pamela Waterbury for bringing to the book her knowledge of and experiences with literature, teaching, and writing and to Rose Casement for contributing her knowledge of the relationship between children's literature and reading. These two women were with me every step of the way—supporting, questioning, conceptualizing, clarifying, editing, and researching. Their input, enthusiasm, and dedication were invaluable.

Diana Mitchell began her love affair with children's literature when her mother read to her such books as *Mrs. Piggle-Wiggle, Mary Poppins,* and *Five Little Peppers and How They Grew.* From the time she learned to read, she was taken to the library each week and allowed to check out four books, a habit she continued through high school. As a twelve-year-old, she joined a classics book club for children, each month receiving books like *Little Women, Treasure Island, Hans Brinker or the Silver Skates, Oliver Twist,* and *Stories from the Arabian Nights.*

Diana took her love of reading to public school teaching. She taught middle school and high school for 30 years and delighted in matching her students' interests with books they would enjoy reading. She loved making good literature available to her students and found ways to use children's literature in her classroom, no matter what grade or subject she taught. One of her fondest memories is of members of her tenth-grade American Literature class persuading her to let them sit cross-legged on the floor as she read picture books to them.

Diana Mitchell

Always viewing herself as a learner, Diana returned to Michigan State University to pursue a doctorate in English. As a graduate student, she began teaching children's literature, young adult literature, reading, and methods classes at the university level, a practice she continued even after she had completed her Ph.D. and returned to her high school classroom. Preparing her dissertation on gender issues in young adult literature opened her eyes to the values embedded in each piece of literature.

Because she enjoys sharing her passions for teaching and literature with others, she became active in the National Council of Teachers of English, serving as president of the Assembly of Literature of the Adolescent of NCTE (ALAN) in 1995, chair of Women in Literacy and Life Assembly (WILLA) in 2000, and a reviewer for the 14th edition of *Booklist* (2001). Co-author with Stephen Tchudi of *Exploring and Teaching the English Language Arts* and with Leila Christenbury of *Both Art and Craft: Teaching Ideas That Spark Learning,* she has also contributed chapters to three books on literature for young adults. She has been on the editorial review boards of *The New Advocate, English Journal,* and *English Education.*

Currently, Diana works as co-director of the National Writing Project at Michigan State University and as an independent consultant to public school districts, speaking mainly about children's literature and how to use it effectively in the classroom.

Children's Literature

An Introduction to Children's Literature

*S*tepping into a library or bookstore filled with children's books is like stepping into a magical world, filled with adventure, amazing people, intriguing places, and beautiful language. Books call out to readers: *Touch me— my glossy pages will entice you. Look at me—my illustrations will transport you. Hear me—my beautiful sounds will delight you and my voices will mesmerize you. Read me—my story will enfold you.* When we open books, touching their smooth pages and sinking into their colors, we become enveloped in the worlds they create as we listen to and learn from their characters.

Books entrance children, too. A toddler will spontaneously dig through a toy collection to drag out a book for a parent to read. The eyes of school-age children light up when they enter a new classroom and discover an array of books, ready for them to explore. Older children will bury themselves for hours with a book in a favorite reading corner. Literature can touch children's lives, as well as teach and entertain them.

What Is Children's Literature?

Although many people define children's literature as any book children read, not all of these books are considered to be literature. Several important characteristics distinguish "kids' books" from children's literature. These include the author's passion, interest, and intention; authenticity; literary merit; the high quality of the illustrations and the effectiveness with which they interact with the text; and the richness of the themes. Obviously, these criteria are subjective, but their consideration nonetheless is important. Excellent children's literature is marked by appealing content and clear writing; the characters are often children, people familiar to children, or animals. The settings generally are places well known to children or places children would love to go. The themes speak to children and their concerns.

Children's literature embraces every genre, including picture books, poetry, realistic fiction, fantasy, historical fiction, biography, informational books, and traditional stories such as myths, fables, and fairy tales. It includes multicultural and international literature across the genres. Much of what children read, however, is not written with children in mind. Christopher Paul Curtis, who won the Newbery Award and the Coretta Scott King Award, never intended to write for children (Curtis, 1997). He wrote the story he had to tell in the voice that seemed best for it. In his first version of the book **The Watsons Go to Birmingham—1963,** he started the story from the point of view of Byron, the older brother. The story didn't work well from that point of view, and so he changed to that of the younger brother, Kenny. Similarly, Newbery Award winner Madeleine L'Engle did not have children in mind when she wrote her award-winning story **A Wrinkle in Time,** which was rejected by more than ten publishers before one saw possibilities in it. According to a television interview, even J. K. Rowling had trouble selling her first book, **Harry Potter and the Sorcerer's Stone,** because publishers said it was too long to be a children's book.

Often, marketing considerations define whether a book is considered a children's book or an adult book. In a children's book, publishers look for young characters, not too many pages, frequent use of dialogue, minimal description, and wide appeal to children. Today, even many picture books, which are traditionally thought of as children's books, are not written strictly with children as their audience. For instance, **The Secret Knowledge of Grown-Ups,** by David Wisniewski, is a satire that older students and adults will enjoy. Some older children read books intended for adults, such as the work of Stephen King. Since the line between children's and adults' literature is sometimes hard to draw, this text will focus on books that have been categorized either by publishers' marketing departments or by libraries as books for children.

What Can You Expect to Find in the Field of Children's Literature?

CD-ROM

The CD-ROM offers descriptions of the writing of many authors listed in the Favorite Authors section. For more examples of authors known for their rich language use, go to Favorite Authors and do a word search for *language.*

The first thing you'll notice about children's literature is the sheer abundance of it. It comes in a variety of shapes, sizes, formats, and genres. Visit any bookstore or children's section of a library and you'll be stunned by the rich selection of books, which offer unlimited possibilities for reading, responding, and teaching. You'll find classics, award winners, and just plain good books, as well as mediocre, poorly written, and poorly conceived books.

Some of the first books you are drawn to may be books you remember from your childhood, many of them classics. *Classics* are defined as books that have withstood the test of time and are favorites of children from generation to generation. Their enduring qualities include universal themes that speak across time and generations, memorable

Although *Charlotte's Web* was originally published 50 years ago, the appeal of Charlotte, the spider, and Wilbur, the pig, is still strong for children today.

(Cover art from *Charlotte's Web* by E. B. White, illustrated by Garth Williams. Used by permission of HarperCollins Publishers.)

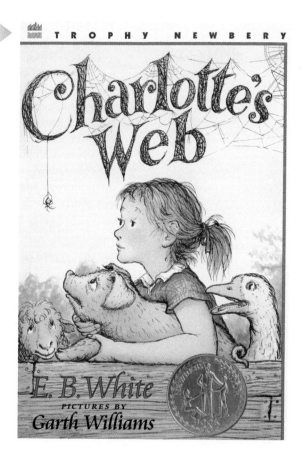

characters that live on in readers' minds, elements that create a strong emotional pull, rich language, and even a memorable rhythm. Such books include *The Wind in the Willows* (1908), by Kenneth Grahame; *The Raggedy Ann Stories* (1920), by Johnny Gruelle; *The Complete Tales and Poems of Winnie-the-Pooh* (1926), by A. A. Milne; *Millions of Cats* (1928), by Wanda Gag; *The Little Engine That Could* (1929), by Watty Piper; *Mike Mulligan and His Steam Shovel* (1939), by Virginia Lee Burton; *Make Way for Ducklings* (1941), by Robert McCloskey; *The Poky Little Puppy* (1942), by Janette Sebring Lowrey; *Goodnight Moon* (1947), by Margaret Wise Brown; *Charlotte's Web* (1952), by E. B. White; *Green Eggs and Ham* (1960), by Dr. Seuss; and *Where the Wild Things Are* (1965), by Maurice Sendak. Books such as these are reprinted because of their constant readership. As years pass, many books are added to the list of those that children turn to again and again. At the same time, some books considered classics by previous generations may lose favor with the current generation of children and slip off the list.

Some especially notable books have a sticker on the cover, signifying receipt of an honor such as the Caldecott, Newbery, or Coretta Scott King award. But because only a small percentage of the more than 5,000 children's books published yearly receive awards, many non-award-winning books are still so engaging that children will embrace them and as adults will share them with future generations. Working with the criteria in Chapter 2 will assist you in determining the literary merit of these books.

Looking at Controversy in Children's Literature

Selecting books for children often includes an element of controversy, as adults' views about what is appropriate for children may clash. Some adults think that children need protection from the harsh realities of life; others believe that letting children explore such topics as loss and death will alleviate their fear of the unknown. The vital questions of who decides what books to produce for children, who makes the decisions about what books to buy for libraries, and how books are selected for use in the classroom are typically ignored. These issues will be addressed in Chapters 2 and 9.

Other issues that arise out of the study of children's literature will be discussed throughout this book. There is controversy about whether people outside a culture should write books about that culture (Chapter 7). Another issue is whether books are simply their words and pictures or whether they contain cultural values and messages (Chapter 6). Although much children's literature takes you away to other times and places, looking beneath the words of the text will often bring you in contact with unexpected issues. Should beautiful award-winning books be eliminated from reading lists because of sexism or racism? Are multicultural and international books important only for the community they describe or for all children in the larger society (Chapter 7)?

Exploring Genre

Although the definitions of genres are not absolute or exclusive of one another, they do provide a framework for categorizing children's literature. *Genre* is a term used to designate the types, or categories, into which literary works are grouped, usually by style, form, or content.

This kind of classification implies that works of the same type have some common characteristics, regardless of time or place of composition, author, or subject matter. Poetry, for instance, is a genre that has a range of specific elements such as the use of rhythm and stanzas, but the subject matter may be almost anything. Dividing literature into genres is simply a way to grapple with a large body of writing and organize our thinking. The term *form* or *format* is sometimes used interchangeably with *genre*, but form is usually the pattern, structure, or organization used to give expression to the content. Although some would categorize picture books as a form of fiction, in this text picture books will be treated as a genre. Picture books are distinguished by specific elements, such as the close connection of the words and the illustrations, and they comprise too large a body of work to be discussed without their own category. You will find common threads as you read through the chapters on the various genres, but there are distinctive characteristics that identify the seven categories.

1. As you begin reading picture books, you'll notice their variety, beauty, and depth. Chapter 2 is intended to help you figure out ways to identify differences in literary and artistic quality by looking at both the text and the art. Chapter 3 focuses on the range of picture books and the characteristics of ABC, counting, and concept books; wordless books; books for the earliest reader; and transitional or chapter books. A thorough look at the purposes for which picture books have been written will alert you to the many reasons children respond so positively to them.

2. Poetry books for children may surprise you, particularly if you haven't been a fan of poetry. In Chapter 5, you will find that not only are the text and pictures closely wed, but themes range from friendship, family, and feelings to historical events and the natural world. By immersing yourself in poetry books and allowing yourself to experience them, you will find poems that speak to you.

3. Traditional literature, which includes folk tales, fairy tales, tall tales, myths, and fables (Chapter 8), is amazing in its variety. You could lose yourself in this genre, in which many excellent books on or from a multitude of cultures have recently been published. The stories contain much cultural information, so the books can be used in many ways with students in the classroom.

4. Realistic fiction and historical fiction are packed with themes to which children can relate. These genres have widespread appeal to children partially because the children can live vicariously through the characters' experiences. Looking at the narrative structures used in realistic fiction and historical fiction will give you a way to organize your thinking about these genres. Evaluative criteria described in Chapter 9 will help you delineate the qualities of excellent books in these areas.

5. Modern fantasy and science fiction, ever popular with the younger set, are now becoming popular with older children, as evidenced by the success of J. K. Rowling's **Harry Potter** series. The appeal of these genres is looked at closely in Chapter 10 and their significance in developing imagination is explored.

6. Nonfiction and informational books (Chapter 11) have benefited from the explosion in the graphic capability of computers. Now, beautiful photographs are found in many of these books. The photos and design add to the accessibility of the information to the reader. Notable contemporary informational books are carefully researched.

7. Biography, often seen as a genre to be read only for reports, also offers much variety in the way stories are written and the kinds of people written about.

CD-ROM

Use the CD-ROM, under Favorite Authors, to find authors who specialize in writing *biographies*.

The Connection Between Children's Literature and Reading

It's important to get children involved in a story so that they can experience what readers do—participate, comment, question, predict, and savor—in short, personally interact with the text and construct meaning from it. If children remain outside a story, they may focus only on decoding without becoming fully engaged readers.

Good books delight children, make them laugh, excite them, intrigue them, mystify them, encourage them to think of themselves as inside the story. Thus, good literature is essential to entice children into the world of reading.

Once children are willing to read, we have to understand what keeps them reading, what pulls them further into books, what pulls them back to books, and what pushes them away from books. Some children come to school or the library eager to read because they have been read to at home and associate being read to with being nurtured and engaging in conversations. What we ask students to do in response to a book can help or hinder their growth as readers.

The relationship between reading and children's literature is reciprocal. Children learn to read by reading, and good literature encourages children to read. Through this reading, they develop an understanding of the process of reading (described in Chapter 4) and in turn become more eager to read good literature.

To get help locating good literature for children, go to **Booktalks—Quick and Simple** at http://nancykeane.com/booktalks/.

The Reading Autobiography

All of your past experiences, both at home and at school, contributed to the kind of reader you are today. What kinds of books call out the deepest responses in you? Which books do you remember the most vividly? What do you remember about being taught to read? What experiences encouraged or discouraged your reading? What were you asked to do with the books you read in school? Did anyone ever give you guidance in your reading?

Everything that happens to you shapes the way you feel about reading. Writing your own *reading autobiography* can give you insight into the way you view the activity of reading. Discussing what drew you to reading and what pushed you away from it can give you insight into how you can best involve your students in reading. Looking at what you read over your years in school can help you be patient when students seem to get stuck in "series" books such as *Goosebumps,* since you may have read series such as *Nancy Drew* or *The Babysitters Club.* One person's reading autobiography might reveal that the writer associates being read to with warmth and nurturing and caring, while another might associate reading with being made to feel stupid by being placed in a low reading group. Still another might associate reading with having to answer hated questions at the end of the piece that asked for the "main idea" of the story.

Reading is much more than decoding words on a page. A willingness to read is vital, and it seems to come about when children are nurtured and helped, not labeled and treated differently.

Different Readers, Different Readings

When we share our views on a book that we love or hate, we are often jolted to find out that others responded in entirely different ways. One person may despise a character we love; another may be bored by a book that we were engrossed in. The uniqueness of each reader's response to a piece of literature is explained by theorist Kathleen McCormick (1994), who says that our perspectives are influenced by our sociocultural background, the roles we play, and our unique viewpoints, formed by our past experiences. Each of us brings all our experiences and memories with us when we read.

As readers, we all have personal histories that include our attitudes about gender, race, religion, values, regional biases, politics, lifestyle, love, education, and so on. Becoming more aware of the facets of our histories that influence the way we read helps us to become critically literate, active readers, alert to the ways our own "repertoires" are embedded within our larger culture.

Being able to talk about how we are situated in our own histories and how they influence the way we "read" a text allows us to support our own reading and see many ways to approach a book. We can think about which part of our social history affects us the most in a particular reading. McCormick's work can help us realize that we are all reading from a certain context and a certain point of view and that we are reading in our own present historical time. These elements will affect and influence our reading. It also can help us to learn why others read differently. By sharing literature reactions with others, we climb into someone else's reading perspective.

Students, too, should understand the perspectives they are reading from so that they can support their right to that reading. For instance, a black South African man who read **The Story of Babar, the Little Elephant,** by Jean De Brunhoff, told Herbert Kohl (1995) that students in his community would not find this an endearing story about an orphaned elephant taken in by a nice, rich, white lady. Students would focus on the fact that a man wearing the clothing of a colonial oppressor (pith helmet and rifle) had needlessly killed an elephant and had never been brought to justice. Because of the experiences in South Africa with dominant colonials who were white supremacists, they also would see the move to clothe the naked elephants as overtly racist and insulting (p. 18). The fact that children from other cultures may react strongly to other elements of the story, such as how sad the death of Babar's mother was, does not invalidate the reading of the South African. Because every reader doesn't see the oppression in the text doesn't mean it's not there.

McCormick's work empowers readers of literature by helping them articulate the importance of context in literature and what contributes to that context for them. With an understanding of the ideas of McCormick, you will be better prepared to listen to what your students see in the books they read, validate the histories they bring to their readings, and help them become engaged readers and lovers of books. Students need a comfortable and supportive learning environment so that they can fully explore their responses and share them with others as they work toward building meaning.

Creating a Community of Readers Through Talk

Most of us need to feel connected to a community; it makes us feel accepted and worthwhile. When we attend a new school, we want to know where to find the bookstore, the advising office, the bathrooms, and the snack bar or coffee shop. More importantly, we want to establish a sense of our identity in the new school. We want comfortable relationships with others—our classmates, our professors. If we feel connected to the community, we no longer have to prove our worthiness every day—our attractiveness, our intelligence, our wittiness. Comfortable relationships make us feel safe and more willing to take risks, ask questions, test our opinions. This sense of ease lets us focus on the more important issue—our learning.

The same is true in a classroom. If we feel we are part of a community, working toward the goal of learning, we feel connected to others and we learn to listen to and value others' opinions. In turn, we feel we can speak freely and not be ridiculed because we have become overly enthusiastic about a book under study. We also want to learn from others. Can they show us another way to look at a character or theme? Creating a community in the classroom is as important in kindergarten as it is at the college level. In such classrooms, students feel they have something to contribute to the class, have the freedom to work with others, and are part of something larger than the individual. The boxed feature Taking a Look at the Research: Creating Classroom Communities provides additional information about the importance of community in the classroom. Here you will also find resources to guide you in developing a classroom community.

Building this sense of community takes time and usually begins with the instructor. The teacher must work to connect with the class and show that student talk is valued. Students then need time to work in small groups, talking with others about responses to books, sharing reading autobiographies, and responding to other group members' ideas. When students see that others value reading and enjoy books enthusiastically, they will feel more ready to participate wholeheartedly.

Creating a community of readers has an even bigger payoff for students than for teachers. They get the opportunity to see how others react to books, thus broadening and enriching their personal views. Talking with others after reading and responding to a book often has surprising effects. After they listened to the views of their classmates, students in classes I have taught have been willing to take a new look at characters they disliked immensely. Talk about books is essential to stretching our own understandings and to the continued pursuit of making meaning. Students will come to see responses to the books they read as "works in progress," not immutable renderings of the meaning of a book. Often, students will mull these works over in their minds and compare characters to other characters they have read about, think about how

Creating Classroom Communities

Creating a community within the classroom begins the moment students arrive on the first day of school. The community is shaped throughout the year, as students grow in their relationships with one another, the teacher, and themselves. Its cohesiveness develops through listening and talking, shared problem solving, and risk taking. In order to create a caring community, individuals must know that within the community there is a commitment that each student will be valued "as a human being, as one who has much to give, much to demonstrate, much to teach others" (Avery, 2002, p. 58). Only within this atmosphere can one expect that children will feel safe to share their responses to the learning they are engaged in. Routman (2000) suggests that a teacher examine the tone of the classroom community by asking, "What would it be like to be a student in this classroom?"(p. 543).

At all grade levels, working to create a caring and respectful community requires establishing predictable routines and clear expectations for community members' behaviors. In order to be effective, these routines and expectations should be developed through discussions within the group itself, in which members define what they want in their classroom community. "It is only when students negotiate acceptable behaviors and routines with the teacher and assume responsibility for putting them into practice that we can effectively teach" (Routman, 2000, p. 539).

Time and space are required for community building. Some teachers set aside an area of their classroom as a meeting space. Taberski (2000) describes this space as the hub of her classroom. Her students gather there at the beginning and end of reading and writing workshop, as well as for a variety of literacy activities including read aloud, shared reading and writing, discussions of text, and mini lessons that demonstrate strategies children might want to employ in their reading and writing. Setting aside time and space for classroom meetings that allow students to share with peers, collaborate, and dialogue—and involve students in establishing the organization and expectations for such meetings—validates the importance of community in the classroom.

Avery, Carol (2002). *. . . And with a Light Touch: Learning About Reading, Writing, and Teaching with First Graders,* 2nd ed. Portsmouth, NH: Heinemann.

Routman, Regie (2000). *Conversations: Strategies for Teaching, Learning, and Evaluating.* Portsmouth, NH: Heinemann.

Taberski, S. (2000). *On Solid Ground: Strategies for Teaching Reading K–3.* Portsmouth, NH: Heinemann.

books are similar thematically, or marvel over an author's use of craft to create a compelling story. In classes where community has been created, books are talked about over and over again and pulled out of the files of students' minds whenever the stories or characters have something to add to a book they are currently reading. Once students have experienced a literary community, they feel cheated when books aren't shared through discussion. The proliferation of adult book clubs reveals how central sharing is to our experience of reading.

Getting Started as a Reader of Children's Literature

The best way to learn about children's literature is to be a reader of children's literature. Read the books, talk about the books, respond to the books, even analyze the books. Read everything you can get your hands on. Share books in class. Haunt the local public library, sampling the various sections of the children's area. Go to the children's section of your local bookstore, sit down, and sample books from the shelves.

Although at first you may want to read those glorious picture books without annotating them, it will stand you in good stead later if you respond to each one, keeping good records of what you read. As a future teacher or librarian, you'll want information about books for your students at your fingertips. At the time you read the book, it may seem you'll never forget it, but after you read hundreds of books, memories of them tend to run together.

Eventually, you'll probably want to develop your own way of keeping track of what you've read, but one way to keep good records is to use the chart in the boxed feature

To see examples of children's book reviews, go to **The Bulletin of the Center for Children's Books** *at www.lis.uiuc.edu/puboff/bccb/.*

Responding to and Analyzing Children's Books

Author:

Title of Book:

Genre (circle one):
picture storybook, poetry, traditional literature, realistic fiction, historical fiction, science fiction, fantasy, informational book, biography, and autobiography

Subject or theme:

Brief summary of plot or format:

How I responded or reacted to the book:

What I want to remember about the book:

Characters:

	Name	M/F	Age	Race	Socioeconomic Class	Actions
Main character						
Main character						
Secondary character						
Secondary character						

Setting (circle one):
rural, urban, suburban, home, school, outside, in a country outside the U.S., other (explain below)

Additional features (circle one):
multicultural, international, strong female character, good role model, written from more than one point of view, literary qualities (such as figurative language, good beginning, good use of dialogue, excellent description), other (explain below)

Possible classroom connection, or how you could foresee using this book in a classroom or library:

Responding to and Analyzing Children's Books. A consistent method for recording what you read along with information about the book allows you to easily retrieve your thoughts and evaluations of books. Some of the suggested categories (gender, age, race, socioeconomic class, and actions of the characters) nudge you to become aware of the values embedded in the books (see Chapter 6 for a fuller discussion of the values in children's literature).

Child Development and the Selection of Children's Literature

Views of child development and how it affects the literature children are drawn to have been greatly influenced by the work of Jean Piaget. Based on his observations of children, Piaget identified four stages of child development. These four stages, according to Piaget, are experienced by children at approximately the same age, and each must be completed before the child can enter the next one.

Applying Piaget's theory of cognitive development to the world of children's literature can help us provide children with books that will enhance their cognitive, emotional, and social development. It must be remembered, however, that children move through the different stages in their own time and that social, motivational, and experiential factors will influence their development.

Piaget's Stages of Development

Piaget's stages of development are sensorimotor (birth to approximately two years), preoperational (approximately two years to seven years), concrete operational (approximately seven years to eleven years), and formal operational (approximately eleven years and older) (Siegler, 1991).

Sensorimotor Stage

In the sensorimotor stage, infants to two-year-olds actively engage with their environment, employing all of their senses to make discoveries of the world. During this stage, the child moves from simple reflexes to more sophisticated intentional actions. Books that interest children in this stage include books that are colorful, that make sounds, and that describe movements the reader and child can do together, as well as books with rhymes, poetry, and songs. For this group, who like to chew what they read and have not yet learned the fine art of turning pages carefully, board books, cloth books, and vinyl books offer an opportunity to hold and manipulate books.

Preoperational Stage

The preoperational stage is characterized by self-orientation, or viewing the world only from one's own perspective. It is in this stage that children develop understandings about the real world, increase their understandings first of themselves and then of those around them, and begin to develop logical reasoning skills (Elliot, Kratochwill, Littlefield, and Travers, 2000). In this stage, in which children develop language rapidly and gradually move away from their egocentricity, they need to continue to manipulate with hands-on experiences. In many ways, it is during this stage that children gather the tools, skills, understandings, and strategies that will allow them to "operate" in the next stage. Books that are appropriate for this stage include everyday stories with characters children can identify with; stories in which relationships with others build family, friendship, and community understandings; stories that use a rich, natural, and authentic language; stories that provide children with opportunities to make predictions; and stories that allow for a variety of active responses such as drama, drawing, conversation, and writing.

Concrete Operational Stage

During the concrete operational stage, children develop the ability to look at situations from another's point of view. "Their thinking has become more logical and more abstract, their attention improves, and their memory becomes more efficient as they develop new strategies" (Elliot et al., 2000). Books that are appropriate for children in this stage are those that relate to different points of view; provide more advanced facts and information; challenge the reader to solve problems, mysteries, or riddles; deal with the diversity within the larger community; expand on notions of family and community; allow for a broader and deeper emotional response to conflict within stories; and have endings that are not always happy. As children's command of text increases, so does their enthusiasm as readers, leading to more self-motivated reading activities.

Formal Operational Stage

In the formal operational stage, logical and abstract thinking can occur. "Adolescents begin to see the particular reality in which they live as only one of several imaginable realities. This leads at least some of them to think about alternative organizations of the world and about deep questions concerning the nature of existence, truth, justice, and mortality" (Siegler, 1991). During this stage, children and young adults are drawn to more complex understandings about themselves and the world around them. Books for students at this stage can be challenging, complex, and thought-provoking. Books may be studied as representations of culture, with discussion of racism, sexism, and other issues of diversity providing for greater awareness of stereotypes.

Piaget's theory has had a significant impact on our understanding of child development. It is not absolute, however. In other words, children are individuals, and although the stages and their characteristics can provide a framework for our pedagogy, we must always respond to the needs of the individual children in our classrooms.

Piaget's Three Processes: Assimilation, Accommodation, and Equilibration

Whatever theories guide our practice, we know that children, in order to learn to their potential, must be provided with an abundance of opportunities and resources from which to construct learning. Piaget describes three processes that are crucial within each stage of development and facilitate the child's progression from one stage to another. The first is assimilation, which is the process of bringing in new information. Accommodation, the second process, refers to the adaptation of one's ways of thinking in light of new experiences. Equilibration encompasses both assimilation and accommodation; it describes the interaction between bringing in new information and adapting to it. During the process of equilibration, the child goes from being satisfied with her or his current understanding of a concept to being aware of its shortcomings, adopting a more sophisticated mode of thought, and eliminating the shortcomings. It is important for teachers to remember: "Assimilation, accommodation, and equilibration all are active processes by which the mind transforms, and is transformed by, incoming information" (Siegler, 1991, p. 24). With this in mind, we need to provide books and experiential opportunities that allow children to continually construct new meanings.

What Makes a Book Accessible?

Books that appeal to children can be found at **ERIC REC Web Resources**, which has links to many other children's and adolescents' literature resources. Find it at http://eric.indiana.edu/www/indexwr.html.

Although most of us are attracted to or repelled by books based on subject matter and genre, we also have unique qualities we look for as we select books. Some of us love languor and richness of description; others of us want to hear people talking and doing almost immediately. Often it's the language that pulls us in or turns us away from a book. Most of us, especially young readers, do not want to feel excluded from a book because the vocabulary is pretentious or difficult. Jargon-filled books make readers outsiders. We want to be respected as readers, not made to feel unintelligent because we don't know the terminology. We want to

Children like to read . . .

Joke books. —Brittany, 2nd grade

Flip books and informational books. —Jessica, 2nd grade

Pop-up books and Arthur books. —Chelsea, 2nd grade

About puppies and hunting. —Drew, 2nd grade

Funny books, interesting books, fairy tales, chapter books, books that I have not read before. I like to read. —Sarah, 2nd grade

Scary books and sports books. —Nathan, 3rd grade

C. S. Lewis. There is action and wonder. —Caleb, 3rd grade

Books that have jokes or famous people in it. —Chris, 4th grade

The Baby Sitters Club so I can try to solve the problem in the story before I read it. —Janae, 6th grade

About African Americans, so I can know more about my ancestors. —Adrik, 6th grade

About cars and engines. That's my hobby. —Dion, 6th grade

Scary books and I like them because they give me goosebumps! —Jerome, 6th grade

Geography books because I can learn more things about the Earth. —Sharren, 6th grade

Biographies because they really happened. —Jasmin, 6th grade

Mystery books and books about space, natural disasters, cars, magic and inventions. —Derrick, 7th grade

Fiction (it's exciting), biography (it's informational), science fiction (it's scary and funny). —Scott, 7th grade

About Renaissance times or knights. —Molly, 7th grade

Books that get to the point and books that make me guess what is going to happen. —Jenny, 7th grade

Fiction books that don't have an unbelievably complex plot. I like simple plots that aren't too hard to understand. —Dori, 7th grade

Fishing and survival stories. —Ben, 7th grade

WWII stories, fantasy, and mystery. —Jon, 7th grade

Science fiction. Aliens and space stuff like that interests me. —Alex, 7th grade

Books about orphans, death, or love books for advice. —Patty, 7th grade

Books that deal with problems that we have now and how the main character in the book solved them. —Emily, 7th grade

Action, adventure, horror. —David, 7th grade

A scary, love, or a mystery story. —Julie, 7th grade

Books about science fiction just because it amazes me. —Emily, 7th grade

(continued)

Children like to read . . .

Action, excitement, adventure, science fiction and some history and biography.
—Kyle, 7th grade

About groups of people or kids that live in the real world and deal with everyday occurrences. —Allison, 7th grade

Mysteries, murders, romance novels, historical novels and books about someone that is sick. —Kim, 7th grade

Outdoor books such as hunting and fishing and mystery and suspense.
—Chris, 7th grade

Sports trivia, adventure, fantasy, and a little bit of history. —Nick, 7th grade

Comics, poem books, and picture books. Word books just don't interest me.
—Jenna, 7th grade

Books about children/teens who don't have all the money but made do.
—Trista, 8th grade

"A child's imagination is a great thing." I would want something that gives details in words not pictures, something I could picture in my head. —Jane, 8th grade

Something adventurous. I hate books that the main characters do nothing but complain all the time. —Jessica, 8th grade

experience the literature, not sit with a dictionary in our hands looking up words. Children's opinions about books they like to read are shared in the boxed feature Children's Voices.

Beginners at anything need to experience success, not failure. Books that offer familiar and natural language to young readers reinforce their confidence in themselves as readers. Experienced or confident readers are willing to work harder to decipher meaning, since they know the rewards they receive from reading. However, new or insecure readers need natural and familiar language in order to learn and practice the strategies that will lead to reading success.

School children also have distinct likes and dislikes, especially about theme or subject matter, that make books inviting or disappointing. But in addition to understanding these individual differences, teachers of children need to be aware of many more issues. Perhaps most important, books need to provide support for students, from the earliest readers to the more mature readers.

How does a book provide support? If you were not aware of the complexity of the reading process, you might think that simply controlling vocabulary would provide enough support for most children. However, this is not the case; there is much more to accessibility than having easily decodable text. Students won't eagerly read what they have no interest in or what they can't understand. Although this sounds like a matter of common sense, teachers often need to work hard to determine what contributes to student interest at a particular grade level and what prevents understanding.

Accessibility in Early Reader Books

The following elements contribute to how accessible an early reader book is to students.

Meaning

For children to make sense of a story, it has to mean something; it has to have a point. Creating text with rigidly controlled vocabulary may make the structure artificial and less

Dick and Jane *and* Henry and Mudge

The early basal readers with which most of us are familiar are represented by the quintessential stories of Dick and Jane. These early basals were written with the sole purpose of controlling vocabulary, in the belief that "language is a bunch of words and learning to read is learning words" (Goodman, 1996). Although vocabulary is an important consideration in writing books for young readers, writers who have focused on the intentional control of vocabulary have often sacrificed authentic syntax and ignored the literary elements that create good literature.

Studying the differences between stories about Dick and Jane and those about Henry and Mudge is an excellent way to see the differences between text that is constructed to control vocabulary and text that is created as literature for young readers. The setting for both texts is the home. The plots revolve around similar everyday events in the children's lives. However, the stories themselves are not similar.

In the beginning of "A Doll for Jane," in the 1951 basal *The New Fun with Dick and Jane* (cited in Kismaric and Heiferman, 1996), Dick calls his father to tell him that Jane will have a birthday soon and to ask him to get a doll that talks. Then Sally, the little sister, tells her mother that Jane will have a birthday soon and Jane wants a doll that talks. By this time in the text, sentences have been repeated almost verbatim several times. For example, in Dick's conversation with his father, he says, "Please get a new doll for Jane. Get a baby doll that talks. Please get a doll that talks" (p. 15). The father and the mother proceed to get identical dolls for Jane, and Dick has one delivered by the mailman. Upon receiving three identical dolls, Jane says, "Thank you, thank you, thank you. This is a happy birthday. A happy, happy birthday for me" (p. 19). Needless to say, this story line would have been just as confusing to young children as it is to us. Why did Dick need to remind their father and mother that it was going to be Jane's birthday? Wouldn't the father and mother have talked about what they were going to select as a gift? And where did Dick get the money to buy a doll and have it sent to Jane?

In *Henry and Mudge and the Best Day of All* (Rylant, 1995), Henry and Mudge say and do interesting things, largely because of their ability to speak outside of the very stilted language of a controlled vocabulary. Mudge is active and endearing. She notices right away that, although Henry's cake is made to look like a fish tank, it indeed smells like a cake. At the end of Henry's birthday party, "Henry and Henry's parents and Henry's big dog sat quietly in the backyard and closed their eyes. They listened to the birds. They rested. And dreamed about birthday wishes on the best day of all" (pp. 38–40). The authentic experiences in the story of Henry's birthday celebration are easily understood by young readers through the text and illustrations. Readers have plenty of opportunities to use cueing systems that involve common grammatical structure and to make predictions from the illustrations about what will happen next and about the vocabulary that they will encounter in the text.

As you select reading material for young readers, keep in mind Goodman's (1996) message: "When you control vocabulary you create artificial and unpredictable texts, whereas authentic texts control their own vocabulary. On the other hand, . . . even uncommon words can be predictable in a given context" (p. 81).

Goodman, K. (1996). *On Reading: A Common-Sense Look at the Nature of Language and the Science of Reading.* Portsmouth, NH: Heinemann.

Kismaric, C., and M. Heiferman (1996). *Growing Up with Dick and Jane: Learning and Living the American Dream.* New York: HarperCollins.

Rylant, C. (1995). *Henry and Mudge and the Best Day of All.* Illus. Suçie Stevenson. New York: Aladdin Paperbacks.

comprehensible; too often, a good story is secondary. Consider the sentence "Run Spot run," which rekindles memories of an early basal text. Not only does it have unauthentic syntax, since this is not how people speak (Goodman, 1996); it is a nonsensical command given to a dog without being embedded in an authentic context. The boxed feature Taking a Look at the Research: *Dick and Jane* and *Henry and Mudge* compares the modern stories of Henry and Mudge with the older ones of Dick and Jane, to demonstrate the importance of authentic context in making stories accessible and interesting to young readers.

Predictability

Predictability is an important element, especially for the earliest readers, who like to be able to discern a pattern so that they can anticipate what will happen next. The pattern might be a question followed by an answer or a rhyme that is repeated over and over. When young children listen to a rhyming story, they can usually supply the last word in a couplet or a quatrain, provided the subject is within the realm of their experience. Another way predictability is enhanced is by establishing the main characters, setting, and problem in the first few pages. Then children can see the main elements in the story and work to understand how all the elements will be played out. After children have been read to for a while, they begin to develop an understanding that stories follow a regular sequence. They can see that problems need resolution, so they begin to think about and guess what might happen.

Young readers also like repetition of actions, phrases, and sentence structure. These predictable structures make stories easier for children to listen to and comprehend. Again, repetition allows children to participate—to be readers, not outsiders to the reading process. Predictable structures also allow authors to introduce surprising or unusual elements successfully within a carefully constructed familiar context, which usually delights children since they love surprises.

Conceptual Information

Young readers have to have conceptual information about the topic in order for a book to be accessible to them. If they have never heard about Arctic winters or how people live in the Arctic, a book that assumes knowledge of the Arctic might not make much sense to them or might make them work too hard to understand. Though based on known conceptual information, the book also needs to contain new information that interests the reader. Students respond positively when a book refers to experiences that they know about. Having some background information gives students a place to put the new information in their minds. If they have never heard of or seen a train station or airport, then vocabulary like *ticket counter, luggage return, conductor, stewardess,* and *boarding passes* will not make much sense to them, and they will need more experiences for it to become part of their language system.

Thus, all readers—even proficient ones but most particularly insecure readers—can benefit from thematic studies that provide background information and connectedness through conceptually related materials and ideas. Classrooms that encourage discussion, questions, and student research offer the curricular support learners need to make sense of texts that might otherwise be too difficult for them.

Room to Make Inferences

Young readers find books more accessible if there is room to make inferences (draw conclusions from facts) and have these inferences confirmed or rejected within the story. For example, a reader might infer that one character will be a good friend based on what he says to another character. Readers draw inferences from the intersections of their lives and the text. They try to figure out how a character will act based on what they know of people or what might happen within the constraints of the setting. Proficient readers go beyond the author's explicit information; they tap into the vast store of knowledge gained from their lives, including experiences with literature. When books make room for inferences, children are drawn into them and work to use what they know to make sense of the text.

Language

Young readers find books accessible if the language is natural for the text and for them. Calling an elephant an elephant, even though the word is a three-syllable one, will not confuse children if the story is indeed about an elephant. Whereas adults may think that children can handle only short, simple words, often it's easier for them to learn the longer, more difficult word as long as it makes sense in the context of the story. Think how frustrated children must feel when they are unable to enter into a story because the language is not language that resonates with them; not being the language of childhood, it is not something familiar that prepares them to read. Students respond to familiar language. If the words chosen by the author seem to speak to the true spirit of childhood, even beginning readers will be able to get involved in the story.

Literary Quality

If the story is well written, the theme is one children can relate to, and the pace keeps the reader turning the pages, the book probably has the literary quality needed to be accessible to children. Something in the plot line must move the story along or add to the overall mood of the book. If the story is poorly organized, if the theme isn't meaningful, if the characters aren't multidimensional, or if the language doesn't ring true, children will have trouble motivating themselves to read further.

Relevance of Illustrations

Drawings that work well to extend and support the text are necessary to make a picture book accessible. The earliest readers can read books somewhat independently if illustrations enable them to do some accurate guessing. When they are not overwhelmed by detail, illustrations support the earliest readers' efforts to focus on the central aspects of the pictures, which contribute to understanding the meaning of the words in the book.

Authentic Social/Cultural Significance

Books are more accessible to children if they can easily identify with the story and discuss similar situations of their own. A book doesn't have to deal with the weighty issues of the world to be authentic; but the issues it discusses must be real to the lives of the children. Children like to hear about others who lose a tooth, who get a new sibling, who worry about doing the wrong thing. While these might not be important issues in adult lives, such situations loom large in the life of a child.

CD-ROM

To find resources on the many aspects of *reading,* go to the References database on the CD-ROM.

As Ken Goodman, noted reading theorist, reminds us in much of his writing, readers must be looking at authentic texts and must be invited to bring to the texts their thoughts, languages, and lives. Reading is a complex activity. The boxed feature Taking a Look at the Research: Literature-Based Reading Programs reflects on the strategies that children use

---

taking a look at the Research

Literature-Based Reading Programs

*L*iterature is the centerpiece of some teachers' reading and writing instruction. They believe that, by reading quality children's literature, not only do children learn to read—they also learn to love reading. The goals of a literature-based reading program are that children will learn to read, that they will understand what they read, and that they will choose to read for pleasure and information (Routman, 2000).

Belief in a literature-based reading program is supported by research on how children read. Researchers have learned about how children read by studying the miscues, or unexpected responses, they make as they read. Studies conducted by Ken and Yetta Goodman in the 1960s indicate that readers use three cueing systems, which work simultaneously to help them read.

The graphophonic cueing system is based on the physical characteristics of individual words. Children look at a word and identify its letters and their sound associations. The syntactic cueing system relies on children's informal understanding of the structure or grammar of language, which they have learned from their experiences as listeners and speakers. Children use familiar sentence structure to make predictions about how the sentence will read. The semantic, or meaning-making, cueing system is invoked as children reflect on their reading, asking, "Does this make

sense?" or "What would make sense here?" in order to self-correct before going forward. They read through the lens of their understanding of their world, with each young reader constructing his or her own meaning while transacting with the text (Goodman, 1996).

When basal readers are written with a controlled vocabulary on the assumption that children will learn to read best if they are introduced to words selectively, slowly, and in isolation, they may not have a familiar syntax. Without a familiar syntax, it is more difficult to make predictions, which are important for reading fluency. Also, the stories often lack the real literary elements that create a rich story and meaning. Goodman (1996) explains that a simplistic view of reading as just a set of words not only produces vacuous text but actually confuses the reader by taking away significant cues for comprehending text. "Authentic texts, on the other hand, not only control their own vocabulary but also have predictable, authentic grammar and thus provide natural grammatical cues to readers" (p. 77).

Goodman, Ken (1996). *On Reading: A Common-Sense Look at the Nature of Language and the Science of Reading.* Portsmouth, NH: Heinemann.

Routman, Regie (2000). *Conversations: Strategies for Teaching, Learning, and Evaluating.* Portsmouth, NH: Heinemann.

when they read. It traces the early investigation of meaning-based reading, which supports the literature-based reading programs used in the classroom today.

Accessibility in Chapter Books

Chapter books get their name from the simple fact that, unlike books for early readers, they are divided into chapters. Children are thrilled to make the move to chapter books because it signals that they are becoming independent readers. The problem with this designation, however, is that it's not clear where it ends, since almost all books read by adults also contain chapters. Some chapter books are transitional and provide continued support through illustrations (these are discussed in Chapter 3). The kinds of chapter books discussed here are the books children read independently from the time they move from transitional books up through the time they are ready for what has been categorized as young adult literature. The following elements contribute to how accessible a chapter book is to students.

Appeal of Topic

Interest is probably the main factor in accessibility of chapter books to students. If students are dying to know more about basketball, they will approach a book on Michael Jordan with zest. If students want to know how other children deal with stepparents in their life, they will approach a book on that subject with interest. Humor also draws students into books. Books with topics that appeal to children include *Because of Winn-Dixie,* by Kate DiCamillo, which begins with a ten-year-old girl's finding and getting to keep a dog; *Stuart Little,* by E. B. White, which tells of a mouse being adopted into a human family; *The Worst Best School Year Ever,* by Barbara Robinson, about misadventures at school; and *Bunnicula: A Rabbit-Tale of Mystery,* by Deborah Howe and James Howe, about the adventures of a talking dog.

Book Appearance and Format

A visually appealing book cover will draw children to a book and entice them to at least consider whether they want to read it. What is written on the back cover is also important, since that is often the thing children read before selecting a book. Thick books with dense type, narrow margins, long paragraphs, and long chapters do not appeal to younger people. These features alone signal that a book may be too hard for them. Chapter books may have a larger format than traditional paperback books and generally run from about 85 pages to 150 pages. The chapters are short, running from a few pages to about 15 pages. Paragraphs are usually no more than five sentences long. Type size is larger than in traditional paperback books, and there is more space between the lines, with fewer lines on a page. All of these features give younger readers breathing space and the feeling that the book is approachable.

Predictability in Structure

Can the reader count on the structure of the story to be predictable, with a beginning, middle, and ending? Younger

Children are drawn to this book because of the humor and the solid relationship between the little girl and her dog.
(BECAUSE OF WINN-DIXIE. Copyright © 2000 Kate DiCamillo. Cover illustration © 2000 Chris Sheban. Reproduced by permission of the publisher Candlewick Press, Inc., Cambridge, MA.)

readers often are not ready for story structures that break the conventions of how a story is normally told. They need to be able to count on the structure that a story of the kind they are reading provides. Mysteries, for instance, usually begin with a problem or a crime. They move to a look at several characters who might be suspects and end with a solution. As readers get more experienced and gain confidence and skill in their reading abilities, they become ready to tackle books that aren't written in a conventional manner.

Room to Make Inferences

None of us wants to have conclusions drawn for us or someone in the book tell us what we should be learning. We stay away from heavy-handed didactic books, preferring to infer the message from the book. Children also prefer and are drawn to books that don't insult their intelligence and that allow them to blend their own thinking into the story. Readers don't want everything spelled out for them; if it is, reading the book is no longer an adventure since someone has already done the reader's work. Readers want to draw their own conclusions based on information and actions and dialogue from the book. This allows the reader to be an active part of the reading process.

Language

Natural-sounding language in familiar sentence patterns, with familiar vocabulary or new vocabulary embedded in an easily understood context, makes books accessible. Younger readers especially are put off by archaic language and elaborate sentence structures with which they have had no experience. Younger readers often lack the patience to overcome the hurdle of antiquated language in order to get to the ideas. Introducing a book like *Great Expectations,* by Charles Dickens, with its rich but long descriptions, antiquated vocabulary, lengthy sentences, and complicated and unfamiliar sentence structures might work against inviting younger children into the literature.

Use of First-Person Narrator

By using the first-person narrative voice, authors control how much of the story the reader hears at a time. First person is the least complicated point of view, because all information comes from one character. There is no jumping around from character to character, and readers know that what they are hearing is coming from one person's point of view. As readers get more experienced, they can easily move to third-person narration and even omniscient narration, where the author has access to the thinking of several characters. The majority of novels for children are written with a first-person narrator.

Literary Qualities

When literature is well written, it is much more accessible to children. If the writing is well organized and easy to follow, if the settings are familiar and vivid, if the themes touch on the lives and interests of students, if the plot is fluid enough that readers want to keep going to see what happens, and if the language is natural sounding, with clear, direct sentences, the book will be one that children will be interested in reading.

Reasons for Reading

Although our experiences with reading are vastly different—some good, others painful—the reasons we choose to read are universal. We read to escape and disappear into books. We read for the sheer pleasure of it. We read to find out new and exciting information. We read to make sense of our lives, to experience new realities, to find answers to the big questions that haunt us. We read because we are enamored with the beauty of literature and how that beauty echoes in our own lives when we read. As parents or older siblings, we watch the children in our families read for the same reasons during their preschool and elementary years. As teachers, we watch our students read for similar reasons. Try to identify the reasons you read as a child and while growing up. Why do you read now?

Work by G. Robert Carlsen, professor of English education and scholar in adolescent literature, may help to shed light on some of the stages you went through and continue to live out as a reader. In his essay "Literature IS . . . ," Carlsen (1974) identifies five roles literature plays in readers' lives and cites key grades in which readers seek each role from literature. The stages of literary appreciation are merely approximations; clearly, the roles overlap and continue to have an impact throughout our lives once we become readers.

Other essays can be found at **Online Journals and Adolescent Literature** *at http://eric.indiana.edu/www/ #JOUR.*

Unconscious Delight

We read for unconscious delight, for the sheer pleasure and joy of entering an imaginary world. Many of us remember being so mesmerized by a book that we hated to have it end, but this unconscious delight is especially evident in young children, for whom reading or being read to is almost magical. Young children and beginning readers have no difficulty entering the world of make believe. A world of talking animals, elves, fairies, dragons, gremlins, and monsters hiding in closets is as real as their everyday world. Although preschool children who are read to obviously enter with ease into this make-believe world, Carlsen identifies this stage as being at its peak in grades three to seven.

Vicarious Experience

Avid readers delight in learning about places, times, and people about which they know little. We long to experience another's reality through books. Historical fiction may give us a glimpse into what our lives would have been like if we had lived during World War II. Books with themes of survival and adventure address our need to experience life vicariously through literature. We can discover what it means to live in a city or on a farm by reading books. Reading permits us to experience emotions of fear or terror that we might not want to experience in real life. Children in grades seven to nine are most often in this stage.

Seeing Oneself

We read to encounter our own realities. We want to see people like us so that we can better understand ourselves and know why we behave as we do. Seeing people who are like us struggle with problems similar to our own helps us to universalize our own experiences. Students in grades nine to eleven identify with this stage.

Philosophical Speculations

We read to make sense of our world and our role in it. Through reading, we encounter "the mystery of the human experience" and struggle with those issues, dilemmas, and questions that have troubled humans from the beginning of existence. We read to make sense of death, love, the loss of love, evil, authority and its abuses, and what it means to be human and act with integrity and courage. Students in grades eleven through fourteen are usually in this stage.

Aesthetic Appreciation

We read for the pleasure we gain from the beauty and craftsmanship in literature. We delight in the richness of its themes and the skill with which they are woven through the work and developed through characters, plot, setting, and language. We admire the unity of a work and in that unity find reassurance that our lives have the same inner harmony. People in grade fourteen and up often experience this stage.

Although these stages overlap, there are clear implications for us as teachers and librarians in the scaffolding that Carlsen has identified. Children do not pick up books primarily for the aesthetic experience of the literature. They do not read to trace foreshadowing, examine metaphor, and identify where the climax of the story occurs. Nor do they read to do story mapping or an analysis of the characters through Venn diagrams. They read primarily for the sheer pleasure of reading; they want to be swept away into the literature.

They also read for all the other reasons we read literature as adults—seeing oneself, philosophical speculation, and aesthetic appreciation.

Not only do children read to gain information, to seek answers, to see themselves and others, and to find hope and meaning in an often confusing modern world; they also read to gain the approval of adults in their lives who value reading. It's important to provide literature and literature experiences that feed children's reading needs at a developmentally appropriate level—both a developmentally appropriate reading level and a developmentally appropriate appreciation level. We should not try to turn them into readers at a more adult stage than is appropriate. If we let them read literature at the level appropriate for their experiences and interests, they will move into the next stage naturally.

What's Changed About Children's Literature Since You Were in Elementary School?

If you haven't read children's literature in the last five to ten years, you may be surprised by the multitude of changes that are now in evidence mainly because of sociopolitical and cultural shifts in our society and because of trends in marketing and technology. Attention to sociopolitical and cultural factors is embedded throughout the text and specifically addressed in Chapter 6.

The Influence of Sociopolitical and Cultural Factors

Children's literature reflects our changing views of children, of the world, and of what literature is and should look like. In fiction, there is a broader view of characterization. Girls are shown in more active roles (*Amazing Grace,* by Mary Hoffman; *Mountain Valor,* by Gloria Houston; and *Sammy Keyes and the Hotel Thief,* by Wendelin Van Draanen). Boys are depicted expressing emotions and nurturing others (*Crazy Lady!,* by Jane Leslie Conly; *Belle Prater's Boy,* by Ruth White; and *Follow the Moon,* by Sarah Weeks). Minority characters are portrayed in a broader range of roles with less stereotyping (*I Hadn't Meant to Tell You This,* by Jacqueline Woodson; *Second Daughter: The Story of a Slave Girl,* by Mildred Pitts Walter; and *Francie,* by Karen English).

Topics continue to broaden but still reflect the hesitancies of our society. For instance, our tangled views of the Arab world often preclude the publishing of fiction about this part of the world (Naomi Shihab Nye's books that focus on Arab families, *Habibi* and *Sitti's Secrets,* are two of the few fictional books published about the Arab world). Our "hands-off" attitude toward books with religious themes is softening (*Armageddon Summer,* by Jane Yolen and Bruce Coville; *The Tent,* by Gary Paulsen; and *I Believe in Water: Twelve Brushes with Religion,* a book of short stories edited by Marilyn Singer). Gradually books with homosexual characters are being published (*Good Moon Rising,* by Nancy Garden; *From the Notebooks of Melanin Sun,* by Jacqueline Woodson; and *Am I Blue? Coming Out from the Silence,* edited by Marion Dane Bauer).

Fiction is still the most prominent genre published, as evidenced by the awarding of the Caldecott and Newbery medals primarily to fiction. The 2001 Newbery winner (*A Year Down Yonder,* by Richard Peck) and all three honor books were fiction. The 2000 Caldecott did go to a nonfiction book (*So You Want to Be President?,* written by Judith St. George and illustrated by David Small), but all the honor books were fiction.

Picture books continue to hold a secure place in the publishing world. As our ideas on what books are appropriate for whom broaden, many more picture books written for older readers are being published. Books for older readers are discussed in Chapter 3.

Many picture books are breaking established conventions to present a "more complex visual image in terms of line, color use and composition, increased use of multiple perspectives, disintegration of the page surface, an altered conceptualization of

To find picture books with positive, powerful women characters, go to *Only the Best for My Child* at www.oz.net/ ~walterh/biblio.html.

the actual page of the book, and a loss of narrative and visual linearity" (Goldstone, 1999, p. 335). Examples of this trend can be found in books illustrated by Jannell Cannon, Peter Catalanotto, David Macauley, Peggy Rathmann, Lane Smith, and David Wisniewski.

The popularity of series books in fiction continues, with themes reflecting the changing, as well as the typical, tastes of children. Visit any bookstore or library and you'll see rows of R. L. Stine's *Goosebumps,* the *American Girl* historical fiction series, and the action-packed *Animorphs* books. Children still like the predictability that series books offer.

High-quality early reader books are being published that allow developing readers to read on their own. Easy-to-read books and series that provide light or humorous reading reflect a trend in school practices away from exclusive reliance on basals, which emphasize controlled or limited vocabulary, to inclusion of trade books (Harris, 1996). Excellent authors of early readers include Betsy Byars and Patricia Reilly Giff.

A new stress on authenticity and research in biography and nonfiction (Fisher, 1997) has made this genre more vigorous and exciting [Kathleen Krull's ***Lives of the Artists: Masterpieces, Messes (and What the Neighbors Thought),*** and Sneed B. Collard III's ***1,000 Years Ago on Planet Earth***]. Instead of being "sanitized," history discusses human frailties. The idea of "heroes" has expanded to include more than just well-known people (***Honoring Our Ancestors: Stories and Pictures by Fourteen Artists,*** edited by Harriet Rohmer). In keeping with the current view that it is natural to learn through mistakes, richer, more accurate information is now included about the history of this country (***Amistad: A Long Road to Freedom,*** by Walter Dean Myers). The advent of literature-based teaching and cross-curricular approaches has increased the demand for well-written nonfiction, which can be used with fiction.

Historical fiction has become more interesting as authors have done increased research on the past in order to portray a particular time as accurately as possible. This increase in accuracy reflects the view that children should be given a full picture of this country's past, blemishes and all (***Dragon's Gate,*** by Laurence Yep; ***Bat 6,*** by Virginia Euwer Wolff; and ***So Far from the Sea,*** by Eve Bunting).

More and better multicultural literature is now available, although it still represents only a small portion of what is published. ***My Heroes, My People: African Americans and Native Americans in the West,*** by Morgan Monceaux and Ruth Katcher, showcases two cultures, describing African Americans and American Indians who played prominent roles in the West. Of the multicultural books published, the largest number focus on African Americans, although there has been a slow increase in books representing American Indians and Asian Americans (Michael Dorris's ***Morning Girl,*** Huynh Quang Nhuong's ***Water Buffalo Days: Growing Up in Vietnam,*** Minfong Ho's ***The Clay Marble,*** and Dia Cha's ***Dia's Story Cloth: The Hmong People's Journey of Freedom***). Part of this increase is due to the strides that have been made in introducing books by authors and artists from diverse cultures into the ranks of publishing (Elleman, 1995).

There has been a burst in the poetry market for children, with many more Latino, Asian American, and African American voices in evidence. Francisco X. Alarcon, Eloise

The bold use of color in the illustrations and the inclusion of subjects of many ethnicities lets readers know that this book will offer a fresh look at the impact ancestors have made.

(Image from *Honoring Our Ancestors: Stories and Pictures by Fourteen Artists.* Reprinted with the permission of the publisher, Children's Book Press, San Francisco, CA. Book project copyright © 1999 by Harriet Rohmer. Individual images copyright © 1999 by Nancy Hom; copyright © 1999 by Maya Christina Gonzalez; copyright © 1999 by Helen Zughaib; copyright © 1999 Stephen Von Mason.)

Greenfield, Nikki Grimes, Juan Felipe Herrera, Pat Mora, Gary Soto, Joyce Carol Thomas, and Janet Wong are among those who have made a significant contribution to widening the repertoire heard in children's poetry (Hade, 2000).

Boundaries between the kinds of literature are being pushed more and more. A blurring of distinctions between genres is becoming apparent with the publication of such books as **The Magic School Bus** series, by Joanna Cole, whose subject matter is science, threaded with fantastical elements.

CD-ROM

Search the CD-ROM References for additional resources on *multiculturalism*.

The Influence of Trends in Marketing and Technology

Advanced technology has led to improvements in many picture books in the area of illustrations (Yolen, 1997). This same technology has allowed for a new emphasis on photos and graphics in nonfiction, making for stunning presentations (Elleman, 1995). However, graphics technology may be overshadowing other considerations that are equally important. Some critics believe that we have let design and appearance factors overpower the content of the books while "going beyond the artistic knowledge of young readers" (Fisher, 1997).

Interactive approaches to books have been developed in reaction to the CD-ROMs and other media being released. Publishers want to give readers something to be involved with, to change, to manipulate. *The Magic Eye* books, which require readers to locate pictures within frames of colored dots, have intrigued both adults and children and have become international best sellers (Elleman, 1995). The rise of audio books has given teachers and parents another way to involve children in literature. *look alike*

More tie-in artifacts, such as lunch boxes and dolls, are being manufactured to accompany books. As the number of publishing houses shrinks, manufacturing of these artifacts rises.

Pop-up, scratch-and-sniff, and paper-engineering products for young children are proliferating. Some fear that these are less literary and more commercial than traditional books (Yolen, 1997).

Production of board books (books printed on cardboard for sturdiness), which toddlers love so much, is increasing. Today's board books offer much more than simple concepts such as colors and objects. Some board books contain images of children of color.

Mass marketing of books in supermarkets, mall bookstores, and drugstores, along with the rise of book clubs in schools, has changed the way books are selected. Before, a teacher or librarian led children to books after explaining their merits. Now, often the appeal of the cover alone sells the book. Some fear that the diversity of published material may decline as distribution lines narrow (Taxel and Ward, 2000).

Because of a tax on warehoused goods, books go out of print quickly if sales aren't high. This often makes it difficult to find a book you loved as a child—or even a book you read about in a review written two years ago (Taxel, 2000).

With the consolidation of publishing houses into a few megacompanies, unknown authors are having a harder time finding a publisher. The tradition of a family-owned publishing house, nurturing and leading along authors and illustrators, has all but disappeared.

Choose several of the following activities to complete:

1. Write about your history as a reader. Include in your reading autobiography answers to some of the following questions:

- What are your earliest memories of reading at home and at school?
- Did you share reading with friends and family?
- What books/authors/subjects did you tend to focus on?
- Which adults most encouraged you as a reader? Why? Discouraged you as a reader?
- In upper elementary school, how did your reading patterns change? Why?
- Do you consider yourself a good reader? Why or why not? What characteristics do good readers have that you would like to develop?
- What roles does reading play in your life now—beyond required reading for classes? Who are some of your favorite authors, and what are some of your favorite books?

2. After sharing parts of your reading autobiographies in a group, create a list of the things that drew you to reading and those that pushed you away. What generalizations can you draw about what contributes to making "readers"? What experiences discouraged people in your group from reading? Did anything surprise you as you shared?

3. Write down in your notebook all the repertoires from which you read (aspects of your personal history or perspective). Share these with your group, and add to your list any mentioned by other group members that you think apply to you. Continue adding to this list as you go through the course so that you get a better understanding of all the parts of your history that affect your reading.

4. What books that you read as a child do you consider to be children's classics? Jot down the titles of books you believe are classics and why you think their appeal is lasting. Share your list with others in your group. What discoveries did you make? Did you agree on what makes a book a classic?

5. Get comfortable in the library with a stack of picture books next to you. Read through ten books, noting what you think makes them accessible to children. Do the pages seem to turn in the right places? Does the text flow naturally when you read it aloud? How does it sound? Do you notice elements of patterned language? Are there sentence or plot structures that make the story predictable? Do the illustrations work with the text and add to the meaning of the story? As you read children's books, use your favorites to formulate statements about what you believe the purpose of children's literature is.

6. One way to build community is to share books you love. Share a favorite story you remember from childhood. Discuss the various repertoires from which you and other members of your group read the book.

7. The boxed feature Taking a Look at the Research: Creating Classroom Communities describes various aspects of creating a classroom community. Think back over your own schooling. In which classes or grades do you remember feeling part of a classroom community? In which classes or grades did you not feel part of a community? Explain to a small group what contributed to these feelings. As a group, come up with a list of dos and don'ts for creating a community in the classroom.

8. Select one website that your group will explore and report back to the class on. If possible, access the site together and then decide which person will familiarize himself or herself with each part of the site. As a group, prepare a written report for the class, explaining what they can find on your site.

CD-ROM

To get a preview of how often group work is offered in the Invitations section, do a word search for *group* under Invitations.

Classroom Teaching Ideas

The best teaching ideas will come from your own interests and needs and the experiences you and your children are having within your unique setting. Many ideas will be spontaneous and teach to the moment. The ones shared here and at the conclusion of each future chapter may be useful, may serve as a springboard for other ideas more perfectly suited to you, or may not be helpful at all. In any case, read, enjoy, and have fun!

1. Have students write or record their own reading autobiographies, in which they share what they remember best about books from their earlier years.

2. Work together with your students to determine what kind of community you want your classroom to be. Talk through and write down rules that will help shape a caring and respectful environment. Remember to keep the rules to a minimum and adhere to them consistently.

3. Share yourself with your students. Perhaps even before school begins, write to your prospective students to introduce yourself. Talk about what interests you, your friends, your pets, your wonderings, and the things you like to do. Include photocopies of photos. Ask your students to bring items about themselves to share during the first days of school. These could include, among other things, photos or favorite toys.

4. Many students make text-to-text connections through their familiarity with authors and illustrators. Select an author or illustrator to study. Have students find as many of the person's works as they can, research biographical material, make a bulletin board display, or bring in foods mentioned or shown in the person's work. Consider having a birthday party on the person's birthday.

Internet and Text Resources

Following are some of the largest websites devoted to children's literature. Several of these will be cited again in the specific chapters to which they pertain. Please note that if a web address is no longer operational, you can often locate the new address by going to a search engine and typing in the name of the site.

1. **American Library Association** provides lists of Best Books for Young Adults, Quick Picks (books for reluctant readers), and information about award-winning books. Find it at

www.ala.org/parents

2. **Booktalks—Quick and Simple** has over 400 booktalks arranged alphabetically by author and book. Go to

http://nancykeane.com/booktalks/

3. **The Bulletin of the Center for Children's Books** contains book reviews, recommended books, in-depth discussions of featured books, and so on. Go to

http://lis.uiuc.edu/puboff/bccb/

4. **Carol Hurst's Children's Literature Site** recommends books, some teaching guides, and activities. Find it at

www.carolhurst.com

5. **The Children's Literature Web Guide** is a great site, packed with information on children's and young adults' books, authors, awards, and many links, even though it hasn't been updated recently. Find it at

www.ucalgary.ca/~dkbrown/

6. **Northwest Regional Educational Library** is another excellent resource, with links to a number of teacher resources. Go to

www. nwrel.org/sky/index.asp?ID=3

7. **ERIC REC Web Resources** provides links to various children's and adolescents' literature resources online. Find it at

http://eric.indiana.edu/www/indexwr.html

8. **Once Upon a Time: A Children's Literature Website** offers readers a myriad of resources. Go to

nova.bsuvc.bsu.edu/~OOmevancamp/clrw.html

9. **Subject Guide to Children's Literature** is an Australian site that allows the searcher to find books, journal articles, Internet sites, and background information. Go to

www.deakin.edu.au/library/srchgdes/SearchChildLit.html

10. **Online Journals on Children's and Adolescents' Literature** also lists special library collections. Find it at

http://eric.indiana.edu/www/#JOUR

References

Carlsen, G. Robert (1974). "Literature IS . . . ." *English Journal 63,* 23–27.

Curtis, Christopher Paul (1997). Keynote address. National Conference of Teachers of English Annual Convention, Detroit, Nov. 20–24, 1997.

Elleman, Barbara (1995). "Toward the 21st Century—Where Are Children's Books Going?" *The New Advocate 8,* 151–165.

Elliot, Stephen N., Thomas R. Kratochwill, Joan Littlefield, and John F. Travers (2000). *Educational Psychology: Effective Teaching, Effective Learning.* New York: McGraw-Hill.

Fisher, Leonard Everett (1997). "From Xenophon to Gutenberg." *The New Advocate 10,* 203–209.

Goldstone, Bette (1999). "Brave New Worlds: The Changing Image of the Picture Book." *The New Advocate 12,* 331–343.

Goodman, Ken (1996). *On Reading: A Common-Sense Look at the Nature of Language and the Science of Reading.* Portsmouth, NH: Heinemann.

Hade, Daniel D., and Lisa Murphy (2000). "Voice and Image: A Look at Recent Poetry. "*Language Arts 77,* 344–352.

Harris, Violet (1996). "Continuing Dilemmas, Debates, and Delights in Multicultural Literature." *The New Advocate 9,* 107–122.

Kohl, Herbert (1995). *Should We Burn Babar? Essays on Children's Literature and the Power of Stories.* New York: The New Press.

McCormick, Kathleen (1994). *The Culture of Reading and the Teaching of English.* New York: Manchester University Press.

Siegler, Robert S. (1991). *Children's Thinking* (2nd ed.). Englewood Cliffs, NJ: Prentice Hall.

Taxel, Joel, and Holly M. Ward (2000). "Publishing Children's Literature at the Dawn of the 21st Century." *The New Advocate 13,* 51–59.

Yolen, Jane (1997). "Taking Time: Or How Things Have Changed in the Last Thirty-Five Years of Children's Publishing." *The New Advocate 10,* 285–291.

Children's Books

Bauer, Marion Dane, ed. (1994). *Am I Blue? Coming Out from the Silence.* New York: HarperCollins.

Brown, Margaret Wise (1947). *Goodnight Moon.* Illus. Clement Hurd. New York: Harper & Row.

Bunting, Eve (1998). *So Far from the Sea.* Illus. Chris K. Soentpiet. New York: Clarion.

Burton, Virginia Lee (1939). *Mike Mulligan and His Steam Shovel.* New York: Houghton Mifflin.

Cha, Dia (1996). *Dia's Story Cloth: The Hmong People's Journey of Freedom.* Stitched by Chue and Nhia Thao Cha. New York: Lee & Low.

Collard, Sneed B., III (1999). *1,000 Years Ago on Planet Earth.* Illus. Jonathan Hunt. Boston: Houghton Mifflin.

Conly, Jane Leslie (1993). *Crazy Lady!* New York: HarperTrophy.

Curtis, Christopher Paul (1999). *Bud, Not Buddy.* New York: Delacorte.

—— (1995). *The Watsons Go to Birmingham—1963.* New York: Delacorte.

De Brunhoff, Jean (1966). *The Story of Babar, the Little Elephant.* New York: Random [1931].

DiCamillo, Kate (2000). *Because of Winn-Dixie.* Cambridge, MA: Candlewick.

Dickens, Charles (1861). *Great Expectations.* Philadelphia: Peterson.

Dorris, Michael (1992). *Morning Girl.* New York: Hyperion.

English, Karen (1999). *Francie.* New York: Farrar, Straus & Giroux.

Gag, Wanda (1928). *Millions of Cats.* New York: Coward-McCann.

Garden, Nancy (1996). *Good Moon Rising.* New York: Farrar, Straus & Giroux.

Grahame, Kenneth (1983). *The Wind in the Willows.* Illus. Ernest H. Shepard. New York: Scribners [1908].

Gruelle, Johnny (1920). *The Raggedy Ann Stories.* Chicago: Volland.

Ho, Minfong (1991). *The Clay Marble.* New York: Farrar, Straus & Giroux.

Hoffman, Mary (1991). *Amazing Grace.* Illus. Caroline Binch. New York: Dial.

Houston, Gloria (1994). *Mountain Valor.* New York: Philomel.

Howe, Deborah, and James Howe (1979). *Bunnicula: A Rabbit-Tale of Mystery.* Illus. Alan Daniel. New York: Avon.

Krull, Kathleen (1995). *Lives of the Artists: Masterpieces, Messes (and What the Neighbors Thought).* Illus. Kathryn Hewitt. San Diego: Harcourt Brace.

L'Engle, Madeleine (1980). *A Wrinkle in Time.* New York: Farrar, Straus & Giroux [1962, Ariel; 1973, Yearling].

Lowrey, Janette Sebring (1942). *The Poky Little Puppy.* Illus. Gustaf Tenggren. New York: Simon & Schuster.

McCloskey, Robert (1941). *Make Way for Ducklings.* New York: Viking.

Milne, A. A. (1988). *The Complete Tales & Poems of Winnie-the-Pooh.* Illus. Ernest H. Shepard. New York: Dutton [1926].

Monceaux, Morgan, and Ruth Katcher (1999). *My Heroes, My People: African Americans and Native Americans in the West.* New York: Farrar, Straus & Giroux.

Myers, Walter Dean (1998). *Amistad: A Long Road to Freedom.* New York: Dutton.

Nhuong, Huynh Quang (1997). *Water Buffalo Days: Growing Up in Vietnam.* Illus. Jean and Mou-Sien Tseng. New York: HarperCollins.

Nye, Naomi Shihab (1997). *Habibi.* New York: Simon & Schuster.

—— (1997). *Sitti's Secrets.* Illus. Nancy Carpenter. New York: Simon & Schuster.

Paulsen, Gary (1995). *The Tent.* San Diego: Harcourt Brace.

Peck, Richard (2000). *A Year Down Yonder.* New York: Dial.

Piper, Watty (1929). *The Little Engine That Could.* Illus. George and Doris Hauman. New York: Putnam [reissued in 1990].

Robinson, Barbara (1994). *The Worst Best School Year Ever.* New York: HarperTrophy.

Rohmer, Harriet, ed. (1999). *Honoring Our Ancestors: Stories and Pictures by Fourteen Artists.* San Francisco: Children's Book Press.

Rowling, J. K. (1997). *Harry Potter and the Sorcerer's Stone.* New York: Scholastic.

Rylant, Cynthia (1995). *Henry and Mudge and the Best Day of All.* Illus. Suçie Stevenson. New York: Aladdin.

Sendak, Maurice (1965). *Where the Wild Things Are.* New York: Harper.

Seuss, Dr. (1960). *Green Eggs and Ham.* New York: Random.

Singer, Marilyn, ed. (2000). *I Believe in Water: Twelve Brushes with Religion.* New York: HarperCollins.

St. George, Judith (2000). *So You Want to Be President?* Illus. David Small. New York: Philomel.

Van Draanen, Wendelin (1998). *Sammy Keyes and the Hotel Thief.* New York: Knopf.

Walter, Mildred Pitts (1996). *Second Daughter: The Story of a Slave Girl.* New York: Scholastic.

Weeks, Sarah (1995). *Follow the Moon.* Illus. Suzanne Duranceau. New York: HarperCollins.

White, E. B. (1952). *Charlotte's Web.* Illus. Garth Williams. New York: Harper & Row.

—— (1945). *Stuart Little.* Illus. Garth Williams. New York: Harper & Row.

White, Ruth (1996). *Belle Prater's Boy.* New York: Yearling.

Wisniewski, David (1998). *The Secret Knowledge of Grown-Ups.* New York: Lothrop, Lee & Shepard.

Wolff, Virginia Euwer (1998). *Bat 6.* New York: Scholastic.

Woodson, Jacqueline (1995). *From the Notebooks of Melanin Sun.* New York: Scholastic.

—— (1994). *I Hadn't Meant to Tell You This.* New York: Bantam Doubleday Dell.

Yep, Laurence (1993). *Dragon's Gate.* New York: Scholastic.

Yolen, Jane, and Bruce Coville (1998). *Armageddon Summer.* New York: Harcourt Brace.

Evaluating and Selecting Children's Literature

Although evaluating and selecting children's books can at first seem like an intimidating and overwhelming task, deciding what to read is important not only for you but also for your students. No one wants to waste time reading mediocre books, especially when one lifetime is hardly enough time to read all the wonderful children's books that have been published. One of the goals of this text is to help you discover what books are worth your and your students' time. Learning why you feel the way you do about particular books will give you more confidence in the choices you make for your students.

Your reactions to the books you choose for your personal reading are based on your own needs, values, experiences, and preferences with respect to style; the same is true of your reactions to children's books. But when, as a teacher or librarian, you are also making choices for students, you want to make sure that you stretch your range of possibilities so that you select books based on the very best criteria possible. If you know little about a subject, your choices are limited. You need to immerse yourself in the world of children's literature. There are, however, ways to fairly quickly come to understand which books are worth your and your students' time. This chapter will help you clarify possible criteria you might use to evaluate books. The boxed feature Children's Voices gives a glimpse of what some middle-grade students like in books.

The Words and the Story

Although responses to books are often organized around the elements of literature (usually thought of as plot, characters, setting, theme, and style, or qualities of writing), this text recommends taking a less structured approach to initial responses. Going through a list of elements in an orderly fashion doesn't mimic the way we actually make choices about books—it's too artificial and discrete. When I set out to evaluate a book, I start by writing down what I like or notice about it. Then, I make generalizations about the process to uncover what I value or think is most important in a book. Finally, I turn to the elements of literature to help me look at the book in its entirety.

Beginning with Response

The Whales' Song, written by Dyan Sheldon and illustrated by Gary Blythe, is one of my all-time favorite books. The words and pictures move me. The grandmother's love for her granddaughter radiates through the illustrations. The words cast a spell as they weave a tale illuminating the importance of spirit and belief. Lilly's grandmother is a kind, wise woman who doesn't allow her spirit to be trampled by great-uncle Frederick. She cherishes her granddaughter and shares her own experiences in the world. Lilly's sense of wonder and love of nature remind me of the child I once was. The pictures of the whales, leaping, jumping, and spinning, leave joy in their wake. In spite of great-uncle Frederick's belief that

THE WHALES' SONG

by Dyan Sheldon   *paintings by* Gary Blythe

Illuminated by moonlight, Lilly gazes at the magical world created by the leaping whales.

(From THE WHALES' SONG by Dyan Sheldon, paintings by Gary Blythe, copyright © 1990 by Dyan Sheldon, text; copyright © 1990 by Gary Blythe, paintings. Used by permission of Dial Books for Young Readers, an imprint of Penguin Putnam Books for Young Readers, a division of Penguin Putnam Inc.)

whales are good only for what they can give to mankind in terms of fuel and food, Lilly sees the magic and beauty of the whales' singing as evidence that whales are much more than their physical bodies. A view of whales as valuable for their beauty, caring, and joyfulness emanates from the book.

The Polar Express, by Chris Van Allsburg, is another favorite book of mine. Its pictures, with the light coming from below, cast an aura of otherworldliness and mystery. The little boy has an experience any child would want. A train pulls up in front of his house to take him to the North Pole. There, he sees Santa Claus and is chosen to receive the first gift of Christmas—a bell. His shock when his parents can't hear its ringing helps us to understand that only those who believe can hear its magical sounds. This book resonates for me because intuitively I've always known that the world is more than its material parts and that people are more than the sum of their jobs and roles. I respond to visions of the world that include beliefs like these—that whales can sing and that sticking with one's own deep feelings and experiences is important.

These two books made me dream and wonder and feel connected to others who don't see the world in the cynical way great-uncle Frederick does in **The Whales' Song.** The language in both of these books is beautiful. Van Allsburg begins, "On Christmas Eve, many years ago, I lay quietly in my bed. I did not rustle the sheets. I breathed slowly and silently. I was listening for a sound—a sound a friend had told me I'd never hear—the ringing bells of Santa's sleigh." The rich language is mesmerizing. Van Allsburg also keeps just the right amount of tension. We're not sure where the little boy is going or what will happen, but we want to know. The ending strikes a chord deep within me, which lingers long after I close the book: "Though I've grown old, the bell still rings for me as it does for all who truly believe."

THE POLAR EXPRESS

A train, its light dimmed by the quietly falling snow, pulls up in front of a house to transport one boy into the experience of a lifetime.

(Cover, from THE POLAR EXPRESS. Copyright © 1985 by Chris Van Allsburg. Reprinted by permission of Houghton Mifflin Company. All rights reserved.)

In a similar way, the language in **The Whales' Song** enchants and lulls: "Lilly's grandmother told her a story. 'Once upon a time,' she said, 'the ocean was filled with whales. They were as big as the hills. They were as peaceful as the moon. They were the most wondrous creatures you could ever imagine.'" The ending kindles a quiet joy and a belief that all life is connected: "Lilly thought she must have been dreaming. She stood up and turned toward home. Then from far, far away, on the breath of the wind, she heard 'Lilly! Lilly!' The whales were calling her name."

In both of these books, I am entranced by the story line and wonder where it will take me. I want Lilly to hear the whales sing, as her grandmother has, though Frederick's strong presence and attitudes make me question whether Lilly will be able to defend her beliefs. In **The Polar Express,** once the boy is at the North Pole and receives his gift, I wonder what will happen next. The plot lines provide tension that makes me read each book to the end.

I am also enamored of **Roll of Thunder, Hear My Cry,** by Mildred D. Taylor, because I feel very connected to the characters—smart, no-nonsense Mama; kindly but strict Papa; sometimes-sassy Cassie. Although surrounded by prejudice and hate, the family members do not let it warp their spirits. The parents teach their children that the people who hate them are ignorant, so the children don't turn their hurt inward, wondering what they have done wrong. Strong families with strong beliefs about themselves and the world I find compelling. I am always trying to figure out how black people survived discrimination and why whites acted as if it were acceptable. Sometimes human beings' behavior stuns me. The tension in the book is constant, beginning with Cassie's confrontation with the teacher over the inferior books given to the children and ending with TJ's being brought to trial. The action never stops.

Cassie gazes straight out at us from Jerry Pinkney's soft watercolor illustration, giving us a hint of her very direct nature.

("25TH ANNIVERSARY COVER" from ROLL OF THUNDER, HEAR MY CRY by Mildred D. Taylor, illustration by Jerry Pinkney. Copyright 1976 by Mildred Taylor, text. Copyright 2001 by Jerry Pinkney, illustration. Used by permission of Dial Books for Young Readers, an imprint of Penguin Putman Books for Young Readers, a division of Penguin Putnam Inc.)

Generalizing the Process

What do my reactions to these books have in common? On what basis do I evaluate books? Emotional impact seems important, as does as the vision the author has of the world. For example, the mood of **The Whales' Song** reverberates; the playfulness of the whales and the timelessness of the water move me, making me want to celebrate the mysteries of the universe. Well-drawn characters are also vital, as are themes that make me think about the books long after I have read them. Themes that involve the resiliency of the human spirit keep me interested. Beautiful language enchants me.

I tend to pay attention to other qualities of writing after I have finished a book. Although I do not specifically think about the setting, I must feel a part of the story's world and "see" the setting, or else engagement with the book is difficult. Envisioning the setting allows me to move around in the world of the characters, seeing the ocean or the North Pole or rural Mississippi. I'm absorbed into books with richly drawn worlds.

The Place of Elements of Literature in Evaluation

Looking at literary elements can help us to see a piece of literature from multiple perspectives and thus experience it more deeply. Probably the first thing we do as readers, before using any other evaluative screen, is decide whether we like a book. Once we have initially connected with a book, we are ready to look at particular literary elements to see whether the book has a universal richness. These elements help us appreciate the craft of the writing.

Although it is important for teachers to know and use the elements of literature in order to select books that will hold up under the scrutiny of children, we all tend to respond holistically on a first read. Then we turn to the elements of literature to see how they can be used to extend our thinking about and evaluation of the book. As you read the following discussion of the elements of literature, think about whether and how each is important to you when you evaluate the merit of a book.

Plot

The plot answers the questions "What is happening in the story?" and "What is the sequence of events?" Some stories have simple and straightforward plots. Others have complex plots that make the reader think and ask questions: Who solves problems? What allows the tension to be dissolved? Herbert Kohl (1995) says, "Studying how tension and dissonance are dealt with in a plot is another way of discovering the role of power relations in a story" (p. 24). For instance, in **The Whales' Song,** although Frederick is ornery and outspoken, he is not able to change the mythic and magical views that Lilly and her grandmother have of the whales. The pace at which the plot unfolds is also important. Stories that flow well keep the reader involved and interested. For some readers, unraveling or solving one plot line doesn't offer enough complexity—they prefer a book to be multidimensional.

Characters

Characterization addresses the questions "Who are these people?" and "Are they believable?" Characters need to be authentic for the reader to connect with them. Readers are looking for multidimensional characters so well developed that they seem to be real people. When characters are flat, given life through stereotyping and predictable actions, readers are not likely to become sufficiently involved with their lives to want to finish the book. Readers seek characters whose humanity touches theirs. Both the grandmother and Lilly in *The Whales' Song* are easy to relate to and believe in, partly because of their sensitivity. It's easy to empathize with the boy in *The Polar Express* and imagine what it would be like going to the North Pole and meeting Santa Claus. In *Roll of Thunder, Hear My Cry,* the characters of Cassie, her mother, and her father are so well developed that it's possible to imagine having whole conversations with them. Characters come to life for us through what they say, their actions, and what others say about them.

Setting

Setting informs the reader of where the story is taking place. It answers the questions "Where am I?" and "What will I see if I walk around here?" Occasionally, the setting is so prominent—for example, when it includes a hurricane, a tidal wave, or a storm—that it almost becomes another character. More frequently, the setting falls into the background, and the reader is not particularly aware of it. Readers know immediately, however, when the setting is not well drawn, because they can't get a sense of where they are. In *The Polar Express,* the language and illustrations evoke a fairy-tale world. In *The Whales' Song,* conversations about the whales and the immediacy of the illustrations of the ocean surround the reader.

Theme

Theme answers the question "What is this story telling me?" Readers want to come away from a story with ideas that they can turn over and over in their mind. The reader may well ask: Have I taken away something of substance by reading the book? Is this something that will help me think about issues within myself? What did I learn about people and society or myself? What kinds of connections to people and society did this book give me? Did this book show me possibilities and make me excited about thinking further about issues? Is the content worth exploring? The theme and the worth of the content are closely intertwined.

Style

Style defines the *qualities of writing,* answering the question "How has this book been written to engage the reader?" Readers often are not aware of the qualities of good writing while they read, but they almost always are jolted by poor or inadequate writing. Hearing the author's voice, the reader realizes that there is someone behind the words. If point of view is not presented effectively, which character is thinking what becomes unclear. Authors who can move smoothly from one point of view to another keep their readers involved. Well-chosen words, rich language, and the skillful use of literary devices make an impact on the reader. Sometimes a beautiful metaphor will take the breath away or cause the reader to linger over the words, savoring the image. Sometimes the richness of the language will stun or simply delight the reader. So, when looking at the qualities of writing, don't simply identify them, but recognize the impact each has on you and how it contributes to the effectiveness of the overall story.

Other Considerations

In addition to the elements of literature, books can also be evaluated on emotional impact, imaginative impact, and vision.

Emotional Impact

Did this book connect you to your own humanity and that of others? Did this piece of literature make an impact on you? The purpose of literature is to make an impact, so if you felt nothing or said "So what?" the book doesn't meet key criteria. If you were moved by the beauty of the language, by the glimpses into the characters' personalities, by the ideas and issues dealt with, or by the actions of the characters, then the book has merit. In ***Roll of Thunder, Hear My Cry,*** Cassie's rage at the injustice she faces from Lillian Jean and the white world becomes our rage.

Imaginative Impact

Books can spark imagination, show possibilities, stretch thinking, pique curiosity, and make the reader think in different ways. Herbert Kohl (1995) identifies the value of this element: "Children's imaginations are lively and are fed by the stories they are told and the images provided them by their culture" (p. 62). Kohl maintains, "Books can be vehicles for sparking utopian and hopeful imaginings" (p. 63). If we don't provide stories that allow young people to "fundamentally question the world as it is and dream it as it might be, resignation, defiance, or the quest for personal success become the only imaginable options . . ." (p. 65).

One of the central characteristics of the imagination is that it crosses borders and categories. The only way we can jump over the boundaries of our own thinking is through imagination, so we need stories that spark it. ***The Polar Express*** makes a strong impact because it not only puts the reader in the center of the little boy's experience, but also makes the reader feel the wonder and beauty of believing in something beyond the self.

Sometimes, this sparking of the imagination can be attributed to plot, character, or theme. But it's much more than any one of these parts—it's the overall quality of the story that makes us wonder or feel awe or think of a million questions we want answered. Since, as Carlsen (1974) pointed out (see Chapter 1), early childhood is a key age for unconscious delight, it's important to offer books that feed the imagination of young students.

Vision

Vision is the view authors have of the world and the people in it, and their attitudes toward both. How are people shown? Are they good or evil? Are they inherently competitive or cooperative? Are some people viewed as less worthy because they are not beautiful or rich, or are all characters portrayed as equal in worth? Does this book connect what happens in the story to "who has the power and how the power is distributed among the characters" (p. 5)? Kohl asks us to look at the way power is represented in the story, "since power relationships in literature reveal the politics of both the story and, frequently, the author. Power relationships also provide examples and models for children of social and moral behavior" (p. 4). In other words, by seeing who makes the decisions, who gives the orders, and who obeys, readers make discoveries about power.

In ***The Whales' Song,*** Frederick, although he is gruff and forceful in his speech, doesn't get the last word. Lilly listens to her gentle grandmother and follows her heart. She doesn't let someone who views the world in utilitarian ways steal her hope and longing for beauty. Thus, power here is somewhat equitably distributed; the overbearing adult doesn't win out. The author's vision of the world encourages children to recognize the importance of their own feelings and not to feel inadequate because someone has a totally different view. Likewise, in ***Roll of Thunder, Hear My Cry,*** the author's vision is of an equitable world where all people can live in peace and not be denied opportunities. The issue of power is, of course, at the forefront, since the story takes place in the 1930s in the South. Although the white people have the upper hand, with the law supporting them, the rightness of this view is challenged throughout the book. An author's vision can have a powerful impact on the reader.

 he Visual

Color leaping off the page. Lines wiggling, waving, or standing straight. Shapes smoothly rounded or abruptly angular. Art includes all of these elements but is much, much more. Art makes an impact on us as we view it, representing one piece of the artist's

To locate books that appeal to children of different age groups, go to **Database of Award-Winning Children's Literature** at www2.wcoil.com/~ellerbee/ childlit.html.

world view and giving us another way to look at the world. Yet, for those of us who are not visual artists ourselves, the idea of evaluating illustrations in books can be intimidating. To evaluate children's literature, we do not need to become art critics; we merely need to learn to trust our own instincts and responses. It is not necessary to know how to name techniques and styles in order to evaluate art. Our descriptions of how the art moves us can provide the beginnings of ways to talk about the art.

Once I asked an artist friend what I was supposed to do when I looked at a picture and what I had to know in order to appreciate art. She told me to start with what moved me and what I noticed about the picture. I now have two beautiful pieces in my living room that I bought for the shapes and the colors. Whenever I look at the abstract shapes in one of the pieces, something pleases me. I can't even name the technique the artist used. All I know is that those colors and shapes put me in touch with deep, deep parts of myself and keep me in touch with my humanness. Now I never buy a painting unless it moves me, adds warmth and beauty to my house, shows me something new every time I look at it, and enriches my life. So, although I am not an artist, I know what I love; I know what moves me and involves me.

As a reader, you too respond to illustrations in books. So we will begin our investigation of art in children's literature with our own responses, considering such issues as whether the pictures please us and make us want to look harder.

Responding to the Visual

First I will tell you what I notice when I look at pictures that attract me or interest me. After responding to a few particular illustrations, I'll make some generalizations about my responses. Then I'll suggest some other ways of responding to art and some ways of understanding what might have elicited a particular response.

I have read many, many Brian Wildsmith books to my children over the years. We all fell in love with his drawings. At first, I couldn't identify why they captivated me, until I described what I saw. His illustrations in *Fishes,* in which the brushstrokes are very obvious, draw me into the pictures. In the picture of "a hover of trout," he uses many shades of blues and purples in the water. Because it's not just a solid blue mass, I feel as if I could find a way to enter into the water. Shadows and openings seem to be created for me. The golds, yellows, and oranges look luminous, as if the fish were lit up by something inside of them. The fish nearer the top seems brighter and has more intense colors, as it is closer to the sun. Their contrasting dark black eyes draw me into their depths, making the fish come alive and giving me an empathy for them as fish. The composition of the fish is balanced, but the fish are moving forward, off the page, and my eye follows them in that direction. The bodies of the fish are covered with red, aqua, and black dots that seem to draw the fish toward me, almost out of the illustration itself. Wildsmith's lines are delicately drawn, adding to the floating quality of the pictures. His pictures are certainly not what would be called realistic or representational because of the blurring of parts of the fish, the obvious strokes, and the way the color seems to be laid on.

In *Mama, Do You Love Me?,* written by Barbara M. Joosse and illustrated by Barbara Lavallee, I immediately notice the shapes and the colors. In the picture of the mother leaning over to receive a hug from her child, the half-elliptical shape makes the mother and daughter seem like one person. Although the art is stylistic, with the faces divided and shaded and the eyes represented by curved lines, this illustration beams with love and affection. The oranges and reds of the mother's dress, which is covered with a cheery flower design and has borders around the neck, sleeves, and bottom ruffle, radiate acceptance and warmth. Even the browns and reddish oranges of the faces are warm and seem to glow. The little girl's positioning—her arms around her mother's neck, her head flung back to receive her mother's kiss, straining on her tiptoes to be as close to her mother as possible—exudes love and trust, suggesting that this child feels completely secure with her mother. This feeling of warmth and the way the artist has positioned the two figures are the most important features of the picture. The doll is a nice touch because it snuggles, with arms flung open, in the little girl's arm and reinforces the feeling of openness to love and affection. The mother,

CD-ROM

To find other books by Brian Wildsmith, go to the CD-ROM database.

Fishes by Brian Wildsmith

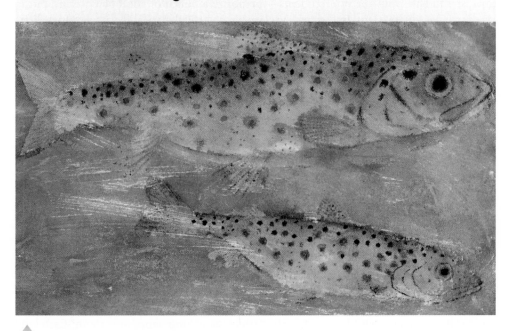

Brian Wildsmith creates a floating, almost ethereal feeling with his use of color, shadows, and brushstrokes.
(Cover illustration from **Fishes** by Brian Wildsmith, by permission of Oxford University Press.)

the child, and the doll all wear similar shoes and leg coverings. These repeated elements serve to show how much the three have in common. The beautiful curving shape of the mother as she bends over the child speaks of softness and yielding. The curve is repeated in the mother's head and arm, the child's head, the doll's head, and even the shoes. There are no sharp, straight lines in the picture to detract from the soothing smoothness. Because the embracing mother and child are right in the middle of the page, nothing takes our eyes away from this display of affection and love. The design of the little girl's dress, with hearts everywhere, reinforces the presence of love. Both mother and daughter are standing on a bluish, shaded area, which holds them together and centered.

In both Wildsmith's and Lavallee's pictures, color adds to the illustrations, as does composition (where objects are placed in a picture). The reader's eye is drawn by the lines and shapes, which also contribute to the impact. The brushstrokes and repeated elements are particularly striking in these two pictures. You may find, however, that you frequently are at a

How much?

Barbara Lavallee's stunning composition and use of line and color create an image bursting with love.
(From *Mama, Do You Love Me?* by Barbara M. Joosse, illustrated by Barbara Lavallee © 1991. Reprinted by permission of Chronicle Books, San Francisco.)

loss for words to describe your reaction to art. The purpose of the following sections is to give you the language to express what you are responding to in the art. By learning the basic vocabulary of art, you also will indirectly acquire another tool for looking at the world. The goal isn't to have you—or your students—memorize a bunch of vocabulary terms, but to open up an evaluative lens. In the same way we use a particular vocabulary to evaluate literature, we can use one for art.

Looking at the Art

When you set out to look at the art in a book, you can learn much by paging through the book quickly, just to get a feel for it. In a quick look through the illustrations, pay attention to colors, lines, shapes, texture, and composition.

Colors

Are the colors bright or dark? How are the pictures shaded? What's in the shadows? Are the colors warm or cool? Do they make the pictures seem joyous or solemn? In **The Painter's Eye,** Jan Greenberg and Sandra Jordan (1991) say, "Paintings filled with intense red, orange or yellow can be exciting or even violent. The duller the color, the softer it seems, as in the blue-grey of dusk or the pale blue of a misty day. Artists use intensity of color to convey mood" (p. 32).

Lines

Are the lines straight, jagged, curved, vertical, thick, thin, long, short, or smooth? Each kind can convey a mood. Horizontal lines may be interpreted as peaceful, depressed, or serene. Vertical lines may be seen as strong, rigid, formal, or even religious. Jagged lines may indicate excitement, anger, or energy, whereas curved lines often are sensuous, organic, or rhythmic, according to Greenberg and Jordan. Brushstrokes also contribute to the overall feel. They can be big and bold or delicate and whispery.

The soft, almost furry quality of this image in *Toby, Where Are You?* emphasizes the gentle, loving nature of the family.
(© 1997 by Teryl Euvremer. Used by permission of HarperCollins Publishers.)

Shapes

Artists use shapes and forms as well as lines to control the direction of our eye movements within an illustration. Curved shapes often represent objects in nature, whereas angular shapes tend to represent man-made objects. According to Greenberg and Jordan (1991), whereas triangles, circles, and rectangles are geometric shapes we're used to seeing in our daily lives, "organic shapes are freer and less defined. These shapes often remind us of animal, human, or natural forms such as a shell or a cloud" (p. 24). Some shapes look strong or dense; others appear soft or floating. Shapes contribute to the overall impression we get from a picture, moving us with their power or inviting us in with their gentleness or softness.

Texture

Do the surfaces of the shapes have a rough, smooth, or soft appearance? When actual material is attached to a canvas, it gives a picture a three-dimensional look. Greenberg and Jordan (1991) say, "Sensing whether the surface is rough or smooth, grainy or gossamer contributes to our feelings about the painting" (p. 30). Because texture appeals to our tactile sense, it can give a strong sensual feeling to artwork. The soft texture of Teryl Euvremer's pictures in *Toby, Where Are You?*, by William Steig, seems to emanate love; we feel almost caressed by the pictures. The smooth texture of Richard Egielski's work in *Buz* adds to the pictures' unreality because nothing can stick to the glossy, impenetrable images. The high gloss doesn't invite us to look deeply *into* the picture—we have to stay on the surface. When a work has a rough texture, we may get a sense of depth. Clearly, texture can have a definite impact on our responses to illustrations.

Composition

Does the placement of objects make them seem to be in harmony with one another? Do they seem unified, or do they stand in contrast or opposition to one another? The sizes of the objects in relation to one another and the perspective from which the picture is drawn are also part of its composition.

In Debra Frasier's *Out of the Ocean,* the balanced, layered composition of the illustrations gives us a feeling of harmony, oneness, and serenity. In *To Market, To Market,* written by Anne Miranda and illustrated by Janet Stevens, the composition of the picture on the eighth page

Janet Stevens's composition captures the chaos and disorder of the situation, since even the goose can't stay on the page.
(Illustration from TO MARKET, TO MARKET by Anne Miranda, illustrations copyright © 1997 by Janet Stevens, reprinted by permission of Harcourt, Inc.)

clearly shows chaos and disharmony. The lady is almost reaching outside the frame of the picture to catch the goose; the pig is partly outside the frame. Nothing appears orderly. As you can see, composition creates distinct impressions in the viewer.

Artists' Media and Materials

After the first quick look-through, you may want to linger over certain pictures that really strike you. Sometimes, knowing the terms for the media and materials the artist used in creating the picture will help you to describe the impression you got from the picture.

Drawing

Artists may draw with pen and ink, pencil or graphite, pastels, or a sharp instrument on scratchboard. The characteristics of each medium affect the impressions it makes.

Pen and ink creates a very defined effect. The strong lines make the objects seem very sure of themselves. Chris Van Allsburg's **Ben's Dream** is drawn in pen and ink, and the lack of color makes the viewer focus more closely on the objects. This medium seems a little more aggressive than other media, as everything has to have an outline and muted areas are rare. However, some artists—like James Stevenson in **"Could Be Worse!"**—use pen and ink and then color the images with watercolors. This creates a softer effect, but the emphasis is still on the outlined shapes. This medium also makes the illustrations look purposeful, as if every single thing in the picture had a definite and important place.

James Stevenson uses the definite lines created by pen and ink to ensure that readers don't miss one thing in this humorous story, which is told largely through the illustrations.
(Cover art from *"Could Be Worse!"* by James Stevenson. Used by permission of HarperCollins Publishers.)

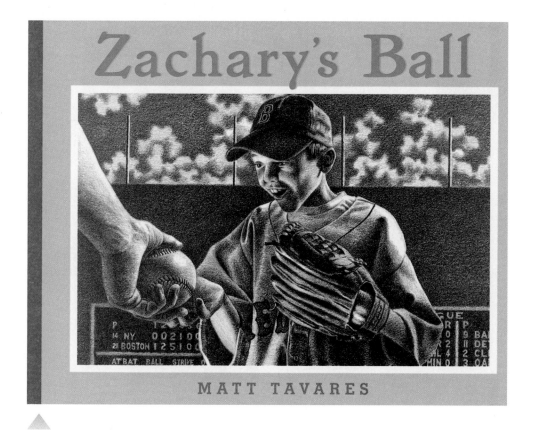

Matt Tavares's use of pencil, with its emphasis on lights and darks, focuses the reader's attention on the emotions the boy is experiencing.
(ZACHARY'S BALL copyright © 2000 Matt Tavares. Reproduced by permission of the publisher Candlewick Press, Inc., Cambridge, MA.)

Pencil or graphite allows for a full range of lights and darks, creating different moods and a sense of depth with shadow. Chris Van Allsburg's **The Garden of Abdul Gasazi** and **Jumanji** offer excellent examples of the sense of depth that can be created. Matt Tavares's use of pencil in **Zachary's Ball** highlights the contrast between light and dark, causing readers to focus on the luminescent expression on the face of the young boy.

Pastels are powdered colors mixed to the desired shade with white chalk and held together with liquids. Because pastels are used in a form that resembles chalk, they have a soft quality and often a muted appearance. Pastels are wonderful for creating moods, as they can so easily be used to suggest subtleties. In **Hoops,** written by Robert Burleigh and illustrated by Stephen T. Johnson, there is a dreamlike quality to the pictures which works well with the text, because readers can imagine themselves in the pictures shooting baskets. Caldecott-winning artist Ed Young often draws in pastels. His drawings in **Lon Po Po: A Red-Riding Hood Story from China** create a mood of danger and foreboding through the muted colors and the floating quality of the soft edges of the illustrations. No harsh, straight lines detract from this illusion. Howard Fine's use of pastels in Margie Palatini's **Piggie Pie!** to achieve a bright effect shows their versatility.

Scratchboard is a technique in which the artist uses a sharp instrument to scratch a picture into a two-layered (usually black-and-white) board. Brian Pinkney does almost all of his work in scratchboard. As he did in **Duke Ellington,** written by Andrea Davis Pinkney, Brian Pinkney often overpaints his illustrations with oil to add color to the sharp black-and-white contrasts. This technique gives the illustrations a rough appearance and implies that everything is not smooth beneath the surface. The deepness of the scratches suggests that they are purposeful and deliberate. The fact that everything is outlined and has a definite shape contributes to a serious mood or tone.

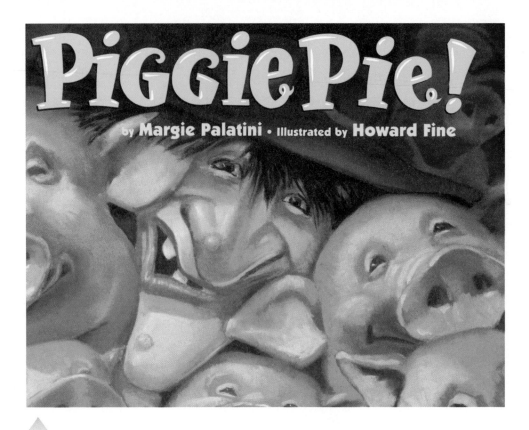

In *Piggie Pie!,* a story of deception, the soft, often blurry look created by the pastels helps mute or hide the truth.

(Cover of PIGGIE PIE! by Margie Palatini, illustrated by Howard Fine. Reprinted by permission of Clarion Books/Houghton Mifflin Co. All rights reserved.)

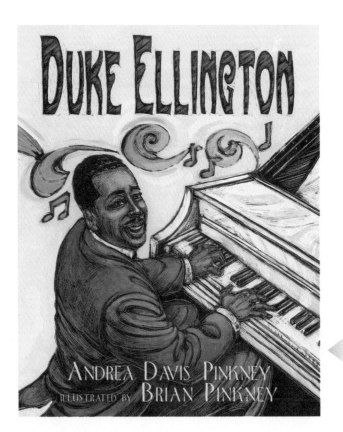

Painting

Painting emphasizes the use of color and tone to convey meaning and emotions. There are many kinds of paints. As Kathleen Horning (1997) explains in *Cover to Cover: Evaluating and Reviewing Children's Books,* each type of paint "begins as a finely ground pigment that is mixed with a different type of binder to adhere to a surface, and as such has its own distinctive properties" (p. 113). Most people will not be able to identify the type of paint used simply by looking at the illustrations, although watercolor seems the most easily distinguishable to me. The reason I am including descriptions of different types of paint is so that when you read in a review that the illustrator used *gouache* or *tempera,* you will be familiar with the term as well as the effects that type of paint can have on a picture.

Gouache (pronounced "gwash") is a type of water-based paint that is used when an "opaque," or solid, even color is

Pinkney's use of scratchboard with its deep, distinct markings helps convey the strength and deliberateness of Duke Ellington's character.

(Illustration reprinted with the permission of Little, Brown and Company from *Duke Ellington* by Andrea Davis Pinkney. Illustrations copyright © 1998 by Brian Pinkney.)

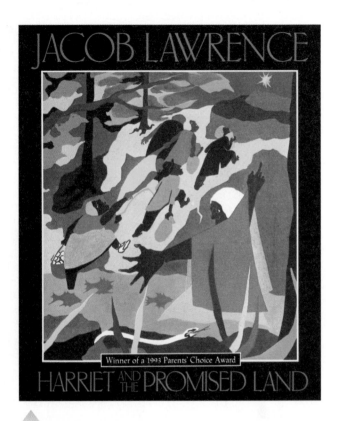

Helen Oxenbury's use of gouache, with the even colors and lack of blurriness, lets viewers directly experience the openness and affection given and received.
(Illustration © 1994 Helen Oxenbury. SO MUCH by Trish Cooke. Reproduced by permission of the publisher Candlewick Press, Inc., Cambridge, MA, on behalf of Walker Books Ltd., of London.)

Jacob Lawrence's use of poster paint in bold primary colors gives a distinct, no-nonsense feel to this painting, leaving no doubt that people are hurrying toward the North Star and away from slavery.
(Reprinted with the permission of Simon & Schuster Books for Young Readers, an imprint of Simon & Schuster Children's Publishing Division from HARRIET AND THE PROMISED LAND by Jacob Lawrence. Copyright © 1968, 1993 Jacob Lawrence.)

wanted. It is powdered color mixed with an opaque white. In **So Much,** written by Trish Cooke and illustrated by Helen Oxenbury, the entire surface of the paper is covered with paint, the lines are distinct, the colors are even, and there are no blurry or muted areas. These qualities give the illustrations a straightforward feel—nothing is hidden; everything is as it is shown. The even, solid quality of the paint gives the illustrations substance, as if you couldn't look through them to find something else. No mystery is implied, consistent with pictures about daily life. Like **More More More Said the Baby,** most of Vera B. Williams's books are done in gouache, with the vivid colors expressing the zest for living of her characters.

Poster paint is a coarser version of gouache in which the color pigment is not as finely ground. I find it difficult to distinguish among gouache, tempera, and poster paint. Jacob Lawrence's **Harriet and the Promised Land,** which is done in poster paint, looks very much like his **The Great Migration: An American Story,** described in the next paragraph.

Tempera is a quick-drying paint that can yield bright, solid colors or can be mixed with water for softer effects. Jacob Lawrence's **The Great Migration: An American Story,** done in tempera, features fully covered surfaces and clearly defined lines, which create a feeling of substance. The often-evident brushstrokes give an impression of scarcity of paint or carelessness in the painting, since everything is not covered evenly. By using this medium, the artist extends the subject of the painting, suggesting the scarcity in the lives of the people migrating North and the carelessness in the way others treated them.

Watercolor is a type of paint that is mixed with water, which decreases its opacity and allows it to appear transparent. Paintings done in watercolors often have a delicate, dreamlike quality. The color may be very uneven; some watercolor paintings even have water spots. It's

CD-ROM

To find illustrators known for their use of watercolor, search for the term *watercolor* in Favorite Authors.

The tempera used in Jacob Lawrence's painting helps convey the contrast between the burdened people, portrayed in solid dark colors, and the birds, flying free in a sparsely colored light blue sky. (*The Great Migration* by Jacob Lawrence. Used by permission of HarperCollins Publishers.)

The delicate effect created by E. B. Lewis's watercolor suggests the fragility of the blossoming relationship between the two young girls.
("Illustrations," copyright © 1998 by E. B. Lewis, illustrations, from THE OTHER SIDE by Jacqueline Woodson, illustrated by E. B. Lewis. Used by permission of G. P. Putnam's Sons, an imprint of Penguin Putnam Books for Young Readers, a division of Penguin Putnam Inc.)

James Ransome's use of oil paint gives a feeling of substance to the relationship between the young girl and her uncle, suggesting that this affection is not shortlived.

(Reprinted with the permission of Simon & Schuster Books for Young Readers, an imprint of Simon & Schuster Children's Publishing Division from UNCLE JED'S BARBERSHOP by Margaree King Mitchell, illustrated by James Ransome. Illustrations copyright © 1993 James Ransome.)

easy to show many shades, either by adding layers of paint or by adding water to the paint after it has been applied to the paper. Watercolor is the most popular medium for picture books because it can so easily express moods and capture the emotions of the characters. Because the shapes need not have definite lines and one color can bleed into the next, watercolor suggests that there is more beneath the surface. The absence of sharp, straight lines conveys a sense of fluidity, the possibility of blending or melding. The blurring suggests permeability— that we, too, can find ways to enter into the picture. The colors are usually muted and gentle, inviting us into the picture. In Jacqueline Woodson's *The Other Side,* E. B. Lewis uses soft, blurred colors and somewhat indistinct images in the distance, suggesting that there is more to the picture, that it goes on and on. Nothing is sharply delineated, so we can go beyond what is on the page to imagine what might be beyond the fence.

Carole Byard's use of acrylic, with its thick, textured surface and evident brushstrokes, suggests that the child picking cotton has a rough, multilayered life that can't be seen at first glance.

(Cover illustration from WORKING COTTON by Sherley Anne Williams. Illustration copyright © 1992 by Carole Byard, reprinted by permission of Harcourt, Inc.)

Oil paint is powdered color mixed with linseed oil. Its heavy look is used to create texture, which gives a sense of depth and substance. Oil paint doesn't seem ethereal; it's not going to disappear, and you can't walk through it. ***Uncle Jed's Barbershop,*** written by Margaree King Mitchell and illustrated by James Ransome, provides a beautiful example of how oil can be used. Highlights on the people's faces, as well as the lines and colors, express a wide range of emotions. The rich jewel-like tones suggest the richness and depth of the lives of the people. The often-evident brushstrokes imply roughness and toughness—the fact that nothing has been smooth or easy.

Acrylic paint is powdered color mixed with water-based plastic. Like oil paint, acrylic paint can be applied thickly to create a textured surface. It is difficult for me to tell the difference between oil and acrylic. In the books I looked at, I did notice that some illustrations done in acrylic, such as Carole Byard's work in ***Working Cotton,*** by Sherley Anne Williams, are blurred or indistinct. Because acrylic has been put on thickly, the cotton in the background of the cover picture almost seems to rise up off the plants. The brushstrokes in the pictures suggest the roughness of the life the characters lead. In ***Something Is Growing,*** by Walter Lyon Krudop, the paint covers the page fully; the people are less distinct, and although the lines are apparent, the tree edges are a bit blurred. These pictures have a flat appearance because the paint does not appear to have been put on thickly.

Printmaking

Printmaking is a time-consuming process that is used only occasionally today because of advances in printing technology. The artist creates a backward image on a surface such as wood, linoleum, metal, or cardboard. This surface is then inked and pressed against paper so that the image is transferred to the paper. Most of the earliest children's books were illustrated with wood prints, but the process is used by only a few artists today. By using wood prints to illustrate ***A Gardener's Alphabet,*** Mary Azarian created substantial images with definite lines. This medium yields a direct look and a very sharp effect.

Collage

Collages are made by attaching bits of paper, cloth, or other materials to a flat surface such as paper. Cut-paper collage often produces crisp pictures with clean lines. Colors are usually solid and uniform, giving illustrations a straightforward look devoid of subtleties. Although the technique sounds simple on the surface, it can be very complex, as Debra Frasier, author and illustrator of ***Out of the Ocean,*** explains in the Illustration Notes at the end of the book. She says, "The illustrations include photocopies of these photographs [of life along the beach], still-life photographs, and two kinds of cut paper—Canson paper for the flat color and hand-embellished pastepaper for the waves." Producing the images incorporating shells, sea glass, and other actual objects took several steps. "Each page of objects was first arranged in a tray of sand and photographed, carefully leaving space for the later addition of other elements. These still-life images were then combined with photographic images of the paper cutouts. Finally, the framed illustrations of the silhouetted figures were added, along with the text."

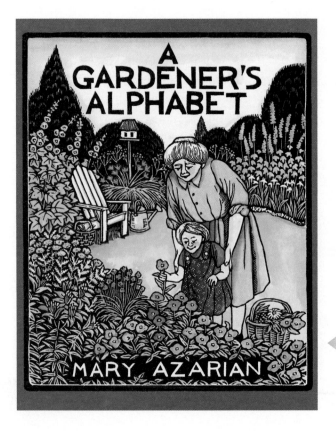

Through distinct lines, which outline every aspect of the image, the woodcuts created by Mary Azarian convey a very definite impression.

(Cover, from A GARDENER'S ALPHABET by Mary Azarian. Jacket Art © 2000 by Mary Azarian. Reprinted by permission of Houghton Mifflin Company. All rights reserved.)

The back and front covers of Frasier's *Out of the Ocean,* done in mixed media collage, include the ocean and cut-paper flowers and waves, all photographed against a box of sand to create a sense of the variety and beauty of the ocean.

(Cover illustration from OUT OF THE OCEAN, copyright © 1998 by Debra Frasier, reprinted by permission of Harcourt, Inc.)

Photography

Most frequently used in nonfiction books, photography has recently found its way into more children's fiction. Photography can give the viewer a feeling of intense realism; sometimes the subjects seem to be looking out at us. *Stranger in the Woods,* by Carl R. Sams II and Jean Stoick, is a photographic fantasy in which wildlife often stares directly out of the page. Capturing these shots obviously took great patience, for the animals are shown coming close to and then nibbling on the vegetable parts of a snowman. In this delightful book, the concept of creating a fictional piece around photographs of wildlife works well.

Mixed Media

Whenever two or more of the above media are employed, the artist is said to be using mixed media. Artists are always exploring the endless possibilities for combining media to create visual effects. Janet Stevens, illustrator of *To Market, To Market,* by Anne Miranda, uses acrylic, oil, pastel, and colored pencil along with photographic and fabric collage elements to create the bright but chaotic effects throughout the book. In *Verdi,* Janell Cannon uses acrylic and colored pencil to help us see the lushness of the jungle habitat. Dom Lee applies encaustic beeswax to paper, then scratches out images, and finally adds oil paint and colored pencil to create the stark but poignant images in *Passage to Freedom: The Sugihara Story,* by Ken Mochizuki. In *Black Cat,* Christopher Myers combines photography with collage, ink, and gouache to create stunning, unusual effects that make the reader want to look closer. Myers began with photographs that he took in Harlem and in his Brooklyn neighborhood. The very textured look created by the mixing of media and the unusual composition of the pictures makes the viewer realize the complexity and depth of the city. It makes us aware that simply by looking at the surface we cannot see the city in all the ways the black cat does.

This information about different media and their effects will become more important to you, and thus be easier to remember, if you have the chance to try some of them for yourself

A PHOTOGRAPHIC FANTASY

Stranger in the Woods

Carl R. Sams II & Jean Stoick

This photograph of deer examining a snowman is so intense that you feel as if you were right there. (Photography © 2000 Carl Sams from *Stranger in the Woods.* Reproduced by permission of Carl Sams.)

Combining photography of the city with ink and gouache paintings allows Christopher Myers to render a complicated, textured view of the city.
(From BLACK CAT by Christopher Myers. Copyright © 1999 by Christopher Myers. Reprinted by permission of Scholastic Inc.)

and see what effects they can produce. Understanding the possibilities of various media can help us as teachers to see how art and words work together to make an impact on readers.

Styles of Artists

Style refers to particular manners of artistic expression that have developed over time and can be defined by broad characteristics. It also refers to the features in an artist's work that make it recognizable and distinctive. Identifying styles is a way to categorize types of art so that we can talk about them more easily.

Artists don't start out thinking about style; they start out thinking about the subject and the impact they want to make. When they set out to illustrate a book, they look for the emotional nuances. Javaka Steptoe (1999) explains that, before he created the illustrations for **In Daddy's Arms I AM TALL: African Americans Celebrating Fathers,** he read each poem over and over again. Then he worked to capture the feeling through his art. David Diaz (1998) talks about looking closely at the art of William Steig and realizing that Steig's technique was subsumed by meaning: "I drew a parallel between what he did and where I was with my background in the super-realist movement. I thought, what's really important here is the essence of what's there, not just the technique" (p. 4).

Understanding the terminology used to describe artists' styles is not essential for appreciating and responding to illustrations in picture books. But this terminology does give us a shorthand with which to discuss the visual in books. If we were struggling to explain why the art in Faith Ringgold's **Tar Beach** was so striking and what was so different about it, we could start by explaining that it was done in the naive style. This label would tell the listener that the pictures were drawn one-dimensionally and simply, often appearing as if they could have been drawn by a child. Knowing the names of styles can help us to explain what we are responding to so that our listeners can picture what we are talking about. The following categories encompass the styles most commonly used in children's picture books.

Realism

Realistic, or representational, style is usually the easiest to recognize, since the artist is working to show things the way they really look. Oftentimes illustrations done in this style have an almost photographic quality. The shapes are recognizable, and the objects are in the proper perspective and proportion. Mike Wimmer's illustrations in **All the Places to Love,** by Patricia MacLachlan, are representative of this style. His artwork is precisely rendered, with great attention to detail. Other artists known for painting realistically are Jerry Pinkney, Floyd Cooper, and Allen Say.

Expressionism

In the expressionistic style, artists represent their emotional, subjective responses to the subject. Abstractions are often used to highlight what artists see as the essence of their reality. This style is widely used in picture books. Excellent examples include the artwork in Sharon Dennis Wyeth's **Always My Dad** (illustrated by Raúl Colón), Vera B. Williams's **A Chair for My Mother,** and Sherry Garland's **The Lotus Seed** (illustrated by Tatsuro Kiuchi).

Impressionism

The impressionistic style was developed by French painters of the nineteenth century who used dabs of color to re-create the sense of constant changes in light and color. Because they were concerned with changing effects, they worked to capture the subjective, sensory impression of a scene or object rather than a sharp, detailed description of it. In impressionistic work, figures might seem blurred or marginal, colors might be placed next to each other to suggest a mingling or mixing of colors. It is as if the contours of reality were softened. E. B. Lewis (whose drawing appears on page 44), Ed Young, and Peter Catalanotto often paint in this style.

This crisp, photo-like painting from *All the Places to Love* is so realistic that viewers have a sense of witnessing this scene filled with obvious warmth and caring.
(COPYRIGHT © 1994 BY MIKE WIMMER. Used by permission of HarperCollins Publishers.)

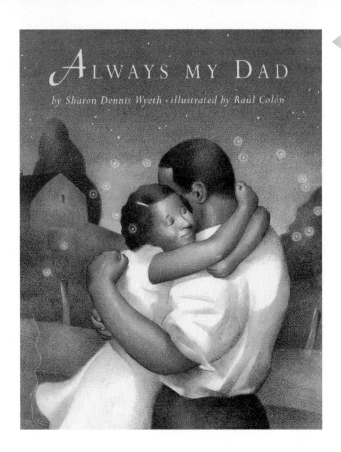

Intense love leaps from this image, done in the expressionistic style.

("Cover illustration" by Raúl Colón, copyright © 1994 by Raúl Colón, from ALWAYS MY DAD by Sharon Dennis Wyeth. Used by permission of Alfred A. Knopf Children's Books, a division of Random House, Inc.)

Surrealism

In the surrealistic style, realistic images are given an unreal or almost dreamlike quality, often through unnatural or unexpected juxtapositions of objects and people. Sometimes the image is photographically represented with very precise details, but what you see couldn't happen. For instance, in Anthony Browne's **Voices in the Park,** the trees and shrubs reflect the characters' outlook and mood. One character sees trees with little foliage, while another sees the same trees bursting with blooms. In David Wiesner's **Tuesday,** we see very realistic frogs on lily pads, except they are flying! So, although the pictures look very real, they are actually surreal because they simply could not happen in the natural world.

Naive Art and Folk Art

Naive and folk art styles are similar in that they are both pre-perspective—that is, all people and objects appear flat and one-dimensional. Naive art simplifies what is seen and experienced. Tomie dePaola's work is largely done in naive style, as is Faith Ringgold's. David Diaz often paints in the naive style, as he does in Eve Bunting's **Smoky Night.** There is much variation in folk art style, since it reflects the aesthetic values of the culture from which it comes. The use of color, stylized patterns, and simple shapes seem to permeate the folk art style.

CD-ROM

To locate illustrators whose style is *surrealistic,* search for the term in Favorite Authors.

Anthony Browne paints surrealistic images in which the objects surrounding a character represent how the character views the world. In this case, the little girl viewing a mother and son on a park bench sees the world in positive, fruitful ways.

(Reprinted from *Voices in the Park,* copyright © 1998 Anthony Browne. Permission granted by Dorling Kindersley, Inc.)

The naive style used in this image by David Diaz, with its flat, one-dimensional people, simplifies what is seen and thus focuses viewers' attention on the emotional content of the picture.
(Cover illustration of *Smoky Night* by Eve Bunting, copyright © 1994 by David Diaz, reproduced by permission of Harcourt, Inc.)

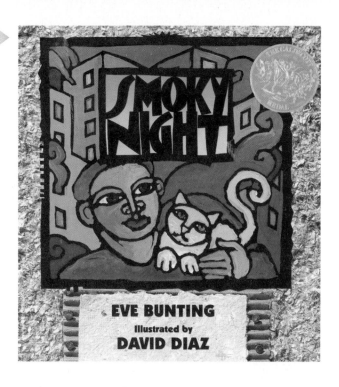

Cartoon Art

Cartoon art is easily recognizable by the use of lines to create exaggerated characters. Cartoon art is used in humorous books and also to lighten a heavy subject. James Stevenson, William Steig, and James Marshall, all masters of this style, use cartoon art to express an amazing range of emotions.

This information on style was provided to help you develop a vocabulary that gives quick ways to talk about illustrations. You have probably already noticed, as you have looked at picture book illustrations, that there is a great deal of overlap in these styles and many illustrations cannot be neatly placed into a category. If this terminology is helpful in describing illustrations, use it. If you find that it interferes with your ability to describe or even respond to a book, don't use it. Sometimes I find myself working very hard to figure out what style a book is drawn in, and I have to admit that this takes me away from the book and isn't productive. So, remember that the point of this information is not to categorize all the picture books you read by style. Artists rarely talk about their style in terms of these categories, which they believe are simply labels overlaid onto their work when it is finished. Using the vocabulary of style is important only if it helps you to describe to yourself and others what you are seeing.

Here are some questions you can ask about illustrations to get at style: Do they have an almost photographic quality? Do the images seem blurry and indistinct, or are they sharp and crisp? Is there a lack of perspective in the pictures, making everything seem flat? Are they cartoonish?

Evaluating the Art

When I evaluate and respond to art in picture books, I first look to see if it invites me in and delights me and makes me want to look closer. Then I look to see how it extends and works with the story. Answering the following four questions is a good place to begin in evaluating the artwork in a picture book.

1. Does it delight and involve you? Babette Cole's books, which she both writes and illustrates, are absolutely delightful. Her whimsical cartoons reflect her rather irreverent attitudes. For instance, in *The Trouble with Mom,* we first see mom wearing a tall, pointy black hat that has a mouse looking off of it and a snake wound around it. Mom also has skull-and-bones earrings, a tattered dress, and unruly hair. On the second full-page spread, we can clearly see that the trouble with mom is that she is a witch, since she takes her child to school on a broomstick!

Richard Egielski's *Buz* is another delightful book. His unusual perspectives, his bright colors, and his clean and uncluttered composing style are very appealing. The pictures on the first pages draw the reader right in. A very large hand holds a spoon that contains not only cereal, but also a bug. The spoon is being put into a very large mouth, and we can see the tonsils as well as the teeth. We wonder right away what will happen to the bug.

Likewise, *To Market, To Market,* written by Anne Miranda and illustrated by Janet Stevens, delights and intrigues the reader immediately. A woman with a large pig in her grocery basket is just something you don't expect to see. The artist surprises us with the look on the pig's face as well as the frazzled actions of the woman shopper. The backgrounds of both the market and the home are done in black and white so that the woman and her pig take center stage.

Wonderful examples of art in children's literature from 1870 to 1920 can be found at Children's Literature—The Art Gallery at www.arts.uwaterloo.ca/ENGL/courses/engl208c/gallery.htm.

Richard Egielski's provocative placement of the bug, Buz, immediately captures the reader's interest and raises questions that beg for an answer. (© 1995 by Richard Egielski. Used by permission of HarperCollins Publishers.)

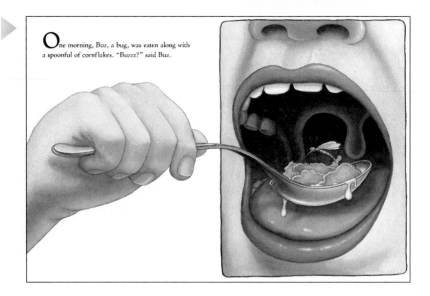

One morning, Buz, a bug, was eaten along with a spoonful of cornflakes. "Buzzz?" said Buz.

How does the artist delight and involve you? Some of the techniques artists use to delight and involve readers include juxtaposing objects and/or kinds of art (putting unlike things next to each other), putting in things we don't expect to see (such as a little girl flying in Faith Ringgold's *Tar Beach*), giving animals human characteristics (as in the work of William Steig and Anthony Browne), using pictures that immediately raise a question (such as the bug sitting on the spoon in *Buz*), showing things from different perspectives (as in Eric Rohmann's art in *Time Flies*), and causing strong feelings to jump out at us (see Dom Lee's little boy with soulful eyes in *Passage to Freedom: The Sugihara Story,* by Ken Mochizuki).

2. Does the artist pick moments that are highly visual? Showing someone in the process of thinking is of little value. As Susan Avanti (in Wolf and Balick, 1999) tells us, if an illustrator can find a way of depicting thought visually, "Even then it cannot be the highest point of action because an illustrator would risk completing it for the reader, instead of enhancing the author's words. We don't want to do it all for them. . . . Additionally illustrators don't want to cover too much. We want to find one moment that can help a reader along the way." She thinks of her task as similar to that of a movie director, because she determines how one line moves into the next or how one scene becomes another: "[W]e are always assessing where would the 'camera' be" (p. 130).

Tatsuro Kiuchi's artwork for Sherry Garland's *The Lotus Seed* does these things. In this story about a family from Vietnam, the first page shows the emperor mourning, with his hand across his face, next to the words "My grandmother saw the emperor cry the day he lost his golden dragon throne." Each picture grabs a few words from the text and illuminates them. Later in the book, when the grandmother once again finds her beautiful lotus and talks to her grandchildren about it, all the reader sees is the beauty of the blossom "unfurling its petals, so creamy and soft." By showing the beauty of the blossom instead of the actions of the characters, the art emphasizes the importance of the flower to the grandmother. Not too much is shown—just enough to make an impact on the reader. The illustrator was very conscious of selecting highly visible moments.

Deciding what image will represent each group of words is one of the most difficult but most creative parts of the illustrator's job. Finding the best moments in the text to illustrate is the mark of an excellent illustrator.

Some of the ways we can tell if an artist has picked the best moments to illustrate are if the illustrations flow seamlessly without jarring us, if the text and the pictures match in mood and tone, and if nothing seems inappropriate or out of place.

3. Does the artwork enhance the author's words? When I think of illustrations that almost tell a story within a story, I think of Sarah Stewart's *The Gardener,* illustrated by

The view of the young emperor, grieving and alone, gives emotional power to the words in the text and is an excellent example of an artist's picking a highly visible moment to illustrate.
(Illustration from THE LOTUS SEED by Sherry Garland, illustrations copyright © 1993 by Tatsuro Kiuchi, reprinted by permission of Harcourt, Inc.)

David Small. The delicately drawn and tinted pictures tell the story of Lydia Grace, who has to live with an uncle in the city because her folks are not making ends meet in the country. The pictures do more than illustrate the text; they augment our understanding of the story. For instance, we can see that her uncle almost always has a scowl on his face. It's obvious from the pictures that the uncle cares for Lydia Grace but doesn't know how to say so or show it. That is why the last picture, unaccompanied by words, is so powerful. At the train station, as she is getting ready to return home after almost a year with him, he kneels down, enfolds her in his arms, and lays his head on her shoulder. The caring he feels toward her comes out in that picture. Another way the illustrator extends the story is by weaving the cat into the pictures even before he is mentioned. Then at the end, again with no mention in the text, we see that Uncle Jim is letting Lydia Grace take the cat back home with her. These illustrations certainly contribute to and deepen the meaning of the story.

Some of the ways an artist can extend the text are by adding details to the picture; adding objects not referred to in the text; capturing the emotional qualities of the story; introducing ethnic or cultural details that support and enrich the text (as is done by such artists as Michael Lapaca and Paul Goble); conveying a definite sense of time, place, or ethnicity (James Ransome's artwork in **Uncle Jed's Barbershop,** by Margaree King Mitchell, does all three); dramatizing what the author tells us about the character (Helen Oxenbury's black-and-white drawings of the baby in Trish Cooke's **So Much** show us his adorable, exuberant personality); and using black-and-white pictures or backgrounds to contrast with color pictures (Chris K. Soentpiet does this in **So Far from the Sea,** written by Eve Bunting, in which the illustrations representing the past are in black and white while those in the present are in color).

4. Is there variety in the work? Does the perspective change? Is the composition different from page to page? **Follow the Moon,** written by Sarah Weeks and illustrated by Suzanne Duranceau, provides a wonderful example of variety. This simply told story takes place entirely on the beach, where a little boy remains with a just-hatched turtle until the turtle knows what he has to do next. The first page consists of text in a frame with a border around it, followed by a gorgeous double-page spread with no words, showing turtles heading into the sea. The next picture focuses directly on the little turtle, who is still partly in his shell. The text is set within a frame with the same border throughout, while the facing pictures extend out to the edges of the page. In the next picture, a little boy is looking down at the struggling turtle as we look down on the boy. Another full-page picture of the turtle still partially in his shell follows. Then we see the little boy up close, looking at the turtle, followed by a double-page spread of the little boy sitting high on his folded-up blanket, looking down at the little turtle, with the water and sky in the background. Next the little boy is rolled up in his blanket, ready to sleep with the turtle, and the angle of the picture makes us feel as if we were lying next to the child. The illustrator keeps our interest by putting each picture at a different distance from us and often giving us a different perspective. Sometimes the turtle is up close, looking right at us, and other times he is shown at a distance. Sometimes we are looking down on the picture, other times we are on the same

David Small's ability to enhance and extend the story through his art is demonstrated in this double-page spread. Occurring after the story told through the text is over, it is a tangible representation of Uncle Jim's love for Lydia.

(Excerpt from THE GARDENER by Sarah Stewart, illustrated by David Small. Pictures copyright © 1997 by David Small. Reprinted by permission of Farrar, Straus and Giroux, LLC.)

level as the picture, and still other times we seem to be looking up into the picture. It amazes me that the artist can keep us so interested in the story and the illustrations when the scene is a rather common one.

What does an artist do to create variety? An artist might create a frame around some pictures but leave other pictures unframed; use borders; mix media from page to page; change where shapes are placed in relation to each other; change where the text is placed in relation to the illustration; change the sizes of the objects from page to page; change the shading or the tones of the colors; or change the size of the illustration itself from quarter page to half page to full page to double-page spread.

Book Awards

A tool often used in selecting books is book awards. Although awards are helpful, it is important to know that selection committees are made up of individuals whose distinct values color their choices of best books. Awards such as the Newbery and the Caldecott carry great weight. They create excitement about a book and help distinguish it from the

Suzanne Duranceau keeps readers interested in this little turtle through her ability to show a range of perspectives, including this closeup of his head with his eye directed at us.
(ART COPYRIGHT ©1995 BY SUZANNE DURANCEAU. Used by permission of HarperCollins Publishers.)

thousands of other books published each year. Because awards put books in the public eye, award-winning books sell better. Almost every bookstore has a section called "Award-Winning Books," which alerts parents and other buyers of books that a committee has put its stamp of excellence on these particular works. This status inspires confidence in teachers, librarians, and other buyers, and thus these books are more often used in the classroom. Two questions come up about classroom use: "What makes these books good?" and "What do these awards mean in terms of what children learn about the world?" Both questions will be addressed in the following discussion.

The Award Selection Process

Just as you and I weigh different factors in our evaluation of books, so too do committees that are selecting an award-winning book. The Caldecott and Newbery awards, the best-known awards for children's books, each have a committee made up of fifteen people who must agree on the selection of a single winner as most outstanding book. Similarly, the Hans Christian Andersen Award committee is made up of fifteen people, representing many countries. Every two years, they give an award internationally for the body of work by a single author.

In reflecting on her four terms as chair of the Andersen Award committee (from 1987 to 1994), Eva Glistrup (1994) explained that each juror comes to the task from a unique perspective, which depends on his or her cultural and professional background, personal taste, view of children and childhood, view of children's literature, and sense of humor or lack of it. Even though aesthetic standards and value structures differ significantly across the different nations and cultural heritages, the group still is able to select a winner.

Juror Maria Antonieta Cunha from Brazil wanted books not only to appeal to children but also to attract and hold her attention. She wanted the aesthetic qualities of the work to take precedence over any moralizing intentions of the author. Originality—surprise, newness, paths never taken before—was important to her. She also believed that characters had to be credible, not stereotyped, and capable of capturing and sustaining the interest of the reader.

Further, the story must not contain prejudices which might lead to a lack of comprehension or respect toward what is different.

Another juror on the same committee, Ruth Mehl of Argentina, sought books that affirmed human values such as peace, understanding, justice, freedom, and the inherent value and richness of differences between races and cultures. The need for love, friendship, and honesty was present in the books she believed were excellent. She wanted to see these values interwoven in a text that brought joy and aesthetic pleasure, that promoted the exercise of critical thinking. Through the promotion of these values, she wanted children to find themselves represented, to have a voice that spoke for them. She wanted stories or poems that made sense, told something truly unforgettable, captured our emotions, and stimulated our reflection. She looked for authors who created characters that became lovable or despicable and went on living with the readers; she wanted these characters to take on some little piece of childhood's predicament so that the reader would gain through vicarious experience. She concluded her discussion by saying: "Finally I would demand from an Andersen Award winner some kind of emotion and magic. I do not know beforehand how this is going to come into play or where it will be appropriate, but I am sure I will recognize the occasion when it comes" (p. 60).

A third juror, Jeff Garrett from the United States, ended his list of criteria by saying: "We need to keep in mind that by giving this award to an individual writer or illustrator we are sending messages to the world about what we see as great writing and illustrative art for children, and only secondarily for ourselves. . . . Finally I think the 'politics' we must be aware of have to do with our perceptions of the social conscience of the author and depth of social and political responsibility this writer imparts to young readers, not the politics represented by a writer's government" (pp. 60–61).

It's easy to see, just from examining the criteria a few members of one committee share, that the impact a book has, the values embedded in it, and the significance of the topic are central. It's also evident that there is no such thing as total objectivity in evaluating books.

Looking at Award-Winning Books

As you can see from the statements made by just three jurors of the Andersen Award committee, each person brings to the committee his or her own experiences and tastes. Thus, committees vary year to year in how they define excellence. Because award winners are held up as models of excellence, they should be able to withstand close scrutiny. One way to judge their merits is to look at them in terms of literary considerations, educational considerations, and sociopolitical considerations.

We can be fairly sure that these award winners have exemplary literary qualities, since that is the major concern of the selection committee. However, as we can see from just a glimpse at the standards that three members of the Hans Christian Andersen Award committee brought with them, educational and sociopolitical qualities are also important. Studies have been done over the years of both Newbery and Caldecott winners, and both have on occasion been found to be lacking in educational and sociopolitical qualities, sometimes even promoting stereotypes.

Peggy Albers (1996) has expressed concern about whether award-winning books attend to the pluralism and democracy that schools strive for. She looked closely at Caldecott literature to see which groups wield power and which ethnic groups are represented and how. She believes that award-winning picture books "need to be examined in light of whose knowledge is considered the best and whose lives are being represented in these books" (p. 269). She looks past the issue of how many times groups are represented and instead examines the representations created. Albers found that the "roles and representations tend to be quite traditional. . . . The roles dominated by white males continue to be more positive and exciting, while many of the roles of females and people of color are traditional, stereotyped, and/or negative" (p. 278).

Although we can count on the literary quality of award-winning books, Albers's research suggests that we have to look carefully at what these books teach about people and whom they show as important. The boxed feature Criteria for Evaluating Award-Winning

Take a look at how Newbery Award winners have been ranked across the years at **Newbery Books Ranked** *at www.acpl.lib.in.us/Childrens_ Services/newberyranking.html.*

Books is intended to provide you with the tools you need to evaluate award-winning books, as well as other books.

Kinds of Awards

Book awards are created to draw attention to books. The best-known awards are the Newbery Award, given to the best-written children's book, and the Caldecott Award, given to the artist of the most distinguished picture book. Both the Newbery and the Caldecott have a long history of favoring the genre of fiction; nonfiction and poetry rarely win. Poetry awards and nonfiction awards have evolved to recognize outstanding books in these genres. Likewise, groups that were not often included as winners and admirers of genres not usually represented have sought to draw attention to the excellent books in their areas by instituting awards.

The Newbery Award is presented by the American Library Association to the author of the book chosen as the most distinguished contribution to American literature for children published the previous year in the United States. The author must be a citizen or resident of the United States. After the winner is chosen, the committee decides whether to name honor books and, if so, how many.

CD-ROM

Award-winning authors cited in Favorite Authors on the CD-ROM can be found by searching for the word *award-winning.*

Criteria for Evaluating *Award-Winning Books*

Literary Considerations:

1. **Plot.** What drives the plot and keeps the reader interested? How do conflicts unfold? Is the plot rich and multilayered? Is the story unforgettable?

2. **Character.** What makes the characters memorable? Will these characters go on living with you? Did you live through a vicarious experience with a character? Is there an absence of stereotyping?

3. **Setting.** Can you enter the setting easily? Is it woven into the story?

4. **Theme.** Are the themes significant ones? Were they worked into the plot, or does the author moralize?

5. **Style—qualities of writing.** Is a strong voice apparent? Does the writing make an impact through careful choice of words, descriptions, dialogue, and figurative language?

6. **Aesthetic qualities.** What is original about this book? What makes it pleasing? Is there some kind of emotion or magic in the book?

Educational Considerations:

1. What do readers learn about people and about the world?

2. What traits of people are emphasized?

3. Whose knowledge is considered best?

4. Does this book introduce your students to groups of people they may not be familiar with?

5. Is the theme one that would involve or interest your students?

6. What could your students gain from reading this book? What do you consider to be extremely strong about the book?

7. What questions do you have about this book as an award winner? Do you believe it merits the award it won?

Sociopolitical Considerations:

1. Which groups are represented in the book? Which are left out?

2. Is a range of characters represented? What kinds of roles do they have?

3. Is a range of socioeconomic levels represented? How is each group represented?

4. Who is shown to have power? What is the power based on?

*For links to the major children's book awards, look at **Children's Book Awards and Other Literary Prizes** at http://falcon.jmu.edu/~ramseyil/awards.htm.*

The Caldecott Award is given by the American Library Association to the artist of the book deemed the most distinguished contribution to American literature for children published the previous year in the United States. The artist must be a citizen or resident of this country. Once the winner is chosen, the committee decides whether to name any honor books and, if so, how many.

The Aesop Prize is awarded by the American Folklore Society to the most outstanding book or books incorporating folklore and published in English for children or young adults. The Aesop Prize committee compiles a useful Aesop Accolade List, an annual roster of exceptional books among Aesop Prize nominees.

The Jane Addams Children's Book Award is given by the Women's International League of Peace and Freedom to recognize the children's book from the preceding year that most effectively promotes the cause of peace, social justice, and world community. Books geared to children of any age, preschool to high school, are eligible, including translations and titles published in English in other countries.

The Américas Award for Children's and Young Adult Literature is sponsored by the National Consortium of Latin American Studies Programs. It is given in recognition of U.S. works of fiction, poetry, folklore, or selected nonfiction (from picture books to works for young adults) published in the previous year in English or Spanish that authentically and engagingly portray Latin America, the Caribbean, or Latinos in the United States. Winners are selected for their distinctive literary quality; cultural contextualization; exceptional integration of text, illustration, and design; and potential for classroom use.

The Mildred L. Batchelder Award was established by the American Library Association to recognize American publishers for issuing quality children's books in translation. The award is given not to the author, illustrator, or translator, but to the publisher. The book must be an outstanding work of literature, it must have a good overall design, the original illustrations must have been retained, and the text must reflect the flavor of the original work and not be unduly "Americanized."

The Pura Belpré Award, established in 1996, is given biennially to a Latino/Latina author and illustrator who best portray, affirm, and celebrate the Latino cultural experience through their outstanding books for children.

The Boston Globe–Horn Book Award is presented jointly by the *Boston Globe* newspaper and the *Horn Book* magazine to recognize excellence in literature for children and young adults. Awards are given to a picture book, a work of fiction, and a work of nonfiction. Like the Newbery and the Caldecott, the award can be given only to a book published in the United States, but unlike the Newbery and Caldecott, it may be given to a book written by a citizen of any country.

The Coretta Scott King Awards, established in 1970, are presented to authors and illustrators of African descent whose distinguished books promote an understanding and appreciation of the "American Dream." Since 1980, this award has been affiliated with the American Library Association.

The NCTE Poetry Award for Excellence was established in 1977 by the National Council of Teachers of English to honor a living American poet for his or her aggregate work. Originally awarded annually, since 1982 it has been awarded only once every three years. The NCTE website has a description of what the group is looking for in the winner: "In short, we're looking for a poet who can write clean, spare lines; use language and form in fresh ways; surprise the reader by using syntax artistically; excite the reader's imagination with keen perspectives and sharp images; touch the reader's emotions. A maker of word events is what we're looking for."

The Scott O'Dell Historical Fiction Award is presented by the American Library Association annually to a work of historical fiction published by a U.S. publisher and set in the New World. This award is named after the highly respected author of children's historical fiction. A list of O'Dell Award winners may be particularly helpful to teachers who want to use children's literature to enhance the social studies curriculum.

The Orbis Pictus Award for Outstanding Nonfiction for Children is given by the National Council of Teachers of English to a nonfiction or informational book that meets their criteria of being outstanding in accuracy, organization, design, and writing. In addition, the book should be useful in the classroom, encourage thinking and more reading, model exemplary expository writing and research skills, share interesting and timely subject matter, and appeal to a wide range of students.

The Edgar Allan Poe Award, instituted in 1945 by the Mystery Writers of America, is given to distinguished works in various categories of the genre. The two categories for children's books are the Best Juvenile and the Best Young Adult mystery.

The Michael L. Printz Award, instituted in 2000 by the American Library Association, celebrates outstanding literature for young adults and honors the late Michael L. Printz, a Topeka, Kansas, school librarian. The winning book, which can be fiction, nonfiction, poetry, or an anthology, must exemplify literary excellence.

The Kate Greenaway Medal, instituted in 1956, is awarded by The [British] Library Association annually for the most distinguished work in the illustration of children's books published in the United Kingdom.

The Carnegie Medal is awarded annually by The [British] Library Association for an outstanding book for children and young people. It was first won in 1936 by Arthur Ransome and has since been won by many of the great names in children's literature, including C. S. Lewis.

The Appendix contains a list of the winners of these awards from 1980 to 2002.

Selecting Books

Selecting books to use with children is a joyous task if you have the time to savor the reading of many books. If you love the literature you use, your passion and excitement will come across to the children, who like to see adults get excited about things! This is one way they have to measure how important things are to you. If you seem blasé about a book, children will get the message that literature isn't important or that it's not worth immersing themselves in. Use books that you love, and your students will love them too.

Katherine Paterson (2001), a Newbery Award–winning author, gives this advice:

- In general, look for plots that grip and satisfy, characters to deeply care about, a world you can believe in, a book worth all the trees that will sacrifice their lives to make it.

- Select a book for the joy of it, not for how you can "use" it. That's just a by-product. The first thing children should learn is the joy of books and what they can do for you.

- Never take anyone else's recommendation about a book you're going to use with students, because you know your kids better than anybody.

- You shouldn't be using a book you don't like or aren't comfortable discussing.

- There's a good reason to choose "hard books" because they give adults and children a place to talk, but only if the adult has carefully read them too. Never stop children from reading difficult books, but always be around when they finish.

In selecting books across the year for classroom use, I ask myself these questions: Do I love or value it? What is my purpose for using it—what is it I want students to know or appreciate? Are my students, with their backgrounds, interests, and age level, the right audience? Am I creating a balance as far as kinds of books selected and kinds of people portrayed? It is important to remember that, through the books we bring into the classroom, we teach students what is important to think about, talk about, write about, and draw.

Value

Every book you share with a child reflects what you value. I want children to be aware of beauty in the world and in their natural surroundings. I want children to be stimulated and amazed by what they read so that they will become even more curious about the world. I want children to learn that this whole world is interconnected and that their actions can have an impact on everyone. I want children to love learning and see its personal value to them. I want them to feel that they are learning for themselves, not for someone else. I want children to be aware of social justice issues and why picking on others or bullying others can end up hurting us all (**Heroes,** by Ken Mochizuki, would effectively do this). I want children to be aware of stereotypical thinking and to see people as individuals, not part of some "other" group. I want children to believe in their own goodness and that they are capable people. I want children to know that they each have individual talents and ways of doing things (**Max Found Two Sticks,** by Brian Pinkney, would be ideal for this).

Purpose

For every book you share with a child, you have a purpose. If it's a book to share with your own child, you may just want her to love reading and enjoy the nurturing that comes through being read to. In schools, these same purposes are still in operation, especially in the early grades. Sometimes the purpose is simply to share illustrations that you like or to read a story that gives you pleasure. Other reasons for selecting books are included below. Choose books

- so that children can learn about themselves and the world.

- to share with children an experience that they may not ever have had, such as going to the ocean.

- so that children can see themselves in books and know that they are OK.

- so that children can see that the world is not made up only of people like them.

- that will encourage children to delight in and love language and writing.

- that will stimulate good talk in the classroom.

- as models of writing.

- that will help children with their reading.

- so that children can see delightful or provocative or beautiful illustrations.

Audience

When you select books, you need to think about your audience. You need to reacquaint yourself with what it means to be a child, to rekindle those feelings of joy and wonder as you read, to think about what you liked and appreciated in a book and what you thought was funny. Books speak to children's reality: that now is everything, that unconscious fears can be overwhelming, that adults are powerful, and that the world is not always a safe place. Songs such as Fred Rogers's "You'll Never Go Down the Drain" and books such as Maurice Sendak's **Where the Wild Things Are** recognize children's fears. My selection of books is based on the needs, interests, and skill levels of the children. It's also based on qualities of the books that lend themselves to thoughtful discussions, discussions that not only enhance the children's enjoyment of the books but also nudge their understanding of concepts and their critical-thinking skills. This interaction with text can allow the teacher to better determine a child's zone of proximal development, thus allowing the teacher and peers to provide the support necessary for each child's learning. In the boxed feature Taking a Look at the Research: Vygotsky and Literature for Children, the summary of Vygotsky's work sheds some light on this aspect of children's interaction with text.

Remember to distinguish between what adults look for and what may delight and engage a child. Children love humor and enjoy seeing adults make mistakes. That's why they like **The Know-Nothings,** by Michele Sobel Spirn, an I-Can-Read book about three

Vygotsky and Literature for Children

*O*ne consideration in the selection and use of children's literature in the classroom is the child's readiness to understand the story content and concepts. Determining what a child is capable of handling in text is part of the ongoing assessment that teachers conduct continually with students. There are some benchmarks in development that, although not specifically applicable to every child, form a framework from which to begin.

The pedagogy of a literature-based practice arises out of the work and theories of Lev Vygotsky, a psychologist whose research took place during the early years of the twentieth century in Russia. Vygotsky began his career studying and critiquing European literature. An avid literary scholar, Vygotsky enjoyed the dialogue that evolved out of the reading of great literature and would have continued to publish a literary magazine if there hadn't been a shortage of paper in Russia at that time (van der Veer and Valsner, 1991). It comes as no surprise, then, that the theories that evolved out of his research as a psychologist should have such an impact on literacy.

First, Vygotsky saw language as the key to literacy and learning. He asserted that thought is determined by language and that "it is through social dialogue with adults and/or more capable peers that language concepts are learned" (Dixon-Krauss, 1996). Based on this theory, then, dialogue is critical. Classroom discussions of children's literature provide opportunities for children to engage in a socially mediated dialogue, which is important for the development of thinking, reading, and problem-solving skills.

Another important aspect of Vygotsky's theory is that of the zone of proximal development (ZPD). The ZPD is where learning takes place; it extends from what a child can do unassisted to what a child can do with assistance. The assistance given can be just a hint, or it can be significant and explicit. Discussions of the literature shared in the classroom offer the teacher the opportunity to work with each child in his or her ZPD. Within a literature-based reading program where reflective discourse is encouraged, each child will have the opportunity to learn not only from the teacher but also from other students.

Dixon-Krauss, Lisbeth (1996). *Vygotsky in the Classroom: Mediated Literacy Instruction and Assessment.* White Plains, NY: Longman.

van der Veer, Rene, and Jaan Valsner (1991). *Understanding Vygotsky: A Quest for Synthesis.* Cambridge, MA: Blackwell.

---

silly adults. Children also like to see children doing things well without adults knowing about it. That's why they like **The Weebie Zone** books, by Stephanie Spinner and Ellen Weiss, in which a boy bitten by his hamster can then understand animal language. Children respond to issues that are important to them. Issues of family, school, and friendship always seem to interest children. When looking at books, look for ways the books can connect to the child, to the child's world, or to other books.

In addition to finding themes and issues that might interest the targeted audience, also work to pick out books that fit with a child's reading level. Books that use words way over the head of the reader will not entice him or her to read further. Books that have some challenging words but have a context or pictures to provide support for the reader will work. Books with highly artificial sentence structure may prove frustrating. On the other hand, children react negatively to overly simplistic, stilted language. In selecting books, think about how the experience children have with the book will affect their reading development and attitudes.

Also ask yourself what the children will learn about themselves and the world through the books you present to them and what you are asking them to think about and pay attention to. Here your notions of children and what you think they are capable of will come into play. Someone who thought that children had no worries and were just happy little people would probably look only for books that wouldn't disturb their universe. But because of television, children are exposed to graphic images of war, natural disaster, violence, and sexuality. Favorite sports figures have AIDs, political figures have sex scandals, and popular actors and actresses discuss substance abuse. Children who see injustice, sexism, poverty, and fighting will be able to talk about very serious issues that are embedded in many aspects of their lives.

Balance

Balance across the year is another important criterion in selecting books. Students need to read in many genres, so bring in poetry books, nonfiction, fairy tales, fantasy, fiction, biographies, and sports books. Students need to read books about and by people of diverse backgrounds, so bring in books about Hmongs, American Indians, Asians, and Africans. Children need to see that the world is made up of people from various economic levels as well as various religious and ethnic backgrounds. Students should read books that do not just show boys and girls in stereotypical activities and roles, so bring in books that depict boys acting in caring ways and books that have girls as active protagonists. Bring in books that show mothers and fathers in nontraditional as well as traditional roles. To encourage students to read about many themes, bring in books about loss, love, pets, relationships, nature, family, and difference. Expose children to a variety of subject matter by finding books about math, social studies and science, as well as language arts. Let students experience many tones in books by bringing in some humorous books as well as some serious ones.

Other Elements to Consider

Although it can seem like a tall order to select books that will work in your classroom, remembering yourself as a child can help. When Ursula Nordstrom (in Marcus, 1998), children's book editor at Harpers, was asked what qualified her for her job, since she had never gone to college or written a book, she replied: "Well, I am a former child, and I haven't forgotten a thing!" (p. xxii). Her confidence and belief in herself and her implied understanding of what children would love in books are apparent.

We too can offer children much by connecting to our past as children and listening to what the children in our lives tell us and show us. Below, two other professionals discuss the elements they use to select books.

Jerome Harste (1998), literacy professor, writer, and National Council of Teachers of English (NCTE) past president, talked in a keynote address about how he and the teachers he works with look for books that will start critical curricular conversations. He encourages teachers to think not just about what concepts they want to teach, but also about what conversations they want kids to have. He says, "Curriculum is a metaphor for lives you want to live and people you want to be. What kind of people do we want to create? Create a classroom that gives our students that vision. Use the disciplines as ways to probe into the questions."

In their quest to involve students in meaningful books that will provoke those critical conversations, Harste and the classroom teachers he works with created the following five categories.

1. They don't make difference invisible, but rather explore what differences make a difference.

2. They enrich our understanding of history and life by giving voice to those who have traditionally been silenced or marginalized.

3. They show how people can begin to take action on important social issues.

4. They explore the dominant systems of meaning in society to position people and groups of people, serving some more than others.

5. They help us question why certain groups are positioned as "others."

Harste's purpose is very clear. He wants children to have meaningful, critical conversations that will put them in touch with their lives and their worlds. His values are also very evident. He wants children to be involved in thinking about people, caring about people, valuing difference, and wondering about our world. Harste offers text examples for each of his categories in the boxed feature Books That Invite Critical Conversations.

From 1996 to 1998, Shelley Harwayne, principal of Manhattan's New School, and her staff reviewed books for *The New Advocate*. The teachers were conscious of purpose as they

Books That Invite Critical Conversations

Understanding differences that make a difference

Bunting, Eve. Illus. David Diaz. *Going Home.*

Fox, Paula. *Radiance Descending.*

Lorbiecki, Marybeth. Illus. K. Wendy Popp. *Sister Anne's Hands.*

Martinez, Victor. *Parrot in the Oven: Mi Vida.*

Steptoe, John. *Creativity.*

Giving voice to those who have been marginalized or silenced

Bunting, Eve. Illus. Chris K. Soentpiet. *So Far from the Sea.*

Coleman, Evelyn. Illus. Tyrone Geter. *White Socks Only.*

Forrester, Sandra. *My Home Is Over Jordan.*

Hansen, Joyce. *Women of Hope: African Americans Who Made a Difference.*

Hirschi, R. Illus. Deborah Cooper. *People of Salmon and Cedar.*

Kaplan, William. Illus. Stephen Taylor. *One More Border: The True Story of One Family's Escape from War-Torn Europe.*

Parker, David L. *Stolen Dreams: Portraits of Working Children.*

Shange, Ntozake. Illus. Michael Sporn. *White Wash.*

Springer, Jane. *Listen to Us: The World's Working Children.*

Tillage, Leon Walter. *Leon's Story.*

Taking social action

Breckler, Rosemary. Illus. Deborah Kogan Ray. *Sweet Dried Apples: A Vietnamese Wartime Childhood.*

Dash, Joan. *We Shall Not Be Moved: The Women's Factory Strike of 1909.*

Fleischman, Paul. *Whirligig.*

McGuffee, Michael. Illus. Edward Sullivan. *The Day the Earth Was Silent.*

Miller, William. Illus. John Ward. *The Bus Ride.*

Mitchell, Margaree King. Illus. Larry Johnson. *Granddaddy's Gift.*

Mochizuki, Ken. Illus. Dom Lee. *Passage to Freedom: The Sugihara Story.*

Winslow, Vicki. *Follow the Leader.*

Understanding how systems of meaning in society position us

Bunting, Eve. Illus. James Ransome. *Your Move.*

Fletcher, Ralph. *Flying Solo.*

Hesse, Karen. *just Juice.*

Jiménez, Francisco. *The Circuit: Stories from the Life of a Migrant Child.*

Levy, Marilyn. *Run for Your Life.*

Lorbiecki, Marybeth. Illus. David Diaz. *Just One Flick of a Finger.*

Mora, Pat. Illus. Raúl Colón. *Tomás and the Library Lady.*

Spinelli, Jerry. *Wringer.*

Thomas, Rob. *Slave Day.*

Wolff, Virginia Euwer. *Bat 6.*

Examining distance, difference, and otherness

Abelove, Joan. *Go and Come Back.*

Ancona, George. *Mayeros: A Yucatec Maya Family.*

Browne, Anthony. *Voices in the Park.*

Dines, Carol. *Talk to Me: Stories and a Novella.*

Fleischman, Paul. Illus. Judy Pedersen. *Seedfolks.*

Walter, Virginia. Illus. Katrina Roeckelein. *Making Up Megaboy.*

Wilson, Nancy Hope. Illus. Marcy D. Ramsey. *Old People, Frogs, and Albert.*

---

selected books that they found worthy of being reviewed. They also asked: Does it open up substantial conversations? Does it contribute to delight in the language? Does its written quality provide models for children?

Their categories demonstrate the myriad goals they have for students throughout the day and the curriculum. "In general, the books are not chunked together because they share a common topic or theme but rather because somehow they called out to teachers or staff to be used in a similar manner in their classrooms" (Harwayne, 1996, p. 62).

In her first column, Harwayne told readers to expect to see such subheadings as

- Leading to Lively Conversations
- Supporting Beginning Readers
- Celebrating Language
- Enriching the Teaching and Learning of Science, Social Studies, and Mathematics
- For Your Poetry Shelf
- Immersing Students in the Spanish Language

The categories that Harwayne and her staff arrived at are not static or finite. "No doubt as we discover new literary treasures, and we design new ways to connect readers and writers with books we will invent new categories. We hope our readers will not view our categories as labels which stop their thinking, but as starting points for their own playful inventing of

*Find lists of books with advice about how to select books at **Basic Reference Tools for Children's Literature** at www.library.arizona.edu/users/ kwilliam/kiddy.html.*

On selecting books . . .

I flip to a page and if it looks good I'll take the book. —Megan, 2nd grade

I take it if the cover has a good drawing on it. —Taylor, 2nd grade

I read the not-true ones, the funny ones, the ones that look exciting. I look inside the book and see if it is good. —Chelsea, 2nd grade

I pick books by what I like. When I get to the library I think of something I like and then find a book about it. At home I pick books by the picture on the cover, by the title, and if it's my favorite. —Drew, 2nd grade

I pick books because I like the pictures, because of the titles, and because other people say they're good books. —Sara, 2nd grade

I pick books that I've watched the movie. —Stephen, 2nd grade

I pick books by looking at the first pages, looking for good words, and flipping through the pages. —Elizabeth, 2nd grade

I just pick a shelf and go to it and pick a book. —TJ, 2nd grade

If it looks interesting, if it doesn't look too hard, and if Kylie likes it too. —Sarah, 2nd grade

I pick books I've already heard before. —Meg, 2nd grade

I pick books because the cover looks cool or by looking at the pictures. —Jacob, 2nd grade

I read the book jackets. —Andy, 3rd grade

I read the back of the book and I open the book to the first page. Either one tells a lot. —Kate, 3rd grade

I either ask someone if it's a good book to read or I read the back of the book. —Steven, 4th grade

Little kids don't read titles to select books. When I take my little brother to the library the first thing he notices is the cover, where a colorful picture will capture his mind. —Jamie, 6th grade

If you pick my book, I don't like it. —Casey, 6th grade

I hate to say it but usually when I select a book I judge it by the cover. —Emily, 7th grade

I tend to go to a familiar author. —Julia, 7th grade

I read the title and if it sounds funny, or adventurous, or mysterious, I flip it over and read the back. If the title doesn't get me then I put it back. —Lori, 7th grade

I go by the catchy cover and if it catches my eye, then the back. I read it but don't judge a book by its cover. —Daina, 7th grade

I look at the beginning and also go by other people's reaction to the book. —Missy, 7th grade

I like ones with an interesting cover that is screaming "Read Me, Read Me." —Katie, 7th grade

Mostly I ask people who have the same interests as me. Other times I open the book and randomly read a page or two. If it is good I start at the beginning and read it. —Jennifer, 7th grade

thoughtful ways to connect with books" (p. 62). And indeed later columns included these subheadings:

- Novels for Older Students
- Fresh Formats for Young Writers
- Books to Grow Up On
- Picture Books Packed with Information
- Appreciating Memoirs and Biographies
- Adding to Our Read-Aloud Chapter Book Shelf
- If You Happen to Be Studying the Moon
- Celebrating City Life
- Books That Celebrate Young Artists and Writers
- Helping Writers See the Potential for Topics Everywhere
- Delighting in All That Is Eerie
- Picture Books for Multicultural Collections
- Books That Encourage Readers to Appreciate Their Natural Environment

Throughout the two years she and her staff did the column, every subhead was crammed with wonderful, useful descriptions of the books, often accompanied by comments by elementary students. As they read and thought about the books, they created new categories to show new ways of thinking that the books stimulated. Learning can never be neatly categorized, because it is complex and multidimensional. As you create your own categories, be sure to give yourself a lot of room for additions, since not every book you choose will fall into a neat category. But also be aware that you have reasons for the books you choose for your classroom and they are based on your beliefs about what is important for children to know.

Children also have various criteria they use when they select their own books, as the boxed feature Children's Voices shows.

Invitations

Choose several of the following activities to complete:

1. Select a stack of picture books from the library. After reading them, rank them from 1 to 10 in terms of how strongly they appeal to you, with 1 being the highest. Describe in your notebook how you feel when you look at each book and what you notice about the language, characters, plot, theme, and illustrations. What is the appeal of each book? What have you discovered about your preferences in picture books? For example, do you prefer funny, psychologically moving, socially provocative, or poetic books?

2. Styles of artwork include realism, surrealism, expressionism, impressionism, naive or folk art, and cartoon art. Form groups and select a style to present to the rest of your group. To prepare for the presentation, look at books in this style in the library and select three to five of the best ones to share with your group. In the presentation, talk about the way you respond to the style you are presenting, discuss what you noticed about it, etc. As group members share other styles, note what draws you to a style and what pushes you away. Why do certain styles seem more appropriate for particular subjects or themes?

3. Choose two picture books that use art effectively. Describe how the art and words work together. Then describe which media or techniques probably wouldn't work for this book and why.

4. Herbert Kohl (1995) said, "There has never been a period in my lifetime when it has been so urgent for children to know that there is more than one way to organize society, and understand that caring and cooperation are not secondary values or signs of weakness so much as affirmations of hope and life" (p. 93). What are Kohl's underlying values? Can you find books in your reading that you think would meet these goals? Create your own list of criteria for selecting books for your classroom. What are the overriding themes you're looking for?

5. Do a study of an artist. Glean information about the artist's style and the media the artist uses by reading several books illustrated by your artist. Evaluate the art, using the criteria in this chapter or other criteria you find more appropriate. Find biographical information on your artist by looking in Pat Cummings's three volume *Talking with Artists* or any other source you can locate. Do a presentation to your whole class, focusing on the major accomplishments or strengths of the artist.

6. Select Caldecott winners from a period of about ten years. Read the books and analyze them in terms of the trends they reflect.

7. Select a book from Harste's list of books that invite critical conversations (p. 63). Discuss it in your group in such a way that critical issues are raised. Record your reaction to the discussion in your notebook. What did this experience make you aware of as far as raising critical issues in a classroom?

8. After reading the research box Vygotsky and Literature for Children, share a memory of a time in your learning when, given assistance by other students or the teacher, you accomplished something you couldn't do before. Can you explain your own ZPD in terms of something you're currently trying to learn?

CD-ROM

To see further examples in Invitations and Classroom Teaching Ideas of how ranking can be used in the classroom, begin your search with the word *ranking*.

Classroom Teaching Ideas

1. To help your students understand that illustrations can convey feelings, have them take out their crayons and draw lines or shapes that would show that they were angry, that they were shy, that they were tired, and that they were happy. Then have them look at the strokes and colors used. Were the strokes thin and delicate or bold and broad? Were the colors soft or loud? Talk about their discoveries and how they can relate this information to the picture books they read.

2. To help students become aware of what influences them when selecting a book, use butcher paper to make a chart (which students could later turn into a graph) with three categories: picture, topic, author. When children select books from the library, ask each one whether they selected the book because of the pictures, because of the topic, or because it was written by an author they knew and liked. Have students add their name to the column corresponding to the factor that influenced them most.

3. After reading a picture book aloud with students, go back through the book with them and do some "picture reading." Ask students to look closely at the pictures to see what kinds of information they can get just from the pictures. Students enjoy commenting on details while they do this.

4. After students have written their own "book" or story, have them illustrate it in the style of an illustrator they admire. Give them time to go through your bookshelves or those in the library, looking for a book illustrated in a style that they would like to use for their own story. This provides students with a real reason to think about many elements of composition, such as whether they want their pictures to have a background, whether they want to put boxes or frames or borders around their pictures (as Jan Brett does) or just have the pictures come to the edge of the page, whether they want to use bright colors (as Eric Carle does) or dark colors, whether they want to use cut paper (as Lois Ehlert does) or paint, whether they want to use watercolor or poster paint. After the illustrations are complete, have the students talk about the choices they made.

5. Bring in a collection of works by different illustrators, and have the children identify the illustrator by the style or medium used. Eric Carle, Jerry Pinkney, Tomie dePaola, Brian Pinkney, Patricia Polacco, and Barbara Cooney are illustrators whose work is well suited for this activity. For added effect, you may wish to bring in Cooney's first book, which illustrates Chaucer's tale ***Chanticleer and the Fox.*** It has a very different style from her later works and will show students that artists can change their style or choice of medium.

Internet and Text Resources

1. Basic Reference Tools for Children's Literature includes lists of books about selecting books in all genres, as well as about using literature in classrooms. Find it at

www.library.arizona.edu/users/kwilliam/kiddy.html

2. David Brown's Website on Children's Literature has a part called Children's Book Awards, which provides links to sites containing the award winners in children's literature. Find it at

www.ucalgary.ca/~dkbrown/ala97.html

3. Children's Book Awards and Other Literary Prizes links not only to the major children's book awards but also to award-winning audiovisual materials, multicultural books, nonfiction, and poetry. Go to

http://falcon.jmu.edu/~ramseyil/awards.htm

4. The Art Gallery allows access to some wonderful art in children's literature from the 1870s to the 1920s. Find it at

www.arts.uwaterloo.ca/ENGL/courses/engl208c/gallery.htm

5. Database of Award-Winning Children's Literature allows users to search for books by ethnicity, genre, age, setting, and so on. It also has links to the award sites. Go to

www2.wcoil.com/~ellerbee/childlit.html

6. Newbery Books Ranked looks at the winners across the years and ranks them from top to bottom. This site could provoke great discussions. Go to

www.acpl.lib.in.us/Childrens_Services/newberyranking.html

7. Smith, Henrietta M. (1999). *The Coretta Scott King Award Book 1970–1999*. Chicago: American Library Association.

8. Association for Library Service to Children (1999). *The Newbery and Caldecott Awards: A Guide to the Medal and Honor Books*. Chicago: American Library Association.

References

Albers, Peggy (1996). "Issues of Representation: Caldecott Gold Medal Winners 1984–1995." *The New Advocate 9*, 267–285.

Carlson, G. Robert (1974). "Literature IS . . . ." *English Journal 63*, 23–27.

Cummings, Pat, ed. (1992). *Talking with Artists: Volume One*. New York: Bradbury.

—— (1995). *Talking with Artists: Volume Two*. New York: Simon & Schuster.

—— (1999). *Talking with Artists: Volume Three*. New York: Clarion.

Diaz, David (1998). "It's All About Process: Talking with David and Cecelia Diaz." *The New Advocate 12*, 1–9.

Glistrup, Eva (1994). "Comparing the Incomparable: The Work of the Hans Christian Andersen Jury, 1987–94." *Bookbird 32*, 55–63.

Greenberg, Jan, and Sandra Jordan (1991). *The Painter's Eye*. New York: Delacorte.

Harste, Jerome (1998). "Supporting Critical Conversations in Classrooms." Lansing, MI: Michigan Council of Teachers of English, Oct. 9, 1998.

Harwayne, Shelley (1996). "Weaving Literature into the School Community." *The New Advocate 9*, 61–74.

Horning, Kathleen (1997). *Cover to Cover: Evaluating and Reviewing Children's Books*. New York: HarperCollins.

Kohl, Herbert (1995). *Should We Burn Babar? Essays on Children's Literature and the Power of Stories.* New York: The New Press.

Marcus, Leonard S., ed. (1998). *Dear Genius: The Letters of Ursula Nordstrom.* New York: HarperCollins.

Paterson, Katherine (2001). "How to Choose Great Books for the Classroom." *NEA Today,* Vol. 19, No. 8 (May 2001), p. 26.

Steptoe, Javaka (1999). "Creating Images That Depict African American Lives." International Reading Association Conference, San Diego, May 2–7, 1999.

Wolf, Dennie Palmer, and Dana Balick, eds. (1999). *Art Works.* Portsmouth, NH: Heinemann.

Children's Books

Abelove, Joan (2000). *Go and Come Back.* New York: Puffin [1998, DK Publishing].

Ancona, George (1997). *Mayeros: A Yucatec Maya Family.* New York: Lothrop, Lee & Shepard.

Azarian, Mary (1999). *A Gardener's Alphabet.* Boston: Houghton Mifflin.

Breckler, Rosemary (1996). *Sweet Dried Apples: A Vietnamese Wartime Childhood.* Illus. Deborah Kogan Ray. Boston: Houghton Mifflin.

Browne, Anthony (1998). *Voices in the Park.* New York: DK Publishing.

Bunting, Eve (1996). *Going Home.* Illus. David Diaz. New York: HarperCollins.

—— (1994). *Smoky Night.* Illus. David Diaz. San Diego: Harcourt Brace.

—— (1998). *So Far from the Sea.* Illus. Chris K. Soentpiet. New York: Clarion.

—— (1998). *Your Move.* Illus. James Ransome. San Diego: Harcourt Brace.

Burleigh, Robert (1997). *Hoops.* Illus. Stephen T. Johnson. San Diego: Silver Whistle.

Cannon, Janell (1997). *Verdi.* San Diego: Harcourt Brace.

Chaucer, Geoffrey (1989). *Chanticleer and the Fox.* Illus. Barbara Cooney. New York: HarperTrophy [1958, Crowell].

Cole, Babette (1983). *The Trouble with Mom.* London: Windmill.

Coleman, Evelyn (1996). *White Socks Only.* Illus. Tyrone Geter. Morton Grove, IL: Whitman.

Cooke, Trish (1994). *So Much.* Illus. Helen Oxenbury. Cambridge, MA: Candlewick.

Dash, Joan (1996). *We Shall Not Be Moved: The Women's Factory Strike of 1909.* New York: Scholastic.

Dines, Carol (1997). *Talk to Me: Stories and a Novella.* New York: Delacorte.

Egielski, Richard (1995). *Buz.* New York: Geringer.

Fleischman, Paul (1998). *Seedfolks.* Illus. Judy Pedersen. New York: HarperCollins.

—— (1997). *Whirligig.* New York: Holt.

Fletcher, Ralph (1998). *Flying Solo.* New York: Clarion.

Forrester, Sandra (1997). *My Home Is Over Jordan.* New York: Lodestar.

Fox, Paula (1997). *Radiance Descending.* New York: DK Publishing.

Frasier, Debra (1998). *Out of the Ocean.* San Diego: Harcourt Brace.

Garland, Sherry (1993). *The Lotus Seed.* Illus. Tatsuro Kiuchi. San Diego: Harcourt Brace.

Hansen, Joyce (1998). *Women of Hope: African Americans Who Made a Difference.* New York: Scholastic.

Hesse, Karen (1998). *just Juice.* Illus. Robert Andrew Parker. New York: Scholastic.

Hirschi, R. (1996). *People of Salmon and Cedar.* Illus. Deborah Cooper. New York: Cobblehill.

Jiménez, Francisco (1998). *The Circuit: Stories from the Life of a Migrant Child.* Albuquerque: University of New Mexico Press.

Joosse, Barbara M. (1991). *Mama, Do You Love Me?* Illus. Barbara Lavallee. San Francisco: Chronicle.

Kaplan, William (1998). *One More Border: The True Story of One Family's Escape from War-Torn Europe.* Illus. Stephen Taylor. Toronto: Groundwood.

Krudop, Walter Lyon (1995). *Something Is Growing.* New York: Atheneum.

Lawrence, Jacob (1993). *The Great Migration: An American Story.* New York: HarperTrophy.

—— (1993). *Harriet and the Promised Land.* New York: Simon and Schuster.

Levy, Marilyn (1996). *Run for Your Life.* Boston: Houghton Mifflin.

Lorbiecki, Marybeth (1996). *Just One Flick of a Finger.* Illus. David Diaz. New York: Dial.

—— (1998). *Sister Anne's Hands.* Illus. K. Wendy Popp. New York: Dial.

MacLachlan, Patricia (1994). *All the Places to Love.* Illus. Mike Wimmer. New York: HarperCollins.

Martinez, Victor (1996). *Parrot in the Oven: Mi Vida.* New York: HarperCollins.

McGuffee, Michael (1997). *The Day the Earth Was Silent.* Illus. Edward Sullivan. Bloomington, IN: Inquiring Voices.

Miller, William (1998). *The Bus Ride.* Illus. John Ward. New York: Lee & Low.

Miranda, Anne (1997). *To Market, To Market.* Illus. Janet Stevens. San Diego: Harcourt Brace.

Mitchell, Margaree King (1997). *Granddaddy's Gift.* Illus. Larry Johnson. Mahwah, NJ: Bridgewater.

—— (1993). *Uncle Jed's Barbershop.* Illus. James Ransome. New York: Simon & Schuster.

Mochizuki, Ken (1995). *Heroes.* Illus. Dom Lee. New York: Lee & Low.

—— (1997). *Passage to Freedom: The Sugihara Story.* Illus. Dom Lee. New York: Lee & Low.

Mora, Pat (1997). *Tomás and the Library Lady.* Illus. Raúl Colón. New York: Knopf.

Myers, Christopher (1999). *Black Cat.* New York: Scholastic.

Palatini, Margie (1995). *Piggie Pie!* Illus. Howard Fine. New York: Hyperion.

Parker, David L. (1998). *Stolen Dreams: Portraits of Working Children.* Minneapolis: Lerner.

Pinkney, Andrea Davis (1998). *Duke Ellington.* Illus. Brian Pinkney. New York: Hyperion.

Pinkney, Brian (1997). *Max Found Two Sticks.* New York: Aladdin [1994, Simon & Schuster].

Ringgold, Faith (1996). *Tar Beach.* New York: Crown.

Rohmann, Eric (1991). *Time Flies.* New York: Crown.

Sams, Carl R., II, and Jean Stoick (2000). *Stranger in the Woods.* Milford, MI: Sams Photography.

Sendak, Maurice (1963). *Where the Wild Things Are.* New York: Harper.

Shange, Ntozake (1997). *White Wash.* Illus. Michael Sporn. New York: Walker.

Sheldon, Dyan (1997). *The Whales' Song.* Illus. Gary Blythe. New York: Puffin [1991, Dial].

Spinelli, Jerry (1997). *Wringer.* New York: HarperCollins.

Spinner, Stephanie, and Ellen Weiss (1997). *The Weebie Zone #3: Born To Be Wild.* New York: HarperTrophy.

Spirn, Michele Sobel (1995). *The Know-Nothings.* Illus. R. W. Alley. New York: HarperTrophy.

Springer, Jane (1997). *Listen to Us: The World's Working Children.* Toronto: Groundwood.

Steig, William (1999). *Toby, Where Are You?* Illus. Teryl Euvremer. New York: HarperCollins.

Steptoe, Javaka (1997). *In Daddy's Arms I AM TALL: African Americans Celebrating Fathers.* New York: Lee & Low.

Steptoe, John (1997). *Creativity.* Illus. E. B. Lewis. New York: Clarion.

Stevenson, James (1987). *"Could Be Worse!"* New York: Morrow.

Stewart, Sarah (1997). *The Gardener.* Illus. David Small. New York: Farrar, Straus & Giroux.

Tavares, Matt (2000). *Zachary's Ball.* Boston: Candlewick.

Taylor, Mildred D. (1976). *Roll of Thunder, Hear My Cry.* New York: Dial.

Thomas, Rob (1997). *Slave Day.* New York: Simon & Schuster.

Tillage, Leon Walter (1997). *Leon's Story.* New York: Farrar, Straus & Giroux.

Van Allsburg, Chris (1997). *Ben's Dream.* Boston: Houghton Mifflin [1982].

—— (1979). *The Garden of Abdul Gasazi.* Boston: Houghton Mifflin.

—— (1981). *Jumanji.* Boston: Houghton Mifflin.

—— (1985). *The Polar Express.* Boston: Houghton Mifflin.

Walter, Virginia (1998). *Making Up Megaboy.* Illus. Katrina Roeckelein. New York: DK Ink.

Weeks, Sarah (1995). *Follow the Moon.* Illus. Suzanne Duranceau. New York: HarperCollins.

Wiesner, David (1991). *Tuesday.* New York: Clarion.

Wildsmith, Brian (1987). *Fishes.* London: Oxford University Press [1968].

Williams, Sherley Anne (1992). *Working Cotton.* Illus. Carole Byard. San Diego: Harcourt Brace.

Williams, Vera B. (1982). *A Chair for My Mother.* New York: Greenwillow.

—— (1997). *More More More Said the Baby.* New York: Tupelo [1990, Greenwillow].

Wilson, Nancy Hope (1997). *Old People, Frogs, and Albert.* Illus. Marcy D. Ramsey. New York: Farrar, Straus & Giroux.

Winslow, Vicki (1997). *Follow the Leader.* New York: Delacorte.

Wolff, Virginia Euwer (1998). *Bat 6.* New York: Scholastic.

Woodson, Jaqueline (2001). *The Other Side.* Illus. E. B. Lewis. New York: Putnam.

Wyeth, Sharon Dennis (1997). *Always My Dad.* Illus. Raúl Colón. New York: Dragonfly.

Young, Ed (1989). *Lon Po Po: A Red-Riding Hood Story from China.* New York: Philomel.

The World of Picture Books

The name *picture books* evokes images of brightly colored, beautifully illustrated books that beg to be read. No matter what our age, most of us still enjoy reading them because of their vibrant pictures, rich and evocative language, and poignant and meaningful themes. Picture books speak to us in the same way photographs do. They touch our emotions, delight our senses, appeal to our whimsy, and bring back memories of our childhood. Picture books invite us to curl up and read them.

The plethora of picture books is both a gift and a bane. It's easy to feel overwhelmed by their sheer number. As you come to know the genre and develop criteria for evaluating books, you will feel more secure about selecting them for your library or your classroom. One of the goals of this chapter is to give you enough information about and examples of picture books that you will be able to tackle this task with confidence.

The ability to evaluate picture books (discussed in Chapter 2) is critical for teachers and librarians because we are expected to use professional judgment in selecting books for our classroom and library. Children trust us to bring in picture books relevant to them and to their lives. Whether as a parent, a friend, a teacher, or a librarian, we can do for one or several children what Kozel (1998) wishes for every child: "I wish that teachers would insist that every little child in our country—rich or poor; black, brown, or white; whatever origin or background—would have the chance to read books not for any other reason than the fact that books bring joy into our lives, not because they'll be useful for a state examination, not because they'll improve SAT scores, but solely because of the intense pleasure that we get from books. If [adults are] not willing to defend the right of every child to enjoy the treasures of the earth, who will?"

Many, many kinds of picture books are produced today. In an effort to give you some meaningful ways to sort them out and think about them, the following categories will be examined: ABC books, counting books, concept books, wordless books, books for the earliest readers, transitional or chapter books, and picture storybooks for older readers. Other categories of picture books exist, such as toy books, participation books, and board books, but the categories included here are the ones most widely used in schools.

Purposes of ABC Books

The phrase *ABC books* sounds so ordinary and straightforward that it's hard to imagine the richness and variety that can be found in these books. Although some are written only to teach the alphabet, many others are written to play with language, present information on a topic, tell a story, or accent the visual.

Teaching the Alphabet

There is no better book than **Brian Wildsmith's ABC** for beginning to teach letter names and the sounds they make as initial letters. The words he has selected to represent the letters and corresponding letter sounds are ones small children would probably know, such as *apple, butterfly, cat, dog,* and *elephant.* But it's his art that will hold the children's attention. The paintings have both depth and luminosity, inviting children to return to the book frequently.

Flora McDonnell's ABC is an exuberant introduction to the alphabet for children. The beautiful color pictures show one very large object or animal along with a small object or animal on each page. The *Dd* page shows dinosaurs and a duck and the *Ll* page a lemon and a ladybug. Humor and wit abound in the juxtaposition of these objects and in the way she portrays them. The dinosaurs appear to be watching the lone duck.

Helen Oxenbury's **ABC of Things** has whimsical drawings that make the reader feel warm and nurtured. Love and caring are embedded in the pages. For instance, on the *Cc* page, a huge *cow* sits on a *couch,* with one leg *crossed* over the other, next to a *cat;* they both look happily at the *crow* bringing in a *cake* with *candles.* The expressions in the eyes of the people and animals bring them to life. Each page has objects familiar to children.

John Burningham's ABC is filled with humorous colored-pencil drawings that invite children to look at them repeatedly. An adorable little boy is in all the pictures, doing unusual things that would appeal to children: riding an *Ostrich;* with a *Parrot* sitting on his head; sticking out his tongue at a *Snake,* which has its tongue out too. Each page has only a single word—the name of the animal—but each picture tells a story.

The illustrators of the best ABC books tap into children's deep needs and wants, as well as into what delights children. They know that a book must be visually interesting to keep children coming back over and over again. When you select ABC books to teach the alphabet and initial sounds to children, be sure that the objects used to illustrate the letters are familiar to children so that they are not trying to absorb too much new information at once.

CD-ROM

For other books by Helen Oxenbury, search the CD-ROM database.

The bright colors and familiarity with the objects and their contrasting sizes make this alphabet book appealing to children. (*Flora McDonnell's ABC* copyright © 1997 Flora McDonnell. Reproduced by permission of the publisher Candlewick Press, Inc., Cambridge, MA, on behalf of Walker Books Ltd., of London.)

Playing with Language

When the sounds of words delight children, they are motivated to want to learn about language and to use language. Language that delights, through the use of such devices as alliteration and rhyming, makes children laugh and feel joyful, eliminating anxiety and self-consciousness about learning. These are prime moments for learning because the filters or blocks are down and new information can be enjoyed and absorbed. Through language play, children gain a heightened sensitivity to the sounds and rhythms of language and become aware of the function and power of words. Books that play with language comprise the largest single category of alphabet books. They can be used to stimulate writing, as well as vocabulary growth and an interest in language.

One of my favorites is Anita Lobel's **Alison's Zinnia,** which is filled with large, gorgeous paintings of flowers. Beneath the painting of the flower, in a long rectangular box, is a girl who will give the flower to another girl, who will do something to or with it. For instance, "Leslie left a Lady's slipper for Maryssa; Maryssa misted a Magnolia for Nancy; and Nancy noticed a Narcissus for Olga." In her author's note, Lobel says, "It took a bit of weeding before I found a way to connect flowers to girls' names. Once I found the verbs, it seemed wickedly simple. Girl—verb—flower. I wrote it A to Z on the plane ride back to New York." The paintings, which took Lobel more than a year, stimulate a desire to know more about flowers and to look closely at those delicate, detailed drawings. Children could use this word pattern as a model for making up their own books on any number of other topics.

Steven Kellogg's **Aster Aardvark's Alphabet Adventure** is a collection of alliterative stories—one for each letter. His skill in both drawing the illustrations and creating the clever and amusing stories invites children to return to the book again and again. A sampling of less than a quarter of this alliterative story reflects how much fun it would be to imitate: "Hermione, a hefty hyperactive hippo, hurt her hip hurling herself into the Hawaiian Hula Hoop Happening."

Other alphabet books focus on rhyme. **Quentin Blake's ABC** rhymes across two pages with such entries as "K is for Kittens, all scratching the chair. L is for Legs that we wave in the air." These rhymes are accompanied by wild, crazy, messy cartoon-like figures. In the *L* picture, the whole family is down on the floor, lying on their backs as they wave their legs in the air. Underwear shows and hairy legs are exposed, as Blake exhibits his sense of the ridiculous!

Books based on alliteration include Graeme Base's **Animalia,** an alphabet book that you can use for a whole year without tiring of it. Each page is resplendent with lush, detailed paintings containing a myriad of things beginning with a particular letter, accompanied by an alliterative sentence for that letter.

ANTICS, by Cathi Hepworth, is a captivating book in which words beginning with every letter of the alphabet have *ant* in them somewhere. *Lieutenant* represents *L,* and the picture shows an ant with a scarf around his neck flying an old World War I plane. *M* is represented by *Mutant,* and a very large ant hovers over an anteater. The zany illustrations alone keep you turning the pages.

Presenting Information Using the Alphabet Scheme

Many alphabet books are packed with fascinating information organized around the letters of the alphabet. Jerry Pallotta is a master at writing alphabet books that easily could be used to introduce students to science concepts or units. In *The Ocean Alphabet Book,* as in all his other books, he writes clear, interesting prose with intriguing information that speaks directly to children. "B is for Bluefish. Everyone loves to catch Bluefish because they love to fight. Their teeth are very, very sharp so don't ever put your fingers in their mouth. C is for Cod. Some grow to be as big as a ten-year-old boy or girl." He keeps his tone upbeat and light, making his books very appealing.

Roger Tory Peterson's ABC of Birds, by Linda Westervelt, shows bright birds from around the globe photographed or painted by this century's foremost birder, who has written many bird field guides. The beautiful language in the text illuminates our knowledge about birds.

Among the alphabet books that could be used in a social studies curriculum is *A Is for Africa,* by Ifeoma Onyefulu, which captures what the people of Africa have in common. One entry is "O is for Ornaments to adorn our bodies. African people love to dress up and look beautiful. In some tribes people wear beaded strands around their waists or across their chests. Body markings are another kind of ornament." Children learn new information in manageable ways.

A Is for Asia, by Cynthia Chin-Lee, gives us glimpses into this area of the globe—which, as the author points out, is one-third of the entire world. We learn that *B* is the letter for *batik, L* is for *lotus,* and *M* is for *monsoon.* Each entry is followed by a few sentences explaining it more fully.

A Gardener's Alphabet, by Mary Azarian, portrays the difficulty and delight of gardening through dazzling, detailed wood prints with strong, clear images related to the theme. Each is accompanied by only a single word for each letter of the alphabet.

A book that teaches children American Sign Language is Laura Rankin's *The Handmade Alphabet.* The hand sign for each letter of the alphabet is paired with a hand holding or pointing to something that begins with that letter. So *A* shows the hand in the "A" position holding asparagus, the "V" signing hand is holding a valentine, and so on. Children will delight in seeing and perhaps learning the whole sign alphabet.

Tomorrow's Alphabet, by George Shannon, is a decidedly different kind of alphabet book. It teaches thinking skills as it pushes readers to figure out why *C* is for *milk* or *E* is for *campfire.* Of course, the answer is that the milk is tomorrow's cheese and the campfire is tomorrow's embers. Readers have to think about how things begin or start. To compile such an alphabet, children would have to think about what things are made of and what they produce.

Telling a Story Using the Alphabet Scheme for Structure

A Long Trip to Z, by Fulvio Testa, has the story embedded in the alphabet structure. In this story, an airplane climbs out of a book and goes on an adventure out of the house and across the world. Each page features a different letter of the alphabet as the plane makes its way.

The ABC Bunny, written by Wanda Gag and illustrated by Howard Gag, is a timeless story, with a rhyming alphabet scheme centered around the activities of a bunny. The pictures of the bunny's adventures convey much of the meaning. "C is for crash, D is for dash, E is for elsewhere in a flash. F is for frog—he's fat and funny. 'Looks like rain,' says he to Bunny."

Doug Cushman's *The ABC Mystery* is a fast-paced chase after an art thief. It begins, "A is the Art that was stolen at night. B is the Butler who sneaks out of sight. C is the Clue that's left in the room. D is Detective Inspector McGroom." The illustrations add depth to the story because they contain clues not mentioned in the text.

Accenting the Visual to Foster Learning

The Graphic Alphabet, a Caldecott Honor book by David Pelletier, is an unusual book in which the illustration of the letter form retains the natural shape of the letter, as well as representing the meaning of the word pictured. For instance, the letter *K* is represented by the word *knot* and the *K* has a knot in its middle. The *M* makes a snow-topped *mountain.* The author is mainly interested in the relationship between the image and the meaning.

Alphabet City, by Stephen T. Johnson, encourages viewers to find the shapes of letters in their surroundings. Johnson wants his paintings to inspire children and adults to look at their surroundings in a fresh and playful way. In the author's note, he says that in doing so "they will discover for themselves juxtaposition of scale, harmonies of shadows, colorful patterns in surface textures, and joy in the most somber aspects of a city, by transcending the mundane and unearthing its hidden beauty." *E* is the side view of a traffic light, *G* is formed from the elaborate ironwork in a street light, and *M* is the two arches of a bridge.

Alphabet books are a source of delight and learning about the alphabet as well as many other things. As you read them, look for other patterns and other purposes.

Purposes of Counting Books

Just as many alphabet books do much more than teach the alphabet, many counting books do much more than teach numbers. Some present information on a topic; others tell a story.

Teaching Numbers

Denise Fleming's **Count!** presents the numbers via the antics of animals—four kangaroos bounce, five giraffes stretch, seven worms wiggle. Each page has the number clearly shown on the left side along with blocks of color so that children can count the blocks of color as well as the animals.

Stephen Kellogg's **Frog Jumps: A Counting Book** is an action-packed, continuous-counting book. Each phrase is repeated before the new number is added. For example, the fifth page says "One frog jumps, two ducks dive, three elephants trumpet, four rabbits run, and five bats bat." The pages get very crowded by the end of the book. Although the pictures are terrific, the pages may be too overloaded to truly teach counting. This would, however, be a wonderful book for students to read along with a teacher to reinforce their counting skills.

The M&M's Counting Book, by Barbara Barbieri McGrath, teaches numbers, six colors, and three shapes through the use of M&M's. It also teaches sets by asking children to arrange the M&M's. This fun, interactive book functions best if the child has M&M's to work with.

Bert Kitchen's **Animal Numbers,** which shows exotic and familiar animals with the specified number of infants, asks the reader to figure out how many babies are in each mother's brood. Beautiful illustrations depict swans, squirrels, lizards, and opossums frequently in unusual positions in relation to the number. The goldfish swim inside the number 8, and salamanders crawl around the number 9.

One Moose, Twenty Mice, by Clare Beaton, uses another device to keep children involved. In each of the photos of the stitched pictures, which also use felt, beads, and buttons, a cat is hiding. Each page asks readers to locate the cat. This book is so playful that children will want to keep reading.

The Crayon Counting Book, by Pam Muñoz Ryan and Jerry Pallotta, has children counting by twos, as well as considering the concepts of odd and even, as they learn about color.

Presenting Information Using the Counting Scheme

Authors use the counting scheme as a way to organize and present information so that it will involve the reader. **Blast Off! A Space Counting Book,** written by Norma Cole and illustrated by Marshall Peck, III, teaches about space travel. Rhymed couplets are accompanied by pictures of child astronauts inside a spaceship. The numbers appear at the sides of the pages, along with dots, arrows, or some other kind of representation so that children have something to count on every page. At the bottom of each page, pertinent information about space is offered.

A counting book set in Africa, *Moja Means One—Swahili Counting Book,* by Muriel Feelings, offers rich learning experiences for all children. The beautiful black-and-white pictures painted by Tom Feelings show many aspects of East African life—musical instruments, market stalls, fish, animals, and clothing.

Waving: A Counting Book, by Peter Sis, set in a large city, shows much about city living. As a little girl and her mother walk down the street, they wave to and receive waves from an ever-increasing number of people. We see bicyclists, mail carriers, police officers on horses, waiters, joggers, Girl Scouts, musicians, tourists, and taxi drivers.

One Horse Waiting for Me, by Patricia Mullins, is a beautiful celebration of horses done in collages of fine tissue and Japanese papers. The evocative language and the stunning artwork invite frequent rereading. Many of these books would make an excellent choice for a read-aloud—a strategy that makes a critical contribution to early literacy skills, as the boxed feature Taking a Look at the Research shows.

taking a look at the Research

The Read-Aloud

Research "confirms that reading aloud positively impacts overall academic achievement as well as reading skills and interest in reading" (Routman, 2000, p. 30). In fact, research over the last twenty years has consistently shown read-aloud to be important to a child's successful reading experience. Yet it is often seen as a peripheral activity, and as the classroom schedule gets tightened by the demands of the day, read-aloud frequently gets omitted.

It is important that we share good children's literature by reading aloud. Routman describes the many ways read-aloud helps a child become a successful reader: Through read-aloud children learn to enjoy books while developing a sense of how stories work, develop a richer vocabulary, learn to make predictions, learn grammatical structure, develop an understanding of literary language, and begin to notice how different writers write (p. 30). It's important to remember that children's understanding of receptive language is beyond their independent reading level and books that might be independently read in third grade may make a wonderful read-aloud for a first-grade class.

In the course of reading aloud, teachers often find opportunities to demonstrate comprehension strategies. For very young children, these strategies may include "reading" the illustrations of a picture book, left-to-right directionality of text, top-to-bottom and left-to-right movement through pages of a book, and using letter/sound relationships to decode beginning and ending sounds (Avery, 2002). Taberski (2000) states that she selects for read-aloud books through which she can demonstrate strategies including stopping and making predictions about what might happen next, demonstrations of story and character mapping, writing to deepen understanding of the story, and creating "Before and After" charts (p. 82). By demonstrating reading strategies during read-aloud, Taberski (2000) feels that teachers can show students that fluent readers use many strategies during the act of reading.

Certainly, demonstrating these strategies is not intended to "basalize" reading. Such demonstrations arise out of the text of the moment and are a natural response to how the story is being read. They should not detract from, but rather actively involve the child in, the story or poem. Teachers know that in the course of a read-aloud activity, many spontaneous responses will add to a rich literary experience. For me, the spontaneity can be the show of emotion as I'm reading. For instance, I cannot read Polacco's *Pink and Say* without crying a little or a lot. It doesn't matter if I am at home, at school, or in a bookstore. Mem Fox (1994) encourages teachers to laugh over funny books, gasp over horror stories, sigh over love stories, and sob over sad stories. Only in doing so can we "help our students to realize that there is some reward, that there are many rewards, to be had from the act of reading" (p. 63). Read-aloud is an opportunity to share some of the best of children's literature throughout all of the grades.

Avery, Carol (2002). . . . *And with a Light Touch. Learning About Reading, Writing, and Teaching with First Graders,* 2nd ed. Portsmouth, NH: Heinemann.

Fox, Mem (1994). *Radical Reflections: Passionate Opinions on Teaching, Learning, and Living.* New York: Harcourt Brace.

Routman, Regie (2000). *Conversations: Strategies for Teaching, Learning, and Evaluating.* Portsmouth, NH: Heinemann.

Taberski, Sharon (2000). *On Solid Ground: Strategies for Teaching Reading K–3.* Portsmouth NH: Heinemann.

Telling a Story Using the Counting Theme for Structure

A fabulously funny counting book is *My Little Sister Ate One Hare,* by Bill Grossman. This rib-tickling story tells all that little sister ate, ending with a surprise twist. The rhythm and the repetitive pattern appeal to children, who want to hear this story again and again.

Little Miss Muffet's Count-Along Surprise, by Emma Chichester Clark, uses the nursery rhyme as the basis for the story but goes beyond the original rhyme. It opens with one spider inviting Miss Muffet to stay. Then she's visited by a large number of animals bringing her things, such as oodles of noodles. This counting book encourages children to have fun with language and rhyme as it builds toward a surprise ending.

When you're not looking . . . A Storytime Book, by Maggie Kneen, doesn't fit into any categories. It seems appropriate for older children, who are developing more sophisticated cognitive skills. This original book asks readers to find objects on each page. On the page for the number 3, beneath the number in a box going down the side of the page, are three tiny elephants. Readers must then find the three elephants on a very crowded toy shelf. We are told that when it gets dark, mischief begins. The picture shows the dolls and animals beginning to move on the shelf. Each page could easily be used as a story-starter.

Purposes of Concept Books

Concept books are generally meant for very young children who are learning about the world. There are two main kinds of concept books—single-dimensional and multidimensional.

Single-Dimensional Concept Books

Single-dimensional concept books take a single concept and show many examples of it. For instance, if the concept was color, the book would portray a multitude of colors. *Growing Colors,* by Bruce McMillan, has large photos of vegetables and fruits, glowing with color. Facing a picture of bright orange carrots on the right-hand page is a picture of what carrots look like when they are in the ground. So, although this book focuses on color in nature, it also shows how fruits and vegetables grow in, on, and above the ground.

Animal Shapes, by Brian Wildsmith, is about shapes of animals, from lions to elephants to jaguars. Wildsmith paints the animal on one page and shows the same shape done in more geometrical cutouts on the facing page.

Tana Hoban, an award-winning photographer, has many concept books, all of high quality and interest to children. Her book *Of Colors and Things* is aimed at children learning their colors and features everyday objects photographed in straightforward but appealing ways. In *So Many Circles, So Many Squares,* the geometric concepts of circles and squares are shown in photographs of wheels, signs, pots, and other familiar objects. After you read this book, you will see circles and squares everywhere and perhaps view the world a little differently. *Exactly the Opposite,* also by Hoban, helps children learn about the concept of opposites through bright, colorful photographs showing opposites side by side.

Another color book is *Who Said Red?,* written by Mary Serfozo and illustrated by Keiko Narahashi. As they delight in the rhythmic text and the imaginative pictures, children learn to relate colors to familiar things. This gorgeous book shows all the commonplace objects that are mentioned in the rhymes. For example, a frog, a leaf, a pickle, and a green bean represent the color green. By connecting the colors to the objects shown, the book gives children many ways to remember what the colors look like.

Denise Fleming's *Lunch* teaches colors through a story line about a mouse who is eating his lunch. Fleming's large, bold, bright pictures will captivate readers as they try to guess what the mouse will eat for each color mentioned.

To locate more books on math, go to **Children's Trade Books in Math** at www.luc.edu/schools/education/csimath/zbib.htm.

The clear, bright photographs involve children by asking them to name what is opposite in each set of pictures.

(Cover art from *Exactly the Opposite* by Tana Hoban. Used by permission of HarperCollins Publishers.)

Multidimensional Concept Books

Multidimensional concept books take a larger concept, such as "picnic," and show all the elements associated with it. In **The Baby's Catalogue,** by Janet Ahlberg and Allen Ahlberg, the whimsical drawings are perfect for the survey of baby life. On each page, a single word is represented by five different pictures: for "babies," one baby is crying, one is sleeping alone, two are sleeping together, one is nursing, and one is looking through the bars of a crib. Various parts of the baby's life are illustrated, including dad, mom, morning, breakfast, toys, lunch, and books. The diversity found in each group of pictures makes this book especially appealing. In addition to being multiethnic, the pictures show dads brushing teeth, changing diapers, making tea, and going to work on a bike. All of the pictures exude love and caring.

Aliki's **Hello! Good-Bye!** is a cheerful book that describes some of the many ways, both verbal and nonverbal, in which people say hello and good-bye. The book is filled with lots of little pictures that show exactly what the words mean. In one section, the text says, "Hello can be said with no words." There are pictures above the words "a wave, a shake, hug, kiss, bow, curtsy, sign, slap, tip [a hat]." When different types of hellos are described, the text states, "A fanfare is a musical hello." And when good-byes are talked about, the most difficult good-bye is not ignored: "Some good-byes are hard to say. A good-bye that lasts forever hurts the most." This book is a mix of playfulness and seriousness. In addition to teaching children that leave-takings and returns are a natural part of life, the book teaches that body language communicates to others.

In the concept book **The Ball Bounced,** by Nancy Tafuri, objects and animals are shown with the actions associated with them. Besides the ball bouncing, we see a cat jumping, water splashing, and a door slamming, as well as many other object–verb combinations. After reading this book, children might be interested in thinking of action words that could go with specific objects.

In *Kente Colors,* written by Debbi Chocolate and illustrated by John Ward, colors are connected to the cloth used and to the culture. The illustrations in this book, which could be used in a study of Ghana, show the Kente cloth costumes of the Ashanti and Ewe people. As they learn about colors through the bright, dazzling pictures, children begin learning about the culture. They also might be interested in learning more about the significance of the cloth. The rhyming pattern adds interest.

Characteristics of ABC, Counting, and Concept Books

Outstanding ABC, counting, and concept books generally share these characteristics:

1. They are uncluttered, giving the young reader a clear, identifiable focus point.

2. Pictures of objects used to illustrate a letter, number, or word are rich in detail so that the intent of the association is obvious. The objects match the letter or word in ABC books and the number in counting books.

3. They are visually interesting, stimulating talk, comments, and questions from the reader.

4. The pictures are easily identified by the young reader, and the vocabulary is age-appropriate using common words.

5. The format is predictable and consistent. In ABC books, the placement of the letter in the word follows a pattern that is easily recognizable to the reader.

6. When they use the alphabet to present a topic, the information included is well researched and accurate.

7. As in other outstanding picture books, the artwork represents the best qualities of the medium or combination of media used and delights and interests children.

Purposes of Wordless Books

Wordless books and nearly wordless books are written to encourage observation of the world around us. While allowing readers to be part of fantastical experiences, they nudge readers to create words for the story. Alexandra Day (1998), author of the wordless *Good Dog, Carl* books, said, "Words would discourage wonder and exploratory thought. Words tie it down. Young children are very willing to enter the game of pushing boundaries." All wordless books require the participation of readers who must create their own words to explain what is happening. Almost all of these books ask us to use our imaginations and stretch our thinking beyond current boundaries. Wordless books have a variety of purposes.

Encouraging Observation and a Closer Look at the World

Anno's USA, by Mitsumasu Anno, could be a history lesson in itself. In the wordless panorama, a lone traveler starts on the West Coast in the present day and journeys across the width of the country as time moves backwards, departing from the East Coast as Columbus's ship *The Maria* appears over the horizon. The pictures contain references to children's books, paintings, and famous buildings, as well as to epic scenes from movies. Children can sort through the many references to figure out which time period in history is shown.

Pat Hutchins's *Changes, Changes,* published more than 25 years ago, is still a popular wordless book. Two dolls start with 27 geometrically shaped blocks and change them into different shapes as circumstances dictate. For instance, when their "house" begins to burn, they turn the blocks into a fire engine to put the fire out. Children may be so intrigued that they'll want to cut out these same shapes in order to see if they can create different structures than the dolls do.

Truck, by Donald Crews, is a concept book that introduces children to the many aspects of trucking, while also nudging them to really look at the world. A big, red truck is shown in traffic among many traffic signs, entering a tunnel, stopping for gas, going through a storm, and so on. The perspective is provocative because it reveals the truck from so many different angles and in juxtaposition to so many different objects. The underlying message is that even a "thing" like a truck is a complicated object whose impact changes depending on the way we look at it.

Encouraging the Creation of Words

Most wordless books encourage readers to create words to go along with the "story" in the pictures. At first glance you may wonder why the author doesn't just tell the reader what he or she had in mind. Alexandra Day (1998), author of the **Good Dog, Carl** books, says that words are simply inadequate to convey the depth of emotion often shown in the illustrations. She feels that the relationship between Carl and the baby is rather mysterious and asks, "How can you put words to it?"

Another good reason for making books wordless is to allow the participation of the reader. Children can read wordless books over and over, practicing the behavior of reading. Because they are not dependent on an adult to construct words, they feel ownership over the meaning of the story. This allows "reading" to become part of the growing-up experience children naturally seek. Mercer Mayer's **Frog** books, including **A Boy, a Dog and a Frog,** are ones that children repeatedly "read."

Eric Carle's **Do You Want to Be My Friend?** is another book in which young children can easily get involved. In his quest to find a friend, a little mouse approaches the tail end of several animals, and children can try to guess what the animal is before turning the page. This device provides an element of surprise throughout, and Carle ends the book with another surprise, which only the most observant will find hints of throughout the story.

John Goodall has created many marvelous wordless books, such as **Paddy Goes Traveling.** His books are known for the half pages between the whole pages that reveal the action quickly and increase suspense.

Dylan's Day Out, by Peter Catalanotto, features a dalmatian who escapes from his home and becomes involved in a soccer game between what he views as penguins and skunks. This imaginative book begins and ends with a few sentences. Dylan's dream of frolicking with pandas and zebras before he finds a way out of the house invites the reader to supply a narrative from Dylan's point of view.

Tomie dePaola's **Sing, Pierrot, Sing: A Picture Book in Mime** and **Pancakes for Breakfast** ask the reader to make sense of the story. Both of these stories have dePaola's light, whimsical touch, as well as surprise endings.

Picnic, by Emily Arnold McCully, shows a little mouse on her way to a family picnic getting bumped off the back end of a truck and left behind. This endearing little mouse, clinging tightly to her pink stuffed mouse, eventually

This story calls out for children to add words in order to tell the story of the little mouse who was left behind.
(Cover from *Picnic* by Emily Arnold McCully. Used by permission of HarperCollins Publishers.)

decides to enjoy her time alone and does just that before her worried family finds her. This book inspires readers to create simultaneous dialogues telling what the little mouse and her family are thinking and saying at each point of the story.

Peter Collington has written many lovely wordless books, including *The Angel and the Soldier Boy* and *The Tooth Fairy.* Because many children believe or want to believe that their toys come to life and that a tooth fairy truly exists, they enjoy providing a narrative or talking about the books.

One of the most somber of the wordless books, *Window,* by Jeannie Baker, depicts a young boy growing and changing as the world outside his window changes dramatically. This book can be used to introduce environmental concerns to the young. The striking collages show the beautiful landscape outside the boy's window going from wilderness to urban blight as he grows up; the collages sear the images into the viewer's mind.

Immersing the Reader in Fantastical Elements

The books that follow deserve a category of their own, for they immerse the reader in fantastical elements as they encourage the creation of a narrative. Many books tap into our imagination, but these books thrust us into the heart of an experience, taking us to the edge of our own dreams and fantasies. David Wiesner's *Tuesday* lets us see frogs invading an ordinary community, floating on lily pads, entering a "normal" house and town, and creating consternation and confusion.

Lily pads floating over a sleeping town startle readers into creating a story to explain what they see happening.

(Cover, from TUESDAY by David Wiesner. Jacket Art copyright © 1991 by David Wiesner. Reprinted by permission of Clarion Books/Houghton Mifflin Company. All rights reserved.)

Raymond Briggs's **The Snowman** shows us a little boy who has the fantastic experience of interacting with a snowman who has come to life. This snowman takes him flying to show him another view of the world. Although the book was published more than 20 years ago, it is still popular because it taps into human longings.

Will's Mammoth, written by Rafe Martin and illustrated by Stephen Gammell, offers another favorite childhood fantasy. In spite of his parents' assurance that mammoths have been gone for over 10,000 years, when Will goes out to play in the deep hills of snow, he finds a mammoth and rides him. Together, they spend the day traveling past many prehistoric sights. When they return, the mammoth reaches through the snow and gives Will a flower, which he sleeps with that night. The lovely paintings, the sympathetic mammoth, and the little boy who enjoys every minute of his adventure make this an unforgettable story.

Ben's Dream, by Chris Van Allsburg, takes the commonplace experience of dozing off while studying (in this case, studying geography) and turns it into a dream. In his dream, Ben finds himself in his house, floating past many of the great monuments of the world. When he is awakened by his friend, he realizes that his friend had the same dream, and he remembers waving to her as her house bobbed past the Great Sphinx in Egypt!

Eric Rohmann engages us in more imaginative wanderings in his Caldecott Honor–winning book **Time Flies,** in which a bird enters a dinosaur museum and then thinks about how he would feel if he were their prey. His wonderings put flesh on the dinosaurs and thrust them all back to prehistoric times, where he narrowly escapes being dinosaur lunch. The rich colors, the unusual perspectives, and the detailed illustrations make reading this book a stimulating experience.

Characteristics of Wordless Books

Outstanding wordless books seem to have several characteristics in common.

1. They almost always have rich pictures, full of details that make readers look carefully on every reading. Readers drink in the illustrations with their eyes, finding just one more thing they hadn't noticed on the first or second or third reading.

2. They use action to develop the characters. The plot shown through the pictures is the driving force that keeps readers turning the pages.

3. They deal with intriguing or interesting themes.

4. The setting is often a big part of the story line. The illustrations must have enough detail to make the place recognizable. Readers have to have enough knowledge to enter and feel comfortable in the story world. This explains why so many fantasies start in a known place, like a child's bedroom or some other part of the house. From there, readers can make leaps into the story world.

5. They demonstrate an expansive vision of the world, in which wanting adventure and using imagination is a normal part of living. When they view the world as an exciting, unfolding place in which we can see and perceive in many different ways, illustrators add to the fascination of the world.

6. They often make a strong emotional impact on the reader, leaving the reader wondering and thinking. Many of these books show people in caring, affirming situations, so readers come away feeling nurtured.

7. Of course, many of these books have a very distinct imaginative impact on us, since they are created for just that reason. But even when wordless books are created mainly to ask us to participate in the story, they require us to use our imaginations in order to enter into the story.

This mouse father with his mismatched pajamas enjoys entertaining his children with stories.
(COPYRIGHT © 1972 by ARNOLD LOBEL. Used by permission of HarperCollins Publishers.)

Characteristics of Books for the Earliest Readers

Although books for the earliest readers do not have the gloriously lush illustrations of many picture books, there is still much to entice the young reader. Series such as *I-Can-Read, Step into Reading,* and *Dell Picture Yearlings* were created to support the child who is starting to read without adult help. Early reader books, probably the first books children will read entirely on their own, share many characteristics.

Uncomplicated Pictures

The pictures, usually done in cartoon style, provide clues to the text. Because the pictures are designed to support the children's reading by providing illustrations of words they may not be familiar with, detail is often minimal. Since the illustrator wants the child to see in the pictures what will be helpful in the reading, extraneous objects and unnecessary backgrounds are not included. The illustrations are still delightful; ***Frog and Toad Are Friends,*** an early reader by Arnold Lobel, has won a Caldecott Honor award. The cartoon style is perfect for these kinds of books, because the strong lines used to create characters and objects make them easy to identify.

Humorous or Delightful Touches

Often the illustrations will delight children by showing them something unexpected, as in Arnold Lobel's ***Mouse Tales,*** where the father mouse is shown with a moustache and mismatched pajama top and bottom. Unexpected things happen, too, such as the wishing well yelling "ouch" every time a coin is thrown into it. Lobel usually draws miniature pictures, which young children adore.

The ***Little Bear*** books, by Else Holmelund Minarik, have whimsical illustrations by Maurice Sendak that endear the characters to the reader. But it isn't just the illustrations that are delightful and humorous; much humor is used in the text itself.

In ***Henry and Mudge in Puddle Trouble,*** by Cynthia Rylant, Henry's father at first is unhappy that Henry and Mudge are rolling around in a puddle of water. But after Mudge shakes himself off all over the father, the father smiles and jumps in the puddle himself, telling Henry, "Next time, ask me along!"

Solid Themes of Interest to Children

Among the themes repeated in many early reader books are the longing for and importance of friendship; adults and children making mistakes and still being accepted; celebration of special events, birthday parties, or Valentine's Day parties; the joy of having a pet; reluctance to go to bed; being afraid or having fears; children being adventurous or creative or doing something unexpected; the need to be nurtured and taken care of; the difficulty of being considered "little"; children having problems with other children; and children's

CD-ROM

To locate authors who are known for humor in their writing, do a word search for *humor* under Favorite Authors.

Booklists of Children's Literature offers lists of books by theme. Go to *www.monroe.lib.in.us/ childrens/children_booklists.html.*

misunderstandings and confusions. Children want to be reassured that what they are feeling or experiencing is not unusual. They want to know that others have the same reactions or feelings—for example, that there are others who are afraid of the dark, as they are.

Short Sentences and Repeated Words

The best early reader books do not have a controlled vocabulary. Rather than restrict themselves to only two-syllable words or words from a prescribed list, they use longer or more difficult words if the words fit the context of the story and if an illustration makes them clear to children. Most of these books have sentences no longer than twelve to twenty words. The authors repeat words over and over again in the context of the story so that they make perfect sense.

In **Silly Tilly's Valentine,** by Lillian Hoban, with text of less than 900 words, *valentine* is repeated 15 times, *snow* (in several forms) is repeated 24 times, *mailbox,* 8; *remember,* 8; *forgot,* 7; and *cupcakes,* 6. It's not just the number of times these words are woven in, but how they are woven in that makes the book accessible to early readers. Hoban is very skillful in introducing new words. The new word is always shown in the illustration, and she finds ways to repeat it several times within a short space. For instance, the first time the word *wipe* is used, the text says: "Wipe your eyes. Tillie wiped her eyes. She wiped the snow from her glasses." The word is used in three adjoining sentences so that children get a chance to say it more than once, thus increasing their chances of remembering it.

Rhyme and Rhythm

Frequent use of rhyme and rhythm makes books easier to read because it makes them more predictable. Some early reader books are downright zany. In such books as **Mr. Brown Can Moo, Can You?** and **The Foot Book,** Dr. Seuss has a rhyme and rhythm so contagious that readers move to the rhythm created by the words. Many early readers depend heavily on rhyme and rhythm because they make reading fun. By making the readers laugh, the author encourages them to keep reading. Because the reader can almost guess what the next word is, rhyming patterns make books more predictable and thus more accessible to early readers, allowing children to feel the success of reading. **The Fat Cat Sat on the Mat,** by Nurit Karlin, is a humorous book done entirely in rhyme, with such text as "One night, when Wilma was out, the fat cat got out of the vat. He went, pit-a-pat, and sat on the mat." Use of the rhyming pattern ending in *at* throughout the book makes it easy for children to figure out what will make the fat cat move from the mat, which is not his.

Alliteration and Plays on Words

Alliteration is found in many parts of **Wizard and Wart at Sea,** by Janice Lee Smith. "Soon Wart fell asleep and started to snore. Soon Wizard was snoring too. Suddenly Wizard heard a scream. 'Help!' yelled Wart. Seagulls swooped around him."

In Nola Buck's **Sid and Sam,** most of the words begin with *s.* "'Sing slower, Sid,' Sam said. Sid sang slower. 'Sing softer, Sid,' Sam said. Sid sang softer." Alliteration motivates children to figure out words, since it makes the tone light and infuses delight into the reading. Playfulness in language makes children less apprehensive about the big job of independent reading.

Frequent Use of Dialogue

Lots of dialogue is used in early readers to carry the plot line forward. Dialogue allows much information to be conveyed in short sentences. For instance, in **Wizard and Wart at Sea,** two-thirds of the sentences in the book are dialogue, which helps keep the action moving.

Grouping of Words in Meaningful Sets

Grouping words in meaningful sets encourages new readers to "chunk," or read phrases instead of just individual words. In **If I Had a Pig,** by Mick Inkpen, the whole book is organized around what could happen if a little boy had a pig. He tells of painting pictures together, making snowpigs, and racing his pig to the park, if he only had a pig. All of these groupings, supported by illustrations, encourage early readers to do more than sound out individual words.

Informative Illustrations

Illustrations carry the heavy load of establishing the characterization as well as the setting. The nature of characters is protrayed through drawings of their facial expressions and actions. For example, in the very beginning level book *Sid and Sam,* written by Nola Buck and illustrated by G. Brian Karas, no reference is made in the words to where the friends meet. We find no physical description of them anywhere, but through the cheerful pictures of the two set in a park and through their actions towards each other, we learn a lot about them and their relationship.

In *The Great Snake Escape,* by Molly Coxe, we read, "One morning Mirabel went to see her friend Maxie." No word clues as to her whereabouts are given, but the pictures fill in this information.

Animals as Characters

Dogs, bears, and mice who demonstrate the characteristics of humans are the main characters in many early reader books. Children can easily relate to animals, and yet these animal characters provide some distance between the child and the characters. It's easier to deal with the difficult issue of being selfish or dishonest or afraid when the character is an animal.

Big Books

Many picture books have been produced as big books—books in oversized format—so that children can follow along, reinforcing recognition of words, as the teacher reads the book aloud. Big books were first introduced by Don Holdaway (1979), who encouraged teachers to enlarge the text and make their own illustrations that they could then share with a group of children. Used with emerging readers, these books are large enough for everyone to see the text and pictures so that together they can follow along as the teacher reads, read the predictable parts as they are repeated during the story, or read the whole story chorally. Teachers can also make observations about features of the text (such as phonetic cueing of initial sounds) or writing conventions (such as use of quotation marks) as part of a mini-lesson. Besides, it's just fun for everyone to share the same text. Some of the books being published in big-book format include *Farmer Duck,* by Martin Waddell; *The First Dog,* by Jan Brett; *Flower Garden,* by Eve Bunting; *The Great Kapoc Tree: A Tale of the Amazon Rain Forest,* by Lynne Cherry; *If You Give a Mouse a Cookie,* by Laura Joffe Numeroff; *The Jacket I Wear in the Snow,* by Shirley Neitzel; and *Magic School Bus: Inside the Earth,* by Joanna Cole.

A Caution

While there are many wonderful, rich easy readers, there are also many that are unnecessarily simplistic and boring. These books have a very limited plot, sing-song language, and flat characterization. Although they are a step up from the *Dick and Jane* books of thirty years ago, they still are disrespectful of children's intelligence and desire for rich language experiences.

Characteristics of Transitional or Chapter Books

Before children are ready for full-fledged novels or longer works of fiction (discussed in the genre chapters), the in-between category of chapter books gives them many choices. These books are usually distinguished by their short chapters, lively topics, and occasional illustrations. Popular authors of transitional or chapter books include Betsy Byars,

Patricia Reilly Giff, James Stevenson, James Marshall, Carla Stevens, Florence Parry Heide, and Elizabeth Levy. In this kind of book you can expect to find several common features.

Black-and-White Illustrations Interspersed Throughout the Text

The illustrations are not intended to provide much of the meaning in the story. Often they just provide a visual to help children "see" the setting or the characters. A few books in this category do have full-color illustrations, such as **Yard Sale,** by James Stevenson, but the purpose of the illustrations is to add interest and visual representations.

Frequent Use of Humor

Since children love to read about funny things, most chapter books use humor to entice children to keep reading. **Flat Stanley,** by Jeff Brown, is a story about Stanley's adventures after he wakes up flat as a pancake. In **The Shrinking of Treehorn,** by Florence Parry Heide, Treehorn's parents hardly notice when he begins to shrink! Much of the humor in these books is based on adults' lack of awareness of the activities in which their children are involved.

Themes That Involve and Delight Children

Many chapter books show children as capable people who should be taken seriously. For instance, Stanley's brother is the one who figures out how to help Stanley become three-dimensional again, and Treehorn takes matters into his own hands to regain his original size. In the **Brian and Pea Brain** series, by Elizabeth Levy, young children in kindergarten and second grade solve mysteries. In the children's series **Polk Street School,** by Patricia Reilly Giff, children both figure out mysteries and learn how to settle conflicts.

Another theme present in many of the books is the importance of being a good neighbor or good friend. This theme is evident in **The Black Cat Club** series, by Susan Saunders, and in **Drew and the Homeboy Question,** by Robb Armstrong. Love and connection to pets, as exemplified by **Tornado,** by Betsy Byars, is a theme very important to children. Understanding people from different cultures is a theme beginning to appear in transitional books. **Premlata and the Festival of Lights,** by Rumer Godden, takes the reader to India to meet a seven-year-old, Prem, who ingeniously helps his poor family.

Structure That Accommodates Young Readers

Not only do transitional books have short chapters (from two to under twenty pages), but the sentences are not as long and complicated as those in full-length novels. Most sentences are no longer than twenty words and are either simple sentences or compound sentences with the noun-verb-object structure. More complex sentence structures are introduced with the use of clauses. Paragraphs range from one sentence to about nine sentences.

Use of Dialogue and Narration

Dialogue is still a prominent part of most of the stories in this category. However, some stories depend on narration rather than dialogue.

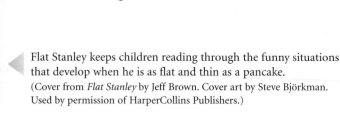

Flat Stanley keeps children reading through the funny situations that develop when he is as flat and thin as a pancake.
(Cover from *Flat Stanley* by Jeff Brown. Cover art by Steve Björkman. Used by permission of HarperCollins Publishers.)

Use of Animals as Characters with Human Characteristics

Although James Marshall's **Rats on the Range and Other Stories** and James Stevenson's **Yard Sale** both feature animals as the cast of characters, transitional books generally have human characters. Sometimes they feature just one animal who can talk or has a special talent—such as the gerbil in **The Weebie Zone** series, by Stephanie Spinner and Ellen Weiss, who by biting the boy gives him the power to understand animals.

urposes of Picture Storybooks

Picture storybooks are books in which the pictures and the text are tightly intertwined. Neither the pictures nor the words are self-sufficient; they need each other to tell the story. The variety of beautiful picture storybooks is staggering. Several categories have been created with which to talk about these books. The categories are not mutually exclusive; most of these books have characteristics of many categories. To demonstrate the range of these books, this section discusses categories that show their purpose or impact on children. Each category will help you think about ways in which these books can be useful in the classroom.

Dealing with Emotions

Picture storybooks can help children to feel nurtured and loved, to understand and accept themselves, and to realize that having emotions such as fear is a part of being human. **Toby, Where Are You?,** by William Steig, tells of the attempt of a furry little animal to have his parents hunt for him in the house to let him know he is important. This book exudes warmth and caring and lets children know that everyone wants to be loved. **The Runaway Bunny,** by Margaret Wise Brown, and **Mama, Do You Love Me?,** by Barbara M. Joosse, both feature a child who asks her mother how she would respond if the child left. Of course, what the child hears makes her happy—the mother expresses unconditional love. In **Koala Lou,** by Mem Fox, a child whose mother has younger children longs for her mother to tell her she loves her, as her mother did when she was little. This very common experience of feeling upstaged or ignored when younger siblings come along is handled with skill and humor. **More More More Said the Baby,** by Vera B. Williams, and **So Much,** by Trish Cooke, show little ones being played with and fussed over by relatives. The illustrations in both these books speak of love and affection and the joy that adults feel in the presence of babies. In **Owl Moon,** by Jane Yolen, an elementary-age child's close relationship with the father unfolds for the reader as the two look for an owl in the dark. All of these books demonstrate that it is natural to want to feel loved.

Understanding and accepting oneself, a multifaceted kind of learning, is part of the work of growing up. In **Chrysanthemum,** by Kevin Henkes, Chrysanthemum learns not to let other children make her feel bad about her name. The important impact a sympathetic and caring teacher can have on a picked-on child is also demonstrated. **Verdi,** by Janell Cannon, shows a beautiful yellow snake who doesn't want to

Five-year-old Emma stands beside her winning entry in an art contest.
(Cover of EMMA'S RUG by Allen Say. Copyright © 1996 by Allen Say. Reprinted by permission of Houghton Mifflin Co. All rights reserved.)

A little girl asks her neighbors and shopkeepers what they have that is beautiful.
(From SOMETHING BEAUTIFUL, by Sharon Dennis Wyeth and illus. by Chris K. Soentpiet, copyright © 1998 by Sharon Dennis Wyeth. Illustrations copyright © 1998 by Chris K. Soentpiet. Used by permission of Random House Children's Books, a division of Random House, Inc.)

grow up and change into a less lively green snake. Over the course of the story, he learns to accept himself and not judge others by how they look. *Leo the Late Bloomer,* by Robert Kraus, depicts a young lion who isn't developing skills as fast as others his age. Luckily, he has a patient, understanding mother to help him through the experience. In *Emma's Rug,* by Allen Say, a very talented young artist learns that the creativity she displays in her paintings comes from within her, not from the rug she has had since she was a baby. And in *Where the Wild Things Are,* by Maurice Sendak, Max learns that he can have emotional outbursts, be "bad," and still be loved.

Children want to know that what they experience and feel is not strange or unusual. Books that assure them that others have fears are *Goodnight Moon,* by Margaret Wise Brown, which shows a child frightened of going to bed, and *Ira Sleeps Over,* by Bernard Waber, which depicts a little boy too embarrassed to bring his teddy bear to a sleepover with his good friend, who also sleeps with a teddy bear. In the very popular *Lilly's Purple Plastic Purse,* by Kevin Henkes, Lilly, who loves school, writes mean things to her teacher when he takes away her purple plastic purse for the day because she is distracting the class with it. The story shows how her parents help her deal with her dilemma and apologize to her teacher.

Learning About the World

CD-ROM

Find historical picture books by *theme* by searching the CD-ROM database.

Picture storybooks dealing with the historical, geographical, and natural world can help children to understand their experiences. Historical picture storybooks abound today. Ann Turner's stunning *Drummer Boy: Marching to the Civil War* gives children a close-up view of one very young boy's experiences in the Civil War. Patricia Polacco's *Pink and Say* relates two boys' experiences in the same time period.

In *The Rock,* by Peter Parnall, respect for nature underscores all that is said as we see the interconnectedness of humans, animals, and the land. *Old Turtle,* by Douglas Wood, is a beautiful story about environmental interdependence and Old Turtle's wisdom in reminding others about the beauty of the fragile earth. *Follow the Moon,* by Sarah Weeks, shows a little boy caring for a small turtle and helping him find his way to his home. Many, many books are written today about caring for the natural world and appreciating its beauty.

Margaret Wise Brown's *The Dead Bird* shows three children burying a bird and creating a ceremony for its burial. This little book introduces children to death in nature and shows how some respond to such a death. On a lighter note, *Livingstone Mouse,* by Pamela Duncan Edwards, is about a mouse who needs to find a home after his mother tells him it's time for him to live on his own. He wants a special place and has heard that China is nice, so he searches in his field for China. After many false starts, he finally finds the home he desires in a china pot, letting children know that while "home" is important, it can be many things. A different aspect of living in the world is shown in Sharon Dennis Wyeth's *Something Beautiful,* in which a little girl who lives in the projects with a graffiti-scarred door asks everyone she knows what they think is beautiful. This book affirms that people can find beauty anywhere around them, especially within other people. Many books in this category can be used in social studies and science curricula, as demonstrated in the boxed feature A Sampling of Picture Storybooks That Can Be Used Across the Curricula.

Learning About People, Relationships, and Feelings

Two books that feature older people are **My Great-Aunt Arizona,** by Gloria Houston, and **Grandpa's Town,** by Takaaki Nomura. In the first book, we see the exuberant Great-Aunt Arizona explaining how she got an education on her own and fashioned her life around a teaching career that inspired many students to travel and fulfill their life dreams. *Grandpa's Town* shows a little boy visiting his grandfather because he is worried that, since his grandmother died, his grandfather will have nothing meaningful in his life. His notions are dispelled when he sees the full, rich life grandfather experiences in his town with his friends. Children can broaden their views of what older people are like through contact with books such as these.

Children can expand their views of the roles of men and women by reading such books as **Mama Is a Miner,** by George Ella Lyon, in which a child talks lovingly about her mother and her demanding job. **Bently and egg,** by William Joyce, shows a male—in this case, a frog—caring for the egg of his duck friend who is called away on family business. Although Bently is at first unhappy with this job, he eventually becomes very involved in caring for the egg and thus very attached to the duckling when he emerges from his shell. In **Tea with Milk,** by Allen Say, a young Japanese woman, raised in California until she was seventeen, goes back to Japan with her parents and cannot adjust to the different view of women held by that culture. When her parents try to arrange a marriage for her, she leaves, goes to the city to work, and eventually meets the man she will marry. This story of Say's mother (and father) gives us a picture of an independent, capable woman in the earlier part of the 20th century.

Many stories show children how people solve problems and get along with other people. In **That Toad is Mine!,** by Barbara Shook Hazen, two boys fight over a toad, lose him, and then resume their friendship. They work through their conflict themselves. In **The Sweetest Fig,** by Chris Van Allsburg, a selfish, mean-spirited man gets his comeuppence when his dog eats the last magic fig and turns the tables on him. In **Chester's Way,** by Kevin Henkes, children see how to be a friend as they watch Chester play with his friends.

Picture storybooks give children a peek into others' family lives, as they see what others do together within the family. An extended family that looks out for each other through hard times is pictured in **Uncle Jed's Barbershop,** by Margaree King Mitchell. When his niece needs an operation, Uncle Jed uses the money he was saving for a barbershop. This beautiful book also shows many other aspects of human behavior, including the importance of "holding fast to dreams." **Daddy Calls Me Man,** by Angela Johnson, gives us a glimpse of what it's like growing up in a family of artists. **Ma Dear's Aprons,** by Patricia C. McKissack, depicts the life of one hard-working single mother from the point of view of her young son. In T. A. Barron's **Where is Grandpa?,** a father explains to his children where his own father is since he died. All of these books show children not only the wide variety of families today, but also how these families handle life, conflicts, and death.

Having Fun

Read-Aloud Books Too Good to Miss, 2000–2001 provides lists of books children will want to hear at www.ilfonline.org/ Programs/Read%20Aloud/ readaloud.htm.

Picture storybooks can help children to learn that the world can be a humorous place and that having fun is a part of living. Some books seem to be written just for the joy and fun they bring to others. One such book written in rhyme, **Mrs. McNosh Hangs Up the Wash,** by Sarah Weeks, shows a woman hanging up just about everything in her house, including herself! **Grandpa's Teeth,** by Rod Clement, plays on the absurd. Grandpa's lost dentures are placed on the Wanted list, and detectives in the city try to locate them. This funny book has zany illustrations, as well as a marvelous surprise ending. In the playful **If You Give a Pig a Pancake,** by Laura Joffe Numeroff, we are shown a series of hilarious things that will happen if you give a pig one pancake. Audrey and Don Wood's **The Napping House,** a rhyming story, is a playful, funny account of what happens when the household all wants to take a nap. The illustrations burst with life and humor. In Anne Miranda's **To Market, To Market,** an old woman goes to market to buy a fat pig, but when she gets him home, he begins to wreck her house. With every additional animal she brings home, it gets worse! This funny rhyming book holds many surprises for the reader. Books in this category often make readers laugh out loud and discover the fun and joy that are part of life.

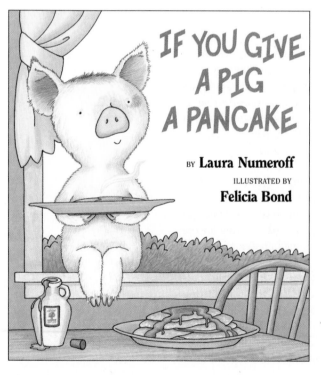

IF YOU GIVE A PIG A PANCAKE

BY **Laura Numeroff**

ILLUSTRATED BY **Felicia Bond**

Stimulating the Imagination

Picture storybooks can help awaken children to the power and pleasure of the imagination. Many books portray the dreams and wishes of children by taking readers off to new places full of wonder. They stimulate imagination, pique curiosity, and fuel the desire to learn and know more. Some books show us new worlds created in the minds of the characters. The lushly illustrated **A Summertime Song,** by Irene Haas, takes us on a journey with Lucy to a birthday party for an owl. Lucy becomes the size of the little animals and can talk to them. She becomes part of their world before finding her grandmother's long-lost doll and returning home, where she regains her human size.

◄ In this circular, outrageous plot, one thing leads to another just because a little girl gives a pig a pancake.
(Cover art from *If You Give a Pig a Pancake* by Laura Joffe Numeroff, illustrated by Felicia Bond. Used by permission of HarperCollins Publishers.)

Several books feature dreams about this world. ***The Wreck of the Zephyr,*** by Chris Van Allsburg, tells the story of why a sailboat is marooned on top of a mountain. Tapping into our desire to experience freedom by soaring on the wind like birds, this book makes us aware of our capabilities and limitations. ***A Dragon in a Wagon,*** by Lynley Dodd, is a delightful rhyming book in which a little girl imagines that her dog has turned into all sorts of wonderful, scary things. Another beautiful fantasy is William Joyce's ***The Leaf Men,*** in which an ill old woman who cannot water her dying garden is helped by the beetles. In their quest to save the garden, they hear the old tale that to call on the help of the leaf men they must go to the top of a tree and call to them. In spite of great perils, the beetles accomplish this task, the leaf men come, and a doll who has lain lost in the garden comes to life to complete the mission of helping the old woman get well.

Two books that give us examples of the imagination in action are ***Cherries and Cherry Pits,*** by Vera B. Williams, and ***Art Dog,*** by Thacker Hurd. In ***Cherries and Cherry Pits,*** a little girl's world is transformed through her imagination and creativity, which are ignited when she draws. In ***Art Dog,*** a security guard in an art museum is not recognized as the artist who expresses his joy and love of life by painting the city. The artists in both these books are shown expressing their personal power as they engage in a pursuit that brings them great pleasure.

Appreciating Beauty

Picture storybooks can help children to experience the wonder and awe of beauty in language and in the visual. Many, many picture books help children to experience the wonder of language. Jane Yolen's ***Nocturne,*** a poetic lullaby illustrated by Anne Hunter, is beautiful to read because she has such a feel for language and such a sense of playfulness. Her love of language, as well as her ability to hear the sounds of language and to pull in or create just the right word, is apparent throughout the book. Hunter's ethereal paintings take us into the night, where we are enfolded by the sounds of Yolen's words.

Book, by George Ella Lyon, ties the beauty of language with the beauty of the visual. Peter Catalanotto's rich-toned watercolors help us feel that we too are inside the book, taking a journey just like the little girl. The words and pictures are wedded perfectly and transport us to the world of imagination that we experience every time we open a wonderful

*Get information on some of these authors and illustrators at the website of **Fairrosa Cyber Library of Children's Literature—Authors and Illustrators.** Find it at www.fairrosa.info/cl.authors.html.*

book. Children remember having such experiences with picture books, as the comments in the boxed feature Children's Voices indicate.

Characteristics of Picture Storybooks for Older Readers

Picture storybooks for older readers are those that can be used from fourth grade up through middle school and beyond. Just because a book is designed for older readers doesn't mean that it can't be used by younger readers. With the help of an enthusiastic teacher or parent or librarian, younger children can appreciate these books. Some of the books mentioned in this section are commonly used by younger children. Picture storybooks for older readers are usually distinguished by a more sophisticated theme, more reflective text, or more academically oriented topic.

Sophisticated Themes or Subject Matter

The Caldecott winner *Snowflake Bentley,* by Jacqueline Briggs Martin, is a biography of a man who spent most of his life photographing snowflakes and revealing their beauty to the world. *Hoops,* by Robert Burleigh, is a poetic description of basketball. *Harlem,* by Walter Dean Myers, is a picture book poem about Harlem. All of these are books whose themes appeal to older readers. Allen Say's *The Sign Painter* is the story of a teenage artist who lands a job as an artist and then realizes that he is not willing to do the kind of commercial art the job requires. He strikes out on his own to live his dream of creating art that is important to him.

Longer and More Reflective Text

Toyomi Igus has written two relatively long and quite reflective picture storybooks, with pictures by Michele Wood. *Going Back Home: An Artist Returns to the South* is about Michele Wood's journey back to the South to capture the history of her African American family in her paintings. This visually stunning book tells the story of each picture both in terms of what it represents in her family and in terms of the symbols used in the paintings. *i see the rhythm* is a visual and poetic introduction to the history of African American music. Not only do the rich tones, lines, and shapes draw us into each era, but Igus's poems capture perfectly the essence of each kind of music. In addition, there is a one- or two-line summary describing each type of music, such as ragtime, swing, or gospel, as well as a brief summary of the events in history that shaped this music. This beautiful book is packed with tantalizing glimpses into African American musical history. *What's the Most Beautiful Thing You Know About Horses?,* by Richard Van Camp, gently prods us into thinking reflectively about these lovely animals, as the narrator asks his friends and family the question in the title. The answers he gets from his family—who, as part of the Dogrib nation, know little about horses because they have always used dogs—are both delightful and profound. George Littlechild's bright, vivid paintings, done in the folk tradition, add an element of playfulness to the book. Because this book pushes readers to think in fresh, positive ways, children find it provocative.

Topics That Relate to Other School Studies

Find books on specific topics or concepts at **Children's Picture Book Database at Miami University** at *www.lib.muohio.edu/pictbks/.*

At the top of the list of academically oriented books that can inspire students to think, research, or write are books that can enrich social studies courses. *Drummer Boy: Marching to the Civil War,* by Ann Turner, and *Pink and Say,* by Patricia Polacco, both show the Civil War from young boys' points of view. The Caldecott winner *Golem,* by David Wisniewski, tells of the year 1580 in Prague, when Jews were being set upon and accused of using the blood of Christian children to make matzoh, the Passover bread. To protect them from angry mobs storming the walls of their ghetto, a Golem, or shapeless man, was created by the chief rabbi. This fascinating legend might encourage students to do research in order to learn more about the persecution of the Jews and the nature of the

On memories of picture books . . .

It's about a dog and little girl and a teacher and a mom but it doesn't have any words in it. I like it because it has a lot of pictures.
—Jessica, 2nd grade

*My favorite picture book is **Outside My Window—Good Day Spider** because this kid liked the duck, the spider, and the dog. The spider said "hello" to the duck and the spider looked sad.* —Ashley, 2nd grade

I can't think of the name of it. It's got a cat in it and the house burns down. I like it because it's got a cat in it. —Sarah, 2nd grade

*The best one I've ever heard of is **Goldilocks.** It has good pictures.* —Elizabeth, 2nd grade

*I like **Hey Al!** because the pictures are colorful and bright.* —Andy, 3rd grade

***Search for Santa's Helpers** because you get to search for elves.* —Amber, 3rd grade

I love Mercer Mayer's books because they have good pictures. —Casey, 3rd grade

***Werewolf of Fever Swamp** because it's scary.* —Nathan, 3rd grade

***There's a Wocket in My Pocket** because it's a tongue twister sort of.* —Amanda, 3rd grade

***Arthur** books make my mind say, "I think this author did a neat job!"* —Jenna, 3rd grade

I liked Eric Carle when I was younger because he did his own artwork. —Jake, 4th grade

*The one picture book that stands out in my memory is **The Little Engine That Could.** It's my favorite book because it reminds me every time I read it about how I need to keep trying. Lots of children's books we read as children we still remember today. They actually help us go through life.* —Jacob, 6th grade

*I loved **Brown Bear, Brown Bear** not because of the words but because of the pictures.* —Joshua, 6th grade

I can't say I remember any picture books but I can remember I liked them when I was little. —Scott, 6th grade

*The book that was called **I Think I Can.** I like it 'cause it tells me not to give up.* —Leon, 6th grade

***Chicka, Chicka, Boom Boom** because when I was in the second grade that was my favorite book.* —Monique, 6th grade

*I remember **Where the Wild Things Are.** I always liked art and the pictures to me were so cool.* —Bridget, 7th grade

I remember Dr. Seuss books when I began reading. What I think I enjoyed the most is how he could use his imagination and how everything rhymed. —Marie, 7th grade

***Rose Blanche** sticks in my mind. I like the unfinished wording and the way the pictures are watercolors and sort of blurry.* —Jeff, 7th grade

***Berenstain Bears** are great. They are colorful and they have a moral. They were great especially when I was young because they helped me understand what not to do.* —Jessica, 7th grade

*My favorite picture book of all time is **If You Give a Mouse a Cookie.** I like this book because it is animals talking and I think it would be cool to meet a talking mouse that wanted a cookie and milk.* —Drew, 7th grade

*I like **Green Eggs and Ham** because I remember how stubborn Sam I Am was.* —Ben, 7th grade

Older readers are drawn to this picture book because of the topic and the illustrations, which pique their interest.

(Reprinted with permission of the publisher, Children's Book Press, San Francisco, CA. *I See the Rhythm* paintings © 1998 by Michele Wood and text copyright © 1998 by Toyomi Igus.)

allegations made against them. Paul Goble's **Death of the Iron Horse** shows an American Indian point of view on the coming of the railroad and what it meant to the native people's way of life. It would be interesting to use this book as a way to talk about point of view and how every instance in history of taking lands can be seen from at least two points of view. Perhaps students studying this time period in history could write about other events from the point of view of the American Indians. Sherry Garland's **The Voices of the Alamo** is the story of the many people who lived on the land surrounding the Alamo or had a hand in fighting there. It is told through poems from the points of view of Indians who first lived there, farmers, Texians (Mexicans who lived in Texas), the military, and many others. Students could work to generate multiple points of view on other historical events or sites.

Students who are learning about Harriet Tubman and her heroic work to save thousands of people from slavery will enjoy two very different accounts of Tubman's accomplishments in Faith Ringgold's **Aunt Harriet's Underground Railroad in the Sky** and Jacob Lawrence's **Harriet and the Promised Land.** In Ringgold's version, a young girl in the present day finds Harriet's railroad in the sky and experiences what escaping slaves did, traveling from safe house to safe house. Ringgold's paintings make the story leap to life. Lawrence's version is written in rhymed verse, accompanied by his rich-hued, stylized illustrations. These two stories cry out to be compared, and students could get involved in looking at which events the artists depicted, which ones they left out, and the impact of each book. These books together show students in very vivid ways how writing about historical events still involves selection and choice on the part of the author; there is no such thing as "just the facts," since the facts to be presented must be selected.

Ringgold's **Dinner at Aunt Connie's House** is another book older readers find interesting. Two children go upstairs at Aunt Connie's house, where the subjects of her paintings of outstanding African American women talk to the children about who they are and what they've done. This marvelous book introduces new information in an interesting way. It provides a good starting point for learning more about the twelve women in the paintings.

An abundance of books are available to introduce or reinforce concepts in science. *Window,* by Jeannie Baker (discussed in the wordless book section), is a book older readers respond to, since they can see so clearly the negative effects of humans' actions on the environment. A book students could use as a starting point for research on how early man lived is Jan Brett's **The First Dog,** set in an Ice Age landscape. **Buddy,** by William Joyce, the true story of a gorilla raised in the New York mansion of Gertrude Lintz, could be used to kick off a unit on animal rights. What happens to Buddy raises many provocative questions students would be eager to explore.

Many picture storybooks can be used to stimulate writing by students. **Tea with Milk,** by Allen Say, could inspire students to unearth the story of how their parents or grandparents met. **Aunt Flossie's Hat (and Crab Cakes Later),** by Elizabeth Fitzgerald Howard, which describes Aunt Flossie's memories of what she experienced as she wore each of her different hats, could lead students to write about memories revolving around an object or memories of aunts and uncles.

The books of Chris Van Allsburg, Jon Scieszka, and Babette Cole are sure to be a hit with older students. Van Allsburg's **The Garden of Abdul Gasazi, Jumanji,** and **The Mysteries of Harris Burdick** all cry out to be viewed closely and repeatedly and talked and written about. These books are nothing short of intriguing. Scieszka's books— **The Stinky Cheese Man and Other Fairly Stupid Tales; Squids will be Squids: Fresh Morals, Beastly Fables; The True Story of the Three Little Pigs by A. Wolf;** and **The Frog Prince Continued**—are riotously funny. They require repeated readings to catch all of the subtleties and humor; they also seem to ask us to create our own tales, just as he does. In combination with his outrageous sense of humor, his breaking of literary conventions

This illustration of two chimpanzees and a surprised girl cries out for an explanation.
(Cover, from JUMANJI. Copyright © 1981 by Chris Van Allsburg. Reprinted by permission of Houghton Mifflin Company. All rights reserved.)

results in highly unusual and entertaining tales. Babette Cole writes and illustrates unconventional, hysterically funny books. *The Trouble with Mom, Winni Allfours,* and *Drop Dead* are all books older students would giggle at. It turns out that mom is a witch, Winnie prefers to be a horse, and Grandad and Gran had very interesting, unconventional lives. These story lines could easily be imitated in students' own tales.

The books mentioned here are only a small sampling of those that could be used with older readers. The best way to find books to use with the older age groups is simply to go to the children's section in the library and sample books.

Favorite Authors and Illustrators of Picture Books

Thousands of picture books are published each year. To help you navigate through the sea of choices until you become familiar with the authors and illustrators and find some you love, I offer the list in the boxed feature Favorite Authors and Illustrators of Picture Books.

Favorite Authors and Illustrators of Picture Books

Aliki creates endearing drawings filled with multiethnic characters in the books she writes, which often deal with the affective.

Graeme Base, author and illustrator, creates books filled with lush, colorful, detailed drawings that beckon readers back to look for what they might have missed the first time through.

Quentin Blake is known for doing humorous, often outrageous drawings in cartoon style, in both his own books and those of others.

Margaret Wise Brown authored some endearing stories, dealing with fears and doubts, that continue to be read to very young children today.

Anthony Browne writes delightful books filled with his exquisitely detailed images, often done in a surrealistic style.

Ashley Bryan, poet and illustrator, creates paintings in the naive style, using bright, bold colors that exude happiness.

Eve Bunting, a very prolific author, writes stories that often touch on the harder "real life" issues such as homelessness, urban riots, and memories of war losses.

John Burningham, author and illustrator, creates delightful picture books that often border on the outrageous.

Janell Cannon, author and illustrator, uses bright colors and clear images to involve the reader in the thoughtful stories she creates.

Eric Carle, author and illustrator, is a master of the cut-paper collage. His books use bright, cheerful colors and sharply delineated illustrations.

Peter Catalanotto, author and illustrator, is a watercolorist whose often-surrealistic illustrations have a dreamlike quality.

R. Gregory Christie is an illustrator known for drama, an effect he achieves through angular representations, outsized heads and hands, and striking perspectives.

Rod Clement's humorous illustrations enhance the reader's enjoyment of the story, whether he is illustrating his own work or a book authored by another.

Babette Cole, author and illustrator, creates zany books with cartoonlike figures. One cannot help but smile at her whimsical characters.

Bryan Collier, author and illustrator, dazzles with his stunning, bold, watercolor and cut-paper-collage compositions. His stylized drawings capture the essence of his subjects.

Barbara Cooney, a Caldecott Award–winning illustrator, also writes lovely books. Simple forms, soft colors, and a sometimes-somber mood characterize her illustrations.

Floyd Cooper, author and illustrator, creates oil-wash illustrations. Some have glowing color, while others are soft and muted. His choices capture the mood of whatever story he is illustrating.

David Diaz, illustrator, is known for the vibrant colors he uses, a collage-like effect, and a naive style.

Leo and Diane Dillon are a husband-and-wife team. They have worked together to create brilliant illustrations for a wide variety of texts authored by some of children's literature's best authors.

Richard Egielski is an author and illustrator. His award-winning illustrations reveal not only a wonderful imagination, but a versatile artistry as well.

Lois Ehlert, author and illustrator, creates cut-paper collage, often embedded with fascinating designs and bright colors.

Mem Fox writes stories for young readers in which the text often has magical repetition, making it predictable and very "readable." The sense that she purposely chooses concise words with a poetic feel permeates Fox's work.

Wanda Gag created the classic story of a little kitten that emerged out of hundreds, thousands, millions, and billions of prospective pets to become part of an elderly couple's home. Her artwork holds up well in today's competitive field of illustrations.

Stephen Gammell is an illustrator and author whose work has a whimsical quality. He can record a fun family get-together but can also convey the mood of a story with a scary or sad theme.

Kevin Henkes, author and illustrator, creates endearing mice in cartoon style and writes about issues near and dear to the hearts of children.

Ronald Himler is an illustrator who works in watercolors. The stories that he illustrates or creates often deal with sensitive issues, and his watercolors capture the dignity of the characters and themes in the text.

Shirley Hughes is an author and illustrator whose books for preschoolers and young readers are well written and entertaining. Her colorful, soft illustrations capture the expressions of the story's characters.

William Joyce is an author and illustrator who, along with illustrating other authors' work, writes creative, fun stories that capture a child's imagination with their bright, colorful, stylized illustrations.

Ted Lewin is a Caldecott Honor–winning illustrator who has worked with many wonderful authors. His beautiful watercolors illustrate this textbook.

E. B. Lewis is an outstanding illustrator whose watercolors are rich in detail and highly luminescent, complementing the texts of leading children's authors.

Leo Lionni is a popular author and illustrator whose work continues to be reprinted. His illustrations are easily recognizable with their cut paper and soft hues.

Arnold Lobel is a prolific illustrator who became an author as well. His stories, characterizing the many aspects of friendship between a frog and a toad, are wonderful texts for early readers.

Thomas Locker, author and illustrator, has won numerous awards for his work. His magnificent realistic paintings are breathtaking, and they capture the essence of the text.

George Ella Lyon, author, is best known for her loving use of language and her willingness to approach subjects in unusual ways.

James Marshall, author and illustrator, illustrates his engaging, humorous stories with delightful cartoon characters.

Robert McCloskey has authored and illustrated some classic children's stories, often set on the East Coast. His subjects range from the life of a family of ducks in a large city to life in a quiet coastal setting.

Barry Moser, book designer and illustrator, creates amazingly beautiful illustrations that reach to the heart of the book.

Helen Oxenbury, author and illustrator, creates whimsical, delightful, cartoonlike characters, using bright, bold colors that capture the essence of the characters.

Margie Palatini is an author whose books delight the young reader. Using dialogue that has been described as riotous, she tickles the funny bone of her readers.

Peter Parnell often illustrates the books of Byrd Baylor, depicting the Southwest in beautiful yellows and oranges against a white background, with finely woven features created with black lines. Illustrating his own New England story led him to use a very different color scheme.

Patricia Polacco illustrates her own stories and poems, which have an extraordinary immediacy. She is known for the breadth of her work across different genres, as well as her inclusiveness of multiracial and ethnic characters in her stories.

Brian Pinkney's work is almost always quickly recognizable. His use of scratchboard is outstanding and captures the feel of the text.

Jerry Pinkney is an amazing watercolorist whose attention to detail, use of soft-hued colors, and authenticity contribute to any book he illustrates.

Chris Raschka, author and Caldecott Honor–winning illustrator, reaches for the never-been-tried-before in his unusual books.

Faith Ringgold, both an author and an illustrator, is known for her naive style and richly colored, detailed pictures, often used in stories that deal with the human desire to be free.

Cynthia Rylant is an author whose themes nudge the boundaries of children's literature. Whether she is writing in prose or in poetry, for

(continued)

older readers or for the very young, her writing finds a way to the heart.

Allen Say, illustrator and author, creates illustrations that have a crisp, photographic quality. His lovely stories are steeped in emotion and human experience.

Jon Scieszka is a zany author whose humorous story lines break literary conventions and make readers pay attention.

Maurice Sendak has authored numerous children's books and illustrated even more. He is best remembered for a story he authored and illustrated about a little boy who imagines a wild adventure after being sent to his room for misbehaving.

Dr. Seuss, often cited as a favorite author/illustrator, made a permanent place for himself in children's literature with his mischievous cat and odd-colored eggs. His books range from simple rhymes creating silly images to books with messages about conservation and life choices.

David Shannon, illustrator and author, often uses bright, splashy colors and cartoonlike characters whose actions children can relate to. When he illustrates for other writers, he demonstrates his range and depth.

David Small, illustrator and author, has a quiet style. His illustrations, usually with soft colors and great attention to detail, wonderfully extend the story.

Chris K. Soentpiet, illustrator for many popular authors, creates stunning images with exciting use of light in his photolike pictures.

William Steig, both author and illustrator, uses a cartoon style and animals with whimsical expressions to make his characters leap to life.

James Stevenson, both author and illustrator, is known for his softly colored cartoons, his gentle characters, and his wit and humor, which make his stories memorable.

Sarah Stewart is a writer who creates gentle, quiet stories, which are often evocative of earlier times.

Ann Turner is an author whose beautiful artistry with words lets her say volumes in just a few words, whether she writes in prose or in poetry.

Chris Van Allsburg is an author and illustrator who uses light masterfully. His surrealistic pictures often startle readers into looking closely at the details.

Rosemary Wells is a versatile author/illustrator who has created many of her own books for young children. Her huggable animal characters, painted in bright colors, live out many stories that young children can relate to.

David Wiesner is an illustrator and author of wordless books that tickle the imagination and create countless texts in the reader's mind. Because of his use of the surreal, interest in his

books extends to the middle school student.

Vera B. Williams, author and illustrator, uses vibrant, rich colors to illustrate her lovely stories, often featuring working-class people.

Mike Wimmer is an illustrator noted for his stunning use of light in pictures that touch the heart of the story.

Jacqueline Woodson is an author relatively new to children's literature. Both her picture books and her young adult realistic fiction tackle difficult issues, opening the way to meaningful discussion with even the youngest readers.

Jane Yolen is a prolific author who writes in a multitude of genres. Her language is always lovely, and she has the ability to wrap the reader in the essence of her stories.

Ed Young, both an author and an illustrator, is known for his soft-hued watercolors and the dreamlike quality of many of his illustrations.

Paul O. Zelinski's strikingly beautiful illustrations have ensured him a place among notable children's literature artists. By retelling and illustrating folk tales, he has brought new beauty and interest to these familiar tales.

ℐnvitations

Choose several of the following activities to complete:

1. What picture storybooks do you remember most clearly from your childhood? Compare your choices to those mentioned in Children's Voices and to those of others in your group. Do any common themes or characteristics pervade your choices?

2. Choose a picture storybook you love, and write a response to it. Then go through the section in Chapter 2 on picture storybooks and analyze your book in terms of purpose, plot variation, vision, setting, characters, and qualities of writing. Feel free to include other characteristics not mentioned. Share your findings with your small group and describe to them all the ways you think this book could be used in a classroom.

3. Choose a favorite author or illustrator and find information about her or him on the Internet, beginning with the sites mentioned in Internet and Text Resources. Share your findings in a small group, explaining what you found out and any insights you gained. Also share what is available on any other sites you found.

4. Bring in a picture book to read aloud to a small group. As each person in the group reads his or her book, jot down your reactions and responses. Then reread Taking a Look at the Research: The Read-Aloud. Looking carefully at Routmann's list (in paragraph two) of ways read-alouds can help a child become a successful reader, write down and then talk about how the books just read can do the things she lists. For example, what could children learn from these books about how stories work?

5. As you read picture books, do one of the following:

- Choose a topic or theme you're interested in and create your own ABC book, using whatever structure or scheme you wish. Share this book with your group and reflect on what you learned about ABC books and about writing.

- Find a wordless book by Anno or Wiesner or another author and create a narrative for it. Share both the book and the narrative with your group. Write a reflection on the experience, focusing on the kind of learning or thinking the book did or did not provoke in you.

- Try to produce an early reader yourself so that you can see how much skill it takes to construct a book with 120–1,000 words that still has a sense of story and engages children. Words have to be selected carefully not only to take into account reading level but also to delight and interest children so as to engage them in the text. Share your results with your group.

6. Have each person in your group select and read ten books in one of the following categories: ABC books, counting books, concept books, or picture books for older readers. Rank the ten books from 1 to 10, with 1 being the best, and explain the reasons for your decisions. Work to generate a list of the characteristics that caused you to rank each book as you did. Was it imaginative/unimaginative pictures? Did the language delight/fail to delight you? Were the illustrations engrossing or too obscure to involve you? Share your findings with your small group.

7. Read ten early reader books in the library. Rank the ten books from 1 to 10, with 1 being the best. Which ones did you personally find most interesting to read? Do any of the characteristics of early reader books apply to or describe the books you read? Did your books have other characteristics that weren't mentioned? What qualities in these books give support to young readers? Did you find books that you did not consider to be of high quality for this genre? Work to name the qualities that put you off. Did you find stereotypes? Did the characters seem uninteresting? Were the illustrations mediocre? Did there seem to be little support for early readers? Share your findings with your group.

8. Read several chapter books and describe how they differ from early reader books. Include themes, types of characters, support for the reading process, and anything else you notice. Also describe any books you found that were flat and uninteresting.

Classroom Teaching Ideas

Imitating the Plot Structures of Picture Books

Concrete writing models allow students to write in new and interesting ways. Encourage students to try one of the following plot structures, instead of always writing stories sequentially. The types of plot structures explained below come from the work of Yvonne Siu-Runyan (cited in McClure and Kristo, 1996).

1. With a circle or turn-around plot, the story begins and ends at the same place. Anita Lobel's *Alison's Zinnia* circles back around, as the little girl on the last page, whose name begins with *Z*, gives a flower to the first girl in the book, whose name begins with *A*. Laura Joffe Numeroff's *If You Give a Pig a Pancake* tells of all the things a pig might demand if you give him just one pancake and ends back in the same place.

2. With a story-within-a-story, there are two stories; one is the vehicle for telling the other. *Home Place,* by Crescent Dragonwagon, tells the story of a family walking in the woods and coming upon the remains of a house. The second story is about the people who once lived there. *Tornado,* by Betsy Byars, an early reader book, tells the story of a family that goes to the cellar because a tornado is sighted. While they wait there, the hired man tells everyone stories from his past, which mainly involve his pets.

3. With a parallel plot, two stories unfold simultaneously. John Burningham's *Come Away from the Water, Shirley* has a parallel plot, with the parents and Shirley experiencing totally different things at the beach. Anthony Browne's *Voices in the Park* actually has four stories going on at once, although each is told in a separate section of the book.

4. With a flashback, a main character in the present tells a story about the past. *The Lotus Seed,* by Sherry Garland, is told mostly in flashback, as a granddaughter describes her grandmother's escape from Vietnam. *Marianthe's Story: Painted Words, Spoken Memories,* by Aliki, is the story of Marianthe telling her class what life was like in her country of origin before she moved to the United States. *Sitti's Secrets,* by Naomi Shihab Nye, relates the memories a little girl has of visiting her grandmother in the Middle East.

5. In a sequential plot, one event follows another. *Inch by Inch,* by Leo Lionni, is the clever story of how an inchworm got along and survived in the world. It is told sequentially, with the inchworm getting away from a predator in the end through quick thinking. *Sylvester and the Magic Pebble,* by William Steig, shows one event after the other. It begins when Sylvester finds a magic pebble, which he then uses to become a rock to escape from a lion; it ends months later when he is finally freed from his rock form.

6. With a cumulative or add-on structure, the preceding events are repeated in order of occurrence each time a new event is added. *My Little Sister Ate One Hare,* by Bill Grossman, is a hilarious tale of all that little sister eats, told using the add-on structure. Each page begins with "My little sister ate one hare" and adds on another disgusting item she ingested. *The Napping House,* by Audrey Wood, also uses this structure, as all the nappers pile on top of each other on the bed. A new napper is added only after the text goes through the whole list of who is already on the bed.

7. With an interlocking plot, each response becomes the beginning for the next sentence. Bill Martin, Jr., uses this pattern in both *Brown Bear, Brown Bear, What Do You See?* and *Polar Bear, Polar Bear, What Do You Hear?* Sue Williams also uses it in her delightful *I Went Walking.*

8. With a question/answer format, a question is asked, then answered. Books with this format include *Mama, Do You Love Me?,* by Barbara M. Joosse, and *Is Your Mama a Llama?,* by Deborah Guarino. These books involve the reader by asking a question, which is answered on the next page.

9. With a repeated refrain, a phrase is repeated throughout the story. In the ever-popular *Chicka Chicka Boom Boom,* by Bill Martin, Jr., and John Archambault, the contagious phrase "Chicka chicka boom boom, will there be enough room?" appears throughout the book. Judith Viorst's *Alexander and the Terrible, Horrible, No Good, Very Bad Day* also repeats the title phrase throughout the story, as we hear about what has gone wrong in Alexander's day.

10. With a surprise ending, the end of the story is unexpected. Creating a surprise ending can be quite an undertaking for a writer. Rod Clement in *Grandpa's Teeth,* Chris Van Allsburg in *The Sweetest Fig,* and David Wiesner in *June 29, 1999* all do it well.

11. A pattern of three may be three characters, three tasks, or three things to overcome throughout the story. This pattern is most common in folk tales and fairy tales. *Wiley and the Hairy Man,* by Judy Sierra, and *Clever Katya—A Fairy Tale from Old Russia,* by Mary Hoffman, both show characters completing three tasks.

12. Familiar sequences around which stories are built include months of the year, days of the week, and holidays. Such stories capitalize on children's familiarity with sequences that are part of their daily lives. Maurice Sendak's *Chicken Soup with Rice: A Book of Months* goes through the months of the year, telling why "All seasons of the year are nice for eating chicken soup with rice." Eric Carle's *The Very Hungry Caterpillar* shows a caterpillar eating his way through food as he goes through his cycle, terminating with his rebirth as a butterfly.

Using Picture Storybooks Across the Curricula

1. Before reading to the class a picture book containing new information about a unit the class is studying, ask them what they know about the topic. After reading the book and allowing sufficient time for response, ask them what they discovered about the topic from the book. For example, if you are studying the South and want students to have information on bayous, you could use this strategy with *Sweet Magnolias,* by Virginia Kroll.

2. Have students interview relatives and friends on how their experiences were different from or similar to the ones read about in a book. For example, after reading *Grandfather's Journey,* by Allen Say, students could interview people about their experiences moving to this country or state or town.

3. Ask children to find in the library a picture book that in some way relates to a unit of study.

4. Ask students to write telegrams or emails to characters, offering encouragement or explaining how they think a situation should be handled and why. One book this strategy could be used with is *Drummer Boy: Marching to the Civil War,* by Ann Turner.

5. Use picture books as models of the kinds of writing you would like your students to do on a topic. For instance, after reading several alphabet books, they could compose their own alphabet book on whatever topic they were studying.

6. Ask students what a character in a book would like to say to the world. What would *Old Turtle,* by Douglas Wood, want to tell us about the way we treat the land? What would Aunt Connie (from *Dinner at Aunt Connie's House,* by Faith Ringgold) want us to be aware of? Students can write these monologues in groups.

7. Have students interview a character, using historical information from the time period of the character or knowledge of a topic from science. For instance, if students were studying the Underground Railroad, they could interview the barefoot man in *Barefoot: Escape on the Underground Railroad,* by Pamela Duncan Edwards.

8. Ask students to think about what gift, either tangible or intangible, a character in a book would most like to have. What would the boy standing by the window in *Window,* by Jeannie Baker, most want? How about Harriet Tubman in *Aunt Harriet's Underground Railroad in the Sky,* by Faith Ringgold?

9. To encourage text-to-text connections, ask children to think of both nonfiction and fiction books that a character in a book would like. For instance, Chrysanthemum, in the book of the same name by Kevin Henkes, might like to read about the Japanese American boy Donnie, who has to deal with a different kind of teasing in *Heroes,* by Ken Mochizuki.

Internet and Text Resources

1. Many children's book authors and illustrators have web pages on the Internet. Some are home pages provided by the authors or illustrators themselves, while others are pages provided by the publishing company to better acquaint you with the author or illustrator and his or her work. One outstanding home page is that of Jan Brett at

www.janbrett.com

This page is user friendly and informative about the author, while at the same time providing activities and ideas one might use in the classroom along with her stories. When you arrive at her site, you are greeted with a variety of different options. Clicking on the site map brings you to choices that include activities related to her books, as well as postcards, bookmarks, and iron-on transfers with pictures of the many characters from her beautifully illustrated books. The assortment of classroom activity pages also include her distinctive artwork. Other authors' web pages can be accessed through the sites listed below.

2. **Learning about the Author and Illustrator Pages,** by Kay E. Vandergrift, provides more than 500 links to the sites of authors and illustrators. Go to

www.scils.rutgers.edu/~kvander/AuthorSite/authora.html

3. **Simon Says Kids.com,** site of publisher Simon & Schuster, will get you to sites of its authors and illustrators. Click on Features, then on Simon Says Kids. Find it at

www.simonsays.com

4. **Young Readers** is Penguin's site, which gets you to its authors and illustrators. Go to

www.penguinputnam.com/

and click on Young Readers.

5. **Literature and Language Sites for Children** contains links to book lists, authors, illustrators, and more. Go to

www.ala.org/parentspage/greatsites/

6. **Fairrosa Cyber Library of Children's Literature—Authors and Illustrators** is yet another site with links to many authors and illustrators. Go to

www.fairrosa.info/cl.authors.html

7. **Children's Picture Book Database at Miami University** lets users search by key words on topics, concepts, and skills. Find it at

www.lib.muohio.edu/pictbks/

8. **Children's Trade Books in Math** provides lists of picture books that teach and reinforce math concepts. Go to

www.luc.edu/schools/education/csimath/zbib.htm

9. **Outstanding Science Trade Books for Students** provides lists of books that can be used in the science classroom. Find it at

www.nsta.org/ostbc

10. **Booklists of Children's Literature** is a site with lists by theme, such as animal stories. Find it at

www.monroe.lib.in.us/childrens/children_booklists.html

11. **Read-Aloud Books Too Good to Miss 2001–2002** provides a wonderful list. Find it at

www.acpl.lib.in.us/Childrens_Services/readalouds.html

12. Benedict, Susan, and Lenore Carlisle (1992). *Beyond Words: Picture Books for Older Readers and Writers.* Portsmouth, NH: Heinemann.

13. Lima, Carolyn W., and John A. Lima (2001). *A to Zoo, Subject Access to Children's Picture Books.* Westport, CT: Bowker.

14. McElmeel, Sharron L. (2000). *100 Most Popular Picture Book Authors and Illustrators: Biographical Sketches and Bibliographies.* Englewood, CO: Teacher Ideas Press.

CD-ROM

Locate more information on *read-aloud* in Classroom Teaching Ideas and Invitations by using the CD-ROM word search feature.

References

Day, Alexandra (1998). "Good Dog, Carl: The Silent Hero of a Successful Series." Presentation to International Reading Association Conference, Orlando, Florida, May 1998.

Holdaway, Don (1979). *The Foundations of Literacy.* New York: Ashton Scholastic.

Kozel, Jonathan (1998). Opening speech, National Council of Teachers of English convention, Nashville, Tennesee, November 1998.

Siu-Runyan, Yvonne (1996). "Connecting Writing, Talk, and Literature." In Amy A. McClure and Janice V. Kristo, eds., *Books That Invite Talk, Wonder, Play.* Urbana, IL: NCTE.

Children's Books

Ahlberg, Janet, and Allen Ahlberg (1982). *The Baby's Catalogue.* Boston: Little, Brown.

Aliki (1996). *Hello! Good-Bye!* New York: Greenwillow.

—— (1998). *Marianthe's Story: Painted Words, Spoken Memories.* New York: Greenwillow.

Anno, Mitsumasu (1983). *Anno's USA.* New York: Philomel.

Armstrong, Robb (1997). *Drew and the Homeboy Question.* New York: HarperTrophy.

Azarian, Mary (1999). *A Gardener's Alphabet.* Boston: Houghton Mifflin.

Baker, Jeannie (1991). *Window.* New York: Greenwillow.

Bang, Molly (1997). *Common Ground: The Water, Earth, and Air We Share.* New York: Scholastic.

Barron, T. A. (2000). *Where is Grandpa?* Illus. Chris K. Soentpiet. New York: Philomel.

Base, Graeme (1987). *Animalia.* Sydney, Australia: Abrams.

Beaton, Clare (1999). *One Moose, Twenty Mice.* New York: Barefoot.

Blake, Quentin (1989). *Quentin Blake's ABC.* New York: Knopf.

Brett, Jan (1988). *The First Dog.* San Diego: Harcourt Brace.

Briggs, Raymond (1989). *The Snowman.* New York: Random.

Brown, Jeff (1996). *Flat Stanley.* Illus. Steve Björkman. New York: HarperTrophy.

Brown, Margaret Wise (1958). *The Dead Bird.* Illus. Remy Charlip. New York: Scott.

—— (1947). *Goodnight Moon.* Illus. Clement Hurd. New York: Harper.

—— (1942). *The Runaway Bunny.* Illus. Clement Hurd. New York: Harper.

Browne, Anthony (1998). *Voices in the Park.* London: DK Publishing.

Buck, Nola (1996). *Sid and Sam.* Illus. G. Brian Karas. New York: HarperTrophy.

Bunting, Eve (1994). *Flower Garden.* Illus. Kathryn Hewitt. San Diego: Harcourt Brace.

Burleigh, Robert (1997). *Hoops.* Illus. Stephen T. Johnson. San Diego: Silver Whistle.

Burningham, John (1997). *Come Away from the Water, Shirley.* New York: Crowell [out of print].

—— (1985). *John Burningham's ABC.* New York: Crown.

Byars, Betsy (1997). *Tornado.* Illus. Doron Ben-Ami. New York: HarperTrophy.

Cannon, Janell (1997). *Verdi.* San Diego: Harcourt Brace.

Carle, Eric (1987). *Do You Want to Be My Friend?* New York: HarperTrophy.

—— (1984). *The Very Hungry Caterpillar.* New York: Putnam.

Catalanotto, Peter (1989). *Dylan's Day Out.* New York: Orchard.

Cha, Dia (1996). *Dia's Story Cloth: The Hmong People's Journey of Freedom.* Illus. Chue Cha and Nhia Thao Cha. New York: Lee & Low.

Cherry, Lynn (1990). *The Great Kapok Tree: A Tale of the Amazon Rain Forest.* San Diego: Harcourt Brace.

Chin-Lee, Cynthia (1997). *A Is for Asia.* Illus. Yumi Heo. New York: Orchard.

Chocolate, Debbi (1996). *Kente Colors*. Illus. John Ward. New York: Walker.

Clark, Emma Chichester (1997). *Little Miss Muffet's Count-Along Surprise*. New York: Doubleday.

Clement, Rod (1997). *Grandpa's Teeth*. New York: HarperCollins.

Cole, Babette (1996). *Drop Dead*. New York: Knopf.

—— (1983). *The Trouble with Mom*. London: Windmill.

—— (1995). *Winni Allfours*. Mahwah, NJ: Bridgewater.

Cole, Joanna (1987). *The Magic School Bus: Inside the Earth*. Illus. Bruce Degan. New York: Scholastic.

Cole, Norma (1994). *Blast Off! A Space Counting Book*. Illus. Marshall Peck, III. Watertown, MA: Charlesbridge.

Collington, Peter (1987). *The Angel and the Soldier Boy*. New York: Knopf [out of print].

—— (1995). *The Tooth Fairy*. New York: Knopf.

Cooke, Trish (1994). *So Much*. Illus. Helen Oxenbury. Cambridge, MA: Candlewick.

Coxe, Molly (1994). *The Great Snake Escape*. New York: HarperTrophy.

Crews, Donald (1980). *Truck*. New York: Greenwillow.

Cushman, Doug (1996). *The ABC Mystery*. New York: HarperCollins.

Day, Alexandra (1985). *Good Dog, Carl*. New York: Simon & Schuster.

dePaola, Tomie (1990). *Pancakes for Breakfast*. New York: HarperCollins.

—— (1983). *Sing, Pierrot, Sing: A Picture Book in Mime*. San Diego: Harcourt Brace.

Dodd, Lynley (1988). *A Dragon in a Wagon*. New Zealand: Mallinson Rendel.

Dragonwagon, Crescent (1990). *Home Place*. Illus. Jerry Pinkney. New York: Macmillan.

Edwards, Pamela Duncan (1997). *Barefoot: Escape on the Underground Railroad*. Illus. Henry Cole. New York: HarperCollins.

—— (1996). *Livingstone Mouse*. Illus. Henry Cole. New York: HarperCollins.

Feelings, Muriel (1971). *Moja Means One—Swahili Counting Book*. Illus. Tom Feelings. New York: Dial.

Fleming, Denise (1992). *Count!* New York: Holt.

—— (1996). *Lunch*. New York: Holt.

Fox, Mem (1988). *Koala Lou*. Illus. Pamela Lofts. San Diego: Harcourt Brace.

Frasier, Debra (1991). *On the Day You Were Born*. San Diego: Harcourt Brace.

—— (1998). *Out of the Ocean*. San Diego: Harcourt Brace.

Gag, Wanda (1997). *The ABC Bunny*. Illus. Howard Gag. New York: Paper Star [1933, Coward-McCann].

Garland, Sherry (1993). *The Lotus Seed*. Illus. Tatsuro Kiuchi. New York: Harcourt Brace.

—— (2000). *The Voices of the Alamo*. Illus. Ronald Himler. New York: Scholastic.

Goble, Paul (1993). *Death of the Iron Horse*. New York: Aladdin.

Godden, Rumer (1999). *Premlata and the Festival of Lights*. New York: HarperCollins.

Goodall, John (1982). *Paddy Goes Traveling*. New York: McElderry [out of print].

Grossman, Bill (1996). *My Little Sister Ate One Hare*. Illus. Kevin Hawkes. New York: Crown.

Guarino, Deborah (1991). *Is Your Mama a Llama?* Illus. Steven Kellogg. New York: Scholastic.

Haas, Irene (1997). *A Summertime Song*. New York: McElderry.

Hazen, Barbara Shook (1998). *That Toad is Mine!* Illus. Jane Manning. New York: HarperCollins.

Heide, Florence Parry (1988). *The Shrinking of Treehorn*. Illus. Edward Gorey. New York: Holiday.

Henkes, Kevin (1997). *Chester's Way*. New York: Mulberry.

—— (1991). *Chrysanthemum*. New York: Greenwillow.

—— (1996). *Lilly's Purple Plastic Purse*. New York: Greenwillow.

Hepworth, Cathi (1996). *ANTICS*. New York: Paper Star.

Hoban, Lillian (1999). *Silly Tilly's Valentine*. New York: HarperCollins.

Hoban, Tana (1990). *Exactly the Opposite*. New York: Greenwillow.

—— (1996). *Of Colors and Things*. New York: Paper Star.

—— (1998). *So Many Circles, So Many Squares.* New York: Greenwillow.

Hoffman, Mary (1998). *Clever Katya—A Fairy Tale from Old Russia.* Illus. Marie Cameron. New York: Barefoot.

Houston, Gloria (1992). *My Great-Aunt Arizona.* Illus. Susan Condie Lamb. New York: HarperCollins.

Howard, Elizabeth Fitzgerald (1995). *Aunt Flossie's Hat (and Crab Cakes Later).* Illus. James Ransome. New York: Clarion.

Hurd, Thacker (1998). *Art Dog.* New York: HarperCollins.

Hutchins, Pat (1971). *Changes, Changes.* London: Bodley Head.

Igus, Toyomi (1996). *Going Back Home: An Artist Returns to the South.* Illus. Michele Wood. San Francisco: Children's Book Press.

—— (1998). *i see the rhythm.* Illus. Michele Wood. San Francisco: Children's Book Press.

Inkpen, Mick (1988). *If I Had a Pig.* Toronto: McClelland & Stewart.

Johnson, Angela (1992). *Daddy Calls Me Man.* Illus. Rhonda Mitchell. New York: Orchard.

Johnson, Stephen T. (1995). *Alphabet City.* New York: Viking.

Joosse, Barbara M. (1991). *Mama, Do You Love Me?* Illus. Barbara Lavallee. San Francisco: Chronicle.

Joyce, William (1997). *Bently and egg.* New York: HarperTrophy.

—— (1997). *Buddy.* New York: HarperCollins.

—— (1996). *The Leaf Men.* New York: HarperCollins.

Karlin, Nurit (1998). *The Fat Cat Sat on the Mat.* New York: HarperTrophy.

Kellogg, Steven (1987). *Aster Aardvark's Alphabet Adventure.* New York: Morrow.

—— (1996). *Frog Jumps: A Counting Book.* New York: Scholastic.

Kitchen, Bert (1987). *Animal Numbers.* New York: Dial.

Kneen, Maggie (1996). *When you're not looking . . . A Storytime Counting Book.* New York: Simon & Schuster.

Kraus, Robert (1971). *Leo the Late Bloomer.* Illus. Jose Aruego. New York: Windmill.

Kroll, Virginia (1995). *Sweet Magnolias.* Illus. Laura Jacques. Charlestown, MA: Charlesbridge.

Lawrence, Jacob (1997). *Harriet and the Promised Land.* New York: Simon & Schuster.

Lionni, Leo (1960). *Inch by Inch.* New York: Astor-Honor.

Lobel, Anita (1990). *Alison's Zinnia.* New York: Greenwillow.

Lobel, Arnold (1970). *Frog and Toad Are Friends.* New York: Harper.

—— (1978). *Mouse Tales.* New York: HarperTrophy.

Lyon, George Ella (1999). *Book.* Illus. Peter Catalanotto. New York: DK Publishing.

—— (1994). *Mama Is a Miner.* Illus. Peter Catalanotto. New York: Orchard.

Marshall, James (1997). *Rats on the Range and Other Stories.* New York: Puffin.

Martin, Bill, Jr. (1983). *Brown Bear, Brown Bear What Do You See?* Illus. Eric Carle. New York: Holt.

—— (1991). *Polar Bear, Polar Bear, What Do You Hear?* Illus. Eric Carle. New York: Holt.

Martin, Bill, Jr., and John Archambault (1989). *Chicka Chicka Boom Boom.* Illus. Lois Ehlert. New York: Simon & Schuster.

Martin, Jacqueline Briggs (1998). *Snowflake Bentley.* Illus. Mary Azarian. Boston: Houghton Mifflin.

Martin, Rafe (1989). *Will's Mammoth.* Illus. Stephen Gammell. New York: Putnam.

Mayer, Mercer (1971). *A Boy, a Dog and a Frog.* New York: Dial.

McCully, Emily Arnold (1984). *Picnic.* New York: Harper & Row.

McDonnell, Flora (1997). *Flora McDonnell's ABC.* Cambridge, MA: Candlewick.

McGrath, Barbara Barbieri (1994). *The M&M's Counting Book.* Watertown, MA: Charlesbridge.

McKissack, Patricia C. (1997). *Ma Dear's Aprons.* Illus. Floyd Cooper. New York: Atheneum.

McMillan, Bruce (1995). *Grandfather's Trolley.* Cambridge, MA: Candlewick.

—— (1988). *Growing Colors.* New York: Lothrop, Lee & Shepard.

Minarik, Else Holmelund (1978). *Little Bear.* Illus. Maurice Sendak. New York: HarperCollins.

Miranda, Anne (1997). *To Market, To Market*. Illus. Janet Stevens. San Diego: Harcourt Brace.

Mitchell, Margaree King (1993). *Uncle Jed's Barbershop*. Illus. James Ransome. New York: Aladdin.

Mochizuki, Ken (1995). *Heroes*. Illus. Dom Lee. New York: Lee & Low.

Mullins, Patricia (1998). *One Horse Waiting for Me*. New York: Simon & Schuster.

Myers, Walter Dean (1997). *Harlem*. Illus. Christopher Myers. New York: Scholastic.

Neitzel, Shirley (1989). *The Jacket I Wear in the Snow*. Illus. Nancy Winslow Parker. New York: Greenwillow.

Nomura, Takaaki (1995). *Grandpa's Town*. Trans. Amanda Mayer Stinchecum. New York: Kane/Miller.

Nye, Naomi Shihab (1994). *Sitti's Secrets*. Illus. Nancy Carpenter. New York: Simon & Schuster.

Numeroff, Laura Joffe (1985). *If You Give a Mouse a Cookie*. Illus. Felicia Bond. New York: HarperCollins.

—— (1998). *If You Give a Pig a Pancake*. Illus. Felicia Bond. New York: HarperCollins.

Onyefulu, Ifeoma (1993). *A Is for Africa*. New York: Cobblehill.

Oxenbury, Helen (1971). *Helen Oxenbury's ABC of Things*. New York: Franklin Watts.

Pallotta, Jerry (1986). *The Ocean Alphabet Book*. Illus. Frank Mazzola, Jr. Watertown, MA: Charlesbridge.

Parnell, Peter (1991). *The Rock*. New York: Macmillan.

Pelletier, David (1996). *The Graphic Alphabet*. New York: Orchard.

Polacco, Patricia (1994). *Pink and Say*. New York: Philomel.

Rankin, Laura (1991). *The Handmade Alphabet*. New York: Dial.

Ringgold, Faith (1992). *Aunt Harriet's Underground Railroad in the Sky*. New York: Crown.

—— (1993). *Dinner at Aunt Connie's House*. New York: Hyperion.

Rohmann, Eric (1994). *Time Flies*. New York: Crown.

Ryan, Pam Muñoz, and Jerry Pallotta (1996). *The Crayon Counting Book*. Illus. Frank Mazzola, Jr. Watertown, MA: Charlesbridge.

Rylant, Cynthia (1996). *Henry and Mudge in Puddle Trouble*. Illus. Suçie Stevenson. New York: Aladdin.

Say, Allen (1996). *Emma's Rug*. Boston: Houghton Mifflin.

—— (1993). *Grandfather's Journey*. Boston: Houghton Mifflin.

—— (2000). *The Sign Painter*. Boston: Houghton Mifflin.

—— (1999). *Tea with Milk*. Boston: Houghton Mifflin.

Scieszka, Jon (1991). *The Frog Prince Continued*. Illus. Steve Johnson. New York: Puffin.

—— (1998). *Squids will be Squids: Fresh Morals, Beastly Fables*. Illus. Lane Smith. New York: Viking.

—— (1992). *The Stinky Cheese Man and Other Fairly Stupid Tales*. Illus. Lane Smith. New York: Viking.

—— (1989). *The True Story of the Three Little Pigs by A. Wolf*. Illus. Lane Smith. New York: Puffin.

Sendak, Maurice (1962). *Chicken Soup with Rice: A Book of Months*. New York: Harper & Row.

—— (1963). *Where the Wild Things Are*. New York: Harper & Row.

Serfozo, Mary (1988). *Who Said Red?* Illus. Keiko Narahashi. New York: McElderry.

Seuss, Dr. (1968). *The Foot Book*. New York: Random.

—— (1970). *Mr. Brown Can Moo, Can You?* New York: Random.

Shannon, George (1995). *Tomorrow's Alphabet*. Illus. Donald Crews. New York: Greenwillow.

Sierra, Judy (1996). *Wiley and the Hairy Man*. Illus. Brian Pinkney. New York: Lodestar.

Sis, Peter (1988). *Waving: A Counting Book*. New York: Greenwillow.

Smith, Janice Lee (1995). *Wizard and Wart at Sea*. Illus. Paul Meisel. New York: HarperCollins.

Spinner, Stephanie, and Ellen Weiss (1997). *Born to Be Wild: The Weebie Zone #3*. New York: HarperCollins.

Steig, William (1969). *Sylvester and the Magic Pebble*. New York: Windmill.

—— (1997). *Toby, Where Are You?* Illus. Teryl Euvremer. New York: HarperCollins.

Stevenson, James (1996). *Yard Sale*. New York: Greenwillow.

Tafuri, Nancy (1989). *The Ball Bounced.* New York: Greenwillow.

Testa, Fulvio (1992). *A Long Trip to Z.* San Diego: Harcourt Brace.

Turner, Ann (1998). *Drummer Boy: Marching to the Civil War.* Illus. Mark Hess. New York: HarperCollins.

Van Allsburg, Chris (1982). *Ben's Dream.* Boston: Houghton Mifflin.

——— (1979). *The Garden of Abdul Gasazi.* Boston: Houghton Mifflin.

——— (1981). *Jumanji.* Boston: Houghton Mifflin.

——— (1984). *The Mysteries of Harris Burdick.* Boston: Houghton Mifflin.

——— (1993). *The Sweetest Fig.* Boston: Houghton Mifflin.

——— (1983). *The Wreck of the Zephyr.* Boston: Houghton Mifflin.

Van Camp, Richard (1998). *What's the Most Beautiful Thing You Know About Horses?* Illus. George Littlechild. San Francisco: Children's Book Press.

Viorst, Judith (1972). *Alexander and the Terrible, Horrible, No Good, Very Bad Day.* Illus. Ray Cruz. New York: Atheneum.

Waber, Bernard (1972). *Ira Sleeps Over.* Boston: Houghton Mifflin.

Waddell, Martin (1992). *Farmer Duck.* Illus. Helen Oxenbury. Cambridge, MA: Candlewick.

Weeks, Sarah (1995). *Follow the Moon.* Illus. Suzanne Duranceau. New York: HarperCollins.

——— (1998). *Mrs. McNosh Hangs Up Her Wash.* Illus. Nadine Bernard Westcott. New York: HarperCollins.

Westervelt, Linda (1995). *Roger Tory Peterson's ABC of Birds.* Illus. Roger Tory Peterson. New York: Universe.

Wiesner, David (1992). *July 29, 1999.* New York: Clarion.

——— (1991). *Tuesday.* New York: Clarion.

Wildsmith, Brian (1981). *Animal Shapes.* London: Oxford University Press [out of print].

——— (1962). *Brian Wildsmith's ABC.* London: Oxford University Press.

Williams, Sue (1990). *I Went Walking.* Illus. Julie Vivas. San Diego: Harcourt Brace.

Williams, Vera B. (1986). *Cherries and Cherry Pits.* New York: Greenwillow.

——— (1990). *More More More Said the Baby.* New York: Greenwillow.

Wisniewski, David (1996). *Golem.* New York: Clarion.

Wood, Audrey (1996). *The Napping House.* Illus. Don Wood. Duluth, MN: Red Wagon.

Wood, Douglas (1984). *Old Turtle.* Illus. Cheng-Khee Chee. San Diego: Harcourt Brace.

Wyeth, Sharon Dennis (1998). *Something Beautiful.* Illus. Chris K. Soentpiet. New York: Doubleday.

Yolen, Jane (1992). *Nocturne.* Illus. Anne Hunter. San Diego: Harcourt Brace.

——— (1987). *Owl Moon.* Illus. John Schoenherr. New York: Philomel.

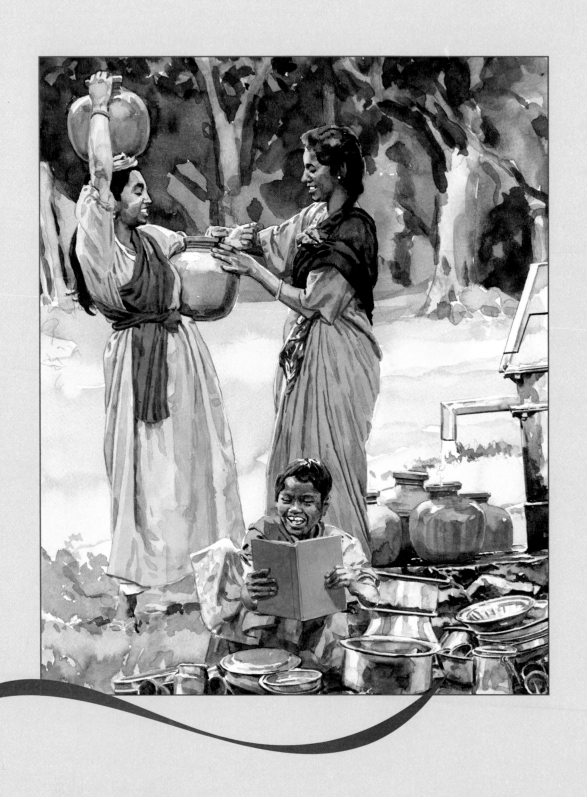

CHAPTER 4

Responding to Books Through Talk, Art, Writing, Drama, Movement, and Music

A kaleidoscope is an object of beauty. After picking it up and feeling its elongated shape, we gaze into its tunnel, where we discover beautiful bursts of color and intricate, complicated shapes. A kaleidoscope gives us new ways to see and to think about light and color. We experience new patterns as shapes split over and over again, shifting into delicate formations, replicating the beauty and complexity of a snowflake. Many kaleidoscopes are objects of art, made with beautiful iridescent glazes on their cases, set in stands crafted from fine old wood. Beauty and inspiration and fresh ways to see the world are the gifts of the kaleidoscope. Imagine analyzing it for its utilitarian value, when its main value lies in what it arouses in the human spirit. It makes us stop, live for the moment, breathe in the stunning sights, see the world anew through slivers of shapes and colors. Its magic makes us feel alive. What it does is enough. It nourishes us as humans, startling us into really looking at the beauty of the world around us by showing us flashes of brilliant colors.

Literature, too, has many of the qualities of the kaleidoscope. It shows us the world through a different lens, gets us in touch with our humanness, takes our breath away, and makes us feel alive. It arouses deep feelings and responses, raises questions about what we know, and expands our ways of thinking. Too often, we treat literature like a cardboard packaging box, to be handled and talked about in terms of qualities of shape, color, size, and utility, forgetting what it does to us, how it moves us.

This chapter focuses on the breathtaking quality of literature. Valuing literature for its own sake means experiencing it fully—reflecting on it and turning it over and over in our minds so that we can see its meaning and its impact on us. The chapter is predicated on a belief in the importance of literature in itself, not merely as a source of information or as a means of teaching vocabulary or story grammar. We must allow our students to take deep breaths and inhale the literature, experiencing it, moving around in it, and seeing how it connects to them, the world, and other texts. The literature itself is on center stage here—and it deserves time.

To treat literature otherwise would be like taking students to a pond surrounded by budding bushes and blooming trees, jumping with fish, covered with frogs on lily pads—a scene teeming with life and beauty—and then using that beautiful vision only to teach science vocabulary words, without letting the children drink in the scene and talk about what they were experiencing. They need to touch the pond in wonder and raise questions about it. Children feel divorced from literature when we ask them to immediately respond to someone else's questions about their reading. They need to linger over it, enjoy it, figure out what it means, and talk about its implications and its impact. Literature strikes at the heart of our humanness and helps us realize that we are not separate and alone; we see our commonality.

Response encourages this kind of meaning-making. This chapter focuses on the many ways to respond to and make meaning of literature through talk, art, writing, drama, movement, and music. Throughout this chapter, I am going to ask you to respond in these forms even if you feel awkward doing so. For only if you have experienced each of these media will you be able to facilitate a variety of learning styles in your own classroom.

What Is Response to Literature?

When we read a work of literature, complex things happen in our head. One piece of our experience might be brought to our consciousness by a particular scene; another piece might be brought to the forefront of our brain by a particular character. The responses elicited in us by a work of literature are like an internal kaleidoscope, with different pieces of our histories and experiences sliding into the "lens" through which we view the literature. Sometimes we see the literature through the pinks and yellows and brilliant reds of our background. Other times we see it through the grays and deep purples and blues. Our own kaleidoscope lens also changes as we share our responses and talk about them. Another's response might tap into something that allows us to see the work through yet another lens. Response isn't something we allow or don't allow in our students. Response happens, and if we build on it, then students will usually want to become more involved in thinking about a book.

Louise Rosenblatt, theorist, scholar, and professor, wrote a ground-breaking book in 1938 called *Literature as Exploration*. In that book, she explains the importance of the reader's finding his or her own meaning in a book. She tells us that the meaning of a book lies in the transaction between the text and the reader. Both of these elements are needed to make meaning. When an author writes a book, she or he can't possibly imagine all the ways readers will interact with and make sense of it. Once the book is out there, readers will find many meanings in it, and the author is shut out of that process.

In a more recent book, *The Reader, the Text, and the Poem,* Rosenblatt (1978) asks us to look at the essence of what we are doing when we use books with children.

> Any sensitivity to literature, any warm and enjoyable participation in the lit-
> erary work, will necessarily involve the sensuous and emotional responsive-
> ness, the human sympathies, of the reader. We shall not further the growth of
> literary discrimination by a training that concentrates on the so-called purely
> literary aspects. We go through empty motions if our primary concern is to
> enable the student to recognize various literary forms, to identify various
> verse patterns, to note the earmarks of the style of a particular author, to
> detect recurrent symbols or to discriminate the kinds of irony or satire.
> Acquaintance with the formal aspects of literature will not in itself insure
> esthetic sensitivity. (p. 52)

Students need to feel that they are accomplishing meaningful tasks and finding some-thing out—not just plodding from story to story or book to book, answering questions and filling out worksheets without trying to make connections or see what literature has to do with understanding life. Meaning and the impact of the literature must be at the center of what we do with students.

Making meaning begins with our transaction with a book and is then extended through our response. Initial responses, of course, aren't enough. We elicit initial responses so that we can work together to create richer meanings, remembering that any book is a conversation among many people. Together, we work to identify pieces of experiences in the book and to see how these pieces relate to each other. The point of response isn't to have everyone share her or his reaction and then close the book. Initial student responses should launch further discussions, which continue the meaning-making journey.

The wonderful thing about using response as the launching point for meaning-making is that it shows us the richness in the literature. None of us can see everything there is to see in a book after one reading. We each pay attention to different things, and when all these different things are brought together, we come away with much more than we could have by reading alone or by hearing just the teacher's interpretation. For instance, when I read **Jacob Have I Loved,** by Katherine Paterson, with a class, student responses focused on parent-child relationships, as well as sibling relationships. They raised many questions that would not have occurred to me: Why didn't Louise ever tell her parents how she felt? How could Louise hate her sister so much? Why didn't Louise try for anything she wanted until the end of the book? Why did Louise want to be like her father and accepted as if she were male? Why was the grandma so rude to everyone? Why was she in the story if everyone thought she was insane? Why didn't the parents realize how much tension there was between the two girls and do something about it? Why do parents sometimes favor one child over another? What is loneliness really? What causes some people to hate so deeply?

These responses were based on the students' desire to know more about people and life. Not only did the questions offer opportunities to discuss real issues that the story tapped into; they also led to discussions of how historical context affects a work of litera-ture. We had opportunities to make meaning together. None of this rich exploring can hap-pen if students aren't provided with occasions to respond and share their responses through talk, art, writing, drama, movement, and music.

Providing Time to Respond

As readers, we focus on our own experiences with a book as we read. We don't think about what others say we are supposed to do. One theorist who looks at reading from

CD-ROM

See examples of how response can be utilized in the classroom by searching Classroom Teaching Ideas and Invitations for the word *response.*

the reader's point of view is Judith Langer (1995). The goal of her research, which took place in classrooms, was to describe what we do as we read and untangle the process of engagement in reading. This work is of the utmost importance because it debunks the belief that readers read only in a linear fashion, going from point A to point B to point C, all following a plot line in the same way, all coming to the same conclusions, and all finishing the story ready to dig into analysis. She revealed that rich and complex thinking is going on in the reader's head. One reader may be transported by a character's actions to a memory of a moment in his own life. Another may be caught up so completely in a character's conflict that she loses track of the order of events. Yet another reader may be so overwhelmed by one image or one scene that all else pales in comparison. Each of these readers will remember the same book very differently, having had a very different experience with it. Langer's work, therefore, makes us aware that worksheets and even specific comprehension questions test only what the teacher notices, not necessarily what the students notice as they read.

Each of us experiences reading in general in a different way. Some people have trouble entering the story world; others are aware of themselves almost as intruders in a story; still others experience the story world the way cinematographers do, seeing each scene in terms of where they'd position the camera for the shot. Examining what we do as we read and sharing our insights with others broadens our views of what happens to readers when they read and helps us see that what we experience does not happen in the same way for everyone. Langer's work explains how a reader actually reads, not how others think a reader should read. An understanding of Langer's work will make you better aware of your own processes and help you shape assignments so that they enhance students' reading, rather than abruptly cutting off or restricting students' thinking through narrowly directed questions. Her work also makes clear the importance of allowing students time to spend in the meaning-making stances described in the following paragraphs.

Langer calls the work a reader does *envisionment*. An envisionment is simply the understanding that the reader has of the text at that moment, whether the text is being read, written, discussed, or tested. Envisionments are subject to change at any time as ideas unfold and new ideas come to mind. This process is sense-making, since meanings shift and grow as the mind creates its understanding of a work. Langer identifies four stances of envisionment that a reader may assume as he or she reads; these are described in the boxed feature Langer's Envisionment Stances.

Langer's work shows that we must not only help students learn how to get into the story world and become engaged in the reading (Stance One), but also allow time for them to think, talk, and speculate about what the book means (Stance Two). This part of the reading process is often ignored in schools, and yet it is the one that many readers enjoy the most! As teachers, we tend to assume that all readers have gotten the same meaning from a particular piece of text, and thus we race ahead of the readers. We jump to Stance Four, asking students to figure out story grammar or plot line or any number of other issues that they usually are not ready to think about until they have had time to sit with the story, listen to others' observations, and let the meaning of the story emerge from the conversation. We often fail to take into account that meaning is not finalized when a story is finished—that, after all, is not the purpose of reading. Meaning is negotiated and added to and reconsidered through classroom talk. Think about how often your ideas on a movie change after you hear another's take on the movie. Langer shows that these envisionments are not static; they are constantly "in process." Students will be much more eager to work in Stances Three and Four if we have given them ample time in Stance Two to respond, think, talk, and consider the text from many angles.

To see how we move around in these stances as we read, see the two boxed features in the next section, where the stances appear in parentheses throughout my response and that of a college student to a picture book. Examining your own movement through the stances as you respond to books will make them concrete and real, helping you to be sensitive to how you can prompt your own students to have full, rich literary

Langer's Envisionment Stances

Langer (1995) sees readers as moving among four stances of envisionment.

In **Stance One, "Being Out and Stepping In,"** we look for clues about what is happening and try to make sense of what the writing will be about. Because we are just entering the story world, we are looking for starting points from which to build an envisionment. We might hook on to a character, be captivated by an action, or fall in love with the narrator's voice.

In **Stance Two "Being In and Moving Through an Envisionment,"** we become immersed in the book and in developing understandings. We bring our personal knowledge to the text to complete ideas and think further about the book. We take new information and, by asking questions about motives, feelings, causes, interrelationships, and implications, use it to go beyond what we already understand. This stance probably is the most satisfying because we get to "muck about" in the text world, wallow in the images, move about in the place and time of the book, and just enjoy reading the book. In this stance, we call upon our knowledge of the text, ourselves, others, life, and the world to elaborate upon and make connections among our thoughts, move understandings along, and fill out our shifting sense of what the piece is about. In this stance, we fill in the gaps the author leaves, figuring out for ourselves what happened in the situations that were suggested but not developed.

Stance Three, "Stepping Out and Rethinking What One Knows," is different from the other stances in that we use our developing understanding, our text world, to add to our own knowledge and experiences. In the other stances, we bring our knowledge and experiences to the text in order to make sense of the text world we are developing. In this stance, the thoughts in our envisionments cause us to shift the focus for a moment from the text world we are creating to what those ideas mean for our own lives. We may be appalled at the behavior of a character and stop to think about whether we have ever acted that way or in what circumstances we might act similarly. We are using the text to reassess and add to the way we think about life and living.

In **Stance Four, "Stepping Out and Objectifying the Experience,"** we distance ourselves from the envisionment we have developed and reflect on it. We analyze and judge what we've been reading and relate the work to other works and experiences. It is in this stance that we can focus on the author's craft, on the text's structure, and on literary elements and allusions. We can become aware of why a particular author or piece holds significance for us and whether we agree or disagree with others' interpretations. In this stance, we become critics, reflecting on what the book means, how it works, and why. If students are allowed to respond to books only in Stance Four, the analytical stance, by teachers who ask just objective questions or questions that the teacher deems important, their love of reading may decline as they climb up the grade-level ladder.

experiences. In the boxed feature Children's Voices on page 114, children's explanations of their involvement with books speak of the importance of Stance Two, Being In and Moving Through an Envisionment.

The Responses of Good Readers

Good readers—those who derive the broadest meaning from texts—respond more fully than do readers struggling to make meaning. Thus, we will look briefly at what good readers do so that we may understand how to provide avenues for response. Although reading is much more than decoding, too often teachers focus on decoding instead of helping readers develop important response skills. In fact, decoding is only the beginning step of the reading process; we engage in a myriad of intellectual and emotional activities when we read.

Fran Claggett (1996) discusses in concrete detail the complex skills involved in reading and responding. She shows that responding is not some "fluffy" activity, devoid of mental rigor, and validates the high levels of mental activity that go into it. Although it's not necessary for your students to analyze their responses, it is important for you as a teacher to understand the array of critical thinking skills involved in responding. Only in this way can you provide appropriate support for your students as they work to develop the skills that good readers exhibit. The following good reading behaviors can be found in even the very earliest readers:

1. Demonstrating intellectual engagement with the text by asking questions, making predictions, and visualizing characters and settings

On becoming immersed in the story world . . .

I like science fiction and mysteries. They make it easy for my mind to see the scene and what's going on and they help my imagination wander.
—Jimmy, 7th grade

Sometimes without even realizing it at the time, I get so caught up in the book at the suspenseful parts that I start to read really fast. I sometimes put myself in the position of the main character. I then think about what I would do if it were me instead.
—Angela, 7th grade

When I read I try to put myself in the characters' shoes, try to think what they think, I try to be them. So the more interesting the book I read is, the more I like it.
—John, 7th grade

I mostly like to read an action type of book. In these books I get so into it that I don't want to stop. I say to myself "I'll stop next page." I never do. I always keep going.
—Jacob, 7th grade

*I read **Redwall** books, **Mossflower** books, and ghost books because they keep you on the edge of your seat.* —Arnie, 7th grade

I don't care for science fiction and fantasy. I can't feel that I'm part of the story when it sounds so fake. —Ashlynn, 7th grade

I like fiction books mostly including dragons or magic. I like them because they draw me in and keep me reading. —Renee, 7th grade

2. Considering cultural or psychological nuances

3. Filling in the gaps by using clues and evidence in the text to draw conclusions

4. Evaluating how the author's ideas fit with one's prior knowledge or experience

5. Challenging the text

6. Demonstrating an understanding of the work as a whole

7. Paying attention to the structure of the text and how parts work together

8. Showing aesthetic appreciation of such features as language use and depth of theme

9. Alluding to or relating specific passages in order to validate ideas

10. Demonstrating emotional engagement with the text

11. Reflecting on the meaning and universal significance of the text

12. Making connections between the text and one's own ideas and experiences

As good readers we use various strategies to help us comprehend and interact with what we read. Every time we read something that is in a new genre or is particularly difficult, we add to our strategies for meaning-making so that we can better understand what we are reading. Like us, students are continually learning how to read. Helping students recognize the reading strategies they use and teaching them new strategies are both vital activities. We all need ways to get the most out of our reading, while keeping the impact of the literature at the center.

Ellin Oliver Keene and Susan Zimmermann (1997) redefine comprehension as new thinking. They point out that teachers already teach children to use webbing and mapping processes to remember significant actions taken by characters. Many of these comprehension tools are primarily enrichment activities. Although they help teachers find out what children remember from their reading, these activities do little to actually change children's thinking while they read. Keene and Zimmermann identified a need to explicitly teach strategies so that students could not only read better but also get more out of their reading. They found that the difference between just talking about books and talking about the thinking processes a proficient reader uses to understand them is subtle but key. They encourage students as young as kindergartners and first-graders to make text-to-self, text-to-world, and text-to-text connections, a self-reflective process that helps readers think as they read. When readers make text-to-self connections, thinking about their own experiences as they read, they understand the story better. For example, when reading a book about a grandfather, readers can more deeply understand the character and his feelings if they think about their interactions with their own grandfathers. These "connection" experiences may cause the children to question the text, which is something else good readers do.

Text-to-world and text-to-text connections also deepen a reading. Children learn to make text-to-world connections as they become more aware of the events of the world through travel, media, and reading. They start to recognize connections between a story they are reading and actual events. Children begin to make text-to-text connections when they associate texts they have read before with the one they are reading. Perhaps the plot or setting is similar or a character reminds them of someone in another story. They may also begin to recognize the work of particular authors or illustrators. What readers already know will change because of what they read. When students focus on their thinking as they read, they are doing more than simply pointing out strategies; they are discovering that thinking helps them understand and interact with the story. They are learning that reading is about making meaning of stories and of their own lives. As mature readers, we usually go through this process unintentionally, silently making text-to-self, text-to-world, and text-to-text connections as we read. This is part of what makes us good readers. Children need to be explicitly taught to do this so that they, too, can understand what they read at deep levels. Understanding what good readers do helps us create meaningful response activities for our students so that they practice good reading strategies.

Initial Responses

Since we all see different things as we read, it isn't appropriate to expect each reader to notice the same details or even view characters in the same way, especially after just a first reading. To get a closer look at the process of how we read and how we make sense of text, let's look at two very different responses to the same book: *We Had a Picnic This Sunday Past,* written by Jacqueline Woodson and illustrated by Diane Greenseid. The boxed feature Response to First Reading of a Book: A Response Log for a Picture Book contains my responses to the picture book as I read it for the first time, including the things I was conscious of noticing and reacting to as I read (see page 116). Then the boxed feature Response to First Reading of a Book: A College Student's Response gives the response of a college student to the same text (see page 117).

The bright colors and smiling faces seem to invite readers to the picnic, too.

No map shows how to write a response log, since we cannot preplan a reader's response. Although the process actually happens very quickly in your head as you read, it would take a long time to write down your responses to every book you read. However, it is rewarding to write down your responses at least once, just to see what's embedded in them. As adults, we need to understand our responses to literature and see how our histories influence our reading.

In my response to the picture book, I react to the use of bright color and the portrayal of people as "real" physically—not just the pencil-thin beauties we see in magazines. I notice the lack of gender and ethnic stereotyping. I respond to the strong women and notice particularly the interactions among the characters and how they treat each other. The fresh, direct language also appeals to me. I feel invited into the story and can locate myself easily within the story.

Reading the college student's response startled me a bit and made me realize that I cannot predict what will attract the attention of others. I have to admit that I hadn't even noticed that quotation marks were not used and that conversations were run together. I was interested in his advice that, for children to understand the book, readers would have to slow their reading down. He assumed that everyone would have a bit of trouble with the book as

Carol Hurst's Children's Literature *site provides teaching ideas on using literature. Find it at www.carolhurst.com/.*

Response to First Reading of a Book

A Response Log for a Picture Book

Jacqueline Woodson, *We Had a Picnic This Sunday Past,* **illustrated by Diane Greenseid.**

[*Note: Langer's (1995) stances, Keene and Zimmermann's (1997) connections, and Claggett's (1996) behaviors are indicated in parentheses.*]

Cover. Wow, I love these bright big colors—the purples, reds, blues, greens, and browns. This looks as if it will be a happy book about a family picnic (Stance 1—getting into the story world). I like that the black woman and girl in the forefront are kind of heavy and that they are smiling and seem glad to be together. The children carrying food in the background with their beads, hats, and baggy pants look and dress like the children I knew at the school where I taught (Stance 2—immersed in the story world; text to self).

In the first picture, Grandma is shown as an active, assertive person who loves being with her granddaughter. The park in the background has people of several shades of color having a nice day in the park. Children are chasing children or playing ball or walking their dogs or reading. Adults are sitting happily under a tree, others are setting up a picnic table with food, and one mother walks a baby (Stance 2—immersed in the story world). Energy leaps off the page. Already this book reminds me of the joy in being together that I found in *Mama, Do You Love Me?,* by Barbara M. Joosse (text to text).

Next, Grandma makes a big show of putting her food out and brags about her granddaughter. It bothers me that she compliments her on being pretty and on the dress that Grandma had made for her (Stance 2—immersed in the story world; cultural and/or psychological nuances, Claggett). Do we ever compliment girls on anything else (questioning, Claggett)? Grandma says, "Got up at four this morning to

make this chicken. Best batch I ever fried" (retelling specific passages to validate ideas, Claggett). She sounds like someone I would like and could relate to because she's so down-to-earth and matter-of-fact and doesn't use language as a barrier to keep others out (Stance 3—stepping out of the story world; cultural nuances, Claggett; text to self).

On the following spread, the big bold picture of Grandma and granddaughter takes up most of the two pages. It's easy to see the affection the child has for her grandma as Grandma is going over how she should behave. Don't we all do that as parents (Stance 3—stepping out; text to self)? Grandma warns her that although Cousin Martha will probably bring the same kind of dried-out pie that she brings each year, the grandchild should eat it so as not to hurt Cousin's feelings. I notice the language here and the colorfulness of the description (Stance 4—analysis). "Says she thinks Cousin Martha scares the stove into baking bad."

This page makes me laugh. Aunt Sadie is shown full of life and energy as she screams when she finds flies on her sweet cob corn. Those corn-on-the-cob pictures make me hungry even if there are plastic flies on them (Stance 3—stepping out)! Then her second cousin's son Jefferson shows how cool he thinks he is with his turned-around baseball cap, sunglasses, oversized shirt, and baggy pants (Stance 2—immersed in the story world). He reminds me of some of the children I had at my school who had that show-off attitude in them (text to self). The rest of the family at the picnic table is having a good time with each other, while other people play in the background. I like it that these children are shown as nonthreatening, neat children. I get so tired of only reading and seeing African Americans portrayed in the media as threats or in crisis (Stance 4—analysis; cultural nuances, Claggett; text to world).

he did, just as I assumed that readers would focus on the strong characters as I did. However, both of us responded to the happy feeling engendered by the bright, bold pictures and to the personalities of the characters. To make concrete what we were saying, we both used specific examples and quotes as we talked about the literature.

You can see, then, that children reading this book or having it read to them would probably have a wide range of reactions. If they were not part of such a warm family group, they might feel attracted to the acceptance emanating from this family gathering. If they were African American, they might enjoy the portrayal of so many people of color in so many ways. Others might notice the friendships and relationships or get hungry just looking at the food. Still other children might be surprised to see people of all colors enjoying the park together, if their only exposure to people of color was on TV. But unless we give students a chance to respond, we will never know the parts of books that seem most significant to them.

As I look over my responses, I see that in just the first half of the book, I have woven my way into and out of all four of Langer's (1995) stances. Reading, indeed, is not done in a linear fashion, starting with Stance One and ending up in Stance Four. I move through the stances recursively in no particular order. Initially I went from Stance One right to Stance Four, then back to Stance Three, then to Two, and back again to Four. If I described my involvement with a whole novel, I would find myself moving through every combination of Langer's four stances. As readers, we need to reflect on our own reading behavior, comparing it to how others read and making generalizations about the best ways to engage readers. Also, we need to be very conscious that each reader's response is unique and vali-

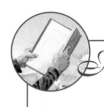

Response to First Reading of a Book

A College Student's Response

Jacqueline Woodson, *We Had a Picnic This Sunday Past,* illustrated by Diane Greenseid.

[Note: Langer's (1995) stances, Keene and Zimmermann's (1997) connections, and Claggett's (1996) behaviors are indicated in parentheses.]

I read the book **We Had a Picnic This Sunday Past.** I'm not exactly sure what I am supposed to cover, so I'll just explain how I felt about it in general.

For starters, I really like the illustrations. The colors Diane Greenseid uses are great—very bright. The combination of bright purples, oranges, and greens works very well. They seem to add to the happy mood of the story (Stance 4—analysis). I also like the way the illustrator treats the "portraits"—they are done in a way that reflects the way one would expect to see the characters (aesthetic appreciation of text, Claggett). For example, when Grandma is being described—blue dress with all those flowers on it—that is exactly how I pictured her (visualizing characters or scenes, Claggett). She has that tremendous purple hat with all the flowers on it, too. In other words, all of the characters seem to have personality (demonstrating emotional engagement, Claggett). I really liked this aspect of the book, and I believe that children will also.

Now although the story is entertaining, I found it difficult to read (Stance 4—analysis). Maybe difficult is not the best word, but I found myself rereading a lot of it. I think it is because dialog is mixed in many of the sentences without the use of quotation marks (Stance 4—analysis). I would be reading along, and would have to stop and say to myself "HUH?" and back up a sentence or two (Stance 1—getting into the story world). Another factor that contributed to this was the author's writing style. It seems to be fragmented, not in complete sentences (Stance 4—analysis). Then add in the fact that there is dialog thrown in without quotation marks to distinguish it and it can be quite confusing. For example: "Pretty-boy Trevor walking into that park with a handful of nothing. Can't eat air, I whispered to Paulette. Don't be a smartie, Grandma said, but you know she was thinking the exact same thing. Cousin Trevor picked daisies as he strutted up, talking about daisies for all the pretty ladies"(relating specific passages to validate ideas, Claggett).

This is exactly as it was written. It is not hard to understand, but I think it would be difficult for a child that this book is aimed at (Stance 4—analysis). They would understand it, but maybe after slowing down and rereading it a few times. The way this book was written—it's like the little girl is talking directly to us—I think this could possibly be a little confusing for a child. It makes for slower reading because it is written differently (Stance 4—analysis). Not that this is necessarily a bad thing, it's just something that I noticed. Maybe a child would like this type of style and would read through it easily, it's just that I didn't (Stance 4—analysis).

I did enjoy the book (especially the illustrations) as well as the overall "bright/happy" feeling that it conveyed.

date these individual reactions. After reading only part of a picture book or novel, I would have difficulty responding in a meaningful way if a teacher asked me to relate key plot details or identify foreshadowing or a character's motivation. Since, like most readers, I do not read in a linear fashion, I would have to explain the bursts and clusters of images that come to me when I think about what I have read. For students, Stances Two and Three can be enhanced through response activities.

When we are reading and responding, we are not aware of the spectrum of sophisticated processes in which we are engaged. By using the categories of Claggett (1996) to look at the way I talked about Woodson's book, I see more clearly what I was doing and what I was working to understand. Included in parentheses in this short response log are the reading behaviors in which I engaged, identified in terms of Claggett's reading performance categories. These categories show the complexities of our reading responses and also help us appreciate more fully the elements of critical thinking and analysis involved as we work simultaneously on many levels of meaning. Claggett's work validates the personal responses students naturally bring to their reading and confirms the importance of encouraging students' instinctive responses to books. We don't need to artificially direct their reading to get them to think in rich and thoughtful ways about literature.

Being aware of Keene and Zimmermann's (1997) theories also helps me understand why I am pulled into the characters and the story. First, since the young people in the story reminded me of students I taught, I felt very connected to them and liked them immediately. This helped me understand how Grandma and her granddaughter viewed them. Then I made a text-to-text connection when the warmth and affection the characters showed toward each other reminded me of **Mama, Do You Love Me?,** by Barbara M. Joosse. The characters' strong caring was reinforced through my connection to the other book. My next text-to-self connection came when I said that I like people who speak plainly and so was drawn to Grandma, who speaks her mind. Because I overlaid on Grandma many of the positive characteristics of people who speak their minds, I saw her positive qualities but also was aware of how some characters might describe her as outspoken. Last of all, I made a text-to-world connection when I became aware that African Americans were not stereotyped in this book. This caused me to look closely at the variety of ways people were characterized and what made each of them unique. Because I actively thought about all these connections as I read, I understood and appreciated the story at a deeper level. Actively thinking about your reading connections will help you elicit richer connections to reading from your students.

CD-ROM

Find other works by Jacqueline Woodson on the CD-ROM database.

Looking at my response in terms of McCormick's work (from Chapter 1), I could see some of the repertoires (a subset of the larger culture's beliefs, values, and ways of understanding the individual and the world) I brought to this reading of Jacqueline Woodson's book. I read the book as a teacher, a female, a daughter and granddaughter, a child of working-class parents, and a believer in the importance of strong families. I also read the book as a social critic and a Caucasian. Although I experienced this as a story about a joyous family picnic, I couldn't help wondering if, as a white woman, I would be welcome at the picnic. I never so keenly realized what it must be like for children not to see themselves in the books they read.

Everything that we are affects the way we read. Just as a turn of the kaleidoscope changes the colors and configurations of the stones, bringing some into prominence, so each of our readings changes the colors and configurations of our histories, bringing different pieces of our repertoires to the forefront.

My response was to a first reading, and I can already think of things I would like to consider more deeply. In other words, responding is a process, not an event. When we are talking to others who have read the same book, this kind of responding comes naturally as we try to figure out what made the book so powerful or why it didn't stack up to other books written by the same author. Being mindful of this process in our own teaching—and not rushing students into analysis or summary activities—benefits our students. They deserve a chance to let a book sit with them, perched on their shoulder like Palmer's pigeon in Jerry Spinelli's **Wringer,** where they can hear its soft coos as it tells them more about itself.

The boxed feature Response to First Reading of a Book: A Sixth-Grader's Response contains the initial response of a sixth-grade student to Mildred D. Taylor's **Roll of**

Response to First Reading of a Book

A Sixth-Grader's Response

Mildred D. Taylor, *Roll of Thunder, Hear My Cry*

The end of the book was very surprising. In the beginning of the book, the author foreshadowed that T. J.'s future was doomed. Near the end, the author left the story in the air. I am encouraged to buy the sequel and see what happened to the Logans. At first, when the cotton caught on fire, I thought the Wallaces or Mr. Granger had set it afire. It never came to my mind that Mr. Logan did it himself to divert everyone's attention from T.J. That's what I really like

about Mr. Logan, he is very smart. I don't know why Mr. Logan saved T. J. though, he didn't like him too much. One thing I really noticed throughout the book was how much Stacey matures. All the things he goes through in the book really change him into a man. I notice a big resemblance between Stacey and his father. Overall, my favorite character had to be Mr. Morrison. When he came into the book, I felt a little more secure. He protected the Logans, and helped them out without taking pay. I hope he is still there in the sequel.

Thunder, Hear My Cry. In this first response, the student notices the characters and how they behave and change. He also enjoys the plot twists, which surprised him. Because he is so taken with the book, he is eager to read more about the family in the sequel. Students don't always notice everything we want them to notice. But by beginning with initial responses, we can build activities and questions that will draw them deeper into the book, not push them away.

Response Through the Arts

Literacy isn't limited to the written word. Broadly defined, literacy is the ability to make and share meaning through all sign systems, including music, art, mathematics, movement, drama, and language (Short and Harste, 1996). Learners mediate the world through these sign systems, which act as lenses that permit us to understand ourselves and our world better (Harste, in Whitin, 1996).

Transmediation—the process of taking understandings created in one sign system, such as language, and moving them into another sign system, such as drama—allows students to create new ideas so that their understandings become more complex. They are not simply doing an activity or presentation from a book, but instead are using these sign systems as tools for thinking about a book and sharing it with others (Spiegel, 1995). Opportunities to use art, music, dance, movement, drama, mathematics, and language need to be available throughout the entire literary experience, not just at the end of it (Short, 2000). As you respond to literature, open the door to all channels of learning and meaning-making. Throw off the restraint of allowing yourself only one kind of response. See what you can find out about literature and yourself from responding in some different ways. Use art, movement, drama, music, and dance to make new discoveries about literature, to open new lines of thinking, and to tap into your own creativity.

Maxine Greene (1995), educator and philosopher, writes eloquently about how important it is to awaken children to the arts as a way of understanding that there are always new directions, possibilities, and opportunities. "This is what we hope to communicate to the young, if we want to awaken them to their lived situations, enable them to make sense, to name their worlds" (p. 150). Dennie Palmer Wolf and Dana Balick (1999), in *Art Works!,* help us understand even more about how children learn through the arts: "The arts teach skills like visual thinking, acute listening, and a sensitivity to metaphor that are well springs—feeding and informing all kinds of understanding. [Not only do the arts] give students sharp-edged tools they can apply outside the studio or off the stage, but they also signal that learning is not a series of distinct classes and topics, but an integrated enterprise" (p. 3).

When students work in the arts, they build their understanding through the work they do. They learn more about literature, for instance, as they grapple with their drawings, their performances, their dances, or their songs. If you create a dance or compose a song in response to a piece of literature, you will never forget that story and the impact it had on you—because the response was performed by your body and your body doesn't forget those kinds of experiences. Learning then becomes part of a whole for students; they see it's for them, not for a teacher. They are learning things directly, not learning about things.

Wolf tells us that even though few of the teachers she worked with "are artists by training, they have all witnessed how the ways of thinking and working that are characteristic of the arts spark an appetite, affection, imagination, attention, and a near fever for quality in their students" (p. 2). Imagination stirs imagination, pushes us to make new connections and new discoveries, and helps us see that we have a big part in our own learning. In contrast, an emphasis on teacher-constructed questions about a story can make students feel constrained and limited in their response to literature and add to their belief that this work is accessible only to literary scholars. Karen Ernst (1994) says, "Students become empowered by the knowledge that they can make meaning; they take charge of their work and can see and know the world as part of their work" (p. 123). Through the use of multiliteracies we deepen our own understanding of literature, which enhances our ability to connect children to literature.

Talk

We make meaning in our lives through talk. We sort things out by talking to others. We change our minds by hearing others talk. We might have disliked a movie but, after talking to others about it, come to see it in a new way. The information we get in our lives comes mainly through talk and listening. Through talk, we create the stories of our own lives—the stories of our past reading and future reading, the stories of what happens to us when we read a poem, a picture book, a novel. We discover what happens to us when we meet characters, what points of view we can see the story from, whom we simply can't relate to. When we share our responses to what we read, we are telling the story of our engagement with the text. Stories make stories. We learn through stories and through hearing others' narratives. Speaking intelligently after hearing a story is at the center of the development of intelligence and the active imagination. Aidan Chambers (1996), author, book critic, and teacher, says, "Talking well about books is a high-value activity in itself. But talking well about books is also the best rehearsal there is for talking well about other things. So in helping children to talk about their reading, we help them to be articulate about the rest of their lives" (p. 2).

In his book *Should We Burn Babar? Essays on Children's Literature and the Power of Stories,* Herbert Kohl (1995) has an essay on teaching the book **Pinocchio,** by Carlo Collodi, to first-graders. He explains the centrality of talk in the classroom:

> By questioning the text the children were encouraged to propose different versions of the story, imagine what the author had in mind, and think about the effect of the book upon themselves not merely as readers but also as males and females and as African Americans and European Americans experiencing the same text in different ways.
>
> . . . My main impulse was to find a way for the class to speak together about interesting and important things and get caught up in ideas. . . . So reading *Pinocchio* wasn't just reading *Pinocchio*. It was my way of introducing my students to the life of the mind, the value of their own experiences and stories, and the courage to raise interesting and challenging questions. It was also introducing them, in a social context, to reading as dialogue with a text, as an act in which their own experience is important and their own mind active. At the same time it was introducing them to studying a text and being able to communicate about ideas. It was about helping them to learn how to value their own and other people's voices. And finally it was a step, within a supportive group, toward helping them internalize the group process and become active intellectuals in their own right. (pp. 102–103)

ARTSEDGE Teaching Materials: The National Arts and Education Information Network *provides links to sites that support arts in education. Go to http://artsedge. kennedy-center.org/teaching_ materials/artsedge.html.*

Eliciting Talk

Talk is an important way to make meaning. In his book *Tell Me: Children, Reading, and Talk,* Aidan Chambers (1996) explores ways to help children respond to books and make sense of them through talk. The whole book is full of wonderfully concrete ideas and clear explanations of how to make talk about books an integral part of the classroom. He explains that children respond well to indirect prompts. Instead of asking children to summarize a story, identify the story elements, or tell why something happened, he suggests a gentler approach that he calls the *three sharings.*

Readers bring meaning to text through conversations and sharings they have with others, according to Chambers (1996). In everyday talk, we usually listen to what others say about an event before we come to any conclusions or make judgments. This listening and talking process is a prominent part of making sense of something and emerges from the conversation. At the beginning of a conversation about an event or movie or book, there is no pre-set meaning. In *Tell Me: Children, Reading, and Talk,* Chambers describes a three-phase approach to sharing what we have read in order to imitate the layering of talk to make meaning. The first he calls "sharing enthusiasms." In this phase, we talk about what we liked, what we thought was funny or sad, or what made us want to keep reading. Then we share what we disliked about the story or what made us less than eager to continue. Chambers points out that sharing our dislikes and disagreements often makes for more interesting and exciting exchanges than a common appreciation of the story.

In a process that Chambers calls "sharing puzzles or difficulties," readers then share the parts of the story they questioned. Some readers may want to discuss what something meant, others may want clarification on a point, and still others may wonder why someone liked a scene that they didn't like. Although friends may not agree on the elements in the story that they question, they will often agree to disagree. These discussions and conclusions do not, according to Chambers, remain static. They change over time as friends revisit the same story at another time, in another place, or with different people. This is true because "in any text, no matter how simple, there is always the possibility of multiple meanings" (p. 10). In this sharing, negotiation of meaning is most obvious.

The last type of sharing Chambers calls "sharing connections" or discovering patterns. It is, he states, a natural part of the human experience to look for connections that will lessen chaos and confusion and bring meaning to text. Story patterns and how one element of a text is connected to another are some of the characteristics that help us create connections and construct meaning. Chambers concludes that, however we share, "booktalk" gives our thoughts and emotions form "stimulated by the book and by the meaning(s) we make together out of its text—the imaginatively controlled messages sent from the author that we interpret in whatever way we find useful or delightful" (p. 12).

This kind of talk can be done through whole-class discussions, in pairs of students, in trios of students, in book groups, or in any number of other imaginative ways. At first it's difficult to accept the idea that all students are not going to come away from a discussion with the various parts of the book nicely wrapped up in a neat package. Approaching literature in this way challenges the stereotypic view that the job of a teacher of literature is to pass on a unified, consistent interpretation to all students. In fact, this is neither possible nor desirable.

Herbert Kohl (1995) advocates this more open-ended approach in his description of a discussion of **Pinocchio** in a first-grade class: "Since the goal is to read and appreciate the tale and not make moral judgments about the children's [in the story] behavior, our talks do not have to be tied up neatly. There's no need to draw final conclusions, write down homilies for the children to parrot, or even come down on the side of good or evil. The intent of discussing the text is to get greater pleasure and understanding from the story" (p. 97). Further, it's essential that students begin doing this work with our support.

CD-ROM

The CD-ROM offers additional resources on talk in References, as well as examples of how it can be used in the classroom in Classroom Teaching Ideas and Invitations. Key in the word *talk* to begin your search.

Children's Talk in Book Clubs

One multi-age first- and second-grade class in a rural area has a teacher who understands literacy and literature. Renee Webster (1996) has her students in book club groups, making meaning from the books she reads them. Webster describes how her students write and talk about books through book clubs:

> Book clubs encourage students to organize their response to a text in a personal way, which stimulates their prior experiences, abilities, and ideas. Conversing through book talks provides students with the experience of sharing a text as more than an exercise in decoding, supporting a belief that the role of a reader goes beyond the reciting of words to discover the multiple interpretations of a text. (p. 42)

The boxed feature First- and Second-Graders Discuss *Henry and Beezus* is a transcript of three first-graders and one second-grader discussing Beverly Cleary's story ***Henry and Beezus.*** The first few minutes of this student-led discussion focus on how Henry actually discovered 49 packages of bubble gum in a vacant lot and the events that led up to the discovery.

Webster points out that we can see from this discussion how the students are moving through the story to construct meaning. In lines 1 through 4, Mary and Ellie work to clarify a description of a vacant lot, which is not a familiar landmark for these rural students. They end up agreeing that it is not exactly an alley but like an alley. In line 6, Mary summarizes her interpretation of Henry's discovery of the gum. Ellie and Ron then begin questioning what actually happens in the story. Their inquiries take the form of restating or describing mental images of what they are trying to learn. These learners take ownership of their learning within a community that demands listening and participation. Webster points out that if a large-group discussion or individual worksheets had been used, these students might never have had the opportunity to scaffold each other's construction of knowledge concerning their understanding of this text.

First- and Second-Graders Discuss *Henry and Beezus*

1. M: He found it in the . . . alley.
2. E: It's not an alley, really.
3. M: It's like one.
4. E: Yeah.
5. M: Henry's dog ran up to chase a cat and . . . he found a package of something and he looked at it and it was gum.
6. E: I don't remember any cat.
7. R: Neither do I.
8. T: I do.
9. M: There was . . .
10. T: A cat.
11. R: I thought that was a dog.
12. E: It was a dog. There was a dog there.
13. R: There was.
14. E: Yeah.
15. T: There was a cat and a dog.
16. M: The dog started chasing the cat and he found the package of something.
17. E: Oh yeah!
18. M: And he opened it and it was gum.
19. T: Neat.
20. E: The dog didn't open it.
21. R: Yeah, the dog didn't open it.
22. T: The dog chased the cat and THEN he found it.
23. R: The dog didn't find it.
24. E: Yes, he did.
25. M: The dog (inaudible)
26. E: The dog found the package.
27. T: Yeah!
28. R: The dog found the cat.
29. E: Yeah, and that was when Henry opened the package and there was gum in there.
30. M: And then he ran to his friend's house and asked for a barrow.
31. R: Ah, no, not a barrow, a . . .
32. ALL: A wagon.

Awareness of the works of Langer (1995) and Claggett (1996) helps us see what these children are doing through their talk. They are in Stance Two (Being In and Moving Through an Envisionment), where they need time to share and build on each other's understandings. They are not yet ready to talk about the story in terms of themselves or to compare it to other stories. We can also see, as Langer points out, that the students each pay attention to different details and don't remember the same things from the story. This kind of book club talk helps them fill in the picture. Their questioning indicates that they are intellectually engaged with the text. They are also filling in gaps by using clues and evidence from the story to draw conclusions. They allude to and relate specific passages to validate their ideas. By deciding that the dog didn't open the package they demonstrate that they are evaluating the story in terms of how the author's ideas fit with their prior knowledge or experience. These children are exhibiting some characteristics of good readers, and they will continue to develop as readers as they are given more occasions to try out behaviors that good readers use.

What Talk Does

> Talk is not only a medium for thinking, it is also an important means by which we learn how to think. From a Vygotskian perspective thinking is an internal dialogue, an internalization of dialogues we've had with others. Our ability to think depends upon the many previous dialogues we have taken part in—we learn to think by participating in dialogues. (Dudley-Marling and Searle, 1991, p. 60)

When students have opportunities such as those just described to talk to each other about books, the understanding comes from within. They've had to think about the book, share responses and questions, pull from their memories pieces of the book, and negotiate meaning with others. Because students are actively involved in this talk, the understandings they come away with are authentic. The talk changes and extends their understanding and teaches them to see through other people's eyes. It shows in a very concrete way that even when we all read the same text, we remember or pay attention to very different things. So this kind of talk enriches all our readings, because it gives us a broader understanding of the many meanings in the text, beyond the ones we found. By examining and weighing possible interpretations through talk, students discover new layers of meaning. One common way to begin this kind of talk in the classroom is through the use of reading aloud. The boxed feature Implementing the Read-Aloud in the Classroom explains the hows and whys of reading aloud to a class (see page 124).

Classroom Read-Aloud Strategies provides even more ideas on implementing this process. Find it at http://clerccenter.gallaudet.edu/ Literacy/readit45.html.

When we read, we see images in our minds—full-blown pictures or flashes of color and shapes. These mental images are what make reading real to us, what make it retrievable, what help us talk about literature. Images have always been a part of the reading process, even though little attention has been paid to them. By talking about these images or sketching them, we can become more closely linked to our reading. But drawing can do even more than that. For too long, we non-artists have not understood the power or the function of art. Now, especially through the work of Karen Ernst, Ruth Shagoury Hubbard, Phyllis Whitin, Dennie Palmer Wolf, and Dana Balick, we are beginning to understand that drawing is another way to make meaning, to process thought, to represent our worlds, and to better understand what we think and feel. It is a vehicle for learning, a tool for expressing and organizing ideas. We have to learn what Karen Ernst (in Hubbard and Ernst, 1996) says kindergartners know naturally: "A picture is a form of expression, holds meaning, and is a story, a poem, a reflection of thinking" (p. 146). We also have to recapture that freedom kindergartners have to just draw. All of us have the capacity for visual expression, even though many of us are frightened by the idea of drawing or sketching.

Implementing the Read-Aloud in the Classroom

There is overwhelming evidence that reading aloud is an important ingredient in the literacy experiences of all readers. Teachers who are committed to including read-aloud in their classroom may be faced with questions about how to implement it. What books are good choices for read-aloud? How does one become proficient at reading aloud?

One of the first things to consider in your selection of a book to read aloud is quality. When you choose a book to be highlighted and shared with the group, you are demonstrating your endorsement of the book. Because you are going to be asking students to respond to the book, the book should be written well, with multidimensional characters, a good plot, an interesting setting, and a theme that a listener is likely to find compelling. Books with well-developed stories provide students with a multitude of ideas that they can relate to and share. These literary qualities can be found at all levels of children's literature. Since many classics fall into this category, many of your choices will probably be what would be described as "tried and true favorites," books that you loved as a child and want your students to have a chance to get to know. Some may come from a list of contemporary award-winning books, selected from the thousands of books published each year.

Academic content will also determine some of the texts you select. Although informational books are most likely to be used to tie in with a theme or unit on which the class is working, books from other genres, including poetry, can bring in a particular richness. Authenticity and accuracy of information are important, regardless of the genre. Although read-aloud is of enormous value as a way to strengthen children's vocabulary and ability to deal with more complex language, not all the books that you select to read aloud should be challenging. In fact, by occasionally reading a book that is at or even below the children's reading level, you may encourage them to select the book for independent reading.

Multicultural literature is great for read-aloud. Having a group share a text and respond together can foster greater understanding of diversity. Teachers need to be sure, however, that books representing different races, cultures, and peoples do not convey stereotypes. Reading aloud books that portray diversity lends credibility to the concept of the inclusion of all people in a respectful community of the world. All classrooms, whether homogeneously grouped or heterogeneously composed, have students who will benefit from being exposed to a wide variety of stories with a balance of male and female protagonists of various backgrounds and ethnicities.

Your own feeling about the book is probably the most influential criterion in selection of a read-aloud text. Your students will know if you are not interested in the book that you are reading; conversely, they will share your enjoyment and excitement about a book that you love. Reading a story that you love will not only share the story, but also demonstrate just how exciting books can be.

Once you have selected a book to use for read-aloud, practice reading it until you feel comfortable with the text. Getting the proper rhythm as you turn the pages and as the story ebbs and flows will require practice. So will phrasing the language in a way that will capture the listener. Practice until you feel comfortable with the text and know how you want to give voice to the characters. Over time, you will accumulate a repertoire of books that you read well. Children will ask you to read them again and again. Repeated rereadings of favorite stories can be beneficial to all children, but particularly those emergent readers who have not had an opportunity to find a favorite story and relish its familiarity.

Since drawing is another way of seeing and knowing, tapping into our rich, complex mental images through drawing encourages a deeper connection to literature. Hubbard (in Hubbard and Ernst, 1996) tells us, "Visual thinking challenges adults to experience things in a new way, enlarges their possibilities for understanding, gives them new tools for reflection, and expands their ideas of what it means to learn and teach" (p. 138). By including a visual response to literature, we can tap into areas that we might not reach through talking or writing. Alan Purves, Theresa Rogers, and Anna Soter, English educators and theorists (cited in Hubbard and Ernst, 1996), tell us, "Visual responses can have the function of unlocking thoughts and feelings in response to literature, enabling us to stand back from the work itself and develop a sense of what we have not yet seen or an angle we have not previously considered" (p. 70).

Since I am the consummate non-artist, I was very surprised by some of my experiences of sketching in response to books. One time I was with a group of teachers and we each sketched our vision of the same crucial scene in the book we were reading. Those drawings gave us fuel for hours of discussion, as we discovered that not only did we view the scene differently but we were all in different places in relation to the scene. We realized whom we felt most closely connected to and whether we saw the events unfold through a character's eyes or through an observer's eyes. Even the little details in our sketches revealed how our own background contributed to the way we envisioned the setting. We all came away from that experience stunned that our sketches held so much meaning and that they told us so much about our connections to the book.

The work of the authors cited in this section has furthered my understanding of how art functions as a meaning-making system. Much of the material in the following sections is drawn from their work.

The Shape Art Can Take in the Classroom

If we are to allow ourselves to explore the many aspects of visual expression, we must be with people who understand its importance and who value it as a way to make meaning. We need to know that drawing is a valuable tool for achieving a deeper understanding of whatever themes or concepts we are exploring in class. We would never draw a response unless we were encouraged to, unless the teacher understood the importance of this kind of meaning-making. That is why Hubbard (in Hubbard and Ernst, 1996), in her college classes, "always make it clear that visual solutions, processes, and experiments are a welcome part of the learning process" (p. 133).

One way we can begin to use visual expression is to sketch pictures of the images that come to us as we read or are read to. This is a particularly good strategy to use when a book is very powerful—when it overwhelms us with emotion and we have no words for the feelings welling up in us. Drawing unearths our response to the literature by giving us a way to start making our thinking concrete. So that students won't feel too intimidated to begin, you might suggest that they jot down a list of the random images that come to mind when they think about the story. Then they can create a visual depiction of the images noted; it might be lines, shapes, stick figures, sketches, or abstractions. Sharing the pictures or images in small groups first gives them a place to begin to talk—a channel for expression. This approach can work well for fiction as well as nonfiction. After reading a book like Marit Kaldhol and Wenche Oyen's **Goodbye Rune,** which deals with a child learning about loss through the death of her best friend, or Katherine Paterson's **Bridge to Terabithia,** on the same topic, it might be a good idea to get crayons out. Drawing shapes, lines, sketches, images, or abstractions might be easier for students than trying to talk when their chests still feel tight with emotion and words are inadequate. Sharon Dennis Wyeth's **Always My Dad,** which shows a little girl longing to have her dad in her life more, is also very emotional; drawing would be a good way to respond to this book. Drawing would also be a good approach to the biography **Richard Wright and the Library Card,** by William Miller, which makes discrimination concrete, and to the historical novel **Drummer Boy: Marching to the Civil War,** by Ann Turner, which shows the horrors a young boy faces in the war.

The images students draw can be starting points to understanding the story or to connecting to the story. This is not to suggest that emotionally powerful books are the only ones that can be responded to through drawing. It is a wonderful strategy to use for any kind of response. Students can draw images that come to them

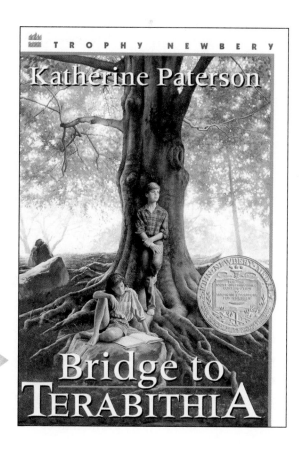

This moving story of a child's death, hard to talk about, may be easier to respond to through drawing.

(Cover art from *Bridge to Terabithia* by Katherine Paterson. COVER ART COPYRIGHT © 1987 BY MICHAEL DEAS. COVER ART COPYRIGHT © 1987 BY HARPERCOLLINS PUBLISHERS. Used by permission of HarperCollins Publishers.)

as they hear or read a story. Hubbard (in Hubbard and Ernst, 1996) reports that second-graders "talked about enjoying the experience of conjuring up and reliving their mental images. When children made that deeper personal connection to the stories they read, they were much more engaged in the book and enjoyed the reading experience" (p. 72). After trying out such drawing responses, you can evaluate whether this is true for you.

Each of us reads for our own purposes, and drawing responses gives us the freedom to shape our own connections with a book. This furthers our sense that the book is truly our own and not a book read for someone else's purpose. When Hubbard was working in a second-grade class, she and the teacher could see that the students who spontaneously drew as part of their responses were much more involved in their reading. So they tried a visual response log, in addition to the literature journals the children already kept. Periodically the children were asked to make two kinds of responses to their favorite section of a book of their choice, drawing and writing what was going on in their mind as they read or heard the story. As the children shared their drawing and writing, they thought of new anecdotes and memories, deepening their connections to different parts of the stories. Through this strategy, children were nudged to make the kinds of connections that could help them become more involved in the reading experience. The major categories of responses elicited through the drawing-writing format were memories of experiences similar to those in the book, memory images of particular details, memory images of other books, sensory images, memories of people they knew, and memories of contexts in which they had read or heard the same story. These responses mirror the connections good readers make to literature.

In one multi-age classroom in which Hubbard worked, she asked children, "How is it different thinking about the book in pictures than writing about it in words?" One eight-year-old told her, "Pictures are more exciting and interesting and I see them in my head." Another student told her that she liked to draw things about the stories she read because "you use your imagination more." The teachers were impressed with how important the talk around their visual responses was to the children's understanding and appreciation of the stories (Hubbard and Ernst, 1996, pp. 79–80). When Hubbard used visual expression with her college graduates, she "saw clearly the power of breaking out of typical literature discussions and venturing into unknown territory: letting images lead to meaning rather than beginning with words" (p. 132).

Using Responsive Drawing

When drawing is done in response to a book, it should be talked about or written about. Ernst (1994) tells us, "Without writing, meanings [of pictures] would have been private; students would have focused on the appearance of pictures or on my interpretations" (p. 51). When she worked with kindergartners, they told her the stories of their pictures. To help her students focus their written responses, she developed the list of questions in the boxed feature Responding to Your Own Pictures. Try answering these questions after you complete your first visual response.

Responding to Your Own Pictures

- What do you see in your picture?
- What do you feel as you look at your picture?
- What is the story in or beyond your picture?
- If you went inside your picture, what would you find?

- What inspired you?
- What surprised you or what did you discover as you worked?

(From Hubbard and Ernst, eds., *New Entries: Learning by Writing and Drawing*, 1996, p. 18.)

After having students produce art in response to literature, hang their pieces around the room. Have others in the class respond to the pictures, explaining what they see, what they think about as they look at the work, what title they might give the piece, and the kind of book for which the drawing was made. In this way, words and pictures will work in partnership as tools to describe meaning.

The Importance of Modeling

In order to encourage students to respond to literature through art, it can be helpful to make explicit how artists make meaning through drawing and painting and how they create their effects. Art should be focused on, techniques demonstrated, elements talked about, and drawings in picture books examined. This background information will project students into the world of art. If the time is taken to teach them the basics of art, they will understand that these are important tools they can use. A word of warning: Like the study of literature, the study of art should be for its own sake, not as a means to memorize tools.

Karen Ernst (1994), language arts teacher turned art teacher, begins with a rehearsal for learning. "We looked at art to understand what real artists do, we studied illustrations to see how words and pictures worked together, and we listened to stories to help inspire and encourage us to open our imaginations" (p. 42). She also demonstrates how to use materials available in the room, talking about and showing picture books done in various media, such as acrylic paints, watercolors, markers, crayons, oil pastels, and drawing pens.

In addition, she brings in the works of poets, illustrators, and writers. Rather than use them prescriptively as story starters or models, she lets them awaken something in students. "I used literature to help my students become concerned with their thinking, build a vocabulary of language and skills in art, use their imagination, avoid realistic depiction, not worry about what pictures looked like" (p. 60). With mini-lessons focused on the techniques used by illustrators, she uses the work of Eric Carle and Leo Lionni to lead students to paint papers and to tear and cut them into collages. For watercolor, she uses **Jackson Makes His Move,** by Andrew Glass; for torn-paper collage, **Mouse Paint,** by Ellen Stoll Walsh; and for cut-paper collage, **The World from My Window,** by S. W. Samton. The children read about the quest of the artist in such books as Cynthia Rylant's **All I See** and Tomie dePaola's **The Art Lesson,** while **Will's Mammoth,** by Rafe Martin, presents the possibilities of imagination to them. An effective workshop provides a balance between modeling the work and giving students a chance to apply that knowledge to their own ideas for projects.

As you read picture books this semester, look for techniques you would like to try. Torn-paper collage is a good place to start, since it doesn't sound intimidating. Montages—the technique of making a single pictorial composition by closely arranging or superimposing many pictures or designs—also seems doable. Many artists use photographs in the background and build up from there.

Another way to appreciate and talk about art is through children's books devoted to the subject of art, books like Pat Cummings's (1992, 1995, 1999) three volumes, **Talking with**

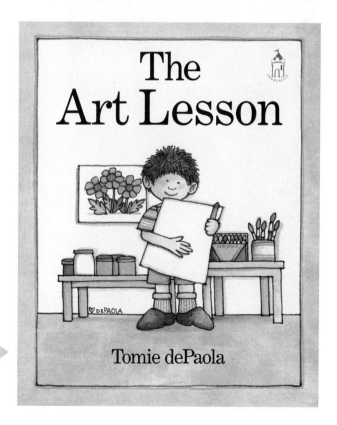

The child's desire to be an artist and his understanding of what artists do may inspire children who love to draw.
(From THE ART LESSON by Tomie dePaola, copyright © 1989 by Tomie dePaola. Used by permission of G. P. Putnam's Sons, an imprint of Penguin Putnam Books for Young Readers, a division of Penguin Putnam Inc.)

Artists; Matthew's Dream, by Leo Lionni; *Linnea in Monet's Garden,* by Christina Björk; *Rembrandt,* by Michael Venezia; and the series *Getting to Know the World's Greatest Artists* and *Art for Children.* Noted nonfiction writer Kathleen Krull has a very engaging book called *Lives of the Artists: Masterpieces, Messes (and What the Neighbors Thought),* illustrated by Kathryn Hewitt.

Writing

Writing is another natural way to respond to literature because it invites us to think about our connection to literature and how literature affects us. After the initial talk or writing response, we can get to the inside of a book or to its impact by writing in a variety of formats. Following are some options for shaping such writing.

1. Change the point of view. Would you like to explore how someone besides the main character felt and thought during the story? Jon Scieszka's classic *The True Story of the 3 Little Pigs!* does just this. We see the entire story from the wolf's point of view, which differs greatly from what the pigs tell us. After reading Natalie Babbitt's *Tuck Everlasting,* write the story from the man-in-yellow's point of view.

2. Focus on issues and themes. Does the idea of home call out a response in you after you have read a book such as *My House Has Stars,* by Megan McDonald, or *Nory Ryan's Song,* by Patricia Reilly Giff? Perhaps you could write a poem about home or write a list of ten things that describe home for you. After reading *Baseball Saved Us,* by Ken Mochizuki, write a tribute to the Japanese who endured the internment camps or write a letter to the editor raising issues about these camps.

3. Connect issues from the story to your own life. After "reading" *Frog and Toad Are Friends,* by Arnold Lobel, write about why you think they were true friends or what you like to do with your friends. Or write about how your own life is different from what is shown in a book.

4. Write about the story in a different genre. Create a poem, write a script, write letters, write lists of things important to characters, write memos from one character to another, write a tall tale or a fairy tale, write about some aspect of the story in a newspaper article or an informational piece.

5. Work to get inside one of the characters. In this kind of writing, the focus is on trying to understand the character more fully. You could write a monologue about how the character likes the way she or he is portrayed in the book, a letter from the main character to several other characters, lists of what the character likes or dislikes about the other characters, an article about the values you think this character finds important, or a diary entry. For instance, after reading *Tar Beach,* by Faith Ringgold, you could explore the values you think the main character holds dear.

6. Extend the story by placing the characters in a new situation or by developing and explaining something that is only suggested. After reading *Charlotte's Web,* by E. B. White, you could write about how

Readers of this story of courage get to know Anne Marie so well that they could write from her point of view or create a script.

Fern would fit in in your elementary school and what kind of friends she might make. Or script out the party your class would like to give for Anne Marie in Lois Lowry's **Number the Stars,** describing the kind of celebration you would have and what you would have her talk about.

7. Connect stories. What does one book remind you of in another? Would the characters have anything to say to each other? Perhaps you could have the ever-so-proper mother in **Voices in the Park,** by Anthony Browne, have a conversation with the woman on the messy side in **To Market, To Market,** by Anne Miranda.

8. Write your own story, inspired by the literature. If reading **The Gardener,** by Sarah Stewart, makes you want to write a story set in a garden, do it. If it makes you want to create a story about a gruff person like her uncle who really is very caring, do it. If it makes you think about the way children can affect adults, write a story probing this issue. Literature is meant to inspire.

9. Produce a writing project. Create a newspaper for the story you have read, with articles based on happenings in the story, interviews of characters in the story, and news briefs about the main events in the story. Create an alphabet scheme, capturing the essence of the book through your choice of words and sentences. After reading **Roll of Thunder, Hear My Cry,** by Mildred D. Taylor, you might come up with an alphabet that begins with "**A** is for the **Anger** that Uncle Hammer had boiling up inside of him." Create a pamphlet that aims to persuade others of the importance of an issue that was central to your character. Include factual information, testimonials, pictures, graphics, and so on. For instance, after reading **The True Confessions of Charlotte Doyle,** by Avi, fifth-graders might create a pamphlet explaining the reasons women should have more life choices. Create a collage, made up of words and pictures cut out of magazines, that gives viewers a distinct impression of what the book is about. Then write about what you selected and why.

CD-ROM

For further ideas on how the *ABC* or *alphabet scheme* can be used in writing, search Invitations and Classroom Teaching Ideas.

When we write in different genres, we bring heightened awareness to our own reading. Writing breeds better readers. Writing also brings our own experiences to the story and helps solidify our connection to the story. Hubbard (1996) found, in a second-grade class, "Even less sophisticated readers were far more likely to choose to write about their books— and to talk about how much they enjoyed them—when they made connections between what they read and their own life experiences" (p. 71).

Providing open-ended options for response is critical if students are to grow as learners. When students are forced into rigid formats and told what to write about, they are being forced to focus on what the teacher experiences or sees as important, not what they see as important. Donald Murray (1982), noted writer and teacher, suggests that students be given four freedoms in writing: ability to find their own subject, their own evidence, their own audience, and their own form. Although this is not always possible on every assignment, if students have control over the format *or* the topic, they usually feel that they are being asked to do something that has meaning for them. For instance, in an assignment involving poetry writing, it works best to have students pick out a topic if a specific form such as a limerick is being asked for or to write in any format they think works best if a specific topic is provided.

Drama

Aidan Chambers (1996) claims that our work as reading teachers includes "helping children engage in the drama of reading, helping them become dramatist (rewriter of the text), director (interpreter of the text), actor (performer of the text), audience (actively responsive recipient of the text), even critic (commentator and explicator and scholarly student of the text)" (p. 5). Drama involves the physical acting out or performance of a piece of literature. In the language arts class, this can take the form of role-playing, scripting and reading aloud (reader's theater), or actually acting out a story.

When we script, role-play, or act out a piece of literature, we increase our comprehension of the literature because we enter into it as a character. Performing parts of scenes provides a forum for discussing a piece of literature, as we learn to express orally a range of meanings and emotions. We understand characters and therefore people better when we role-play, or "try on," their actions, seeing how it feels to do or say what the character did. When we create our own script from a piece of literature, we learn how to select its essence and how to get the meaning and tone across to others. Creating and performing a script is fun and highly motivational because others will see our performance and respond to it.

Scripting

Scripting usually involves selecting a scene or chapter from a book, eliminating extraneous material from it, and adding a narrator to set the scene and provide transitions or information that the characters do not speak in dialogue. Scripting changes the format of the writing into all speaking parts.

A chapter selected for a reader's theater script should have the following characteristics:

Reader's Theater Scripts and Plays for the Classroom not only shows how to produce scripts but also provides some scripts. Go to www.teachingheart.net/ readerstheater.htm.

- The characters are interesting and quickly understood through their dialogue.

- The dialogue carries the action, leaving little need for supplementary information.

- The writing is clear and concrete, yet rich in the choice and placement of words.

- The scene will encourage others to want to change parts and seek other interpretations of the material.

- The scenes will stir the imagination and interest of the listeners.

Other characteristics you might look for include the following:

- The depth of emotion or characterization will be better understood through performance.

- The scene will be a good introduction to the rest of the book.

- The scene will give listeners a better understanding of an historical period, a contemporary problem, the people of another culture, or a new genre of literature.

- The scene will introduce listeners to an author or a series, enticing them to do more reading.

When you respond to a book by creating a reader's theater script, your goal is to capture the essence of the book or its conflicts through the chapter you select to script. If the script is read aloud, you will feel the power of performance, of hearing the words spoken with emotion. Short scripted pieces of stories should make us wonder what will happen to characters, how a problem will be resolved, or what will happen next and thus make us want to read the whole story.

Many novels do not lend themselves to easy adaptation without significant rewriting. Oftentimes, to unleash the power of a scene, you will have to leave out great hunks of the writing so as to uncover the essence of the scene for your listeners. If the narrator seems to have a very heavy reading load, you might consider using more than one narrator to keep the pacing lively. The Internet resources at the end of the chapter provide sites where scripts are available.

Role-Playing

Role-playing thrusts us inside a piece of literature, as we work to think and speak like the character we are playing. When a character is puzzling to you, when you would like to figure out why she reacted as she did to another character, find a partner and role-play the parts. In a two-person role-play, each person is forced to think of explanations for the actions and attitudes of his or her character—to think like the character. Or, if everyone in the class has read the same book, you could take the part of a character and be interviewed by the whole class, answering questions as that character. Interviewers might ask how you feel about taking care of your brother, whether you think your parents were fair, and so on. Another way to role-play is simply to have students enact the story, as the boxed feature The Drama Connection illustrates.

Using drama builds understanding and involvement. Seeing, doing, or touching helps us understand. Drama also provides the opportunity to repeat and review. When you have trouble understanding a characterization, role-play can help you figure out the character's thinking. Through involvement in drama, students cease being observers of a conflict in a text. Instead, they become active agents and participants in a real human dilemma, using language to work toward resolution of that dilemma.

To experience the power of role-play, find a scene in a book that puzzles or troubles you and start role-playing. Books that work well for role-playing or scripting include **The Giver** and **Number the Stars,** both by Lois Lowry; **Red Scarf Girl: A Memoir of the Cultural Revolution,** by Ji Li Jiang; **Ella Enchanted** and **Dave at Night,** both by Gail Carson Levine; **Freak the Mighty,** by Rodman Philbrick; **Bud, Not Buddy** and **The Watsons Go to Birmingham—1963,** both by Christopher Paul Curtis; **Tuck Everlasting,** by Natalie Babbitt; and **Roll of Thunder, Hear My Cry,** by Mildred D. Taylor.

The Drama Connection

It is always amazing when children who have been quoted in their school reports as hating reading fall in love with read-aloud and enthusiastically interact with text. This was the case in Rose Casement's (1998) classroom of children diagnosed with severe behavioral and emotional disabilities. Early years in skill-and-drill literacy programs had convinced them that they could not read. For many of them, **The Frog and Toad** stories by Arnold Lobel were a captivating segue into text. One day, as the teacher and students gathered on the floor for a read-aloud, Julia picked **Frog and Toad Are Friends** (1970) and Casement read the chapter called "The Story." Julia sat where she could see the text; as Casement read, she stopped and Julia filled in the words. This oral-to-print literacy teaching strategy promotes a focus on meaning, or the semantic cueing system. Julia responded enthusiastically.

In the story, Toad goes through several antics, trying to get an idea for a story. Everyone in the class cracked up when Toad stood on his head and later when he poured water on his head. They almost fell out of their seats when he hit his head on the wall. No one wanted to let go of the story.

Julia suddenly remembered that the class the year before had done a dramatization of another **Frog and Toad** story, "Spring." It was her idea to dramatize **Frog and Toad Are Friends,** and Casement suggested that the class focus on the part where Frog tells Toad the story they have created through their own actions.

Julia's four classmates joined in the excitement of the play. The teacher quickly turned to the story for possibilities. After the initial casting of Frog and Toad, the real work began. "OK, who will be the water?" "Who will be the wall?" And then there was the role of the narrator. As the play commenced, the water dutifully splashed, and the wall did its best to just stand flat. The part of the narrator was filled with each child in turn, some of whom could read the entire story and others who required various degrees of support from Casement. Everyone played his or her part and readily switched as they re-performed the story. Not only did everyone have fun; the students also saw the text come alive and realized that they could interact with it in a way that was meaningful for them. As Jeffrey Wilhelm (1997) suggests in *You Gotta BE the Book: Teaching Engaged and Reflective Reading with Adolescents,* using drama with reluctant and less proficient readers "may help such students enormously as we come to more fully understand actual processes of making meaning through reading" (p. 112).

The story plays that these students performed involved community building as part of the production. Each of the parts, even those that might have seemed mundane, had some fun aspect. The wall, after all, wasn't such a bad part when one remembered that Toad, as part of the story, was to pretend to hit his head on it. But the "lead roles" and "secondary roles" and even the role of a flat wall didn't seem to matter. It was being part of the drama that counted.

Interestingly, for the students in Casement's classroom, drama not only enhanced their engagement with text but also improved their interactions with the other students in the class. The activity of story play—and the requirements that came with it of active participation and consideration for others—helped build community.

Movement or Kinesthetic Learning

Sometimes "we limit learning to the area from the nostrils up—no talking, no moving, no fidgeting. Yet children need to use their bodies and space" (Trussell-Cullen, 1999). Children love to move. This is the way they explore their world and react to it. They jump for joy, stomp their feet in anger, dance their exuberance, and walk out their energy. They use their bodies to play, to communicate, and to express emotions. They are all fluent in this nonverbal, physical language when they begin elementary school. The norm, however, has been to disregard this language of theirs; instead of channeling it constructively, teachers expend all of their energy trying to prevent children from expressing their physicality. Susan Griss (1998), author of *Minds in Motion: A Kinesthetic Approach to Teaching Elementary Curriculum,* tells us that while "bodily-kinesthetic intelligence is recognized as one of our multiple intelligences, it is one of the more undervalued in the schools." She says, "Learning, in a physical language—a language that includes kinesthetic activities, creative movement, and dance—is wonderfully natural to most children" (p. 2).

She suggests that children be asked to depict a scene from a story by creating sculptures made of still, posed bodies. This kind of kinesthetic teaching reflects the natural language of children. When we give them permission to "speak" this language in the classroom, our students will amaze us with their abilities to interpret, express, and analyze ideas through movement.

Griss gives a very powerful example of the levels of learning we can internalize through the use of our bodies. She begins by asking a group to tell her which medium they think sound travels through the fastest—solid, liquid, or gas. Once they have expressed their opinions, the group is divided into three lines to participate in a kind of relay race, each line representing either a solid, a liquid, or a gas. The liquid group is lined up one behind the other so that they each will have to take a couple of steps to touch the person in front. The solid group is lined up so that they can touch the person in front without extending their arms fully. The gas group is lined up so that each person will have to run several steps to reach the next person in line. When everyone is set and a signal is given, the last person in each line taps the shoulder of the person in front of him or her to pass the sound wave along. When the tap reaches the first person in line, that person yells out "solid," "liquid," or "gas." The solid group gets done first, and the gas group finishes last. Now, when she asks her opening question, they can not only answer correctly but also explain what density has to do with the rate at which sound waves travel. Because they have done this exercise physically, the information will be indelibly stored in their brains. Information learned physically is information that is not forgotten.

Kinesthetic teaching makes subject matter accessible by concretizing the abstract. It involves children in the creative process and develops higher-level thinking and social skills. It provides an affirmative means for self-expression. Griss tells us that if we follow the maxim "teach from the known to the unknown," we will understand the value of allowing children to learn from their bodies (p. 14). "Children who learn through their muscles viscerally remember information that they might otherwise forget" (p. 23).

Using Movement in Response to Literature

A kinesthetic approach can be used if the topic offers at least one of the following three points of access (Griss, 1998, p. 15):

1. There is a possibility for creative interpretation.

2. Kinesthetic elements of motion, time, space, or shape are present.

3. Authentic dance forms can be extrapolated from the topic.

Any subject that involves some sort of drama or emotion can probably be interpreted by children through movement.

Susan Griss (1998) structures the form of her dance lessons to reflect the content of the reading lessons. To learn about main idea, her students did "theme dances: rain dance, planting dance, animal dances." To focus on details, they did "mirror dances, carefully observing their partners." To understand the importance of sequence, they created "pattern dances in which the order of the dance was significant." To emphasize drawing conclusions, they "interpreted Aesop's fables through dance" (p. xii).

Kinesthetic perceptions and responses are much more natural for elementary school children than for older people, who have lost much use of the language of movement. When we expand our concept of learning to include physical language, "we broaden children's access to comprehension. In particular, creative movement—the improvisation of interpretative movements—is an excellent way to engage children with literature" (p. 6).

Griss (1998) uses the story of **Swimmy,** by Leo Lionni, to illustrate how creative movement can express a specific story's setting, plot, theme, and character development. Children are invited to become part of the story, entering the ocean habitat and following the sequence of exciting and sometimes tragic events while they hear the story read aloud. As they become involved in acting out the drama of the story, they feel and express Swimmy's emotional responses. In this story in which a school of small fish learn to swim together in the shape of a large fish as a way to protect themselves, children "will feel the surge of collective power as they group together to fool their bigger sea predators" (p. 6). This active participation allows children's "kinesthetic intelligence [to] clarify principles and information that may elude them in other languages of learning" (p. 6).

Kinesthetic learning can reveal to students aspects of themselves of which they had no awareness. Griss tells us, "By dancing the attributes of wind, from gentle breezes to wild hurricanes and forceful tornadoes, timid children can express their physical power, while aggressive children can find the peacefulness of being soft, of floating" (p. 7). Seeing these hidden qualities emerge, teachers will find their perceptions and expectations of children expanding.

Structuring Kinesthetic Elements

Griss recommends using one of four elements to structure kinesthetic experiences: motion, shape, space, or time. When kinesthetic elements are being used, it often works well to have one person supply the narrative by reading or telling the story as the participants move.

Motion

If Lilly in **The Whales' Song,** by Dyan Sheldon, were to dance a whale dance, what would it look like? Students can spin, jump, twist, and turn as the whales do to express their exuberance.

Through movement in groups of four, capture the mood of a book such as **We Had a Picnic This Sunday Past,** by Jacqueline Woodson. Each group can perform its moves and see whether the other groups can interpret what these moves mean.

Improvise the feelings a poem elicits from you—perhaps a dance of the wind, a dance of fear, a dance of freedom. If your class gets into movement and begins to feel comfortable with it, you might ask someone in the class with dance experience to show you how to repeat your moves to make up a full-length dance.

Another possibility is to use body movement to demonstrate three encounters that a character had in a story.

Shape

Groups can make static shapes or move together. Students enjoy making tableaux—still poses—of scenes in a book. What would it have looked like when all the animals and the lady went to market together at the end of **To Market, To Market,** by Anne Miranda? A few students can make the shape of the "beautiful pink lotus unfurling its petals" in **The Lotus Seed,** by Sherry Garland, or the whole class can make the shape of one snowflake after reading **Snowflake Bentley,** by Jacqueline Briggs Martin.

Space

Space involves height, width, and depth. What would it be like to live on a prairie or in a city, to be on the *Mayflower,* to hide in the room that Anne Frank's family did? To experience what it was like for the characters, figure out how much space Anne's family had and put the appropriate amount of students in the space. To capture the increasing aloneness the plastic ducks must have felt when boxes of them fell into the ocean in *Ducky,* by Eve Bunting, have the whole class start out as ducks in a small space and then drift apart.

Time

The time reflected in a kinesthetic approach can be time lapsed or time passing. For instance, you could clap your hands, stomp your feet, slap your legs, or make mouth sounds to indicate the pace or tempo of a chapter in a book. This is a good way to make students aware of how action builds in a book and is especially fun to do with a mystery. Or you could figure out the pattern or rhyme of a book and move to that pattern or rhyme. What beat does each chapter have? If it's a fast beat, you could tap your feet quickly. As the book slows down, your tapping or clapping could slow down.

Since it can be very intimidating to get in front of a class alone, have students do things in groups. Start with an obvious reading, such as the poem "The Dance of the Thirteen Skeletons," by Jack Prelutsky, in *Nightmares—Poems to Trouble Your Sleep.* Get in a circle and move clockwise as someone reads the poem. When you get to the lines "and they danced in their bones/their bare, bare bones," dance like skeletons, with that loose-limbed look.

Pantomime is another way to ease reluctant participants into movement. Different class members or groups might take turns pantomiming scenes or actions from a book that the whole class has read. The rest of the class has the job of guessing what the pantomime is about.

Music

Another little-used avenue to literature response is music and song. Teachers who have not had experience singing in groups or in public may feel intimidated by the idea of singing publicly. In her book *Lasting Impressions,* Shelley Harwayne (1999), elementary school principal and writer, admits that she felt hesitant about using music but decided: "Children deserve an opportunity to tap into the music of their lives. They had a right to sing." She arranged to make time for music using students' favorite singers, and they "began to listen to tapes and records and sing along joyfully, regularly, and with gusto in the classroom" (p. 114).

From exposure to music they learned to write "original lullabies, jazz chants, and blues songs. They were then able to bring rhythm, repetition, and cadence to their poetry and prose." She continued to experiment with bringing music into their lives:

> I could press a button on a tape player and have students write with music in the background. I could surround students with songs that have been published in picture book format and invite them to do the same. [See Ashley Bryan's illustrations in *What a Wonderful World,* by George David Weiss and Bob Thiele.] I could help students select music to accompany a read-aloud. I could invite students to realize that there are stories attached to songs that have been important in their lives. (p. 113)

By starting slowly and gradually becoming comfortable with music and singing, Harwayne extended to her students another way to learn. Even as neophytes we can bring music into our classrooms. Singing and making music are ways to make meaning in the classroom and to connect to and extend literature. If singing and songs are an integral part

See **Creating Music,** a site where children can create their own music, at www.creatingmusic.com/contours/index.html.

of your class, it will not be a great stretch for children to pick songs or tunes that they think speak to a story they have read.

Once students are used to singing in class and have a repertoire of songs from which to choose, it becomes easier to encourage response to literature through song. Think back to all the songs, tunes, and rhymes you knew as a little kid. These might include "To Market, To Market to Buy a Fat Pig," "Twinkle, Twinkle Little Star," "Row, Row, Row Your Boat," "Ring Around the Rosie," "The Eensy, Weensy Spider," "I'm a Little Tea Pot," "The ABC Song," "Shake Them Halloween Bones," and "London Bridge Is Falling Down." Think of the melodies to these songs. Could you make up a short song, using one of these melodies that would speak to a story or character in a book you have read?

Here are other ways to use music to respond to literature:

- Select music that you think goes with a story. Play it in class, explaining why you selected it or asking students to figure out how that piece could be connected to a story they have read.

- Design a CD collection for a character, being sure that the collection includes music that explains as many aspects as possible of the character.

- After reading a novel, figure out how you would divide the book into sections. Then select a piece of music that you think captures the feel or tone of each section. Record the pieces. If possible, do voice-overs explaining what is happening in the novel during the piece of music and why you feel the piece of music fits the section of the novel.

CD-ROM

For examples in Invitations and Classroom Teaching Ideas of how music can be used with literature, key in the words *music, song,* and *sing.*

The Affective in Literature

Feelings and emotions surround everything we do. When you are using literature, opportunities will come up naturally to deal with issues about which your students will have strong feelings. Herbert Kohl (1995) used **Pinocchio,** by Carlo Collodi, to "discuss the limits of mischief and the development of empathy" (p. 98). He believes, "Stories, delightful in themselves, are also powerful vehicles for the discussion of sensitive issues in a non-emergency situation" (p. 98). So before students have the chance to pick on other students about their name, read **Chrysanthemum,** by Kevin Henkes, with your students to show them how others feel when teased about their name. **Leo the Late Bloomer,** by Robert Kraus, can help children understand that everyone doesn't learn to do things at the same time—that everyone has her or his own internal calendar. Kohl puts it succinctly: "Stories become tools to approach and investigate these issues with students. They provide problems at a distance, moral dilemmas to discuss and examine, rather than conflict situations to be resolved" (pp. 98–99).

When a book deals with a sensitive issue such as the loss of a friend or how a child responds to divorce, it is important to encourage talk on the issue, not let it go in silence. Silence implies fear and dread and suggests that the issue is too horrible or shameful to discuss. When students know

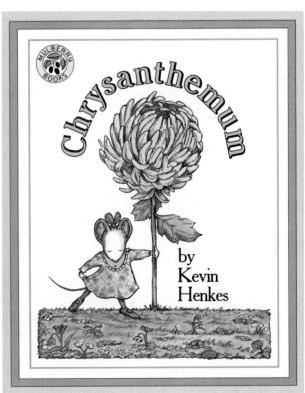

Chrysanthemum loves her name until others start to tease her about it.

(Cover art from *Chrysanthemum* by Kevin Henkes. Used by permission of HarperCollins Publishers.)

that we are comfortable discussing issues that touch on the emotions, they will usually be comfortable too.

We will do in our classrooms only what we are comfortable doing and only what we know how to do. That is why it is so important to be a genuine practitioner of the outlets we want children to explore. If we want them to draw in response to literature, we have to feel comfortable drawing. If we want them to role-play in response to literature, we have to feel comfortable role-playing. If we want them to be doers and active participants in their learning, we have to be doers and active participants too.

Through the arts and the multiliteracies approach, children can see in concrete ways that *they* are in charge of their own learning—that to learn means to create and find places for information. Learning no longer means simply adopting someone else's view of the world. If we want to involve all of our students, including children outside the mainstream culture, in meaningful learning, we must use all the avenues available. If children are able to use the strengths they bring to school, they will not be as resistant to learning.

Invitations

Choose several of the following activities to complete:

1. Aidan Chambers (1996) says, "The meaning of a story for that group of readers emerges from the conversation." Think of a book you've discussed in your small group or in a whole-class discussion. What new realizations or interpretations did you come up with?

2. After a group discussion on a common book, reflect on your discussion in terms of Chambers's three sharings approach.

3. Choose one or more of the following responses to complete. By the end of the semester, have several kinds of responses to literature collected in your portfolio. If one response is a performance, write up a summary of it or put a tape of it in your portfolio. Reflect on how the response form gave you new understandings of the books.

- Create a collage or some other kind of visual response to a book. Share your art with your group and elicit their response to what you have created.

- Create an abstract representation of a book to accompany a reflective essay on the book.

- Choose one or more of the writing options mentioned in this chapter as a way to respond to a book you read. Share the writing in your small group, explaining whether the option got you deeper into the book and/or caused you to see different aspects of the book.

- Role-play a character in a book you have all read by letting your small group ask you questions as if you were the character.

- In your small group, select a scene from a story that raises many issues about the character and her/his intentions or motives. Role-play the scene, with members of the group adopting characters' personas. By making up your own words and adding to what the character said in the story, what realizations did you come to about the character?

- With others in your small group, create a tableau of a scene in a book you read that you think is significant. Elicit responses from viewers as to what they thought you were portraying and the impact the tableau had on them.

- Using one of the kinesthetic elements (motion, shape, space, or time), create a "performance" based on a story or poem your group has read. Talk and write about the experience.

- Carry out one of the music options described in this chapter or another one of your own. Share it with your small group or the whole class.

4. Look through books you have read to get ideas for art, writing, drama, movement, and music responses. Write up ten suggestions and share them with your small group.

5. After you have responded to several books or novels, look for evidence of Langer's four stances in your work. What do you notice about yourself as a reader? Do you seem to stay in one stance longer than the others? Share your findings with your small group. Discuss whether your school work has emphasized the stance you spend a lot of time in. Can you make any generalizations that may help you as a teacher?

Classroom Teaching Ideas

1. After students have read a book such as **Koala Lou,** by Mem Fox, encourage them to make bag puppets to represent the characters in the book and perform their interpretation of the story for the whole class.

2. After reading a book such as **Tacky the Penguin,** by Helen Lester, students can write a rap about what happened in the story and perform it for the class.

3. After reading a book such as **Follow the Drinking Gourd,** by Jeanette Winter, students can make drums out of coffee cans and oatmeal boxes, decorate them, and compose a rhythm and a chant to retell the main events in the story. They can practice beating out the rhythm in time with the chant and then perform for the class.

4. After reading a book such as **The Tale of Rabbit and Coyote,** by Tony Johnston and Tomie dePaola, students can use chalk on a large piece of butcher paper to draw a mural interpreting the story. When they present the mural to the class, they can explain the choices they made.

5. After reading the picture book version of **The Story of Ruby Bridges,** by Robert Coles, students can dramatize the story. They can figure out the script (perhaps with the help of an aide or parent volunteer), get a few costumes and props (if you have a costume box in your room), and then act the story out for the class.

6. After reading **Six Crows,** by Leo Lionni, students can create a game board, a game picture, game cards, and

rules that reflect how the farmer and the crows learned to get along. Once they complete the work, they can teach the rest of the class how to play.

7. Students can create interview questions after reading a book such as **Now One Foot, Now the Other,** by Tomie dePaola. In this story, a little boy thinks about how his grandfather helped him in so many ways and how, now that his grandfather is ill, he is doing the same for his grandfather. The interview questions might focus on what children do for their grandparents and vice versa or on some other aspect of the grandparent/grandchild relationship. After creating the questions, students can arrange to go to other classrooms to interview students. They should then present their findings to their class.

8. After reading a book such as **Who Sank the Boat?,** by Pamela Allen, students can extend the theme of the story by creating a game show. Contestants should be called upon to answer questions about what would sink and what would float.

9. After reading a book, students can write new words about the events in the book to the tune of a well-known song and sing the song to the class.

10. To help students develop an awareness of their own comprehension, ask them to make text-to-self connections, text-to-world connections, and text-to-text connections as they read. Show them how these connections can help them understand a book better.

Internet and Text Resources

1. **ARTSEDGE Teaching Materials: The National Arts and Education Information Network** provides links in an effort to get the arts and education together. Find it at

   http://artsedge.kennedy-center.org/teaching_materials/artsedge.html

2. **Reader's Theater Scripts and Plays for the Classroom** gives detailed steps for producing scripts as well as many reproducible scripts. Go to

   www.teachingheart.net/readerstheater.htm

3. **Reader's Theater/Language Arts for Teachers** provides a variety of scripts arranged by title. Find it at

   http://hometown.aol.com/rcswallow/index.html

4. **Classroom Read-Aloud Strategies** provides a set of seven strategies to use when reading aloud. Find it at

   http://clerccenter.gallaudet.edu/Literacy/readit45.html

References

Casement, Rose (1998). "The Impact of a Holistic Literacy Learning Environment for Children with Severe Multiple and Emotional/Behavioral Disabilities." Unpublished dissertation. University of Maine.

Chambers, Aidan (1996). *Tell Me: Children, Reading, and Talk*. York, ME: Stenhouse.

Claggett, Fran (1996). *A Measure of Success: From Assignment to Assessment in English Language Arts*. Portsmouth, NH: Heinemann.

Cummings, Pat, ed. (1992). *Talking with Artists—Volume 1*. New York: Bradbury.

—— (1995). *Talking with Artists—Volume 2*. New York: Simon & Schuster.

—— (1999). *Talking with Artists—Volume 3*. New York: Clarion.

Dudley-Marling, Curt, and Dennis Searle (1991). *When Students Have Time to Talk*. Portsmouth, NH: Heinemann.

Ernst, Karen (1994). *Picturing Learning*. Portsmouth, NH: Heinemann.

Greene, Maxine (1995). *Releasing the Imagination: Essays on Education, the Arts, and Social Change*. San Francisco: Jossey-Bass.

Griss, Susan (1998). *Minds in Motion: A Kinesthetic Approach to Teaching Elementary Curriculum*. Portsmouth, NH: Heinemann.

Hansen, Jane (1998). *When Learners Evaluate*. Portsmouth, NH: Heinemann.

Harwayne, Shelley (1999). *Lasting Impressions*. Portsmouth, NH: Heinemann.

Hubbard, Ruth Shagoury, and Karen Ernst, eds. (1996). *New Entries: Learning by Writing and Drawing*. Portsmouth, NH: Heinemann.

Keene, Ellin O., and Susan Zimmermann (1997). *Mosaic of Thought: Teaching Comprehension in a Reader's Workshop*. Portsmouth, NH: Heinemann.

Kohl, Herbert (1995). *Should We Burn Babar? Essays on Children's Literature and the Power of Stories*. New York: New Press.

Langer, Judith (1995). *Envisioning Literature: Literary Understanding and Literature Instruction*. New York: Teachers College Press.

Murray, Donald M. (1982). *Learning by Teaching: Selected Articles on Writing and Teaching*. Portsmouth, NH: Boynton/Cook.

Rosenblatt, Louise (1996). *Literature as Exploration*. New York: Modern Language Association [1938].

—— (1978). *The Reader, the Text, and the Poem*. Carbondale, IL: Southern Illinois University Press.

Short, Kathy, and Jerry Harste, with Carolyn Burke (1996). *Creating Classrooms for Authors and Inquirers*. Portsmouth, NH: Heinemann.

Short, Kathy G., Gloria Kauffman, and Leslie H. Hawn (2000). "'I Just Need to Draw': Responding to Literature Across Multiple Sign Systems." *The Reading Teacher 54*, 160–171.

Spiegel, M. (1995). "More Than Words: The Generative Power of Transmediation for Learning." *Canadian Journal of Education 20*, 455–475.

Trussell-Cullen, Alan (1999). "Traditional Tales: Portfolios from the Past—Time Capsules for the Future." Presentation to International Reading Association Conference, San Diego, May 2–7, 1999.

Webster, Renee (1996). "Literacy: A Never-Ending Story." *The Language Arts Journal of Michigan 12*, 40–44.

Whitin, Phyllis (1996). *Sketching Stories, Stretching Minds: Responding Visually to Literature*. Portsmouth, NH: Heinemann.

Wilhelm, Jeffrey D. (1997). *You Gotta BE the Book: Teaching Engaged and Reflective Reading with Adolescents*. New York: Teachers College Press.

Wolf, Dennie Palmer, and Dana Balick, eds. (1999). *Art Works!* Portsmouth, NH: Heinemann.

Children's Books

Allen, Pamela (1990). *Who Sank the Boat?* New York: Coward McCann.

Avi (1990). *The True Confessions of Charlotte Doyle.* New York: Orchard.

Babbitt, Natalie (1975). *Tuck Everlasting.* New York: Farrar, Straus & Giroux.

Björk, Christina (1985). *Linnea in Monet's Garden.* Illus. Lena Anderson. New York: R & S.

Browne, Anthony (1998). *Voices in the Park.* New York: DK Publishing.

Bunting, Eve (1997). *Ducky.* Illus. David Wisniewski. New York: Clarion.

Cleary, Beverly (1983). *Henry and Beezus.* Illus. Louis Darling. New York: Morrow.

Coles, Robert (1995). *The Story of Ruby Bridges.* Illus. George Ford. New York: Scholastic.

Collodi, Carlo (1914). *Pinocchio.* Philadelphia: Lippincott.

Curtis, Christopher Paul (1999). *Bud, Not Buddy.* New York: Delacorte.

—— (1995). *The Watsons Go to Birmingham—1963.* New York: Delacorte.

dePaola, Tomie (1989). *The Art Lesson.* New York: Putnam.

—— (1988). *Now One Foot, Now the Other.* New York: Putnam.

Fox, Mem (1988). *Koala Lou.* Illus. Pamela Lofts. San Diego: Voyager.

Garland, Sherry (1993). *The Lotus Seed.* Illus. Tatsuro Kiuchi. San Diego: Harcourt Brace.

Giff, Patricia Reilly (2000). *Nory Ryan's Song.* New York: Delacorte.

Glass, Andrew (1982). *Jackson Makes His Move.* New York: Frederick Warne.

Henkes, Kevin (1991). *Chrysanthemum.* New York: Greenwillow.

Jiang, Ji Li (1997). *Red Scarf Girl: A Memoir of the Cultural Revolution.* New York: HarperCollins.

Johnston, Tony (1994). *The Tale of Rabbit and Coyote.* Illus. Tomie dePaola. New York: Putnam.

Joosse, Barbara M. (1991). *Mama, Do You Love Me?* Illus. Barbara Lavallee. San Francisco: Chronicle.

Kaldhol, Marit, and Wenche Oyen (1987). *Goodbye Rune.* Trans. Michael Crosby-Jones. New York: Kane/Miller.

Kraus, Robert (1971). *Leo the Late Bloomer.* Illus. Jose Aruego. New York: Windmill.

Krull, Kathleen (1995). *Lives of the Artists: Masterpieces, Messes (and What the Neighbors Thought).* Illus. Kathryn Hewitt. San Diego: Harcourt Brace.

Lester, Helen (1988). *Tacky the Penguin.* Illus. Lynn Munsinger. Boston: Houghton Mifflin.

Levine, Gail Carson (1999). *Dave at Night.* New York: HarperCollins.

—— (1997). *Ella Enchanted.* New York: HarperCollins.

Lionni, Leo (1991). *Matthew's Dream.* New York: Knopf.

—— (1988). *Six Crows.* New York: Knopf [out of print].

—— (1963). *Swimmy.* New York: Knopf.

Lobel, Arnold (1970). *Frog and Toad Are Friends.* New York: HarperCollins.

Lowry, Lois (1993). *The Giver.* Boston: Houghton Mifflin.

—— (1989). *Number the Stars.* Boston: Houghton Mifflin.

Martin, Jacqueline Briggs (1998). *Snowflake Bentley.* Illus. Mary Azarian. Boston: Houghton Mifflin.

Martin, Rafe (1989). *Will's Mammoth.* Illus. Stephen Gammell. New York: Putnam.

McDonald, Megan. (1996). *My House Has Stars.* Illus. Peter Catalanotto. New York: Orchard.

Miller, William (1997). *Richard Wright and the Library Card.* Illus. Gregory Christie. New York: Lee & Low.

Miranda, Anne (1997). *To Market, To Market.* Illus. Janet Stevens. San Diego: Harcourt Brace.

Mochizuki, Ken (1993). *Baseball Saved Us.* Illus. Dom Lee. New York: Lee & Low.

Paterson, Katherine (1977). *Bridge to Terabithia.* New York: Crowell.

—— (1980). *Jacob Have I Loved.* New York: Crowell.

Philbrick, Rodman (1993). *Freak the Mighty.* New York: Scholastic.

Prelutsky, Jack (1976). *Nightmares—Poems to Trouble Your Sleep.* Illus. Arnold Lobel. New York: Greenwillow.

Ringgold, Faith (1991). *Tar Beach.* New York: Crown.

Rylant, Cynthia (1988). *All I See.* Illus. Peter Catalanotto. New York: Orchard.

Samton, Sheila White (1985). *The World from My Window.* New York: Crown.

Scieszka, Jon (1989). *The True Story of the 3 Little Pigs!* Illus. Lane Smith. New York: Penguin.

Sheldon, Dyan (1991). *The Whales' Song.* Illus. Gary Blythe. New York: Dial.

Spinelli, Jerry (1997). *Wringer.* New York: HarperTrophy.

Stewart, Sarah (1997). *The Gardener.* Illus. David Small. New York: Farrar, Straus & Giroux.

Taylor, Mildred D. (1976). *Roll of Thunder, Hear My Cry.* New York: Dial.

Turner, Ann (1998). *Drummer Boy: Marching to the Civil War.* Illus. Mark Hess. New York: HarperCollins.

Venezia, Michael (1988). *Rembrandt.* San Francisco: Children's Book Press.

Walsh, E. S. (1989). *Mouse Paint.* San Diego: Harcourt Brace.

Weiss, George, and Bob Thiele (1995). *What a Wonderful World.* Illus. Ashley Bryan. New York: Atheneum.

White, E. B. (1952). *Charlotte's Web.* Illus. Garth Williams. New York: Harper & Row.

Winter, Jeanette (1992). *Follow the Drinking Gourd.* New York: Knopf.

Woodson, Jacqueline (1997). *We Had a Picnic This Sunday Past.* Illus. Diane Greenseid. New York: Hyperion.

Wyeth, Sharon Dennis (1995). *Always My Dad.* Illus. Raúl Colón. New York: Knopf.

The Delights of Poetry

Poetry is a natural language for children. As babies, many of us were tucked into bed to the soothing sounds of poetry and song. As toddlers, we delighted in the Mother Goose rhymes our parents read to us. As children, we recited rhymes as we skipped rope or played Red Rover, Red Rover, and we repeated the jingles we heard on television.

The experience of hearing rhyming words and hearing the same sounds repeated over and over again was satisfying and fun. Children love poetry because it makes them feel happy or bouncy or jiggly. They like to join their voices with others as they play with repetition, rhythm, and rhyme. The zest for words, the sounds they make together, and the patterns they create follows children to school.

Although poetry can work its magic on adults and cast a spell over us too, it sometimes evokes feelings of insecurity and dread, depending on the kinds of school experiences we've had. Some of us have had arid, deadly encounters with poetry; others have no memory at all of reading poetry in school. Poetry comes alive for us only when we find poets who speak to our experience, whose work resonates in our hearts and minds. We need to fall in love with a poem in order to share our passion for poetry with students. The world of poetry is one of immense beauty, depth, and range. The intent of this chapter is to help you recapture that love of rhyme, rhythm, and repetitive sounds that you experienced in your early years and to take you on a journey into the wide, delightful, and extraordinarily beautiful world of children's poetry. My guess is that you will find it speaks to you even more clearly and joyfully as an adult!

To help you explore the genre, this chapter will discuss what poetry is and does, how it communicates feelings and ideas, what special kinds of poetry exist, and what some common themes are in children's poetry. The chapter will also explore ways of sharing poetry with students in classrooms and the resources that are available for you as teacher.

What Is Poetry?

Like anything magical, poetry is slippery and elusive and thus very hard to define. Children's poet Lilian Moore (in Cullinan, 1996) says, "Poetry should be like fireworks, packed carefully and artfully, ready to explode with unpredictable effects" (p. 47). Emily Dickinson described her test of poetry in this way: "If I read a book and it makes my whole body so cold that no fire can warm me, I know that is poetry. If I feel physically as if the top of my head were taken off, I know that is poetry. These are the only ways I know it is. Is there another way?" (in Hodgins and Silverman, 1985, p. 277).

Poetry is more than its "meaning." It is distilled language, using metaphors and images to touch the imagination, memory, and emotions. It is word sounds and rhythm. The sequence of words works through suggestion, leaving space for us to envision that which is actually suggested. Good poetry often makes the ordinary seem extraordinary and gives us glimpses of truth and beauty. We delight in it; we feel the verse. Sometimes we laugh with it, enjoying the sense of humor.

Poems can send messages about how people feel and act—the way we treat others, what we are doing to our universe. Poems tell us that we are not alone—that others experience the same feelings of fear, sadness, jealousy, and joy. As X. J. Kennedy and Barbara Kennedy (1982) point out, poems can also make us laugh, tell stories, and start us wondering. Laughter connects us to other people and helps us experience joy in the moment. Through the telling of stories, we see what others have experienced, we learn of journeys we weren't aware of, and we connect to other times and places. Poems that make us wonder propel us to learn. What makes the stars twinkle? What makes each snowflake different? Poetry can open new worlds and experiences to us.

A Pocketful of Rhymes has poems kids will love. Find it at www.hometown.aol.com/ Bvsangl/pocket.html.

Approaching Poetry

Poetry is meant to be enjoyed. Read poetry for the fun of it, for the beauty of it. Give yourself permission to savor it. Find poems that move or delight you. Throw out old expectations that poetry is a puzzle to be figured out or analyzed syllable by syllable.

Bring heaps of poetry books into your classroom. Have everyone find one poem that she or he loves and read it to the class. Poetry appreciation becomes contagious when readers share short pieces in which they delight.

Use poetry as an appetizer or a dessert. Don't feel that it has to be the main course, the center of your lesson plans. Have students find poems that go with a picture book or a chapter book. Let them read the poems and explain the connection.

Celebrate poetry—its sounds, language, and meaning. Read to the class lines that move you or make you laugh. Sit back and appreciate the power of poetry. Watch how a few words, carefully chosen with attention to sound, rhyme, rhythm, and meaning, can produce such an impact. Fit poetry in around the edges of your classroom by beginning each day by having a student read a poem he or she has selected.

Spend time with poetry, keeping in mind that nothing is expected from you but a response. Become comfortable with it, knowing that nothing is demanded from you but a reading. Don't treat poems gingerly. As Eve Merriam (1964) says, "Bite right in." Poems are not delicate structures that need to be handled with care. They are strong, sturdy creations that beg to be read and savored. They're resilient and become better with use.

Just as you read a picture book for the pure enjoyment of it, feel free to do the same with poetry. Find poems you love, poems that speak directly to your heart. Once you experience the power of poetry to evoke a response, once you stop feeling that you must get the right meaning, once you learn to relax and enjoy the subtleties of the craft without having to stop and identify them, then you can start to delight in poetry and make it a part of your classroom.

Listening to the Sounds of Poetry

Surround your students with the sounds of poetry. Read poetry to them at the beginning of the day, in the middle of the day, at the end of the day, any time at all. Have them clap to it, tap to it, snap to it, move with it, and sway with it. Encourage them to recite it, chant it, and sing it.

Let them feel the alliterative sounds wash over them; let them delight in those rhyming end sounds. Let them savor the long, slow vowel sounds of *oo, o,* and *ee.* Poetry is meant to be heard. Don't let your students miss those soft, soothing sounds; those hard, heavy sounds; those purring sounds; and those alluring sounds. Poetry is most accessible to children through their ears.

Ashley Bryan (2001), poet and artist, said that he learns what poetry means by "listening to poems being read again and again." He practices reading poems aloud until he can hear the voice. "We have to work out poetry by the way it looks on the page, but it has to be heard. Poetry is only words until you go over and over it again and hear the voice and rhythm."

When Bryan reads poetry, he pays attention to every syllable and figures out how it should be said—whether it should be drawn out or cut off. He says that by reading poetry aloud we can open up the whole range of the play of the voice and show children the power that the voice contains. When Bryan reads poetry, it hollers, squeals, and rumbles. He makes it soft and soothing, low and somber, or high and excited. The sounds coming off his tongue can be soft, hard, fast, or staccato. We can feel the poem's cadences, its beat, its rhythm. When poetry is read this way, we can hear the play and variation and magic of the voice; we can hear what the voice can do. Bryan encourages us to "Hear what language does. Open up the sound of the poem. Open up the spirit of the voice." He suggests that teachers have children read poems expressively, focusing on what the words are asking them and working on the voice they hear in the poem.

Selecting poetry children love jumpstarts this performance process. Bring in **Where the Sidewalk Ends,** by Shel Silverstein, and laugh along with the children while they hear or perform his outrageous, humorous poems on topics dear to their hearts, such as "For Sale," about a sibling selling his sister. Bring in Douglas Florian's pithy poems and hear the magic in his choice of concise words. Read Jack Prelutsky's scary tales during Halloween and shiver along with your students. Read Dr. Seuss for the strong rhythm and rhyme and for his unique words and unusual word order. Read Eloise Greenfield for the beauty and poignancy of her words.

CD-ROM

Find more works by Douglas Florian on the CD-ROM database.

Reading poetry is a joyous affair. Images wash over us, creating kaleidoscopes of color. Our senses may be tantalized by the smell of freshly cut fields, the buzz of bees, or the clang of church bells. Hearing poetry read can be lesson enough. We don't always have to analyze it or teach specific terminology through it. The simple act of reading a poem aloud celebrates words, sounds, language, and life.

Encourage students to memorize and then recite snippets of verses they love to hear. Encourage children to read poems chorally. Let children savor the playfulness of nonsense poems, limericks, and clerihews.

Keep poetry books in the room and regularly ask students to select a poem to read to the class. Make poetry a classroom affair. Show your delight in it so that children will be free to express their joy. Include on your shelves thin books of poetry, tall books of poetry, and fat books of poetry. Bring in poetry on every topic imaginable. Read poems to celebrate spring, read poems to recognize the importance of ordinary things, read poems to introduce topics, and read poems for the sheer joy of it.

Celebrating Poetry

Enjoying poetry isn't a matter of understanding but of experiencing. A poem captures an experience, a moment, a thought—and becomes that thing for us. Unfortunately, school experiences with poetry have made many people believe that they need to dissect a poem in order to understand it. Poetry will never move you or speak to you if you see it as a puzzle to be figured out. It isn't something that can be made whole by taking the pieces apart and putting them together again. Dissecting and analyzing won't make you a lover of poetry.

Poetry is best experienced in layers. Let a poem work on you in the way a piece of music works on you. Let it get inside your body and mind until it becomes the very experience itself. Children instinctively do this with poetry. From the earliest ages, they get caught up in reciting with their parents nursery rhymes like "Itsy Bitsy Spider" and "Patty Cake." Whether it's Mother Goose or Dr. Seuss or sing-song poems recited on the playground or street to the beat of the jump rope, children respond to poetry—word pictures, word music, repeating beats, comparisons, and fresh language. Very young children respond to rhymes without conscious effort; they do not need to make sense of them. They live the rhymes with their whole bodies, their hands, their faces. Watch babies hold their mother's or father's hands as together they imitate the spider walking up the water spout or the baker rolling out the dough. The experience is integral to the meaning.

As with any meaningful activity, the more skilled and involved we become, the richer the experience. This doesn't mean that we should expect young readers of poetry to understand the various aspects of craftsmanship that make a poem work. But as teachers, we want to understand these characteristics so that we are better able to connect students with meaningful and beautiful poems. As you explore the genre of poetry, you'll discover an abundance of poems that speak to you and will speak to your students.

The Characteristics of Poetry

Why do some poems explode inside our heads while others just create a soft humming? For most of us, it's what a poem says—the message it conveys. But equally important is how its message is conveyed—how the poem stirs us or moves us. Poets use language in a particular way to create an experience of a poem. It is these qualities of poetry that make some poems sing for us and others merely hum.

Imagery

The images are the word pictures that a poet paints to make the details concrete and help a reader see, hear, smell, and touch the experience of the poem. Effie Lee Newsome, in "Violets," lets us "see" the flowers:

> The sunflowers wear great gold farm hats,
> The poppies red silk hoods.
> But violets wear their bowed heads bare
> On highways or in woods.

(Copyright © 1999 by Rudine Sims Bishop from *Wonders: The Best Children's Poems of Effie Lee Newsome*, compiled by Rudine Sims Bishop. Published by Boyd Mills Press, Inc. Reprinted by permission.)

Rhyme

Poets repeat sounds at the end of lines to create a particular rhythm or sound. This sound is pleasing because it gives us a sense of anticipation, a sense of order, and a sense of closure. It satisfies our notion of rightness. Most rhymes are in couplets, like William Blake's "Tyger Tyger, burning bright/In the forests of the night." But there are variations of rhyme schemes that often make the lines seem to talk back to each other. Sometimes the second and fourth lines rhyme; sometimes only the last lines in a stanza rhyme. In addition to end rhyme, there is internal rhyme, in which words within the line rhyme.

CD-ROM

Locate authors and poets who use rhyme in their work by searching for *rhyme* under Favorite Authors.

Rhythm

Even poems that don't use rhyme have rhythms that intensify the reader's experience of the poem, either making it pleasing to the ear or enhancing its meaning. Rhythm and beat allow us to feel life forces coursing through us, get caught up in the beat of the poem, and feel the poem, not just hear it. One nonrhyming poem that is very rhythmic is Christopher Myers's **Black Cat.** Although one rhyming verse is repeated several times throughout the book, Myers seems to achieve the rhythmic quality mainly by beginning the majority of lines with present participles—words ending in *-ing*. This gives the poem the feel of continuous motion, as we hear the black cat sauntering, sipping, dancing, ducking, listening, chasing, and tiptoeing. Nothing is capitalized, nor is any punctuation used except in the repeated verse. This enhances the sense of continuous motion, as we fall into the black cat's rhythms.

Sound Devices

Onomatopoeia (using words that sound like the objects they refer to), alliteration (repeating the same initial sounds), consonance (repeating the same consonant sounds within or at the end of words), and assonance (repeating of the same internal vowel sounds) are all devices poets use so that we can hear how a word's softness or hardness or longness or shortness relates to its meaning. This section of **Listen to the Rain,** by Bill Martin, Jr., and John Archambault, is packed with sound devices:

> Listen to the rain,
> the singing of the rain,
> the tiptoe pitter-patter,
> the splish and splash and splatter.
> Listen to the rain,
> the roaring pouring rain,
> the hurley-burley
> topsy-turvy
> lashing gnashing teeth of the rain,
> the lightning-flashing
> thunder-crashing
> sounding pounding roaring rain,
> leaving all outdoors a muddle,
> a mishy mushy muddy puddle.

(LISTEN TO THE RAIN by Bill Martin Jr. and John Archambault, © 1988 by Bill Martin Jr. and John Archambault. Reprinted by permission of Henry Holt and Company, LLC.)

The devices used include onomatopoeia ("the tiptoe pitter-patter"); alliteration ("the splish and splash and splatter"); consonance ("soun**d**ing poun**d**ing roaring rain"), where the hard *d* sounds emphasize the hardness of the rain; and assonance ("Listen to the rain,/the r**oar**ing p**our**ing rain"), where the emphasis on the long *oar* sound emphasizes the drawn-out nature of the downpour.

Sensory Details

Poets use details of the senses to help a reader see, hear, smell, touch, and even taste. In ***Listen to the Rain,*** when Bill Martin, Jr., and John Archambault say, "leaving all outdoors a muddle,/a mishy mushy muddy puddle," we can almost feel that mud squishing through our toes.

Figurative Language

Poets use similes, metaphors, personification, and other nonliteral descriptions to "provide clarification and intensity of thought," according to Mary Oliver (1998) in *Rules for the Dance: A Handbook for Writing and Reading Metrical Verse* (p. 67). Figurative language, which is at the heart of many poems, is present in the form of personification, simile, and metaphor in this Maya Angelou poem:

> ### I Love the Look of Words
>
> Popcorn leaps, popping from the floor
> of a hot black skillet
> and into mouth.
> Black words leap,
> snapping from the white
> page. Rushing into my eyes. Sliding
> into my brain which gobbles them
> the way my tongue and teeth
> chomp the buttered popcorn.
>
> When I have stopped reading,
> ideas from the words stay stuck
> in my mind, like the sweet
> smell of butter perfuming my
> fingers long after the popcorn
> is finished.
>
> I love the book and the look of words
> the weight of ideas that popped into my mind
> I love the tracks
> of new thinking in my mind.

("I Love the Look of Words" by Maya Angelou, copyright ©1993 by Maya Angelou, from SOUL LOOKS BACK IN WONDER by Tom Feelings. Used by permission of Dial Books for Young Readers, an imprint of Penguin Putnam Books for Young Readers, a division of Penguin Putnam Inc.)

Line Breaks and White Space

Another way poets make meaning is through the use of empty space and printed lines. By directing us where to pause and where to rush on, poets use line breaks to emphasize meaning. In Maya Angelou's poem, the way she separates adjectives from their noun and nouns from their prepositional phrase tells us what to pay attention to or give weight to. For instance, when she ends the line with "white," she makes us pause and wonder what will come after it. In the last stanza, when she ends the line with "tracks," the pause before "of new thinking in my mind" makes us experience the impact of reading on her.

Repetition

Poets often use the same phrases or words over and over again for emphasis and rhythmic pleasure. David McCord's "Five Chants, III" reads:

> The pickety fence
> The pickety fence

Give it a lick it's
The pickety fence
Give it a lick it's
A clickety fence
Give it a lick
It's a lickety fence
Give it a lick
Give it a lick
With a rickety stick
Pickety
Pickety
Pickety
Pick

(From ONE AT A TIME by David McCord. Copyright © 1952 by David McCord. By permission of Little, Brown and Company (Inc.).)

Compact Language

Poets distill language so that we get the essence of an experience. Sometimes the words bump into each other to create an impression. Douglas Florian is a master at distilling language. Although the poem "The Beaver" is but four words long, every word is packed with imagery and meaning:

Wood-chopper
Tree-dropper
Tail-flopper
Stream-stopper.

(Reprinted with permission of Harcourt, Inc. from *Mammalabilia: Poems and Paintings,* by Douglas Florian. Copyright © 2000 Douglas Florian.)

The Many Types of Poetry

Poetry comes in many shapes and sizes. The types most often used with children are narrative poems, lyric poems, poems with special forms (including limericks, haiku, cinquains, and clerihews), free verse, concrete poetry, and nursery rhymes.

Narrative Poems

Narrative poems tell a story. Gary Soto often writes poetry in a narrative form, as he does in "Sarape" from **Canto Familiar.** It begins

It's itchy
Against my skin,
This sarape
In the backseat
Of our Chevy,
Faded Aztec rainbow
That was a hand-me-down
From a friend
Of a friend
That Papi no longer remembers.

(Reprinted with permission of Harcourt, Inc. from *Canto Familiar,* by Gary Soto. Copyright © 1995 Gary Soto.)

Diane Siebert's lovely picture book–length poem **Sierra,** the story of the mountain ranges, is told from the point of view of the mountain. It describes how the mountain was formed millions of years ago, what activities it views, and its worries about its future.

PoetryTeachers.com is packed with information on poems, poetry writing, and poetry teaching. Find it at www.poetryteachers.com.

Lyric Poems

Lyric poems evoke an emotion or mood. Thoughts and feelings are expressed in direct and intense ways. The majority of lyric poems, like Sara Holbrook's "Alone," express a single mood:

> Alone
> Doesn't have to be sad
> like a lost-in-the-city dog.
>
> Alone
> doesn't have to be scary
> like a vampire swirled in fog.
>
> Alone
> Can be slices of quiet,
> salami in between
> a month of pushy hallways
> and nights too tired to dream.
>
> Alone
> doesn't have to be
> a scrimmage game with grief.
> Alone
> doesn't have to argue,
> make excuses or compete.
> Like having nothing due,
> sometimes.
> Alone
> is a relief.

(Text copyright © 1996 by Sara Holbrook from *I Never Said I Wasn't Difficult* by Sara Holbrook. Published by Boyds Mills Press, Inc. Reprinted by permission.)

Poems with Specific Forms

Poems with a specific number of lines and syllables per line include limericks, haiku, cinquains, and clerihews. A limerick is five lines long and has the rhyme scheme AABBA; this means that the first, second, and fifth lines rhyme and the third and fourth lines rhyme. Usually the first, second, and fifth lines are longer, with about eight or nine syllables, while the third and fourth lines have about six syllables. X. J. Kennedy's **Uncle Switch: Loony Limericks** is filled with examples such as this one:

> When a thirsty mosquito in flight
> Whistles down in the dead of the night
> To our uncle's sleep couch,
> The poor insect cries, "Ouch!"
> And starts scratching an Uncle Switch bite.

(Copyright © 1997 by X. J. Kennedy. Limerick appears in *UNCLE SWITCH* by X. J. Kennedy, published by Margaret K. McElderry Books, an imprint of Simon & Schuster Children's Publishing. Reprinted by permission of Curtis Brown, Ltd.)

A haiku has five syllables in the first and last line and seven syllables in the middle line and usually is about nature. The last line generally captures the essence of the subject or offers a surprise. "Washing the Dog: A Haiku," by Jane Yolen, is an example:

> The dog was filthy
> Still she shook off our soapsuds:
> Bubbles in the grass.

(Text copyright © 1995 by Jane Yolen from *Water Music* by Jane Yolen. Published by Wordsong/Boyds Mills Press, Inc. Reprinted by permission.)

The cinquain, a popular form for children to write, is composed of five lines, none of which have to rhyme. The syllable count is two for the first line, four for the second line,

CD-ROM

To learn what other genres Jane Yolen writes in, do a word search for her name on the CD-ROM.

six for the third line, and eight for the fourth line, ending with two for the last line. In **One at a Time,** David McCord shares this cinquain:

> Pen, ink,
> table, paper,
> an idea, a first line,
> more lines, changes, great long pauses,
> A poem.

(From ONE AT A TIME by David McCord. Copyright © 1952 by David McCord. By permission of Little, Brown and Company (Inc.).)

The clerihew is a four-line poem that offers a fact in the first two lines and shares a reaction in the second two. The first and second lines rhyme with each other, as do the third and fourth. This one by David McCord comes from the same collection as the cinquain:

> Samson, you might say
> Had long hair for his day.
> What horrid thoughts we harbor
> For the first lady barber!

(From ONE AT A TIME by David McCord. Copyright © 1952 by David McCord. By permission of Little, Brown and Company (Inc.).)

Free Verse

Free verse is poetry that is arranged on the page in the shape of a poem but is written without stanzas or rhyme. The poem often has other characteristics of poetry, such as figurative language, sound devices, and repetition. **Home Place,** a picture storybook by Crescent Dragonwagon, is written in free verse. It begins:

> But still they come up, these daffodils
> in a row; a yellow splash
> brighter than sunlight, or lamplight, or butter,
> in the green shadow of the woods.
> Still they come up, these daffodils,
> cups lifted to trumpet
> the good news
> of spring . . .

(Reprinted with the permission of Simon & Schuster Books for Young Readers, an imprint of Simon & Schuster Children's Publishing Division from HOME PLACE by Crescent Dragonwagon. Text copyright © 1990 Crescent Dragonwagon.)

Concrete Poetry

Concrete poetry takes the shape of the object being described. J. Patrick Lewis's **Doodle Dandies: Poems That Take Shape** is filled with concrete poetry. "Dachshund" looks like this:

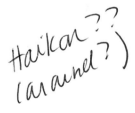

(Reprinted with the permission of Atheneum Books for Young Readers, an imprint of Simon & Schuster Children's Publishing Division from DOODLE DANDIES, by J. Patrick Lewis. Text copyright © 1998 J. Patrick Lewis.)

Another remarkable collection of concrete poetry is *Flicker Flash,* by Joan Bransfield Graham. Many of Douglas Florian's poems are also written in the shape of the subject.

Nursery Rhymes

Nursery rhymes often provide a child's earliest exposure to poetry. These well-loved rhymes, part of our oral tradition, are full of sense and nonsense and can become springboards to fuller and richer experiences with poetry later in childhood. A fuller discussion of nursery rhymes takes place in Chapter 8, Traditional or Folk Literature.

Why Use Poetry in the Classroom?

In the introduction to *Side by Side: Poems to Read Together,* Lee Bennett Hopkins (1988), poet and anthologist, stresses the importance of poetry in children's lives:

> I have seen how poetry has enhanced the lives of children anywhere and everywhere, giving them familiar sounds and quiet music that only children continue to hear. Poetry comes naturally to those discovering the magic of language. Pictures develop inside young minds, stretching imaginations, evoking fresh visions, generating smiles, reflections, and satisfaction. I have said it many times. I shall say it over and over again: Poetry should flow freely in the lives of children; it should come to them as naturally as breathing; for nothing—*no thing*—can ring and rage through hearts and minds as does this body of literature. (unpaged)

Echoing Hopkins's view, Northrup Frye, literary theorist, believes that experiencing the rhythms of verse, which reflect the child's own bodily rhythms, in a sense teaches the child the basics of using language. He considers it significant that the first selections "read" by a child—long before he or she goes to school—are likely to be the jingles of television commercials. He wonders why, in elementary school, we don't capitalize on this and use these familiar jingles as early reading material. When we are steeped in rhythmic language like that of nursery rhymes and advertising jingles, language reflecting our bodily rhythms, he believes that we are more likely "to develop a speaking and prose style that comes out of the depths of personality and is a genuine expression of it" (in Sloan, 1998, p. 72).

Although poetry doesn't need a utilitarian value to be valuable in the classroom, understanding what poetry can do and how it can be used may give you the incentive to use it with children. Children find joy in playing with sounds and language, which stimulates their interest in reading. Kathy Perfect (1999), a classroom teacher, claims that poetry is a genre especially suited for struggling or unmotivated readers. She explains,

> Rhyme in the form of playground games, music, and other cultural play makes the link between oracy and literacy a natural one. . . . The playfulness or poignancy of words, the ability of language to hold us almost captive in its intensity, beauty, or genius, is particularly apparent in poetry. . . . Poetry's frequent repetition, rhyme, and predictable language make children eager participants in oral and choral readings. (pp. 728–730)

She believes that these joyful experiences with the spoken word can make students enthusiastic about reading not just more poetry, but other genres as well. Many books tap into this playfulness with language, including *What in the World?,* by Eve Merriam; *Surprises,* an *I-Can-Read* book with poems selected by Lee Bennett Hopkins; Douglas Florian's *Laugh-eteria: Poems and Drawings* and *Bing Bang Boing: Poems and Drawings;* and Mary Ann Hoberman's *The Llama Who Had No Pajama.*

Poetry can be used to enhance topics being talked about in class. Such poetry can convey information and integrate facts while delighting the senses and evoking emotion. If children are studying insects in science, what better way to provoke talk and interest than by bringing in Douglas Florian's *Insectlopedia: Poems and Paintings?* His humorous, pithy

For more ways to involve children in poetry, go to *The Academy of American Poets: Teaching Tips* at *www.poets.org/npm/teachtip. cfm.*

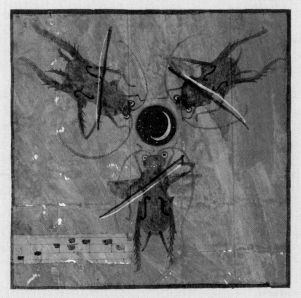

INSECTLOPEDIA

POEMS AND PAINTINGS BY

DOUGLAS FLORIAN

Reading these delightful poems about insects could inspire children to want to learn more about them. (Jacket illustration from INSECTLOPEDIA. Jacket illustrations copyright © 1998 by Douglas Florian, reprinted by permission of Harcourt, Inc.)

look at 21 different insects through short poems and entertaining drawings will allow children to see these insects through new eyes.

Poems can bring many voices and views into the classroom, often on the same topic. *Cats Are Cats,* compiled by Nancy Larrick, lets children hear what 43 different poets have to say about cats—how they regard them, what they notice about them, and what they think is important about them. Bringing in new voices can allow students to hear the ideas and feelings of someone who rarely has the opportunity to have her or his ideas heard. All children need a chance to both see reflections of themselves in poems and learn about others. Poetry collections that give children in parallel cultures a chance to see themselves in poems include the National Museum of the American Indian's *When the Rain Sings: Poems by Young Native Americans; The Rainbow Hand: Poems About Mothers and Children,* by Janet S. Wong; *Brown Honey in Broomwheat Tea,* by Joyce Carol Thomas; *My Man Blue,* by Nikki Grimes; and *Confetti: Poems for Children,* by Pat Mora.

Poetry can whet students' appetites for learning more about the subjects of the poems. Reading *All by Herself,* biographical poems about 14 girls who made a difference, by Ann Whitford Paul, may interest students in learning more about the lives of these girls or other women who made a difference. Sharing Jane Yolen's poems in *Sacred Places,* about sites around the world that are considered sacred by various cultures, may stimulate students to learn more about the history of these sites.

Poetry can also be used as a model for writing. As a prelude, children must read and hear excellent poems in many formats, such as those reprinted in this chapter. Children love using the format and phrasing of an existing poem to create a new poem on a different topic. The boxed feature Encouraging Students to Write Poetry gives specific ideas for involving children in writing poetry, using a poem as a model (see page 152).

Encouraging Students to Write Poetry

Poetry is an ideal genre for student writing. Because the format is short and the language imaginative, it is a natural form of writing for children, who are at their most creative stage in thinking and using language vividly and playfully. Published poems can be used as models to spur students on and provide structure so that the activity does not seem overwhelming. As with any writing activity, students should not be required to write a poem without prewriting guidance and activities. For example, students shouldn't be expected to produce a haiku on demand, even though the format seems relatively easy to explain. Much preteaching needs to go into introducing the form. Many examples should be read and discussed. Students can find their favorites, collect them in a book, and illustrate them. By working with the form so intimately, they will begin to understand it. The teacher can then share a haiku she or he has written. Only then should students be encouraged to write their own, using the principles of haiku writing—three lines with syllable counts of 5, 7, 5; a theme of nature; and an unexpected surprise in the last line.

"This Is Just to Say," by William Carlos Williams (in *The Collected Poems of William Carlos Williams: Volume I, 1909–1939,* edited by A. Walton Litz and Christopher McGowen), can be used as a model for older students, who can be asked to write a poem apologizing for something they really aren't sorry for having done. List poems provide a wonderful structure for students. Using the prompt "I remember . . . ," they can write a list poem capturing childhood memories, with each line a different memory. Other triggers for creating poems work equally well. In response to an exhibit of Romantic paintings in an art museum, fifth- and sixth-graders were encouraged to write "invitation poems." Sensory details in each of the paintings were discussed, and then the teacher shared a poem she had written in response to a landscape photograph she had blown up. Students then chose one painting and wrote "An Invitation," in which they invited the viewer into the painting to explore its sensory images.

To encourage students to write about color, bring in Mary O'Neill's *Hailstone and Halibut Bones* or *Out of the Blue: Poems about Color,* by Hiawyn Oram, so that they can see how others approach the topic. Then challenge children to choose a color and create their own poems.

These are just a few of the many poetry-writing activities that students can do. Any of the books listed in this chapter will offer useful models for you and your students. Support young poets in their work by surrounding them with good poetry and celebrating their efforts at language play.

The following books are especially helpful for elementary teachers who want to encourage students to write poetry:

Heard, Georgia (1999). *Awakening the Heart: Exploring Poetry in Elementary and Middle School.* Portsmouth, NH: Heinemann.

—— (1989). *For the Good of the Earth and the Sun.* Portsmouth, NH: Heinemann.

Kennedy, X. J., and Dorothy Kennedy (1989). *Knock at a Star: A Child's Introduction to Poetry.* Boston: Little, Brown.

Koch, Kenneth (1973). *Rose, Where Did You Get That Red?* New York: Random.

—— (1970). *Wishes, Lies and Dreams; Teaching Children to Write Poetry.* New York: Chelsea.

Koch, Kenneth, and Kate Farrell (1985). *Talking to the Sun: An Illustrated Anthology of Poems for Young People.* New York: Metropolitan Museum of Art and Holt.

Ziegler, Alan (1984). *The Writing Workshop,* Vol. 1 and Vol. 2. New York: Teachers and Writers Collaborative.

How Children Connect to Poetry

Using poetry with children not only can have a positive impact on curricular interest and achievement but also can enrich children's lives. Nikki Grimes (2000), children's author and poet, believes that poetry has an impact on children partly because it's "portable. A poem can be memorized or sung, or, as it were, carried in the back pocket of the mind" (p. 33). Knowing poetry gives children the power to speak and memorize the words of others. It gives them control over written words, which become theirs, not just marks on a page. Saying or reading aloud a poem allows it to enter their minds, hearts, and bodies. As they say the poem, they feel it, and move with its rhythm and beat. One little girl whom Grimes met in a school explained that she liked "Sweet Blackberry," from Grimes's *Meet Danitra Brown,* because "whenever I read it, it makes me feel beautiful" (p. 33). Poetry can have this effect on children, making them feel beautiful and acceptable and special or, if they are not represented, left out. If poetry has a visible presence in the classroom, children

Floyd Cooper's glowing paintings lovingly complement Thomas's beautiful poems about a young girl's family, self, and heritage.

(Cover art from *Brown Honey in Broomwheat Tea* by Joyce Carol Thomas. Cover art by Floyd Cooper. Used by permission of HarperCollins Publishers.)

can adopt poems that are special to them. We need in our classrooms poems that can help children celebrate themselves and their strengths, poems that speak to who our children are. Today the marketplace offers a vast collection of poetry books that can make every child feel beautiful and special.

Poetry also speaks in the language of young children. As Barbara Harrison and Gregory Maguire (1987), noted children's literature experts, remind us, "Young children are in the most poetic time of their lives, stretching and inventing words and creating curious and intriguing metaphors and rhymes" (p. 391). Norma Farber (in Harrison and Maguire, 1987) enlarges on this notion, while warning that we must help children keep their natural poetic ability:

> Children tell us small poems long before they command the technique and habit of prose. . . . Songs and game-poems and Mother Goose are early childhood's daily fare of natural food. A cleavage may develop between useful, real speech and the language of vivid images, of intense emotion. Alienation may follow. They discard the old plaything, that musical toy—poetry. Let us intervene. Let us keep that birthright vital in the mind and memory and in the mouth and ear of our children. Let us take up armfuls of poems signaling the years from the Queen of Hearts to King Lear. Let us speak poems aloud at home, in the school, in the library, in the open, wherever they may resound. Let us ourselves memorize them, or at least their memorable lines, so that readily and ear to ear we may share them with young listeners, swiftly, urgently, on any pretext, at the drop of a reminder. (pp. 393–394)

Encourage students to browse through poetry books and share their favorites in small groups or as a class. Ashley Bryan (1996) reinforces the importance of reciting poetry: "Poetry is an oral art. Hearing a poem is as necessary to the art of poetry as hearing a song is necessary to the art of song. To know song only from sight-singing music is as limited an experience as knowing poetry only from sight-reading the words" (p. 222). Children respond to the oral and love to be part of orchestrated choral readings of poems. Because they can feel and hear the poetry, they make a connection to it. Some of my favorite classroom memories are of children reciting together David McCord's "The Pickety Fence" from **One at a Time** and chanting "What Night Would It Be?" from **You Read to Me, I'll Read to You,** by John Ciardi. They were totally immersed in the experience, moving their bodies to the beat of the words and expressing the exuberance and joy they felt from making music together.

Once children have become captivated by poetry, they are ready to try more sophisticated poetry and will willingly work to make it their own. In the hands of a skillful or enthusiastic teacher, sophisticated poetry is not beyond the reach or appreciation of even young students. Moving students to another level in the kinds of poetry used in the classroom calls for teacher modeling. Taking advantage of Vygotsky's zone of proximal development, teachers can aid children in moving beyond what they can do on their own to what they can accomplish with the help of others.

Give poetry a prominent place in your classroom, letting children hear it frequently. Slip it into the small spaces of the day, and let it work its magic on your students. Children share some of their thoughts on poetry in the boxed feature Children's Voices.

Children's Voices

Children like poetry because . . .

It's funny. —Drew, 2nd grade

It rhymes, is funny and crazy. —Janae, 6th grade

It sounds musical to my ears. —Trent, 6th grade

It comes from the heart. —Brentin, 6th grade

It's sweet and loving when I hear it. —Aloushia, 6th grade

I can make a rap out of it. —Angel, 6th grade

It is very deep. —Jasmin, 6th grade

The rhyme is fun. —Kent, 7th grade

A lot of thought is put into it. I like poems that relate to emotion and feelings.
—Chris, 7th grade

It's just thought. It doesn't have to have a plot or a main character. It's just itself.
—Camille, 7th grade

Poetry is soft and soothing to listen to. —Molly, 7th grade

It tells a story in a couple paragraphs or less. —Brittany, 7th grade

I like how they put feelings and emotions in a different point of view and make you see something so significant that it has a totally new meaning. —Maria, 7th grade

Funny, zany poems that make me laugh. —Jenny, 7th grade

Poems appeal to me when they point out certain things about something.
—Samantha, 8th grade

How Poetry for Children Reflects a Changing World

Poetry, like other genres, reflects the changing sociocultural landscape of society, as well as its changing views of childhood. Contemporary poetry for children reveals trends in what is considered important to share with children, as well as what subject matter is considered appropriate for them to explore.

1. Poetry is directed more toward children's experience. Many poems have as their topic school, siblings, feelings, childhood experiences, pets, or friends. The world isn't presented to children so that they can see what it is like; it is shown from the child's point of view. This trend is easier to see if you compare a book of poetry written today to poetry written before 1950, such as the well-loved *A Child's Garden of Verse,* by Robert Louis Stevenson.

2. Poetry is written by a broader array of people, including children. More ethnically diverse poets are being published today, although the number still does not reflect the demographics of this country. Poems written in two languages are also being published; these collections are mentioned in Chapter 7. Children's voices are appearing more frequently, often in collections dealing with the hard social issues that are part of their lives.

CD-ROM

To find poets from diverse backgrounds, go to Favorite Authors and key in *poem.*

Collections of children's poetry include *Salting the Ocean: 100 Poems by Young Poets,* selected by Naomi Shihab Nye; *Quiet Storm: Voices of Young Black Poets,* selected by Lydia Omolola Okutoro; the National Museum of the American Indian's *When the Rain Sings: Poems by Young Native Americans; The Palm of My Heart: Poetry by African American Children,* edited by Davida Adedjouma; *I Heard a Scream in the Street: Poetry by Young People in the City,* selected by Nancy Larrick; and *Reach for the Moon,* by Samantha Abeel, a student who is dyslexic. Publication of children's poetry indicates the importance of looking at how children perceive their world: Their voices help us learn.

3. Poetry deals with more social concerns, such as abuse, environmental issues, poverty, urban issues, violence, and racism. The troubling aspects of society are shared with children, not hidden from them. For example, Eve Merriam's *The Inner City Mother Goose* includes poems on war, the ghetto, and hate. The publishing of these poems reflects the belief that it is better to bring issues out in the open, instead of keeping them in the shadows and pretending they don't exist. Children fear the unknown and the ignored more than they fear harsh truths that are dealt with openly.

4. Poetic forms have loosened and broadened. No longer are most poems written in stanzas with tight rhyme schemes. Poems are likely to be arranged on the page in a pattern that captures the essence of the content of the poem, such as Arnold Adoff's *Love Letters.* With *Joyful Noise: Poems for Two Voices, I Am Phoenix: Poems for Two Voices,* and *Big Talk: Poems for Four Voices,* Paul Fleischman has popularized poems written in more than one voice. Another collection written for two voices is *Farmer's Garden: Rhymes for Two Voices,* by David Harrison. These collections demand an oral reading in order to experience the full impact of the poems. Poems written in free verse, in the shape of the subject, and as lists are appearing with more regularity.

5. Collections of poetry about people's lives are being published regularly. Biographical poems help us view a person's life in a fresh way or let us see the high points of a person's

The colorful cover with talking children signals readers that the poems will be lively and light. (Cover art from BIG TALK: POEMS FOR FOUR VOICES. Text copyright © 2000 Paul Fleischman; illustrations copyright © 2000 Beppe Giacobbe. Reproduced by permission of the publisher Candlewick Press, Inc., Cambridge, MA.)

Skillful poets bring the lives of famous Americans to life in just a few short stanzas.

(Cover art from *Lives: Poems About Famous Americans* edited by Lee Bennett Hopkins, illustrated by Leslie Staub. Used by permission of HarperCollins Publishers.)

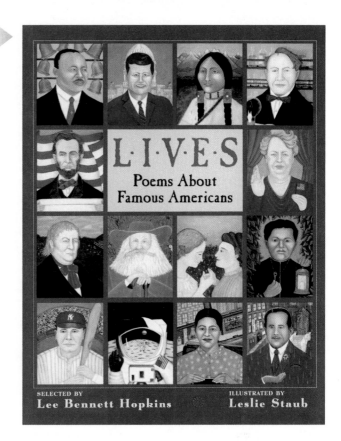

life. Biographical poems are no longer written only about people viewed as great heroes. Today's collections include lesser-known people whose lives are celebrated through poetry. This trend reflects the opening up of society and inclusion of more people.

Latino Rainbow: Poems About Latino Americans, by Carlos Cumpian, includes poems about singer Linda Ronstadt, physicist Luis Alvarez, farm worker organizer Cesar Chavez, baseball hall-of-famer Roberto Clemente, folksinger Joan Baez, and Ellen Ochoa, the first Latina astronaut. *Believers in America: Poems about Americans of Asian and Pacific Islander Descent,* by Steven Izuki, features Kristi Yamaguchi, U.S. Olympic ice skater, and Daniel Inouye, U.S. senator. *Lives: Poems About Famous Americans,* selected by Lee Bennett Hopkins, includes poems about Eleanor Roosevelt, Walt Whitman, Babe Ruth, Rosa Parks, and John F. Kennedy. *Freedom Like Sunlight: Praisesongs for Black Americans,* by J. Patrick Lewis, includes poems on Wilma Rudolph and Louis "Satchmo" Armstrong. *All by Herself,* by Ann Whitford Paul, is another excellent biographical collection.

6. Artwork is being meshed with the poetry, giving many poetry books the appearance of a picture book. Pictures are now more than ever what draws children to books and makes books attractive to them. Brilliantly hued covers of poetry books shout, "Read me, read me." Good examples of enticing artwork are the dazzling photographs by Lisa Desimini in both *Touch the Poem,* by Arnold Adoff, and *Doodle Dandies: Poems That Take Shape,* by J. Patrick Lewis, and the delightful illustrations by Maya Christina Gonzalez in *Laughing Tomatoes and Other Spring Poems* and *From the Bellybutton of the Moon and Other Summer Poems,* both written by Francisco X. Alarcon. In many poetry books, the illustrations pick up the mood and tone of the poems so that children can see at a glance what kind of poetry is included. An example is *Night Garden: Poems from the World of Dreams,* written by Janet S. Wong and illustrated by Julie Paschkis, in which the paintings reflect the glowing colors that can fill our everyday dreams. The illustrations signal that this book is not about scary dreams or nightmares, but about ordinary dreams.

What Kinds of Poetry Books Can You Expect to Find?

Poetry is packaged in many forms. Poetry anthologies, filled with many poems by a variety of people, abound. But other kinds of poetry books exist too. Sometimes a picture book contains only one illustrated poem. Sometimes a poem or series of poems in a book tells a single story. Sometimes a book of poetry is organized around a single theme or poet.

A Single Illustrated Poem

Picture books that contain only one poem make excellent read-alouds and easily involve children. *City Dog,* written and illustrated by Karla Kuskin, lets readers share in the adventures of a city dog who enjoys the excitement of discovering the countryside. As always,

Colorful photos throughout Arnold Adoff's collection add to the exuberance of the poems.
(Cover art from TOUCH THE POEM illustrated by Lisa Desimini. Cover art copyright © 2000 by Lisa Desimini. Reprinted by permission of Scholastic Inc.)

Kuskin's verse is evocative, crisp, and fun. **Sun Song,** by Jean Marzollo, is told in rhyming quatrains, each addressed to the sun as it follows its path on a summer day. The glorious illustrations by Laura Regan will make this book a favorite with young readers or listeners. Other books with single poems include **Listen to the Rain,** by Bill Martin, Jr., and John Archambault, and Christopher Myers's **Black Cat.**

Stopping by Woods on a Snowy Evening, written by Robert Frost and illustrated by Susan Jeffers, is a picture-book version of the famous poem. The exquisite details and sweeping backgrounds of frosty New England scenes contribute to the beauty of this evocative poem. Another picture-book version of a poem is e.e. cummings's **hist whist,** illustrated by Deborah Kogan Ray. The vibrant illustrations of this richly onomatopoeic poem bring to life the sights and sounds of the haunting Halloween night.

A Poem or Series of Poems Telling a Story

Poems may tell a story through rhymed verse or free verse. **Prowlpuss,** by Gina Wilson, is the rhymed story of a tough-looking cat and his nighttime prowlings. **Home Place,** by Crescent Dragonwagon, is a poem written in free verse about a family on a hike who finds an abandoned house and imagines what the family who lived there was like. The intricate delicacy of the watercolors by Jerry Pinkney works with the words to encircle us with color and beauty. **Meet Danitra Brown,** by Nikki Grimes, a series of poems about Danitra, lets us know about the activities and thoughts of this exuberant girl.

Collections Built Around a Single Theme or Poet

The fact that many poetry books have been built around a common theme or single poet makes selection easier for the teacher. If you want poetry to complement and enrich

Kristine O'Connell George's website is filled with her poetry and other delights. Go to www.kristinegeorge.com/.

The rough-looking cat on the cover sets the stage for this story poem about a cat's nighttime wanderings.

(PROWLPUSS. Text copyright © 1994 Gina Wilson; illustrations copyright © 1994 David Parkins. By permission of the publisher Candlewick Press, Cambridge, MA, on behalf of Walker Books Ltd., London.)

classwork on families, you could use *Families: Poems Celebrating the African American Experience,* selected by Dorothy S. Strickland and Michael R. Strickland, or *Relatively Speaking: Poems about Family,* by Ralph Fletcher. Collections built around the theme of music include *Call Down the Moon: Poems of Music,* selected by Myra Cohn Livingston, and *My Own Song and Other Poems to Groove To* and *Poems That Sing to You,* both collections selected by Michael R. Strickland. Two noteworthy collections built around a specific animal are *Mice Are Nice,* compiled by Nancy Larrick, and *Little Dog Poems,* by Kristine O'Connell George. Lee Bennett Hopkins's *Yummy! Eating Through a Day* contains poems all about food. There are collections built around sports, nature, holidays, and many other subjects.

Some collections use poetry to bring to light a little-known topic. Many new poetry books combine poetry with basic information on a given subject. Thomas Locker's *Home: A Journey Through America* acquaints us with the many landscapes of America. His luminous paintings accompany poems written about the many places we call home. In Shonto

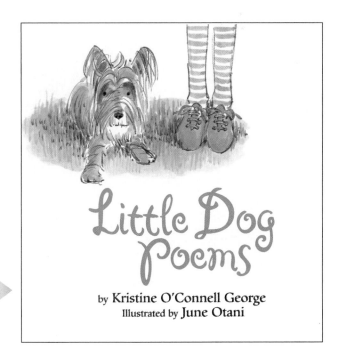

This endearing dog draws readers into George's collection of poetry all about little dogs.

(Cover, from LITTLE DOG POEMS by Kristine O'Connell George, illustrated by June Otani. Jacket illustrations copyright ©1999 by June Otani. Reprinted by permission of Houghton Mifflin Company. All rights reserved.)

Begay's **Navaho: Visions and Voices Across the Mesa,** deeply personal poems and paintings weave a magnificent portrait of Navajo life that brims with a spirit of love and hope. **Bone Poems,** by Jeff Moss, is a collection of fresh, funny, and off-beat poems inspired by the bones of dinosaurs and early mammals on display at the American Museum of Natural History.

Collections intended to introduce children to one of the "adult poets" provide a wonderful way to acquaint children with some of the best of the masters. **Don't You Turn Back: Poems by Langston Hughes,** selected by Lee Bennett Hopkins, speaks of the basic elements and emotions of life. This timeless collection is priceless. Paul Laurence Dunbar's **Jump Back, Honey: The Poems of Paul Laurence Dunbar** is filled with poems that children will love. All are illustrated by Ashley Bryan and other distinguished African American artists, who contribute to the power of this collection.

Boshblobberbosh: Runcible Poems for Edward Lear was written by J. Patrick Lewis to honor the world that Lear created with his fantastical verses, such as "The Owl and the Pussycat," and other nonsense poems, songs, and limericks. Whenever Lear was at a loss for words, he simply made up new ones. Many of these delightful poems are about the life of Lear. They make the reader want to read everything Lear has written to see how his poems match up to those of Lewis. A Newbery winner that introduces children to William Blake is Nancy Willard's **A Visit to William Blake's Inn: Poems for Innocent and Experienced Travelers.** Willard wrote these magical poems about life at an imaginary inn, run by William Blake himself.

Anthologies with Poems on Varied Topics by Various Authors

For poetry resources that can be used across the curriculum, see **ISLMC Poetry for Children** at http://falcon.jmu.edu/%7eramseyil/poechild.htm.

Given the large number of wonderful collections that exist, it is difficult to pick just one for the home or classroom. **Sing a Song of Popcorn: Every Child's Book of Poems,** selected by Beatrice Schenk de Regniers, Eva Moore, Mary Michaels White, and Jan Carr, has nine themed sections, beginning with "Fun with Rhymes." Nine Caldecott Medal artists drew the colored illustrations throughout, making this a visually stunning collection. **Talking to the Sun: An Illustrated Anthology of Poems for Young People,** selected by Kenneth Koch and Kate Farrell to surprise and please young people, includes paintings from the Metropolitan Museum of Art. Poems and art have been carefully matched to achieve maximum impact and pleasure for the reader/viewer. **A Jar of Tiny Stars: Poems by NCTE Award–Winning Poets,** edited by Bernice E. Cullinan, is packed with children's favorites by ten well-loved poets. **Words of Wisdom: A Treasury of African-American Poetry and Art,** selected by Belinda Rochelle, contains 21 poems and stunning illustrations by a range of African American poets and artists. **Salting the Ocean: 100 Poems by Young Poets,** selected by Naomi Shihab Nye, focuses on young people's views of the world, in poems written by children in grades one through twelve.

Because the world of poetry is so expansive, poems can be found on just about any topic and mood imaginable. This aspect of poetry makes it the perfect choice to accompany almost any activity in the classroom. The boxed feature Common Themes and Curricular Connections shows the range of content in poetry today. For space reasons, only a few books are mentioned in each category, but many more can be found at any library or bookstore.

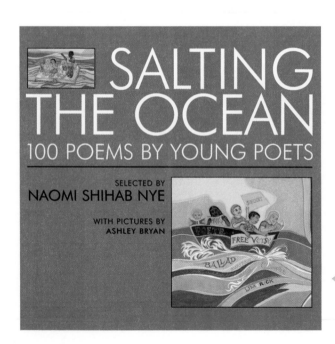

These 100 poems written by young poets shine with truth and passion.

(Cover art from *Salting the Ocean: 100 Poems by Young Poets* by Naomi Shihab Nye. Cover art by Ashley Bryan. Used by permission of HarperCollins Publishers.)

Common Themes and Curricular Connections

Friendship and family

Rolling Harvey down the Hill, by Jack Prelutsky, focuses on the friendships and antics of a funny, but real, bunch of boys. *Brown Angels: An Album of Pictures and Verse,* by Walter Dean Myers, is a charming collection of photos and poems celebrating children. *I Like You, If You Like Me: Poems of Friendship,* selected by Myra Cohn Livingston, is a collection of 90 poems that reflect a diversity of feelings and thoughts about friends and the importance of friendship. Javaka Steptoe's *In Daddy's Arms I AM TALL: African Americans Celebrating Fathers* is a lovely collection of poems about fathers, accompanied by Steptoe's stunning collages. Denizé Lauture's picture-book poem *Father and Son* is a warm portrayal of a father and son who revel in each other's company. *Isn't My Name Magical? Sister and Brother Poems,* by James Berry, features a sister and brother team who write poems about all aspects of their lives. Mary Ann Hoberman's *Fathers, Mothers, Sisters, Brothers: A Collection of Family Poems* covers all family members!

Holidays

One good way to squeeze more poetry into the classroom is to read poems written for holidays. Halloween is a popular time of year with children, and there is an abundance of poetry written about this scary holiday. *Boo! Halloween Poems and Limericks,* written by Patricia Hubbell and richly illustrated by Jeff Spackman, will be a hit with students. *Halloween Hoots and Howls,* by Joan Horton, a collection of very humorous poems, encourages students to get out their pencils and try to emulate many of the formats, such as "The Recipe for Goblin Punch." *The Headless Horseman Rides Tonight: More Poems to Trouble Your Sleep,* by Jack Prelutsky, has scary poems that students will love on mummies, zombies, and banshees. Christmas is another holiday much written about. *Celebration Song: A Poem,* by James Berry, is a book-length poem in which Mary tells one-year-old Jesus the story of his birth. Set against a Caribbean background, this poem resonates with the cadences of the West Indies. *Festivals,* by Myra Cohn Livingston, contains 14 lovely story poems about festivals around the world, from Las Posadas in Mexico to Tet Nguyen-Dan in Vietnam. This book can be used and appreciated throughout the year.

Home or place

In *My Mexico~México Mío,* Tony Johnston takes us on a sensory journey through the streets of Mexico with her poems. *Home: A Collaboration of Thirty Distinguished Authors and Illustrators of Children's Books to Aid the Homeless,* edited by Michael J. Rosen, features a variety of poems exploring home. Angela Johnson's *The Other Side: Shorter Poems,* a collection of poems about growing up in Shorter, Alabama, is written in a simple, honest, and thoughtful way. *Is Somewhere Always Far Away? Poems about Places,* by Leland B. Jacobs, offers poems about the country, the city, make-believe, and home. *Street Music: City Poems,* by Arnold Adoff, captures the energy of the city through poems about city sights and the noises and rhythms of the city.

Just for fun

This category includes poetry that is often humorous and always fun to hear and say. Shel Silverstein's ever-popular *Where the Sidewalk Ends* tops the list. Most of what Jack Prelutsky writes would fit this category, including *The Dragons Are Singing Tonight.* John Ciardi's wonderful rhymes in such books as *Someone Could Win a Polar Bear* and *You Read to Me, I'll Read to You* continue to delight children. N. M. Bodecker's nonsense poems in such books as *Let's Marry Said the Cherry* and *Hurry, Hurry Mary Dear* have charmed children for almost 30 years. Roald Dahl's *Dirty Beasts* and *Revolting Rhymes* enthrall children because of Dahl's outrageous sense of humor. The rhymes and wordplay evident in Karla Kuskin's *The Sky Is Always in the Sky* and *Dogs & Dragons, Trees & Dreams* make children want to hear more by Kuskin. Eve Merriam makes us feel her joy in the sounds of language in such books as *Higgle Wiggle: Happy Rhymes, You Be Good & I'll Be Night: Jump-on-the-Bed Poems,* and *Blackberry Ink.*

Moods and feelings

Sara Holbrook is wonderful at writing from a kid's perspective about the moods, feelings, and situations children encounter. Her books include *The Dog Ate My Homework, Am I Naturally This Crazy?, Walking on the Boundaries of Change: Poems of Transition,* and *I Never Said I Wasn't Difficult.* Judith Viorst's *If I Were in Charge of the World and Other Worries: Poems for Children and Their Parents* and Brod Bagert's *Let Me Be . . . the Boss: Poems for Kids to Perform* also speak directly to children. Nikki Grimes's *A Dime a Dozen* explores the pains and pleasures of being who you are, while she expresses the hopes, fears, joys, and sorrows of growing up in *Something on My Mind.*

Poetry for performance

Two books of particular note are *I Am Phoenix: Poems for Two Voices* and *Joyful Noise: Poems for Two Voices,* both by

(continued)

Paul Fleischman. Both books are written for two people to read aloud and so are perfect for performance. *It's Show Time: Poetry from the Page to the Stage,* by Allan Wolf, is filled with scripted poems and hints on enhancing student performance. Poems written from the point of view of children are also marvelous ones to perform. One such collection is Brod Bagert's *Let Me Be . . . The Boss: Poems for Kids to Perform.* Of course, any poems that are rhythmic or have a definite rhyme scheme work well too.

Sports

If sports-loving children need an enticement to read poetry, these books will do the trick. *Extra Innings: Baseball Poems,* selected by Lee Bennett Hopkins, is filled with energetic poems, illustrated with brilliant paintings by Scott Medlock. Arnold Adoff's *The Basket Counts* is packed with his exuberant poems about young people playing basketball. *Hoops,* by Robert Burleigh, is a picture book–length poem about playing a game of basketball. *For the Love of the Game: Michael Jordan and Me,* by Eloise Greenfield, is a lovely poem comparing Michael Jordan's love of the game of basketball to love of the game of life.

Science connections

Since both scientists and poets are close observers of nature, poetry makes a natural complement to science.

Natural world

Lee Bennett Hopkins's *Spectacular Science: A Book of Poems* contains poems about science and the questions it suggests. *Once Upon Ice: And Other Frozen Poems,* poems selected by Jane Yolen, shows students the power and beauty of ice in its many different configurations. Myra Cohn Livingston's *Sky Songs,* illustrated by Leonard Everett Fisher, is a stimulating and beautiful collection of poems that challenge our minds and enrich our visions of the universe. The poems Jane Yolen has selected for *Mother Earth, Father Sky: Poems of Our Planet* pay tribute to our fragile world. Frank Asch's *Cactus Poems* is about the desert, while his *Sawgrass Poems: A View of the Everglades* puts us in the heart of the Everglades in Florida. Kristine O'Connell George's *Old Elm Speaks: Tree Poems* engages us to view trees in original ways through poems laced with humor and imagination.

Animal world

Douglas Florian's *In the Swim: Poems and Paintings* and *On the Wing: Bird Poems and Paintings* will delight youngsters who are learning about fish or birds. *Weird Pet Poems,* compiled by Dilys Evans, and *Words with Wrinkled Knees: Animal Poems,* by Barbara Juster Esbensen, playfully involve students in new ways to think about animals. Alice Shertle's *How Now, Brown Cow?* is a collection of poems exclusively about cows. Some show us the cow's point of view, some remind us of the many aspects of a cow's life, and some simply make us laugh out loud. *The Originals: Animals That Time Forgot,* by Jane Yolen, is a book of story poems that intrigue and inform as we learn about animals that have hardly changed over centuries.

Social studies connections

Celebrating life/people/diversity

Joseph Bruchac's *The Circle of Thanks: Native American Poems and Songs of Thanksgiving* will help students understand that for American Indians, every day is a day to give thanks. *The Tree Is Older Than You Are: A Bilingual Gathering of Poems and Stories from Mexico,* edited by Naomi Shihab Nye, gives readers a taste of the everyday aspects of this culture. The poems in *All the Colors of the Race,* by Arnold Adoff, are written from the point of view of a child who has a white father and a black mother. *Bein' with You This Way,* by W. Nikola-Lisa, celebrates the diversity among people. *Canto Familiar,* by Gary Soto, focuses on the pleasures and woes that Mexican American children experience growing up.

Historical events

Ann Turner's *Grass Songs* reveals the intensity of the pioneer experience for the women who journeyed west. Many of the poems are in the voice of real women whose writings Turner read. Exposure to poems such as these gives children a more balanced view of what actually happened during the westward movement. *I Have Heard of a Land,* by Joyce Carol Thomas, is a book-length poem inspired by Thomas's family's westward journey to Oklahoma. This lovely poem is the story of black settlers surviving and thriving, a story not often told in history books. *The Ballad of the Pirate Queens,* by Jane Yolen, is based on two women who were arrested and tried in England in 1720 on charges of being pirates.

Selecting Poetry for the Classroom

As you select books of poetry to bring into the classroom, take into consideration what you know about your children and what you want to accomplish. You might want to answer the questions in the boxed feature Criteria for Evaluating Poetry.

In bringing poetry into the classroom, variety is essential. You don't want children to think that there is only one kind of poem, or only one subject written about in poetry, or

Criteria for Evaluating *Poetry*

1. **Appeal and impact.** Will the poem interest children? Can you see them becoming involved in the poetry? Do you think it will have an impact on them because of the power of the words, the topic or theme, or the presentation?

2. **Purpose.** Does the poem meet the purpose for which you want to use it? Does it infect children with a joy for language? Does it make them want to perform it? Does it enhance a topic? Will it make them want to know more?

3. **Complexity.** How understandable is the poetry? Will it be accessible to your students in terms of content, language, and structure?

4. **Uses of poetic elements.** Does the poem offer surprises? Is the language fresh or used in unusual and satisfying ways? Does the rhyme or rhythm give the poem an infectious quality? Does the figurative language provide clear ways to view the topic?

5. **Visual images.** Do the pictures complement and extend the words? Do the illustrations make the tone of the poetry collection obvious? In other words, if the poems are scary, can you tell from the illustrations? Are the illustrations ones children will want to look at more than once?

---

only one characteristic that marks all poems. So when selecting poems, keep in mind the categories in the boxed feature Ensuring Variety in the Poetry Selected for the Classroom.

It is often difficult to know where to begin to select poetry for your classroom. The boxed feature Favorite Authors and Anthologists of Children's Poetry provides a bit of information on some people you can count on to provide high-quality writing and strong appeal to children.

Ensuring Variety in the Poetry Selected for the Classroom

1. Mood and tone. Bring in funny poems, serious poems, sad poems, happy poems, poems that will soothe, and poems that will elicit hand-clapping.

2. Form. Bring in narrative poems, lyric poems, concrete poems, and poems written in specific formats. Bring in long poems and short poems.

3. Content. Bring in poetry about friendship, family, the moon, ice, animals, and counting. Use poetry with math, with science, with social studies, in conjunction with books read, and just for fun.

4. Poetic characteristics. Bring in poems with rhyme, without rhyme, with rhythm, in free verse, with strong images, with repetition, with onomatopoeia, with figurative language, and with sound devices.

5. Purpose. Bring in poetry that calls forth stories and experiences, poetry that opens students' eyes to new ways of seeing, poetry that validates what they are experiencing, poetry that creates a mood, poetry that shows them the wonder and beauty in a subject, poetry written in response to literature, and poetry that uses language in unusual ways.

6. Visual images. Bring in poetry illustrated in a variety of ways so that children can enjoy a range of images and artistic styles and media. Beautiful art can call out an even deeper response to the poetry and add to the children's delight.

7. Range of difficulty. Bring in poetry that is fun and easy to experience, as well as poetry that may at first seem just beyond the children's reach. *Talking to the Sun: An Illustrated Anthology of Poems for Young People,* edited by Kenneth Koch and Kate Farrell, is filled with every kind of poem and would be a good choice to broaden the range of sophistication in the poems read to a class. Another collection that can be used for the same purpose is Nancy Willard's *Step Lightly: Poems for the Journey.* When children read "Child on Top of a Greenhouse," by Theodore Roethke, they will fall in love with his work and want to hear more.

Arnold Adoff writes often unrhymed poems, which can be tender or outrageous or poignant, with an exuberant attitude.

Gwendolyn Brooks writes direct poems, in plain language, that speak to the heart and spirit.

John Ciardi writes whimsical, humorous poems that delight readers.

Barbara Juster Esbensen loves to play with the intricacies of language and challenge her readers to think about words and discover subtleties and shades of meaning in them. Joy of language is evident in all her poetry.

Aileen Fisher's ebullient spirit is reflected in the strong rhythm and rhyme of her poetry, which surprises us, makes us smile, and carries us away to other places.

Douglas Florian, both an artist and a poet, illustrates his books with the same wit, humor, and directness that mark his delightful poetry.

Nikki Giovanni, a nationally acclaimed poet, writes for both children and adults. Her directness, her use of the language, and the truths embedded in each poem make her work both accessible and popular.

Eloise Greenfield, a poet best known for *Honey I Love,* writes strong rhythmic verses packed with feelings.

Nikki Grimes's exuberant poems leap from the page to enfold us in her characters and her places.

Mary Ann Hoberman writes strongly rhymed, witty, informative verse that speaks to the concerns and interests of children.

Sara Holbrook writes poems about everyday feelings and situations that upper elementary and middle school students can relate to. Her bouncy rhymes, humor, and surprises keep students interested.

Lee Bennett Hopkins is both a poet and an anthologist. In his writing and selection of poems for children, he is always on the mark.

Langston Hughes, beloved poet from the Harlem Renaissance, is known for his short poems that speak directly to the human heart.

Karla Kuskin is a prolific poet who uses rhythm and rhyme to involve her readers in poems that focus on everyday experiences while giving us new ways to look at the world.

Nancy Larrick, anthologist, creates collections of poetry with proven kid appeal.

J. Patrick Lewis delights in trying his hand at many forms, such as tongue twisters, haiku, shape poems, limericks, and plays on words. He invites us to wrap our tongues around challenging sounds.

Myra Cohn Livingston, poet and anthologist, uses lovely language and strong images to create moods, draw us pictures, and help us see the world in new ways.

David McCord's work, imbued with rhythm and rhyme, continues to delight children.

Eve Merriam's joy in the sounds of language is evident in each of her delightful, exuberant poems.

Pat Mora uses fresh language and occasional Spanish words in her poetry, which often focuses on everyday happenings.

Jack Prelutsky is a master of rhymed verse. His collections, laced with humor, are favorites of children.

Alice Shertle evokes moods and plays with sounds as she surprises and delights children with topics they care about.

Shel Silverstein, known to most children for his rhyme and humor, speaks to the essence of childhood in his poems.

Gary Soto, who writes in many genres, often focuses his poetry in gentle, humorous ways on family and experiences of growing up.

Joyce Carol Thomas writes gentle poems that touch readers' hearts and spirits.

Janet Wong tells of life's common experiences in new ways in her sometimes sarcastic, sometimes funny, but always sensitive poems.

Jane Yolen's feel for language and sound permeates her poetry. Her fresh images and coined words often stun and surprise readers.

Invitations

Choose several of the following activities to complete:

1. Read several collections of poetry for children and decide which categories your favorite poems fit into. Do they make you laugh, tell stories, send messages, start you wondering, or share feelings? What other categories would you add to this list? What do you respond to in a poem? What delights you? Bring in five favorite poems from different categories to share with your group.

2. Spend an hour browsing through poetry collections for children. Select five that you think are the strongest and bring them to class to share with your group. As a group, give a Critics Award to the best poetry collection. What criteria did you use? Share the award-winning book with the class.

3. As you read poetry collections, do one or more of the following:

- Choose a poem that a character in a novel you've read would like. Share the poem with your group and explain why you think the poem speaks to the character.

- Choose a favorite poem and make a collage of words and pictures showing your reaction to it.

- Create a visual response to a poem, using a medium such as torn paper, collage, photography, or watercolor.

4. Make an anthology of your favorite poems. Write an introduction to the collection and illustrate it. Perhaps you'll want to arrange the collection thematically. Share your collections at a poetry coffee house.

5. As a group, try the following activities:

- Find a poem to act out in a small group. ***Casey at the Bat,*** by Ernest Thayer, would work well.

- Create a musical tape to accompany a reading of poems.

- After reading ***Joyful Noise: Poems for Two Voices,*** by Paul Fleischman, make your own collaborative poems.

CD-ROM

See ideas for visual responses by doing a word search for *draw* and *art.*

Classroom Teaching Ideas

1. Read poetry aloud in your classroom each day for no other reason than to enjoy it.

2. Since emotion can often ignite vivid words and images, give children an opportunity to reflect on past or present emotional moments and quickly record words and short phrases that come to mind. Offer time for them to weave these pieces together until they sound just right to the children.

3. After introducing poems in two (or three) voices, encourage students to work in pairs to create a poem in two voices. Suggest that they share a topic that they feel some passion for, although not necessarily one they agree on. Take time to record words and short phrases related to this topic and together decide when the voices will be together and when they will be separate. Allow time for students to present their poem to the class if they choose to do so.

4. Have children contribute to a class poetry book or collect and publish their own poems.

5. Since poetry is well suited for mini-lessons, use that format with a small group to work on reflecting on and revising their own poetry. Ask students to find the action words in their poems and underline them. Are there other words they might want to use instead to better convey what they intended? As with other writing, the decision is theirs.

6. Ask students to find a poem (from the library or your bookshelves) that in some way relates to a book read in science, social studies, or math.

Internet and Text Resources

1. A Pocketful of Rhymes is full of poems for kids. Find it at

www.hometown.aol.com/Bvsangl/pocket.html

2. PoetryTeachers.com is packed with information on poetry, poetry writing, and poetry teaching. Go to

www.poetryteachers.com

3. Bob's Byway: Glossary of Poetic Terms does just what its name implies. Find it at

www.poeticbyway.com/glossary.html

4. ISLMC Poetry for Children provides elementary and middle school teachers with resources that can be used across the curriculum. Find it at

http://falcon.jmu.edu/%7eramseyil/poechild.htm

5. Kristine O'Connell George's website is inviting and kid-friendly. Go to

www.kristinegeorge.com/

6. Poetry Month: The Academy of American Poets is a site where you can look up a particular poem or poet, as well as ideas on celebrating National Poetry Month. Find it at

www.poets.org/npm

7. The Academy of American Poets: Teaching Tips provides creative suggestions for making poetry a more important part of school life. Go to

www.poets.org/npm/teachtip.cfm

8. Heard, Georgia. *Awakening the Heart: Exploring Poetry in Elementary and Middle School.* Portsmouth, NH: Heinemann, 1999. Tools, examples, and stories useful for implanting poetry in the classroom and the hearts of children.

9. Hopkins, Lee Bennett. *Pass the Poetry, Please!* 3rd ed. New York: HarperCollins, 1998. Indispensable help in selecting poetry, involving children in poetry, and integrating poetry into the classroom.

10. Koch, Kenneth. *Rose, Where Did You Get That Red?* New York: Random, 1973. Wonderful ideas for introducing classic poems to children.

11. Koch, Kenneth. *Wishes, Lies, and Dreams: Teaching Children to Write Poetry.* New York: Vintage, 1971.

12. Larrick, Nancy. *Let's Do a Poem: Introducing Poetry to Children.* New York: Delacorte, 1991. A handbook full of lively ideas on how to bring children and poetry together in imaginative and interactive ways.

References

Bryan, Ashley (1996). "The Sound of the Voice in the Printed Word." In Amy A. McClure and Janice V. Kristo, eds., *Books That Invite Talk, Wonder, and Play.* Urbana, IL: NCTE.

—— (2001). Speech at the National Council of Teachers of English Spring Conference, Birmingham, Alabama, March 29–31, 2001.

Grimes, Nikki (2000). "The Power of Poetry." *Booklinks, 9,* 32–35.

Harrison, Barbara, and Gregory Maguire, eds. (1987). *Innocence & Experience: Essays and Conversations on Children's Literature.* New York: Lothrop, Lee & Shepard.

Hodgins, Francis, and Kenneth Silverman, eds. (1985). *Adventures in American Literature.* San Diego: Harcourt Brace.

Kennedy, X. J., and Barbara Kennedy (1982). *Knock at a Star: A Child's Introduction to Poetry.* Illus. Karen Ann Weinhaus. Boston: Little, Brown.

Oliver, Mary (1998). *Rules for the Dance: A Handbook for Writing and Reading Metrical Verse.* Boston: Houghton Mifflin.

Perfect, Kathy (1999). "From Rhyme and Reason: Poetry for the Heart and the Head." *The Reading Teacher 52,* 728–737.

Sloan, Glenna (1998). "Poetry and Linguistic Power." *Teaching and Learning Literature 8,* 69–79.

Children's Books

Abeel, Samantha (1994). *Reach for the Moon.* Illus. Charles R. Murphy. Duluth, MN: Pfeifer-Hamilton.

Adedjouma, Davida, ed. (1996). *The Palm of My Heart: Poetry by African American Children.* Illus. R. Gregory Christie. New York: Lee & Low.

Adoff, Arnold (1982). *All the Colors of the Race.* Illus. John Steptoe. New York: Beech Tree [out of print].

—— (2000). *The Basket Counts.* Illus. Michael Weaver. New York: Simon & Schuster.

—— (1997). *Love Letters.* Illus. Lisa Desimini. New York: Scholastic.

—— (1995). *Street Music: City Poems.* Illus. Karen Barbour. New York: HarperCollins.

—— (2000). *Touch the Poem.* Illus. Lisa Desimini. New York: Blue Sky.

Alarcon, Francisco X. (1998). *From the Bellybutton of the Moon and Other Summer Poems.* Illus. Maya Christina Gonzalez. San Francisco: Children's Book Press.

—— (1997). *Laughing Tomatoes and Other Spring Poems.* Illus. Maya Christina Gonzalez. San Francisco: Children's Book Press.

Asch, Frank (1998). *Cactus Poems.* Illus. Ted Lewin. San Diego: Harcourt Brace.

—— (1996). *Sawgrass Poems: A View of the Everglades.* Illus. Ted Lewin. San Diego: Harcourt Brace.

Bagert, Brod (1992). *Let Me Be . . . the Boss: Poems for Kids to Perform.* Illus. G. L. Smith. Honesdale, PA: Boyds Mills/ Wordsong.

Begay, Shonto (1995). *Navaho: Visions and Voices Across the Mesa.* New York: Scholastic.

Berry, James (1994). *Celebration Song: A Poem.* Illus. Louise Brierley. New York: Simon & Schuster.

—— (1999). *Isn't My Name Magical? Sister and Brother Poems.* Illus. Shelly Hehenberger. New York: Simon & Schuster.

Bishop, Rudine Sims, ed. (1999). *Wonders: The Best Children's Poems of Effie Lee Newsome.* Illus. Lois Mailou Jones. Honesdale, PA: Boyds Mills.

Bodecker, N. M. (1976). *Hurry, Hurry, Mary Dear.* Illus. Eric Blegvad. New York: Atheneum.

—— (1974). *Let's Marry Said the Cherry.* New York: Atheneum [out of print].

Bruchac, Joseph (1996). *The Circle of Thanks: Native American Poems and Songs of Thanksgiving.* Illus. Murv Jacob. Mahwah, NJ: BridgeWater.

Burleigh, Robert (1997). *Hoops.* Illus. Stephen T. Johnson. San Diego: Harcourt Brace.

Ciardi, John (1970). *Someone Could Win a Polar Bear.* Illus. Edward Gorey. New York: Lippincott.

—— (1962). *You Read to Me, I'll Read to You.* Illus. Edward Gorey. New York: HarperTrophy.

Cullinan, Bernice E., ed. (1996). *A Jar of Tiny Stars: Poems by NCTE Award–Winning Poets.* Illus. Andi MacLeod. Honesdale, PA: Boyds Mills.

cummings, e. e. (1989). *hist whist.* Illus. Deborah Kogan Ray. New York: Crown [out of print].

Cumpian, Carlos (1994). *Latino Rainbow: Poems About Latino Americans.* Illus. Richard Leonard. Chicago: Children's Press.

Dahl, Roald (1986). *Dirty Beasts.* Illus. Quentin Blake. New York: Puffin.

—— (1982). *Revolting Rhymes.* Illus. Quentin Blake. New York: Knopf.

de Regniers, Beatrice Schenk, Eva Moore, Mary Michaels White, and Jan Carr, eds. (1988). *Sing a Song of Popcorn: Every Child's Book of Poems.* Illus. Marcia Brown et al. New York: Scholastic.

Dragonwagon, Crescent (1993). *Home Place.* Illus. Jerry Pinkney. New York: Aladdin.

Dunbar, Paul Laurence (1999). *Jump Back, Honey: The Poems of Paul Laurence Dunbar.* Illus. Ashley Bryan et al. New York: Jump at the Sun/Hyperion.

Esbensen, Barbara Juster (1997). *Words with Wrinkled Knees: Animal Poems.* Honesdale, PA: Wordsong/Boyds Mills.

Evans, Dilys (1997). *Weird Pet Poems.* Illus. Jacqueline Rogers. New York: Simon & Schuster.

Feelings, Tom (1993). *Soul Looks Back in Wonder.* New York: Puffin.

Fleischman, Paul (2000). *Big Talk: Poems for Four Voices.* Illus. Beppe Giacobbe. Boston: Candlewick.

—— (1985). *I Am Phoenix: Poems for Two Voices.* Illus. Ken Nutt. New York: Harper.

—— (1988). *Joyful Noise: Poems for Two Voices.* Illus. Eric Beddows. New York: Harper.

Fletcher, Ralph (1999). *Relatively Speaking: Poems about Family.* Illus. Walter Lyon Krudup. New York: Orchard.

Florian, Douglas (1994). *Bing Bang Boing: Poems and Drawings.* San Diego: Harcourt Brace.

—— (1997). *In the Swim: Poems and Paintings.* San Diego: Harcourt Brace.

—— (1998). *Insectlopedia: Poems and Paintings.* San Diego: Harcourt Brace.

—— (1999). *Laugh-eteria: Poems and Drawings.* San Diego: Harcourt Brace.

—— (2000). *Mammalabilia: Poems and Paintings.* San Diego: Harcourt Brace.

—— (1996). *On the Wing: Bird Poems and Paintings.* San Diego: Harcourt Brace.

Frost, Robert (1978). *Stopping by Woods on a Snowy Evening.* Illus. Susan Jeffers. New York: Dutton.

George, Kristine O'Connell (1999). *Little Dog Poems.* Illus. June Otani. New York: Clarion.

—— (1998). *Old Elm Speaks: Tree Poems.* Illus. Kate Kiesler. New York: Clarion.

Graham, Joan Bransfield (1999). *Flicker Flash.* Illus. Nancy Davis. Boston: Houghton Mifflin.

Greenfield, Eloise (1997). *For the Love of the Game: Michael Jordan and Me.* Illus. Jan Spivey Gilchrist. New York: HarperCollins.

Grimes, Nikki (1998). *A Dime a Dozen.* Illus. Angelo. New York: Dial.

—— (1994). *Meet Danitra Brown.* Illus. Floyd Cooper. New York: Mulberry.

—— (1999). *My Man Blue.* Illus. Jerome Lagarrigue. New York: Dial.

—— (1978). *Something on My Mind.* Illus. Tom Feelings. New York: Dial [out of print].

Harrison, David L. (2000). *Farmer's Garden: Rhymes for Two Voices.* Illus. Arden Johnson-Petrov. Honesdale, PA: Boyds Mills.

Hoberman, MaryAnn (1991). *Fathers, Mothers, Sisters, Brothers: A Collection of Family Poems.* Illus. Marylin Hafner. Boston: Little, Brown.

—— (1998). *The Llama Who Had No Pajama: 100 Favorite Poems.* Illus. Betty Fraser. San Diego: Harcourt Brace.

—— (1994) *My Song Is Beautiful: Poems and Pictures in Many Voices.* Boston: Little, Brown.

Holbrook, Sara (1996). *Am I Naturally This Crazy?* Honesdale, PA: Boyds Mills.

—— (1996). *The Dog Ate My Homework.* Honesdale, PA: Boyds Mills.

—— (1996). *I Never Said I Wasn't Difficult.* Honesdale, PA: Boyds Mills.

—— (1998). *Walking on the Boundaries of Change: Poems of Transition.* Honesdale, PA: Boyds Mills.

Hopkins, Lee Bennett, ed. (1969). *Don't You Turn Back: Poems by Langston Hughes.* New York: Knopf [out of print].

——, ed. (1993). *Extra Innings: Baseball Poems.* Illus. Scott Medlock. San Diego: Harcourt Brace.

——, ed. (1999). *Lives: Poems About Famous Americans.* Illus. Leslie Staub. New York: HarperCollins.

——, ed. (1988). *Side by Side: Poems to Read Together.* Illus. Hilary Knight. New York: Simon & Schuster.

——, ed. (1999). *Spectacular Science: A Book of Poems.* Illus. Virginia Halstead. New York: Simon & Schuster.

——, ed. (1984). *Surprises.* New York: HarperTrophy.

——, ed. (2000). *Yummy! Eating Through a Day.* Illus. Renée Flower. New York: Simon & Schuster.

Horton, Joan (1999). *Halloween Hoots and Howls.* Illus. Joann Adinolfi. New York: Holt.

Hubbell, Patricia (1998). *Boo! Halloween Poems and Limericks.* Illus. Jeff Spackman. Tarrytown, New York: Marshall Cavendish.

Izuki, Steven (1994). *Believers in America: Poems about Americans of Asian and Pacific Islander Descent.* Illus. Bill Fukuda McCoy. Chicago: Children's Press.

Jacobs, Leland B. (1993). *Is Somewhere Always Far Away? Poems about Places.* Illus. Jeff Kaufman. New York: Holt [out of print].

Johnson, Angela (1998). *The Other Side: Shorter Poems.* New York: Orchard.

Johnston, Tony (1996). *My Mexico~México Mío.* Illus. F. John Sierra. New York: Philomel.

Kennedy, X. J. (1997). *Uncle Switch: Loony Limericks.* Illus. John O'Brien. New York: McElderry.

Koch, Kenneth, and Kate Farrell, eds. (1985). *Talking to the Sun: An Illustrated Anthology of Poems for Young People.* New York: Metropolitan Museum of Art and Holt.

Kuskin, Karla (1994). *City Dog.* New York: Clarion.

—— (1980). *Dogs & Dragons, Trees & Dreams.* New York: HarperTrophy [out of print].

—— (1998). *The Sky Is Always in the Sky.* Illus. Isabelle Dervaux. New York: Geringer.

Larrick, Nancy, ed. (1988). *Cats Are Cats.* Illus. Ed Young. New York: Philomel.

——, ed. (1970). *I Heard a Scream in the Street: Poetry by Young People in the City.* New York: Evans.

—— (1990). *Mice Are Nice.* Illus. Ed Young. New York: Philomel.

Lauture, Denizé (1992). *Father and Son.* Illus. Jonathan Green. New York: Paperstar.

Lewis, J. Patrick (1998). *Boshblobberbosh: Runcible Poems for Edward Lear.* Illus. Gary Kelley. San Diego: Harcourt Brace.

—— (1998). *Doodle Dandies: Poems That Take Shape.* Illus. Lisa Desimini. New York: Atheneum.

—— (2000). *Freedom Like Sunlight: Praisesongs for Black Americans.* Illus. John Thompson. Mankato, MN: Creative.

Litz, A. Walton, and Christopher McGowen, eds. (1986). *The Collected Poems of William Carlos Williams: Volume I, 1909–1939.* New York: New Directions.

Livingston, Myra Cohn, ed. (1995). *Call Down the Moon: Poems of Music.* New York: McElderry [out of print].

—— (1996). *Festivals.* Illus. Leonard Everett Fisher. New York: Holiday.

——, ed. (1987). *I Like You, If You Like Me: Poems of Friendship.* New York: McElderry.

—— (1984). *Sky Songs.* Illus. Leonard Everett Fisher. New York: Holiday.

Locker, Thomas (1998). *Home: A Journey Through America.* San Diego: Harcourt Brace.

Martin, Bill, Jr., and John Archambault (1988). *Listen to the Rain.* Illus. James Endicott. New York: Holt.

Marzollo, Jean (1995). *Sun Song*. Illus. Laura Regan. New York: HarperCollins.

McCord, David (1974). *One at a Time*. New York: Little, Brown [out of print].

Merriam, Eve (1985). *Blackberry Ink*. Illus. Hans Wilhelm. New York: Morrow.

—— (1997). *Higgle Wiggle: Happy Rhymes*. Illus. Hans Wilhelm. New York: Mulberry.

—— (1996). *The Inner City Mother Goose*. Illus. David Diaz. New York: Simon & Schuster.

—— (1964). *It Doesn't Always Have to Rhyme*. New York: Atheneum.

—— (1998). *What in the World?* Illus. Barbara J. Phillips-Duke. New York: Harper Festival.

—— (1996). *You Be Good & I'll Be Night: Jump-on-the-Bed Poems*. Illus. Karen Lee Schmidt. New York: Mulberry.

Mora, Pat (1996). *Confetti: Poems for Children*. Illus. Enrique O. Sanchez. New York: Lee & Low.

Moss, Jeff (1997). *Bone Poems*. Illus. Tom Leigh. New York: Workman.

Myers, Christopher (1999). *Black Cat*. New York: Scholastic.

Myers, Walter Dean (1993). *Brown Angels: An Album of Pictures and Verse*. New York: HarperCollins.

National Museum of the American Indian, ed. (1999). *When the Rain Sings: Poems by Young Native Americans*. New York: Simon & Schuster.

Nikola-Lisa, W. (1994). *Bein' with You This Way*. Illus. Michael Bryant. New York: Lee & Low.

Nye, Naomi Shihab, ed. (2000). *Salting the Ocean: 100 Poems by Young Poets*. Illus. Ashley Bryan. New York: Greenwillow.

——, ed. (1995). *The Tree Is Older Than You Are: A Bilingual Gathering of Poems and Stories from Mexico*. New York: Simon & Schuster.

Okutoro, Lydia Omolola, ed. (1999). *Quiet Storm: Voices of Young Black Poets*. New York: Jump at the Sun.

O'Neill, Mary (1989). *Hailstones and Halibut Bones*. Illus. John Wallner. New York: Doubleday.

Oram, Hiawyn (1993). *Out of the Blue: Poems about Color*. Illus. David McKee. New York: Hyperion.

Paul, Ann Whitford (1999). *All by Herself*. Illus. Michael Steirnagle. San Diego: Browndeer.

Prelutsky, Jack (1993). *The Dragons Are Singing Tonight*. Illus. Peter Sis. New York: Greenwillow.

—— (1980). *The Headless Horseman Rides Tonight: More Poems to Trouble Your Sleep*. Illus. Arnold Lobel. New York: Greenwillow.

—— (1980). *Rolling Harvey down the Hill*. Illus. Victoria Chess. New York: Greenwillow.

Rochelle, Belinda, ed. (2000). *Words of Wisdom: A Treasury of African-American Poetry and Art*. New York: HarperCollins.

Rosen, Michael J., ed. (1992). *Home: A Collaboration of Thirty Distinguished Authors and Illustrators of Children's Books to Aid the Homeless*. Illus. Aliki et al. New York: Zolotow.

Shertle, Alice (1994). *How Now, Brown Cow?* Illus. Amanda Schaffer. San Diego: Browndeer.

Siebert, Diane (1991). *Sierra*. Illus. Wendell Minor. New York: HarperTrophy.

Silverstein, Shel (1974). *Where the Sidewalk Ends*. New York: Harper & Row.

Soto, Gary (1995). *Canto Familiar*. Illus. Annika Nelson. San Diego: Harcourt Brace.

Steptoe, Javaka (1997). *In Daddy's Arms I AM TALL: African Americans Celebrating Fathers*. New York: Lee & Low.

Stevenson, Robert Louis (1905). *A Child's Garden of Verse*. Illus. Jesse W. Smith. New York: Scribners.

Strickland, Dorothy S., and Michael R. Strickland, eds. (1994). *Families: Poems Celebrating the African American Experience*. Honesdale, PA: Boyds Mills.

Strickland, Michael R., ed. (1997). *My Own Song and Other Poems to Groove To*. Honesdale, PA: Boyds Mills.

——, ed. (1993). *Poems That Sing to You*. Honesdale, PA: Boyds Mills.

Thayer, Ernest (1901). *Casey at the Bat*. New York: Amsterdam.

Thomas, Joyce Carol (1993). *Brown Honey in Broomwheat Tea*. Illus. Floyd Cooper. New York: HarperCollins.

—— (1998). *I Have Heard of a Land*. Illus. Floyd Cooper. New York: HarperCollins.

Turner, Ann (1993). *Grass Songs*. Illus. Barry Moser. San Diego: Harcourt Brace [out of print].

Viorst, Judith (1981). *If I Were in Charge of the World and Other Worries: Poems for Children and Their Parents*. Illus. Lynn Cherry. New York: Atheneum.

Willard, Nancy, ed. (1998). *Step Lightly: Poems for the Journey*. San Diego: Harcourt Brace.

—— (1981). *A Visit to William Blake's Inn: Poems for Innocent and Experienced Travelers*. Illus. Alice Provensen and Martin Provensen. San Diego: Harcourt Brace [out of print].

Wilson, Gina (1994). *Prowlpuss*. Illus. David Parkins. Cambridge, MA: Candlewick.

Wolf, Allan (1990). *It's Show Time: Poetry from the Page to the Stage*. Asheville, NC: Poetry Alive!

Wong, Janet S. (2000). *Night Garden: Poems from the World of Dreams*. Illus. Julie Paschkis. New York: McElderry.

—— (1999). *The Rainbow Hand: Poems About Mothers and Children*. Illus. Jennifer Hewitson. New York: McElderry.

Yolen, Jane (1995). *The Ballad of the Pirate Queens*. Illus. David Shannon. San Diego: Harcourt Brace.

—— (1996). *Mother Earth, Father Sky: Poems of Our Planet*. Illus. Jennifer Hewitson. Honesdale, PA: Boyds Mills.

—— (1997). *Once Upon Ice: And Other Frozen Poems*. Illus. Jason Stemple. Honesdale, PA: Wordsong/Boyds Mills.

—— (1996). *The Originals: Animals That Time Forgot*. Illus. Ted Lewin. New York: Philomel.

—— (1996). *Sacred Places*. Illus. David Shannon. San Diego: Harcourt Brace.

—— (1995). *Water Music*. Illus. Jason Stemple. Honesdale, PA: Boyds Mills.

The Context of Children's Literature

Context refers to situation, environment, circumstance, or setting. When we are immersed in a familiar environment or context, like our home, its trappings are almost invisible to us. When someone we don't know very well comes to visit, our view changes dramatically. Suddenly, we see clutter, and every flaw is highlighted. At this point, we're looking at our place of residence through a new lens—a fresh and more critical lens. Our familiarity with our home allows us not to see its flaws. That view of our home is partly accurate, and there is nothing wrong with it—but it is not the whole picture. Our home also has the flaws and imperfections we see when we look at it through the new lens of another person's perspective. Of course, this more dispassionate and critical perspective is not the whole picture of our house either.

A similar limitation of perspective occurs in our reading; we see only part of the picture. When we read, we read through our own lens, which is fine. However, the students in our classes are not reading through our perspective; they are reading through their own lenses. As teachers, we need to try to see the literature we use in the classroom through as many lenses as we can. We need to read through the richest, most complex perspective available to us, so that, by choosing the best literature available to share with them, we can help our students do the same thing. This chapter provides tools to help you see literature more fully—not just through your familiar stance, but through fresh and more critical eyes.

In addition to widening our own lenses as readers, we also have to be aware that books written for children incorporate assumptions and world views that reflect the circumstances in which they were created—the context. For children's literature, this context includes the author's world view, the time period in which the book was written, publishing parameters at the time, contemporary notions of children's literature, and, of course, societal attitudes. In order to be conscious of what we are teaching through children's books and how these books can affect children, we must keep in mind the context in which they were written and look closely at what implied or hidden ideas these books contain. Through literature, children are taught what society values, even though those values may not be explicitly stated. It is important to be aware of all the implied messages books contain, because they may validate or change the way children see themselves and the world.

How Books Can Affect Children

Herbert Kohl (1995), who writes widely about educational issues, describes the deep impact books have on children:

> I believe that what is read in childhood not only leaves an impression behind but also influences the values, and shapes the dreams, of children. It can provide negative images and stereotypes and cut off hopes and limit aspirations. It can erode self-respect through overt and covert racism or sexism. It can also help young people get beyond family troubles, neighborhood violence, stereotyping and prejudice—all particulars of their lives that they have no control over—and set their imaginations free. (pp. 61–62)

Books validate for children that their lives are normal and that they are part of the culture. If they see dogs and cats in books, they accept them as appropriate animals to have for pets. If they see only two-parent families, they might begin to question whether something is wrong with their single-parent family. If they see only houses with white picket fences, they may come to believe that living in an apartment or in a city neighborhood is less acceptable. Even though I lived in a two-parent family, I remember thinking that something was wrong with my family because we were not like the perfect family in *Dick and Jane* stories. In that family, no one ever argued, no one ever had a temper tantrum, and no one ever worried about money. Everyone seemed happy all the time. I knew my family wasn't like that, and I worried that something was wrong with my family. Children expect the world as they know it to be represented in some of the books they read. If they see no reflections of themselves or the world they live in, they begin to wonder about themselves.

Not only does literature reflect society; it also helps shape society by suggesting that the institutions and people it shows are reflective of the norm. Children take what is written in books very seriously. They believe that books show truth—that the words would not be in print if they weren't true. Thus, if people of color are shown only in subservient roles, children internalize that view. If only women are shown doing housework, they believe that is the natural order. Children learn from books what behaviors are considered appropriate for males and females, children and adults. Books serve as a touchstone to which children compare their realities and from which they form their sense of the world. When adults select books and formulate ways to discuss books, they need to be aware that children see books as reflecting how the world really is and should be.

The views of educator, theorist, and author Louise Rosenblatt are discussed extensively in *Literature as Exploration,* first published in 1938 and reprinted in 1996. She points out that children are not aware of all the things they take away from literature or even the things they select to pay attention to. In her discussion of the interaction of the reader and the text, Rosenblatt (1996) says, "The reader is . . . immersed in a creative process that goes on largely below the threshold of awareness. . . . [The reader] is not aware of the individual responses or of much of the process of selection and synthesis that goes on as his eyes scan the page" (p. 54). Thus, teachers and adults need to find ways to make students aware of how and why they form impressions about a book.

The first step in looking at what our society values and what it teaches children through the books written for them is to examine our own assumptions and beliefs. Before we can see with a fresh or critical eye, we have to be aware of what makes up a world view and what it means to look at the world through one.

CD-ROM

To learn about the many aspects involved in using literature in the classroom, as reflected in this text's References, do a CD-ROM word search for *literature.*

Recognizing Our Own World Views

At birth, not only are we stamped with the genetic patterns of our parents, which determine our physical characteristics; we also are born into belief systems about the way people behave; what's appropriate for girls and boys; how to view people of our own race and those of other races, religions, and cultures; and what to think about people who live in a different kind of environment, such as the city, the farm, the suburbs, or the mountains. Children come to school wrapped in the amniotic sac of their culture and their family. If school validates their background by building learning around their culture and their class, they assume that this picture reflects the world. If school does not validate their background, they become aware that they are different, and they may not know how to enter into the belief system and assumptions that undergird the educational system.

When we are surrounded by people who view the world as we do, we believe that our views are natural and normal. For instance, most of us are immersed in the belief in hierarchical institutions such as school, church, and government. We view some people in these institutions as more important than others and as capable of knowing more than others. We believe that a hierarchy with one person at the top is the normal structure for institutions. At school, the principal is in charge, teachers are next in line, and students are at the bottom of the hierarchy. We call this hierarchical view of the world a "common sense" view because it is the view we know best.

The Limits of Our Ability to "See"

My world view was influenced by the books I read and what I was taught in school. I never questioned beliefs that reflected the Western view of the world. I learned that Columbus "discovered" America, never wondering why the indigenous people who already lived here didn't count. In history texts, I learned that westward expansion was a good thing because the land would be inhabited by people who were "civilized," bringing "progress" to the area. I accepted the idea that progress was measured in terms of material wealth, buildings, and technology, without examining the assumptions beneath this belief—that connections to other people, spiritual growth, and living in harmony with the earth were not important components of progress.

At that time (late 1950s), I still was not aware of the racism and sexism that were rampant in our society. In the early 1960s, when I went to college, I didn't wonder why females could not wear slacks to class at Michigan State University or why teaching, nursing, and secretarial careers were the only professions really open to women. That's just the way it was. I didn't wonder why I lived only a few miles from Detroit but never saw any people of color in my suburb. I didn't realize that I was, in fact, surrounded by racism.

Now, some 40 years later, I can look back and easily see how racism and sexism were embedded in the fabric of our society. Even the books I read as a child, I can now see, were blatantly racist. But when I read such books as the *Bobbsey Twins* series, I found nothing out of the ordinary in them. No one pointed out the racial stereotypes. I didn't "see" them with a critical perspective. For instance, in *The Bobbsey Twins in Eskimo Land,* by Laura Lee Hope, one such passage reads:

> Black Dinah, the jolly old cook of the Bobbsey family, came in from the kitchen just then with a plate of home-made cookies in her hand.
> [Responding to a picture Flossie had drawn] "All dat ice an' snow look like wintah, an' no mistake. An' what's dis here thing?" she asked, pointing to the igloo. "One ob dim iggles Ah hears tell about?"
> Flossie chuckled, and even Nan had to laugh.
> "Not iggle, Dinah—igloo," the taller girl corrected. (p. 2)

Although now the book's obvious depiction of the children as superior to their servant jumps out at me, I didn't notice it as a child. The demeaning dialect, which seems to be a white person's idea of how black servants would speak, didn't seem unusual to me, since I had never met anyone black and never heard any dialect other than a Midwestern Caucasian one. Nor did I notice that the only roles black people had in this series were as servants or workers in menial jobs.

The concept of racism was foreign to me as a child. I assumed that I led a "normal, average" life, not realizing that "normal" is actually based on constructs that are gradually developed by a society. We all carry around with us a set of assumptions; we see the world through the lens of these assumptions. Thus, it is very difficult to extricate ourselves from society's precepts and get a different look at the world. One intent of this chapter is to help you uncover some of your own assumptions so that you can be aware of them in your teaching. The process is like looking at your home through someone else's eyes so as to see it more freshly. But the intent is also to help you see other world views so that you can understand how people different from you might react to portrayals in books—to give you a glimpse of the racism, sexism, and classism that are sometimes present in books written for children. Our job as teachers is to reach as many of our students as possible. To do this, we need to be aware of when and why students feel shut out of a classroom or a book and the implications this feeling may have for their education and their sense of the world.

How World Views Affect Reading

Readers take from society, both consciously and unconsciously, a belief system about themselves and about their culture. This belief system creates around them a bubble through which they view the world. Because they are inside the bubble, they often are not aware of the colorings and shadings that the bubble casts on whatever they view through it. As Kathleen McCormick (1994) writes, "[Since] we read a text in our own time, not in the time in which it was written, . . . we read it with questions, anxieties and interests that come into existence because of our own particular places in history" (p. 80).

She explains further, "A text is always a site of struggle: it may try to privilege [validate] a particular reading position as 'natural,' but because readers are subjects in their own histories, they may not produce that seemingly privileged reading" (p. 69). Readers are not absolutely autonomous either. Because of this lack of autonomy, "Like the texts they read, they too are sites of struggle, caught up in cultural determinants that they did not create and in which they strive to make meaning" (p. 69). Thus, as a reader today, I often view literature through the bubble, or perspective, of being a parent. Themes of family, communication, abandonment, and sibling relationships leap out at me, even though they may be secondary to another theme.

Oftentimes teachers expect students to just look at the purpose for which the author wrote the book and not respond from their own histories. For example, if students reading *The Indian in the Cupboard,* by Lynne Reid Banks, were offended by the stereotypical portrayal of the Indian, a teacher might say that the author didn't mean anything by that portrayal and tell students not to react to things the author didn't consciously intend. The teacher might suggest that they focus on the literary elements or the story grammar and not discuss those disturbing issues, thus telling students that those issues have nothing to do with literary quality. That is what McCormick means by a privileged reading. Too often teachers expect students to read in only one way—their way. We must realize that students bring their full histories, experiences, and feelings with them when they read. If we expect students to find and create meaning in their reading worlds, we must let them start with their own experiences and responses.

Children's Literature as More Than a Story

Beneath the surface of the words and pictures, children's books contain an array of information and messages. Among the elements embedded in literature are the author's world view, societal constructs, and evidence of society's attitudes about such issues as racism, sexism, and classism.

Because all these elements are present in books, when we read books to children we are telling them what is important in the world and what to pay attention to in our culture. Through books, we are exposing them to a belief system that we have validated as important. When we share books, they assume that we value what the books emphasize. We are passing on to them ways to see themselves, other people, and the world.

The Author's World View

Literature is written by people firmly embedded in a particular culture, society, gender, race, and often religion. From the author's place at the intersection of these entities, a book is created. Authors notice things that they have learned are important; many don't see the things that their particular society does not value. The content of books directly reflects the society in which the books are produced. For instance, in **Grandpa's Town,** by Takaaki Nomura, a man and his grandson go to the bath house to enjoy the company of the other men in town. This book was published in Japan, where men bathing together is viewed as a normal activity—a view that would not prevail in an American setting. Indeed, the book is about a grandson bonding with his grandfather through an activity based on comradeship and community.

In addition to reflecting the society, authors' and artists' world views also reflect what they personally view as important enough to write about or draw. Babette Cole, for instance, loves to challenge our stereotypical views of people. In **Drop Dead,** she explodes every stilted notion we have of old people by showing Gran and Grandad as adventurous risk-takers with a great sense of humor. In **Prince Cinders,** she turns the Cinderella story on its head. The book starts with a princess looking for the prince she is enamored with and ends with Prince Cinders's big, hairy, and obnoxious brothers turning into house fairies, who spend their time doing housework. Because writers and artists draw from their own experiences, they often put women and men only in traditional roles or show only white, middle-class children. Until about 30 years ago, social and economic logistics made it difficult for women and minorities to get published, so little was written by or about them. As our culture extends authorship, this picture is changing. We need to remember, and remind our students, that all authors write from a point in time and that there is *always* a person beneath the words, a person whose attitudes and belief systems are reflected in his or her books.

Societal Constructs

Literature, like every other cultural artifact, carries embedded messages based on the constructs of the society. In Western thinking, for example, the concept of a hierarchy is used to explain the universe. The fact that those above have dominance over those lower on the ladder leads to the belief that humans have dominance over animals. But the whole idea of a hierarchy is nothing more than a theoretical construct—a concept put together to explain how the parts of the world work together and to explain who is in charge.

When we became grandparents we retired

Gran and Grandad are active, fun-loving seniors in this irreverent story by Babette Cole.
(From DROP DEAD by Babette Cole, copyright © 1996 by Babette Cole. Used by permission of Alfred A. Knopf Children's Books, a division of Random House, Inc.)

Not all cultures and societies use the same constructs to explain the universe, and many don't see the universe as a hierarchy. For instance, in the picture book *Father Sky and Mother Earth,* by Oodgeroo, an Aboriginal woman in Australia, the earth and its plants and animals are seen as entities helping each other. The book says,

> Rock created Mountains and Hills to protect his servants [Trees, Birds, Animals, Reptiles, and Insects] from the cold winds of Gale, Cyclone and Tornado. And Tree created Plants and Grass and Flowers. And Animals, Reptiles and Insects created more Animals, Reptiles and Insects. And so on. . . . And they were all very happy creating and balancing and loving and living and helping one another. (p. 16)

Vestiges of Racism, Sexism, and Classism

CD-ROM

Do a word search for *racism* to see how this issue surfaces in Invitations, References, and works by Favorite Authors.

As a country, we pride ourselves on providing opportunities for everyone and treating everyone in an equal manner. We believe that we are a classless society because movement from one class to another is possible. Yet because we each see through our own world view, it is difficult to determine how prevalent racism, sexism, and classism are in our society. And, of course, whatever is in the society at large is reflected in books. The racism, sexism, or classism found in books today is rarely intentional. However, if we don't know how to see situations and events through others' eyes, how do we recognize inherent racism, sexism, and classism? How do we know what will offend people? How do we know when others will feel that they have been wrongly or unfairly portrayed? Many times, the majority truly has no idea of what is offensive; this understanding does not come easily or all at once.

Just after I had studied stereotypes of American Indians and thought hard about *The Indian in the Cupboard*, by Lynne Reid Banks, I went to a work session of a national organization. Three of us were selecting proposals for programs about literature for an upcoming conference. One of the women in the group turned to me and said: "Can you believe it! This person wants to present a session on Southern literature and the impact that losing a war has had on the South. She claims the South is the only section of the country that has lost a war on its own soil."

I sat silent, stretching to figure out why this was offensive. Fortunately, the woman continued, "I'm sure American Indians don't feel that way, or the Mexicans who lived on and lost their land in areas like Arizona and New Mexico."

I was truly taken aback, because I had caught myself in a limited world view. History books tend to only "count" wars that involve primarily white people. No name has been given to the seizing of American Indian lands. The taking of Mexican land in the Treaty of Guadalupe-Hidalgo often isn't counted as a war on "our own land" because the land was taken from people of color.

The intent of this chapter is to uncover some of the ways in which we have been trained to "see." An important part of the process is to look at scenarios through others' eyes, just as we might look at our house through someone else's eyes. As teachers, we must keep in mind that just because something is not offensive to us does not mean it won't offend our students and their families. Remember, as McCormick tells us, that we all have different histories and experiences.

According to Audre Lorde (1992), poet and critic, "Racism/sexism/classism is the belief in the inherent superiority of one race/gender/class over all others and thereby the right to dominance" (p. 402). Racism, sexism, and classism seem to be built on expectations, selection, and power. Those who view a group through a distorted or incomplete prism have expectations about how members of that group will behave. Women might be seen as emotional, and thus disqualified from making tough decisions that must be based on a "rational" or logical approach. People in parallel cultures (a term Virginia Hamilton [in Harris, 1996] offered as a replacement for *minority cultures* because it is less hierarchical) might be seen as lazy or less intelligent, and thus disqualified from positions of power. People living in poverty might be seen as unmotivated, disorganized, and dependent, and thus not suited for positions of power. Selection comes into play because only limited instances, actions, or behaviors are selected to define these groups, from the broad array of actions individuals in these groups exhibit. Thus, the major element in racism, sexism, and classism is power—the need on the part of the people who hold power to preserve it. They disenfranchise others to keep themselves in charge. Yet people who accept racist, sexist, or classist views are not always aware that these attitudes rest on power relationships. It takes looking closely at all these isms to see the structure of power needs beneath them, since these needs are so tightly built into our society's constructs that they are practically invisible.

It is hard to get a grasp on sexism because it surrounds us and is inherent in the foundations of most aspects of our belief systems. One quick way to uncover a modicum of awareness of sexism is to select a few assumptions and expectations that we have for women and apply them to men. So imagine with me . . .

At birth he was beautiful—long lashes, symmetrical features, a full head of hair. Relatives and friends crowded around him, oohing and aahing about how handsome he was. As he grew older, he received constant attention for his looks and his outfits. "How darling! Look at those precious little buttons on his little vest. Doesn't that make him look handsome!" He liked to move and scoot after things. However, when he was quiet, just looking around or holding his stuffed animals, his parents would gush, "What a sweet, well-behaved child. Isn't he darling!"

As he grew and started to toddle around, he was curious, as all children are, picking up objects, getting into cupboards, and generally working to make sense of his world. At night, he hugged his teddy bear tight.

But the constant chorus of comments he heard from his parents told him what was important—how he looked, how docile he was, and how much he hugged his

For ideas on reducing bigotry and intolerance in schools, check out **Teaching Tolerance** at www.splcenter.org/teachingtolerance//tt-index.html.

teddy bear. "What a good little father he will make," he heard as he walked holding his teddy bear tightly. So out of all the behaviors he displayed, his family (and society) selected the ones they found pleasing and those were the ones for which he got attention and rewards.

When he went to school, he was harshly reprimanded for any slight misbehavior and told, "I can't believe a handsome boy like you would act that way." The girls around him got to roughhouse, and all he heard from his teacher was "Girls will be girls."

He also found out it was all right for girls and their parents to make fun of boys. If a girl threw a ball poorly at her Little League game she was chastised for "throwing like a boy." Gradually he got the message: Boys couldn't do much physically; they were too clumsy and uncoordinated. He and his friends begged their parents to come to see them play ball at the park. They promised they'd come, but when they didn't think he was around, he heard them say, "The games the boys play are so slow. Girls' games are fast-paced and exciting." And parents and neighbors continued to come in droves to see the girls play.

As he grew and developed, his body became well defined and muscular. All the girls ogled and said rude things to him in the hall. When he asked them to stop, they told him they didn't mean anything by it—they were just one hundred percent all-girl and very interested in boys and their bodies. When the comments increased, he talked to his parents, who told him he should be proud to have a body that girls pay attention to—then he wouldn't have any trouble getting a woman. This seemed very important to everyone. He noticed that when the kids at school started to pair up, the boys picked by girls suddenly went up in status. His friend became "Annie's boy," and all the other boys seemed jealous of his "achievement."

When sexism is taken out of its familiar casings and shown in a different light, it appears ridiculous and shocking. Yet when the scenario is applied to a female, these same attitudes seem natural because our society has built constructs that support sexism. Of course, these constructs imply a certain "place" for men and for women, based on who is seen as most important or most powerful.

Sexism doesn't cut only one way. Males are as affected by gender expectations as females. Men are expected to take charge; to be brave, strong, athletic, rational, and responsible; and to know how to fix cars. If boys are thin and sensitive, enjoy classical music, and loathe sports, they are not easily accepted by their peers. Sexism limits choices for both sexes by making assumptions about how a person should be based solely on gender.

Just as we have used role reversal as a way to reimage and better understand sexism, we can imagine a scenario in which our current racial hierarchy is toppled. Imagine, if you will, a world in which the darker your skin, the more power you have. What expectations would people have for those with the darkest skin? What expectations would they have for people with the lightest skin? Where would you fall in this hierarchy? How would your world be different than it is now?

Or imagine reversing the way we view rich and poor people. No longer would society believe that material worth determines human worth and dignity. The rich would be seen as preoccupied with hoarding material wealth for themselves, while the poor would be seen as interested in pursuing a simple life so that all could share the earth's resources. People living simply would be elevated to a heroic status for living in a way that takes into consideration the entire community and their need for resources. Those who lived extravagantly would be viewed as selfish, concerned only with themselves and not with what is best for the world. When people in different economic situations are discussed in this way, it is easy to see that the classifications of poor and rich are defined behaviorally, not economically. But when we read of the poor or see them portrayed in the media, we may not notice that the terms *poor, working class,* and *underclass* hide judgmental baggage. It is important to look closely at how groups are being portrayed in order to uncover the way they are being defined.

The only way to learn how our words and actions affect people is to pay attention to how people react to us and ask them for advice and feedback. If we are to create a community of

The unearthly, celestial qualities of the story are suggested by this intriguing cover image.

(Jacket design from A WRINKLE IN TIME, by Madeleine L'Engle. Copyright © 1962, renewed 1990 by Madeleine L'Engle Franklin. Reprinted by permission of Farrar, Straus and Giroux, LLC.)

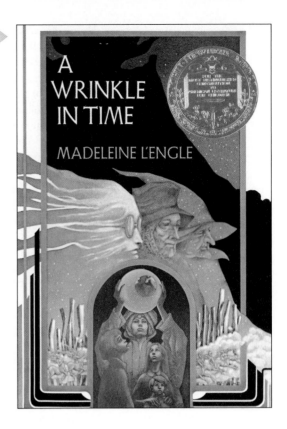

learners in our classrooms, we must be aware of and gently address the issues of racism, sexism, and classism as they arise in class. (See one way a first-grade teacher dealt with stereotypes on pages 186–187.)

Uncovering Stereotypes in Children's Books

The beliefs embedded in some texts are so prominent that we notice them even when we are not consciously looking for them. For instance, the spiritual basis of Madeleine L'Engle's *A Wrinkle in Time* would be hard to miss because of the central emphasis on good and evil. But identifying underlying beliefs in books is not always that easy. Answering the questions in the boxed feature Criteria for Evaluating the Beliefs Beneath the Writing can help the process along, making it easier to at least begin to approach the depths of the text.

If answering this set of questions for a particular book reveals extensive evidence of racism, sexism, or classism, you could then use other tools to look more closely at stereotypes and other distortions. Several other tools—boxed sets of questions on race, gender, and class—appear later in the chapter.

Recognizing Stereotypes

For those outside a culture or class, it is difficult to know what is offensive to those in it. For instance, we may not immediately understand American Indians' negative reactions to the counting book *The Ten Little Rabbits*, by Virginia Grossman and Sylvia Long, which shows rabbits dressed as American Indians performing such activities as sacred ceremonies. One way to begin to think about portrayals is to ask ourselves how we would feel if we were portrayed that way. Would we be offended if a counting book had figures of people of our race or ethnicity to count? Would we feel we were being viewed as nothing more than objects? How would Christians react if a rabbit minister or priest were administering communion to rabbit parishioners? How would they react if Mary, Joseph, and Jesus were

*For **Native American Indian Resources**, go to www.kstrom.net/ isk/mainmenu.html.*

Criteria for Evaluating **the Beliefs Beneath the Writing**

As you read books, you can ask these questions to get a look at the beliefs and assumptions imbedded in the writing:

1. Who or what was included and who or what was left out of the scope of the book?

2. What information does the author assume the reader knows?

3. What attitudes are shown toward people, animals, and even the land?

4. Who has the power? How is this power shown?

5. What is shown as being important or good?

shown as rabbits in the nativity scene, with a halo around the little rabbit's head? Christians might feel that having a little animal take the place of an important figure belittled their sacred ceremonies and beliefs. Putting yourself in someone else's place is a beginning, but it is not always enough. For example, most white people would see nothing wrong with the portrayal of Timothy, a black man, in *The Cay,* by Theodore Taylor. Timothy is shown as an admirable character who cares deeply about the white boy, so what's to object to? What majority members may not easily see is that black characters who are depicted as admirable are usually allowed those traits when they are shown helping white people in some way. Comparing the bias with gender stereotypes makes it easier to see. How would women feel if the only admirable female characters were those shown waiting on or caring for men? This portrayal limits and distorts female behavior. Certainly women do other admirable things that could be written about. The same is true for people of color; many portrayals limit and distort who they are.

Authors and illustrators can not foresee everything that those they write about and draw would find offensive, but they can check out their portrayals with someone who is part of the culture or group. Authors and illustrators cannot be naive about the impact of their books on readers. Neither can we, as teachers, be naive about the impact of books on our students.

Because we are encapsulated by our culture and class, it is hard for us to see beyond our own background. The lists in the boxed features here, by providing concrete criteria, can provide some help. Criteria for Evaluating Children's Books for Racism and Sexism is from the Council on Interracial Books for Children. It offers specific things to look for in terms of racism and sexism. Criteria for Evaluating Bias Toward American Indians on page 182, adapted from Slapin and Seale's (1998) book on American Indians, points out the different forms stereotyping of that group takes. Criteria for Evaluating Gender Stereotyping, on page 183, is a list I created to expand on the gender stereotypes covered by the Council on Interracial Books for Children. I also created the list on classism, Criteria for Evaluating the Presence of Class or Socioeconomic Bias, found on page 184. These lists offer concrete ways to locate examples of bias in books. It isn't necessary to use more than one list per book, as that could be repetitive and tedious.

---

*C*riteria for Evaluating *Children's Books for Racism and Sexism*

These ten quick ways to analyze children's books for racism and sexism are adapted from the Council on Interracial Books for Children.

1. **Check the illustrations.** Look for stereotypes— oversimplified generalizations about a particular group, race, or sex, which usually carry derogatory implications. Some infamous stereotypes of blacks are the happy-go-lucky, watermelon-eating Sambo and the fat, eye-rolling "mammy"; of Chicanos, the sombrero-wearing peon and the fiesta-loving, macho bandito; of Asian Americans, the inscrutable, slant-eyed "Oriental"; of American Indians, the naked savage or "primitive brave" and his "squaw"; of Puerto Ricans, the switchblade-toting teenage gang member; of women, the completely domesticated mother, the demure doll-loving little girl, and the wicked stepmother. Look for variations that in any way demean or ridicule characters because of their race or sex.

Look for tokenism. If there are racial minority characters in the illustrations, do they look just like whites except for being tinted or colored in? Do all minorities look stereotypically alike, or are they depicted as genuine individuals with distinctive features?

Who's doing what? Do the illustrations depict minorities in subservient and passive roles or in leadership and action roles? Are males the "doers" and the females the inactive observers?

2. **Check the story line.** Look for these subtle forms of bias.

What is the standard for success? Does a minority person need "white" behavior standards to "get ahead"? Is "making it" in the dominant white society projected as the only ideal? To gain acceptance and approval, do persons of color have to exhibit extraordinary qualities? In friendships between white and nonwhite children, is it the child of color who does most of the understanding and forgiving?

How are problems resolved? Examine the way problems are presented, conceived, and resolved in the story. Are minority people considered to be "the problem"? Are the oppressions faced by minorities and women represented as related to social justice? Are the reasons for poverty and oppression explained, or are they accepted as inevitable? Does the story line encourage passive acceptance or active resistance? Is a particular problem that is faced by a racial minority person or a female resolved through the benevolent intervention of a white person or a male?

What roles do women have? Are the achievements of girls and women based on their own initiative and intelligence, or are they due to their good looks or their relationships with males? Are sex roles incidental or critical to characterization and plot? Could the same story be told if the sex roles were reversed?

3. ▶ **Look at the lifestyles.** Are minority persons and their setting depicted in such a way that they contrast unfavorably with the unstated norm of white middle-class suburbia? If the minority group in question is depicted as "different," are negative value judgments implied? Are minorities shown exclusively in ghettos, barrios, or migrant camps? If the illustrations and text attempt to descibe another culture, do they go beyond oversimplifications and offer genuine insights into another lifestyle? Look for inaccuracy and inappropriateness in the depiction of other cultures. Watch for instances of the "quaint natives in costume" syndrome (most noticeable in areas like clothing and custom, but extending to behavior and personality traits as well).

4. ▶ **Weigh the relationships between people.** Do the whites in the story possess the power, take the leadership, and make the important decisions? Do racial minorities and females of all races function in essentially supporting roles?

How are family relationships depicted? In black families, is the mother always dominant? In Hispanic families, are there always lots of children? If the family is separated, are societal conditions—unemployment, and poverty, for example—cited among the reasons for the separation?

5. ▶ **Note the heroes.** For many years, books showed only "safe" minority heroes—those who avoided serious conflict with the white establishment. Minority groups today are insisting on the right to define their own heroes (of both sexes), based on their own concepts and struggles for justice.

When minority heroes do appear, are they admired for the same qualities that have made white heroes famous or because what they have done has benefited white people? Ask this question: Whose interest is the hero really serving?

6. ▶ **Consider the effects on a child's self-image.** Are norms established that limit any child's aspirations and self-concept? What effect could it have on black children to be continuously bombarded with images of the color white as the ultimate in beauty, cleanliness, virtue, and so on, and the color black as evil, dirty, menacing, and so on? Does the book counteract or reinforce this positive association with the color white and negative association with the color black?

What happens to a girl's self-image when she reads that boys perform all of the brave and important deeds? What about a girl's self-esteem if she is not "fair" of skin and slim of body?

In a particular story, is there one or more persons with whom a minority child can readily identify to a positive and constructive end?

7. ▶ **Check the author's and illustrator's biographical material.** Analyze the biographical material on the jacket flap or the back of the book. If a story deals with a minority theme, what qualifies the author and illustrator to deal with the subject? If the author and illustrator are not members of the minority group being written about, is there anything in their backgrounds that would specifically recommend them as the creators of this book?

8. ▶ **Check out the author's perspective.** No author can be wholly objective. All authors write out of a cultural, as well as a personal, context. Children's books have traditionally come from authors who were white and who were members of the middle class, with one result being that a single ethnocentric perspective has dominated children's literature in the United States. Read carefully to determine whether the direction of the author's perspective substantially weakens or strengthens the value of his or her written work. Is the perspective patriarchal or feminist? Is it solely Eurocentric, or do minority cultural perspectives also receive respect?

(continued)

9. **Watch for loaded words.** A word is loaded when it has insulting overtones. Examples of loaded adjectives (usually racist) are *savage, primitive, conniving, lazy, superstitious, wily, crafty, docile,* and *backward.*

   Look for sexist language and adjectives that exclude or ridicule women. Look for use of the male pronoun to refer to both males and females. While the generic use of the word *man* was accepted in the past, today it is outmoded.

10. **Look at the copyright date.** Books on minority themes—usually hastily conceived—suddenly began appearing in the mid-1960s. There followed a growing number of "minority experience" books to meet the new market demand, but most of these were still written by white authors, edited by white editors, and published by white publishers. They therefore reflected a white point of view. Not until the early 1970s did the children's book world begin to even remotely reflect the realities of a multiracial society. The new directions resulted from the emergence of minority authors writing about their own experiences. Unfortunately, this trend has been reversing, as publishers have cut back on such books.

    Nonsexist books, with rare exceptions, were not published before 1973. The copyright date, therefore, can be a clue as to how likely the book is to be overly racist or sexist, although a recent copyright date, of course, is no guarantee of a book's relevance or sensitivity. The copyright date only reflects the year the book was published. It usually takes about two years from the time a manuscript is submitted to the publisher to the time it is actually printed and put on the market. This lag meant very little in the past, but in a time of rapid change and changing consciousness, when children's book publishing is attempting to become "relevant," it has become increasingly significant.

Criteria for Evaluating *Bias Toward American Indians*

The following criteria are adapted from Beverly Slapin and Doris Seale (1998).

1. Is the vocabulary demeaning? Are terms like *squaw, papoose, chief, redskin, savage,* and *warrior* used?

2. Do the Indians talk like Tonto or in the "noble savage" tradition?

3. Are the Indians all dressed in the standard buckskin, beads, and feathers?

4. Are Indians portrayed as an extinct species, with no existence as human beings in contemporary America? This is the whole "vanishing Indian" concept.

5. Is Indian humanness recognized? Do animals "become" Indians simply by putting on "Indian" clothes and carrying a bow and arrow? Do children "dress up like Indians" or "play Indian" as if "Indian" were a role that one could assume, as one can dress up like a doctor or cowboy or baseball player? For comparison, do animals or children also dress up as African Americans or play Italians?

6. Do American Indians appear in alphabet and counting books as objects that are counted?

7. Do American Indian characters have ridiculous imitation "Indian" names, such as "Indian Two Feet" or "Little Chief"?

8. Is the artwork predominately generic "Indian" designs or has the illustrator taken care to reflect the traditions and symbols of the particular people in the books?

9. Is the history distorted, giving the impression that the white settlers brought civilization to native peoples and improved their way of life? Are terms like *massacre, conquest, civilization, customs, superstitions, ignorant, simple, advanced,* and *dialects* (instead of languages) used in such a way as to demean native cultures and achievements and indicate the superiority of European ways?

10. Are Indian characters successful only if they realize the futility of traditional ways and decide to "make it" in white society?

11. Are white authority figures, such as teachers and social workers, able to solve problems of native children that native authority figures have failed to solve? (Are there any native authority figures?)

12. Are women perceived as subservient drudges? Or are women shown to be the integral and powerful part of native societies that they are?

13. Finally, and most importantly, is there anything in the book that would make an American Indian child feel embarrassed or hurt to be what he or she is? Can the child look at the book and recognize and feel good about what he or she sees?

Criteria for Evaluating *Gender Stereotyping*

1. Look at the words and pictures used to depict males and females. What personality characteristics or attributes are considered to be important to each gender? Who is active/passive; stable/unstable; courageous/afraid; selfless/selfish; rational/emotional; a risk taker/a complier; aggressive/not aggressive; challenging/obedient; in little need of friends/in great need of friends; competitive/nurturing (frequently viewed as opposites in society)? What personality characteristics are valued for females/males and which lead to achievement and success outside the home? Who seems to be the most intelligent? the most sensitive? the most emotional? What does this show about what we expect of males and females?

2. Look at what males and females are shown doing. Who takes action? Who is more passive? Who takes the lead in making decisions? Who protects the other from "danger"?

3. What brings about disapproval for males? for females? What are males/females apologetic for? Who criticize themselves?

4. How are fathers and mothers portrayed? What is expected of them? Who is blamed for a family's unhappiness?

5. Who seems to be in charge or the more important one in a relationship?

6. Would this character have changed if the author had decided to use a female/male for this part?

7. How does the language in the story reinforce gender expectations? Are females described as "beautiful" and men as "strong"? Are females complimented on their looks? shown to be always concerned with their physical appearance? What does this tell us about what is valued in males and females?

8. Which characters get to do the most interesting things and seem to have the most interesting plans for the future? What do females/males get status or importance from? Are females shown as achieving or finding happiness only in relationship to males? Is having a man seen as the supreme female achievement?

9. Do females speak indirectly and try hard not to offend males while males speak directly? Are females openly criticized? Who questions, interrupts, or initiates conversation?

10. Are females viewed primarily as caretakers of others? Are additional female interests subordinate? Is the realm of nurturing and emotional support left to the female? Are females shown to be at their best when most domesticated?

11. Are males shown to be highly valued and raised with different expectations than females? Are male interests shown as being more important than female interests? Is deference given to the male whose activities are highly valued?

Criteria for Evaluating *the Presence of Class or Socioeconomic Bias*

When people with few economic resources are written about or shown in illustrations, consider the following questions.

1. Is the vocabulary demeaning?

2. Are they viewed with contempt, as undeserving and at fault for their economic situation?

3. Are they shown as dirty and unkempt, not paying attention to their personal appearance?

4. Are they viewed as disorganized and impulsive, concerned only with the present?

5. Do the illustrations compare them unfavorably to the "norm" of the middle class?

6. Are middle- or upper-class authority figures shown solving the problems of the working class or poor?

7. Are they seen as successful only if they embrace the values of the middle and upper class?

8. Are they depicted only in settings that contrast unfavorably with the unstated norm of middle-class suburbia? If they are shown as "different," are negative value judgments implied?

9. Is it implied that they lack firm internal values?

10. Is it implied that they are squandering their resources?

11. Are they shown as not taking proper care of their children and not interested in education?

12. Are they portrayed as bigoted and narrow in their thinking, with tendencies toward violence?

13. Would the portrayal be hurtful to a child in the working class or living in poverty?

Rooting Out Some Examples of Stereotypes

In reading a book for any purpose—reviewing, pleasure, possible use with students—I always allow myself an initial response. The first time through Lynne Reid Banks's *The Indian in the Cupboard*, I just read it, responding in the ways I normally would. Even though I knew there were stereotypes in it, I tried to read it just to get involved in the story. The story has many attractive features, including the appealing main character, the responsibility he feels for the "little people," and the suspense when Omri brings both miniature people to school and is called to the principal's office. In spite of these qualities, it was hard not to notice the bias, beginning with the title of this well-loved children's book. The words "The Indian" assume that "Indian" is descriptive in itself and represents a whole race. When the plastic figures of whites were mentioned, they were given job titles such as soldier, cowboy, or doctor. Imagine if a book referred to a plastic "Italian" or a plastic "white" or a plastic "black." Reaction would be strong or confused.

When I had finished reading *The Indian in the Cupboard*, I used the list from *Through Indian Eyes: The Native Experience in Books for Children*, edited by Beverly Slapin and Doris Seale (1998), to locate other stereotypes. (See the boxed feature Applying the Criteria: Evaluating Bias Toward American Indians.) If I hadn't known whether the book contained racism, sexism, or classism, I might have used the list by the Council on Interracial Books for Children as a starting point. Then, if the answers to the questions indicated the presence of racism, sexism, or classism, I might have used one of the other lists. For an example in which this process is applied to the well-known and acclaimed picture book **The Polar Express,** by Chris Van Allsburg, see the boxed feature Applying the Criteria: Evaluating the Beliefs Beneath the Writing on page 186. It reveals some messages that we need to be aware of in this classic Christmas story.

CD-ROM

Find other books by Chris Van Allsburg on the CD-ROM database.

Applying the Criteria *Evaluating Bias Toward American Indians*

Here's what I found when I applied the criteria from Beverly Slapin and Doris Seale (1998) to *The Indian in the Cupboard*, by Lynne Reid Banks.

1. **Demeaning vocabulary.** Loaded, racist words and phrases used by the cowboy to describe the Indian include "Ya red varmint. Ah'll have yer stinkin' red hide for a sleepin' bag," followed by "redskin," "dirty savages," and "th' only good Injun's a daid Injun." None of these racial insults are ever acknowledged.

2. **Talk.** The Tonto-like talk was everywhere. Omri was surprised that the Indian didn't talk English like the Indians in the movies did. Little Bear's talk throughout made him seem less intelligent.

3. **Dress.** Although Little Bear was said to be an Iroquois, a nation from the Great Lakes area, he wore no shirt, had a feather in his headband, and generally dressed like the Plains Indians from much warmer areas.

4. **Extinct species.** All the way through the story there was no recognition or talk of American Indians still being very much a part of American life today.

5. **Humanness.** Although Little Bear was allowed some human characteristics, "Indian" was seen primarily as a role. It was assumed that the "nature" of the Indian was to kill, fight, and be superstitious. The way the cowboy was portrayed was also quite negative and

basically a caricature of a cowboy. But the whole story was peopled with "nice" white people, so it may have balanced out this one negative portrayal. This was not true for the "Indian," who was the only representative of all American Indian peoples and the myriad tribal groups in this country.

7. **Names.** He was called Little Bear. Most grown men are not called "little" anything.

9. **History distorted.** This was very present in the book. Little Bear's native culture and achievements were demeaned through Omri's attitude toward Little Bear's spiritual beliefs and through the generally caricatured view of his life.

10. **White authority figures.** Omri was shown as the only one capable of solving the problems of Little Bear. At one point, Omri thinks, "What mattered was that Little Bear should be happy. For that, he would take on almost anything." This seemed to be almost like a Great White Father, swooping in to take care of the childlike natives.

11. **Women.** The female selected by Omri for Little Bear was shown as subservient and concerned only about male needs.

12. **Impact on American Indian children.** Native children would probably be mortified by the portrayal of Little Bear, especially as he was presented as a representative of all American Indians.

What Does All This Mean?

When books contain stereotypes or don't seem to include all of the children in our classes, should we exclude these books from our classroom? No. If a book is rich in other literary aspects, using it offers an opportunity to help students increase their awareness of how people are portrayed and question the assumptions made about boys and girls, people in parallel cultures, and people in different classes. Part of a teacher's task is to recognize some of the more obvious beliefs and attitudes embedded in literature, in order to select for students pieces of literature that will invite them in, not alienate them or make them uncomfortable. By analyzing what books do and do not contain, teachers can work to include books that represent a wide range of peoples and cultures and socioeconomic classes. Teachers need to open up these areas for discussion in their classes, as well as try to balance the portrayals in books in the curriculum throughout the year.

For example, analyzing **The Polar Express** could help the teacher be more sensitive to the need for prereading discussions. The other kinds of celebratory traditions that take

Applying the Criteria *Evaluating the Beliefs Beneath the Writing*

The Polar Express, by Chris Van Allsburg.

1. Who or what was included and who or what was left out of the scope of the book? Upper-middle-class lifestyle is included; other socioeconomic levels are left out. Santa Claus and his relationship to Christmas are included; other celebratory traditions are left out. A white, upper-middle-class male child's experience with Christmas is included. The idea of magic and belief is included in terms of Santa Claus, while knowledge of parents as gift source is left out.

2. What information does the author assume the reader knows? The story of Christmas and Santa Claus. Familiarity with mountains and forests and wolves. Awareness of upper-middle-class lifestyle.

3. What attitudes are shown toward people, animals, and even the land? It's normal for children to question the existence of Santa Claus. Children can expect to be taken care of by adults. Adults are solicitous of children and want to be of help.

4. Who has the power? How is this power shown? Adults have the power—especially Santa Claus, who is appreciated or adored by the elves and children. The waiters on the train are not shown as having power, while the conductor is shown as being in charge. The little boy has more power or importance than the other children.

5. What is shown as being important or good? A belief in Santa Claus. Living in a big, beautiful house with rooms completely decorated and coordinated. Wearing beautiful nightclothes to bed and owning robes and slippers. Having a Christmas tree and celebrating Christmas. Getting lots of presents for Christmas. Boys are more important than girls. Girls' roles are to care for and show concern for others, so when the little boy is upset at the loss of the bell, it's only girls who respond to him. Girls are shown only in passive roles, except when they show concern for the main character. Men with swarthy complexions are shown waiting on children and are clearly servants.

place at the same time of year as Christmas might be discussed, to make children aware that other traditions exist. Children could be asked when they've been waited on and what the occasion was. The subject of who waits on people could also be broached, to broaden the view that only people of color are waitpeople. Even talking about houses—what's in them, how different people decorate them, what allows some people to afford bigger houses, and so on—can do much to allay the discomfort children may feel if they realize that their house is not nearly as grand as the one pictured. Sometimes simply raising these issues is enough to help children realize that they are not the only ones who don't have the kind of life that is portrayed in the book.

Some people might ask, "Why not let children remain innocent for a while and read stories about people who live well and enjoy life without questioning them?" Herbert Kohl (1995) answers this concern well when he points out, "There are many ways to live well, and it's important to show children that you don't have to be rich to live well, that living well is not simply a matter of being able to buy things and have other people take care of your everyday needs" (p. 25).

A more direct approach to dealing with stereotypes is demonstrated by Paula Rogovin (1998) in her book *Classroom Interviews.* In her first-grade class, she began a study on American Indian History and Culture by asking her students what they knew about American Indians. Their list included the following: Indians wear feathers, kill children, fight, dance, live in tepees, use bows and arrows, do war whoops (p. 32). Rogovin saw that the list was full of stereotypes and misinformation but did not criticize the children; instead, she asked where they got their information. They mentioned movies on television, teachers, family members, friends, and pictures. She very gently asked them, "Did you know that sometimes our information is wrong?" Many children were astounded, but she reassured them that that was not their fault because sometimes movies showed the wrong information. She explained a few aspects of the culture, telling them that although many American Indians did use bow and arrows, they used them mainly to hunt, not to kill people. "If we say that all American Indians use bows and arrows to go around killing people, that is not true. That is a stereotype" (p. 39). The students discussed this and decided that they could not believe everything they saw in the movies. From there, they watched different versions of the segment of Peter Pan showing Peter meeting the Indians. The children looked for stereotypes. One student wrote in his notebook, "Stereotypes are a kind of a lie. Like if I would say every Indian wears feathers, that would be a stereotype. And you can't use stereotypes because it hurts people's feelings. And if you told one, you would feel bad after you told it" (p. 40). Obviously, this teacher does a wonderful job of addressing issues head on and helping students not only understand stereotypes but also understand the need to question sources. Rogovin suggests that with older children, the study of misinformation and stereotyping could be extended by having them work on checking multiple sources and challenging sources of information.

Joel Taxel (1981) would agree that the kind of work Rogovin does with her students is very important because of the subconsciousness of the process. He explains: "Stereotypes, particularly with young children, do not register at the conscious level unless they are raised as an issue. Stereotypic attitudes are probably 'imprinted' at an unconscious level through repeated exposure to many books, films, television shows, and, of course, parental and peer group attitudes" (p. 15).

When we don't raise these issues, when the reading or talking is uncritical, there is always the chance that the book or movie or talk will change the way the child looks at and relates to the world. Thus, teachers must be aware of the racism, sexism, and classism in books in order to help students become aware of them and not accept the prevailing view that society seems to hold of gender, people in parallel cultures, and the poor and working class. Not talking about race, gender, and class stereotypes is just another way of perpetuating racism, sexism, and classism, since it allows the status quo to remain firmly in place. Sometimes middle-grade children do notice stereotypes, as the boxed feature Children's Voices shows.

Adults cannot effectively facilitate or encourage in young people work that they themselves have not already done. We need to have done the thinking and self-reflection about these issues before we can have genuine conversations in the classroom.

Learning from the History of Children's Literature

Part of the context of children's literature is the time period in which it was written. From the literature of each historical period, we can locate attitudes toward children, as well as attitudes toward every other aspect of life and society. By looking at what is published for children, we can see what a society thinks about who children are, what they can handle, what can be expected of them, and what is important for them to pay attention to. The purpose of this section is to look at what we can learn about children's literature from changes over the years and to think about the implications these changes have for our ability to look critically at children's literature today.

Changes in Children's Books Through the Years

Much of the early history of children's literature in the United States is grounded in the white culture. Both American Indians and blacks maintained rich oral traditions that were not part of written children's literature, for cultural and political reasons. We will look briefly at the more than two centuries of children's literature in the United States to see what kind of changes occurred as the times, attitudes, and technology changed.

What stereotypes have you ever noticed in your reading?

In the **Outsiders** *there were a lot of stereotypes, and in Mildred Taylor's books blacks are also labeled.* —Danielle, 6th grade

The only stereotype I noticed was a long time ago. The author only used blonde people and the "bad guy" was brunette. —Chris, 7th grade

Take Indians, for example. They aren't cowboy-killing bad guys. They are very respectful to the land, animals, and people who aren't trying to kill them or take their land. —Jeff, 7th grade

I have noticed that black people all are shown as having some sort of problem in books. —Allison, 7th grade

I've read a book that stereotyped cheerleaders as blonde, ditzy preps, and that's not true at all. I know; I'm a cheerleader myself. —Lori, 8th grade

Yes, when people didn't like someone because of their weight or how they looked. —Samantha, 8th grade

Yes, I have noticed racism and sexism, as well as other things. —Monica, 8th grade

No, I have not heard a stereotype because I never knew about it. —Angel, 6th grade

Do you choose to read books about people of other races than your own?

When I read a book, it doesn't matter what race or color they are. —Aaron, 6th grade

I read books about any races; it doesn't matter to me. —Tiffany, 6th grade

I don't care what race the character is; I will still read the book. —LaQuisha, 6th grade

I like to read about all people and not be a racist. Beth Lee is white, and I like her writing. —Ticia, 6th grade

I have read many books by people with different races other than mine. —Donnell, 6th grade

I normally choose books of any race since most of them are white (and I'm black). —Dorothy, 6th grade

When I read a book, it's sometimes not my race. But it doesn't matter to me. —Jasmin, 6th grade

Purpose

Children's literature written by the Puritans in the colonies was designed solely to instruct. The colonists were religious dissenters who had left their homes in Europe, and they wanted their children to accept their beliefs and carry them on to the next generation. Therefore, it was essential that the children learn about religion from books, in addition to learning from their parents. From the early 1800s to the middle of the century, children's literature moved away from the overtly religious as more stories were published, but it was still morally instructive.

After the American Civil War, as the book business continued to grow, it finally became accepted that literature for children must entertain, especially if it was to sell (Hunt, 1995, p. 126). Views of childhood also changed. Children were no longer seen as little adults who should be concerned only with adult matters as they prepared for a life of work. In her essay "Go, and Catch a Falling Star: What Is a Good Children's Book?" (in

Harrison and Maguire, 1987), Ethel Heins says, "The eighteenth-century doctrine of original sin turned into the nineteenth-century cult of original virtue—or innocence—in the child" (p. 525). Childhood became separate from adult life and was given a value of its own.

The conventions that dictated the attitudes and purposes of literature for children remained remarkably stable until about the middle of the 20th century. The growth in publishing was very rapid, but changes in the content of books came more slowly.

Children's literature "absorbed and recorded the major changes in the American outlook: a slow shift from the Puritan preoccupation with spiritual meaning, to a more generalized Protestant concern for personal morality, and from that moralism to a largely secular interest in social behavior," writes Peter Hunt (1995). He also tells us, "The literature changed as American attitudes to children and childhood changed" (p. 129). Thus, each period of our history redefined what was "good literature" for children as the culture changed.

Although instructing and entertaining certainly are still purposes, other purposes implicit in children's books today include nurturing, consoling, broadening world views, challenging ideas, boosting self-concept, and helping children see the normalcy of the experiences they go through.

Topics

Since children's literature reflects contemporary society, the topics found in books have broadened as attitudes in society about what's appropriate for children have changed. No longer is children's literature as sanitized as it was 50 years ago. Then, no mention was made of bodily functions; of subjects thought to upset children, such as death; or of subjects adults had trouble dealing with, such as sexuality. However, now it seems we have a different taboo. In a 1998 article co-written with Jane Yolen about their book *Armageddon Summer,* Bruce Coville says,

> . . . I think that the last taboo in children's books these days, and one that needs
> desperately to be shattered, is religion. . . . we should not ignore the reality of
> children's lives, which is that most of them do indeed think a great deal about
> matters of faith, of the spirit. . . . If we refuse to acknowledge this in our books
> for young readers, we leave a glaring hole in our work, and deny the truth of
> their own lives. (p. 57)

Despite this taboo, which may be reflective of an area with which our society has trouble, the subjects books discuss are more wide ranging than ever before. We read stories about one-parent families, about abuse, about alcoholic parents, and about accepting oneself.

Language

Books have often been viewed as the repositories of language and culture. "Imperfection in language or deviance from the social norms was not allowed. Slang did not appear in books before the 1960s for children, and the language remained quite formal" (Hunt, 1995, p. 65).

Today this type of restricted language is hard to imagine. In 1953, in a letter to one of her authors, Ursula Nordstrom (in Marcus, 1998), children's book editor at Harper, gave us a peek at how high the expectations were. One reviewer of a book said that she "likes the book but is concerned about the use of 'gee' and 'by holy saints'" (p. 65).

The relaxed and often colorful language used today reflects a much more relaxed view of what is appropriate. In *Wizard and Wart at Sea,* by Janice Lee Smith, we find, "'A curse and worse!' yelled Wizard." In *Toby, Where Are You?,* by William Steig, we read, "Where on earth is that little rascal?" and "So where the dickens is he?" Even comparisons can be spicy. In *Noel the First,* by Kate McMullan, Noel thinks that the two girls trying to outperform each other in a dance "looked more like a pair of killer whales going after the same sardine."

Kinds of Characters, Heroes, and Behavior

In the early part of the 19th century, children were shown learning to obey, learning to be unselfish, and learning to be careful in their actions. No mischievous children who were

To compare themes and subject matter in earlier children's literature, go to **Children's Literature, Chiefly from the Nineteenth Century,** at www.sc.edu/library/spcoll/kidlit/kidlit/kidlit.html.

unrepentant or unchanged were shown. In the last part of the 19th century and the first part of the 20th century, Horatio Alger books were popular. In these books, a hard-working, honest, respectful boy is shown climbing the ladder to success and achieving the American dream of social and economic advancement.

One "bad boy" who did appear was Tom Sawyer, but he had redeeming qualities such as being likable! Girls seemed to like the more daring females in **Little Women,** by Louisa May Alcott; **Anne of Green Gables,** by Lucy Maud Montgomery; the **Betsy-Tacy** novels, by Maud Hart Lovelace; and **Daddy-Long-Legs,** by Jean Webster, either because the girls were spirited, outspoken, and honest and pushed the rules governing proper behavior or because they tried to resist domestic servitude.

Editors from publishing houses had an impact on what was published. One editor who wanted to provide the very best books for children was Ursula Nordstrom of Harper. She wanted originality and honesty in books, and so she was willing to have characters who would not always be admired. One such character was Max, the mischievous child who is sent to his room in Maurice Sendak's **Where the Wild Things Are.** Reviewers wondered about the example Max set for children and worried that the monsters would frighten children badly. But Nordstrom believed that the book was revolutionary not only because it was "the first complete work of art in the picture book field, conceived, written, illustrated, executed in entirety by one person of authentic genius. But *Wild Things* is written from the inside out. . . . [It] is the first picture book to recognize the fact that children have *powerful* emotions, anger and love and hate and only after all that passion, the wanting to be 'where someone loved him best of all'" (Marcus, 1998, p. 177). Once the ground was broken by one publishing house, it was much easier for other houses to follow. But it took strong, determined editors like Nordstrom to publish books that adults criticized. In a letter to one of Harper's salespeople, Nordstrom pulled no punches. With respect to a grumpy buyer who disliked Ruth Krauss's book **How to Make an Earthquake,** she said, "Krauss books will not charm those sinful adults who sift their reactions to children's books through their own messy adult maladjustments" (Marcus, 1998, p. 71).

Genres

In the early colonial days, most books for children came from England. Some publishing was done in America, but the books written here were serious-minded ones, such as sermons, catechisms, doctrinal treatises, history, natural history, biography, and maps (Hunt, 1995, p. 104).

Before the end of the 19th century, children's reading was emphatically not intended to encourage fantasy or imagination, because it was viewed as dangerous for children to think imaginatively without adult guidance. After reading fantasy, children might have the audacity to question concepts adults were teaching them!

Even nonfiction in the 18th century was at least as concerned with values as with fact. One ground-breaking event, which signaled a new way to conceive of this genre, was the publication of a book called **Orbis Pictus** in England. In this book by John Amos Comenius, which contained all the information he thought a child should know, the illustrations were as important as the text, furthering what the reader could learn. Because the book was not published in the still-very-Puritan colonies in America, marrying illustrations to text took longer to gain ground in America.

Today nonfiction is flourishing, especially in picture books, partly because photographs and drawings can be produced so easily. The blending of text and illustrations makes the information very accessible to and interesting for the young reader. Interest is further heightened by the authors' use of a narrative or storytelling style.

Another notable contribution to children's literature came in 1744, with John Newbery's idea to design a book that would entertain children as well as teach them. This English bookstore owner and publisher designed and published **A Little Pretty Pocket-Book,** which taught children the alphabet.

Now, of course, fiction is very popular, and fantasy is widely accepted. Inclusion of children's literature across the curriculum has made biography, historical fiction, and traditional literature more popular. Within each genre, there is more breadth and depth. New formats are being created within the genres because of advances in technology. Walter Dean Myers's **Monster** uses the handwriting of the main character in many chapters, a feature that would not have been possible years ago. Pop-up books, such as **The Movable Mother Goose,** by Robert Sabuda, can be produced easily now that modern technology has made it possible to engineer the paper in such a way that pictures pop up when a page is opened.

Attitudes Toward Difference

Today, authors and publishers try to be sensitive to portraying characters in realistic ways so as not to stereotype them. However, attitudes that are common in society, but can still be seen as racist, sexist, or classist, sometimes slip into books unintentionally, as in the earlier example of *The Indian in the Cupboard,* by Lynne Reid Banks. Blatant racism is no longer tolerated in children's literature. But this was not always true. For instance, Nathaniel Hawthorne, known best as the author of the classic *The Scarlet Letter,* was allowed to be racist, perhaps because what he said reflected the prevailing attitude at the time. In *Parley's Universal History on the Basis of Geography,* published in 1837 and intended for children, Hawthorne casually dismissed the non-Protestant, non-Western world, telling young Americans that "no country has ever been happy or well governed where Mohammedanism prevailed" and "the whole Chinese are great fibbers" (in Hunt, 1995, p. 114). His beliefs about people who are different are right out in the open.

Who Is Left Out and Who Is Included?

As mentioned earlier in the chapter, the kinds of people who are included in books are frequently the ones the writers know about. Thus, in the first half of the 19th century, much was written about white, middle-class families and children, since the majority of the authors being published were from New England or Middle Atlantic states and were white, Protestant, and middle-class. The children's literature from this period reflected an agreed-upon "moral framework" (Hunt, p. 112).

But in the early years of the 20th century, as immigrants poured through Ellis Island and became part of the city school systems, some authors consciously tried to include immigrants as characters in their books. One such author was Lucy Fitch Perkins, whose 26 **Twins** books published between 1911 and 1935, such as **Belgian Twins,** helped create "mutual respect and understanding between people of different nationalities" (Hunt, 1995, p. 242). These books included immigrant children as the main characters and were aimed at helping children recognize the commonalities of humans, no matter what immigrant group they were part of.

CD-ROM

To find authors of different ethnicities, go to Favorite Authors and key in a particular ethnicity, such as *Asian American.*

The influence of the writers' own lives and locations on their work continued after the turn of the century, when many of the new writers lived in cities. Stories of urban life, which had not been seen in children's literature earlier, became common (Hunt, 1995, p. 115). Not only did writers include more accurate city details; they also wrote about the realities of the city. Many of these realities, such as the existence of slums and poverty, were unpleasant ones that had traditionally been excluded from children's literature.

However, positive portrayals of working-class families who cared about each other were usually missing from the literature. Children were shown in middle-class families and in single-family dwellings. This is only now gradually changing with such books as Cynthia Rylant's **The Relatives Came,** which shows a close and caring family leading evidently happy lives, even though the relatives sleep on the floor when they visit. According to Herbert Kohl (1995), Vera B. Williams's books **A Chair for My Mother, Something Special for Me,** and **Music, Music for Everyone** "portray working people with dignity, present an image of collective and compassionate living, and . . . are unique in primary school literature through their presentation of a complex and loving view of life within a multiracial and multicultural working-class community" (p. 79).

Books that included American Indians, immigrants, and blacks were generally stereotypical. It wasn't until the 1960s that authentic books on black experiences slowly began to appear. Up to this time, characters were mainly white, and few pictures even included

A loving working-class family and their neighborhood are painted in bold colors that suggest the vibrancy of their lives.

(From *A Chair for My Mother,* by Vera B. Williams. Used by permission of HarperCollins Publishers.)

children of color. A notable exception was *The Brownies' Book,* a magazine written for "the children of the sun" by black adults in 1920 and 1921. The goal of the magazine was to publish stories, poems, and songs that challenged racial stereotypes, built pride, and socialized black students. It was published by W. E. B. DuBois, rather than a mainstream publisher, and lasted only two years. Because it was rarely read by those beyond the target audience, white librarians and teachers were not aware of its existence. In 1996, ***The Best of The Brownies' Book,*** edited by Deanne Johnson-Feelings, was published by Oxford University Press so that the magazine's place in children's literature could be made known.

As criticism mounted in the 1970s about the roles of females in children's books, authors started to show girls as more than passive observers, thrilled just to be noticed by a male. That trend has continued, although boys are still the main characters far more often than girls. Other current trends include presenting characters with disabilities, stepparents, blended families, characters of different sexual orientation, and interracial dating, as well as matters of faith. The boxed feature Taking a Look at the Research discusses representations not often found in children's books today.

See ***Books about Children with Disabilities*** at *www.math.ttu.edu/ ~dmettler/dlit.html.*

Book Appearance

If you pick up a book printed in the 1930s or 1940s, you will at once know that it is an older book, based solely on its appearance. Color was very time-consuming to produce, so even the illustrations from this time period are in black and white.

Until recently, an illustrator would have to make a black base drawing, with three overlays for the three additional colors. It was a long, expensive process, and so books were not nearly as colorful as they are today. Even today, when a page is printed, it must go through the press once for every color used. So if a page has even a touch of red, it must go through the press once to put the red ink on and once to put the black ink on. Today four-color

Inclusion and Exclusion

Traditional representations in children's literature of an idyllic family structure have gradually given way to candid depictions of divorce, single parenting, blended families, and foster and adoptive families. Even issues of abuse and homelessness now appear occasionally in literature for children. For the most part, these books have been seen as enriching the literature selection possibilities and a welcome reflection of the variety of family structures and issues that exist in our culture today. They, indeed, give our students more authentic and meaningful text which they can relate to their own lives.

One family relationship that continues to be, for the most part, excluded is one in which there are same-gendered parents. While there are certainly children who are living in households with two moms or two dads, they are unlikely to see their families represented in classroom children's literature collections. Although books are available that depict these families, fear of censorship or teachers' personal displeasure or self-censorship is likely to keep them out of the classroom. It is hard to know how many thousands of children are living in loving families with gay or lesbian parents, siblings, or other family members but, as this act of exclusion demonstrates, "often remain invisible for the whole school experience" (Henkin, 1998, p. 81).

In young adult literature, *Am I Blue? Coming Out from the Silence,* edited by Marion Dane Bauer (1994), is a collection of original stories, by leading children's literature authors, that depict a wide range of gay and lesbian themes. In the introduction, Bauer expresses the concern of many when she speaks of the significant number of teenagers who attempt suicide because of fears associated with their gay or lesbian sexuality. Worried about the lack of information and support for these young people, she states that it is the intention of this collection "to tell challenging, honest, affecting stories that will open a window for all who seek to understand themselves or others" (p. ix).

Bauer, Marion Dane, ed. (1994). *Am I Blue? Coming Out from the Silence.* New York: HarperCollins.

Henkin, Roxanne (1998). *Who's Invited to Share? Using Literacy to Teach for Equity and Social Justice.* Portsmouth, NH: Heinemann.

(which means just about every shade, since the four colors can be combined) books are very common. Although the presses still have to make four runs, the burden is off the illustrators to make four separate layers for each page that has color. Now that modern technology, with its scanners and separators, can do the bulk of the work, producing colored picture books has become the norm. And typography has improved so much that changing a font usually just requires a click of the mouse. The downside to all this wonderful technology seems to be that the occasional author and publisher depend on impressing readers with spectacular visuals rather than the story. In years past, only stories deemed to be of excellent quality were considered worthy of the added expense of color.

Changes in Views of Children Through the Years

By looking at the kinds of books that are published for children, we can see what a society thinks children's function is. The Puritans viewed children mainly through the lens of their religious beliefs, seeing the stain of original sin on every child. They were eager to have their children lead the kind of lives that would bring them eternal salvation and saw children's learning about Puritan beliefs as the main function of childhood. There was little time for frivolous things such as games or books for entertainment (if such a thing had existed), since children had to take their salvation seriously. The only books children in the Puritan colonies had put in their hands were those that could further this otherworldly end.

One interesting aspect of the books the Puritans used to instruct children is that they did make some concessions to the way children learn best. Realizing how much more easily verse was memorized than prose, the Puritans wrote doctrine in verse for the young. *The New England Primer* was illustrated, since children were understood to like and learn from pictures.

By 1870, books for children had become much more than instructional. The shift to novels that were interesting and attractive to the young, as well as wholesome, reflected a change in views toward children. Once the overwhelmingly Puritan ethic softened, books began to focus on social behavior, since children were still seen as impressionable and not quite ready to handle books without a clear message of what was and was not acceptable in society. In the early part of the 20th century, children were expected to be purposeful and take on adult responsibilities early. Books on this side of the Atlantic reflected that somber, utilitarian approach, while fantasy and fairy tales were popular in England, where many children had a more prolonged childhood.

Today children are viewed as having psyches that must be tended to with care. We view childhood as a special time when children should not be burdened with adult responsibilities. This is a time for them to play, learn, and enjoy themselves. We understand that learning takes place in many ways, and so we try to provide children with experiences through which they can learn, such as a visit to a zoo. We know that this is a time when children develop a sense of right and wrong, and we want to provide them with good models. Today's books reflect our views of childhood, and so they nurture, console, boost self-esteem, help children see the normalcy of the experiences they go through, provide role models for them, and teach them concepts about the world in interesting ways.

Invitations

Choose several of the following activities to complete:

1. Look for good books for young people that are not written from the perspective of the virtues of individualism, competition, and capitalism. Look for books for young people that question the economic and social views of our society. If you find such books, note these qualities in your responses to them.

2. Work to unearth the assumptions on which you have built your belief system. What facts and experiences do you include in your opinions or judgments about members of the opposite sex, about people of a race different from your own, about people who belong to a different kind of church than you do, about people who have different political persuasions than you do? Can you trace the origin of these assumptions? Making your belief system explicit will not only help you understand your responses to books, but also allow you to explore your beliefs. Although these are subjects that are difficult to talk about with others, if you can find one other person in your class whom you feel you can trust, share your responses with that person. What did you learn?

3. Think back to something you read in the past that you can now see has other dimensions, such as racism or classism or sexism. Suppose you identified with the group presented in an unflattering manner in the book; how would you feel? As you read books this semester, be aware of which books make you feel like an outsider or an insider. What is it about the books that causes you to react that way?

4. Select a picture book or novel to analyze in terms of racism, sexism, or classism, using the criteria in this chapter.

5. Herbert Kohl (1995) says,

> The stories we provide to youngsters have to do with personal challenge and individual success. They have to do with independence, personal responsibility and autonomy. The social imagination that encourages thinking about solidarity, coop-

eration, group struggle, and belonging to a caring group is relegated to minority status. Healthy community life and collective community-wide struggles are absent from children's literature and the stories most children encounter on TV, in film, or at home. (p. 62)

As you read books for this course, look at them in terms of Kohl's quote and report what you find. Which books do you think are appropriate for children? Which ones do you see as inappropriate? What can you learn from these responses about your views of children and what you think they are capable/incapable of understanding?

6. Magazines can be particularly good barometers of social change, reflecting current attitudes of the society toward children. Go to a library and look through the current year's issues of a magazine for children, noting what topics are written about in fiction and nonfiction. Or look at a series for children like the *Berenstain Bears*. Analyze how the culture has changed over the past ten years by comparing the ways gender and social issues are handled.

7. Imagine that the only artifacts you had to learn about this culture were stacks of picture books. What could you tell about this culture? What's important to us? What do we value? What is happening in the culture? Who has the power? If you have access to a special collection in your library, look through several children's books from another time period, noting all the things that are different. What view of life do these books paint?

CD-ROM

Locate other references to *culture* in Favorite Authors and References by using the word search feature.

❮❮❮❮❮❮❮❮❮❮❮❮❮❮

Classroom Teaching Ideas

1. To heighten awareness of stereotypes, select one book that you know has stereotypes in it and one that does not. Read both books to your class. After students discuss how women or the aged or people in parallel cultures were portrayed differently in the books, explain to them what makes a stereotype. As the children respond to the books they read throughout the year in their book logs, ask them to notice and point out stereotypes or unfair portrayals.

2. Every time you read a book aloud to your class, as part of the follow-up discussion ask students to think about whom this book is leaving out. What people are not represented? This kind of ongoing discussion throughout the year will keep students sensitized about whom books exclude and whom they represent.

Internet and Text Resources

1. **Teaching Tolerance** is the site for the Southern Poverty Law Center. The mission of the center is to reduce hate, bigotry, and intolerance in schools. Find great resources at

www.splcenter.org/teachingtolerance//tt-index.html

2. **Books about Children with Disabilities** provides titles and sometimes brief descriptions of books that include children with CP, hearing impairments, spinal cord injuries, spina bifida, progressive illnesses, and communications disorders, as well as mental illnesses and learning disabilities. There are also links to sites featuring trade books for siblings of children with disabilities. Find it at

www.math.ttu.edu/~dmettler/dlit.html

3. **Brave Girls and Strong Women Booklist** is a site with annotated lists of books from small publishers. Find it at

www.members.aol.com/brvgirls/bklist.htm

4. **Books for Girls** offers booklists on topics of interest to girls. Go to

   www.girlpower.gov/girlarea/books/

5. **Children's Literature, Chiefly from the Nineteenth Century** contains pictures from early children's books, along with brief descriptions. The site would be ideal for the viewer who wants to compare themes and subject matter of earlier literature to those of present-day children's literature. Find it at

   www.sc.edu/library/spcoll/kidlit/kidlit/kidlit.html

6. **Native American Indian Resources** contains stories, art, herbal knowledge, native books, and an online bookstore. Find it at

   www.kstrom.net/isk/mainmenu.html

References

Council on Interracial Books for Children (no date). "10 Quick Ways to Analyze Children's Books for Racism & Sexism." CIBC pamphlet.

Harris, Violet (1996). "Continuing Dilemmas, Debates, and Delights in Multicultural Literature." *The New Advocate 9,* 107–122.

Harrison, Barbara, and Gregory Maguire, eds. (1987). *Innocence and Experience: Essays and Conversations on Children's Literature.* New York: Lothrop, Lee & Shepard.

Hunt, Peter, ed. (1995). *Children's Literature: An Illustrated History.* New York: Oxford University Press.

Kohl, Herbert (1995). *Should We Burn Babar? Essays on Children's Literature and the Power of Stories.* New York: New Press.

Lorde, Audre (1992). "Age, Race, Class, and Sexism: Women Redefining Difference." In Paula S. Rothenberg, ed., *Race, Class, and Gender in the United States.* New York: St. Martin's.

Marcus, Leonard S., ed. (1998). *Dear Genius: The Letters of Ursula Nordstrom.* New York: HarperCollins.

McCormick, Kathleen (1994). *The Culture of Reading and the Teaching of English.* New York: Manchester University Press.

Rogovin, Paula (1998). *Classroom Interviews.* Portsmouth, NH: Heinemann.

Rosenblatt, Louise (1996). *Literature as Exploration.* New York: Modern Language Association [1938].

Slapin, Beverly, and Doris Seale, eds. (1998). *Through Indian Eyes: The Native Experience in Books for Children.* Berkeley, CA: Oyate.

Taxel, Joel (1981). "Cultural Theory and Everyday Educational Life." Paper presented at the annual meeting of the American Educational Research Association, April 15, 1981.

Yolen, Jane, and Bruce Coville (1998). "Two Brains, One Book; or How We Found Our Way to the End of the World." *Booklinks 8,* 54–58.

Children's Books

Alcott, Louisa May (1994). *Little Women.* New York: Tor [1868].

Banks, Lynne Reid (1980). *The Indian in the Cupboard.* Illus. Brock Cole. New York: Delacorte.

Cole, Babette (1996). *Drop Dead.* London: Jonathan Cape, Random.

—— (1987). *Prince Cinders.* New York: Putman & Grosset.

Comenius, John Amos (1968). *Orbis Pictus.* London: Oxford University Press [1659].

Grossman, Virginia, and Sylvia Long (1991). *The Ten Little Rabbits.* New York: Chronicle.

Hawthorne, Nathaniel (1895). *The Scarlet Letter.* Boston: Houghton Mifflin.

—— (1837). *Parley's Universal History on the Basis of Geography.* London: Goodrich.

Hope, Laura Lee (1936). *The Bobbsey Twins in Eskimo Land.* New York: Grosset & Dunlap.

Johnson-Feelings, Deanne, ed. (1996). *The Best of the Brownies' Book.* New York: Oxford University Press.

Krauss, Ruth (1954). *How to Make an Earthquake.* Illus. Crockett Johnson. New York: Harper [out of print].

L'Engle, Madeleine (1973). *A Wrinkle in Time.* New York: Farrar, Straus & Giroux.

Lovelace, Maud Hart (2000). *Betsy-Tacy.* Illus. Lois Lenski. New York: HarperTrophy [1940, Crowell].

McMullan, Kate (1996). *Noel the First.* Illus. Jim McMullan. New York: HarperCollins.

Montgomery, Lucy Maud (1981). *Anne of Green Gables.* New York: Bantam [1908, L. C. Page].

Myers, Walter Dean (1999). *Monster.* Illus. Christopher Myers. New York: HarperCollins.

New England Primer, The (1824). Newark: Benjamin Olds [1795].

Newbery, John (1744). *A Little Pretty Pocket-Book.* Self-published.

Nomura, Takaaki (1991). *Grandpa's Town.* Trans. Amanda Mayer Stinchecum. New York: Kane/Miller.

Oodgeroo (1981). *Father Sky and Mother Earth.* Sydney, Australia: Jacaranda.

Perkins, Lucy Fitch (1917). *Belgian Twins.* Boston: Houghton Mifflin.

Rylant, Cynthia (1986). *The Relatives Came.* Illus. Stephen Gammell. New York: Simon & Schuster.

Sabuda, Robert (1999). *The Movable Mother Goose.* New York: Little Simon.

Sendak, Maurice (1963). *Where the Wild Things Are.* New York: Harper.

Smith, Janice Lee (1995). *Wizard and Wart at Sea.* Illus. Paul Meisel. New York: Harper.

Steig, William (1997). *Toby, Where Are You?* Illus. Teryl Euvremer. New York: HarperCollins.

Taylor, Theodore (1995). *The Cay.* New York: Camelot [1967, Avon Flare].

Van Allsburg, Chris (1985). *The Polar Express.* Boston: Houghton Mifflin.

Webster, Jean (1995). *Daddy-Long-Legs.* New York: Puffin [1912, Century].

Williams, Vera B. (1982). *A Chair for My Mother.* New York: Greenwillow.

—— (1984). *Music, Music for Everyone.* New York: Greenwillow.

—— (1983). *Something Special for Me.* New York: Greenwillow.

Yolen, Jane, and Bruce Coville (1998). *Armageddon Summer.* New York: Harcourt Brace.

Multicultural and International Literature

*M*ulticultural books can be as vibrant as ***Uncle Jed's Barbershop,*** by Margaree King Mitchell, which sings with family caring and community. They can be as startlingly beautiful as ***The Dragon Prince: A Chinese Beauty & the Beast Tale,*** by Laurence Yep with Kam Mak's luminous illustrations. They can be as poignant as Allen Say's ***Emma's Rug,*** which depicts a five-year-old's fear and uncertainty. They can be as packed with fascinating information as ***Black Hands, White Sails: The Story of African-American Whalers,*** by Patricia C. McKissack and Fredrick L. McKissack. They can sing with joy, the way the illustrations by Ashley Bryan do in ***Sing to the Sun.*** They can lift us off the page with beautiful language, the way ***Meet Danitra Brown,*** by Nikki Grimes, does. They can make us laugh and cry, the way ***The Watsons Go to Birmingham—1963,*** by Christopher Paul Curtis, does.

Multicultural literature has the richness, depth, beauty, and variety of any category of literature. It is represented in every genre, including picture books, realistic and historical fiction, traditional literature, fantasy, nonfiction, and poetry.

Although multicultural literature should be integrated into the curriculum and used as other books in other genres are used, it is treated separately here so that we can closely examine books and authors who can be considered multicultural. This chapter is designed to show in concrete ways the importance of using such literature, to help you get to know what literature is available, and to encourage you to think about the issues embedded in the use of multicultural literature.

What Is Multicultural Literature?

In the broadest sense, multicultural literature could include every book because every book comes from the point of view of a culture and every book can be read from multiple points of view based on gender, socioeconomic class, ethnicity, and so on. Some ethnic groups, especially those from Europe, have had a continuous presence in children's literature. We all have heard of the Grimm brothers, Hans Christian Andersen, and the tales of King Arthur.

In the interest of diversity and equity, the focus in this chapter is on literature about and/or by historically underrepresented groups, whose faces and stories and histories are missing from much of our literature. As early as 1941, Charlemae Rollins, African American librarian and activist, raised her voice for more positive examples of blacks and black culture in children's books. This issue began to be addressed after Nancy Larrick (1965) in "The All-White World of Children's Literature" also pointed out this lack in the field. By defining multicultural literature as literature that calls attention to peoples and voices not traditionally written about or included in the body of literature most frequently taught, we can focus on filling in the part of the picture that is missing. In this country, this group is composed of people of color, including African Americans, Mexican Americans/Latinos, Asian Americans, and American Indians. This definition of multicultural literature does not include international literature, which will be addressed later in this chapter, because international literature does not focus on the issues of the multiple cultures in our nation.

Reasons for Using Multicultural Literature

Rudine Sims Bishop (1997), noted African American professor of children's literature, often talks about how literature serves as a mirror and a window for the reader. As a mirror, it shows children reflections of themselves; as a window, it shows them what other people are like. Too often children of color experience literature only as a window, while white children experience it only as a mirror. It is, of course, important that all of the children in our classrooms see people who look like them in literature, as well as people who don't look like them. Although superficial and not in itself enough, representation of their ethnicity is what children first notice when they read a book.

Benefits of Multicultural Literature for Children from Parallel Cultures

Faith Ringgold, noted artist and author, tells us on the book jacket of *The Invisible Princess* that, while reading to her granddaughters one day, she was asked why there were no African American princesses in stories. When she realized the truth in their question, she remedied the situation by writing *The Invisible Princess.* In this story, Mama and Papa Love have a child, the Invisible Princess, who saves them and the

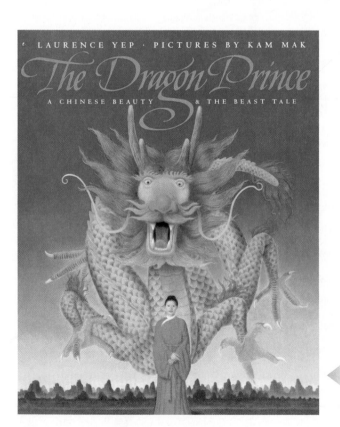

Kam Mak's stunning illustrations make Laurence Yep's adaptation of "Beauty and the Beast" an unforgettable adventure.
(Cover art from *The Dragon Prince* by Laurence Yep. Cover art copyright © 1997 by Kam Mak. Used by permission of HarperCollins Publishers.)

other plantation slaves from their cruel master so that they can all find happiness in the Invisible Village of Peace, Freedom, and Love. This story, written in response to her granddaughters' question, underscores the importance of seeing ourselves in representations of the world that we encounter, be it in television, books, movies, or magazines.

Philip Lee (1999), one of the founders of Lee & Low, a publishing company with a specific focus on multicultural themes, explained how this lack of representation affected him. He told of growing up in Hong Kong, where 98 percent of the population was Chinese. But because Hong Kong was then ruled by the British, "all things Anglo were better than Chinese." The commercials, the movies, and everything else surrounding him shouted out that blonde was better. Although living "in a place rich with role models, we were reminded every day that Chinese wasn't as good." As a teenager, Lee moved to California and was eager to assimilate. He even bleached his hair blonde. "How powerful," he says. "I wanted to be someone other than myself ethnically." Because he understood how important it was for children to see themselves in the media, specifically in books, and because he was conscious of what was missing, he established his company.

Benefits of Multicultural Literature for All Children

While it is easy to understand why multicultural literature is important for people in parallel cultures, sometimes it is harder to see why this literature is so vitally important for all students. The promise of multicultural literature is "not just that we will learn about other cultures but that we will learn about ourselves" (Aronson, 1996, p. 32). The achievements of others tell us something about who we are, for if others can achieve, part of the reason is that attitudes—including ours—in society have made room for this kind of achievement. Consistently reading and discussing a wide range of multicultural books has important benefits for all children.

Enjoying Good Literature

Children can enjoy multicultural literature simply because it is good literature. Good literature is a work of art that invites readers into an aesthetic or "lived through" experience. Of prime importance in selecting books is considering the literary merit of a book. Publisher Philip Lee (1999) explains that, in looking for multicultural books to publish, the first thing his company looks at is "whether or not it's a good story. Does it have believable characters, a compelling plot, and a satisfying ending—all the same elements that make any book a good read? If it doesn't read well, it won't be published." It is the literary qualities of multicultural books that have been responsible for their winning both the Newbery Award (**M. C. Higgins, the Great,** by Virginia Hamilton; and **Bud, Not Buddy,** by Christopher Paul Curtis) and Newbery Honor awards (**The Watsons Go to Birmingham—1963,** by Christopher Paul Curtis; **Yolonda's Genius,** by Carol Fenner; **Dragon's Gate,** by Laurence Yep; **The Dark-Thirty: Southern Tales of the Supernatural,** by Patricia C. McKissack; and **Somewhere in the Darkness,** by Walter Dean Myers, among others). Artistic excellence has secured the Caldecott Medal for David Diaz for **Smoky Night,** by Eve Bunting; Allen Say for **Grandfather's Journey;** Ed Young for **Lon Po Po: A Red-Riding Hood Story from China;** Leo Dillon and Diane Dillon for **Why Mosquitoes Buzz in People's Ears: A West African Tale,** by Verna Aardema, and for **Ashanti to Zulu: African Traditions,** by Margaret Musgrove, as well as several Caldecott Honor awards.

Gaining Information and Knowledge

By seeing in multicultural literature stories of the diverse citizens who live in the United States, children can gain information and knowledge. This nation has been filled with people of color from the beginning. Native American peoples have lived in what is now the United States since ancient times. Many African Americans were enslaved and brought here in the 17th century. Mexicans lived on the land that was then known as Northern Mexico and is now the Southwest of the United States. Asians came to this country in the last part of the 19th century and were largely restricted to the dangerous work of completing the Transcontinental Railroad. Since these peoples' land and/or labor helped found this country, their histories are part of America's story and their faces and stories belong in books for

At the **Multicultural Pavilion,** find research, activities, and links to other multicultural websites. Go to http://curry.edschool. virginia.edu/go/multicultural/.

Use the CD-ROM database to see the many genres Laurence Yep writes in and create a list of his books.

Find lists of award-winning books on the CD-ROM.

children. Using multicultural literature helps children understand that being American is a matter of where one was born or one's legal status, not how one looks. Through books, we can give children access to the whole picture, showing them that there are Asian Americans, Latinos, African Americans, and American Indians who are part of America's history and who contribute today to this country's beliefs, identity, and values.

Expanding World Views

The varying perspectives offered by multicultural literature can expand children's world views. Many students are not aware that there is more than one way to view the world, people, and events. Multicultural literature helps them understand the existence of multiple viewpoints in very concrete ways. Stories like **Home to Medicine Mountain,** by Chiori Santiago, and **My Name Is SEEPEETZA,** by Shirley Sterling, show American Indian children's reactions to being forced by law to attend schools that sought to erase their native culture. In these books, we also see the point of view of the people who ran these schools.

Through experiencing such books, children discover viewpoints other than the EuroAmerican one. They learn that there is never only *one* story—one objective or true way to look at things. To any given issue or event, we each bring our cultural background and experiences and point of view. One way to help students see this is to use several books on Christopher Columbus's landing in the Americas. Most show the story from Columbus's point of view, but an increasing number—including Michael Dorris's **Morning Girl**—tell the

Readers are taken as far back as 1500 for glimpses of the various peoples who inhabited the place now called Texas.
(From VOICES OF THE ALAMO by Sherry Garland, illustrated by Ronald Himler. Illustration copyright © 2000 by Ronald Himler. Reprinted by permission of Scholastic Inc.)

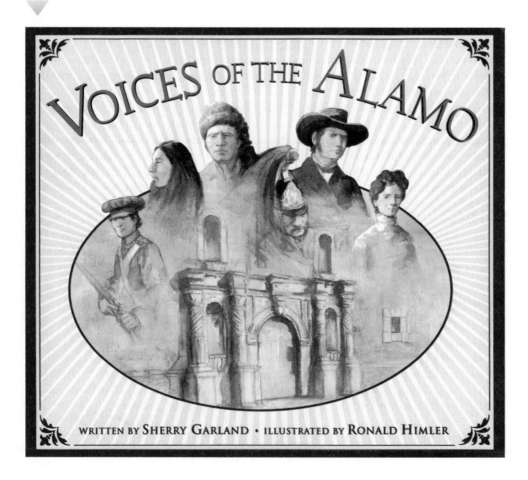

story of Columbus's landing from the point of view of the native people on the shore. By reading Sherry Garland's picture book *Voices of the Alamo,* children can hear the many voices of people over time who inhabited the area where the Alamo was built, and then perhaps talk about the range of views and why there is a difference in the way people think.

Appreciating Cultural Diversity

Through multicultural literature, children can develop an appreciation of and respect for cultural diversity. Children who are members of the majority have always found mirrors in books. Too often they have not been exposed to the views of people of color. Thus, they cannot discover views they can respect, admire, and love. Rudine Sims Bishop (1992) explains that, when they see only people like themselves in books, they get an "exaggerated sense of their own importance. . . . [They are also] denied the benefits of books as windows onto worlds and people different from, and yet similar to, themselves" (p. 20). Thus, they do not have opportunities to develop "a full understanding of what it means to be human, of their connections to all other humans in a world populated by a wide variety of people and cultures" (p. 20).

What better way to address this than by reading multicultural literature? Valerie Flournoy's *The Patchwork Quilt,* illustrated by Jerry Pinkney, shows the centrality of the family reflected in the work on the quilt. *Tea with Milk,* by Allen Say, demonstrates the difficult choice a young Japanese American woman has to make about her future. Gary Soto's *Chato's Kitchen,* an amusing story about a cat who invited a family of mice to dinner, captures the flavor of life in East L.A. culture. A novel with an American Indian as the main protagonist is Joseph Bruchac's *The Heart of a Chief.* Sixth-grader Chris Nicola is shown as a fully developed character concerned about a wide variety of issues, including the stereotyping of American Indians. It takes courage, but he works to help his fellow classmates understand how he feels. In response to a fellow classmate's question about Thanksgiving, he says, "It's kind of funny in a grim way" (p. 109). He goes on to ask his classmates to "Think of what it's like for an Indian kid to go to a school where they're dressing the other kids up in phony Indian costumes with eagle feather headdresses made of paper and cardboard. You feel like they're making fun of your whole culture" (p. 109).

Pat Mora (1998), Latina author and poet, says we need to put literature to work as an art form "that moves readers to hear another human's voice, and thus to experience the doubts, fears, and joys of a person who may not look or sound at all like us" (p. 283).

Another aspect of diversity that can be celebrated through multicultural literature is language diversity or bilingualism. With the growing number of Spanish-speaking people in this country, books are beginning to be published with the story or poems in both Spanish and English. One such picture book for older readers is *It Doesn't Have To Be This Way: A Barrio Story,* by Luis J. Rodríguez. The poetry of Francisco X. Alarcon (see Chapter 5) and Gary Soto is often published in both languages, side by side on the page. Other books are enriched by the inclusion of phrases or vocabulary in the language of the culture being written about. Julia

Use *Bilingual Books for Children* as a resource. Find it at www.ala.org/alsc/bilingual_books_for_children.html.

This is a compelling story, written in both Spanish and English, of a young boy's encounter with the world of gangs, a world the author knows firsthand.

(*It Doesn't Have To Be This Way: A Barrio Story/No tiene que ser así: Una historia del barrio,* story by Luis J. Rodríguez and illustrations by Daniel Galvez. Reprinted with the permission of the publisher, Children's Book Press, San Francisco, CA. Story copyright © 1999 by Luis J. Rodríguez. Illustrations copyright © 1999 by Daniel Galvez.)

Alvarez has written a chapter book, *How Tía Lola Came to ~~Visit~~ Stay,* that is liberally sprinkled with Spanish words and phrases. Many of Gary Soto's books include this feature. When readers see the two languages in print, non–Spanish speakers may gain respect for the ability of others to speak more than one language, while Spanish speakers may feel pride that their home language is being represented.

Promoting Critical Inquiry

Confrontation with the equity issues embedded in multicultural literature can nudge children toward critical inquiry. Children usually have to be helped to question portrayals in literature and to see the subtext, or what lies beneath the surface. Children in the majority culture often are not conscious of racism (the false belief that some races are superior and other races are inferior) and its insidious effects on its targets. One book that touches on the institutional nature of racism is Faith Ringgold's *Tar Beach,* in which Cassie talks about how her dad can't join a union because his father was not a member. She says, "Well, Daddy is going to own that building, 'cause I'm gonna fly over it and give it to him. Then it won't matter that he's not in their old union, or whether he's colored or a half-breed, like they say" (unpaged). Children could easily be drawn into a discussion of how they'd feel if one of their parents were treated this way and why people treat other people this way. What are they assuming about other groups of people? Where do these impressions come from?

Another book that allows children to see how racism hurts is Ken Mochizuki's *Heroes,* in which a young Japanese American boy, Donnie, always has to be the enemy in the games he plays with his friends. One boy "repeated how I always had to be the enemy when we played war because I looked like them." When Donnie protests, telling them that his dad and uncle had been U.S. war heroes, the children reply, "How could your dad or uncle be in our army?" Donnie says that he hates being the enemy, but "Still, it was better than having no friends." Racism and stereotyping are very evident in this book, and children could be drawn into discussions of its effects on Donnie and why the other children make the assumptions they do about him. Where did Donnie's friends get this information? Have they themselves ever seen books with Japanese American families in them? Why is Donnie treated as such an outsider?

Encouraging children to think about how people are depicted in literature and whose point of view is represented is one way to help them begin inquiring critically into all the books and textbooks they read. As Paula Rogovin does with her first-graders (see Chapter 6), you can help children see that the way people of color are viewed is often based on stereotypes, misinformation, or lack of information. Children's varied attitudes toward reading multicultural literature are reflected in the boxed feature Children's Voices.

The Variety of Multicultural Books

In *Reading Against Racism*, Rudine Sims Bishop (1992) identifies four types of multicultural literature: consciously interracial books, "people are people" books, books on the distinctive experience of being within a particular cultural group, and books on coping with racism and discrimination. Multicultural books of all these types exist in every genre of children's literature—picture books, poetry books, and realistic fiction, as well as nonfiction books and biographies. In the boxed feature Multicultural Literature Across Genres, the suggested books in each genre are organized by type. The lists are intended to give you a taste of the abundance of multicultural literature available so that you can integrate it into the curriculum.

Consciously Interracial Books

By "simply including pictures of various and diverse children participating in whatever activity is being depicted" or by focusing on people of different backgrounds interacting with each

Yes! I do like it [multicultural literature]. If I were reading a book about Philipino people, I would like to learn more about them, because my step-mom is Philipino. I like to read about any race. —Lisa, 4th grade

I read a biography and I enjoyed it a lot. I like the biography about Rosa Parks and it was great. —Donnell, 4th grade

*I like to read about characters my own age or from different cultures that live in worlds different from mine. I like **Shabanu, Red Scarf Girl,** and **Dangerous Skies.*** —Carlyn, 7th grade

Most of the books I read have characters from other cultures or races. —Christine, 7th grade

I like books about different cultures. —Fia, 7th grade

I don't care about what race they are, just as long as it's interesting. —Chris, 7th grade

Yes, I enjoy reading about other races. —Samantha, 8th grade

Sometimes especially about how a white and black person got along during slavery. —Dan, 8th grade

I choose to read a book because it interests me, not because of the race of the characters or author. —Hannah, 8th grade

I don't look for multicultural books specifically, but if one sounds good or is recommended to me I have no problem reading it. —Monica, 8th grade

I like to read when Jewish people were in danger with the Nazis around. —Angela, 8th grade

other, some books "project a vision of a multicultural, multiracial society" (Bishop, 1992, p. 23). An example is **Brown Bear, Brown Bear, What Do You See?,** written by Bill Martin, Jr., and illustrated by Eric Carle, which shows children of many colors in school.

"People Are People" Books

Some books feature children of color but make no attempt to reflect a culture distinct from the shared dominant one. The children could be members of any cultural group within the larger society. An example is **Ten, Nine, Eight,** by Molly Bang, which features a black child and her father at bedtime. Done well, this kind of book has the merit of depicting its characters positively as participants in the "mainstream," capturing the universal experiences we all share.

Books on the Distinctive Experience of Being Within a Particular Cultural Group

In books that deal directly with the distinctive experience of being a human being within a particular cultural group, integration is not the focus, even if there are characters from other cultures. Ways in which the distinct culture is reflected may range from a "subtle incorporation of values and attitudes in an otherwise 'people are people' story, to a reflection of distinctive language patterns, to a conscious effort on the part of the author to portray some particular aspect of the specific culture" (Bishop, 1992, p. 24). Examples are Virginia Hamilton's **M. C. Higgins, the Great** and Rosa Guy's **The Friends.** Bishop cautions

Multicultural Literature Across Genres

Picture books

Consciously interracial books

Books that are consciously interracial show a world filled with people of all colors. *Miz Berlin Walks,* written by Jane Yolen and illustrated by Floyd Cooper, is about the relationship between an elderly white woman and a young black girl. *What a Wonderful World,* by George David Weiss and Bob Thiele, shows children's faces of many colors. Aliki's books, such as *My Visit to the Aquarium,* are always filled with representations of people of many ethnic groups and colors.

"People are people" books

"People are people" books focus on the commonality of experiences across cultures. *Emma's Rug,* by Allen Say, is about a small Japanese American girl who is struggling with a belief in herself and her art. *Always My Dad,* by Sharon Dennis Wyeth, is the story of African American children who long for their dad. *More More More Said the Baby,* by Vera B. Williams, is a collection of three stories about adults loving babies, all of whom are from different racial backgrounds. *Daddy Calls Me Man,* by Angela Johnson, is the story of a young African American boy's life with his artist parents. *Max Found Two Sticks,* by Brian Pinkney, tells of an African American boy's love of drumming. While all of these picture books show children of color, none of them focus on specifics about their culture.

Books about the distinctive experience of being within a particular cultural group

In *Uncle Jed's Barbershop,* by Margaree King Mitchell, we see a close-knit family working together and helping each other in the face of discrimination. *Working Cotton,* written by Sherley Anne Williams and illustrated by Carole Byard, pictures one family's day in the cotton fields. *Tar Beach,* by Faith Ringgold, gives a little girl's view of the world of her family. In *The Lotus Seed,* by Sherry Garland, we see the importance of the lotus seed to the Vietnamese grandmother. In *It Doesn't Have To Be This Way: A Barrio Story,* by Luis J. Rodríguez, a young boy becomes involved in the activities of his local gang and is forced by events to decide whether or not to be part of it. *Friends from the Other Side,* by Gloria Anzaldúa, tells how a young boy and his mother are helped by a Mexican American girl after they cross over to Texas. *Jingle Dancer,* by Cynthia Leitich Smith, shows Jenna, who badly wants to be part of the traditional jingle dance, working to secure enough jingles so that her dress will sing at the upcoming powwow. *SkySisters,* by Jan Bourdeau Waboose, tells of the night journey of two Ojibway sisters to see the SkySpirits, or Northern Lights. *Arctic Stories,* by Michael Arvaarluk Kusagak, describes what life is like in the Arctic for a small girl called Agatha. All of these stories show us the characters immersed in their culturally distinctive environments.

Books on coping with racism and discrimination

In Andrea Davis Pinkney's *Dear Benjamin Banneker,* Banneker, although born free, never stops working for the freedom of his people. *The Invisible Princess,* by Faith Ringgold, describes how the princess could deal with the discrimination of the time by becoming invisible. *Richard Wright and the Library Card,* by William Miller, shows the lengths Wright had to go to in order to check out library books. In *Baseball Saved Us,* by Ken Mochizuki, a little boy emerges from the internment camps only to face more discrimination. *Virgie Goes to School with Us Boys,* by Elizabeth Fitzgerald Howard, tells of the Quaker school black children attended after the Civil War because they were not allowed into public schools. In *Momma, Where Are You From?,* by Marie Bradby, a mother tells her daughter about her life in the segregated South.

Poetry

Books about the distinctive experience of being within a particular cultural group

Most multicultural poetry books display elements of a specific cultural group; books in this category include *Laughing Out Loud, I Fly: Poems in English and Spanish,* by Juan Felipe Herrera; *Canto Familiar,* by Gary Soto; *Cool Salsa: Bilingual Poems on Growing Up Latino in the United States,* edited by Lori M. Carlsen; *My Name Is Jorge: On Both Sides of the River,* by Jane Medina (all about the Mexican American experience); *Good Luck Gold and Other Poems,* by Janet S. Wong (on the Asian American experience); *Soul Looks Back in Wonder,* by Tom Feelings; *Pass It On: African-American Poetry for Children,* edited by Wade Hudson (on the African American experience); *Thirteen Moons on Turtle's Back,* a collection of storytelling poems by Joseph Bruchac and Jonathan London; *When the Rain Sings: Poems by Young Native Americans,* edited by the National Museum of the American Indian (on the American Indian experience); and *19 Varieties of Gazelle: Poems of the Middle East,* by Naomi Shihab Nye (on the Arab experience).

Nonfiction and biography

Books about the distinctive experience of being within a particular cultural group

Nonfiction books written about a specific people include *Bowman's Store: A Journey to Myself,* by Joseph Bruchac; *Under the Royal Palms: A Childhood in Cuba,* by Alma Flor Ada; *Sacajawea,* by Joseph Bruchac; *Fiesta Fireworks* and *Barrio: José's Neighborhood,* both by George Ancona; *Ininatig's Gift of Sugar: Traditional Native Sugarmaking,* by Laura Waterman Wittstock; *Clambake: A Wampanoag*

Tradition, by Russell M. Peters; and *Songs from the Loom: A Navajo Girl Learns to Weave,* by Monty Roessel.

Books on coping with racism and discrimination

Books that directly address racism and discrimination include *Bound for America: The Forced Migration of Africans to the New World,* by James Haskins and Kathleen Benson; *Now Is Your Time: The African-American Struggle for Freedom* and *Amistad: A Long Road to Freedom,* both by Walter Dean Myers; *Desert Exile: The Uprooting of a Japanese-American Family,* by Yoshiko Uchida; *Warriors Don't Cry: A Searing Memoir of the Battle to Integrate Little Rock's Central High,* by Melba Pattillo Beals; *At Her Majesty's Request: An African Princess in Victorian England,* by Walter Dean Myers; *Osceola: Memories of a Sharecropper's Daughter,* edited by Alan B. Govenar; *My Name Is SEEPEETZA,* by Shirley Sterling; *Letters from a Slave Girl: The Story of Harriet Jacobs,* by Mary E. Lyons; *Sojourner Truth: Ain't I a Woman?,* by Patricia C. McKissack and Fredrick L. McKissack; *Through My Eyes,* by Ruby Bridges; and *Leon's Story,* by Leon Walter Tillage.

Traditional stories

Books about the distinctive experience of being within a particular cultural group

Traditional stories that focus on one culture and its view of the world include *When the Chenoo Howls: Native American Tales of Terror,* by Joseph Bruchac and James Bruchac; *Uncle Remus: The Complete Tales,* by Julius Lester; *The Adventures of Brother Sparrow, Sis Wren and Their Friends,* by Virginia Hamilton; *Moaning Bones: African-American Ghost Stories,* by Jim Haskins; *The Ch'I-Lin Purse: A Collection of Ancient Chinese Stories,* by Linda Fang; *The Lizard and the Sun/La Lagartija y El Sol: A Folktale in English and Spanish,* by Alma Flor Ada; and *Golden Tales: Myths, Legends, and Folktales from Latin America,* by Lulu Delacre.

Historical fiction

Books about the distinctive experience of being within a particular cultural group

Books that provide a picture of a specific time period within a specific culture include *Morning Girl, Sees Behind Trees,* and *Guests,* by Michael Dorris; *Dragonwings,* by Laurence Yep; and *Children of the Longhouse* and *Arrow Over the Door,* both by Joseph Bruchac.

Books on coping with racism and discrimination

Books on coping with racism and discrimination include *In the Time of the Wolves,* by Eileen Charbonneau; *Dragon's Gate* and *The Journal of Wong Ming-Chung: A Chinese Miner,* both by Laurence Yep; *Roll of Thunder, Hear My Cry,* by Mildred D. Taylor; *A Jar of Dreams,* by Yoshiko Uchida; and *Shota and the Star Quilt,* by Margaret Bateson-Hill.

Realistic fiction

Books about the distinctive experience of being within a particular cultural group

More and more realistic fiction today shows what it's like being part of a particular cultural group. Books in this category include *Yang the Third and Her Impossible Family,* by Lensey Namioka; *Cousins* and *Second Cousins,* by Virginia Hamilton; *The Heart of a Chief,* by Joseph Bruchac; *Thief of Hearts* and *The Case of the Lion Dance (Chinatown Mystery No. 2),* both by Laurence Yep; *The Window,* by Michael Dorris; *Have a Happy* and *Justin and the Best Biscuits in the World,* both by Mildred Pitts Walter; *Fast Sam, Cool Clyde, and Stuff,* by Walter Dean Myers; and *Zeely, The House of Dies Drear,* and *Bluish: A Novel,* all by Virginia Hamilton.

Books on coping with racism and discrimination

Books that deal with issues of discrimination and racism include *F Is for Fabuloso,* by Marie G. Lee; *Yang the Second and Her Secret Admirers,* by Lensey Namioka; and *The Bracelet,* by Yoshiko Uchida.

Short stories

Books about the distinctive experience of being within a particular cultural group

The following collections of stories, written by an author from that culture, include many cultural elements: *My Land Sings: Stories from the Rio Grande,* by Rudolfo Anaya; *Salsa Stories,* by Lulu Delacre; *El Bronx Remembered: A Novella and Stories,* by Nicholasa Mohr; *Tales from Gold Mountain: Stories of the Chinese in the New World,* by Paul Yee; *Gone from Home,* by Angela Johnson; *145th Street: Short Stories,* by Walter Dean Myers; and *Turtle Meat and Other Stories,* by Joseph Bruchac.

Fantasy

Books about the distinctive experience of being within a particular cultural group

Most fantasy by people of color incorporates some elements that make the culture distinctive. Books in this category include *Justice and Her Brothers, Dustland, The Gathering,* and *Sweet Whispers, Brother Rush,* all by Virginia Hamilton, and *Dragon of the Lost Sea,* by Laurence Yep.

This delightful counting book portrays characters of color as visible parts of society, although it does not deal with any distinctive experiences of this group.

(Cover art from *Ten, Nine, Eight* by Molly Bang, copyright © 1983. Used by permission of HarperCollins Publishers.)

readers not to generalize from a story to a whole culture. She points out, "The experience of any one group is not monolithic. Reflecting 'the black experience' in the USA, for example, does not mean that a book must be set in the inner city and feature characters who are economically poor" (p. 24).

Books on Coping with Racism and Discrimination

The most powerful books about racism and discrimination set in the United States are the historical novels of Mildred D. Taylor. Ruby Bridges's autobiography ***Through My Eyes*** fits in this category too, as it shows how Ruby and her family coped with the physical, emotional, and economic costs of integrating a school. Ruby talks movingly about her discovery that people were yelling ugly things because of the color of her skin.

Favorite Authors and Illustrators of Color

In selecting multicultural books, it helps to know the names of authors and illustrators who produce high-quality books. The list in the boxed feature Favorite Authors and Illustrators of Color provides a sampling and should not be construed as an exhaustive list.

The Issue of Writing Outside One's Culture or Race

One of the biggest issues in multicultural books is whether the people written about are authentically represented. One way to resolve the authenticity issue is to have only people who are part of a culture write about it. Although this would provide readers with "insider" insights and perceptions, it is an overly simplistic solution to a complex issue.

Many prolific, well-respected authors are offended by the suggestion that they cannot write a book that accurately represents a culture outside of their own. With careful research and immersion in a culture, they believe that they have the ability to write from many perspectives. Jane Yolen

Each poem appears in both English and Spanish, encouraging readers to compare the languages and to appreciate the differences.

(Cover art from *Laughing Out Loud, I Fly: Poems in English and Spanish* by Juan Felipe Herrera, illustrated by Karen Barbour. Used by permission of HarperCollins Publishers.)

Favorite Authors and Illustrators of Color

African American

Carole Byard, award-winning illustrator, creates pictures with an impressionistic quality, which contribute to the mood and emotions evoked by the story.

Floyd Cooper, illustrator and author, is best known for his glowing watercolor paintings and stunning biographies of African American notables.

Niki Daly, South African author and illustrator, is known for his picture books filled with gentle watercolors, which draw readers deeper into the story.

Leo and Diane Dillon, renowned husband and wife illustrators, produce rich, sophisticated drawings that have been described as opulent, magical, and a feast for the eyes.

Sharon Draper, author, writes poetry and novels that older elementary and middle schools students can relate to.

Tom Feelings, illustrator, creates hauntingly beautiful paintings for the books he illustrates.

Eloise Greenfield, author, writes picture books and poems that glow with love.

Nikki Grimes, poet and author, writes with a zest and feeling that bring us into the heart of her poems and stories.

Virginia Hamilton, author, writes beautiful fiction, nonfiction, traditional tales, and fantasy. Her careful use of language and feel for rhythm and sound qualities make her works a joy to read.

Angela Johnson, author, writes poetry, picture books, and novels. Her use of language is notable.

Julius Lester, author, paints beautiful pictures with his words when he writes novels, nonfiction, picture books, and traditional tales.

E. B. Lewis, illustrator, is known for his evocative watercolors, often based on extensive research to guarantee accuracy.

Patricia McKissack, author, always writes with passion, whether her genre is historical fiction, biography, fiction, or nonfiction. Much of her work is a beautiful tribute to those who have helped clear the way to freedom and dignity.

Christopher Myers, illustrator and poet, has won acclaim with his first two books.

Walter Dean Myers, author, has garnered many awards for his poetry, short stories, novels, photo picture books, and nonfiction books.

Andrea Davis Pinkney, author, uses an energetic, expressive style to tell her stories.

Brian Pinkney, illustrator, is best known for his bold use of the scratchboard technique in his handsome, distinctive illustrations.

Jerry Pinkney, illustrator, paints luminous but delicate-looking watercolors for the multitude of books he illustrates for children.

Faith Ringgold, author, artist, illustrator, and quilter, is known for her colorful paintings in the naive style.

Synthia Saint James, artist, is known for the bold, bright colors in her cut art.

Javaka Steptoe, illustrator, develops his designs three-dimensionally, using objects, paper collage, and other materials.

John Steptoe, author and illustrator, is known for his groundbreaking work in bringing images and stories of African American children into the literature. He writes with compassion and illustrates in vibrant, glowing colors that emanate warmth and beauty.

Mildred Pitts Walter, prolific author, puts her storytelling talents to work in the tales, picture books, novels, and nonfiction she writes.

Jacqueline Woodson, author, writes novels, poetry, and picture books that burst with life.

Sharon Dennis Wyeth, author, writes picture books and novels, which often include biracial children.

American Indian

Joseph Brubrac, Abenaki storyteller and author, writes novels, nonfiction, picture books, and traditional tales. He is well known for his work on the *Keepers of the Earth* series.

Louise Erdrich, author, is best known for her novels for adults but has begun to write novels for children.

Michael Arvaarluk Kusagak, Inuit author, writes his tales of the Arctic in a simple, direct way, reflective of a storyteller's style.

Michael Lacapa, Hopi and Apache illustrator and author, is known for using strong lines and bold geographic shapes in his illustrations.

George Littlechild, Plains Cree artist, illustrates children's books with vibrant multimedia collage paintings that feature startling, wide-awake colors.

(continued)

Cynthia Leitich Smith, a mixed-blood member of the Muscogee (Creek) Nation, features contemporary Indian life in both her picture book and her first novel.

Virginia Driving Hawk Sneve, Rosebud Sioux author, writes in a quiet, uncomplicated manner. In addition to writing Native American folk tales, she has produced a series of books called *First American Books,* which explain the background of many native nations.

Clifford Trafzer (Richard Red Hawk), author, writes mainly nonfiction for older readers, although he does have a few books for early elementary children.

Asian American

Sook Nyul Choi, Korean American author, writes poignant, moving novels and picture books based on her experiences in escaping from Japanese rule and being an immigrant in a new country.

Yangsook Choi, Korean American illustrator, captures the mood and period of the books she illustrates. She paints spare yet elegant pictures, in colors ranging from vivid to muted.

Sheila Hamanaka, Japanese American artist and author, writes picture storybooks, nonfiction, and folk tales. Her dramatic, vibrant illustrations are done in watercolor, oil, and even paper collage.

Minfong Ho, Thai American author, writes charming rhythmic poems, as well as picture books and novels based on experiences in Thailand and Cambodia.

Benrie Huang, Taiwan-born artist, has illustrated more than twenty-five picture books. Her illustrations are often rounded and soft-toned, and her compositions offer a variety of perspectives.

Dom Lee, Korean American illustrator, is known for his evocative illustrations. Expressive faces, often done in sepia tones, give his pictures the quality of old photographs.

Huy Voun Lee, Cambodian illustrator and author, is known for her masterful use of pattern. She creates visually captivating illustrations with cut-paper collage and rich details.

Jeanne M. Lee, Chinese American author and illustrator, often retells tales and illustrates them in brilliant colors with stylized drawings.

Marie G. Lee, Korean American author, writes sensitive stories about adjusting to life in a new country and surviving as an ethnic minority.

Grace Lin, Chinese American illustrator, is known for her lively, color-saturated paintings.

Ken Mochizuki, Japanese American author, has written award-winning picture books dealing with the racism that Japanese Americans have had to face.

Lensey Namioka, Japanese American author, writes poignant, funny stories dealing with family situations, which often involve conflict over the pull of two cultures.

Ching Yeung Russell, Chinese American author, writes loosely autobiographical novels and picture books that are filled with rich cultural details of China in the 1940s.

Allen Say, Japanese American author and illustrator, focuses mainly on picture books. He began as an illustrator of others' work but now writes and illustrates his own books.

Chris Soentpiet, Korean-born illustrator, creates richly detailed, dramatic illustrations that are beautifully lit and strongly realistic.

Yoshiko Uchida, Japanese American author, writes lively stories, which often portray the pain of rejection as well as the spirit of determination.

Janet Wong, Chinese Korean American poet, touches the heart of human experience with her sometimes funny, sometimes sarcastic, always sensitive poems.

Paul Yee, Chinese Canadian author, writes hard-hitting, honest short stories, novels, and picture books, which often focus on aspects of life as an ethnic minority.

Laurence Yep, Chinese American author, is a prolific storyteller who writes beautifully in many genres, including realistic and historical fiction, fantasy, picture books, and short stories.

Ed Young, Chinese American illustrator, has won the Caldecott Medal for his complex use of color and shadow. His impressionistic compositions capture the emotional content of the scenes.

Latino/Chicano

Alma Flor Ada, Cuban American author, captures the authentic flavor of Latin culture in her folk tales, poetry, and novels. She also writes picture books based on inventive versions of fairy tales.

Francisco X. Alarcon, award-winning Chicano poet and educator, has written three collections of seasonal poems for young people, all of which are playful, moving, and inspirational.

Rodolfo Anaya, Mexican American author and renowned storyteller, although mainly a writer for adults, also writes lyrical folk tales and picture books for children.

Lulu Delacre, Puerto Rican American author, writes evocative, often touching stories, well integrated with cultural details.

David Diaz, Mexican American illustrator and Caldecott winner, is known for his use of bold colors, his innate sense of design, and his naive-style incandescent illustrations.

Carmen Lomas Garza, renowned Chicana illustrator, often uses cut-paper art in her vibrant narrative paintings, which sing out with pride in her Mexican American heritage.

Susan Guevara, illustrator, creates paintings that beg to be pored over for their detailed, richly colored depictions.

Juan Felipe Herrera, a bilingual poet and picture book author, writes poetry that can be understood more with the heart than with the head and lyrical prose that often speaks to the new immigrant experience.

Nicholasa Mohr, Puerto Rican American author, touches the heart of Puerto Rican pride with her many novels about growing up.

Pat Mora, Latina author, writes picture books, poetry, and novels that sparkle with love and respect for her Mexican heritage.

Luis J. Rodríguez, Chicano author, has turned to writing children's books. His books about what an immigrant child faces have a strong sense of immediacy.

Enrique O. Sanchez, illustrator, uses warm glowing colors and stylized figures, which make his work eye-catching and evocative.

Gary Soto, Mexican American author, writes poetry, short stories, picture books, and novels evocative of his experiences in the Mexican American community.

(1997) says, "When a child at a bookstore where I was giving a reading asked me, 'You are Jewish, so how come you can write *Hark! A Christmas Sampler*?' I answered: 'I have written murder mysteries, too'" (p. 289).

Rudine Sims Bishop (1992) believes, "The issue of perspective—when evaluating books about people of color—is often over-simplified to the question of whether whites can or should write about people of color" (p. 31). She points out that this issue is made more complicated by the subtle way attitudes are formed and synthesized in each of us: "Unfortunately, writers who are members of non-dominant groups are not immune from having absorbed some of the negative attitudes held about their own group by others, and these stereotypic attitudes towards their own group will be reflected in their work" (p. 31). Bishop suggests, "Some white writers, from their own vantage point, can create works about blacks that are positive and noteworthy" (p. 31). For her, "The race of the author is not the point—the perspective of the author is what matters" (p. 31). Ultimately, the success of a book will be determined by "how effectively it succeeds in fulfilling the author's purpose or in satisfying the readers' needs" (p. 31).

Philip Lee (1999), publisher, agrees with Bishop: "The ethnicity of the authors and artists is an important factor, but by no means do we feel that it is a requirement." Lee & Low has published multicultural stories by authors and illustrators from both within and outside the culture of the story. In an interview with Sloan (1999), Lee says, "Our experience has shown us that the same background authors/artists can often bring an additional personal identification to the story. However, it would be wrong to assume that they are automatically experts in their ethnic heritage" (p. 30).

Lee offers *Baseball Saved Us* as an example. Author Ken Mochizuki, a Japanese American born and raised in Seattle, had parents who were sent to the internment camp in Minidoka, California. Since "he was not born until after their internment, he had to spend a great deal of time researching historical articles and interviewing members of the Japanese American baseball league to achieve a historically authentic story in spite of his ethnic heritage" (p. 30).

Lee explains that the illustrator, Dom Lee, was selected not only because of his powerful imagery but also because he is a big sports fan. Being from Korea, he knew little about the internment history. "So he too went searching for factual materials, working with the Baseball Hall of Fame and studying the photographs of Ansel Adams, who was the only person officially allowed to take pictures of the camps" (p. 30). After Lee received Ken's manuscript and Dom's sketches, he contacted former internees in the New York area for fact-checking. They were able to offer comments that led to changes in the text and the art. "Clearly, even with an all Asian American team of a Japanese American author, a Korean American illustrator, and a Chinese American editor, we had to do extensive research to ensure the authenticity of *Baseball Saved Us*" (p. 30). The resulting story was not only an Asian American story but also a sports story.

Dom Lee's moving illustrations add power to the story of how baseball provided Japanese American children with a purpose while they endured injustice and hardships in internment camps during World War II.

(*Baseball Saved Us* text copyright © 1993 by Ken Mochizuki. Illustrations copyright 1993 by Dom Lee. Permissions arranged with LEE & LOW BOOKS INC., New York, NY 10016.)

Writers who step beyond their lived experiences need to carefully research and explore the cultural group they portray in order to avoid perpetuating stereotypical images and erroneous cultural information. When an author writes outside of his or her culture, careful research, respect for the people being written about, immersion in the culture, and a willingness to seek out people from the subject group to read the manuscript are key.

Using Multicultural Literature in the Classroom

Finding high-quality, appropriate multicultural literature isn't enough. While it is important to use books that give an honest view of the diversity that exists in America, if we don't discuss the literature in a meaningful way with our students, the literature may have little impact. Here are some guidelines for discussing multicultural literature.

1. Discuss the content of the literature. Teaching skills through multicultural literature without discussing what is in the text does little to help children understand other people. Use the books to open up children's minds and cultivate their respect and appreciation for other cultures.

2. Share commonalities (how people are alike), but also talk about differences. After reading *We Had a Picnic This Sunday Past,* by Jacqueline Woodson, ask children to describe their family gatherings. If their family had a picnic, what range of people might be invited? What kinds of food would be served? How would their picnics be different? What did they learn about this African American extended family and what is important to them? Reading books about people of color should lead to reflection that might eventually change children's perspective on others.

3. Out of respect for the culture, don't simplify it by looking only at food, fashion, folklore, and festival. Daphne Muse (1999), African American writer and educator, says, "The tourist approach to literature—relating to people as if they lived in a travel poster—undermines the fact that these people have values, intellect and standards" (p. 12). To understand how the tourist approach reduces a culture to an almost unrecognizable caricature, imagine teaching EuroAmerican culture in another country by looking at McDonald's hamburgers (food), blue jeans and sneakers (fashion), stories of the wild west (folklore), and the celebration of Halloween (festival), with no mention of democratic values. Although these items are certainly a part of our culture, they in no way come close to representing the richness and depth of that culture.

The boxed feature Taking a Look at the Research: Listening to the Voices of Those You Wish to Include discusses other issues raised by the use of multicultural literature in the classroom (see page 214).

Evaluating Multicultural Literature

As with any literature, literary qualities must be considered before we decide whether a multicultural book merits a place in our classroom. Multicultural books also have to be looked at in terms of sociopolitical considerations, since we would not want to provide children with erroneous or distorted perceptions of a culture. In addition, educational considerations come into play, as we must look at our purpose for teaching the book.

Literary Considerations

The literary elements are plot, character, setting, theme, and writing style (see Chapter 2):

1. Is the plot engaging?

2. Are the characters well developed?

3. Does the setting connect to the story?

4. Is the theme rich and interesting to students?

5. Will the writing be pleasing to children?

Educational Considerations

1. What educational purpose is the book intended to serve?

2. What seems to be the purpose of the book?

3. Who is the implied audience?

4. Does the book have the potential to promote critical discussions?

5. Does the book illuminate differences or provide factual information about people and their way of life?

Sociopolitical Considerations

1. How are the characters depicted? Are they complex individuals or simple stereotypes? Are a range of characters represented? Does the description ring true in terms of physical appearance, behaviors, attitudes, values, language, beliefs, way of life, and culture?

*For resources, go to the **Annotated Bibliography of Children's Literature Focusing on Latino People, History, and Culture** at http://clnet.ucr.edu/ Latino_Bibliography.html.*

CD-ROM

To locate authors known for their strong characterizations, do a word search for *character* under Favorite Authors.

taking a look at the Research

Listening to the Voices of Those You Wish to Include

Merely including different ethnicities, religions, races, family groups, and abilities in the literature is not helpful if negative stereotypes are presented about any group. As Debbie Reese (1996) describes in her work on American Indian literature for young children, many books actually perpetuate stereotypes and misrepresent American Indians. For example, often texts suggest that American Indians no longer exist and misguide students into thinking that all American Indians wear buckskin and feathers and live in teepees. Such misrepresentation encourages children to overgeneralize and ignores the complex cultures of the over 500 diverse groups included in the term *American Indian* (Reese, 1996). Similarly, it is not uncommon for Africa to be referred to as a single country, rather than a continent with over 50 countries, each of which has distinctly different political, cultural, and spiritual traditions.

Combatting the stereotypes and overgeneralizations that surface in children's literature is an issue in representations of all cultural, racial, religious, ability, and family groups. To ensure that stereotypes are not woven through a story, it is important to check texts for authenticity before sharing them with children. Texts should be historically accurate and have rich, multidimensional characters.

Relying on books that have earned honors and awards is not enough to ensure the absence of stereotypes. Some past winners of the prestigious Newbery Award, for example, reflect the racial and ethnic prejudices of their day. For example, in the 1927 medal winner *Smoky, the Cowhorse*, by Will James, the first Latino minor character is portrayed as thieving and inhumane. In *Daniel Boone*, by James Daugherty, the 1940 winner, Daniel refers to American Indians as "savages." The same term is used to describe black minor characters in the 1941 winner, *Call It Courage*, by Armstrong Sperry (Gillespie, Powell, Clements, & Swearingen, 1994).

Reese (1996) offers teaching suggestions and positive strategies for including American Indian themes in the classroom. She encourages choosing themes that will help children develop an understanding of the cultures, spiritual practices, and contemporary lives of many different tribes and selecting well-written stories with authentic characterizations, plots, and settings.

In order to include multicultural children's literature in our classrooms without perpetuating stereotyping, we must seek out and listen to the thoughts and feelings of those who are being portrayed in the books. All too often, groups who are not the object of the offending stereotype are slow to notice it and react defensively when concern is expressed. Sometimes these voices are difficult to hear because we want to defend our attachment when some favorite piece of children's literature is attacked. But the benefits of incorporating multicultural children's literature in the classroom are easily outweighed by the negative effects of using books that demonstrate stereotypes. How can we, as teachers, say that prejudice and discrimination are wrong but continue to teach works that perpetuate through stereotype?

Gillespie, C. S., J. L. Powell, N. E. Clements, and R. A. Swearingen (1994). "A Look at the Newbery Medal Books from a Multicultural Perspective." *The Reading Teacher 48*, 40–50.

Reese, Debbie (1996). *Teaching Young Children about Native Americans* (Report No. DERR93002007). Champaign, IL: Clearinghouse on Elementary and Early Childhood Education (ERIC Document Reproduction Service No. EDO-PS-96-3).

2. How is the family depicted? Who is missing and who is included?

3. Who are the heroes of the story? What do they accomplish?

4. How do the characters resolve the dilemma they face? What is the role of family and close friends? Are majority characters always the saviors?

5. Is the diversity of the cultural community (color, socioeconomic level, urban/rural) evident?

6. Who wrote the story? Who did the illustrations? What does the book jacket or Author's Note say about their familiarity with the culture?

In the boxed feature Applying the Criteria: Evaluating Sociopolitical Considerations, these criteria are applied to *Francie,* by Karen English. The book was a Coretta Scott King Honor winner in 2000.

Applying the Criteria *Evaluating Sociopolitical Considerations*

Francie, by Karen English.

Synopsis: Francie, by Karen English, is written from the point of view of an African American girl in eighth grade in the South sometime before 1960. It shows Francie, her community, her school, and the segregated town she lives outside of. Francie cares deeply about her hard-working mom, her sometimes pesky little brother, and her dad, who is in Chicago working as a Pullman porter to make enough money to bring the family north. Francie is smart but often outspoken, especially around white people. When the 16-year-old boy she has tutored in reading is being hunted by the townsfolk for supposedly attacking a white man, she tries to help and gets embroiled in more than she counted on. Because of the overt racism and because Francie's mom knows that Francie's passion and caring will get her in trouble in the South, her mother decides to move to Chicago on the money she has saved.

1. **How are the characters depicted?** We see many kinds of black people and many kinds of white people in this novel. Francie and her mom, whom we get to know best, are shown as complex, multidimensional characters. We get a clear picture of how Francie's mom has to behave around white people to get along. The descriptions of dress, hair, attitudes, behaviors, values, and language ring true for the time period and locale. The mother is clearly respected by the children and takes the switch to them when she thinks it's necessary. Within the black community in the book, we see differences in temperament, behavior, and social class. Francie's family is poor but values education and work, focuses on keeping their house and clothes very clean, and is shown as very respectable. Jesse Pruit, the boy who wants to start school at age 16, is from a very poor motherless family which doesn't see any benefit to an education. Francie considers him poor. We see one gossipy neighbor, as well as an aunt who is helped by many relatives and friends because she is ill after giving birth.

2. **How is the family depicted?** Francie's dad is not living with the family, but they get letters and money from him. Her brother's best friend has both a father and a mother in the home. Because the story focuses on Francie, we see more of her and her mother than anybody else.

3. **Who are the heroes of the story?** Francie is viewed as a hero because she tries to help the wrongly accused boy. Her mother is also seen as a hero for working seven days a week to keep the family together while she saves to go to Chicago to join her husband. She is also shown helping her neighbors when they need help. Jesse is also a hero of sorts because he has the wits to escape the whites who hunt him and eventually make it to California.

4. **How do the characters resolve the dilemma they face?** Francie resolves her dilemma with one white girl who treats her terribly by being clever and figuring out how to subtly put the girl in her place. She resolves the dilemma of helping her starving friend, Jesse, by providing food and support for him when she can. Mama resolves her own dilemma of wanting to be in Chicago with her husband by working seven days a week and somehow saving money for railroad tickets. Family and close friends are an important part of this story. We see how members of the black community help each other and how close friends are integral to their lifestyle. Although one white girl is shown being helpful at figuring out how to get Francie's brother and friend back home after they've been accused of helping the fugitive, her role isn't pivotal.

5. **Is the diversity of the cultural community (color, socioeconomic level, urban/rural) evident?** Although most of the community is extremely poor because discrimination allows them no equitable work opportunities, there is diversity of skin color and occupations, as well as some socioeconomic variations.

6. **Who wrote the story? What does the book jacket or Author's Note say about her familiarity with the culture?** The book jacket had no picture or other information indicating that the author was African American. However, before I knew she was indeed African American because only African Americans are given the Coretta Scott King Award, I had figured it out from the fact that her writing so beautifully captures the intimacy of the day-to-day life this family led. Also, Francie's comments about trying to manage her hair and the attitudes of the people rang true to me.

Because this book presents a warm, intimate, non-stereotypical view of Francie and her family, it could be a good choice to use in the classroom. But before that decision can be made, other educational considerations have to be examined.

Francie, a Coretta Scott King Award winner, tells of an inventive and courageous 13-year-old who faces life in a racist society head on.
(Jacket design by Tim Hall from FRANCIE by Karen English. Copyright © 1999 by Karen English. Reprinted by permission of Farrar, Straus and Giroux, LLC.)

International Books

Wonderful books are published all around the world. As the world becomes smaller and countries come to depend on each other for global solutions to global problems, we must educate students to be world citizens. Only if they have a broad understanding of the multitude of world cultures can they make informed decisions about the future. Because they are written in a different voice from a different perspective, translated books provide understanding that cannot be gained from books written by someone from our culture about another culture. When authors within a country write books for children in that country, they write differently than they would if they were writing for an American audience.

In 1967, noted librarian Mildred L. Batchelder (cited in Dickman, 1999) powerfully made the case for international children's literature:

> When children know that they are reading in translation the same stories that children in another country are reading, a sense of nearness grows and expands. Interchange of children's books between countries, through translation, influences communication between the peoples of these countries, and if the books chosen for traveling from language to language are worthy books, the resulting communication may be deeper, richer, more sympathetic, more enduring. (p. 22)

Since international stories are also about different cultures, international literature has the same benefits as multicultural literature. But through its focus on other countries, international literature can also do other things.

International literature can show children cultures in the present. Although children may have read folk tales about old Japan or old Ireland, often they don't know what these countries are like today. They don't have any idea how children in other countries spend their time. Books that show children in the present include *I'm José and I'm O.K.,* by Werner Holzwarth (Bolivia); *Nina Bonita,* by Ana Maria Machado (Brazil); *Will Goes to the Post Office,* by Olof Landstrom and Lena Landstrom (Sweden); and *I'll Take You to Mrs. Cole,* by Nigel Gray (Great Britain).

By revealing the complexity of the people and culture, international literature can bring other countries to life for children and cut down on stereotyping and ungrounded assumptions. With only blurry, indistinct impressions of different parts of the world, children may not even know that other people drive cars or have technology. Lack of knowledge may lead children to assume that other countries are not modern. Particularly notable for offering a peek into life in other countries are *The Tiny Kite of Eddie Wing,* by Maxine Trottier (Canada); *Paul and Sebastian,* by René Escudié (France); *The Park Bench,* by Fumido Takeshita (Japan); *Grandpa's Town,* by Takaaki Nomura (Japan); *Goodbye Rune,* by Marit Kaldhol (Norway); *The Mats,* by Francisco Arcellana (Philippines); *Jon's Moon,* by Carme Solé Vendrell (Spain); *Brush,* by Pere Calders (Spain); and *A Bicycle for Rosaura,* by Daniel Barbot (Venezuela).

By building interest in other countries, international literature can motivate children to pay closer attention to the geographical and historical content often found in textbooks. Reading excellent stories about the people in a particular place can pave the way to greater interest when children confront the place in textbooks. Books that make places and people

For an abundance of links, go to **Multicultural and International Literature Links** *at http://home. earthlink.net/~elbond/ multicultural.htm.*

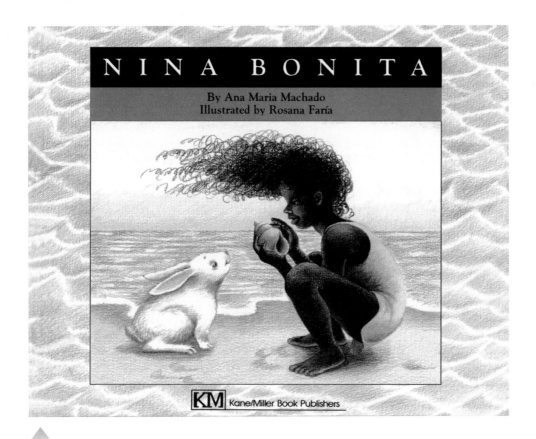

N I N A B O N I T A

By Ana Maria Machado
Illustrated by Rosana Faría

KM Kane/Miller Book Publishers

Nina Bonita is about a young girl living in today's Brazil who is admired for her dark skin color.
(From *Nina Bonita* by Ana Maria Machado, illustrated by Rosana Faría. American text copyright © 1996 Kane/Miller Publishers. All rights reserved. Used by permission of Kane/Miller Book Publishers.)

come alive include *Star of Fear, Star of Hope,* by Jo Hoestlandt (France); *The Red Comb,* by Fernando Picó (Puerto Rico); *Shin's Tricycle,* by Tatsuharu Kodama (Japan); *My Place,* by Nadia Wheatley and Donna Rawlins (Australia); and *Waiting for the Rain: A Novel of South Africa,* by Sheila Gordon (South Africa).

Which Countries Do International Books Come From?

The majority of international books come from English-speaking countries with similar traditions (Canada, Great Britain, Australia, and New Zealand). Oftentimes we're not even aware that books come from another country because they seem so solidly a part of our literature. Young readers are often familiar with the works of Shirley Hughes (Great Britain), Mem Fox (Australia), Margaret Mahy (New Zealand), and Brian Wildsmith (Great Britain). Older readers know the works of Graeme Base (Australia) and Anthony Browne (Great Britain). Although very different in topic and theme from U.S. books, books from South Africa do find their way here because English is one of the languages of that country.

A significant number of children's books from Japan, a country with a particularly well-established literary tradition, are translated into English and published in this country. Mitsumasa Anno's books such as *Anno's Journey* and *All in a Day* are very popular here. *Hiroshima No Pika,* by Toshi Maruki, is an award-winning book from Japan. France, Sweden, Switzerland, Germany, and the Netherlands are some of the countries in Western Europe from which we draw many children's books. We also get books from Israel and Greece, and some books from parts of Africa and South and Central America are now being offered in translation.

*Find a list of recent international honor books at **International Board on Books for Young People** at www.ibby.org/Seiten/ 03_archiv.htm.*

According to Susan Stan (1999), a children's literature expert who has done research on international books, few of the children's books coming out of Russia and China would be considered appropriate for sale in this country, largely because political conditions there dictate that books be published to instruct or indoctrinate. Little literature comes from Africa and India because the multiple languages and lower literacy rates make it difficult to internally support the costs of publishing. Since "the size of the book buying market, the literacy rates, the reading habits of a people, and the wealth of the nation are all critical factors in supporting an ongoing indigenous publishing program, publishing any children's books seems to be an impossible task wherever some or many of these elements are missing" (Stan, 1999, p. 171).

Another concern Stan addresses is that international fare is not reflective of the world's literature for children, since "most of the children's literature from outside our borders comes from places with people who see the world much as we do and is then edited to conform even more strictly to our world view" (p. 175). Fortunately, such a tendency has not prevented some distinctly "other" books from making it into publication, such as *Pheasant and Kingfisher,* by Catherine Helen Berndt; *The Friends,* by Kazumi Yumoto; *Linnea in Monet's Garden,* by Christina Björk; *The Red Comb,* by Fernando Picó; and *Winter Rescue,* by W. D. Valgardson. These books "do not repackage the world into a form most comfortable for American readers but take them on new journeys into unfamiliar and exciting territories" (p. 176).

Kane/Miller, a publisher specializing in translated children's books, does offer books from distinctly different points of view and books that describe life in the present in a foreign country, but these are a small part of their total offerings. The company carries books from Australia, Belgium, Bolivia, Brazil, Canada, England, France, Germany, Ghana, Italy, Japan, the Netherlands, Norway, the Philippines, Spain, Sri Lanka, Sweden, and Venezuela. When a book is translated, Kane/Miller takes care to keep the foreign flavor of the book instead of Americanizing it. Ken Miller (2000), one of the publishers, explained that when the book *Brush,* by Pere Calders, was published in England, the publishers there changed the name of the dog to Scamp and the name of the little boy to Joey. Kane/Miller kept the original names of Turco and Little Sala.

BRUSH

By PERE CALDERS
Illustrated by CARME SOLÉ VENDRELL

KM Kane/Miller Book Publishers

Which International Books Get Selected?

To see what is available in international literature, many publishers go to the big, international book fairs that take place in Frankfurt, Germany; Bologna, Italy; and Harare, Zimbabwe. According to Carl Tomlinson (1999), who has done extensive work on international literature, the negotiation and bidding for rights to publish books begin at these fairs. Given the extra expense to the publisher of translating a book written in another language, editors want to be sure that the books they sign will appeal to readers here. According to Hoyle (1994), often the jacket is changed to make the book more marketable in the United States; sometimes new interior illustrations are drawn as well. Publishing books from other countries involves risk on the part of publishers, since historically translated books have not sold well in this country.

First published in Spain, this story shows how Little Sala deals with his family's decision to get rid of his dog, who chews everything in sight.

(From *Brush* by Pere Calders, illustrated by Carme Solé Vendrell. American text copyright © 1986 Kane/Miller Book Publishers. All rights reserved. Used by permission of Kane/Miller Book Publishers.)

What do publishers look for in international literature? Generally speaking, according to Stan (1999), American publishers are most likely to publish international books that have won awards in their country of origin—books that can be considered "the best." They also look for universal story lines and generic settings that could be construed as American. Kane/Miller often selects books that would not normally be published here because our culture avoids discussion of the topics written about. For instance, because American publishers are squeamish about publishing books discussing body parts or body functions, Kane/Miller carries the series from Japan called **My Body Science,** with such titles as **The Holes in Your Nose** and **All About Scabs,** by Genichiro Yagyu. They also publish the Australian book **Welcome With Love,** by Jenni Overend, in which a family helps Mom deliver her baby at home.

Another Kane/Miller book, **Good Bye Rune,** by Marit Kaldhol, deals with the difficult emotions of grief and sorrow. This book handles these disturbing subjects with honesty and love. Harcourt Brace translated and published **Rose Blanche,** by Roberto Innocenti and Christophe Gallaz, which shows a young child becoming aware of the hunger in the concentration camps and reacting to that need. The harsh realities shared in these two books are not often found in books for children written and published in the United States. Perhaps as teachers, librarians, and parents demand more books that face tough issues and the difficult parts of history, authors will write such books and publishers will publish them.

Invitations

Choose several of the following activities to complete:

1. In your notebook, list the children's trade books (non-textbooks) you remember reading as a child. How many of those books were written by or about someone from another ethnic group or culture? What does this suggest to you? Share your results in a small group. Read the statements made by children in the boxed feature Children's Voices on page 205. Do any surprise you?

2. In your notebooks, explore why you think it's important to use multicultural literature in the classroom. What concerns or questions do you have? After discussing these topics in small groups, return to your notebooks and reflect on what you discovered through the discussion.

3. Form a small group and have each member choose a different multicultural group. After reading five novels or picture books about your multicultural group, create an annotated bibliography of your reading. Make copies for your group. When you share the annotations, discuss what you have learned through your reading.

4. Read three multicultural novels from different cultures and evaluate them using the criteria listed in this book. Share the results with your group.

5. Find ten multicultural picture books on the same culture. Rank them from 1 to 10, with 1 being the best. Form a group with students who have read books on other cultures. Share your favorite three books, using criteria discussed in this chapter to explain why they are the most successful.

CD-ROM

To see examples of how to use the strategy of listing, search Invitations and Classroom Teaching Ideas for the word *list* or *listing*.

6. In a small group, create a readers theater presentation for a favorite multicultural novel. Share it with the class.

7. Read ten international picture books, and then choose your favorite to read aloud to a small group. In your notebook, discuss what you learned from this experience.

Classroom Teaching Ideas

1. To develop understanding about the great diversity within the American Indian cultures, have students research the histories of several tribes from different areas of the United States. Try to get information from the various councils of tribal elders.

2. To develop an understanding of the difference between historical and contemporary culture, gather an assortment of books on the African American experience and create a timeline showing the historical placement of the stories. Do the same with American Indian or Latino/Latina books.

3. Create an international bulletin board with a map of the world at the center. Select books from or about different countries as read-alouds. After each reading, find the country on the map and put the title of the book near it. You may wish to use a highlighter to distinguish between books from that country and books written here using that country as a setting. Older readers could browse and read independently to contribute to the board.

4. Keep an investigator file. As you become more aware of the sometimes casual stereotypical characteristics that continue to be present in children's literature, have children record what they find that they think belongs in the classroom "detective" file box.

Internet and Text Resources

1. Multicultural Kids Education Network provides teacher activities, multicultural literature, and links to other helpful resources. Find it at

www.johnpizz.com/multiculturalkids/home

2. Multicultural Pavilion includes a thread to an online discussion board, a multicultural evaluation checklist for websites, online articles for research, and awareness activities for self-development and the elimination of prejudice. Go to

http://curry.edschool.virginia.edu/go/multicultural/

3. Myths and Fables from Around the World has beautifully illustrated myths and fables. Find it at

www.afroam.org/children/myths/myths.html

4. Children's Library, the site of the Boulder Public Library, has a series of pages on multicultural literature, including Chapter Books about Jewish Life, African-American Fiction and Nonfiction and Picture Books, Asian-American Picture Books to 3rd Grade, Asian-American Fiction and Nonfiction 3rd Grade up to Young Adult, and Native American Picture Books up to 3rd Grade. Find it at

www.boulder.lib.co.us/youth/booklists

5. Cynthia Leitich Smith's Multicultural Children's and Young Adult Books provides multicultural book reviews at

www.cynthialeitichsmith.com/newreadingb.htm#multiculturalism

6. Making Multicultural Connections Through Trade Books provides multicultural book reviews at

www.mcps.K12.md.us.curriculum/socialstd/MBDBooks_Begin.html

7. Multicultural Book Review provides multicultural book reviews at

www.isomedia.com/homes/jmele/joe.html

8. Bishop, Rudine Sims (1994). *Kaleidoscope: A Multicultural Booklist for Grades K–8.* Urbana, IL: NCTE.

9. Kruse, Ginny Moore, and Kathleen T. Horning (1997). *Multicultural Literature for Children and Young Adults.* Madison, WI: Cooperative Children's Book Center, University of Wisconsin—Madison. This annotated bibliography of books by and about people of color, published between 1991 and 1996, presents the best multicultural literature, arranged in 16 sections by theme or genre.

10. Day, Frances Ann (1997). *Latina and Latino Voices in Literature for Children and Teenagers.* Portsmouth, NH: Heinemann.

11. Day, Frances Ann (1994). *Multicultural Voices in Contemporary Literature: A Resource for Teachers.* Portsmouth, NH: Heinemann.

12. Harris, Violet J., ed. (1997). *Using Multiethnic Literature in the K–8 Classroom.* Norwood, MA: Christopher-Gordon.

13. Susag, Dorothea M. (1999). *Roots and Branches: A Resource of Native American Literature—Themes, Lessons, and Bibliographies.* Urbana, IL: NCTE.

14. Tomlinson, Carl, ed. (1999). *Children's Books from Other Countries.* Lanham, MD: Scarecrow.

References

Aronson, Marc (1996). "No Renaissance Without Openness: A Philosophy of American Multiculturalism." *Bookbird 36,* pp. 27–32.

Bishop, Rudine Sims (1992). "Children's Books in a Multicultural World: A View from the USA." In Emrys Evans, ed., *Reading Against Racism.* Philadelphia: Open University Press.

—— (1997). "Selecting Literature for a Multicultural Curriculum." In Violet J. Harris, ed., *Using Multiethnic Literature in the K–8 Classroom.* Norwood, MA: Christopher-Gordon.

Dickman, Floyd (1999). "I Can't Believe It's a Translation." *Booklinks 8,* 22–26.

Hoyle, Karen Nelson (1994). "Studies in Metamorphosis: Illustrating the Andersen Award Winners." *Bookbird 32,* pp. 23–28.

Larrick, Nancy (1965). "The All-White World of Children's Literature." *Saturday Review,* September 11, 1965, 63–65.

Lee, Philip (1999). "A Publisher's Responsibility in Creating Multicultural Books for Children." IRA Annual Convention, San Diego, May 2–7, 1999.

Miller, Ken (2000). Conversation at NCTE Spring Convention, New York, March 16–18.

Muse, Daphne (1999). "New Voices, New Visions." *Teaching Tolerance 15,* 11–15.

Mora, Pat (1998). "Confessions of a Latina Author." *The New Advocate 11,* 279–290.

Rollins, Charlemae (1941). *We Build Together: A Reader's Guide to Negro Life and Literature for Elementary and High School Use.* Chicago: NCTE.

Sloan, Glenna (1999). "Multicultural Matters: An Interview with Philip Lee of Lee & Low Books." *Journal of Children's Literature 25,* 28–33.

Stan, Susan (1999). "Going Global: World Literature for American Children." In Rudine Sims Bishop, ed., *Theory into Practice.* Columbus, OH: Ohio State University.

Tomlinson, Carl, ed. (1999). *Children's Books from Other Countries.* Lanham, MD: Scarecrow.

Yolen, Jane (1997). "Taking Time: Or How Things Have Changed in the Last Thirty-five Years of Children's Publishing." *The New Advocate 19,* 285–291.

Children's Books

Aardema, Verna (1975). *Why Mosquitoes Buzz in People's Ears: A West African Tale.* Retold by Verna Aardema. Illus. Leo Dillon and Diane Dillon. New York: Dial.

Ada, Alma Flor (1999). *The Lizard and the Sun/La Lagartija y El Sol: A Folktale in English and Spanish.* Illus. Felipe Dávalos. New York: Yearling.

—— (1998). *Under the Royal Palms: A Childhood in Cuba.* New York: Atheneum.

Aliki (1993). *My Visit to the Aquarium.* New York: HarperCollins.

Alvarez, Julia (2001). *How Tía Lola Came to ~~Visit~~ Stay.* New York: Knopf.

Anaya, Rodolfo (1999). *My Land Sings: Stories from the Rio Grande.* Illus. Amy Córdova. New York: Morrow.

Ancona, George (1998). *Barrio: José's Neighborhood.* San Diego: Harcourt.

—— (1998). *Fiesta Fireworks.* New York: Lothrop, Lee & Shepard.

Anno, Mitsumasa (1999). *All in a Day.* New York: Philomel.

—— (1997). *Anno's Journey.* New York: Paperstar [1978, Cleveland: Collins-World].

Anzaldúa, Gloria (1993). *Friends from the Other Side.* Illus. Consuelo Méndez. San Francisco: Children's Book Press.

Arcellana, Francisco (1999). *The Mats.* Illus. Hermès Alègré. New York: Kane/Miller.

Bang, Molly (1983). *Ten, Nine, Eight.* New York: Greenwillow.

Barbot, Daniel (1991). *A Bicycle for Rosaura.* Illus. Morella Fuenmayor. New York: Kane/Miller.

Bateson-Hill, Margaret (1998). *Shota and the Star Quilt.* Lakota text by Philomine Lakota. Illus. Christine Fowler. New York: Larousse Kingfisher Chambers.

Beals, Melba Pattillo (1995). *Warriors Don't Cry: A Searing Memoir of the Battle to Integrate Little Rock's Central High.* New York: Pocket.

Berndt, Catherine Helen (1994). *Pheasant and Kingfisher.* Illus. Arone Raymond Meeks. Greenvale, NY: Mondo.

Björk, Christina (1985). *Linnea in Monet's Garden.* Illus. Lena Anderson. New York: R & S Books.

Bradby, Marie (2000). *Momma, Where Are You From?* Illus. Chris K. Soentpiet. New York: Orchard.

Bridges, Ruby (1999). *Through My Eyes.* New York: Scholastic.

Bruchac, Joseph (1998). *The Arrow Over the Door.* Illus. James Watling. New York: Dial.

—— (1997). *Bowman's Store: A Journey to Myself.* New York: Dial.

—— (1996). *Children of the Longhouse.* New York: Dial.

—— (1998). *The Heart of a Chief.* New York: Dial.

—— (2000). *Sacajawea.* San Diego: Silverwhistle.

—— (1992). *Turtle Meat and Other Stories.* Duluth, MN: Holy Cow!

Bruchac, Joseph, and James Bruchac (1998). *When the Chenoo Howls: Native American Tales of Terror.* Illus. William Sauts Netamuxwe Bock. New York: Walker.

Bruchac, Joseph, and Jonathan London (1992). *Thirteen Moons on Turtle's Back.* Illus. Thomas Locker. New York: Philomel.

Bryan, Ashley (1996). *Sing to the Sun.* New York: HarperTrophy.

Bunting, Eve (1994). *Smoky Night.* Illus. David Diaz. San Diego: Harcourt Brace.

Calders, Pere (1986). *Brush.* Illus. Carme Solé Vendrell. Trans. Marguerite Feitlowitz. New York: Kane/Miller.

Carlsen, Lori M., ed. (1994). *Cool Salsa: Bilingual Poems on Growing Up Latino in the United States.* New York: Holt.

Charbonneau, Eileen (1994). *In the Time of the Wolves.* New York: Tom Doherty.

Curtis, Christopher Paul (1999). *Bud, Not Buddy.* New York: Delacorte.

—— (1995). *The Watsons Go to Birmingham—1963.* New York: Delacorte.

Daugherty, James (1939). *Daniel Boone.* New York: Viking.

Delacre, Lulu (1996). *Golden Tales: Myths and Legends from Latin America.* New York: Scholastic.

—— (2000). *Salsa Stories.* New York: Scholastic.

Dorris, Michael (1996). *Guests.* Illus. Ellen Thompson. NY: Hyperion.

—— (1992). *Morning Girl.* New York: Hyperion.

—— (1996). *Sees Behind Trees.* New York: Hyperion.

—— (1997). *The Window.* Illus. Ken Robbins. New York: Disney.

English, Karen (1999). *Francie.* New York: Farrar, Straus & Giroux.

Escudié, René (1988). *Paul and Sebastian.* Illus. Ulises Wensell. Trans. Roderick Townley. New York: Kane/Miller.

Fang, Linda (1994). *The Ch'I-Lin Purse: A Collection of Ancient Chinese Stories.* Illus. Jeanne M. Lee. New York: Farrar, Straus & Giroux.

Feelings, Tom (1993). *Soul Looks Back in Wonder.* New York: Puffin.

Fenner, Carol (1995). *Yolonda's Genius.* New York: McElderry.

Flournoy, Valerie (1985). *The Patchwork Quilt.* Illus. Jerry Pinkney. New York: Dial.

Garland, Sherry (1993). *The Lotus Seed.* Illus. Tatsuro Kiuchi. New York: Harcourt Brace.

—— (2000). *Voices of the Alamo.* Illus. Ronald Himler. New York: Scholastic.

Gordon, Sheila (1995). *Waiting for the Rain: A Novel of South Africa.* New York: Walker.

Govenar, Alan B., ed. (2000). *Osceola: Memories of a Sharecropper's Daughter.* Illus. Shane W. Evans. New York: Jump to the Sun.

Gray, Nigel (1992). *I'll Take You to Mrs. Cole.* Illus. Michael Foreman. New York: Kane/Miller.

Grimes, Nikki (1994). *Meet Danitra Brown.* Illus. Floyd Cooper. New York: Lothrop, Lee & Shepard.

Guy, Rosa (1973). *The Friends*. New York: Holt, Rinehart and Winston.

Hamilton, Virginia (1996). *The Adventures of Brother Sparrow, Sis Wren and Their Friends*. New York: Scholastic.

—— (1999). *Bluish: A Novel*. New York: Blue Sky.

—— (1990). *Cousins*. New York: Philomel.

—— (1980). *Dustland*. New York: Scholastic.

—— (1981). *The Gathering*. New York: Scholastic.

—— (1984). *The House of Dies Drear*. New York: Aladdin.

—— (1978). *Justice and Her Brothers*. New York: Scholastic.

—— (1974). *M. C. Higgins, the Great*. New York: MacMillan.

—— (1998). *Second Cousins*. New York: Scholastic.

—— (1982). *Sweet Whispers, Brother Rush*. New York: Putnam.

—— (1968). *Zeely*. New York: Simon & Schuster.

Haskins, Jim (1998). *Moaning Bones: African-American Ghost Stories*. Illus. Felicia Marshall. New York: Lothrop, Lee & Shepard.

Haskins, Jim, and Kathleen Benson (1999). *Bound for America: The Forced Migration of Africans to the New World*. Illus. Floyd Cooper. New York: Lothrop, Lee & Shepard.

Herrera, Juan Felipe (1999). *Laughing Out Loud, I Fly: Poems in English and Spanish*. Illus. Karen Barbour. New York: HarperCollins.

Hoestlandt, Jo (1995). *Star of Fear, Star of Hope*. Illus. Johanna Kang. Trans. Mark Polizzotti. New York: Walker.

Holzwarth, Werner (1999). *I'm José and I'm Okay*. Illus. Yatiyawi Studios. Trans. Laura McKenna. New York: Kane/Miller.

Howard, Elizabeth Fitzgerald (1999). *Virgie Goes to School with Us Boys*. Illus. E. B. Lewis. New York: Simon & Schuster.

Hudson, Wade, ed. (1993). *Pass It On: African-American Poetry for Children*. Illus. Floyd Cooper. New York: Scholastic.

Innocenti, Roberto, and Christophe Gallaz (1996). *Rose Blanche*. Trans. Martha Coventry and Richard Graglia. San Diego: Harcourt Brace [1985].

James, Will (1926). *Smoky, the Cowhorse*. New York: Scribner.

Johnson, Angela (1997). *Daddy Calls Me Man*. Illus. Rhonda Mitchell. New York: Orchard.

—— (1998). *Gone from Home*. New York: DK Publishing.

Kaldhol, Marit (1987). *Goodbye Rune*. Illus. Wenche Oyen. Trans. Michael Crosby-Jones. New York: Kane/Miller.

Kodama, Tatsuharu (1995). *Shin's Tricycle*. Illus. Noriyuki Ando. Tran. Kazuko Hokumen-Jones. New York: Walker.

Kusagak, Michael Arvaarluk (1998). *Arctic Stories*. Illus. Vladyana Langer Zkrykorka. Toronto: Annick.

Landstrom, Olof, and Lena Landstrom (1994). *Will Goes to the Post Office*. Illus. Olof Landstrom. Trans. Elisabeth Dyssegaard. New York: R & S Books.

Lee, Marie G. (1999). *F Is for Fabuloso*. New York: Camelot.

Lester, Julius (1999). *Uncle Remus: The Complete Tales*. Illus. Jerry Pinkney. New York: Dial.

Lyons, Mary E. (1992). *Letters from a Slave Girl: The Story of Harriet Jacobs*. New York: Scribner.

Machado, Ana Maria (1996). *Nina Bonita*. Illus. Rosana Faría. Trans. Elena Iribarren. New York: Kane/Miller.

Martin, Bill, Jr. (1992). *Brown Bear, Brown Bear, What Do You See?* Illus. Eric Carle. New York: Holt [1964].

Maruki, Toshi (1980). *Hiroshima No Pika*. New York: Lothrop, Lee & Shepard.

McKissack, Patricia C. (1992). *The Dark-Thirty: Southern Tales of the Supernatural*. Illus. Brian Pinkney. New York: Knopf.

McKissack, Patricia C., and Fredrick L. McKissack (1999). *Black Hands, White Sails: The Story of African-American Whalers*. New York: Scholastic.

—— (1992). *Sojourner Truth: Ain't I a Woman?* New York: Scholastic.

Medina, Jane (1999). *My Name Is Jorge: On Both Sides of the River*. Illus. Fabricio Vanden Broeck. Honesdale, PA: Wordsong.

Miller, William (1997). *Richard Wright and the Library Card*. Illus. R. Gregory Christie. New York: Lee & Low.

Mitchell, Margaree King (1993). *Uncle Jed's Barbershop*. Illus. James Ransome. New York: Simon & Schuster.

Mochizuki, Ken (1993). *Baseball Saved Us*. Illus. Dom Lee. New York: Lee & Low.

—— (1995). *Heroes*. Illus. Dom Lee. New York: Lee & Lowe.

Mohr, Nicholasa (1993). *El Bronx Remembered: A Novella and Stories*. New York: HarperCollins.

Musgrove, Margaret (1976). *Ashanti to Zulu: African Traditions*. Illus. Leo Dillon and Diane Dillon. New York: Dial.

Myers, Walter Dean (1998). *Amistad: A Long Road to Freedom*. New York: Dutton.

—— (1988). *Fast Sam, Cool Clyde, and Stuff*. New York: Viking.

—— (1999). *At Her Majesty's Request: An African Princess in Victorian England*. New York: Scholastic.

—— (1991). *Now Is Your Time: The African-American Struggle for Freedom*. New York: Scholastic.

—— (2000). *145th Street: Short Stories*. New York: Delacorte.

—— (1992). *Somewhere in the Darkness*. New York: Scholastic.

Namioka, Lensey (1998). *Yang the Second and Her Secret Admirers*. Illus. Kees de Kiefte. Boston: Little, Brown.

—— (1996). *Yang the Third and Her Impossible Family*. Illus. Kees de Kiefte. New York: Yearling.

National Museum of the American Indian, ed. (1999). *When the Rain Sings: Poems by Young Native Americans*. New York: Simon & Schuster and the Smithsonian Museum.

Nomura, Takaaki (1991). *Grandpa's Town*. Trans. Amanda Mayer Stinchecum. New York: Kane/Miller.

Nye, Naomi Shihab (2002). *19 Varieties of Gazelle: Poems of the Middle East*. New York: Greenwillow.

Overend, Jenni (2000). *Welcome With Love*. Illus. Julie Vivas. New York: Kane/Miller.

Peters, Russell M. (1992). *Clambake: A Wampanoag Tradition*. Illus. John Madama. Minneapolis: Lerner.

Picó, Fernando (1995). *The Red Comb*. Illus. María Antonia Ordóñez. Mahwah, NJ: Bridgewater.

Pinkney, Andrea Davis (1994). *Dear Benjamin Banneker*. Illus. Brian Pinkney. New York: Harcourt.

Pinkney, Brian (1994). *Max Found Two Sticks*. New York: Simon & Schuster.

Ringgold, Faith (1999). *The Invisible Princess*. New York: Crown.

—— (1991). *Tar Beach*. New York: Crown.

Rodríguez, Luis J. (1999). *It Doesn't Have To Be This Way: A Barrio Story*. Illus. Daniel Galvez. San Francisco: Children's Book Press.

Roessel, Monty (1995). *Songs from the Loom: A Navajo Girl Learns to Weave*. Minneapolis: Lerner.

Santiago, Chiori (1998). *Home to Medicine Mountain*. Illus. Judith Lowry. San Diego: Children's Book Press.

Say, Allen (1996). *Emma's Rug*. Boston: Houghton Mifflin.

—— (1993). *Grandfather's Journey*. Boston: Houghton Mifflin.

—— (1999). *Tea with Milk*. Boston: Houghton Mifflin.

Smith, Cynthia Leitich (2000). *Jingle Dancer*. Illus. Cornelius Van Wright and Ying-Hwa Hu. New York: Morrow.

Soto, Gary (1995). *Canto Familiar*. Illus. Annika Nelson. San Diego: Harcourt Brace.

—— (1995). *Chato's Kitchen*. Illus. Susan Guevara. New York: Putnam & Grosset.

Sperry, Armstrong (1940). *Call It Courage*. New York: Macmillan.

Sterling, Shirley (1992). *My Name Is SEEPEETZA*. Vancouver: Douglas & McIntyre.

Takeshita, Fumido (1989). *The Park Bench*. Illus. Mamoru Suzuki. Trans. Ruth A. Kanagy. New York: Kane/Miller.

Taylor, Mildred D. (1976). *Roll of Thunder, Hear My Cry*. New York: Dial.

Tillage, Leon Walter (1997). *Leon's Story*. Illus. Susan L. Roth. New York: Farrar, Straus & Giroux.

Trottier, Maxine (1996). *The Tiny Kite of Eddie Wing*. Illus. Al Van Mil. New York: Kane/Miller.

Uchida, Yoshiko (1993). *The Bracelet*. Illus. Joanna Yardley. New York: Philomel.

—— (1984). *Desert Exile: The Uprooting of a Japanese-American Family*. Seattle: University of Washington Press.

—— (1981). *A Jar of Dreams*. New York: Atheneum.

Valgardson, W. D. (1995). *Winter Rescue*. Illus. Ange Zhang. Toronto: Groundwood.

Vendrell, Carme Solé (1999). *Jon's Moon*. New York: Kane/Miller.

Waboose, Jan Bourdeau (2000). *SkySisters*. Illus. Brian Deines. Toronto: Kids Can Press.

Walter, Mildred Pitts (1989). *Have a Happy*. Illus. Carole Byard. New York: Lothrop, Lee & Shepard.

—— (1988). *Justin and the Best Biscuits in the World*. Illus. Catherine Stock. New York: Lothrop, Lee & Shepard.

Wheatley, Nadia, and Donna Rawlins (1994). *My Place*. New York: Kane/Miller.

Whelan, Gloria (1996). *Indian School*. Illus. Gabriella Dellosso. New York: HarperCollins.

Williams, Sherley Anne (1992). *Working Cotton*. Illus. Carole Byard. New York: Harcourt Brace.

Williams, Vera B. (1990). *More More More Said the Baby*. New York: Greenwillow.

Wittstock, Laura Waterman (1993). *Ininatig's Gift of Sugar: Traditional Native Sugarmaking*. Illus. by Kale Kakkah and Michael Dorris. Minneapolis: Lerner.

Woodson, Jacqueline (1997). *We Had a Picnic This Sunday Past*. Illus. Diane Greenseid. New York: Hyperion.

Wong, Janet S. (1994). *Good Luck Gold and Other Poems*. New York: McElderry.

Wyeth, Sharon Dennis (1995). *Always My Dad*. Illus. Raúl Colón. New York: Knopf.

Yagyu, Genichiro (1998). *All About Scabs*. Trans. Amanda Mayer Stinchecum. New York: Kane/Miller.

—— (1994). *The Holes in Your Nose*. New York: Kane/Miller.

Yee, Paul (1999). *Tales from Gold Mountain: Stories of the Chinese in the New World*. Illus. Simon Ng. Toronto: Groundwood.

Yep, Laurence (1998). *The Case of the Lion Dance (Chinatown Mystery No. 2)*. New York: HarperCollins.

—— (1982). *Dragon of the Lost Sea*. New York: Harper & Row.

—— (1997). *The Dragon Prince: A Chinese Beauty & the Beast Tale*. Illus. Kam Mak. New York: HarperCollins.

—— (1993). *Dragon's Gate*. New York: Scholastic.

—— (1975). *Dragonwings*. New York: Harper & Row.

—— (2000). *The Journal of Wong Ming-Chung: A Chinese Miner (My Name Is America)*. New York: Scholastic.

—— (1995). *Thief of Hearts*. New York: HarperTrophy.

Yolen, Jane (1991). *Hark! A Christmas Sampler*. New York: Putnam [out of print].

—— (1997). *Miz Berlin Walks*. Illus. Floyd Cooper. New York: Philomel.

Young, Ed (1989). *Lon Po Po: A Red-Riding Hood Story from China*. New York: Philomel.

Yumoto, Kazumi (1996). *The Friends*. Trans. Cathy Hirano. New York: Farrar, Straus & Giroux.

CHAPTER

Traditional or Folk Literature

We learn through stories, just as we learn through our experiences in life. Sometimes stories are easier to learn from than real-life situations because stories offer more distance from the experience. We can see ourselves and our actions in the characters and the problems they encounter, and yet we have enough distance that we feel safe in exploring the difficulties these make-believe characters confront.

Folk literature speaks to universal experiences of what it means to be human. These seemingly simple stories allow us to reexperience, on a psychological level, universal issues in our lives. In *Tell Me a Tale: A Book about Storytelling,* Joseph Bruchac (1997), storyteller, author, and poet, explains what these kinds of stories have meant to him: "Few things have helped me understand the world better than a good story. . . . Stories helped me grow, and stories helped me gain insight. . . . Stories helped me overcome my problems and stories taught me many things: that I didn't have to be ashamed when I was afraid, that I could learn to be brave, that there were times for sorrow and times for joy, that things were always going to change and that some things—like love and courage, hope and faith—were unchanging" (p. xi).

The stories Bruchac learned so much from are the folk stories he heard as he was growing up. He says, "Stories, like trees, have roots. They are rooted in our words and in our world" (p. 5).

What Is Traditional or Folk Literature?

Although the terms *folk tales, legends, fairy tales, tall tales, fables, myths, trickster tales, creation stories,* and *pourquoi stories* are familiar to most people, the distinctions among them are unclear. Figuring out what they have in common and how they are different is difficult. Reading over 150 books to write this chapter, I often felt like the man in Allen Say's **Under the Cherry Blossom Tree: An Old Japanese Tale,** who has a cherry tree growing from his head. All these kinds of stories were swirling around in my head like tangled tree branches growing into and around each other. When I found the term *folk expression* in my reading, the tangle started to unsnarl. I could see that all the types of literature called "traditional" were some form of folk expression, and most of them came out of the oral tradition, since they were first told aloud.

Bruchac offers a clear explanation: "Folklore is traditional knowledge passed along by word of mouth within a small isolated community of people." He points out that this knowledge may be conveyed through "songs, games, ways of speaking, and lore about such things as the weather or medicine, as well as myths and legends" (p. 5). Because these tales started as spoken stories, all are set in a time long ago, all have flat or stereotypical characters who generally represent specific human qualities, all have linear or single plot lines, and all are embedded with lessons or truths. When we tell a story aloud, we can't possibly create a full picture of a person or keep more than one plot line going. Although these types of folk stories each have unique conventions and formats that will be explained in this chapter, understanding the purpose for these tales and the truths in them is much more important than being able to categorize them by type. And no matter what kind of traditional tale we are talking about, the purpose is the same: to teach lessons through stories.

Folklore and Culture

Although the cultural connection may not be immediately apparent, stories and rhymes reflect the culture as it was at the time of their origin. For instance, many people are familiar with the refrain "Ring around the rosie/Pocketful of posies/Ashes, ashes/We all fall down," but no one can be sure of its meaning. Its origin has come to be folklore itself. Some people, believing that it describes sores and death from disease, say it originated during the Bubonic Plague. Others, for the same reason, say it describes a 19th-century smallpox epidemic. Still others say it is nothing more than the words to a party game.

Writers cannot help but impart to a traditional story their views and understandings of the world. For instance, when the Grimm brothers began collecting oral tales in Germany and putting them in writing, they wrote them from the perspective of early 19th-century Europe and its values. Because their views of women were colored by those of their society, the majority of their stories feature very passive women. For example, in the Grimm version of "Rapunzel," the heroine waits for help from a prince. In earlier versions of the same tales, female heroines were much more active in determining their fate. **Petrosinella: A Neopolitan Rapunzel,** by Diane Stanley, was based on an Italian version of this story, written 200 years earlier than the Grimm brothers' version. This Italian version, which came directly from the oral tradition, shows a much more active heroine who has a hand in orchestrating her escape from the tower. Paul Zelinsky, who wrote and illustrated the Caldecott Medal–winning **Rapunzel,** includes the following comment in "A Note about Rapunzel" at the end of his book: "Although the Grimm brothers purportedly created their collection to preserve ancient stories in a pure state, untouched by literary influence, the history of 'Rapunzel' shows how far from this goal the reality actually fell." So just as modern stories always reflect the author's world view, so do the stories that are passed down to us.

Excellent collections of traditional stories often include a Foreword, Afterword, or Author's Notes directed to the reader. It is heartening that so many authors are concerned about the accuracy of their tales and want to let their readers know if parts of the stories or illustrations are not consistent with the culture they are portraying. When authors outside the culture write folk tales, they often explain their connection to the culture and how they immersed themselves in the culture to capture cultural beliefs in the stories. The books that contain such notes are often the best ones in terms of authenticity. Watch for explanatory notes as you read in this genre; they can be an indication of the accuracy of the text.

Mother Goose Rhymes

Most people do not think of the Mother Goose rhymes they heard as a child as folk literature. (John Newbery's use of *Mother Goose* as the title of a collection of rhymes and jingles began its association with highly rhythmic nursery rhymes, even though Charles Perrault first used the name as a title of a collection of stories.) However, because these rhymes have been handed down over the centuries, they are a form of folk expression. Peter and Iona Opie, world authorities on children's games and rhymes, worked continuously for nearly 40 years (until his death in 1982) studying and writing about children's lore and literature. The Opie Collection of Children's Literature is a repository for rhymes and versions of rhymes that have been handed down through the generations. This collection of over 20,000 items, housed at Oxford University, includes not only 800 children's books published before 1800, but later stories, picture books, children's magazines, and comics. Any book edited by an Opie is a treasure in itself. Not only does Iona Opie's introduction explain the purpose and importance of the rhymes, but her joyous language makes us eager to jump in. In her introduction to *My Very First Mother Goose,* Opie says that for centuries Mother Goose "has been gathering rhymes that will help people along the bumpy road of life . . . suggest[ing] that mishaps might be funny rather than tragic, that tantrums can be comical as well as frightening, and that laughter is the cure for practically everything" (unpaged).

CD-ROM

To identify other artists who use bright, bold colors in their illustrations, search for the word *color* or *bright* or *bold* under Favorite Authors.

In an Opie book meant especially for schoolchildren, *I Saw Esau: The Schoolchild's Pocket Book,* edited by Iona and Peter Opie and illustrated by Maurice Sendak, playful rhymes are coupled with serious ones. In the introduction, Iona Opie says:

> They were clearly not rhymes that a grandmother might sing to a grandchild on her knee. They have more oomph and zoom; they pack a punch. Many are directly concerned with the exigencies of school life: the need for a stinging reply when verbally attacked; the need for comic complaints in the face of persecution or the grinding drudgery of schoolwork; the need to know some clever rhymes by heart, with which to win popularity. They pass from one child to another without adult interference. . . . The best antidote to the anxieties and disasters of life is laughter; and this children seem to understand almost as soon as they are born. If laughter is lacking, they create it; if it is offered to them, they relish it. (unpaged)

Rosemary Wells's endearing animal drawings make this a Mother Goose book that will be read over and over again. (Illustration © 1996 Rosemary Wells. MY VERY FIRST MOTHER GOOSE selected and compiled by Iona Opie. Reproduced by permission of the publisher Candlewick Press, Inc., Cambridge, MA.)

Go to *Mama Lisa's House of Nursery Rhymes* for the text of many traditional Mother Goose rhymes at www.mamalisa. com/house/.

This attitude comes through clearly in the verses selected for the volume, perhaps because the editors were so sure about their purpose. Reading these rhymes brings back childhood memories of chanting "It's raining, it's pouring/The old man is snoring . . . ," "I asked my mother for fifty cents/To see the elephant jump the fence . . . ," the retaliation verse "Sticks and stones/May break my bones/But words will never hurt me," and the lamentation "Nobody loves me/Everybody hates me/Going in the garden/To eat worms." As adults we often forget children's pleasure in coupling the serious and the playful; the Opies remind us not to overlook how important nursery rhymes can be for children.

The Nursery Treasury: A Collection of Baby Games, Rhymes and Lullabies, selected by Sally Emerson, harks back to those delightful years when we played baby games such as "Knock at the Door, Ring the Bell . . ."; recited nursery songs such as "Humpty Dumpy," "Little Boy Blue," and "Little Jack Horner"; and acted out such songs as "I'm a Little Teapot" and "The Wheels on the Bus." The collection also includes rhymes to introduce letters of the alphabet, days of the week, months of the year, and numbers (with such rhymes as "One two/Buckle my shoe"). Story rhymes (including "Mary Had a Little Lamb") and lullabies are other categories in this book, whose soft colored pictures, by Colin MacLean and Moira MacLean, add to its appeal.

Harry Bornstein and Karen L. Saulnier's *Nursery Rhymes from Mother Goose: Told in Signed English,* illustrated by Patricia Peters with sign line drawings by Linda C. Tom, is unique in that it is accessible to hard-of-hearing children. On each double-page spread, a full-page picture is faced by the rhyme, followed by the rhyme in sign language. This beautifully illustrated book, with hints of humor throughout, is a treat for both hard-of-hearing children and those with hearing.

Old Mother Hubbard: A Nursery Rhyme, illustrated by David A. Johnson, is devoted to a single nursery rhyme. This inventive interpretation of the rhyme features a well-off older woman who dotes on her darling dog, giving him the best of everything.

In *Babushka's Mother Goose,* by Patricia Polacco, the traditional rhymes have been rewritten to feature Russian characters and scenes. Polacco tells us, "My Babushka [grandmother] reshaped tales so they reflected her own heart and homeland, the Ukraine."

Recapture some of the joy and delight you felt as a young child by sampling many of these charming books. As the boxed feature Taking a Look at the Research indicates, rhymes make wonderful read-alouds for children, helping them become aware that words are made up of sounds.

Tongue Twisters, Puns, Proverbs, and Street Rhymes

The tongue twisters, puns, proverbs, and street rhymes that are passed on mainly through the oral tradition are a type of folk expression. Such folk expressions continue to be created today by children playing games, as well as by adults who pass on urban legends—those stories which "really happened to a friend of a friend of a friend." Such stories often relate to ghostly hitchhikers or people who had to pay exorbitant fees for a cake or cookie recipe they asked to have at a restaurant.

Moses Supposes His Toeses Are Roses and Seven Other Silly Old Rhymes, retold and illustrated by Nancy Patz, includes many tongue twisters you may remember, including

A tooter who tooted his flute
Tried to tutor two tooters to toot.

Alvin Schwartz, in *A Twister of Twists, a Tangler of Tongues,* shares tongue twisters from around the world. From the United States comes "Old, oily Ollie oils oily autos," and from France comes "Six cents for these sausages?" Reading tongue-twister books takes time; you need to stop and say each one aloud. Listening to these sounds rolling off the lips and tongue is just pure fun and invites children to play with language and listen to its sound.

Books that collect street rhymes almost seem to jump up and down, begging for our attention. And with good cause. Exuberant books such as *Miss Mary Mack and Other*

Learning Phonemic Awareness Through Children's Literature

Research is often cited to show that phonemic awareness is among the consistent predictors of reading success. Unfortunately, there is a great deal of confusion about just what phonemic awareness is. Although some people think that phonemic awareness is synonymous with phonological awareness, it is, in fact, only one aspect of phonological awareness. Phonological awareness also includes awareness of words within sentences and of syllables within words. Some people also confuse phonemic awareness with phonics, though clear distinctions can be made (Opitz, 2000). While phonics is the sound/letter connection, phonemic awareness is the awareness that words are made up of individual sounds. As Opitz (2000) points out, "A person can be phonemically aware yet unable to identify a single letter of the alphabet!" (p. 8). In short, phonemic awareness is a child's ability to determine how many sounds are in a particular word.

Many kindergarten students come to school having gained phonological awareness in informal home settings. Nursery rhymes, poems, songs, and stories told at bedtime have already created interest in, and understanding of, many aspects of spoken language. Children's literature provides wonderful experiences to continue that learning in the classroom. Teachers who believe in incorporating learning into a whole language experience believe that phonemic awareness is not an end in itself but rather a part of the child's literacy experience (Avery, 2002; Routman, 2000). Instead of presenting worksheet skill and drill exercises, they intentionally teach phonemic awareness in the context of a literacy-rich environment, where regular talk about words is fun and engaging. Thus, rather than being left with fragments of skills taught in isolation and quickly forgotten, children learn strategies to better understand the texts they are being read or reading themselves.

Opitz (2000) describes how phonological awareness activities, which include phonemic awareness, can be part of children's "print-rich environment that affords them with many opportunities to participate in authentic reading and writing experiences" (p. 13). Such activities include working with rhyming texts, alliterative texts, repetitive texts, single-poem picture books, poetry collections, and song texts.

Avery, Carol (2002). *. . . And with a Light Touch. Learning about Reading, Writing, and Teaching with First Graders,* 2nd ed. Portsmouth, NH: Heinemann.

Opitz, Michael (2000). *Rhymes and Reason: Literature and Language Play for Phonological Awareness.* Portsmouth, NH: Heinemann.

Routman, Regie (2000). *Conversations: Strategies for Teaching, Learning, Evaluating.* Portsmouth, NH: Heinemann.

Children's Street Rhymes, by Joanna Cole and Stephanie Calmenson, have hand-clapping rhymes and ball-bouncing rhymes:

> A, my name is Alice,
> And my husband's name is Al.
> We come from Alabama,
> And we sell apples.

The book includes counting-out rhymes like

> One potato,
> two potato

and

> The sky is blue
> How old are you?
> Nine.
> One, two, three, . . .

just-for-fun rhymes like

> Birdie, birdie in the sky
> Why'd you do that in my eye?
> Gee I'm glad that cows don't fly

teases and comebacks like

> Liar, liar
> Pants on fire!
> Nose as long
> As a telephone wire

and spelling rhymes.

In *Anna Banana: 101 Jump-Rope Rhymes,* Joanna Cole tells us that the subjects of these rhymes are satisfyingly down-to-earth, ranging from the commonplace of the table ("Two little sausages frying in the pan") to family squabbles ("John broke a tea cup/and blamed it on me") to girl meets boy ("Ice cream soda, Delaware punch/Spell the initials of your honeybunch"). Some rhymes give directions for actions to perform, while shorter rhymes often are simply introductions to counting the number of jumps ("Cinderella, dressed in yellow/Went downstairs to kiss her fellow/How many kisses did she give?"). Reading these rhymes stirs memories of the days when we enjoyed language and rhyme with abandon.

Folk Tales

At **Absolute Whootie: Stories to Grow By,** find folk tales on specific themes. Go to www.storiestogrowby.com.

Today when people are unsure about some aspect of human behavior, such as how to communicate better with their significant other, they turn to self-help books, TV talk shows, support groups, or professional therapists. In times past, however, stories were the major vehicle for passing along knowledge about how to live successfully, as well as for passing along spiritual beliefs and information about the world. These stories took many forms, including folk tales, fairy tales, fables, legends, and myths. In this text, I will categorize as a folk tale any story that does fall into one of the more specific categories of fairy tales, fables, legends, myths, or tall tales.

All folk tales were written for a similar purpose—to share the beliefs of the culture and its explanation for things in order to help people live happily and successfully. The differences come in what the stories show about a culture. To really see what a folk tale says about a culture, you can use the questions in the boxed feature Criteria for Evaluating Folk Tales. What else do you notice as you read folk tales?

Criteria for Evaluating *Folk Tales*

1. What does the culture see as the sources of power (for example, strength, wisdom, experiential knowledge, scientific knowledge, wealth, cleverness)?

2. What ethical codes or values are promoted?

3. What do images of heroes and heroines look like? What does this tell us about how males and females are viewed?

4. How are animals and nature and the earth thought of or considered?

5. What assumptions are made about the world? Are people viewed as good or bad? Are individuals more important than the community? Is competition or cooperation emphasized?

6. Whom or what is looked to for wisdom (for example, people, animals, nature, religion, science)?

7. What is the place of spirituality in the culture?

8. How important is the accumulation of material possessions?

9. How much emphasis is placed on the beauty of the world, music, art, or movement?

Folk Tales as a Reflection of World Views

To see how a culture's world view and values are embedded in its folk tales, let's look at folk tales from two different cultures—those of the Japanese and those of the North American Indians. Although there are hundreds of separate American Indian nations on this continent, their literature shares some commonalities that we can explore.

Japanese Folk Tales

Reading one Japanese folk tale after another provides glimpses of a Japanese cultural world view. Although many of these tales were written by non-Japanese and thus contain views colored by the outsider perspective, all are by people who immersed themselves in the culture. In the collection *Mysterious Tales of Japan,* by Rafe Martin, the tales seem gentler and the action not as vigorous as in folklore from other countries. In his extensive, interesting notes to the reader, Martin observes that the culture "retains, even today, a fundamental respect for the Invisible." He explains that the tradition came from a blending of Shintoism, the original religion of Japan, and Buddhism.

> Shinto maintains that clouds, mountains, rocks, ponds, trees and animals all have Spirit, or Kami, power. . . . Buddhism, specifically Zen Buddhism, emphasizes that all forms of life are One and yet . . . [each is] completely itself and unique. Compassion for every living thing permeates the Buddhist vision of reality. These two strands come together in the stories of Japan and . . . carry with them a special awareness of the fleeting yet haunting beauty we know from life. (unpaged)

Some of these same elements are reflected in *Under the Cherry Blossom Tree: An Old Japanese Tale,* retold by Allen Say, a writer born in Japan. This rather funny story features a rich, greedy landlord who owned the land and all the houses in a village. "He was so mean babies cried at the sight of him." He had a cherry tree growing from his head, but he "was too stingy to see a doctor and too mean to be embarrassed." Eventually he pulled the cherry tree out of his head and was left with a large hole, which filled up with water and was quickly populated by fish. The neighbor boys would wait until he was asleep in the afternoons and then go fishing, putting the ends of their lines in his head. One day he woke up, began chasing the boys, tripped, and flipped over. His feet went into his head and he disappeared, creating a lovely pond for the village. The lesson seems to be that money doesn't buy happiness, so be kind, generous, and happy. The story has a sensitivity to the beauty of nature, as well as mystery and moral significance.

A story that emphasizes inner power is *The Stonecutter: A Japanese Folk Tale,* by Gerald McDermott, who is not Japanese but who immersed himself in the culture. He writes about a humble stonecutter who, at first, is content with his work, pleasing the spirit of the mountain. However, over time, Tasuku becomes less happy about being himself and desires to become increasingly powerful. He changes from being a prince to being the sun to being the clouds to being a mountain. Then, a stonecutter begins cutting his face.

Under the Cherry Blossom Tree
An Old Japanese Tale · Retold by Allen Say

Japanese humor and wisdom sit side by side in this story about what happened to a grumpy landlord.
(Cover, from UNDER THE CHERRY BLOSSOM TREE by Allen Say. Jacket art © 1974 by Allen Say. Reprinted by permission of Houghton Mifflin Company. All rights reserved.)

Through Tasuku we learn that we can never be invulnerable, that there is always something or someone who has power over us.

Tsubu, the Little Snail, by Carol Ann Williams, another non-Japanese writer, is the story of a childless elderly couple who pray for a son. The Water God sends them a snail boy, who grows up to marry a noble's daughter. One day she loses him on the way to the spring festival. Because her love causes her to search everywhere without caring what anyone thinks of her, when she finds him later that day, his shell cracks and the son of the Water God emerges. The author tells us in her note that, although the details in this tale vary, the message always stays the same: "Life is sacred. No matter how insignificant it may seem, it is to be loved and respected. It is also a source of joy." The origins of this story are in Shintoism, with its "emphasis on recognizing the fundamental mystery at the heart of all things."

Since cultures reflect their values and concerns in their stories, we see both universal and unique characteristics of cultures in their folk tales. These Japanese folk tales give us hints about some of the important aspects of the Japanese culture as three Anglo writers and one Japanese writer see it.

American Indian Folk Tales

One of the best ways to learn about the native peoples of America is through the abundance of culturally authentic American Indian folk tales that exist today. The multitude of nations that make up the group referred to as American Indians, while certainly not all the same, do have some beliefs in common.

CD-ROM

Search the CD-ROM database for other books by Joseph Bruchac.

On the front cover flap of *Between Earth and Sky: Legends of Native American Sacred Places,* Joseph Bruchac, an Abenaki writer, talks about American Indian traditions. He states that in American Indian tradition, "All is sacred and legends exist to help us understand our lives. Stories from the land speak to us, can tell us of wisdom, can tell us of power, can tell us of the world that surrounds us. Listen." In this book, through the guidance of his uncle and the retelling of various American Indian legends, a young boy learns that everything living and inanimate has its place and should be considered sacred and given respect. The notes offer a clear idea of some essential values within the cultures and give us a measure of how representative the book is of the cultures.

Paul Goble, although not American Indian, writes with knowledge and reverence about their cultures and beliefs. In *Her Seven Brothers,* he retells the Cheyenne legend in which a girl and her seven chosen brothers become the Big Dipper. It tells us, "In the old days . . . there were more people who understood animals and birds." The young girl and her younger brother understand animals. This story about giving and being in touch with the spirit reflects a culture that validates and respects such communication. The collecting of possessions is not emphasized, as the people are shown living in tepees with their dogs and a few minimal possessions. This type of story is often viewed as an explanation tale, which tells how something happened; but looking closely, we see that it is also a story about living and what is valued in life.

Antelope Woman: An Apache Folktale, by Michael Lapaca, reveals why Apaches honor all things great and small. Lapaca, both the artist and the author, makes use of his cultural roots (Apache, Hopi, and Tewa) and artistic training to develop stories filled with the beautiful designs and patterns found in pottery and basketry in the Southwest.

Shingebiss: An Ojibwe Legend, retold by Nancy Van Laan, a nonnative author, teaches the power of perseverance and resourcefulness through the story of a duck in the cold North. This duck bravely challenges the Winter Maker and manages to find enough food to survive. The Author Notes once again give us important information. Van Laan says that the Ojibwe "perceive nature to be their teacher. They closely watched birds and animals to see how to survive the harsh climate. They believe every living thing imparts a sacred teaching."

These few stories about American Indians reflect reverence toward the earth and animals and a belief in a spiritual power. They offer a sense of some of the values held by American Indian peoples, as well as a glimpse at how they view the world.

Shingebiss, known for his determination and grit, is given a very definite look through the lines of the woodcuts.

(Cover, from SHINGEBISS by Nancy Van Laan. Jacket art © 1997 by Betsy Bowen. Reprinted by permission of Clarion Books/Houghton Mifflin Company. All rights reserved.)

Comparing Versions of a Folk Tale

Many of the folk tales written today are based on past stories or songs. Every writer and every illustrator make choices about what to emphasize in the tales they write and illustrate. The choices they make may alter the tale slightly or change it a great deal, depending on how they interpret the plot, characters, setting, theme, and structure. Comparing two versions of the same tale can yield interesting insights; the boxed feature Criteria for Evaluating More Than One Version of the Same Tale provides the criteria for doing so.

In the boxed feature Applying the Criteria: Evaluating Two Versions of a Yiddish Folk Tale on page 236, two folk tales are then compared. Both use as sources Yiddish songs the authors heard as young children. Steve Sanfield's *Bit by Bit* is based on the song "If I Had a Little Coat," while Simms Taback's *Joseph Had a Little Overcoat,* a 1999 Caldecott Honor Medal winner, is based on the song "I Had a Little Overcoat." Both tell the tale of a man who is able to make something out of little by transforming a cherished worn-out overcoat into other pieces of clothing. As each item becomes worn out, the man transforms it into something new, until eventually he is left with nothing material, but he has the ability to make art by retelling his experience through story. While the two tales have only slight variations in plot, the differences in characters, setting, theme, and structure show how much an individual author's or illustrator's unique approach alters a common folk tale.

Criteria for Evaluating More Than One Version of the Same Tale

1. **Plot.** What is the sequence of events in the story? Do the plots differ? How might the different versions appeal to children of different ages?

2. **Characters.** How are the characters portrayed? What details (either visual or textual) contribute to the characterization? Are there any differences that change our understanding of the characters?

3. **Setting.** Where does the story take place? What do you learn about the culture from the details of the setting? Is this different for the tales being compared?

4. **Theme.** What is the message? What values are shown as important? Is the theme the same in each version?

5. **Style or language.** What do you notice about how the writer uses language? How does it differ in each tale?

6. **Structure.** What is the framework from which the story is narrated? Is it a simple chronological retelling, or does it have a more complex structure, such as a story within a story, flashbacks, or multiple narrators?

7. **Visual elements.** How is the art used to develop, contribute to, and extend the story? Is it done differently in the different versions?

Applying the Criteria *Evaluating Two Versions of a Yiddish Folk Tale*

Comparison of *Joseph Had a Little Overcoat,* by Simms Taback, and *Bit by Bit,* by Steve Sanfield.

1. **Plot.** *Joseph Had a Little Overcoat* is the simpler version of the song. It tells the story of how Joseph alters his shabby overcoat into first a jacket, then a vest, a scarf, a necktie, a handkerchief, and finally a button, which he loses. "Now Joseph had nothing. So Joseph made a book about it." Joseph's quick decision explicitly tells the reader, "You can always make something out of nothing." In *Bit by Bit,* the narrator, who introduces himself as a storyteller, tells the story of Zundel. When Zundel's first overcoat wears out, he is able to earn enough pennies to buy a new cloth which has "red threads and gold threads and blue threads and green threads" to make a new one. When his new coat becomes shabby, he, too, finds enough left of the beautiful cloth to turn it into first a jacket, then a vest, a cap, a pocket, and finally a button. When Zundel realizes that there is nothing left of the button, the narrator realizes that he can retell the story over and over. In this story within a story, Zundel gradually ages and has his own family. The greater complexity of Sanfield's plot would be lost on very young children, while older children would begin to see the changes in Zundel as they read the story.

2. **Characters.** Characterization is simpler in *Joseph Had a Little Overcoat.* Joseph is a flat character who expresses no emotions and remains a consistent age throughout the book. In *Bit by Bit,* not only do we have more characters (the narrator, a wife, and a son), but Joseph's character is more complexly developed. The reader sees him change over time from a young single man to a married man to a father. More significantly, he reveals more feelings, expressing sadness by crying when his old clothing wears out, before he realizes that he can make something new out of the worn item.

3. **Setting.** Both books use folklike setting details, which suggest the Yiddish origins of the tale. Taback, in his illustrations in watercolor, gouache, pencil, ink, and collage, vividly portrays village life. Through details like the art on the walls of the home and the newspaper headlines, the observant older reader is immersed in cultural details such as Yiddish folk sayings and words. The die-cut holes used to reveal what Joseph intends to make next would appeal especially to young children. While *Bit by Bit* also shows aspects of village life, Susan Gaber's illustrations are less vibrant and give a less complex view of the culture. Her portrayal of Zundel's wife almost suggests an Asian woman.

4. **Theme.** Both tales are optimistic and positive, showing the values of thriftiness, positive thinking, and approaching difficulties creatively. The value of telling stories as a means of making meaning is emphasized in both books.

5. **Style or language.** The simpler style of *Joseph Had a Little Overcoat* is also carried out through the language. Taback uses only a line or two on each page to help develop the plot: "So he made a vest out of it" shows Joseph in his new vest on one page, while "and danced at his nephew's wedding" appears on the next page. Sanfield's language in *Bit by Bit* is not only more complex, with a stanza on each page, but also more musical and more repetitious. Zundel, who loves the button more than his coat, jacket, vest, cap, or pocket, "wore it in the morning and he wore it at night."

6. **Structure.** In *Joseph Had a Little Overcoat,* the title page tantalizes the reader with the promise of a mystery about Joseph's overcoat ("He wore the coat for a long time and then something happened to it") and a moral ("and there's a moral, too!"). The framework is Joseph's story. *Bit by Bit* provides a story within a story. The reader learns not only about Zundel's life and thriftiness but also about the narrator's discovery that, if we pay attention, stories can be told from others' lives. This story within a story would be a difficult structure for very young children to grasp.

7. **Visual elements.** In these tales, the visual contributes to the setting and characterization. In *Bit by Bit,* the visual is more refined artistically. In *Joseph Had a Little Overcoat,* it is more like folk art.

The Organization of Folk Tale Collections

To get a peek at the range of folk tales available, let's look at a few different types of collections. Many collections revolve around a single theme or element; other collections are organized around a specific kind of tale; still others come from a specific country or region.

Single Theme or Element

One collection of stories echoing a theme is *Giants: Stories from Around the World,* by Paul Robert Walker, in which people outwit a giant through cunning and bravery. The stories range from "Jack and the Beanstalk" from England to "The Cannibal's Wonderful Bird" from South Africa to "David and Goliath" from ancient Israel. Each of the seven stories is followed by notes from the author explaining where he got the story, what resources he used, and any changes he made.

Jane Yolen's *Not One Damsel in Distress: World Folktales for Strong Girls* contains stories of brave females from around the world. These thirteen stories—from as many countries or cultures—inspire, entertain, and encourage readers to be brave. The extensive end notes explain where the stories came from and what changes Yolen made, if any. *Grandmothers' Stories: Wise Woman Tales from Many Cultures,* retold by Burleigh Mutén, gives us stories about benevolent, resourceful, independent older women who are respected in their cultures. *Mother and Son Tales,* by Josephine Evetts-Secker, looks at mother/son relationships across cultures.

Tooth Tales from around the World, by Marlene Targ Brill, is an unusual book that shows how different cultures view losing teeth and where the idea of a tooth fairy originated. Young children will love this book, which relates the diverse folk practices surrounding the losing of a tooth.

CD-ROM

If you are attracted to books with strong themes, do a word search on *theme* under Favorite Authors to find authors known for use of strong underlying concepts in their works.

Specific Kind of Tale

The trickster tale is a very popular category for collections, probably because people love to read about an underdog outsmarting those who have the power. In *The Barefoot Book of Trickster Tales,* Richard Walker tells us that tricksters are "those engaging characters who use all kinds of cunning tactics to overcome the seemingly insurmountable odds that are stacked against them." His collection includes stories from Asia, England, Bengali, Russia, Switzerland, Turkey, and Ghana, as well as from African Americans and American Indians. By comparing the stories, we learn about each culture or group of people.

Virginia Hamilton has a collection of trickster tales called *A Ring of Tricksters: Animal Tales from America, the West Indies, and Africa,* illustrated by Barry Moser. According to Hamilton, trickster tales were brought from Africa to the southern United States and the Caribbean West Indies. There, the Africans added new tales that reflected the many different animals they encountered in their new lands. But, "All of these new tales kept the pattern of the African trickster tales in which a resourceful animal hero having human traits used deceit and sly trickery, and often magic, to get what it needed from bigger and stronger animals" (unpaged). The language Hamilton uses invites us to read

These stories of strong women from around the world take their place alongside the already-known tales of male courage. (Cover illustration from NOT ONE DAMSEL IN DISTRESS: WORLD FOLKTALES FOR STRONG GIRLS by Jane Yolen, illustrations copyright © 2000 by Susan Guevara, reprinted by permission of Harcourt, Inc.)

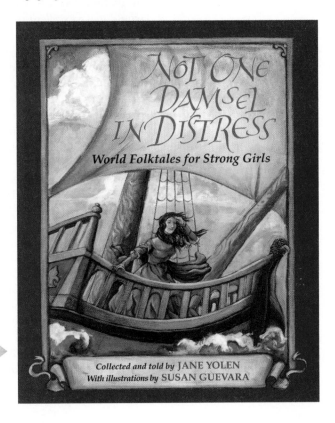

these tales aloud: "One dance-in, the gator children were having themselves a good, slam-tail, sway-back time." The design of this book and the illustrations by Barry Moser make it even more inviting, especially the perspective of many of the drawings—a leopard drapes itself across two pages, a chameleon lies on its back across the top of two pages, and an elephant holds a rabbit high in its trunk across two pages.

Specific Country or Region

A group of tales collected by region is *Folk Tales and Fables of the Middle East and Africa,* by Barbara Hayes. The paintings by Robert Ingpen, of almost photolike quality, add stunningly different interpretations to the tales. From the Middle East come "David and Goliath," "Aladdin and the Wonderful Lamp," and "Joseph Who Dreamed the Truth." From Africa come "The Proud Princess," "The Cunning Man," "The Clever Monkey," and "Tricky Mr. Rabbit."

In *Golden Tales: Myths, Legends, and Folktales from Latin America,* Lulu Delacre shares stories from thirteen countries and four native cultures. In her wonderfully informative end note, she tries to give us a feel for this varied group of people whom we tend to lump together as Latin Americans.

Why Lapin's Ears Are Long: And Other Tales from the Louisiana Bayou, by Sharon Arms Doucet, is a collection of tales featuring the Trickster Lapin. We learn that the stories were born in Senegal and Gambia in Western Africa, came to America in slave ships, were translated into French, and mingled with elements of European folk tales. One story begins, "On the banks of a Louisiana bayou, not so very long ago . . . ." Then we meet the familiar Trickster, who was not big and strong, but was clever and crafty.

In the outstanding collection *The People Could Fly: American Black Folktales,* Virginia Hamilton tells us that these "folktales of animals, fantasy, the supernatural, and desire for freedom [were] born of the sorrow of the slaves, but passed on in hope." In her Author's Note, she explains that folk tales offered a creative way for an oppressed people to express their fears and hopes to one another. This collection of tales is particularly magnificent because of the gorgeous illustrations by Leo Dillon and Diane Dillon. With such language as "The little animals held a sit-down talk, and one by one and two by two and all by all, they decide to go see Bruh Bear and Bruh Rabbit," it's easy to see that these stories would make excellent read-alouds.

In Julius Lester's collection *Further Tales of Uncle Remus: The Misadventures of Brer Rabbit, Brer Fox, Brer Wolf, the Doodang, and Other Creatures,* illustrated by Jerry Pinkney, the tales sing and almost seem to jump off the page. "But when his head bought him trouble deeper than what he'd counted on, he called on his feet, because that's where he kept his lippity-clip and his blickety-blick." Language like this makes these tales just plain fun to read.

You will be able to uncover even more riches in the area of traditional literature if you spend time with this genre. Children respond to the lessons that folk tales teach, as the boxed feature Children's Voices indicates.

Legends are a part of folklore. They are magical stories that are presumed to relate to actual persons, events, and places. Many people think of them as historical accounts, even though the basic historical facts generally have been embroidered upon and may even be questionable. Several regional legends have become part of popular tall tales, discussed later in this chapter. A legend refers to specifics and history ("There once was . . ."), while a tale refers to a fanciful, never-never land ("Once upon a time . . . "). The English stories of King Arthur and the Knights of the Round Table and those of Robin Hood and his band of outlaws are examples of legends, which often express the hopes and desires of a people. In the story of King Arthur, the ideas of chivalry and English standards of honor are expressed, while Robin Hood tells of the hopes of people to overcome oppression and misrule. The Swiss have the legend of William Tell, who shot an apple off his son's head. Duncan Emrich (1972) says that Americans have several kinds of legends. Some stem from greatness (Washington, Lincoln, John Henry, Babe Ruth), some from romanticized outlawry (Jesse James, the Daltons), and some from disaster (the *Titanic,* the Chicago fire, the Trail of Tears, the Great Depression). Legends can be looked at through the same lens as folk tales, using the questions in the boxed feature Criteria for Evaluating Folk Tales on page 232.

Fairy Tales

Fairy tales "are folktales, not necessarily about fairies. They are about the unusual, the different, and the fantastical, and they give accounts of magical and enchanting events," says Virginia Hamilton in ***Her Stories: African American Folktales, Fairy Tales, and True Tales.*** Fairy tales often have magical elements in them; often are set in castles and kingdoms; have stock characters such as ogres, witches, stepmothers, and princesses, who exemplify specific qualities such as good or evil; and usually begin with "Once upon a time" and end with "They lived happily ever after." "Little Red Riding Hood," for instance, is classified as a fairy tale. It includes a crafty talking wolf, a sweet old grandmother, and an innocent little girl going on an errand of goodness. Although deciding just what is classified as a fairy tale can be confusing, the more important issues are what the tale is saying, how it reflects universal human experiences, and what it shows about a culture.

Fairy tales are some of the most popular stories in our culture. Every time a movie version of a fairy tale is made, the tale gains popularity and attention. Since fairy tales meet some deep-felt needs in people, the route I will take in this discussion is to look at what makes them important to people. As you read fairy tales, I encourage you to focus your attention on the questions in the boxed feature Criteria for Evaluating Fairy Tales on page 240, because they give us so much cultural information.

Fairy tales have traditionally been thought of as children's stories, but adults can find many truths in them too, as the analysis in the boxed feature Applying the Criteria: Evaluating the Content of "Rapunzel" reveals. Each fairy tale provides information about society's values, both past and present, as well as glimpses of parts of ourselves.

Since fairy tales are laden with subtle messages, you should look closely at the fairy tales you use with children to identify the implicit messages. It is also interesting to compare versions of the same fairy tale across cultures. Ed Young's *Lon Po Po: A Red-Riding Hood Story from China,* a Caldecott winner, is a Chinese version of the Little Red Riding Hood story. Rafe Martin's *The Rough-Face Girl* is the Cinderella story told through an American Indian perspective. The websites listed at the end of this chapter can lead you to more such tales from various cultures.

Fairy Tale Variants

Fairy tale variants are retellings of known fairy tales, with new elements added, a different twist, or a fresh point of view. It's fascinating when an author can figure out a way to take an original fairy tale whose ending we all know and yet make it so compelling it's difficult to put down. One such book, Donna Jo Napoli's *Zel,* based on the Rapunzel story, is imaginative, intriguing, and masterfully written. Napoli deserves these plaudits because of her skill at writing and her willingness to plumb the psychological depths of the main characters. *Ella Enchanted,* by Gail Carson Levine, was so well received it won a Newbery Honor award. The story involves us in the life of Ella (Cinderella), who was given the gift of obedience by her fairy godmother with startling and sometimes amusing results. *I Was a Rat,* by Philip Pullman, tells what happened to one rat who remained in his human form after the ball. Throughout the story, we see glimpses of Cinderella in her new life. Robin McKinley's magical *Beauty: A Retelling of the Story of Beauty & the Beast* is a well-known variant of the Beauty and the Beast story. Monica Furlong's version of the Robin Hood legend in *Robin's Country* is both lively and evocative, as readers romp through Sherwood Forest.

---

*C*riteria for Evaluating *Fairy Tales*

1. **Lessons and/or truths.** What truths does this story tell? What is the message to each person in the tale? What is it saying to the parents? What is it saying to the children? What is it saying to the foils like a witch or a monster?

2. **Societal values.** What societal values are embedded in the story? What is it telling us about how to become part of society?

3. **Positive human qualities.** What human qualities are admired?

4. **Negative human qualities.** What human qualities are not admired?

5. **Elements used to frame the story and make it more palatable or believable.** Why was the story framed as it was, using a faraway place or a stepmother or a beast?

6. **Applying the fairy tale to today's world.** How is the story valuable to us today?

7. **Parts of ourselves reflected in the characters.** What parts of ourselves do we see reflected in the characters?

Applying the Criteria *Evaluating the Content of "Rapunzel"*

Summary: "Rapunzel" is told in many versions, but they all show a sorceress who threatens to withhold the fresh rapunzel, or lettuce, from the pregnant woman stealing it from her garden unless the woman promises to give up her child when it is born. The sorceress raises the child in a tower so that she will not be influenced by anyone else or pay attention to anyone else. A prince finds Rapunzel, is captivated by her, and learns how to ascend the tower. When the sorceress finds out, she throws the prince to the ground, where he is blinded by thorns. She banishes Rapunzel, who later is reunited with her prince. Rapunzel's tears of love at the sight of the prince restore his vision, and the two live happily ever after.

1. **Lessons and/or truths.** People who are imprisoned physically, mentally, or emotionally will not freely give love to their imprisoner. Power does shift, and those who feel powerless can gain power. To the parents: Don't solve problems with short-term solutions that don't take into account the long-term consequences. To the witch: By sheltering a child excessively or limiting a child's life experiences you lose the child in the long run. Trying to fill your loneliness by obtaining "companionship" through duplicity or magic simply doesn't work. You gain friends and keep loved ones by showing them who you are and allowing them choices. Using magic or illusions to get what you want doesn't pay off. Is it worth losing a child simply because she violated your sexual and/or social mores with the choices she made? To the child: You may have a period of powerlessness in your life. However, as you grow older, and often with the help of others, you will eventually gain control over your life. Be patient, don't rail against your life, find beauty and happiness wherever you can. Patience and serenity can be virtues.

2. **Societal values.** It is foolish of parents to bargain away their child. Happiness can be found through love. Pairing of males and females in marriage is seen as expected and desirable. Females are expected to be beautiful and often need saving. Love can be transforming and cure ills such as the prince's blindness. Children are expected to find a life apart from their parents and caregivers and eventually take care of themselves.

3. **Positive human qualities.** Patience, caring, fortitude, persistence.

4. **Negative human qualities.** Selfishness, self-centeredness, greed, anger, violence.

5. **Elements used to frame the story and make it more palatable or believable.** The frame refers to the consistent elements we find in fairy tales, such as the wicked stepmother, the beast, or the far-away setting. At the time the tales were created, these elements helped people to see the message in the story, since the framing of the story was based on assumptions in the culture—for example, a biological mother would not harm her own child, marriage was the major goal for women, and so on. Stories show a male saving a female and the couple ending up marrying and living happily ever after probably because it's a story format people were used to; thus, they could "hear" what was said in the story. If the story appeared to break the conventions of the genre, people might be suspicious and not understand what was said. Perhaps there was a witch in this story so that parents could hear the message more clearly. If Rapunzel had been locked up by her own parents, it would have been much more difficult for parents to see the effects of this imprisonment on the child because they would have related too closely to Rapunzel's parents. Using a witch objectifies the experience enough that parents can hear what the story says. We can recognize the witch parts of ourselves.

6. **Applying the fairy tale to today's world.** In those days, love and marriage were shown as the be-all and end-all. This raises questions for the listener: What other goals do people have today? What do men work toward? What do women work toward? What are other kinds of goals? Is getting married the best thing that can happen to a person? Do married people have other goals? Do children ever feel "imprisoned" by their families?

7. **Parts of ourselves reflected in the characters.** I can identify with Rapunzel, who was locked up and kept away from the world. As a teenager, I felt locked up by my parents' belief system, as most teenagers do. As a parent, I can understand the desire that the witch had to shelter children from the world, allowing them to be exposed only to my values, which I view as good ones. Of course, I didn't act on this desire.

◁ Ella's mysterious smile invites readers to uncover her secret.
(Cover art from *Ella Enchanted* by Gail Carson Levine. Used by permission of HarperCollins Publishers.)

Females in Fairy Tales

Fairy tales written about other times and places often portray male and female figures in stereotypical ways, showing females as subservient and passive. Thus, teachers and parents sometimes hesitate to use them for fear of diminishing what a little girl thinks she can accomplish. As more and more research is done on tales around the world, writers are unearthing tales that feature strong and even daring women. One such tale is ***Rimonah of the Flashing Sword: A North African Tale,*** by Eric A. Kimmel, an Egyptian version of "Snow White." When Rimonah is taken by the huntsman to be killed, she escapes and goes to live with the Bedouin in the desert, where she becomes skilled with the dagger and sword. When her stepmother pursues her, Rimonah cleverly escapes. The second time she is not as lucky and is plunged into a deep sleep, only to be awakened by a prince. This story emphasizes how fearless and brave Rimonah is.

In ***Clever Katya: A Fairy Tale from Old Russia,*** by Mary Hoffman, Katya is portrayed as a clever child able to solve the Tsar's riddles. This not only helps her father but ultimately is beneficial to her. In the Author's Note, Hoffman tells us that originally this tale was called "The Wise Little Girl" and featured a nameless heroine. Hoffman explains that she likes the story because "the weak get the better of the strong, the child of the adult, and the female of the male." She further notes that the three tasks set by the Tsar are consistent with the tradition in folklore of using the number three.

Another book about an active female who does her own problem solving is ***Count Silvernose: A Story from Italy,*** by Eric A. Kimmel. This girl is the oldest and least pretty of three daughters, but smart and clever. When her two sisters are left for dead in Count Silvernose's castle, she goes to his home as a servant and not only rescues her sisters but also manages to get rid of the evil Count Silvernose.

Children have very strong feelings about fairy tales, as their comments in the boxed feature Children's Voices indicate. On your own, examine the messages about males in fairy tales. How are they characterized? What are they admired for?

See ***Cinderella Variants*** to find more than 100 variants of the fairy tale at www.acpl.lib.in.us/ Childrens_Services/cinderella.html.

 Tall Tales

Tall tales are very much a part of the American folk tradition. They may be based on a real person whose exploits are exaggerated or on someone totally imaginary. Characters include Paul Bunyan, Johnny Appleseed, Pecos Bill, Joe Magarak, and the Swamp Angel. Although tall tales may be wild, humorous, exaggerated stories, they contain a kernel of truth. While making us laugh, they also show us what it means to be quick-witted or brave and how to overcome adversity. The truths contained in these tales are more significant than how real or fictional a particular story is.

Tall tales generally share the characteristics shown in the boxed feature Criteria for Identifying Tall Tales on page 244. Examples of these characteristics taken from several tales are shown in the boxed feature Applying the Criteria: Identifying Characteristics of Tall Tales.

As with other forms of traditional literature, background notes provided by the authors are valuable for understanding the times and conditions that gave birth to tall tales. In ***Mike Fink,*** Steven Kellogg explains that extraordinary strength was needed to work on keelboats

Children's Voices

On reading fairy tales . . .

I like "Cinderella" because I like her dress. —Taylor, 2nd grade

My favorite is "Once Upon a Time." They're my favorite, with "Sleeping Beauty" and other girl stuff. —Elizabeth, 2nd grade

I like "Jack and the Beanstalk" because it is weird that Jack can hold on the stalk and not fall off. —Kate, 3rd grade

I like "Peter Pan." It has magic. —Richard, 3rd grade

When I was little, I read stories like "Cinderella," "Snow White," "Hansel and Gretel." What I like about "Cinderella" is that Cinderella went into a carriage and went off with the prince. What I like about "Snow White" is that she sang and danced with animals. What I like about "Hansel and Gretel" is that they came to their cottage with jewelry. —Jayne, 4th grade

I read them to my sister and for myself, once in a while. Everyone has to fantasize. —Craig, 6th grade

In them, the good guy always wins and the bad guy always gets what he deserves, so they always make you feel good. —Alison, 6th grade

I like to read fairy tales because they let me know I can dream. —Patrice, 6th grade

The sweet princess would always get her prince. —Tessa, 7th grade

I like fairy tales with a weird twist at the end. —Hailey, 7th grade

I used to like fairy tales but now they are too babyish. —Becky, 7th grade

They are always too farfetched to be remotely true. —Natalie, 7th grade

They always seem to turn out perfect. It was comforting when I was little. —Aaron, 7th grade

Fairy tales always have to do with cool things like magic, animals, and people. They always end with a happy ending, and begin with once upon a time. I like them. —Katie, 7th grade

I remember reading fairy tales when I was little. They each had a moral and gave you something good to read about. —Carolyn, 7th grade

I remember them when I was little reading them and pretending I was in it. —Hanna, 7th grade

I don't read many fairy tales anymore, but I did when I was younger. I really liked them and every so often I will take them off my bookshelf and read them. I enjoy reading them because they are so magical and make-believe, so they are fun to read. —Julia, 7th grade

I remember writing fractured fairy tales after reading them. I did like them because they were so fun to listen to and read. —Dustin, 8th grade

Criteria for Identifying *Tall Tales*

1. ▶ Are the physical attributes of the hero exaggerated?

2. ▶ Are the accomplishments of the hero exaggerated?

3. ▶ Is there an emphasis on winning and competition?

4. ▶ Is colorful language used?

5. ▶ Are humor and a light tone present?

6. ▶ Is the hero helpful?

7. ▶ Is the storytelling creative, often including explanations of geographic features made by the hero?

Applying the Criteria *Identifying Characteristics of Tall Tales*

1. ▶ **Are the physical attributes of the hero exaggerated?** Many tall tales tell what these heroes were like as babies. In *Swamp Angel,* by Anne Isaacs, we hear that there "was nothing about the baby to suggest that she would become the greatest woodswoman in Tennessee. The newborn was scarcely taller than her mother and couldn't climb a tree without help." Steven Kellogg tells us that Mike Fink "hated being shut up indoors, and so when he was only two days old he ran away from home." About John Henry, Julius Lester says, "That baby jumped out of his mama's arms and started growing." Audrey Wood, in *The Bunyans,* says that Paul was "taller than a redwood tree, stronger than 50 grizzly bears and smarter than a library full of books."

2. ▶ **Are the accomplishments of the hero exaggerated?** We hear in *Sally Ann Thunder Ann Whirlwind Crockett,* by Steven Kellogg, that "Sally Ann continued to astonish folks throughout her childhood. When she was one year old, she beat the fastest runner in the state." Paul Bunyon "raced with deer and wrestled with the grizzlies," according to Kellogg.

3. ▶ **Is there an emphasis on winning and competition?** In Steven Kellogg's *Mike Fink,* Mike could pole his keelboat up the Mississippi faster than any other man. In *Keelboat Annie: An African American Legend,* by Janet P. Johnson, Annie Christmas says, "I'll wager I can pole a keelboat faster than any ten of your keelboat captains put together. And to make things interesting, I'll beat them going both downstream and upstream."

4. ▶ **Is colorful language used?** We hear that the Swamp Angel "snored like a locomotive in a thunderstorm." In *John Henry,* Julius Lester writes about the boulder John will remove: "This was no ordinary boulder. It was as hard as anger . . . ."

5. ▶ **Are humor and a light tone present?** In Kellogg's *Paul Bunyan,* "Paul built a colossal flapjack griddle. The surface was greased by kitchen helpers with slabs of bacon laced to their feet." In *John Henry,* when the road crew planted dynamite, "That dynamite made so much racket, the Almighty looked over the parapets of Heaven and hollered, 'It's getting too noisy down there.'"

6. ▶ **Is the hero helpful?** Annie Christmas takes care of bullies who bother others, Paul Bunyan clears land so that settlers can live there, John Henry hammers a tunnel through the mountain for a railroad, and Swamp Angel kills a mighty grizzly bear who was bothering the settlers.

7. ▶ **Is the storytelling creative, often including explanations of geographic features made by the hero?** In Kellogg's *Paul Bunyan,* "Paul's great ax fell from his shoulder, gouging a jagged trench, which today is known as the Grand Canyon." The Swamp Angel dragged the pelt of the mammoth grizzly to her new home in Montana and placed it in front of her cabin: "Nowadays, folks call it the Shortgrass Prairie."

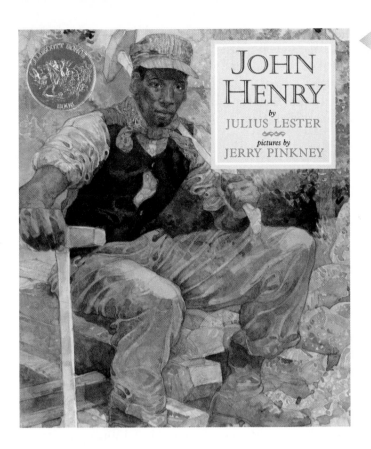

John Henry's deeds are shown to great advantage through the powerful language of Julius Lester and the watercolors of Jerry Pinkney, which burst with Henry's energy.
(From JOHN HENRY by Julius Lester, illustrated by Jerry Pinkney. Copyright 1994 by Julius Lester, text. Copyright © 1994 by Jerry Pinkney, illustrations. Used by permission of Dial Books for Young Readers, an imprint of Penguin Putnam Books for Young Readers, a division of Penguin Putnam Inc.)

because of the need to pole against the current on the return trip up the Mississippi. "Proud of their grit, the crewmen competed vigorously [to be] the strongest man on board. They loved to boast about the dangers they'd faced and the critters they'd licked; and they were convinced that a keelboatman could outdo anybody at anything" (unpaged).

Although most tall tales entertain and some inspire, they also tell us a great deal about this country's culture and what is considered important. Reading these tales makes it evident that this country prizes bigness. The value placed on things large and sprawling perhaps comes from the taming of what this nation considered to be a vast "unsettled" land. The tall tales also emphasize individual accomplishments rather than cooperation or community—the individual is primary. Competition and winning are also featured, with one person emerging as the biggest, strongest, or fastest, often at the expense of another. No mention is ever made about the human connection to the earth; it is viewed as something to be used, not something that gives to us. Paul Bunyan cut down trees wherever he found them. Animals are also seen as something to be used, not something to be treated with reverence. Pecos Bill used a rattlesnake for a whip. These tales, like the tales from the European tradition, mention only physical and material qualities—those things you can feel or touch. Little reference is made to spiritual and emotional realms. Characters learn from people and their actions, not from nature or a higher power.

This country seems to admire human qualities like strength, generosity, kindness, helping others, proving oneself, and being daring. Physical abilities are respected. Families are shown as being important. What else do you notice that tall tales demonstrate about our culture's values?

CD-ROM

To find more books illustrated by Jerry Pinkney, use the CD-ROM database.

Fables

Fables are simple, traditional tales with a moral or lesson. The characters in fables are usually animals that behave like humans. The animals act as abstractions, making the characters impersonal. When readers don't distance themselves from the characters by denying that they share the characters' qualities, they can more clearly see what the fable is telling them. It is always easier to hear or absorb a lesson if we don't feel it's directly about us.

Many fables contain much human wisdom and teach valuable lessons. "The North Wind and the Sun," in *Aesop's Fables,* reminds us that "persuasion is better than force," while "The Wolf in Sheep's Clothing," also in *Aesop's Fables,* reminds us that "pretending to be what you are not can bring trouble." Bruchac (1997) points out that tall tales address understanding:

> Those who cannot see beyond the surface are often fooled. One of the oldest
> stories about being fooled by not seeing deeply is the Aesop's fable of the fox and

Locate the text of more than 600 fables at **Aesop's Fables Online Collection** *at www.aesopfables.com.*

the grapes. If we do not look at things with understanding, we cannot really see other people, we only see a reflection of ourselves. A person who cannot see the wisdom in others often turns out to be the one who is a fool. (p. 42)

Books of fables vary in their presentation, purpose, and impact. At the top of my list is Jane Yolen's *A Sip of Aesop,* because Yolen has turned the fables into delightful verses. Even the morals are in verse. For example, from the "The Hare and the Tortoise," we read the first of six verses,

"Slowpoke, lowpoke,"
Called the hare.
"You no-go-poke
Anywhere."

This is followed by the moral,

If naps and laps
You do confuse,
Then you are surely
Bound to lose.

(From A SIP OF AESOP by Jane Yolen. Copyright © 1995 by Jane Yolen. Reprinted by permission of Scholastic Inc.)

Yolen's playful, pithy poems and Karen Barbou's bright, colorful paintings make this a book you'll want to return to. The freshness of the language makes the "truisms" startling, while the rhyme scheme may even inspire you to try your hand at turning a fable into a poem.

With its appealing, humorous illustrations and wonderfully told stories, it is easy to see why *Fables,* by Arnold Lobel, won the Caldecott Medal. *Seven Blind Mice,* a Caldecott Honor Medal winner, is an original fable written and illustrated by Ed Young. First we see each part of the elephant as it really is, and then the next page reveals it as the blind mouse experiences it. The stunning, bold colors contrast sharply with the black background, making the entire book a visual treat. The moral—"Knowing in part may make a fine tale, but wisdom comes from seeing the whole"—has many applications to our lives today.

Myths

Myths are ancient stories which often explain how things came to be long ago. Myths include stories of gods and goddesses from ancient Greece, creation stories from around the world, and stories of religious beliefs and rituals. In her introduction to *In the Beginning—Creation Stories from Around the World,* Virginia Hamilton says:

[Myths] are the truth to the people who believe in them and live by them. They give people guidance and spiritual strength. . . . Myths were created by people who sensed the wonder and glory of the universe. Lonely as they were, by themselves, early people looked inside themselves and expressed a longing to discover, to explain who they were, why they were, and from what and where they came. (unpaged)

Paying attention to the vast range of myths can make us respectful of other cultures and beliefs. New stories of the sacred are told every day. These stories, past and present, explain how the world came to be and how people succeeded in it. Myths often show the outward journey of a hero to his own inner journey. Clyde Ford (2001), scholar and writer, explains that myths come from the same realm as dreams; they speak to our psyche and our soul. To get to this dimension of a myth and uncover the deep wisdom in it, readers have to look beneath the words. For example, the deeper wisdom contained in a myth about a hero who gives up his life for others might be that we must let our erroneous beliefs die so that other parts of ourselves can survive.

Gerald McDermott (1999), Caldecott winner for *Arrow to the Sun: A Pueblo Indian Tale,* strongly believes in the power of myth. He tries "to find the emotional and spiritual

*At **Mythology,** find myths organized in categories. Go to www.windows.ucar.edu/ cgi-bin/tour_def/mythology/ mythology.html.*

center of folk tales and myths to give to the new generation. The outer myth may be fantastical but at its inner core is truth." He explains, "Tales tell the drama of the inner life. Stories were guideposts to how to become part of society but they get lumped as pourquoi stories [stories of explanations of how things happened]. It's the spirit core that makes them live." McDermott believes that these stories still live today because they contain metaphors for what we all go through in creating or re-creating ourselves.

What's in a Myth?

McDermott's words remind us that categorizing tales as trickster tales, noodlehead tales, pourquoi tales, creation tales, fairy tales, tall tales, and myths is not what is meaningful. While these labels do describe the surface features of the tales or myths, they don't address the essence of what is within the story. It's this essence—the emotional and spiritual center—that we must uncover if we are to learn the truths contained in the story.

As you look at myths, one way to grasp some of what is being implied is to ask the questions in the boxed feature Criteria for Analyzing Myths.

In the boxed feature Applying the Criteria: Analyzing Two Myths on page 248, these questions are used to examine *Raven: A Trickster Tale from the Pacific Northwest,* by Gerald McDermott, and *Cupid and Psyche,* a Greek myth, by M. Charlotte Craft.

The Organization of Myth and Creation Books

Books containing myths and creation stories are organized in several ways. Some revolve around a specific kind of myth or story, usually from a religious tradition; others contain only a single myth; still others focus on individual aspects of mythology, such as giants or gods and goddesses.

A Specific Kind of Myth or Story

Mary Pope Osborne's *Favorite Greek Myths* retells twelve Greek myths. Her graceful language and ear for story—along with Troy Howell's illustrations, which put a face on these seemingly ethereal figures—make this an outstanding collection. Osborne's notes at the end of the book clear up confusion about Greek and Roman deities by explaining their origins. Most of the stories involve transformation—gods, goddesses, and mortals changing their shapes to become different things.

A book dealing with religious stories from the Christian and Jewish traditions is Barbara Diamond Goldin's *Journeys with Elijah: Eight Tales of the Prophet.* The beautifully written stories are enhanced by the dazzling paintings of Jerry Pinkney. In her Author's Note, Goldin explains that Elijah is part of Jewish folklore in Europe, Asia, and Africa, as well as being part of the folklore of Christianity and Islam. She explains that Elijah, a symbol of hope, represents goodness and justice. "He is a helper and friend to those in need, a teacher of lessons, a master of disguises and surprises. He is immortal, able to appear at any

*C*riteria for Analyzing *Myths*

1. What is shown as important to people?

2. What actions are taken to secure what is important?

3. What human qualities or actions are viewed as positive?

4. What human qualities or actions are viewed as negative or bring punishment?

5. What is implied about spiritual or supernatural power?

6. What is the universal message of the myth?

1. **What is shown as important to people?** In *Raven,* by Gerald McDermott, people long to be out of the darkness and have light in their lives. Raven wants to bring to the world the light that he sees coming from the lodge house of the Sky Chief. There is a desire for spiritual enlightenment which can only be gotten from the gods. In *Cupid and Psyche,* by M. Charlotte Craft, love is seen as important to people, as something people long for.

2. **What actions are taken to secure what is important?** Raven figures out a way to trick the Sky Chief and his daughter by being born through the daughter. As the beloved grandchild of the Chief, he is allowed to open the box containing the sun, which he then snatches and brings to the people of the world. In *Cupid and Psyche,* Psyche first has to go to a mountaintop to see if she is indeed to be the wife of a god. Then she has to prove her trust by never looking upon Cupid but only being with him in darkness. When she fails to do this, his mother Venus gives her four tasks, which test her worthiness.

3. **What human qualities or actions are viewed as positive?** In *Raven,* cleverness is elevated, as is the willingness to figure out a plan and stick with it. In *Cupid and Psyche,* listening to your heart and your experience is seen as positive. Trust is also elevated.

4. **What human qualities or actions are viewed as negative or bring punishment?** In *Raven,* there are no negative examples. In *Cupid and Psyche,* violating the trust of a loved one is deemed punishable. Also, jealousy and envy are viewed negatively.

5. **What is implied about spiritual or supernatural power?** In *Raven,* we see that the gods have things that are desirable to humans—things that humans could benefit from having. We also see that effort has to be made to get these things from the gods; they are not simply handed to humans. All of this implies that the gods have powers superior to man's. In *Cupid and Psyche,* we see that the gods have the power and can interfere at any time with the lives of humans. Even though the gods are very powerful, they can still have failings, such as the envy that Venus suffered.

6. **What is the universal message of the myth?** In *Raven,* we find that we all long to "see" and have light in our lives, whether it be spiritual or physical, and our job is to share that light with others in the world. Another message is that we can succeed against the more powerful. In *Cupid and Psyche,* we learn that revenge can backfire. (When Venus tries to get Cupid to make Psyche fall in love with someone ugly, her own son, Cupid, is pierced by his own arrow.) We also learn to trust our own experiences and feelings and not let others interfere, especially those who are motivated by envy.

---

time, in any place, to any person" (unpaged). Julius Lester's *When the Beginning Began: Stories about God, the Creatures, and Us,* written in a much lighter tone, contains stories that touch our spirit and take us to a more reflective place within. In Chapter 3, "Sun and Moon," when the angels are trying to grapple with the many forms God can take and are frustrated because they can't be sure whether or not they are talking to God, Sara has a thought-provoking response. She says, "Maybe it just means we should talk to everyone as if it was God" (p. 12).

A Single Myth

Stolen Thunder: A Norse Myth, by Shirley Climo, is the retelling of a single myth. In this story, the god of Thunder wants to recover his stolen hammer, which he needs to make thunder. Together with his advisor, he concocts a scheme in which he disguises himself as a bride. The luminous pictures by Alexander Koshkin add to the book's interest and charm.

The Marriage of the Rain Goddess: A South African Myth, by Margaret Olivia Wolfson, tells of a rain goddess looking for a husband. When she finds a potential husband,

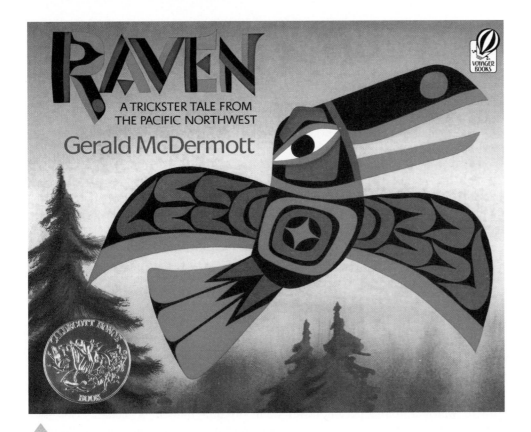

Through vibrant images and careful attention to language, Gerald McDermott aims to capture the truth that is at the inner core of every myth.

(Cover illustration from RAVEN: A TRICKSTER TALE FROM THE PACIFIC NORTHWEST, copyright © 1993 by Gerald McDermott, reprinted by permission of Harcourt, Inc.)

she decides to test him. But he is not fooled. He tells the disguised goddess that, along with "the bright gleam of rivers, ponds, lakes and seas," he can see in her eyes "the power of one who greens the earth and nourishes the crops. Such power surpasses the charm of well oiled skin and the jingling of bracelets of cowry shells" (unpaged). In making this statement about external beauty, the myth says much about the importance of soul in a spouse.

The single tale **Pegasus, the Flying Horse,** retold by Jane Yolen, follows the familiar folk tale pattern in which the hero is set tasks likely to kill him and yet accomplishes them all with the aid of a magical helper, winning the hand of the king's daughter. In this story, however, the hero, who loves the thrill of riding a flying horse, suffers an unheroic death because he's so taken with the idea that he can be one of the gods and live on Mount Olympus. The vivid paintings of Li Ming and Yolen's way with words make this a satisfying retelling.

The lore surrounding the prophet Elijah is brought to life through the blending of Barbara Goldin's text and Jerry Pinkney's paintings.

(Cover illustration from JOURNEY WITH ELIJAH: EIGHT TALES OF THE PROPHET by Barbara Diamond Goldin, illustrations copyright © 1999 by Jerry Pinkney, reproduced by permission of Harcourt, Inc.)

Individual Aspects of Mythology

In her introduction to *Mythical Birds & Beasts from Many Lands,* Margaret Mayo tells us that for thousands of years people have believed that fabulous birds and beasts exist. They've told stories about the animals' special power, appearance, and realms. This collection includes tales of the European unicorn, the North American thunderbird, the Chinese dragon, and the Aztec-inspired feathered snakes. It is interesting to look at what characteristics various cultures give their beasts, how they interact with the beasts, and what the beasts do or give to the cultures.

The One-Eyed Giant: And Other Monsters from Greek Myths, by Anne Rockwell, devotes two pages to each kind of monster, including the Cyclops, Medusa, the Minotaur, and the Centaur. Aliki's *The Gods and Goddesses of Olympus* is the story of how the "awesome Olympians earned their thrones on Olympus." The lovely pictures and the clearly written text make this a good introduction to the major Greek gods.

These books and more are in the folklore section of the library. Browse through them and see what discoveries you make.

Heroes in Folk Literature

Folk tales, fairy tales, tall tales, fables, and myths often portray heroes. The hero's journey has been described in literature throughout the ages. Often it is part of a coming-of-age story in which a young person leaves home to find himself or herself. This is a common theme in stories, probably because each of us must take this journey. Whether or not we physically leave home, we must separate from our parents, look within ourselves, and figure out what values or beliefs are truly our own.

Joseph Campbell (1988), a famous author who writes about myths and legends, calls this part of life the hero's journey. That journey, which is like a circle, starts out when a young man or woman leaves home to seek his or her fortune. Along the way, obstacles arise. The hero or heroine overcomes these obstacles, learns from the experience, and then continues on. Eventually the hero or heroine returns home, strengthened by the experience and ready to help his or her family and people. In his explanation of Campbell's cycle, Bruchac (1997) says:

> Most stories about heroes or heroines have these four parts:
>
> *Departure.*
>
> *Difficulty*—faces obstacles, hardships including evil people, threats by monsters, and abandonment.
>
> *Discovery*—finds a way to overcome obstacles. Doing this, he or she gains power or is given a special gift.
>
> *Return*—the hero or heroine goes back home, often using what he or she has gained to help the people. (p. 45)

We all have different definitions of what makes a person or an action heroic. The boxed feature Characteristics of a Hero summarizes what Joseph Campbell (1988) says about heroes in Chapter 5 of *The Power of Myth,* to help you look at the array of characteristics considered heroic.

The hero cycle appears in such stories as Eric A. Kimmel's *Count Silvernose,* Mary Hoffman's *Clever Katya: A Fairy Tale from Old Russia,* Carol Ann Williams's *Tsubu, The Little Snail,* and even Paul Zelinsky's *Rapunzel.* People in the legends of William Tell,

The following characteristics are adapted from Joseph Campbell (1988):

- A hero gives his or her life to something bigger than himself or herself—some higher end.

- A hero performs a courageous act, either physical or spiritual.

- A hero is usually someone from whom something has been taken or who feels there's something lacking in the normal experience available or permitted to members of his or her society.

- A hero embarks on a series of adventures to recover what is lost or to discover some life-giving information.

- A hero usually moves out of the known, conventional safety of his or her own life to undertake a journey.

- A hero undergoes trials and tests to see if he or she has the courage, the knowledge, and the capacity to survive.

- A hero has to achieve something.

- A hero's journey usually consists of a departure, a fulfillment, and a return.

Robin Hood, and King Arthur have many of the characteristics of heroes. As you read traditional literature, look for evidence of the hero cycle and the characteristics considered heroic.

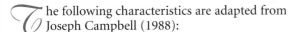

Evaluating Traditional Literature

Each genre has unique qualities that make it necessary to alter or add to the criteria used to evaluate other books. In Chapter 2, the text of books is evaluated mainly in terms of plot, characters, setting, theme, style or qualities of writing, emotional impact, imaginative impact, and vision. Some of these criteria do not play as important a part in traditional literature, however, since plots are usually linear and one-dimensional, characters are often stereotypical and flat, and the setting is "long ago." One additional element that is important in traditional literature is a respect for and understanding of the culture being written about. The text must be truthful and faithful to the original story. With folk tales, we must think about whether there is anything that would embarrass or hurt a child of that culture and whether or not the book fosters cultural stereotypes. This element will be called respect for the culture.

The visual aspects of a book should be looked at in terms of the four questions in Chapter 2:

1. Does it delight and involve you?

2. Does the artist pick moments that are highly visual?

3. Does the artwork enhance the author's words?

4. Is there variety in the work in terms of perspective and composition?

But accurate representation of the people and culture is also essential. Oftentimes illustrators of books on American Indians show a mishmash of "generic Indian" designs, oblivious to the fact that there are many American Indian nations, each with its own designs and traditions. It is always easier to trust in the authenticity of the book when the illustrator and author talk about the ways they've worked to be true to the culture. In the boxed feature Criteria for Evaluating Traditional Literature on page 252, this artistic element is called accurate visual representation.

Criteria for Evaluating *Traditional Literature*

1. **Plot.** Is there enough detail to make the plot interesting? Are plot elements presented in such a way that the reader is kept interested?

2. **Characters.** Are we given as full a picture of the characters as is possible in this genre? Do we find out enough about the characters to spark an interest in them? Do the details help us envision the characters?

3. **Setting.** How are we taken to that long ago or faraway place? Do details and images make us feel that we are in another time and place?

4. **Theme.** What is the truth or lesson here? Is it an important or worthwhile one? What are its implications?

5. **Style—qualities of writing.** Is the voice strong? Is the point of view easy to listen to and respond to? Is there richness of language and skillful use of literary devices? This criterion is especially important in traditional stories.

6. **Emotional impact.** Do you feel something as you read? Are you moved by the language? Can you feel the essence of the story?

7. **Imaginative impact.** Does the story stretch your thinking, pique your curiosity, make you leap over the boundaries of your own thinking, or help you see possibilities?

8. **Vision.** What view of people and the world is shown? How is power distributed? What is valued? Is equity an issue?

9. **Respect for the culture.** Has the author taken the time to do adequate research? (Often Author's Notes or the inside book flap will give you this information.) Are the portrayals of people consistent with what you know of the culture? If the author changed a story, is that indicated somewhere?

10. **Accurate visual representation.** Do the illustrations give you the feel of the culture? Are stereotypes avoided? Do any pictures appear to ridicule or make fun of the culture? See whether the illustrator explains the kind of research he or she has done.

Favorite Authors and Illustrators of Traditional Tales

Because so few authors write only traditional stories, the list in the boxed feature Favorite Authors and Illustrators of Traditional Tales is short. Most of these authors have several traditional stories in publication. The list is intended merely as a starting point, as you begin to explore the very large field of traditional literature.

Favorite Authors and Illustrators of Traditional Tales

Alma Flor Ada retells traditional tales and also writes wonderfully creative stories in which nursery rhyme or fairy tale characters exchange charming letters.

Joseph Bruchac is a natural storyteller who is at his best in telling American Indian tales. His love and reverence for the culture are apparent in his careful choice of language and selection of detail.

Shirley Climo, a writer who relishes finding and retelling stories from around the world, uses vivid language to bring the stories to life. Her source notes are an excellent resource for the reader.

Paul Goble, author and illustrator, has a characteristic style in which he retells American Indian legends and folk tales. In his illustrations, children can readily identify the clear and crisp features against an often white background.

Barbara Diamond Goldin's retellings are filled with love and respect for both the reader and the story. She often retells stories about Jewish holidays and American Indian folk tales.

Virginia Hamilton, a writer in many genres, is especially skilled at writing traditional literature. Her ear for dialect and her joy in using language make her stories wonderful read-alouds.

Eric A. Kimmel, a renowned storyteller and folklorist, writes, retells, and adapts stories from around the world, using precise and often colorful language.

Julius Lester writes with zest and humor, using language in loving ways to retell tales.

Rafe Martin, a professional storyteller, has written many lovely tales. He brings his stories to life through drama and through his belief that stories pass on the realities of the human heart.

Gerald McDermott writes with elegant simplicity, evoking the power of myth through his passion for getting to the heart of a myth through his retelling.

Robin McKinley's retellings of fairy tales are notable for her beautiful use of language, her ability to create mystery and suspense with a known plot, and her creation of lush, detailed, magical settings.

Donna Jo Napoli creates lovely, fresh retellings of fairy tales. Her complex characterizations give readers new ways to think about characters' actions and motivations.

Mary Pope Osborne adds her magic to retellings of tales. With her clean, straightforward language and passion, she makes these tales interesting and understandable.

Nancy Van Laan's desire to understand the intent of each story before she re-writes it allows her to capture the tone and flavor through her word choice and characterization. Her well-detailed source notes are a bonus.

Jane Yolen is a storyteller whose ability to spin a story is almost unmatched. Her use of details helps us land right in the settings she creates. Her imagination seems unlimited, and her tales always have a freshness about them.

Invitations

Choose several of the following activities to complete:

1. Choose a fairy tale such as "Snow White," "Sleeping Beauty," "Hansel and Gretel," "The Ugly Duckling," "The Emperor's New Clothes," "Rumpelstiltskin," "Little Red Riding Hood," "Three Little Pigs," or "The Billy Goats Gruff." Examine the lessons and truths in it, as well as the human qualities admired and not admired. What societal values are embedded in the tale? Share your findings with your group.

2. Read a book of Mother Goose rhymes and explain their appeal and any lessons or messages you think they impart to children. What features of the rhymes teach or reinforce phonemic awareness (see Taking a Look at the Research). Discuss your findings. Which Mother Goose rhymes were your favorites as a child?

3. After you have read several fairy tales, folk tales, or legends that contain both male heroes and female heroines, compare the heroes to the heroines. What do they do to achieve heroic status, what motivates them, what qualities are they applauded for? Are men usually cruel through their strength while women are cruel through magic or through demanding hard work of children?

4. After reading many fables, bring to class a list of morals that you feel are still timely today. Which fables have importance to your life? Compare your list to the lists of others in your group and try to compile a "Top Ten" list of the group's favorite morals.

5. Read several folk tales and fairy tales, and list patterns you find, such as three siblings or three tasks to be accomplished. Share your list with your group and compile a whole-group list that includes all the patterns found.

6. Read eight to ten folk tales from a specific cultural or ethnic group or geographic area— for example, Irish, Italian, Russian, British, German, Ethiopian or North African, Chinese, Korean, Vietnamese, Latin American, South American, Mexican, or Inuit. Look for commonalities in the tales, using the questions in the boxed feature Criteria for Evaluating Folk Tales or other categories you develop. Share your findings with group members who have read about different areas, and see what you can discover about each culture, group, or area.

7. Read several versions of a fairy tale or folk tale from different cultures. Compare the language, the illustrations, and what the author seems to emphasize, noting any differences in the impact the books have on you. Share your findings with your group.

8. Look for evidence of either the hero cycle or the characteristics of heroes in the folk tales, fairy tales, tall tales, and myths you have read. In which kinds of folk tales do you find the most heroes? Share your findings with your group.

9. Read several specific kinds of folk tales from several cultures—for example, creation stories or trickster tales. What similarities do you see? What differences do you notice? Share your findings with your group.

10. Think about what you remember about reading fairy tales and folk tales as a child. Compare your memories and reactions to those in the boxed feature Children's Voices.

Classroom Teaching Ideas

1. To personalize the genre of folk literature for young children, ask your students to talk to their parents about traditions in their family. Did their parents sing them songs that had been passed down from an older generation? Were they read nursery rhymes and fairy tales or told family stories? Have students share these stories, songs, rhymes, and books with the class. This can be an especially good way to tap into diversity in the class and celebrate it.

2. Ask children in groups or as a whole class to choose a folk tale or a fable and turn it into a poem or a song.

3. Find several versions of the same fairy tale, tall tale, or folk tale, and have children compare the versions and write or tell why they are drawn to a certain version.

4. If you read many folk tales on one culture, ask your students to create an alphabet book of the culture.

5. On a bulletin board, create a Kids Care Corner where students write messages to their friends, family, and community, showing how they can apply messages in folk tales and fables to their lives today. For instance, after reading a fable that showed the folly of greed, a student could write a note to a sibling explaining how he or she will try to share toys more.

6. Have students write a readers theater script for a modern day "Cinderella" or other familiar fairy tale and perform it for the class. Older students might focus on changing or reversing male and female roles in the script. This should encourage lots of conversation about gender expectations.

7. Read aloud to your class several fables from a collection. Divide the students into groups and ask each group to think about the fables in terms of what characteristics they share. Compare the lists. Ask children in the groups to write a modern fable, adopting a moral they have already heard or one they create.

8. In order to help children recognize what they may be absorbing from fairy tales, have them look at the characters in terms of what they would like/dislike about being each of the characters. They could talk about the best/worst thing about being the prince, the fairy godmother, the stepmother, the father, and so on.

Internet and Text Resources

1. **Grimms' Fairy Tales** contains a collection of the stories of Jacob and Wilhelm Grimm. Find it at

    www.nationalgeographic.com/grimm/index2.html

2. **Folklore, Myth and Legend** contains a wealth of Internet sources on folklore, myth, and legend, with links to various sites. Many of the sites listed contain several versions or variants of the same story, such as "Cinderella" or "Little Red Riding Hood." Go to

    www.acs.ucalgary.ca/~dkbrown/storfolk.html

3. **Mythology** shows commonalities across cultures in myths, which are organized in such categories as sun, earth, and moon. If you want to learn about the links between myths, this is the site. Go to

    www.windows.ucar.edu/cgi-bin/tour_def/mythology/mythology.html

4. **Nursery Rhyme Time** looks at nursery rhymes in relation to fourteen categories, including literature, language development, and even bulletin board ideas. Find it at

    www.sbcss.k12.ca.us/sbcss/specialeducation/ecthematic/rhymes

5. **Mama Lisa's House of Nursery Rhymes** is a colorful site which provides the text of many traditional Mother Goose nursery rhymes. Go to

    www.mamalisa.com/house/

6. **Reading Zone—Myths and Fables** contains a collection of worldwide myths and fables. Go to

    www.ipl.org/cgi-bin/youth/youth.out

7. **Cinderella Variants** lists more than 100 variants of the fairy tale. Find it at

www.acpl.lib.in.us/Childrens_Services/cinderella.html.

To find Little Red Riding Hood variants, use the same address but change "cinderella" to "redridinghood."

8. **Aadizookaanag—Traditional Stories, Legends, and Myths** is a lovely site with stories from the cultures of indigenous peoples. Find it at

www.kstrom.net/isk/stories/myths/html/

9. **Folklore and Mythology Electronic Texts** provides oodles of complete texts. Find it at

www.pitt.edu/~dash/folktexts.html/#1

10. **Aesop Fables Online Collection** provides texts of over 600 fables! Go to

www.aesopfables.com

11. **AbsoluteWhootie: Stories to Grow By** contains a selection of fairy tales and folk tales from around the world that speak to such themes as courage, justice, and kindness. Go to

www.storiestogrowby.com

References

Bruchac, Joseph (1997). *Tell Me a Tale: A Book about Storytelling*. San Diego: Harcourt Brace.

Campbell, Joseph (1988). *The Power of Myth*. New York: Doubleday.

Emrich, Duncan (1972). *Folklore on the American Land*. Boston: Little, Brown.

Ford, Clyde (2001). Speech at Spring Conference of National Council of Teachers of English. Birmingham, Alabama, March 29–31.

McDermott, Gerald (1999). "Traditional Fantasy in Picture Books." IRA Annual Convention. San Diego, May 2–7, 1999.

Children's Books

Aesop (1967). *Aesop's Fables*. Illus. Arthur Rackham. New York: Franklin Watts.

Aliki (1994). *The Gods and Goddesses of Olympus*. New York: HarperCollins.

Bornstein, Harry, and Karen L. Saulnier, eds. (1992). *Nursery Rhymes from Mother Goose: Told in Signed English*. Illus. Patricia Peters. Signline drawings by Linda C. Tom. Washington, DC: Kendall Green.

Brill, Marlene Targ (1998). *Tooth Tales from around the World*. Illus. Katya Krenina. Watertown, MA: Charlesbridge.

Bruchac, Joseph (1996). *Between Earth and Sky: Legends of Native American Sacred Places*. Illus. Thomas Locker. San Diego: Harcourt Brace.

Climo, Shirley (1994). *Stolen Thunder: A Norse Myth*. Illus. Alexander Koshkin. New York: Clarion.

Cole, Joanna, ed. (1989). *Anna Banana: 101 Jump-Rope Rhymes*. Illus. Alan Tiegreen. New York: Morrow.

Cole, Joanna, and Stephanie Calmenson (1990). *Miss Mary Mack and Other Children's Street Rhymes*. Illus. Alan Tiegreen. New York: Morrow.

Craft, M. Charlotte (1996). *Cupid and Psyche*. Illus. K. Y. Craft. New York: Morrow.

Delacre, Lulu (1996). *Golden Tales: Myths, Legends, and Folktales from Latin America*. New York: Scholastic.

Doucet, Sharon Arms (1997). *Why Lapin's Ears Are Long: And Other Tales from the Louisiana Bayou*. Illus. David Catrow. New York: Orchard.

Emerson, Sally, ed. (1988). *The Nursery Treasury: A Collection of Baby Games, Rhymes and Lullabies*. Illus. Moira MacLean and Colin MacLean. New York: Doubleday.

Evetts-Secker, Josephine (1999). *The Barefoot Book of Mother and Son Tales*. Illus. Helen Cann. New York: Barefoot.

Furlong, Monica (1998). *Robin's Country*. New York: Knopf.

Goble, Paul (1988). *Her Seven Brothers*. New York: Bradbury.

Goldin, Barbara Diamond (1999). *Journeys with Elijah: Eight Tales of the Prophet*. Illus. Jerry Pinkney. San Diego: Harcourt Brace.

Hamilton, Virginia (1995). *Her Stories: African American Folktales, Fairy Tales, and True Tales*. Illus. Leo Dillon and Diane Dillon. New York: Blue Sky/Scholastic.

—— (1991). *In the Beginning: Creation Stories from Around the World*. Illus. Barry Moser. San Diego: Harcourt Brace [1988].

—— (1985). *The People Could Fly: American Black Folktales*. Illus. Leo Dillon and Diane Dillon. New York: Knopf.

—— (1997). *A Ring of Tricksters: Animal Tales from America, the West Indies, and Africa.* Illus. Barry Moser. New York: Blue Sky/Scholastic.

Hayes, Barbara (1998). *Folk Tales and Fables of the Middle East and Africa.* Illus. Robert R. Ingpen. New York: Chelsea.

Hoffman, Mary (1998). *Clever Katya: A Fairy Tale from Old Russia.* Illus. Marie Cameron. New York: Barefoot.

Isaacs, Anne (1994). *Swamp Angel.* Illus. Paul O. Zelinsky. New York: Dutton.

Johnson, David A. (1998). *Old Mother Hubbard: A Nursery Rhyme.* New York: McElderry.

Johnson, Janet P. (1998). *Keelboat Annie: An African American Legend.* Illus. Charles Reasoner. Mahwah, NJ: Troll.

Kellogg, Steven (1992). *Mike Fink.* New York: Morrow.

—— (1984). *Paul Bunyan.* New York: Morrow.

—— (1995). *Sally Ann Thunder Ann Whirlwind Crockett.* New York: Morrow.

Kimmel, Eric A. (1996). *Count Silvernose: A Story from Italy.* Illus. Omar Rayyan. New York: Holiday.

—— (1995). *Rimonah of the Flashing Sword: A North African Tale.* Illus. Omar Rayyan. New York: Holiday.

Lapaca, Michael (1996). *Antelope Woman: An Apache Folktale.* Flagstaff, AR: Northland.

Lester, Julius (1990). *Further Tales of Uncle Remus: The Misadventures of Brer Rabbit, Brer Fox, Brer Wolf, the Doodang, and Other Creatures.* Illus. Jerry Pinkney. New York: Dial.

—— (1994). *John Henry.* Illus. Jerry Pinkney. New York: Dial.

—— (1999). *When the Beginning Began: Stories about God, the Creatures, and Us.* Illus. Emily Lisker. San Diego: Silverwhistle.

Levine, Gail Carson (1997). *Ella Enchanted.* New York: HarperCollins.

Lobel, Arnold (1980). *Fables.* New York: Harper.

Martin, Rafe (1996). *Mysterious Tales of Japan.* Illus. Tatsuro Kiuchi. New York: Putnam.

—— (1992). *The Rough-Face Girl.* Illus. David Shannon. New York: Putnam.

Mayo, Margaret (1997). *Mythical Birds & Beasts from Many Lands.* Illus. Jane Ray. New York: Dutton.

McDermott, Gerald (1974). *Arrow to the Sun: A Pueblo Indian Tale.* New York: Viking.

—— (1993). *Raven: A Trickster Tale from the Pacific Northwest.* San Diego: Harcourt Brace.

—— (1999). *The Stonecutter: A Japanese Folk Tale.* New York: Econo-Clad [1975, Viking].

McKinley, Robin (1978). *Beauty: A Retelling of the Story of Beauty & the Beast.* New York: Harper & Row.

Mutén, Burleigh (1999). *Grandmothers' Stories: Wise Woman Tales from Many Cultures.* Illus. Sian Bailey. New York: Barefoot.

Napoli, Donna Jo (1996). *Zel.* New York: Dutton.

Opie, Iona, ed. (1996). *My Very First Mother Goose.* Illus. Rosemary Wells. Cambridge, MA: Candlewick.

Opie, Peter, and Iona Opie, eds. (1992). *I Saw Esau: The Schoolchild's Pocket Book.* Illus. Maurice Sendak. New York: Walker.

Osborne, Mary Pope (1991). *Favorite Greek Myths.* Illus. Troy Howell. New York: Scholastic.

Patz, Nancy (1983). *Moses Supposes His Toeses Are Roses and Seven Other Silly Old Rhymes.* San Diego: Harcourt Brace.

Polacco, Patricia (1995). *Babushka's Mother Goose.* New York: Philomel.

Pullman, Philip (1999). *I Was a Rat.* New York: Knopf.

Rockwell, Anne (1996). *The One-Eyed Giants: And Other Monsters from Greek Myths.* New York: Greenwillow.

Sanfield, Steve (1995). *Bit by Bit.* Illus. Susan Gaber. New York: Philomel.

Say, Allen (1974). *Under the Cherry Blossom Tree: An Old Japanese Tale.* New York: Houghton Mifflin.

Schwartz, Alvin (1972). *A Twister of Twists, a Tangler of Tongues.* Illus. Glen Rounds. New York: Lippincott.

Stanley, Diane (1995). *Petrosinella: A Neopolitan Rapunzel.* New York: Dial.

Taback, Simms (1999). *Joseph Had a Little Overcoat.* New York: Viking.

Van Laan, Nancy (1997). *Shingebiss: An Ojibwe Legend.* Woodcuts by Betsy Bowen. Boston: Houghton Mifflin.

Walker, Paul Robert (1995). *Giants! Stories from Around the World.* Illus. James Bernardin. San Diego: Harcourt Brace.

Walker, Richard (1998). *The Barefoot Book of Trickster Tales.* Illus. Claudio Muñez. New York: Barefoot.

Williams, Carol Ann (1995). *Tsubu, the Little Snail.* Illus. Tatsuro Kiuchi. New York: Simon & Schuster.

Wolfson, Margaret Olivia (1996). *The Marriage of the Rain Goddess: A South African Myth.* Illus. Clifford Alexander Parms. New York: Marlow.

Wood, Audrey (1996). *The Bunyans.* Illus. David Shannon. New York: Blue Sky/Scholastic.

Yolen, Jane (2000). *Not One Damsel in Distress: World Folktales for Strong Girls.* Illus. Susan Guevara. San Diego: Starwhistle.

—— (1998). *Pegasus, the Flying Horse.* Illus. Li Ming. New York: Dutton.

—— (1995). *A Sip of Aesop.* Illus. Karen Barbour. New York: Blue Sky/Scholastic.

Young, Ed (1989). *Lon Po Po: A Red-Riding Hood Story from China.* New York: Philomel.

—— (1992). *Seven Blind Mice.* New York: Scholastic.

Zelinsky, Paul (1997). *Rapunzel.* New York: Dutton.

Realistic and Historical Fiction

eer pressure. Choices. Divorce. Friendship. Death of a pet. Death of a grandparent. Moving. Loss of friends. Sibling rivalry. Survival in the wilderness. Falling in love. Solving a mystery. Overcoming adversity. Sports adventures. Family closeness. Coping with disabilities. Adoption. Problems with growing up. Although these topics appear unrelated, explorations of these themes set in contemporary times are grouped together under the umbrella term *realistic fiction* because they deal with real-life issues children experience. Books in this genre are often avenues for understanding one's own situation, meeting people who are similar to people one knows, and seeing how other people negotiate their lives. The focus on life's experiences makes this genre very appealing to children, who are eager to learn more about people and how they handle life's situations. This chapter will deal separately with historical fiction because, although it is a kind of realistic fiction, its emphasis on accuracy and authenticity raises different issues.

What Is Realistic Fiction?

The classification *realistic fiction* is assigned to stories that are convincingly true to life and that help children examine their own lives, empathize with other people, and see the complexity of human interaction. But exactly what does *real* mean and how real can realistic fiction be? When students are asked to assess this genre in terms of how realistic it is, they often respond only in terms of their own experiences, claiming that people they know don't act that way. Oftentimes they judge realism by imagining their friends and family in the roles of the characters. Behavior that is realistic to one person may seem far fetched to others. Gordon Korman (2000) says that he often begins stories with a real event and yet that tends to be the part of the story that seems unbelievable. He tells about visiting a school where a first-year teacher was teaching his students where their food comes from by having them raise a chicken in class, feed it, take it home on weekends, and then eventually have it killed and eat it. Korman could immediately see the problem with this "lesson plan"—the children would become too attached to the chicken to want to eat it. When he put this incident in one of his books and invented the rest of the story, readers complained that the chicken incident didn't seem realistic!

How real is too real if this genre is supposed to mirror real life? First of all, since moving the story along is the primary consideration, much of real life must be left out. Readers usually don't need to see in detail the showering, dressing, eating, and hygienic habits of characters. A more controversial issue is the realism of topics in realistic fiction. Should children read about death, cancer, and AIDS? Should they read about violence and abuse? Should they read about corruption and cruelty? Should they read about diverse families, such as families with two mothers or two fathers? Today all of these issues are being written about, but some parents don't want their children exposed to such realism (see the discussion on censorship later in this chapter). One standard that seems to permeate children's realistic stories is whether the ending offers hope or is uplifting in some way. Robert Cormier has been criticized because his books for older readers seem not to offer hope. Writers for younger children almost always hold out hope. Betsy Byars (2000) said, "I could never write anything that depresses me." She is an irrepressible person, however, who by nature seems to see the positive side of things, and that is reflected in her books even though they deal with tough issues. At bottom, then, realistic fiction is a genre that deals with the experientially true, tempered by both the author's view of life and what the public will accept.

The Appeal of Realistic Fiction

Realistic fiction is a genre of great appeal, as evidenced by the large number of Newbery Awards given to realistic fiction books. We like to meet other people whom we can relate to, whom we can learn from, and whom we can laugh with. Realistic fiction is appealing and valuable to children for a variety of reasons:

1. They can learn about human behavior and how people interact and get along with each other.

2. They can laugh with others in books and learn to laugh at themselves a little.

3. They can meet people who are experiencing the same feelings and emotions that they are and use these characters' experiences as a guide in handling challenges in their own lives, such as death, divorce, and moving.

4. They can learn about people who have different experiences and living conditions and thus can see that the whole world does not live as they do.

5. They can participate vicariously in events and activities that they may never actually experience, such as living in the woods, fighting for their homes, or climbing a mountain.

6. They can find out what it's like to live in another place, such as Appalachia, New York City, or the Cholistan Desert in Pakistan.

7. They can take an active part in solving a mystery and feel that they are helping to change the balance in the world between good and evil.

8. They can be delighted by heartwarming and life-affirming stories and good writing.

Types of Realistic Fiction

Realistic fiction is a broad category that includes many kinds of books. Among the most popular are adventure stories, animal stories, family stories, growing-up stories, books on social issues, humor, mysteries, romances, school stories, and sports stories. Children have definite ideas on the kinds of realistic fiction they prefer, as the boxed feature Children's Voices shows (see page 262).

Adventure Stories

Many people love the idea of adventure—of participating in an event or undertaking marked by risk or excitement. For some, going on a roller coaster and believing life will end momentarily is enough adventure. Other people actually go white water rafting or parasailing or mountain climbing. Most of us, however, would rather read about others participating in adventures. Then, from the safety of our own homes, we can watch others undertake dangerous adventures, witnessing vicariously as they fight wars or survive in the wilderness.

Gary Paulsen writes compelling adventures of survival, such as **Hatchet** and **Canyons.** Will Hobbs puts readers squarely in the center of dangerous situations in **Far North, Ghost Canoe,** and **Downriver. The Shark Callers,** by Eric Campbell, pits the protagonists against a massive tidal wave in shark-infested waters.

Adventure involving risks is largely absent from early readers mainly because many young children cannot separate themselves from the characters and thus find adventure stories too frightening. However, chapter-book adventures do exist, including **The Righteous Revenge of Artemis Bonner,** by Walter Dean Myers, in which a young man goes West to avenge the murder of his uncle, and the **Danger Guys** series. In **Danger Guys and the Golden Lizard,** by Tony Abbott, the protagonists engage in mildly risky adventures, facing dangerous Land Rover rides, a plane crash in the jungle, and the jaws of an alligator.

Animal Stories

Almost every child has had positive experiences with animals and loves to read stories that have animals in them. We love animals because they are soft to pet, respond to us with soulful looks, and live totally in the present, allowing play and fun to take precedence in their lives. We believe that our own animals care deeply about us and are very attuned to us. We love their loyalty, their patience, their wish to spend as much time as possible with us. They make us feel special and needed. We recognize that our animals need us, too,

Nathan and Lighthouse George paddle through treacherous waters, both literally and metaphorically, in this mystery adventure.
(From *Ghost Canoe* by Will Hobbs. Cover art copyright © 1997. Used by permission of HarperCollins Publishers.)

Go to **Book Lists at the RT Library** to find lists of books about school, survival, and more at www.gti.net/rocktwpl/booklist.html.

On realistic fiction . . .

I like books that can really happen but don't. Realistic books are easier to think about, understand, and have feelings for. But if they really haven't happened, authors can add anything they want as they go along.
—Jennifer, 7th grade

I like to read realistic fiction that has happened or can happen. It's neat to put yourself in characters' shoes and knowing what you did in the book could really happen.
—Kelli, 7th grade

I like to read about real life because I like to compare my life to the character's.
—Luis, 7th grade

I like to read about characters that are in trouble and are trying to get out of their situation. —Katie, 7th grade

On adventure books . . .

Gary Paulsen is my favorite author. He writes a lot of adventure novels that keep you on the edge of your seat and make you feel lucky you don't have to go through what the characters go through. —Michael, 7th grade

I like something adventurous or with a twist at the end or something that tells about kids my age with problems that relate to mine. —Hailey, 7th grade

In survival stories it's interesting how they do the things they do like survival skills and different tactics, also some things they learn from mistakes. —Ben, 7th grade

Gary Paulsen in **Hatchet**, **Brian's Winter**, **The River**, *and* **Brian's Return** *brilliantly describes nature, Brian's activities in the woods, and how he lives.* —Matt, 8th grade

On humor . . .

My favorite author is Roald Dahl because he is funny and seems like he knows how to end a book or when to end a book. —Keith, 7th grade

If I were to remember anything out of a book it would be the part that makes me laugh. —Brittany, 7th grade

I like funny books read aloud to me. —Derrick, 7th grade

On mystery . . .

I like Nancy Drew books because they are exciting and scary. —Shelby, 3rd grade

I like dramas and mysteries. I like the suspense and outcomes. —Erin, 7th grade

I like mysteries because you never know what's going to happen. —Jenny, 7th grade

I like mysteries to be read to me. —Michael, 7th grade

On sports books . . .

I like sports books because I play sports and I like to keep up to date on facts about sports players and sports. —Billy, 7th grade

On my own I like to read sports books because I play sports and they are interesting to me. —Madison, 7th grade

and we give them our time and are generous in ways that we might not be with siblings. For all these reasons, we have a passion for animal stories.

You may remember reading an animal story that tugged at your heartstrings or made you cry. Every time I read *Where the Red Fern Grows,* by Wilson Rawls, to my middle school students, I cried when Old Dan and Little Ann died. Maybe you remember *Sounder,* by William H. Armstrong; *Shiloh,* by Phyllis Reynolds Naylor; or *Stone Fox,* by John Reynolds Gardiner.

Realistic animal stories are written even for the youngest readers. *Biscuit,* the first title in an early reader series by Alyssa Satin Capucilli, features a darling yellow puppy who doesn't want to go to bed yet. Chapter books featuring animal stories include *A Dolphin Named Bob,* by Twig C. George; *Tornado,* by Betsy Byars; and *There's an Owl in the Shower,* by Jean Craighead George.

Family Stories

Sometimes family stories are called problem novels because they often deal with family problems such as divorce. Students enjoy reading about other people experiencing the same things they are. They get to see how others handle these things and, most of all, know that they are not the only ones in the world who are dealing with this issue or feeling this way. Students respond to family books because they can see that the characters experience feelings of confusion, insecurity, anger, and loss and then adjust.

Dear Mr. Henshaw, by Beverly Cleary, shows children coping with the emotional loss caused by divorce. Many books deal with several themes at once. In *The World of Daughter Maguire,* by Sharon Dennis Wyeth, Daughter is trying to understand what being biracial means as she copes with her parents' potential divorce. *Plain City,* by Virginia Hamilton, shows the main character dealing with being biracial as well as accepting that her father was psychologically damaged. The stories of Cynthia Voigt, in such books as *Homecoming,* focus on Dicey and her brothers and sisters as they cope with a mentally ill mother and an absent father. In *Belle Prater's Boy,* by Ruth White, the boy must cope with the disappearance of his mother as his cousin learns to accept the death of her father. *Joey Pigza Loses Control,* by Jack Gantos, focuses on the antics of Joey, a hyperactive child, when he comes to visit his grandmother and alcoholic father for the summer. Laurence Yep's *Child of the Owl* portrays twelve-year-old Casey learning to appreciate her Chinese heritage when she's sent to live with her grandmother in Chinatown because her father's illness prevents him from caring for her.

Growing-Up Stories

Growing-up stories portray the struggles young people go through with friends, identity, and ethical issues. Beverly Cleary's *Ramona* stories, Lois Lowry's *Anastasia Krupnik,* and Christopher Paul Curtis's *The Watsons Go to Birmingham—1963* are among the best known and loved. *The Baby-Sitters Club* series, by Ann M. Martin, showcases friendship and the issues of being part of a group. *Wringer,* by Jerry Spinelli, poignantly portrays a young boy dealing with peer and community pressure to kill pigeons as part of a community fund-raising event. *The Great Gilly Hopkins,* by Katherine Paterson, shows young Gilly trying to understand what family is as she moves in and out of foster home experiences. *Maniac Magee,* by Jerry Spinelli, tells of the growing-up years of Maniac, after the death of his parents, when he

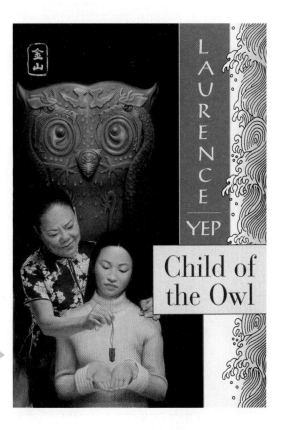

Paw Paw's affection for her granddaughter and patience in teaching her about their Chinese culture permeate this story, which focuses on Casey's adjustment to living away from her father.
(Cover art from *Child of the Owl* by Laurence Yep. Used by permission of HarperCollins Publishers.)

becomes something of a hero because of his unusual feats. For many children, growing up includes dealing with the death of someone close to them. **Walk Two Moons,** by Sharon Creech, shows Salamanca coming to accept the death of her mother. In **Crazy Lady!,** by Jane Leslie Conly, a young boy is coping with the death of his mother as he learns how to accept a mentally retarded boy.

Growing up also includes dealing with sexuality. The ever-popular **Are You There God? It's Me, Margaret,** by Judy Blume, talks about girls' body changes. In **The Goats,** by Brock Cole, two young people are confronted with their own sexuality when they are stripped and left on an island by other campers. Other books look at understanding one's sexual identity. **Annie on My Mind** and **Good Moon Rising,** both by Nancy Garden, are stories of girls coming to accept their homosexuality.

Other growing-up stories tell of the impact of moving to a different city or country. In Naomi Shihab Nye's **Habibi,** the Arab American protagonist moves from the United States to Israel, where she deals with cultural and language changes and sees evidence of prejudice and hatred.

Books on Social Issues

Some realistic fiction deals with issues beyond the scope of everyday family interactions. These issues include abuse, alcoholism, drug use, homelessness, homophobia, poverty, racism, sexism, and violence. More resources than the family itself can provide are required to address these issues, which have societal implications.

Books that deal with the gritty theme of family abuse include **I Hadn't Meant to Tell You This** and **Lena,** by Jacqueline Woodson; **Uncle Vampire,** by Cynthia D. Grant; **Max the Mighty,** by Rodman Philbrick; **When She Hollers,** by Cynthia Voigt; and **What Jamie Saw,** by Carolyn Coman. In **Freak the Mighty,** by Rodman Philbrick, Max has to come to terms with witnessing his father killing his mother.

The plight of a homeless father and his son is seen in Eve Bunting's picture book **Fly Away Home.** In Jacqueline Woodson's **From the Notebooks of Melanin Sun,** Melanin, a high school boy, is trying to figure out what it means to him to have a lesbian mom. Woodson's **If You Come Softly** deals with parent issues, school issues, and ultimately the violence in our society, through the love story of Jeremiah and Ellie. The persistence of racism is confronted in Suzanne Fisher Staples's **Dangerous Skies.** Coping with being the only Korean family in town is depicted in Marie G. Lee's **Necessary Roughness. Bearstone,** by Will Hobbs, shows Cloyd trying to hold onto his Native American culture as he moves from foster home to foster home.

Humor

Michael Cart (1995), writer and critic, claims, "Humor is the Rodney Dangerfield of literary forms: It gets no respect" (p. 1). Yet, according to Barbara Elleman (2000), scholar and critic, "Funny picture books are not only good for kids but encourage them to think creatively and read more." She believes that because children's lives are often so structured, they are taught things step by step. Humor helps them think outside the box and do such things as play with words: "Giggles can affect children in many positive ways." Dan Gutman (2000), creator of witty and entertaining books for middle grade readers, echoes some of Elleman's concerns: "Kids want to laugh, but comedy gets a bad rap. People assume it doesn't require much work and is not of high quality." Gordon Korman

To find authors who write about social issues, search Favorite Authors for the key word *issues*.

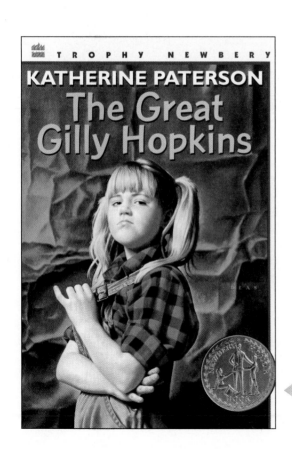

It takes a special person to understand and penetrate the tough exterior that Gilly Hopkins presents to the world.

(Cover art from *The Great Gilly Hopkins* by Katherine Paterson. Used by permission of HarperCollins Publishers.)

(2000), writer of humorous novels such as ***The Chicken Doesn't Skate,*** points out that a funny book is usually the one book that will turn reluctant readers into readers. Another writer of humor, Paula Danziger (1999), explains that she deals with "serious issues and uses comedy to make those issues more bearable.... Humor is touching.... It gets close to feelings. It can make us feel better—almost like a caress of understanding—or it can really hurt—like a stiletto in your heart" (p. 29). Betsy Byars writes about growing-up issues in extraordinarily funny ways in such books as ***Bingo Brown and the Language of Love.***

Humor abounds in picture books such as Margie Palatini's ***Moosetache, Ding Dong Ding Dong,*** and ***Piggie Pie!;*** Babette Cole's ***The Trouble with Mom;*** and David Wisniewski's ***Tough Cookie*** and ***The Secret Knowledge of Grown-Ups.*** Early readers such as ***A Know-Nothing Birthday,*** by Michele Sobel Spirn, and ***Wizard and Wart at Sea,*** by Janice Lee Smith, let kids laugh as they read. Chapter books that will keep kids chuckling and reading include ***The School Bus Driver from the Black Lagoon,*** by Mike Thaler; ***Play Ball, Amelia Bedelia,*** by Peggy Parish; ***The Time Warp Trio,*** by Jon Scieszka; and ***The Shrinking of Treehorn,*** by Florence Parry Heide. Chris Lynch's ***Babes in the Woods: The He-Man Women Haters Club #3*** and Paula Danziger's ***Amber Brown*** series bubble over with humor. Other writers of humorous books include Judie Angell, Beverly Cleary, Ellen Conford, Helen Cresswell, Louise Fitzhugh, Stephen Manes, Barbara Park, Daniel Pinkwater, Barbara Robinson, and Barbara Wersba.

Mysteries

From the ***Nancy Drew*** and ***Hardy Boys*** series to today's crop of whodunnits, young people love mysteries. Part of the thrill of mystery reading is trying to figure out who did it before the characters do. This kind of book requires active reading and thinking and evaluating, as the reader must decide which clues are worth paying attention to.

This kind of book demands a lot of the author, too. Betsy Byars (2000), who won an Edgar Award for one of her mysteries, says, "Mysteries are the most structured of the genres to write." When she writes mysteries, she draws an actual map. Jean Lowry Nixon (2000) explains that making young detectives realistic is at the core of writing mysteries for young people. The young person has to be a believable character and have a strong motive to want to solve the mystery. Kids like to know that kids are clever enough to pick up a clue that police miss. Nancy Werlin (2000) believes that the world of the mystery is highly moral, with its emphasis on right and wrong, good and evil: "The world of mystery says the truth must be found and right must be restored." Byars offers another reason for the popularity of mysteries. She feels that detective stories are "one way we can deal with violent death—we can make sense of it with human intelligence." Perhaps this explains why the genre is so popular with children.

Many early reader books, such as ***Detective Dinosaur: Lost and Found,*** by James Skofield, introduce children to the genre. These are followed up by chapter books such as Betsy Byars's ***The Seven Treasure Hunts;*** the ***Chet Gecko*** mysteries, by Bruce Hale, such as ***The Chameleon Wore Chartreuse;*** the ***Sammy Keyes*** books, by Wendelin Van Draanen, such as ***Sammy Keyes and the Hotel Thief;*** the ***Encyclopedia Brown*** series, by Donald J. Sobel, such as ***Encyclopedia Brown Solves Them All;*** and the ***Carmen Sandiego*** mystery series, published by HarperTrophy. Other mysteries include ***The Westing Game,*** by Ellen Raskin; ***The Case of the Lion Dance,*** by Laurence Yep; and ***Mr. Was,*** by Pete Hautman. If students like mysteries, refer them to authors such as Jay Bennett, Lois Duncan, and Jean Nixon Lowery.

*Find plans for using mysteries in the classroom at **Kids Love a Mystery.com** at http:// mysterynet.com/learn*

CD-ROM

If you like *mysteries* because they are *compelling,* do a word search in Favorite Authors for either word to find the names of more authors who write compelling stories/mysteries.

Romances

Everyone wants to be cared about. In about sixth or seventh grade, some boys and girls start wanting attention that takes on romantic overtones. They want someone to care for them in a special way. At this age, the search for romance is often played out, especially for girls, in romance novels. The *Sweet Valley High* series, with over 100 titles, is often the first kind of romance novel girls read. The focus of these novels is on how important it is for a girl to be accepted by a boy. More developed romance novels usually use romance as the frame for the story, while the protagonist deals with other issues.

In *The Melinda Zone,* by Margaret Willey, Melinda is working out her feelings about her relationship with each of her divorced parents as she gets involved with Paul. It isn't the end of the story when Paul asks her out; it's the beginning. In *Thwonk,* by Joan Bauer, growing-up issues are embedded in a hilarious story of a girl who makes her dreamboat fall in love with her and then realizes what a bore he is. *Motown and Didi,* by Walter Dean Myers, is the story of two teens struggling with family issues but finding strength in the caring of the other person. In *Whistle Me Home,* by Barbara Wersba, Noli and TJ seem like soul mates until Noli finally realizes that TJ is gay. She has to figure out whether a relationship without romance is doable for her. These four novels have multiple plot lines, well-developed characters, and substantial themes within the romance format.

School Stories

Because children spend at least six hours each weekday in school, they have intimate knowledge of the setting and the workings of school. They love to hear school stories, which tend to be humorous and show characters doing things they might like to do. One popular picture book is *Miss Nelson is Missing,* by Harry Allard, which shows how one teacher dealt with an unruly class. Early readers such as *Arthur's Back to School Day,* by Lillian Hoban, calm students' fears of returning to school. Patricia Reilly Giff's chapter books, *The Kids of the Polk Street School,* offer stories of school experiences—such as losing library cards and making friends in *Say "Cheese."* Douglas Evans's *The Classroom at the End of the Hall* exaggerates events in a third-grade classroom. Andrew Clements's *Frindle* and *The Landry News* are humorous stories of fourth- and fifth-graders and their amazing undertakings. Many of Gordon Korman's humorous books are set in school, such as *Beware the Fish!* in which the students take action when they hear their school may close.

Sports Stories

Sports books are stories much like any other realistic story except that the framework on which the story is based is a sport instead of a mystery or a romance or an adventure. One chapter-book series popular with kids is Bruce Brooks's *The Wolfbay Wings,* about a hockey team. Embedded in stories such as *Barry* are traditional growing-up issues, such as getting good grades and being part of a team. The coaches in these books are pretty low key and encourage the kids to enjoy playing.

Another popular sports writer for younger kids is Matt Christopher, who is known for his fast-paced, action-packed stories, such as *The Kid Who Only Hit Homers.* Will Weaver's sports stories for older readers are meaty and satisfying. His baseball series about Billy Baggs, which includes *Striking Out, Hard Ball,* and *Farm Team,* has won many awards. John H. Ritter's baseball novels offer older readers a look at societal and family issues. In *Choosing Up Sides,* Luke has to decide whether his left-handedness is a mark of the devil, as his preacher father believes, or a gift for powerful pitching, as his uncle believes. In *Over the Wall,* the angry Tyler learns much about the Vietnam War and about healing in his bid to make the Little League All-Stars.

Using the sports story format to move his stories forward, Will Weaver focuses on father-son relationships and their importance to the mental and emotional health of the son.

(Cover art from *Hard Ball* by Will Weaver. JACKET ART © 1998 BY MICHAEL KOELSCH. JACKET © 1998 BY HARPERCOLLINS PUBLISHERS. Used by permission of HarperCollins Publishers.)

Using sports as a frame, David Klass writes compelling stories in such novels as **Wrestling with Honor** and **Danger Zone,** which are packed with issues of growing up and identity. Chris Lynch also has sports books for older readers, including **Iceman** and **Shadow Boxer,** both of which deal with family and relationship issues. Well-written books such as these can oftentimes lure otherwise reluctant readers into pleasurable reading experiences.

Themes and Formats of Realistic Fiction

Realistic fiction—whether in the form of picture books, chapter books, or novels—is packed with themes. Sometimes it's helpful to think about realistic fiction in terms of themes if you want to bring to your class books that can reach students going through a specific experience, such as the death of a loved one. Themes can also be the umbrella with which to focus a unit. In the boxed feature A Sampling of Realistic Fiction on page 268, books related to various themes are described.

It is also useful to think of realistic fiction in terms of narrative voice, to ensure that students are exposed to a variety of formats. Although first and third person still predominate in realistic fiction, contemporary authors have devised creative ways to use these voices.

First-Person Narrative

In fiction, events are frequently shown through the eyes of a narrator. Although this approach precludes the author from showing anything that the narrator does not either experience or have someone else tell her or him, there is an immediacy and closeness to events when one person is telling the story. Readers can identify with narrators, since they know exactly how they think and feel. In Paula Danziger's **Amber Brown Sees Red,** the first page says, "I, Amber Brown, am going through a growth spurt. Either that or the mirror's getting smaller." Some authors intersperse letters into a first-person account in order to hear from another character, as Patricia MacLachlan does in **Sarah, Plain and Tall.** Other times the entire story is told through letters or diary entries.

Third-Person Narrative

When a story is told in the third person, we can see the broad sweep of the story right away because we don't have to wait for the first-person narrator to show it to us. In Florence Parry Heide's **The Shrinking of Treehorn,** we hear immediately that something unusual is happening to the main character, Treehorn: "The first thing he noticed was that he couldn't reach the shelf in his closet that he had always been able to reach before, the one where he hid his candy bars and bubble gum" (p. 2).

Alternating or Multiple Narrators

To give readers access to two points of view, some writers choose to alternate viewpoints from chapter to chapter. Margaret Willey's **Facing the Music** alternates between fifteen-year-old

Palmer cannot admit to his own family, let alone his friends, how much he abhors the yearly town activity that so many approach with joy and relish.
(Jacket art for *Wringer* by Jerry Spinelli. JACKET ART COPYRIGHT © 1997 BY CLIFF NIELSEN. JACKET COPYRIGHT © 1997 BY HARPERCOLLINS PUBLISHERS. Used by permission of HarperCollins Publishers.)

A Sampling of Realistic Fiction

Awareness of other cultures

Namioka, Lensey. *April and the Dragon Lady.*
A young Chinese American teenager finds out about the demands of family when her grandmother comes to live with her. Readers learn much about the interworkings of the family.

Nye, Naomi Shihab. *Habibi.*
This story takes us to the West Bank, where we see one Arab family from America learning to live in a culture with sharp divisions between Jews and Arabs.

Staples, Suzanne Fisher. *Shiva's Fire.*
We become immersed in the culture of India and the dreams of Parvati, a young girl who wants to be a dancer.

Changes in family

Bunting, Eve. *The In-Between Days.*
Eleven-year-old George has difficulty when his father begins to date again, many years after his mother's death.

———. *Train to Somewhere.* Illus. Ronald Himler (picture book).
A young girl, still believing that her mother will come to the orphanage for her, is put on a train with other orphans in hope of finding a new family.

Holt, Kimberly Willis. *When Zachary Beaver Came to Town.*
A young boy learns much about himself the summer his mother leaves to become a singer and the largest boy in the world is on display in his Texas town.

MacLachlan, Patricia. *Journey.* Illus. Barry Moser (picture book).
A young boy must come to terms with the fact that, although his mother is gone, he is still part of a family.

Sachs, Marilyn. *Another Day.*
Fourteen-year-old Karin must cope with the feelings of rejection surrounding her parents' divorce.

Say, Allen. *Allison* (picture book).
Allison, born to Japanese parents and adopted in the United States, has to come to terms with her adoption.

Death or loss

Barron, T. A. *Where Is Grandpa?* Illus. Chris K. Soentpiet (picture book).
A father explains the death of his own father to his children.

Coman, Carolyn. *Tell Me Everything.*
As she struggles to accept the death of her mother and repress memories of what her mother was really like, Rox keeps calling the boy whom her mother died trying to rescue.

Coville, Bruce. *My Grandfather's House.* Illus. Henri Sorensen (picture book).
A young boy asks, "Where did Grandpa go when he died?" and is answered in various ways by different people in his life.

Kaldhol, Marit. *Goodbye Rune.* Illus. Wenche Oyen (picture book).
A very young child grieves for her best friend, who drowned.

Rylant, Cynthia. *Missing May.*
A young girl and her guardian learn how to live without May, the woman central to both of their lives.

Talbert, Marc. *A Sunburned Prayer.*
A young boy comes to understand that praying hard cannot prevent his beloved grandmother from dying.

White, Ruth. *Belle Prater's Boy.*
Cousins Woodrow and Gypsy deal with their own losses over the summer they spend together.

Friendships/relationships

Giff, Patricia Reilly. *Lily's Crossing.*
Ten-year-old Lily, whose father is away in World War II, develops a deep, honest friendship with a boy who has escaped from the Nazis and is also haunted by loss.

Problems at home

Draper, Sharon M. *Forged by Fire.*
A young teenager tries to save his half-sister from her abusive father.

Haddix, Margaret Peterson. *Don't You Dare Read This, Mrs. Dunphrey.*
In a journal she does not want her English teacher to read, a young girl who's been abandoned by both parents details her struggle to support herself and her younger brother.

Illness/disabilities

Philbrick, Rodman. *Freak the Mighty.*
A very large boy who can't read teams up with a very small boy who is a genius but whose outer body has stopped growing. The results are funny and touching.

Williams, Carol Lynch. *If I Forget, You Remember.*
A young girl's life changes the summer before seventh grade, when her grandmother who has Alzheimer's moves in with her family.

Inner conflicts

Spinelli, Jerry. *Wringer.*
A boy knows he must refuse to kill pigeons for a fundraiser, no matter what his friends and family say.

Staples, Suzanne Fisher. *Dangerous Skies.*
Buck tries to figure out how to be supportive of his friend Tunes when she is unjustly accused of murder. Assumptions are made about her in the community because of her race.

Survival

George, Jean Craighead. *Julie and the Wolves.*
A young girl survives in the Arctic because she is befriended by wolves.

Koller, Jackie French. *A Place to Call Home.*
A teenager must find a way to take care of her little sister and baby brother after their mother disappears.
O'Dell, Scott. *Island of the Blue Dolphins.*
A young girl survives alone on an island for 17 years.
Woodson, Jacqueline. *Lena.*
Two very young girls hit the road to escape an abusive father.

Strong families

Curtis, Christopher Paul. *The Watsons Go to Birmingham—1963.*
After tragedy hits, Kenny retreats into himself and is brought back out through the efforts of his family, especially his older brother.
Fenner, Carol. *Yolonda's Genius.*
Yolonda makes sure that others understand the genius that lies within her little brother's musical ability.
Flournoy, Valerie. *The Patchwork Quilt.* Illus. Jerry Pinkney (picture book).
From scraps of family clothing, Tanya helps her grandmother make a quilt to tell the story of the family's life.
Mitchell, Margaree King. *Uncle Jed's Barbershop.* Illus. James Ransome.
During the Great Depression, family members pull together in the face of poverty and discrimination and help each other.
Steig, William. *Pete's a Pizza* (picture book).
To cheer up a young boy who is having a bad day, his parents treat him like a pizza.
Stewart, Sarah. *The Gardener.* Illus. David Small (picture book).
During the Great Depression, Lydia Grace's uncle takes her in until her parents can support her again.
Wyeth, Sharon Dennis. *Always My Dad.* Illus. Raúl Colón (picture book).
Although three children wish their dad lived with them, they realize that his love is always there, even when he isn't.

Being uprooted

Aliki. *Marianthe's Story: Painted Words, Spoken Memories* (picture book).
A little girl who recently immigrated from Greece struggles to fit in at school, where she can communicate only through her art.
Garland, Sherry. *The Lotus Seed.* Illus. Tatsuro Kiuchi (picture book).
A little girl tells the story of her immigration from Vietnam.
Namioka, Lensey. *Yang the Third and Her Impossible Family.*
Yingmai changes her name to Mary to be more acceptable to her American classmates and wishes her stubborn family wouldn't hold on to their Chinese customs.
Say, Allen. *Grandfather's Journey* (picture book).
Grandfather, who immigrated to the United States from Japan, always misses the place in which he isn't currently living.

Prejudice/discrimination

Garland, Sherry. *Song of the Buffalo Boy.*
A young Vietnamese girl with an unknown American father is treated poorly in her village because of her parentage. After escaping to the big city with the buffalo herder she loves, she must decide whether to remain in Vietnam or go to America to search for her father.
Lorbiecki, Marybeth. *Sister Anne's Hands.* Illus. K. Wendy Popp (picture book).
At a parochial school in the 1950s, the presence of a black teaching nun is a source of controversy.
Wolff, Virginia Euwer. *Bat 6.*
Racism erupts after World War II when a Japanese American girl, just returned from an internment camp, plays softball with her sixth-grade teammates.

Lisa and her older brother Mark so that readers can see the same events from two different perspectives. In **Seedfolks,** Paul Fleischman, a master at presenting multiple points of view, tells the story of a city neighborhood's community garden through the eyes of the many people who want to grow food there. The variety of narrators, from immigrants to long-time residents of apartments across from the park, gives us glimpses into many lives and views of life.

Other Formats

Mel Glenn has now written two mysteries in the form of a series of poems. In **Who Killed Mr. Chippendale? A Mystery in Poems,** the murder is described from the points of view of students and teachers. Careful reading reveals the killer. **Nothing But the Truth,** by Avi, is written in documentary format, with memos, letters, newspaper articles, and dialogue in lieu of a narrator. This format forces the reader to ask how anyone can know the "whole truth." In **Monster,** by Walter Dean Myers, diary entries of a boy in prison are interspersed with the movie script he imagines could be made from his trial. **Make Lemonade,** by Virginia Euwer Wolff, is a story told through prose poems. As you read books in different formats, it is interesting to think about whether the format is limiting or whether it opens up the story in new ways.

CD-ROM

Walter Dean Myers writes in a wide range of genres. Use the CD-ROM database to create a list of his books.

Realistic Fiction Series Books

Go into the children's section of any bookstore or library and you will see rows and rows of series books. They range from *Goosebumps* to *Sweet Valley High, The Baby-Sitters Club,* and *Nancy Drew.* Can these books be considered good literature? Why are they so popular with children? What can we learn from their success? Should we make students choose other kinds of books?

Most adults would probably agree that, because the books in these series are written quickly and often by different authors, the quality may be lacking. Others worry about the implications on girls' social development of being exposed to *Sweet Valley High* books, which promote male acceptance as being supreme. R. L. Stine also comes in for criticism. Roderick McGillis (1995) is blunt: "I think of Stine's books as camp because they are so artificial, so formulaic, so predictable, so repetitive, so bad" (p. 1). Yet he compares their popularity to that of comics and serial movies in earlier generations.

Children seem to love the books because they find familiar patterns and know what to expect. Thus, these books can be soothing to children, who often turn to their favorite series books when they're upset or need comfort. They retreat to their room and get involved in a world in which they have no responsibilities and no conflicts. Also, these books often show children doing things on their own, such as solving mysteries. Children love seeing this independence from adults, since most children would like to have more control over their own lives.

In my 30 years of classroom teaching, I found it best to engage students in the underlying issues in the books—to try to get them to look beneath the surface instead of forbidding their reading choices. Children seem to read and read in a series until at some point they outgrow it and go on to something different. Scolding children for reading something from which they get so much pleasure is counterproductive if our aim is to nourish lifetime readers. By making their own selections, children are developing critical standards for what makes a book good, even if these standards are different from our own. We have to respect this stance and encourage children to read on their own, while also continuing to bring a variety of literature into the classroom.

The Threat of Censorship

> Censorship can exist even in countries that profess themselves democracies, perhaps in more subtle forms. When the voices of those with darker skins, less money, funny accents, and different religious affiliations or sexual preferences are excluded from our curriculums, when they are not on the shelves in libraries, when they are refused entry into our canons or our understanding of ourselves as a nation, then we have less than the full story of who we really are. (Julia Alvarez, 1998, p. 39)

As teachers and librarians, we are all role models, whether we want to be or not. The literature we choose to use in class or in the library may or may not validate the wide range of diversity in this country, as mentioned in the quote above. Whom do we include and whom do we leave out through our selection of books? Unfortunately, because of fear of censorship, not all of us feel free to choose what we think is best for our students. This thorny issue has several faces. Sometimes it takes the form of one parent's not wanting her child to read an all-class book. Sometimes it takes the form of parents' demanding that a book be removed from a school library's shelves. Sometimes it takes the form of a principal's quietly instructing teachers not to use a particular book again. Other times it takes the form of self-censorship, when teachers or librarians don't buy books they fear might be found objectionable. Certainly, as teachers, we must be mindful of community standards and not flout them by bringing in several books on an issue likely to be inflammatory in the community.

We all know that any parent has the right to determine what his or her child can read. In a case where a parent objects to a book used in class, a teacher simply substitutes another book for the child. In some instances, however, parents demand that a book be removed entirely from a school because they believe it is dangerous or not good for any children. Such is the case with the furor over the oft-read *Harry Potter* books, by J. K. Rowling. Some parents object to the portrayals of witches and warlocks, feeling they undermine Christian values. The would-be censors also look askance at the way the adults—especially the Muggles (those who don't believe in magic)—are portrayed, feeling it undermines adult authority. Those who study censorship cases have found that many parents do not want their children to learn to question anything, believing it is an affront to their authority and their values. On the other side of the issue, many educators may not think that they themselves have a political agenda, but they do because they believe in intellectual curiosity and questioning.

Getting involved in a head-on conflict about the use of a particular book is not an experience any teacher should seek, and there are plenty of books that will not hit the hot buttons of the community. However, we have an obligation to our students to find a whole range of books that represent the best literature available in our world today. Teachers can feel secure in their book choices if they have read several reviews of a book and can explain what children will gain from the book and why the book has literary merit. It is also helpful if a book selection policy, including a list of criteria used for book selection, is in place in the school. Such a policy might include statements explaining why literature is taught and how books are chosen for each class, as well as a statement supporting the teacher's right to choose supplementary materials and to discuss controversial issues insofar as they are relevant. Procedures for Book Selection (updated in 1982), which can be found on the National Council of Teachers of English (NCTE) website at www.ncte.org, suggest that schools can benefit from having a committee to help other language arts teachers find exciting and challenging books of potential value to students in that school. If, in spite of these kinds of book selection procedures, complaints do arise, many school districts use the NCTE form, which requires that a parent have read the whole book before the complaint is processed. This form can be accessed at www.ncte.org/positions/right.html. Other guidelines and information on censorship are also housed at this site at www.ncte.org/censorship. The American Library Association website offers information on the topic at www.ala.org/alaorg/oif/intellectualfreedomandcensorship.html.

Although it is not surprising that books dealing with issues that are highly controversial in our society, such as death and sexuality, are targets of censorship, censorship extends much deeper. It centers on the issue of free thought. John Stewig (1994) points out that self-censorship reaches far beyond the particular question of presenting lesbian and gay male parents in books: "Censorship concerns intellectually curiosity. Do we want to encourage children to wonder about their world? Do we value children asking questions about topics that interest them, or do we only want inquiry with which we as adults are comfortable?" (p. 189).

Evaluating Realistic Fiction

Realistic fiction can be evaluated on the same criteria used to evaluate other genres, except that plot, character, and theme are looked at in slightly different ways, as shown in the boxed feature Criteria for Evaluating Realistic Fiction on page 272. Then, in the boxed feature Applying the Criteria: Evaluating Realistic Fiction, these criteria are applied to *Getting Near to Baby,* by Audrey Couloumbis.

What Is Historical Fiction?

Historical fiction is a time machine into the past. It gives readers passage on the Oregon Trail, or onto a Civil War battlefield. They can eat beans and pan bread

Criteria for Evaluating *Realistic Fiction*

1. **Plot.** Do the strands of the plot work well together? Does anything seem too coincidental? How is the conflict presented—subtly or all at once? What effect does this have on the story?

2. **Character.** Do the characters ring true? Do they seem like people you've met? Are the characters individualized, or do they have a sameness about them? Is there variety in the kinds of people you meet in the story? Are their personalities revealed through their actions and words and the reactions of others?

3. **Setting.** Is the setting vivid enough that you can imagine being there? Are you comfortable in the setting, or are there elements that jar you out of it? Is the setting woven into the story or presented all at once? Does the setting illuminate the story and add to its impact? Does the setting complement or extend the story, or does it contrast with the people and ideas presented in the story?

4. **Theme.** Are the themes well integrated with the other elements of the story? Do they seem too ponderous or obvious? Are they presented in a didactic way? Do the themes grow out of the story naturally? Are they significant?

5. **Style—qualities of writing.** Does the language bring you in contact with the characters? Does figurative language bring the characters, setting, and plot to life? Does the dialogue sound natural and reveal character?

6. **Emotional impact.** Do you care about the characters and what happens to them? Does the story connect you to your own humanness and that of other people? Does the story make you laugh or make you feel happy or sad? Does the story linger with you, making you want to rethink and reexperience parts of it?

7. **Imaginative impact.** Does the story make you think about the characters in other situations? Do you think about what will happen to the characters next, when the story is over? Does the story spark your imagination, sending your mind off in many directions? Do you imagine what it would be like if you were in the situation the main character was in?

8. **Vision of the author.** What does the author see and feel about people and their connection to each other and to the world? Do you share the author's view of the world as it is presented through the characters?

9. **Realistic elements.** What elements make this story realistic, even if it is outside of your experience? Does the wisdom offered ring true? Does it offer believable insights into human nature? Do the characters behave in ways that are understandable or believable, given their background? Does the setting seem appropriate to the story and the characters?

Applying the Criteria *Evaluating Realistic Fiction*

Getting Near to Baby, by Audrey Couloumbis, a 2000 Newbery Honor book.

Synopsis: Thirteen-year-old Willa Jo and seven-year-old Little Sister come to stay with Aunt Patty and Uncle Hod while their mother recovers from the death of Baby. Although Willa Jo and Aunt Patty are constantly at odds, their time together is healing. At times poignant and at other times funny, this story gives us glimpses of a family trying to cope with the death of a child.

1. **Plot.** The story is told in the present when Willa Jo and Little Sister are sitting on the roof of their aunt's home. Through flashbacks, we discover how the two girls came to be sitting on the roof. We get involved in the lives of the girls and their mother, of Aunt Patty, and of the Fingerses, a large family across the street. Subplots revolve around the catastrophes that, according to Aunt Patty, are brought on because of the girls. Each subplot reveals something about either Willa Jo or Aunt Patty, who are the

main characters. The conflicts in the story are presented gradually. We first see the girls bringing their aunt unhappiness by sitting on the roof. Then we find out that Little Sister hasn't spoken since Baby died. We learn how and why Aunt Patty took the girls home with her and how she lives so differently from her sister, Noreen. Yet the major conflict in the story—how each person deals with Baby's death—unfolds slowly throughout the book. This gradual unfolding adds suspense to the plot but also seems realistic, since grieving and resolving relationships are processes that do not happen suddenly.

2. **Character.** We have all met bossy people like Aunt Patty, who insists that everyone walk only on the plastic runners over the carpet in her house. We recognize young teens who tell it like it is, as Willa Jo does when she says to the young Bible camp teacher, "Mrs. Weeds, if left to herself, would've had better sense than to make us sit under that tree once we found there were ticks in the grass" (p. 107). These characters come to life as individuals. We see Noreen, the dreamy-eyed artist who paints pictures of her dead child as an angel in heaven. We meet the Fingers family and the oldest daughter, Liz, who says, "Don't be embarrassed by honest feelings, that's what my mama would say." We meet Uncle Hod, who surprises us with his gentleness and wisdom.

3. **Setting.** The author makes the setting vivid by using many sensory details to help us get the feel of the place. When Willa Jo is on the roof, she thinks: "I inch across the roof that feels like it has been sprinkled with coarse salt, liking the way the scratchy surface clutches at the fabric of my shorts, clings to my skin" (p. 4). We see the run-down little cabins that the Fingers family members live in, both through the eyes of Aunt Patty and through the eyes of Willa Jo. When the children dig into the walls of the cave, we can feel and smell the dirt all around us. The author doesn't waste time on details of settings that are of no importance to the story. For instance, when the girls are sent to Bible camp, no picture is given of the place itself. We only hear in detail about sitting under the tree with the ticks on the ground, because that is the part of the camp that is significant to the story. No descriptions are given of the playing fields or the surroundings, because they are simply not needed. The setting does illuminate the story by bringing the characters and events into focus. When we are in Noreen's house before the girls go to stay with their aunt, we see the chaos of the house, which gives us an idea of Noreen's emotional state. When we are in Aunt Patty's immaculate house, we learn much about her and why her house is so important to her. When we are in the cave and over at the Fingerses' cabins, we get glimpses of a family that puts people first. All the settings are closely connected to the characters and reveal the characters to us.

4. **Theme.** Although the major theme is coping with loss, it is very well integrated into the story and there is still room for lightness and fun. The author never becomes didactic, telling us how death should be handled or experienced. She shows us many faces of grief through her portrayals of Noreen, the silent Little Sister, the outspoken Willa Jo, and the blustery Aunt Patty. The theme of loss flows in and out of the story, leaving room for the themes of making friends, the importance of family, the difficulty of relationships, discovering what's important in life and what's not, and the importance of caring. These themes are all significant because they are what life is about.

5. **Style—qualities of writing.** The writing in this story is spare and powerful. When Willa Jo is on the roof watching the sun rise, we read: "A thin rim of orange-red, so deep and strong my heart almost breaks with the fierceness of that color" (p. 2). Throughout the story, each character's language reflects his or her personality. After Aunt Patty buys the clothes she likes for her nieces and declares them cute as a button, Willa Jo thinks, "I have never in my life wanted to be cute as a button" (p. 11). The natural-sounding talk among the characters throughout the book is also a strength of the writing.

6. **Emotional impact.** These characters just wormed their way into my heart. By the end of the book, I even cared about brusque Aunt Patty when she revealed how hard it was for her to watch her own younger sister suffer so much. I also liked her when she could admit that she was wrong and that she did occasionally jump to conclusions. It became clear why Uncle Hod let Aunt Patty boss him around. Willa Jo is so clearly etched she becomes unforgettable. She cares so deeply about Little Sister and her mother and has such a strong sense of herself that she sees the world clearly. Each time I read the scene where Baby dies, I am moved to tears. Because the sparse, powerful language suggests so much more than it says, readers have room

(continued)

for their own grief. The message that appearance pales in comparison to the substance of a person is important for all readers.

7. **Imaginative impact.** So much is left unsaid that readers can imagine many scenarios involving the characters. The open-endedness evokes many questions. What will happen with the cave the Fingers family is digging? Will they discover something underground that will halt their progress? How is the uncle who was in Vietnam doing? What does the Fingers family do to embrace him? Will Aunt Patty change as a result of her experience with her nieces?

8. **Vision of the author.** The author shows the deep connections that unite people. She knows that children can be cruel to each other, especially if they've been brought up to believe that they are somehow better than other people. She also knows the immense capacity children have to be kind and connected with each other. Although we see many gossipy, curious neighbors who find a reason to come over to the cul-de-sac to get a glimpse of the children on the roof, the author deals with them in a kind way, implying that they are lonely or have little to do. The author focuses on the positive in people while acknowledging the negative. Her view of the world is refreshing.

9. **Realistic elements.** The wisdom in this story, often conveyed through the words of Willa Jo, makes it seem very realistic. When Aunt Patty is overly concerned about finding friends for her nieces, Willa Jo thinks: "She didn't seem to know that friends aren't something one person picks out for another, like flowers at a shop" (p. 38). The girls' reactions when their aunt outfits them in clothes of her choice remind me of my own children's incredulousness when I tried to pick out something I thought they should like to wear. People's reactions to the fact that Little Sister didn't speak after the death of Baby also seem very realistic. Most characters, in their frustration with not being able to help Little Sister, think she should be shocked out of it or put in situations where she will be forced to speak. Judging people on outward appearances is fairly typical of most of us. Aunt Patty concludes that the Fingers children are not suitable to play with because of the appearance of their house and the fact that they are allowed to play in the dirt. This author appears to be a very good student of life, watching people and capturing their attitudes and beliefs in the story.

---

with the Forty-Niners, or choke through a dust storm during the Great Depression. Readers can go skinny-dipping with President John Quincy Adams in a chilly Potomac River at dawn, catch Teddy Roosevelt's children in the act of climbing lampposts in Lafayette Square, smell the sweat of youngsters helping their parents fell trees for their new homestead in the territories, and even listen in on their complaints. Historical fiction sets a story within the overview of an earlier period, emphasizing extraordinary events or historical figures, or just gives a feeling for what life could have been like in "the good old days." (Karr, 2000, p. 30)

At **Children's Library,** *find a series of websites on different aspects of historical fiction. Go to www.boulder.lib.co.us/ youth/booklists/booklists_ historical.html.*

At its best, historical fiction is both good fiction and good history. There is general agreement about what makes good fiction: a compelling plot, well-developed characters, important themes, a setting readers can easily enter, and writing that makes the story flow effortlessly. There are, however, different views about what makes good history (Is point of view a factor? Is there such a thing as objectivity?) and what kind of history school children should be exposed to (some want children to hear only about the positive aspects of our past). Wendy Saul (in Meltzer, 1994) reminds us that professional historians encourage students to reflect on the following key issues: What is worth knowing? Who is a reliable source? What facts in a given document are emphasized or ignored? Whose sense of "normal" is evident in the description or re-creation of events? Whose values? Whose perceptions of time? Whose perceptions of pleasure or pain?

This sense of inquiry has not always been apparent in historical fiction for children. Jean Fritz (1998) said that when she started writing historical fiction, children were to be "protected from grimness of present or past. History didn't require original research. Stories were told in general ways." As a result, the stories that were written often came across as lifeless and smacked of sameness. Only the positive qualities of a historical figure were revealed. Children were not given a chance to see that heroes could grow through mistakes. In an effort to make this historical fiction interesting, writers used dialogue. But all the characters sounded like the "good" boy next door when they were given words to say. Fritz refused to put in dialogue she couldn't absolutely document. She could document that Paul Revere said "damn," and so she used it in her book about him. One boy wrote to tell her that this was the first history book he believed! Fritz believes that historical fiction writers today show more respect for children, for research, and for accuracy. Much of the historical fiction written today is lively, intriguing, suspenseful, and full of people readers can connect to, flaws and all.

What historical fiction is depends on who is defining it. For school children, the past is any year before they were born; it may even include the years they were babies and toddlers. For adults, the present stretches much further back; almost no one views the years they themselves were school children as "historical" ones. Books published or set in a time period 25 or more years ago have often been moved into the category of historical fiction simply because children today have no awareness or memories of those times.

The Appeal of Historical Fiction

Historical fiction is filled with dramas and adventures of people in times past. What can children get out of historical fiction that they can't get from the study of textbook history? Why are children interested in reading historical fiction?

Historical fiction can enrich the lives of readers by helping them do the following:

1. Vicariously experience events and feelings as they were experienced by the people of the time.

2. Understand that there are universal truths, such as the need to be loved and cared for.

3. See that people not only had different clothing and living conditions but also had different beliefs—for example, that children were the property of their parents and that disfigured or handicapped people were to blame for their condition.

4. See many interpretations of the same period in history and understand that people view events from their own point of view, embedded in their own circumstances. For example, Patriots and Tories viewed the Revolutionary War very differently and would write about it in different ways.

5. Discover core values in the lives of others, as well as see examples of many people of courage.

6. Understand the prejudices and biases of another time period and thereby have more insight into our own society.

7. See what they have in common with people in other times and realize that all people have problems and challenges.

8. Develop an awareness that when and where people live influences who they are.

9. Satisfy their curiosity about the past by becoming involved in well-written, compelling stories.

10. Experience in an immediate and compelling way historical events or details that otherwise might seem boring and academic.

Children have definite views on the value of historical fiction, as the boxed feature Children's Voices indicates (see page 276).

On historical fiction . . .

I don't like them because they're boring. —Wright, 6th grade

I like reading historical fiction. I enjoy reading what happened in history and how people dealt with the problems they faced. —Christi, 7th grade

Historical fiction is interesting because it happened, so it has many facts, but has enough fiction to be creative. —Shannon, 7th grade

I mostly read about girls in history who went through an important time. —Jan, 7th grade

I think that if I know what it was like so long ago, I will know more about today and how it came to be this way. —Elizabeth, 7th grade

I read historical fiction because it's learning about something that's half truth and half fiction. —Savontae, 7th grade

My favorite author is Karen Hesse 'cause I like the book she wrote, **Out of the Dust.** —Rachael, 7th grade

I really enjoy historical fiction. I find fascinating the triumphs and troubles that the characters go through. My favorite historical fiction book is **My Brother Sam Is Dead.** —Elizabeth, 8th grade

I read historical fiction about times long ago. And books that have completely different settings than where and when we live. It's like an escape. —Eric, 8th grade

I read some of it, it tells me about ways others deal with problems. —Beth, 8th grade

I like that I can read them and learn about historical events, but the characters don't have to be so boring as actual people. —Emily, 8th grade

Types of Historical Fiction

The germ of an idea for a historical story often comes from the life of the writer; historical fiction writer Joan Blos calls such a story a fictionalized memoir. If the idea comes from stories the writer's family told, the story is a fictionalized family story. Other historical stories are based on research.

Fictionalized Memoirs

Fictionalized memoirs are based on the author's memories of an earlier time. Often the author takes an incident and shapes a story around it. Other times, he or she writes of lived-through events such as the Holocaust but changes things slightly to keep the sense of story.

    Lily's Crossing, by Patricia Reilly Giff, is an example of a story created around the memories of the author. In a letter to her readers at the end of the book, Giff explains that she remembers the summer of 1944, the time period of the story. She also remembers how friendship added comfort and joy to her life. So in this story with created characters, she evokes that time and place and lets readers live through those days of World War II in America. Ching Yeung Russell bases **Child Bride** on her childhood growing up in China. In **Sing for Your Father, Su Phan,** Fay Tang, with Stella Pevsner's assistance, writes a fictionalized account of her childhood as a Chinese girl living in Vietnam during the war. **So Far from the Bamboo Grove** and its sequel, **My Brother, My Sister, and I,** by Yoko Kawashima Watkins, present the compelling fictionalized autobiography of Yoko's Japanese family, caught in Korea when World War II ends. Although the book was written as fictionalized autobiography, it is now thought of as historical fiction because it takes place many years before the lifetimes of present-day school children.

Fictionalized Family Stories

Many writers have been fortunate enough to come from storytelling families and hear family stories from their earliest days. Gloria Houston, writer of picture books and novels, uses her family history in **Mountain Valor,** the story of a twelve-year-old girl who masquerades as a boy and enters the Civil War to preserve her family's safety. It is based on a true event in the life of Matilda Houston, a great-great aunt. **Sarah, Plain and Tall,** by Patricia MacLachlan, is also based on a true event in the author's family history. Mildred D. Taylor's stories of the Logan family come from her father's storytelling. She dedicates **Roll of Thunder, Hear My Cry** "to the memory of my beloved father who lived many adventures of the boy Stacey and who was in essence the man David."

Fictionalized Stories Based on Research

Milton Meltzer's (1994) passion for setting the record straight and giving voice to people often left out of history has been the impetus for his historical fiction. He loves the challenge of uncovering the stories of people from earlier times. His **Underground Man** started as a biography of Calvin Fairbanks, a white man who rescued slaves from the South, but ended as a work of fiction.

Two brothers step off the boat from China in 1865 hoping to realize their dreams, unaware of the harsh life and injustices in store for them.
(From COOLIES by Yin, illustrated by Chris Soentpiet, copyright © 2001 by Yin, text. Copyright 2001 by Chris K. Soentpiet, illustrations. Used by permission of Philomel Books, an imprint of Penguin Putnam Books for Young Readers, a division of Penguin Putnam, Inc.)

Writers of historical fiction generally feel an affinity for research. Cynthia DeFelice (1998) describes the work of researching her books as incredible, wonderful, and "actually, well, fun. I get to play detective, digging for clues to the truth about the past. I get to play the role of my main characters, and feel what he or she experiences" (p. 34). This zest for research surfaces in well-researched, well-written books like **Pharaoh's Daughter: A Novel of Ancient Egypt,** by Julius Lester, and **Letters from Vinnie,** by Maureen Stack Sappéy, about the teenage girl who began sculpting the statue of Abraham Lincoln that stands in the Rotunda of the Capitol today. **Coolies,** by Yin, the story of brothers from China who work on the railroad going West, grew out of the author's desire to know more about the Chinese contribution to American history. Excellent research is at the heart of good historical fiction.

Themes and Formats of Historical Fiction

Although events surrounding wars seem to produce the most books, historical fiction can be found about almost any time period in United States history. Historical novels can also be found on ancient times, medieval times, and times of European exploration in North and South America. Because historical fiction is based on people who contributed to their culture's history, it is rich in the drama of life. It works on multiple levels and can be used as more than a social studies component. Many of the themes found in realistic books are also present in historical fiction—for example, centrality of family, importance of real friends, dealing with people with different values, resisting peer pressure, resisting social pressure, the individual's role in making choices, courage, survival under difficult circumstances, loyalty, importance of a belief in one's self, resisting oppression, the place of delayed gratification, responding to hate, overcoming circumstances in your early life, figuring out what's important or worthwhile in life, and prioritizing one's goals. In the boxed feature A Sampling of Novels of Historical Fiction, several titles not already mentioned in this chapter are suggested for each time period, with the major themes indicated in parentheses.

The same variety that is found in themes also characterizes formats. No longer are stories told only as straight narratives. Now you can find diaries, journals, letters, two narrators in alternating chapters, and even prose poems and time travel stories. These increasingly creative and unusual formats add interest and keep the plot moving.

Diaries, Journals, and Letters

The advantage of diaries, journals, and letters is the direct connection the reader can make with the protagonists. Readers are drawn into their lives and issues immediately. On the second page of **North by Night: A Story of the Underground Railroad,** by Katherine Ayres, sixteen-year-old Lucinda, who helps her family with their underground railroad station, says, "Drat the president anyway. Papa voted for him. President Fillmore is a Northern man, a New Yorker. So how could he let us down?" She is discouraged about the fugitive slave law that brought suffering to so many. We can clearly hear her voice and feel what she feels. Joan Blos's **A Gathering of Days: A New England Girl's Journal, 1830–32** also gives instant access to the character and engages readers quickly.

First-Person Narrative

Many historical novels use the first-person point of view but are not written in diary or letter format. Since first-person narrative limits the events the reader can see to only those the narrator sees and since a person can be in only one place at one time, this point of view doesn't allow as much latitude as third-person narrative. Of course, writers can overcome this difficulty by doing such things as having another character report back to the narrator on events he or she has witnessed, as Gail Carson Levine does so effectively in **Dave at Night.**

A Sampling of Novels of Historical Fiction

 *I*mportant themes appear in parentheses after each description.

Ancient Egypt

Lester, Julius. *Pharaoh's Daughter: A Novel of Ancient Egypt.*
In this fictionalized account of the Biblical story, an Egyptian princess rescues a Hebrew baby who becomes a prophet of his people. (Loyalty, courage, resisting social pressure, dealing with people with different beliefs.)

Asia

Namioka, Lensey. *Ties That Bind, Ties That Break.*
When a five-year-old girl in China in the early part of the 20th century refuses to have her feet bound, her life is forever affected. She must eventually find her own way in life, which leads her to America. (Resisting social pressure, courage, survival under difficult circumstances.)

Pre-Columbian

Talbert, Marc. *Heart of a Jaguar.*
Balam, a Mayan boy, prays with his people for relief from the drought they are experiencing. This is a unique glimpse into the jungle-shrouded world of the ancient Mayas. (Centrality of family/community, individual's role in making choices, prioritizing one's goals.)

Middle Ages

Barrett, Tracy. *Anna of Byzantium.*
Anna is groomed to be queen of the Byzantine Empire, but when she displeases her grandmother, everything changes. Eventually she is exiled for the rest of her life to a convent, where she writes an eleven-volume epic about the life of her father. (Individual role in making choices, figuring out what's important in life, the lure of power.)

Temple, Frances. *The Beduins' Gazelle.*
In 1302, two cousins of the nomadic Beni Khalid tribe who are betrothed become separated by political intrigue between warring tribes. (Centrality of family, loyalty.)

——. *The Ramsay Scallop.*
Fourteen-year-old Eleanor, unhappy at her betrothal to a man she hardly knows, obeys the village priest and goes on a religious pilgrimage with her intended. Both learn of the world and of each other. (Centrality of family, loyalty, growing through experience.)

Early days in North America

Dorris, Michael. *Sees Behind Trees.*
An American Indian boy with poor eyesight learns through his adventures and trials with an old warrior that he has the power to "see" beyond what others can see. (Courage, importance of a belief in self.)

Dyer, T. A. *A Way of His Own.*
A young lame boy from a nomadic tribe, abandoned by his family, must survive a harsh winter with a girl stolen from another tribe. (Courage, dealing with people of different values, survival.)

Garland, Sherry. *Indio.*
As teenage Ipa happily prepares for her wedding day, she is captured. Brutal changes face her as the Spanish begin their conquest of the native people along the Texas border. (Courage, survival, dealing with people of different values, resisting oppression.)

Vick, Helen Hughes. *Walker of Time.*
A Hopi boy travels 800 years back in time to help his people in a time of drought and illness. (Courage, survival, centrality of family, individual's role in making choices.)

Colonial days

Hansen, Joyce. *The Captive.*
Kofi, an African prince, is captured in his homeland and taken to America, where he eventually figures out a plan to free himself. (Survival, resisting oppression, picture of two cultures.)

O'Dell, Scott. *Sarah Bishop.*
Sarah's life in America with her father and brother is turned upside down when the Revolutionary War begins, and she flees to the wilderness to survive. (Resisting social pressure, courage, survival under difficult circumstances.)

Rinaldi, Ann. *Broken Days (The Quilt Trilogy).*
In the early 19th century, a half-Shawnee girl claims to be the daughter of the Chelmsford daughter kidnapped more than 20 years before. (Survival, prejudice, individual's role in making choices.)

Walter, Mildred Pitts. *Second Daughter: The Story of a Slave Girl.*
Aissa, the teen sister of the girl who challenged the Massachusetts law on slavery, struggles against a system that views her as property. (Courage, survival, resisting oppression, individual's role in making choices.)

Whelan, Gloria. *Once on This Island.*
While their father is away fighting the British in the War of 1812, young Mary and her older brother and sister must run the farm on Michigan's Mackinac Island. (Loyalty, courage, determination.)

Victorian England

Pullman, Philip. *The Ruby in the Smoke.*
In this compelling mystery, 16-year-old Sally journeys into the underworld and poverty of Victorian London to try to solve the puzzle of her father's death. (Dealing with people with different values, resisting social pressure, courage, survival under difficult circumstances.)

Civil War era

Houston, Gloria. *Bright Freedom's Song: A Story of the Underground Railroad.*
In the years before the Civil War, Bright learns that her parents, yeoman Southern farmers, are providing a safe house for the underground railroad. Will she be courageous

(continued)

enough to help "the bundles" to safety, too? (Centrality of family, individual's role in making choices, courage, loyalty, resisting oppression.)

Paulsen, Gary. *Soldier's Heart.*

Fifteen-year-old Charley is eager to enlist to fight in the Civil War. But the physical horrors and mental anguish he experiences make him heartsick and change his mind about fighting. This poignant story shows how what we now call "post-traumatic stress syndrome" ate away at the life and mind of this young man, ending with his early death after the war. (Courage, figuring out what's important and worthwhile in life.)

Yep, Laurence. *Dragon's Gate.*

Building the transcontinental railroad immediately after the Civil War, the teenager Otter and his relatives and countrymen must deal with blizzards, the dangers of working in the mountains with explosives, and the inhuman working conditions and poor treatment at the hands of their employer. Otter and his uncle make a difference by organizing a strike and then saving the workers from avalanches by risking their own lives. (Centrality of family, dealing with people with different values, resisting social pressure, survival under difficult circumstances, resisting oppression and prejudice.)

Early 20th century

Bunting, Eve. *SOS Titanic.*

At 15, Barry O'Neill is journeying aboard the *Titanic* to join his wealthy parents in New York. He becomes involved with others from his Irish village who are very poor and traveling in steerage. Through his efforts, some of them are saved. We very clearly see the social restrictions enforced between the lower and upper classes throughout the voyage. (Centrality of family, resisting social pressure, courage.)

Meyer, Carolyn. *Gideon's People.*

Isaac, an Orthodox Jewish boy, wakes up in the home of an Amish family after being injured in an accident on his dad's wagon. Although he and Gideon, a teen in the home in which he is staying, seem very different, they find out that they both long to live differently than their families. At 16, Gideon finally has the courage to break loose. (Importance of family, dealing with people with different values, resisting social pressure, courage.)

Porter, Tracey. *Treasures in the Dust.*

Through the stories of eleven-year-old Annie and Violet, we learn of the hardships endured by their families when dust storms, drought, and the Great Depression hit rural Oklahoma. (Importance of family and friends, survival under difficult circumstances.)

Rostkowski, Margaret I. *After the Dancing Days.*

After World War I, Annie volunteers to work at a hospital for badly wounded veterans, and there she meets a badly disfigured young man. This relationship causes her to redefine the word *hero* and question the conventional ideas of patriotism. (Resisting social pressure, individual's role in making choices, importance of a belief in one's self, resisting societal attitudes against disfigured people.)

World War II

Greene, Bette. *Summer of My German Soldier.*

Patti is twelve and Jewish in a small town in Arkansas when German prisoners are brought there. She helps an escapee, seeing him as a human, not a Nazi, and brings the wrath of the town down upon herself. (Dealing with people with different values, resisting social pressure, courage, responding to hate and prejudice.)

Magorian, Michelle. *Good Night, Mr. Tom.*

When Willie is evacuated from London along with other children to escape the incessant German bombing, he ends up at the home of a crotchety old man, who comes to love Willie and recognize that he is an abused child. (Importance of caring, individual's role in making choices, survival under difficult circumstances.)

Mazer, Norma Fox. *Good Night, Maman.*

Karen Levi and her older brother manage to escape from Nazi France to the United States aboard the *Henry Gibbins*. They are settled at Fort Ontario in upstate New York with other refugees. They learn about life as displaced persons as they cope with the immensity of their losses. (Dealing with death, courage, survival.)

Richter, Hans Peter. *Friedrich.*

A young German boy recounts the fate of his best friend, a Jew, during the Nazi regime. (Courage, survival under difficult circumstances, dealing with oppression and prejudice.)

Wolff, Virginia Euwer. *Bat 6.*

Sixth-grade girls on the local softball teams of two Oregon communities tell of their experiences on the teams, which illustrate the communities' struggle to deal with the aftermath of World War II and their attitudes toward the Japanese who have returned to their homes after spending time in U.S. internment camps. (Importance of real friends, resisting peer pressure, courage, facing prejudice.)

Civil Rights era

Davis, Ossie. *Just Like Martin.*

Following the deaths of two of his classmates in a bomb explosion at his Alabama church, fourteen-year-old Stone confronts racism and learns about nonviolence as he organizes a children's march for civil rights. (Centrality of family and community, fighting racism and oppression, responding to hatred and prejudice, importance of a belief in one's self, courage.)

Third-Person Narrative

The freedom to show events from more than one point of view can be important in historical novels. Also, the third-person perspective allows the author to write about people and events the main character doesn't directly experience. In Patricia Beatty's **Charley Skedaddle,** we can see more of the events than Charley does. Before describing the action, the narrator steps back and explains the fear of most Virginians of getting lost in the thick forest: "As soldiers moved forward, picking their way through the forest where twisting vines and thickets tore at their bodies and small trees grew so close to each other that it was impossible to squeeze through, their progress was slowed" (p. 76).

Time Travel

Another way writers lure readers into historical fiction is through the device of time travel. Stories start in the present with modern characters and modern problems and then thrust the characters into another time period. This device is especially effective in historical fiction because hints that a character in the past is connected to a character in the present can be used to increase suspense. Well-received and well-reviewed time travel books include Jane Yolen's **The Devil's Arithmetic** (Holocaust), Janet Lunn's **The Root Cellar** (Civil War), Ruth Park's **Playing Beatie Bow** (Victorian Australia), and Helen Hughes Vick's **Walker of Time** (Hopis in 1250).

Other Formats

Writers of historical fiction don't feel obligated to tell stories in conventional ways. In Paul Fleischman's award-winning **Bull Run,** the 16 main characters each have several brief chapters, written as monologues. None of the characters speak to each other in this riveting look at one battle in the Civil War. Another award-winning book, **Out of the Dust,** by Karen Hesse, is in the form of a prose poem, whose language leaves a powerful impact on the reader.

Other historical novels are written from two viewpoints, given in alternate chapters. Carolyn Meyer's **Where the Broken Heart Still Beats** uses the journals of Lucy Parker, a cousin, to tell the story of how Cynthia appears to her white family. Alternate chapters are told from the point of view of the woman who was "rescued" by her people after living happily as an Indian for 25 years. This format allows the reader to clearly see the culture clash and difference in values. In **Steal Away Home,** by Lois Ruby, chapters alternate between the first-person account of a child in the days of the underground railroad and the third-person narrative of a girl in the present who is trying to solve the mystery of the skeleton she found in a sealed-off part of her house.

*H*istorical Fiction Picture Books

Historical fiction isn't written just for students who can read independently. On the market today are many picture books of historical fiction that can be read aloud to young students or used as independent reading for older students. **Christmas in the Big House, Christmas in the Quarters,** a well-researched

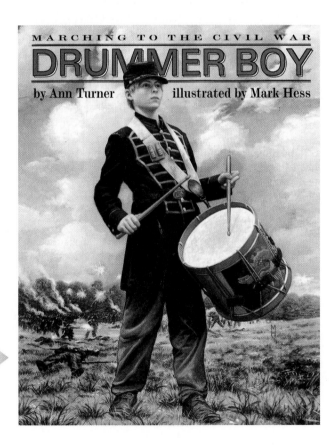

This poignant story of a young boy who "sees things no boy should ever see" thrusts readers into the heart of war and stimulates a desire to know more about the Civil War.

(Cover of *Drummer Boy: Marching to the Civil War* by Ann Turner. Art copyright © 1998 by Mark Hess. Used by permission of HarperCollins Publishers.)

Locate current event themes and lessons at the website of **The New York Times for Teachers** at www.nytimes.com/ learning/teachers/lessons/archive. html.

story by Patricia and Fredrick L. McKissack, tells of a Christmas celebration on a pre–Civil War plantation. **Drummer Boy: Marching to the Civil War,** by Ann Turner, and **Pink and Say,** by Patricia Polacco, are both set in the Civil War. Elizabeth Fitzgerald Howard's **Virgie Goes to School with Us Boys** is the story of a Quaker school for black children after the Civil War. Allen Say's **Grandfather's Journey** is one immigrant's experience of coming to this country in the early part of the 20th century. **Baseball Saved Us,** by Ken Mochizuki, tells of the Japanese internment camps during World War II. **If a Bus Could Talk: The Story of Rosa Parks,** by Faith Ringgold, describes the beginning of the civil rights movement. Picture books can be found on many topics in history. For more examples, take a look at the boxed feature A Sampling of Historical Fiction Picture Books.

A Sampling of Historical Fiction Picture Books

Ancient Egypt

Bunting, Eve. *I Am the Mummy Heb-Nefert.* Illus. David Christiana.
A mummy on display in a museum recalls her past life in ancient Egypt as the lovely wife of the pharaoh's brother.

Columbus's landing

Yolen, Jane. *Encounter.* Illus. David Shannon.
A Taino boy on the island of San Salvador recounts the landing of Columbus and his men in 1492.

Pre–Civil War

Hooks, William H. *Freedom's Fruit.* Illus. James Ransome.
Based on a tale told to the author as he was growing up in rural North Carolina, this story is about Mama Marina, a slave woman and conjurer who casts a spell on her daughter in order to earn her freedom by fooling her master.
Hopkinson, Deborah. *Birdie's Lighthouse.* Illus. Kimberly Bulcken Root.
When her father becomes ill during a severe storm off the coast of Maine in 1855, ten-year-old Birdie keeps the light burning.
———. *Sweet Clara and the Freedom Quilt.* Illus. James Ransome.
A young slave stitches a quilt with a map pattern, which guides her to freedom in the North.
Siegelson, Kim L. *In the Time of Drums.* Illus. Brian Pinkney.
Mentu, an American-born slave boy, watches his beloved grandmother, Twi, lead the insurrection at Teakettle Creek of the Ibo people arriving from Africa on a slave ship. This lyrically told tale speaks strongly of the desire for freedom in every human soul.
Turner, Ann. *Nettie's Trip South.* Illus. Ronald Himler.
A ten-year-old northern girl visits Richmond, Virginia, and encounters the awful realities of slavery when she sees a slave auction.
Van Leeuwen, Jean. *Nothing Here But Trees.* Illus. Phil Boatwright.
A pioneer family carves out a new home amidst the densely forested land of Ohio in the early 19th century.

Post–Civil War

Bradby, Marie. *More Than Anything Else.* Illus. Chris K. Soentpiet.
In this story, based on an early incident in the life of Booker T. Washington, we see him working in the salt mines with his father and dreaming about the day he can learn to read.
Lester, Julius. *Black Cowboy Wild Horses: A True Story.* Illus. Jerry Pinkney.
Bob Lemmons, a former slave, displays his legendary tracking skills as he singlehandedly brings in a herd of mustangs.

Late 19th century

Bunting, Eve. *Train to Somewhere.* Illus. Ronald Himler.
In this poignant, beautifully done story set in the late 19th century, Marianne travels westward on the orphan train in hope of being placed with a caring family.
Howard, Ellen. *The Log Cabin Quilt.* Illus. Ronald Himler.
When Elvirey and her family move to a log cabin in the Michigan woods, something even more important than granny's quilt pieces makes the new dwelling home. The hard work involved in raising a cabin and moving to a new area is emphasized.
Kalman, Esther. *Tchaikovsky Discovers America.* Illus. Laura Fernandez and Rick Jacobson.
A fictional little girl, Jenny, writes to her best friend about her meetings with Tchaikovsky when he comes to America in 1891. The illustrations show details of life at this time, and we get glimpses of Tchaikovsky and what he did on this documented trip to America.
Lasky, Kathryn. *She's Wearing a Dead Bird on Her Head!* Illus. David Catrow.
This is a fictionalized account of the activities of Harriet Hemenway and Minna Hall, founders of the Massachusetts Audubon Society, a late-19th-century organization that would endure and have an impact on the bird-protection movement.
Levitin, Sonia. *Nine for California.* Illus. Cat Bowman Smith.
Amanda, along with her four siblings and her mother, travels by stagecoach from Missouri to California to join her father. In this funny, heartwarming tale, mother saves the day whenever crises arise.

Turner, Ann. *Dakota Dugout*. Illus. Ronald Himler.
A grandmother describes to her granddaughter life in a sod house on the Dakota prairie, sharing the joys as well as the difficulties.
———. *Red Flower Goes West*. Illus. Dennis Nolan.
On the journey to California, a family nurtures the one thing Mother would not leave behind—a red geranium from her own mother's garden. As it survives river crossings and wagon jouncings, it becomes symbolic of the family's ability to survive.

Early 20th century

Hall, Donald. *The Milkman's Boy*. Illus. Greg Shed.
After 1915, people stopped keeping cows in their backyards and depended on horse-drawn wagons to deliver fresh milk to them. This story shows what it took for one family to maintain its milk delivery service.
Lasky, Kathryn. *Marven of the Great North Woods*. Illus. Kevin Hawkes.
To keep him away from the influenza epidemic of 1918, a young boy is sent to a logging camp in Duluth, Minnesota, where he finds a special friend.
Lee, Milly. *Earthquake*. Illus. Yangsook Choi.
Following the earthquake of 1906, a Chinese American family hurrying from its San Francisco home meets others trying to make their way to safety.
Littlesugar, Amy. *Tree of Hope*. Illus. Floyd Cooper.
Florrie's parents both work hard at menial jobs to make ends meet during the Great Depression. Florrie wishes that the Lafayette Theater in Harlem would reopen so that her Daddy could reach his dream and act again.
Moss, Marissa. *True Heart*. Illus. C. E. Payne.
This story, based on the history of women who worked on the railroad, tells of a young girl at the turn of the century who accomplishes her dream of becoming an engineer when the male engineer is injured and can't drive his train.

World War II

Borden, Louise. *The Little Ships: The Heroic Rescue at Dunkirk in World War II*. Illus. Michael Foreman.
A young English girl and her father take their fishing boat and join scores of other civilian vessels crossing the English Channel to rescue Allied troops stranded on the beach at Dunkirk by Nazi fire.
Hunter, Sara Hoagland. *The Unbreakable Code*. Illus. Julia Miner.
A young Navajo boy does not want to leave the reservation when his mom marries a man from Minnesota. His grandfather shows the quiet pride of a Navajo code talker as he explains to his grandson how the Navajo language, faith, and ingenuity helped win World War II. He reminds his grandson that he, too, has something to take off the reservation—the unbreakable code.
Lee, Milly. *Nim and the War Effort*. Illus. Yangsook Choi.
Nim, a little Chinese American girl, works hard collecting newspapers for the war effort so that she can prove herself as she proves her loyalty.

In historical fiction picture books, the illustrator carries much of the burden of telling the story. E. B. Lewis (2000), artist and illustrator, says that the "author provides the seed while the artist is the sun needed to make the story grow." The drawings must be accurate if the illustrator is to contribute effectively to the story and its authenticity. Lewis explains the extensive research he undertakes for each book he illustrates, not only researching the geography of a place in the picture collections of the library but actually going to Ethiopia when he couldn't envision the setting. He says, "I want kids to be transported to other places through the perfect match of text and image."

Authenticity sometimes presents unusual problems for illustrators of historical picture books. Philip Lee (1999), book publisher, explained the dilemma Dom Lee faced in illustrating **Baseball Saved Us**, by Ken Mochizuki. Through researching the Japanese internment camps, Lee found that the guards at these camps actually wore old World War I uniforms, even though the internment occurred during World War II. The artist and publisher had to decide whether to be totally accurate at the expense of confusing their readers. They decided to use World War II uniforms for the sake of clarity.

Historical Fiction Series Books

Series books have become some of the most popular books of historical fiction among children and have spurred an interest in historical fiction. Children seem to like the predictability of the diary format and the guarantee that the book will get them in touch with another time in this country's history through the eyes of a person their age. *Dear America,* one popular series, includes books by many of this country's best writers, such as Ann

Rinaldi, Kristina Gregory, and Kathryn Lasky. Books in this series about people of different ethnicities are often written by authors of that ethnicity, such as Laurence Yep and Walter Dean Myers.

Children tend to think of these stories as "real." Oftentimes it is difficult to even find out whether or not these series books are fiction. Early volumes in the *Dear America* series and currently published volumes in the *American Diaries* series only indicate in small print on the copyright page that the book is fiction. (Now the *Dear America* series does have on the cover page an indication that the character is fictional.) Although generally well written, historical fiction series books are sometimes packaged in misleading ways, so readers believe that they are reading an actual diary of a child who lived in the time period of the book. Most of these books do not list sources from which the author drew, and none of them have acknowledgments or an author's note about the process of writing the book. In spite of these factors, these books have stimulated interest in reading historical fiction and usually give readers a good look at other times and places.

*The Dear America series has its own website. **Dear America: Official Website** is at www.scholastic.com/ dearamerica/index.htm.*

The Challenges of Writing Historical Fiction

Since writers of historical fiction focus on the events and issues of distant time periods, not only do they have the job of writing a compelling story, they have the additional task of doing sufficient research to make their stories authentic and lively. They can't get carried away and bury the story under the weight of all they've learned. They have to be judicious in the selection of the details. They have to decide whether they need to add characters, change the ages of characters, and combine events that happened in diverse places. They face the challenging job of making sense out of all their research. After all, the primary sources they use do not all represent one consistent view nor do they necessarily suggest the meaning beneath the events. The responsibilities of historical fiction writers are numerous.

Researching

What does it take to gather information for a story? Katherine Ayres says in an author's note of her research for **North by Night: A Story of the Underground Railroad,** "To help me write Lucinda's letters and those of young men who admire her, I read real letters of young courting couples." Next she studied slavery from Northern and Southern perspectives, using original slave narratives and abolitionists' writing. "I found a book with yellowing pages, written in 1856, about fugitive slaves who escaped to Canada. I read newspapers' reward notices for runaway slaves." She also visited the tombstone of a four-year-old slave child.

In writing the story of **Trouble's Daughter: The Story of Susanna Hutchinson, Indian Captive,** Katherine Kirkpatrick even had to learn about another language. Her activities during the three years she spent writing the book included "listening to Lenape language tapes, auditing a college course in archaeology, reading Dutch documents in translation, finding old maps, and hiking and kayaking through the area" (p. 244).

Stories of more recent times often rely heavily on other people's memories. In the acknowledgments to **Dave at Night,** which is set in the 1920s, Gail Carson Levine gives thanks to

> Irving Aschheim for sharing the bounty of his encyclopedic memory; to Michael Stall and Hyman Bogen for helping me understand asylum life; to Jim Van Duyne for explaining the mysteries of classic luxury cars; to Steve Long of the Tenement House Museum for answering my questions about the Lower East Side and for directing my research into productive channels; to Kenny Dasowitz of the New York Transit Museum for telling me about travel by trolley and train in a younger New York City; to Nedda Sindin for her help with Yiddish and for her memories of New York City in the twenties . . . .

The stories of authors' research paths often parallel the stories they uncover.

Cynthia DeFelice (1998), writer of historical fiction, likens research to a skeleton that the author fleshes out to create an historical novel: "A skeleton without blood and muscle and skin is not a complete human being; but without the bones, the rest has no form or strength" (p. 30). She goes on to explain, "Facts alone don't make a story; yet historical fiction that isn't based on fact simply won't stand up" (p. 30). Jill Paton Walsh (in Harrison and Maguire, 1987), writer of many novels of historical fiction, enjoys the research. She believes that the past is more accessible than the present: "You can read private letters and diaries, which would be intolerable conduct toward your contemporaries. It is nearly as intolerable to eavesdrop and certainly intolerable to put real people directly into your books" (p. 269). Thus, we can access the past through the library, while we are isolated in the present.

Keeping the Story First

When writers engage in research, they find out much more than they could ever use in a single story. In a conversation about his book **Heart of a Jaguar,** the story of a Mayan boy in the 13th century, Marc Talbert explained that his first draft was so full of history and facts that it was hard to see the story (personal interview, November 1995). His editor reminded him not to write a complete history of the Mayan people but to focus on what was necessary to tell the story of this young boy and his decision to be sacrificed.

Elizabeth George Speare (in Sipe, 1997) explains that every detail in historical fiction must do double duty: "It must not only add to the reader's sense of the historical setting but also contribute to the story" (p. 247). Writers of historical fiction are not historians, who can consider an exhaustive number of causes for a historical event and range over a huge geographical area, analyzing large, complicated events. Fictional text often deals in miniatures, which imply or symbolize larger social and cultural forces, as when the interactions of a few characters indicate a broad societal theme.

Lois Lowry (in Sipe, 1997) says she "can't write well about 'huge events' such as World War II" (p. 252); but she can find the details of everyday life which exemplify and evoke these events in such novels as **Number the Stars**. Fiction streamlines and simplifies so that the plot is clear and easy to follow and reaches a satisfying resolution.

Distinguishing Facts from Fiction

Authors such as Mildred Pitts Walter make very clear to readers which parts of their story are fact and which are fiction. In a Historical Note at the end of **Second Daughter: The Story of a Slave Girl,** Walter says that the sister Bett in the story is fictional. She also explains that she uses slave names that existed in records, but for most slaves no record of names was found. Although she included in her story the names of actual outstanding black contemporaries of the main character Elizabeth, she has "no indication that they ever met" (p. 213). Carolyn Meyer, in **Where the Broken Heart Still Beats,** took "the key facts of the history of Cynthia Ann Parker and used them as a framework on which to fashion the story of her life, as it could have been. Lucy Parker, her brothers and sisters, and her journal are my fictional inventions" (p. 194).

Creating Meaning in Events

Like historians, writers of historical fiction not only *see* meaning in events and chains of events, they also *create* meaning. Joyce Hansen (in Sipe, 1997), writer of historical fiction, believes that the writer must impose her own interpretation and actively construct history. She writes of finding much contradictory information in the historical records and learning that "history is made up of individual stories shaded by individual perceptions and experiences" (p. 246). Thus, it was necessary for her to take authorial responsibility for the shape of her story, in the same way a historian would.

In general, according to Sipe (1997), authors seem to accept history as a construction and go on to debate the degree to which history may be flexibly interpreted to meet the needs of the present. One debate centers around the way females in past times are portrayed.

They are often shown as having freer choices than their cultures would have offered. A case in point is the independence of the protagonist in Karen Cushman's *Catherine, Called Birdy*. MacLeod tells us, "Birdy's repeated resistance might have drawn much harsher punishment than she got," since children were considered little more than chattel (p. 30).

Retaining Authenticity

Writers of historical fiction want to present the past authentically but face obstacles with which they must grapple in order to do so. First, staying true to the record and times is of the utmost importance, but authors do not always know the whole story. Second, language issues come into play. If an author uses the authentic language of the time, will modern readers have the patience to interpret it? Third, writers know that they are products of today and as such see the world in different ways than the people they write about did.

Staying True to the Record and Times

While writers agree that the historical facts in a story must be correct, they must figure out how to fill in the gaps left by research. How do they check their own accuracy? One of Jill Paton Walsh's (in Sipe, 1997) rules is based on the distinction between "known not to be true" and "not known to be true":

> Now I do not think any intellectually honest person should have anything to do with the "known not to be true." The "not known to be true" is quite another matter. The "not known to be true" is the whole point of writing historical novels. What sources lack, imagination will supply. (p. 247)

Handling Language

Writers of historical fiction have to deal with the important question of how authentic they can make the language in historical novels without losing young readers, who may not be engaged by characters who speak very differently from themselves. If the language is too antiquated, children will have difficulty understanding it.

Gloria Houston explains her use of a mountain dialect in **Mountain Valor** as a means of mirroring this disappearing dialect of 18th-century English, used until recent times by Appalachian Mountains residents. "Its similarity to black English in some instances reflects a common linguistic heritage" (p. 239). She goes on to explain that she strives for historical accuracy by phonetically spelling the archaic pronunciations (*holp* for *help*) to enrich the dialogue.

Patricia Beatty tells in her author's note why she writes in dialect in **Charley Skedaddle**, a story set in the Civil War in the mountains of Virginia. She explains that for young readers who are not familiar with reading or hearing dialect and may find it difficult "I have toned down the speech of my mountaineers to an approximation of the way they very likely would have sounded in 1864. I have not used *tarnal* and *bodacious* and other words and expressions that would need defining" (p. 185).

Authors of historical fiction work to find language solutions, since they want to capture the spirit of the times without overburdening their readers with unfamiliar words and sentence structures. On the other hand, they know it can be jarring to use excessively contemporary language in a historical novel. Rosemary Sutcliff (in Sipe, 1997), who often writes of medieval times, tries to "steer a middle course between archaic language and modern colloquialism." That often involves the subtle changing or transposing of just one word: "'I beg your pardon' is changed into 'I ask your pardon'" (p. 246).

An especially problematic area involves racial terms that were used in the time period but are offensive today. At the beginning of their novel **With Every Drop of Blood: A Novel of the Civil War,** the Collier brothers, James Lincoln and Christopher, have a note "About the Use of the Word 'Nigger' in This Book." Part of it says,

> Regrettably, the most common term for blacks has been, for well over two hundred years, nigger, a corruption of the word Negro. Until recent decades most whites in the North and virtually all in the South regularly employed this term, although in the North at least they might avoid using it in front of black people. . . . It is therefore impossible to completely avoid the term in a book of this kind,

if we are to be historically accurate; many of the kinds of people portrayed here would have used that term, and not others. We hope readers will understand that we do not approve of the word, but have used it in order to present an accurate picture of black-white relations during the Civil War period. (p. ix)

Looking Back Through the Author's Lens

Joan Blos (in Sipe, 1997) "recognizes that interpretations of past events can change because the author's own personality and her social and cultural context (like the historian's) determine, in part, what perspective the author will take on the past" (p. 245). Christopher Collier (in Sipe, 1997), a professional historian and writer, says that all written history is interpretation, and novelists present their own historical interpretation, whether they are conscious of it or not.

Even 20 years ago, children always read the story of Christopher Columbus's landing in Central America from the European point of view. Today, they are provided with other ways to view this event. Jane Yolen's **Encounter** portrays a very different Columbus than children are used to seeing. The story, told from the point of view of a Taino boy, focuses on the greed of those who landed. Michael Dorris's **Morning Girl,** about the lives of the Tainos, shows the fullness of their culture before the arrival of Columbus. The story ends with a young girl viewing the landing of Columbus and his men.

Katherine Paterson (in Harrison and Maguire, 1987), reflecting on her own writing about ancient Japan, is mindful of the fact that she is looking at the events of ancient Japan through her Western 20th-century mind. She "sifts them and creates the characters who allegedly took part in them. . . . I have not written a Japanese novel. I've written quite a Western novel which happens to be set in Japan" (p. 264).

The Effects of Distortion

Although it is understood that events and their causes have to be simplified in historical fiction, critics have concerns about what children are learning from these books. Anne Scott MacLeod (1998) worries about truth: "A literature about the past that makes overt rebellion seem nearly painless and nearly always successful indicts all those who didn't rebel: it implies, subtly but effectively, that they were responsible for their own oppression" (p. 32). She encourages us to remember that people of the past were not today's people in different clothing; they saw the world differently and approached human relationships differently. "Even if human nature is much the same over time, human experience, perhaps especially everyday experience, is not" (p. 33).

Herbert Kohl (1995) expresses discomfort with the way individuals are often presented to children as having acted alone to make big changes. He cites the case of Rosa Parks. In Montgomery, the boycott had been planned and organized by the African American community before Rosa Parks was arrested. It was an event waiting to take place, waiting for someone who had the respect of the community and the strength to deal with the racist police force. Rosa Parks was such a person, and because the plan was in place the boycott could be mobilized quickly. Parks had been very actively working toward civil rights before the boycott. Kohl points out, "When the story of the Montgomery bus boycott is told merely as a tale of a single heroic person, it leaves children hanging. . . . Not every child can be a Rosa Parks but everyone can imagine her- or himself as a participant in a boycott" (p. 47).

Evaluating Historical Fiction

In evaluating historical fiction, it is not always possible to gain from the content of the book enough information to determine the accuracy of the work. Oftentimes, acknowledgments, forewords, afterwords, and author's notes are not present, yet the information is top-notch. A case in point is Paul Fleischman's **Bull Run,** a Newbery Award winner. All he tells us is that all the facts are accurate although the characters are largely fictional ones. Whether because of the publisher's decision or the author's, many books meant for elementary children simply do not contain information on authenticity, and we cannot be expected to know so much about each time period that we can spot inauthenticity. If in doubt about the historical accuracy of a book, consult book reviews in journals or on the Internet. Sometimes you just have to trust your own instincts and assume that you can spot obvious inaccuracies. If the language seems too modern or strained, if characters seem like today's youth in old-fashioned clothes, if the history is smothering the story, this is probably not a book you should share with your class.

It is delightful to find author's notes and other indications of how authors went about constructing the story, what details they changed or added, and how they dealt with the language issues; it is unfortunate that that information is not always available. But the fact that there is not enough information in the book to address the first two evaluative criteria in the boxed feature Criteria for Evaluating Historical Fiction does not mean that a book is unfit for use. Publishers seem more willing to publish explanatory material than ever before, and I hope this trend continues because such information enriches the experience the reader has with the book.

As the evaluation in the boxed feature Applying the Criteria: Evaluating Historical Fiction shows, the book *The Road to Freedom: A Story of the Reconstruction,* by Jabari Asim, does not meet all the criteria. Yet the book is still a good choice for classroom use, because the issues in the book are very worthy ones and the book is well written. Almost nowhere else do we hear the voices of ex-slaves and experience the day-to-day difficulties of their lives. The lack of sources could be dealt with by challenging students to find resources that verify the information in the book, by either looking on the Internet, going to the library, or contacting the author.

Criteria for Evaluating *Historical Fiction*

1. Is fact distinguished from fiction?

2. From the inside jacket flap, acknowledgments, or author's note, can you get a sense of the research the author did and learn what sources were used?

3. Do the action and plot develop out of the time period? If the book could be set in any other time period with the same conflicts present, it's not historical fiction.

4. Do the characters jump to life and make the reader feel connected to them? Do they express attitudes and beliefs consistent with the time period?

5. Are the historical setting and events woven into the story in seamless ways, or do the characters spout history lessons?

6. Are the themes significant ones?

7. Does the writing bring the story to life?

8. Is the story authentic in language, details, and spirit of the times?

Applying the Criteria *Evaluating Historical Fiction*

The Road to Freedom: A Story of the Reconstruction, by Jabari Asim. I chose this book, which has not been scrutinized by critics, in order to mimic the situation many teachers will be in when they are selecting historical fiction for their classes.

Synopsis: Ezra Taplin is ten when the Union soldiers arrive at the North Carolina plantation to set him, his father, and the rest of the slaves free. These soldiers force the ex-slaves to go to Roanoke to be resettled and to work for the Union army. At the end of the war, Ezra and his dad go to Charleston, where there is a settlement of blacks who were born free. One of this group, Thaddeus Cain, is willing to help the Taplins establish a new life.

1. **Is fact distinguished from fiction?** No. Nowhere in this book, one of the series called *Jamestown's American Portraits,* is there any indication that it is fiction. On the back cover, along with a picture of the author, is the information that he is a poet, critic, and fiction writer. No mention is made of what parts of the story were based on fact.

2. **From the inside jacket flap, acknowledgments, or author's note, can you get a sense of the research the author did and learn what sources were used?** No. Nothing is mentioned about sources. There are, however, five pictures from the time of the story, including a picture of black troops in uniform, two pictures of the ruins of cities in South Carolina, and a picture of Frederick Douglass. In the story are passages from Douglass's writings, as well as excerpts from black newspapers, which I take as indications that much research was done. Also, the descriptions of the city, how the ex-slaves lived, and the issues they were concerned with seem to be steeped in research because they appear accurate.

3. **Do the action and plot develop out of the time period?** The action and plot come out of the time period because they relate to the struggle of ex-slaves to find a way to make a living as they deal with the racist and repressive "Black Codes." Also, we see how many people place ads in black newspapers, hoping to find relatives who had run away or been sold away. The only part of the plot line that strained credibility a bit was on the very last page, when Ezra's mother, who had been gone since he was two, pulled up in a wagon and the family was reunited. While this event is within the range of the possible, it just seems to make the ending too pat.

4. **Do the characters jump to life and make the reader feel connected to them? Do they express attitudes and beliefs consistent with the time period?** The story is told through the eyes of Ezra, a likable boy. While I could get a good sense of Ezra's father, Thaddeus Cain, and his friend Cinda, I didn't feel closely connected to any of the characters. The characters, however, did seem to express attitudes and beliefs of the time period. It was hard to read about how thrilled Ezra was when a white man first spoke kindly to him. He reveled in his feelings of acceptance. Because this is a period not often written about

from the point of view of the freed slaves, I had never thought about how deeply many slaves internalized the belief that they were inferior. The other attitude that seemed consistent with the times was the insistence of some Southern whites that they would never accept blacks as equals. This story showed how very difficult each step of "emancipation" was.

5. **Are the historical setting and events woven into the story in seamless ways, or do the characters spout history lessons?** Throughout the book, the events are woven into the story very tightly. The only time a character had the burden of "telling" history was in the second chapter from the end, when Ezra summarized in about four pages all the actions blacks in southern states were taking to resist the discrimination and oppression of those who did not view blacks as equals.

6. **Are the themes significant ones?** Yes. This story makes evident what the struggle for freedom involved. The information on the struggles of blacks at the time is rarely mentioned in other books I've read. Themes of inferiority versus superiority, speaking up in the face of oppression and death, and importance of family to a people who had been at the mercy of their masters all make this book a provocative one.

7. **Does the writing bring the story to life?** I found the writing to be excellent. The device of opening the book with an old man looking back on his early days of freedom is effective. The language, rich with description, allowed me to see the farm, the island, and the city.

8. **Is the story authentic in language, details, and spirit of the times?** The story seems very authentic, even though this is not a view of the Reconstruction period that we hear often. It is especially interesting to see how the author handled the language issue, since he was writing from the point of view of an uneducated ex-slave. Much of the narration is in the mind of the narrator, and that is written in standard English. Dialect is used only in dialogue and only if the character spoke in dialect. Thaddeus Cain, a very educated black man, speaks in standard English. The author never uses the word *nigger,* but instead has Northern troops refer to black males as *boys* or *coloreds.* The language choices the author made work for this book, as they involve us in the burning equity issues of the time.

Since more books are written in the genre of realistic and historical fiction than in any other, I have had to limit my list of favorite authors. To do otherwise would be to create an unwieldy list, which would not be as useful.

Favorite Authors of Realistic and Historical Fiction

Joan Bauer often focuses on the growing-up experiences of memorable female characters, whom readers get to know well through details, dialogue, and humor.

Marian Dane Bauer writes stories for the younger set that are sensitive, evocative, and unforgettable. She involves her characters in some of life's biggest challenges, such as dealing with divorce and death.

Judy Blume continues to delight readers with tales of growing up, puberty, and coping with siblings. Always laced with humor, her stories keep the reader involved.

Betsy Byars's exuberance for life comes through in her stories for children. While she often writes about sensitive issues, she does so with humor and honesty.

Beverly Cleary writes with clarity, sensitivity, and humor. She tackles many of the prickly issus of childhood with aplomb.

Carolyn Coman gets inside the minds of her characters, sharing their fears, doubts, and hopes in sensitively written books marked by excellent dialogue.

Bruce Coville's warmth, humor, and sensitivity come bursting through in all of his books. His choices of themes and situations demonstrate his deep understanding of the world of the child.

Christopher Paul Curtis writes with humor and compassion. By putting endearing characters in memorable situations, his books bring to light social issues such as racism and discrimination.

Paula Danziger specializes in using humor to capture and keep readers' attention in her sensitive stories of growing up.

Lois Duncan writes compelling mysteries that often have a touch of the supernatural in them.

Paula Fox writes with honesty and clarity about issues that face young readers. Her characterization is especially notable; readers feel a deep empathy for characters facing issues such as loss and lack of courage.

Nancy Garden creates layered stories that ring with emotional honesty as characters face challenging issues such as accepting their own sexuality.

Patricia Reilly Giff offers her young readers a wide range of reading experiences. Her tales of school experiences are humorous and sensitive; her stories of earlier times are evocative and memorable.

Cynthia D. Grant writes powerful novels dealing with social issues such as abuse. Her strong characterization and compelling plot lines bring these issues home to the reader.

Margaret Peterson Haddix, a versatile writer who is as comfortable writing fantasy as she is writing realistic fiction, creates stories with strong plots and memorable characters.

Virginia Hamilton, a writer in almost every genre, creates mysteries and growing-up stories with intriguing plot lines and characters with depth.

Will Hobbs crafts amazing adventure/survival stories, which demonstrate his familiarity with the wild and his skill in making readers care about characters.

Gordon Korman, one of the funniest writers around, creates deliciously involving stories, often about kids getting into trouble.

Julius Lester, a master wordsmith, uses his love of language to bring historical and realistic tales to life.

Gail Carson Levine, a highly inventive writer who constantly amazes her readers with the variety in her works, is noted for involving plot lines, the ability to create memorable settings, and characters who jump to life.

Jean Nixon Lowery is a master crafter of spellbinding mysteries. Her young detectives are provided with both a motive and the resources for an investigation, and her plots are ingenious in their twists and turns.

Lois Lowry exhibits a capacity to write on a wide range of topics and in several genres. Some of her books for young readers humorously explore issues of family life, while others more soberly explore issues in society.

Carolyn Meyer writes both historical and realistic fiction in which characters jump to life, their issues become our issues, and the settings are well drawn.

Walter Dean Myers, a writer in many genres, writes with honesty, an ear for dialogue, compassion for his characters, and a sensitivity to issues of importance to his audience.

Lensey Namioka creates endearing characters and interesting plot lines. She offers readers an inside view of life in the homes of Chinese American children, as her characters deal with issues of childhood and acceptance.

Phyllis Reynolds Naylor is difficult to categorize as a writer because she writes so many different kinds of books. But whether she's writing about an endearing dog or travel through time, her plot development is superb, her characters are memorable, and her themes keep swirling through the reader's head long after the book is finished.

Katherine Paterson writes so beautifully that many of her books have become children's classics. She evokes settings readers can relate to, characters they care about, and plots that become etched in their minds.

Gary Paulsen is a master at crafting words that quickly involve the reader in the world of his characters. His plots, which often focus on adventure and survival, keep readers on the edge of their seats.

Richard Peck writes effectively for a range of ages. Whether he is writing a mystery, a time travel story, or a story about a sensitive social issue, he has a great ear for dialogue and an ability to capture the foibles and joys of human behavior.

Daniel Pinkwater's sense of humor and the absurd permeates his hilarious stories, which often have serious themes at the core.

Kathryn Reiss weaves us into the worlds she creates through her words. Her plot lines are fascinating, her ability to evoke a particular time period is outstanding, and her characters deal with issues that become real to readers.

Ann Rinaldi writes historical fiction so realistically that the reader feels part of the time and connected to the characters. Her research is notable, and she always provides engrossing plot lines.

Jerry Spinelli is a master storyteller who remembers being a kid and writes compellingly about the many aspects of childhood and adolescence. Humor is part of all his

books, although he writes stories with many different tones.

Suzanne Fisher Staples specializes in stories with compelling plots, well-developed characters, and easily entered settings, often in other countries. Much of the material for her novels was gathered during her time as a wire service correspondent in India.

Cynthia Voigt creates characters who resonate with readers, issues that readers care about, and compelling plot lines that keep readers reading. Her use of language is notable.

Virginia Euwer Wolff writes in a fresh way, often taking risks in format (prose poem, multiple points of view) to achieve the effect she is after. Her plots are fascinating, her language is beautiful, the issues she tackles are memorable, and her characters are ones that remain with us long after the book is finished.

Jacqueline Woodson knows how to touch the heart as she crafts stories with characters we care passionately about, issues that strike a chord in us, and plots that involve us.

Laurence Yep is another author who writes in many genres. His stories of children learning about their Chinese heritage are wonderful, as are his stories of historical fiction.

ℐnvitations

Choose several of the following activities to complete:

1. Have each member of your small group choose a different theme in realistic fiction—for example, death, family, pets, fears, or friendship—and find ten picture books on the topic. Rank the books from 1 to 10, with 1 being the best. What criteria influenced your ratings? Share your reactions to the top two or three books with your group. What aspects of the theme does each explore?

2. Choose a controversial topic—for example, abuse, violence, or homosexuality—and read a novel that explores that theme. In your notebook, discuss why you would or would not use this novel with students. What are the literary and thematic merits of the

novel? Discuss the extent to which you believe children should be exposed to realistic issues. Why? Share this information with your small group.

3. Choose a realistic novel that, although frequently taught, is often controversial (for example, Katherine Paterson's **Bridge to Terabithia**). With a partner, role-play a scene in which a parent criticizes the book and you defend it.

CD-ROM

Other examples of dramatizing books can be found under Classroom Teaching Ideas and Invitations by searching for the key terms *dramatize, role-play, present,* and *readers theater.*

4. Read realistic novels from three of the following areas—survival, sports, humor, mystery, horror, or romance. Evaluate the quality of these books. What appeal might these topics have? In a small group, share the best book you read and discuss its thematic and literary value.

5. Choose two historical novels that deal with the same time period or event—for example, Revolutionary War, Civil War, Holocaust, or civil rights movement—and compare them. What do you learn about the period from each? What design decisions did the authors make? Using the criteria for assessing historical fiction, explain which you prefer.

6. Choose a favorite historical novel and become the main character. Talk about the story to your group or the class, using props or artifacts.

7. Each member of your small group should read a different historical novel from a different time period. Prepare a panel discussion of the main characters in which you compare their experiences in the novels and their attitudes toward issues of today. Present this discussion to the class.

8. Collect ten historical fiction picture books. Rank them from 1 to 10, with 1 being best. What made some more appealing than others? To what extent did the illustrations, characterizations, and stories influence your decisions?

9. Read **Johnny Tremain,** by Esther Forbes, and **My Brother Sam Is Dead,** by James Lincoln Collier and Christopher Collier. What attitudes toward war are presented in the two novels? How might the different historical times in which the authors wrote the books have influenced those attitudes? What are the implications for influences on the writing of historical fiction?

Classroom Teaching Ideas

1. Put up a timeline in the classroom. Make it long and large enough so that, whenever children read a historical fiction book, the name of the book can be placed on the line. At the end of the school year, children can observe whether their reading was concentrated on certain periods of time. If there are clusters in one time period, is it because the class was studying an event such as the Civil War or did students gravitate there for some other reason? What might be some possible reasons?

2. Have students share realistic fiction books that describe lives like their own lives, lives very different from their own lives, how they wish their lives could be, or how they're glad their lives are not.

3. Have students find in a book a character who reminds them of a friend, a neighbor, a teacher, or a parent. How is this person like the character in the book? How is this person different?

4. After they read a realistic novel, have students articulate the literary elements. What was the plot? What was the setting? What was the theme? Who were the characters? Did they seem real? Which elements seemed most important and least important to the story? How did they like the book as a whole?

Internet and Text Resources

1. Children's Library, the site of the Boulder Public Library, has a series of websites on different aspects of historical fiction, including Medieval and Renaissance Fiction, Colonial Period, Revolution Fiction, Civil War Fiction, Pioneer and Frontier Life, World

War II Chapter Books, World War II Picture Books, American Internment Camps, and The Holocaust. Find it at

> www.boulder.lib.co.us/youth/booklists/booklists_historical.html

2. **Database of Award-Winning Children's Literature** allows users to search for books by age of child and historical period. Go to

> www2.wcoil.com/~ellerbee/childlit.html

3. **Book Lists at the RT Library,** the site of the Rockaway Township Free Public Library in New Jersey, has book lists on Classics for Children and Young Adults, Historical Fiction, Horror & Supernatural Fiction for Young Adults, School Days, Survival Fiction, and more. Go to

> www.gti.net/rocktwp/booklist.html

4. **The New York Times for Teachers** provides lesson plans related to current events. Find them at

> www.nytimes.com/learning/teachers/lessons/archive.html

5. **Dear America: Official Website** offers a list of all the books in this historical series, timelines, and discussion guides for the books, as well as information on the authors. Go to

> www.scholastic.com/dearamerica/index.htm

6. **Kids Love a Mystery.com** lets teachers use kids' love of mysteries to encourage them to write and solve mysteries. The site includes lesson plans and mini-mysteries. Go to

> www.mysterynet.com/learn

7. Edinger, Monica, and Stephanie Fins (1998). *Far Away and Long Ago: Young Historians in the Classroom.* York, ME: Stenhouse. Practicing elementary teachers share how they involve students in history and historical fiction.

References

Alvarez, Julia (1998). "Ten of My Writing Commandments." *English Journal 88,* 36–41.

Byars, Betsy (2000). "President's Symposium on Mystery Through Literature." IRA Annual Convention, Indianapolis, Indiana, April 30–May 5, 2000.

Cart, Michael (1995). *What's So Funny? Wit and Humor in American Children's Literature.* New York: HarperCollins.

Danziger, Paula, and Elizabeth Levy (1999). "Talking about Humor Writing." *Booklinks 8,* 29–31.

DeFelice, Cynthia (1998). "Research: The Bones Beneath the Flesh of Historical Fiction." *Booklinks 8,* 30–34.

Elleman, Barbara (2000). "Taking Funny Books Seriously: A Reviewer and Book Selector Discusses Criteria for Evaluating Humorous Books for Children." IRA Annual Convention, Indianapolis, Indiana, April 30–May 5, 2000.

Fritz, Jean (1998). "Writing About History in the 1950s and 1960s." IRA Annual Convention, Orlando, Florida, May 3–8, 1998.

Gutman, Dan (2000). "Keep Them Laughing: Writing Humorous Chapter Books." IRA Annual Convention, Indianapolis, Indiana, April 30–May 5, 2000.

Harrison, Barbara, and Gregory Maguire, eds. (1987). *Innocence & Experience: Essays and Conversations on Children's Literature.* New York: Lothrop, Lee & Shepard.

Karr, Kathleen (2000). "The Time Machine: Writing Historical Fiction." *Booklinks 9,* 30–33.

Kohl, Herbert (1995). *Should We Burn Babar? Essays on Children's Literature and the Power of Stories.* New York: The New Press.

Korman, Gordon (2000). "Keep Them Laughing: Writing Humorous Novels for Middle Graders and Older Readers." IRA Annual Convention, Indianapolis, Indiana, April 30–May 5, 2000.

Lee, Philip (1999). "A Publisher's Responsibility in Creating Multicultural Books for Children." IRA Annual Convention, San Diego, May 2–7, 1999.

Lewis, E. B. (2000). "Getting the Details Right: Creating Illustrations for Books Set in Other Times and Places." IRA Annual Convention, Indianapolis, Indiana, April 30–May 5, 2000.

MacLeod, Anne Scott (1998). "Writing Backward: Models in Historical Fiction." *HornBook Magazine,* Vol. 74, No. 1, pp. 26–33.

McGillis, Roderick (1995). "R. L. Stine and the World of the Child Gothic." *Bookbird 33,* 15–21.

Meltzer, Milton (1994). *Non-Fiction for the Classroom.* New York: Teachers College.

Nixon, Jean Lowry (2000). "President's Symposium on Mystery Through Literature." IRA Annual Convention, Indianapolis, Indiana, April 30–May 5, 2000.

Sipe, Lawrence (1997). "In Their Own Words: Authors' Views on Issues in Historical Fiction." *New Advocate 10,* 243–258.

Stewig, John (1994). "Self-Censorship of Picture Books about Gay and Lesbian Families." *The New Advocate 7,* 184–192.

Werlin, Nancy (2000). "President's Symposium on Mystery Through Literature." IRA Annual Convention, Indianapolis, Indiana, April 30–May 5, 2000.

Children's Books

Abbott, Tony (1996). *Danger Guys and the Golden Lizard.* Illus. Joanne Scribner. New York: HarperTrophy.

Aliki (1998). *Marianthe's Story: Painted Words/Spoken Memories.* New York: Greenwillow.

Allard, Harry (1985). *Miss Nelson is Missing.* Illus. James Marshall. Boston: Houghton Mifflin.

Armstrong, William H. (1969). *Sounder.* Illus. James Barkley. New York: Harper & Row.

Asim, Jabari (2000). *The Road to Freedom: A Story of the Reconstruction.* Lincolnwood, IL: Jamestown.

Avi (1991). *Nothing But the Truth.* New York: Orchard.

Ayres, Katherine (1998). *North by Night: A Story of the Underground Railroad.* New York: Delacorte.

Barrett, Tracy (1999). *Anna of Byzantium.* New York: Delacorte.

Barron, T. A. (2000) *Where Is Grandpa?* Illus. Chris K. Soentpiet. New York: Philomel.

Bauer, Joan (1995). *Thwonk.* New York: Delacorte.

Beatty, Patricia (1987). *Charley Skedaddle.* New York: Morrow.

Blos, Joan W. (1979). *A Gathering of Days: A New England Girl's Journal, 1830–32.* New York: Aladdin.

Blume, Judy (1970). *Are You There God? It's Me, Margaret.* Englewood Cliffs, NJ: Bradbury.

Borden, Louise (1997). *The Little Ships: The Heroic Rescue at Dunkirk in World War II.* Illus. Michael Foreman. New York: McElderry.

Bradby, Marie (1995). *More Than Anything Else.* Illus. Chris K. Soentpiet. New York: Orchard.

Brooks, Bruce (1999). *Barry (Wolfbay Wings #11).* New York: Laura Geringer.

Bunting, Eve (1991). *Fly Away Home.* Illus. Ronald Himler. New York: Clarion.

—— (1997). *I Am the Mummy Heb-Nefert.* Illus. David Christiana. San Diego: Harcourt Brace.

—— (1994). *The In-Between Days.* New York: HarperTrophy.

—— (1996). *SOS Titanic.* San Diego: Harcourt Brace.

—— (1996). *Train to Somewhere.* Illus. Ronald Himler. New York: Clarion.

Byars, Betsy (1991). *Bingo Brown and the Language of Love.* Illus. Cathy Bobek. New York: Puffin.

—— (1991). *The Seven Treasure Hunts.* Illus. Jennifer Barrett. New York: HarperTrophy.

—— (1996). *Tornado.* Illus. Doron Ben-Ami. New York: HarperTrophy.

Campbell, Eric (1993). *The Shark Callers.* San Diego: Harcourt Brace.

Capucilli, Alyssa Satin (1996). *Biscuit.* Illus. Pat Schories. New York: HarperCollins.

Christopher, Matt (1972). *The Kid Who Only Hit Homers.* Illus. Harvey Kidder. Boston: Little, Brown.

Cleary, Beverly (1983). *Dear Mr. Henshaw.* Illus. Paul O. Zelinsky. New York: Dell.

Clements, Andrew (1996). *Frindle.* Illus. Brian Selznick. New York: Aladdin.

—— (1999). *The Landry News.* Illus. Salvatore Murdocca. New York: Simon & Schuster.

Cole, Babette (1983). *The Trouble with Mom.* London: Windmill.

Cole, Brock (1987). *The Goats.* New York: Farrar, Straus and Giroux.

Collier, James Lincoln, and Christopher Collier (1974). *My Brother Sam Is Dead.* New York: Scholastic.

—— (1994). *With Every Drop of Blood: A Novel of the Civil War.* New York: Delacorte.

Coman, Carolyn (1993). *Tell Me Everything.* New York; Farrar, Straus and Giroux.

—— (1995). *What Jamie Saw.* Arden, NC: Front Street.

Conly, Jane Leslie (1993). *Crazy Lady!* New York: HarperTrophy.

Couloumbis, Audrey (1999). *Getting Near to Baby.* New York: Putnam.

Coville, Bruce (1996). *My Grandfather's House.* Illus. Henri Sorensen. New York: Bridgewater.

Creech, Sharon (1994). *Walk Two Moons.* New York: HarperCollins.

Curtis, Christopher Paul (1995). *The Watsons Go to Birmingham—1963.* New York: Delacorte.

Cushman, Karen (1994). *Catherine, Called Birdy.* New York: Clarion.

Danziger, Paula (1997). *Amber Brown Sees Red.* Illus. Tony Ross. New York: Putnam.

Davis, Ossie (1992). *Just Like Martin.* New York: Simon & Schuster.

Dorris, Michael (1992). *Morning Girl.* New York: Hyperion.

—— (1996). *Sees Behind Trees.* New York: Hyperion.

Draper, Sharon M. (1997). *Forged by Fire.* New York: Simon & Schuster.

Dyer, T. A. (1981). *A Way of His Own.* Boston: Houghton Mifflin.

Evans, Douglas (1996). *The Classroom at the End of the Hall.* Illus. Larry Di Fiori. Arden, NC: Front Street.

Fenner, Carol (1995). *Yolonda's Genius.* New York: McElderry.

Fleischman, Paul (1993). *Bull Run.* Illus. David Frampton. New York: HarperCollins.

—— (1997). *Seedfolks.* Illus. Judy Pedersen. New York: HarperCollins.

Flournoy, Valerie (1985). *The Patchwork Quilt.* Illus. Jerry Pinkney. New York: Dutton.

Forbes, Esther (1943). *Johnny Tremain.* Illus. Lynn Ward. Boston: Houghton Mifflin.

Gantos, Jack (2000). *Joey Pigza Loses Control.* New York: Farrar, Straus & Giroux.

Garden, Nancy (1982). *Annie on My Mind.* New York: Farrar, Straus & Giroux.

—— (1996). *Good Moon Rising.* New York: Farrar, Straus & Giroux.

Gardiner, John Reynolds (1980). *Stone Fox.* New York: HarperCollins.

Garland, Sherry (1995). *Indio.* San Diego: Harcourt Brace.

—— (1993). *The Lotus Seed.* Illus. Tatsuro Kiuchi. San Diego: Harcourt Brace.

—— (1992). *Song of the Buffalo Boy.* San Diego: Harcourt Brace.

George, Jean Craighead (1974). *Julie and the Wolves.* New York: HarperTrophy.

—— (1995). *There's an Owl in the Shower.* Illus. Christine Herman Merrill. New York: HarperTrophy.

George, Twig C. (1996). *A Dolphin Named Bob.* Illus. Christine Herman Merrill. New York: HarperTrophy.

Giff, Patricia Reilly (1997). *Lily's Crossing.* New York: Delacorte.

—— (1985). *Say "Cheese."* Illus. Blanche Sims. New York: Dell.

Glenn, Mel (1996). *Who Killed Mr. Chippendale? A Mystery in Poems.* New York: Dutton.

Grant, Cynthia D. (1993). *Uncle Vampire.* New York: Atheneum.

Greene, Bette (1999). *Summer of My German Soldier.* New York: Puffin [1973, Dial].

Haddix, Margaret Peterson (1997). *Don't You Dare Read This, Mrs. Dunphrey.* New York: Aladdin.

Hale, Bruce (2000). *The Chameleon Wore Chartreuse: A Chet Gecko Mystery.* San Diego: Harcourt Brace.

Hall, Donald (1997). *The Milkman's Boy.* Illus. Greg Shed. New York: Walker.

Hamilton, Virginia (1993). *Plain City.* New York: Blue Sky/Scholastic.

Hansen, Joyce (1994). *The Captive.* New York: Scholastic.

Hautman, Pete (1996). *Mr. Was.* New York: Simon & Schuster.

Heide, Florence Parry (1971). *The Shrinking of Treehorn.* Illus. Edward Gorey. New York: Dell.

Hesse, Karen (1997). *Out of the Dust.* New York: Scholastic.

Hoban, Lillian (1996). *Arthur's Back to School Day.* New York: HarperTrophy.

Hobbs, Will (1989). *Bearstone.* New York: Atheneum.

—— (1991). *Downriver.* New York: Atheneum.

—— (1996). *Far North.* New York: Morrow.

—— (1997). *Ghost Canoe.* New York: Morrow.

Holt, Kimberly Willis (1999). *When Zachary Beaver Came to Town.* New York: Holt.

Hooks, William H. (1996). *Freedom's Fruit.* Illus. James Ransome. New York: Knopf.

Hopkinson, Deborah (1997). *Birdie's Lighthouse.* Illus. Kimberly Bulcken Root. New York: Atheneum.

—— (1993). *Sweet Clara and the Freedom Quilt.* Illus. James Ransome. New York: Knopf.

Houston, Gloria (1998). *Bright Freedom's Song: A Story of the Underground Railroad.* San Diego: Silver Whistle.

—— (1994). *Mountain Valor.* Illus. Thomas B. Allen. New York: Philomel.

Howard, Elizabeth Fitzgerald (2000). *Virgie Goes to School with Us Boys.* Illus. E. B. Lewis. New York: Simon & Schuster.

Howard, Ellen (1996). *The Log Cabin Quilt.* Illus. Ronald Himler. New York: Holiday.

Hunter, Sara Hoagland (1996). *The Unbreakable Code.* Illus. Julia Miner. Flagstaff, AZ: Rising Moon.

Kaldhol, Marit (1987). *Goodbye Rune.* Illus. Wenche Oyen. Trans. Michael Crosby-Jones. New York: Kane/Miller.

Kalman, Esther (1994). *Tchaikovsky Discovers America.* Illus. Laura Fernandez and Rick Jacobson. New York: Orchard.

Kirkpatrick, Katherine (1998). *Trouble's Daughter: The Story of Susanna Hutchinson, Indian Captive.* New York: Delacorte.

Klass, David (1996). *Danger Zone.* New York: Scholastic.

—— (1989). *Wrestling with Honor.* New York: E. P. Dutton.

Koller, Jackie French (1995). *A Place to Call Home.* New York: Aladdin.

Korman, Gordon (1980). *Beware the Fish!* New York: Scholastic.

—— (1996). *The Chicken Doesn't Skate.* New York: Scholastic.

Lasky, Kathryn (1997). *Marven of the Great North Woods.* Illus. Kevin Hawkes. San Diego: Harcourt Brace.

—— (1995). *She's Wearing a Dead Bird on Her Head!* Illus. David Catrow. New York: Hyperion.

Lee, Marie G. (1996). *Necessary Roughness.* New York: HarperCollins.

Lee, Milly (2001). *Earthquake.* Illus. Yangsook Choi. New York: Farrar, Straus & Giroux.

—— (1997). *Nim and the War Effort.* Illus. Yangsook Choi. New York: Frances Foster.

Lester, Julius (1998). *Black Cowboy Wild Horses: A True Story.* Illus. Jerry Pinkney. New York: Dial.

—— (2000). *Pharaoh's Daughter: A Novel of Ancient Egypt.* San Diego: Silver Whistle.

Levine, Gail Carson (1999). *Dave at Night.* New York: HarperCollins.

Levitin, Sonia (1996). *Nine for California.* Illus. Cat Bowman Smith. New York: Orchard.

Littlesugar, Amy (1999). *Tree of Hope.* Illus. Floyd Cooper. New York: Philomel.

Lorbiecki, Marybeth (1998). *Sister Anne's Hands.* Illus. K. Wendy Popp. New York: Dial.

Lowry, Lois (1989). *Anastasia Krupnik.* New York: Bantam [1979, Houghton Mifflin].

—— (1989). *Number the Stars.* Boston: Houghton Mifflin.

Lunn, Janet (1981). *The Root Cellar.* New York: Scribner.

Lynch, Chris (1997). *Babes in the Woods: The He-Man Women Haters Club #3.* New York: HarperCollins.

—— (1994). *Iceman.* New York: HarperCollins.

—— (1993). *Shadow Boxer.* New York: HarperCollins.

MacLachlan, Patricia (1991). *Journey.* Illus. Barry Moser. New York: Delacorte.

—— (1985). *Sarah, Plain and Tall.* New York: Harper & Row.

Magorian, Michelle (1999). *Good Night, Mr. Tom.* New York: Econo-Clad [1981, Harper & Row].

Mazer, Norma Fox (1999). *Good Night, Maman.* San Diego: Harcourt Brace.

McKissack, Patricia, and Fredrick L. McKissack (1994). *Christmas in the Big House, Christmas in the Quarters.* Illus. John Thompson. New York: Scholastic.

Meltzer, Milton (1990). *Underground Man.* New York: Harcourt Brace.

Meyer, Carolyn (1996). *Gideon's People.* San Diego: Harcourt Brace.

—— (1992). *Where the Broken Heart Still Beats.* San Diego: Harcourt Brace.

Mitchell, Margaree King (1993). *Uncle Jed's Barbershop.* Illus. James Ransome. New York: Simon & Schuster.

Mochizuki, Ken (1993). *Baseball Saved Us.* Illus. Dom Lee. New York: Lee & Low.

Moss, Marissa (1999). *True Heart.* San Diego: Silver Whistle.

Myers, Walter Dean (1999). *Monster.* Illus. Christopher Myers. New York: HarperCollins.

—— (1984). *Motown and Didi.* New York: Viking.

—— (1992). *The Righteous Revenge of Artemis Bonner.* New York: HarperCollins.

Namioka, Lensey (1994). *April and the Dragon Lady.* San Diego: Browndeer.

—— (1999). *Ties That Bind, Ties That Break.* New York: Delacorte.

—— (1995). *Yang the Third and Her Impossible Family.* Boston: Little, Brown.

Naylor, Phyllis Reynolds (1991). *Shiloh.* New York: Atheneum.

Nye, Naomi Shihab (1997). *Habibi.* New York: Simon & Schuster.

O'Dell, Scott (1978). *Island of the Blue Dolphins.* New York: Laurel Leaf.

—— (1999). *Sarah Bishop.* New York: Econo-Clad [1980, Houghton Mifflin].

Palatini, Margie (1999). *Ding Dong Ding Dong.* Illus. Howard Fine. New York: Hyperion.

—— (1997). *Moosetache.* Illus. Henry Cole. New York: Disney.

—— (1995). *Piggie Pie!* Illus. Howard Fine. New York: Clarion.

Parish, Peggy (1972). *Play Ball, Amelia Bedelia.* Illus. Wallace Tripp. New York: Harper & Row.

Park, Ruth (1982). *Playing Beatie Bow.* New York: Atheneum.

Paterson, Katherine (1977). *Bridge to Terabithia.* New York: Crowell.

—— (1978). *The Great Gilly Hopkins.* New York: Crowell.

Paulsen, Gary (1999). *Brian's Return.* New York: Delacorte.

—— (1996). *Brian's Winter.* New York: Delacorte.

—— (1990). *Canyons.* New York: Delacorte.

—— (1987). *Hatchet.* New York: Bradbury.

—— (1991). *The River.* New York: Delacorte.

—— (1998). *Soldier's Heart.* New York: Delacorte.

Pevsner, Stella, and Fay Tang (1997). *Sing for Your Father, Su Phan.* New York: Clarion.

Philbrick, Rodman (1993). *Freak the Mighty.* New York: Blue Sky/Scholastic.

—— (1998). *Max the Mighty.* New York: Blue Sky/Scholastic.

Polacco, Patricia (1994). *Pink and Say.* New York: Philomel.

Porter, Tracey (1997). *Treasures in the Dust.* New York: HarperTrophy.

Pullman, Philip (1985). *The Ruby in the Smoke.* New York: Knopf.

Raskin, Ellen (1978). *The Westing Game.* New York: Dutton.

Rawls, Wilson (1961). *Where the Red Fern Grows.* New York: Doubleday.

Richter, Hans Peter (1970). *Friedrich.* New York: Holt, Rinehart & Winston.

Rinaldi, Ann (1995). *Broken Days (The Quilt Trilogy).* New York: Scholastic.

Ringgold, Faith (1999). *If a Bus Could Talk: The Story of Rosa Parks.* New York: Simon & Schuster.

Ritter, John H. (1998). *Choosing Up Sides.* New York: Philomel.

—— (2000). *Over the Wall*. New York: Philomel.

Rostkowski, Margaret I. (1999). *After the Dancing Days*. New York: Econo-Clad [1985, Harper & Row].

Ruby, Lois (1994). *Steal Away Home*. New York: Macmillan.

Russell, Ching Yeung (1999). *Child Bride*. Illus. Jonathan T. Russell. Honesdale, PA: Boyds Mills.

Rylant, Cynthia (1992). *Missing May*. New York: Orchard.

Sachs, Marilyn (1997). *Another Day*. New York: Dutton.

Sappéy, Maureen Stack (1999). *Letters from Vinnie*. Asheville, NC: Front Street.

Say, Allen (1997). *Allison*. Boston: Houghton Mifflin.

—— (1993). *Grandfather's Journey*. Boston: Houghton Mifflin.

Scieszka, Jon (1991). *The Time Warp Trio: Knights of the Kitchen Table*. Illus. Lane Smith. New York: Puffin.

Siegelson, Kim L. (1999). *In the Time of Drums*. Illus. Brian Pinkney. New York: Hyperion.

Skofield, James (1996). *Detective Dinosaur: Lost and Found*. Illus. R. W. Alley. New York: HarperTrophy.

Smith, Janice Lee (1995). *Wizard and Wart at Sea*. Illus. Paul Meisel. New York: HarperCollins.

Sobel, Donald J. (1968). *Encyclopedia Brown Solves Them All*. Illus. Leonard Shortall. New York: Scholastic.

Spinelli, Jerry (1990). *Maniac Magee*. Boston: Little, Brown.

—— (1997). *Wringer*. New York: HarperTrophy.

Spirn, Michele Sobel (1998). *A Know-Nothing Birthday*. Illus. R. W. Alley. New York: HarperTrophy.

Staples, Suzanne Fisher (1996). *Dangerous Skies*. New York: Farrar, Straus & Giroux.

—— (2000). *Shiva's Fire*. New York: Farrar, Straus & Giroux.

Steig, William (1998). *Pete's a Pizza*. New York: HarperCollins.

Stewart, Sarah (1997). *The Gardener*. Illus. David Small. New York: Farrar, Straus & Giroux.

Talbert, Marc (1995). *Heart of a Jaguar*. New York: Simon & Schuster.

—— (1995). *A Sunburned Prayer*. New York: Simon & Schuster.

Taylor, Mildred D. (1976). *Roll of Thunder, Hear My Cry*. New York: Dial.

Temple, Frances (1996). *The Beduins' Gazelle*. New York: HarperTrophy.

—— (1994). *The Ramsay Scallop*. New York: HarperTrophy.

Thaler, Mike (1999). *The School Bus Driver from the Black Lagoon*. Illus. Jared Lee. New York: Avon.

Turner, Ann (1985). *Dakota Dugout*. Illus. Ronald Himler. New York: Macmillan.

—— (1998). *Drummer Boy: Marching to the Civil War*. Illus. Mark Hess. New York: HarperCollins.

—— (1987). *Nettie's Trip South*. Illus. Ronald Himler. New York: Macmillan.

—— (1999). *Red Flower Goes West*. Illus. Dennis Nolan. New York: Hyperion.

Van Draanen, Wendelin (1998). *Sammy Keyes and the Hotel Thief*. New York: Knopf.

Van Leeuwen, Jean (1998). *Nothing Here But Trees*. Illus. Phil Boatwright. New York: Dial.

Vick, Helen Hughes (1993). *Walker of Time*. Tucson, AZ: Harbinger.

Voigt, Cynthia (1981). *Homecoming*. New York: Atheneum.

—— (1994). *When She Hollers*. New York: Scholastic.

Walter, Mildred Pitts (1996). *Second Daughter: The Story of a Slave Girl*. New York: Scholastic.

Watkins, Yoko Kawashima (1994). *My Brother, My Sister, and I*. New York: Bradbury.

—— (1986). *So Far from the Bamboo Grove*. New York: Lothrop, Lee & Shepard.

Weaver, Will (1995). *Farm Team*. New York: HarperTrophy.

—— (1998). *Hard Ball*. New York: HarperCollins.

—— (1993). *Striking Out*. New York: HarperTrophy.

Wersba, Barbara (1997). *Whistle Me Home*. New York: Holt.

Whelan, Gloria (1995). *Once on This Island*. New York: HarperCollins.

White, Ruth (1996). *Belle Prater's Boy*. New York: Farrar, Straus & Giroux.

Willey, Margaret (1996). *Facing the Music*. New York: Delacorte.

—— (1993). *The Melinda Zone.* New York: Bantam.

Williams, Carol Lynch (1998). *If I Forget, You Remember.* New York: Delacorte.

Wisniewski, David (1998). *The Secret Knowledge of Grown-Ups.* New York: Lothrop, Lee & Shepard.

—— (1999). *Tough Cookie.* New York: Lothrop, Lee & Shepard.

Wolff, Virginia Euwer (1998). *Bat 6.* New York: Scholastic.

—— (1993). *Make Lemonade.* New York: Holt.

Woodson, Jacqueline (1995). *From the Notebooks of Melanin Sun.* New York: Blue Sky/Scholastic.

—— (1994). *I Hadn't Meant to Tell You This.* New York: Bantam Doubleday Dell.

—— (1998). *If You Come Softly.* New York: Putnam.

—— (1995). *Lena.* New York: Delacorte.

Wyeth, Sharon Dennis (1995). *Always My Dad.* Illus. Raúl Colón. New York: Knopf.

—— (1994). *The World of Daughter Maguire.* New York: Delacorte.

Yep, Laurence (1998). *The Case of the Lion Dance.* New York: HarperCollins.

—— (1977). *Child of the Owl.* New York: HarperCollins.

—— (1993). *Dragon's Gate.* New York: HarperCollins.

Yin (2001). *Coolies.* Illus. Chris K. Soentpiet. New York: Philomel.

Yolen, Jane (1988). *The Devil's Arithmetic.* New York: Viking.

—— (1992). *Encounter.* Illus. David Shannon. San Diego: Harcourt Brace.

Modern Fantasy and Science Fiction

Fantasy connects well to the lives and the play of children. Children go in and out of worlds of make-believe, in which animals and toys talk and in which they become something other than themselves. Oftentimes their fantasy life is as real to them as their real life. Children don't have a difficult time believing in fantasy because they recognize that the world has many unseen elements—feelings, wonder, tensions, dreams, fears, hopes, wishes, and longings. Magic seems natural to them, a way to go beyond the boundaries of their very small worlds. It is no wonder they love books filled with little people, talking animals, and live toys, such as *The Borrowers,* by Mary Norton; *Alice in Wonderland,* by Lewis Carroll; *Charlotte's Web,* by E. B. White; *The Complete Tales & Poems of Winnie-the-Pooh,* by A. A. Milne; *The Wind in the Willows,* by Kenneth Grahame; *Raggedy Anne Stories,* by Johnny Gruelle; *The Wonderful Wizard of Oz,* by L. Frank Baum; and *The Tale of Peter Rabbit,* by Beatrix Potter. These stories speak of their deepest hopes, dreams, emotions, and fears and take them to exciting and new places. Fantasy provides a vision that other genres don't offer.

Authors of fantasy are well aware of the existence of wonder, that "great excitement that is a mixture of astonishment and delight" (Cooper, in Harrison and Maguire, 1987). Yet most children abandon fantasy when adults stop reading to them. Then they mainly read realistic fiction and informational books—perhaps trying to figure out how to get along in the world, how to crack those seemingly secret codes of behavior so that they can be accepted by others. Sometime in middle school many students find or rediscover that part of themselves that believes in the vision fantasy offers, and they begin reading *The Dark Is Rising* series, by Susan Cooper; *The Chronicles of Narnia,* by C. S. Lewis; and *The Chronicles of Prydain,* by

Lloyd Alexander. They allow the smoldering embers of their love of fantasy to burst back into flame.

Because fantasy can enrich the early lives of children, it is important to think about your own attitudes about fantasy, which you will bring to the children you teach. Are you comfortable with fantasy, or do you believe it is silly? Do you think it is a genre all children can enjoy? In my 30 years in the classroom, I have found that teachers' attitudes toward books and materials have a very real impact on the way children respond. By finding books in this genre that you can actively enjoy along with your students, you'll give your students an opportunity to find joy in this genre too. Some children explain how they view fantasy in the boxed feature Children's Voices.

What Is Fantasy?

For information and surprises, go to *The Wonderful Wizard of Oz Website* at www.eskimo.com/~tiktok/index. html.

Lloyd Alexander (in Harrison and Maguire, 1987), notable fantasy writer, gives a simple, straightforward definition of fantasy: "If the work contains an element of the impossible (at least as we currently understand the world), we classify it as fantasy; . . . if its events could indeed physically happen in the real world, we classify it as realism." He adds, however, that such classification is "simply a categorical convenience" (p. 195). Alexander's definition confirms that genres slide together, making it difficult to separate them. Events that seem very real may cause one person to identify a book as realistic, while others would categorize it as fantasy because it includes talking animals, which are viewed as an impossibility. Even novels that take us way back in time can seem real, probably because the writers make the transition seem so effortless with their vivid descriptions.

The genre of fantasy includes high fantasy, time travel, magic in everyday life, fantastical worlds, animals that talk and think, battles of good against evil, and even historical fantasy. The characteristics that distinguish one kind from the other are important only because they provide an indication of what kind of experience you'll have with that kind of book. Do you like having one foot in the real world and one foot in the world of magic and seeing how the two worlds exist side by side? Do you want to go to fresh, new worlds, where you can see how they organize their society, what customs they have, and what they consider "normal" and thus see our own world in much clearer ways? Do you like to get involved in time slips, in which one character goes to another time? Do you like to wonder whether people in eras before or after us are speaking to us? Do you enjoy the feeling of being able to do something few other people can

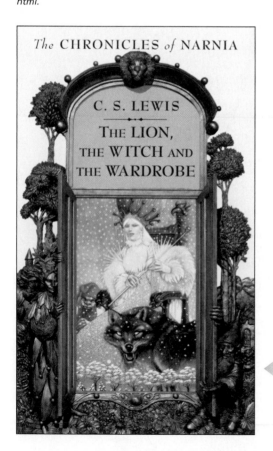

The Lion, the Witch and the Wardrobe, one of the best-loved of *The Chronicles of Narnia,* takes children into the heart of Narnia, where the forces of good and evil are at odds.
(Cover art from *The Lion, the Witch and the Wardrobe* by C. S. Lewis. COVER ART COPYRIGHT © 1994 CHRIS VAN ALLSBURG. COVER COPYRIGHT © 1994 BY HARPERCOLLINS PUBLISHERS. Used by permission of HarperCollins Publishers.)

Children's Voices

On fantasy . . .

It leaves you with wonder. —Jonah, 6th grade

It sparks your imagination and gives you the feel for creativity. —Allison, 7th grade

I love the fact that anything can happen. —Elizabeth, 7th grade

I guess I'm somewhat of a dreamer. Fantasy worlds are perfect without problems and troubles. —Carlyn, 7th grade

It gives you a chance to "escape reality." You can really use your imagination. —Julie, 7th grade

They take me to a whole different world and my imagination can think of anything. They take me away from all my thoughts and problems. —Joseph, 7th grade

I like fantasy because of how they [heroes] do what they do and fight against unbeatable odds. —Sam, 7th grade

These types of books bring me to another world. In this world I'm anyone I want to be. I can imagine a different time and place. Fantasy also gets my imagination going. —Georgia, 8th grade

I enjoy fantasy because I sometimes like to picture myself anywhere but in the world today. —Liz, 8th grade

Brian Jacques is one of my favorite authors because his stories are woven together with information they give. I also like J. K. Rowling because she does not give information if it is not part of the story. —Brian, 8th grade

*In **Mossflower** there's a badger named Bella. She's a leader. She protects her people. So do I.* —Amie, 8th grade

*I like **Harry Potter.** They have a lot of adventure and it really has some heart-throbbing moments.* —Steven, 4th grade

J. K. Rowling is my favorite author because of her immense use of detail, her funny yet serious way of telling the story. —Annie, 6th grade

*I thought that **Harry Potter's** Hermione was an awful lot like me. That was a light, fun read and I will always be jealous of the characters.* —Sara, 7th grade

On horror . . .

***Goosebumps** books are "funny-scary and quick and easy to read. I can finish one in an hour. . . . When you read **Goosebumps,** you can talk to other children who've read them and find out that they're scared about things, too. Also when you read about monsters and ghosts, you imagine what they look like in your mind even though you've never seen them in the real world, so you really have to use your imagination. This is a good thing."* —Rachel (cited in Rud, 1995/1996, p. 24)

*I like scary books such as **Fear Street, Terror Academy,** and **Goosebumps.*** —Jon, 7th grade

I read horror mostly because I love the way you get so involved in the story that you can't put it down. To me, I feel I'm actually in the story. —Katie, 7th grade

do, such as talk to animals, transport yourself from one place to another through a magic spell, or become part of the world of toys? All of these kinds of experiences are available through the magical genre called fantasy.

The Appeal of Fantasy

Find out more about this popular series at the **Harry Potter** page on Scholastic's website. Go to www.scholastic.com/harrypotter/home.asp.

Whether they acknowledge it or not, most people appreciate fantasy. Why else would they go in droves to see such movies as *Star Wars, Jurassic Park, Close Encounters of the Third Kind,* and *ET?* Why else would hotels have no thirteenth floor? Why else would newspapers print daily horoscopes? Why else would J. K. Rowling's **Harry Potter** books be at the top of the bestseller list week after week, month after month? Because our society sees reason as the opposite of and more desirable than emotion, however, people are often apologetic about their love of the magical and mysterious. They think of fantasy as an add-on, an extra, almost an unneeded appendage in their lives. After all, Freud, the grandfather of psychology, believed that fantasy was an escape from real life, and this theory worked its way into popular thought. Freud would certainly not consider fantasy to be of any essential importance. Luckily, some of his successors have taken issue with his theory about fantasy and demonstrated its positive aspects.

Fantasy can channel actions into the verbal rather than the physical. Psychologist Melanie Klein explains that when life appears futile and meaningless, creative activity reduces mental stress (in Harrison and Maguire, 1987, p. 54). Bruno Bettelheim (in Harrison and Maguire, 1987, p. 55) says that children under stress are able to battle through their problems only if they can fantasize about future achievements—even in an exaggerated and improbable way. If a child for some reason is unable to imagine her or his future optimistically, arrested development results. Jerome L. Singer (in Harrison and Maguire, 1987, p. 54) points out that the low-fantasy child reveals much action and little thought; the high-fantasy child is more highly structured and creative and tends to be verbally, rather than physically, aggressive. Stimulating children's minds through fantasy can help them cope with issues in their lives in imaginative, not physical, ways.

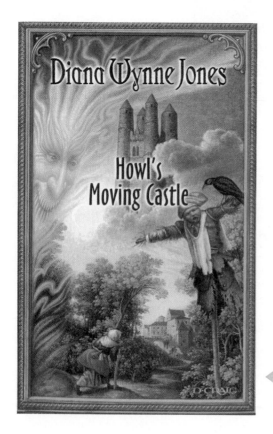

Fantasy can help fuel hope. Imagination helps us to hope, to envision things as they could be. If we could see only who we are now and how we live now, without imagining how things could be different, we would be without hope. If we saw only bleakness and despair around us, how would we know there could be another kind of existence if our imagination didn't let us fly above our present reality and see possibilities? In such books as ***Howl's Moving Castle,*** by Diana Wynne Jones, we see the hero's journey, the tests she survives, and her return. Seeing ourselves as the hero gives us hope that we too can accomplish wonderful feats.

Fantasy can make a difference in the way we see things. As people age, they tend to become deadened to their surroundings, even taking the beauty of nature for granted. Think about how differently young children and adults take a walk. Adults stroll along, while young children leave nothing unexplored. They look and question. They know that the world is filled with amazing information, and their curiosity drives them. They believe that almost anything is possible. By providing literature that stretches the imagination, we can perhaps help children retain their curiosity, keeping their minds flexible so that they'll be willing to stretch

◀ In this warm-hearted, witty fantasy, Sophie, turned into an old woman by a witch, finds that seeking her fortune involves bargaining with the heartless Wizard Howl. (Cover art from *Howl's Moving Castle* by Diana Wynne Jones. Used by permission of HarperCollins Publishers.)

out and grab concepts that seem just out of reach. Keeping the imaginative muscles flexed helps children think about familiar things in unaccustomed ways.

Fantasy can help us grapple with the essential questions of the universe, for which there are no observable answers. Some people turn to fantasy because it taps into their deep inner longing to understand phenomena that science and religion have been unable to explain to everyone's satisfaction. Erich Fromm suggests (in Harrison and Maguire, 1987) that acceptance and understanding of this other world are contained in the subconscious mind, which he calls the storehouse of a "forgotten language . . . the common origin of dream, fairy tales, and myth" (p. 178). It has been suggested that this subconscious mind Fromm alludes to, which we carry around within us and sometimes let ourselves experience, may be a genetic intelligence of things the human race has known since the earliest days. As Natalie Babbitt (in Harrison and Maguire, 1987) describes it, "true fantasy" is not a new creation but "is distilled and interpreted—from impressions that go far back into prehistory, impressions that, so far as we can tell from the study of folktales, are common to us all whatever our age and nationality" (p. 174). Babbitt believes this other world that is deep within our subconscious will always be somewhere; because no matter how we may try to deny it, our need for it is large. Patricia Lee Gauch (1994) writes that the creation of the best fantasy involves probing the wisdom of "that dark and secret place in the human psyche," as well as using the intellect. "Fantasies have common recurring elements because the terrain of the human psyche is universal, or, as Jung argued, 'the journey reflects a collective human experience'" (p. 162). Given that we all have to answer the same essential questions about our lives, Gauch says, "If literature does, in fact, provide a map for living, there is no map more powerful for the developing individual, more full of humanity, than fine fantasy" (p. 166).

Fantasy can help empower us to become who we wish to be. Especially in quest or high fantasy, we live through the trials of the heroes; we experience their decision making and the consequences of those choices. We hurt when they hurt, we are thrilled when they are thrilled; we are defeated when they are defeated; and we are victorious when they are victorious. This kind of fantasy asks us to go within, to dwell in those shadowy places in our heart and mind. Through fantasy, we can get to know ourselves better: what we're capable of, what fears hold us back, what we'd like to accomplish, what things are near and dear to our heart, and what issues we're willing to take a stand on. In this age of media scrutiny, when all the blemishes of contemporary and historical heroes are publicized, children need to see figures of heroic dimension. Fantasy can help empower them to be the people they want to be by giving them models for facing their deepest fears and accepting challenges they aren't sure they're capable of. By inhabiting this inner territory, we can all become more aware of that which we are capable of.

Fantasy can help us learn about and understand people. Bruce Coville's ***Jennifer Murdley's Toad*** provides an excellent illustration of what judging people on their appearance can bring. Through magic and humor, Coville shows that the worth of a person rests on much more than his or her outer covering or body. Children like books that help them understand the complexities of human behavior so that they can be more successful in negotiating their way through life.

Fantasy can allow us to vicariously have experiences that make us special. When students read stories of magic in everyday life, they can envision something exciting happening to them—such as getting a talking dog. This makes them special, giving people a way to relate to them and recognize in them qualities that they had never seen. Fantasy helps readers to feel deep inside, "if only someone really knew me, knew all the exciting thoughts and ideas I have, knew how much fun I could be." When the characters in Edward Eager's ***Knight's Castle*** become little people along with Roger's toy soldier, they are called on to display the kind of courage and inventiveness that most children are never called on to display. They have found a way to demonstrate who they really are and who they can be. In our ordinary-seeming lives, we often feel that we don't have a chance to show our promise or true ability.

Fantasy can reveal truths about life. At the core of much fantasy literature lies a gleaming nugget of truth, which is obscured in our regular world. Being in an imaginary world has the effect of lifting us up above our world so that we can clearly see these nuggets, which are usually covered by our fears or by the blinders we develop within a culture.

Lyra learns some uncomfortable truths about life as she journeys to the North to solve the mystery of the missing children.

("Cover illustration" by Eric Rohmann, copyright © 1996 by Eric Rohmann, from THE GOLDEN COMPASS by Philip Pullman. Used by permission of Alfred A. Knopf Children's Books, a division of Random House, Inc.)

Because our society is not comfortable with the idea of death, we tend to fear it and miss the truths death holds. *Tuck Everlasting,* by Natalie Babbitt, in which one family lives forever, asks readers to think about the purpose of dying—how it fits into the natural order of things and is part of the rhythm of life. Readers of *The Golden Compass,* by Philip Pullman, might question whether religious organizations could be involved in far-reaching schemes to protect their own power at the expense of the people.

Fantasy can make life more diverting and interesting. Reading fantasy takes us away from the humdrum of daily existence and gives us interesting things to think about. It provides an escape when we need one. Who wouldn't rather live in a world peopled by flying dragons or wizards-in-training? Who wouldn't rather be neutralizing the "threads" spewed by the Red Star so as to save the world from fires and great destruction? Who wouldn't rather be able to see what mere Muggles cannot? Given how many alternatives we have in our complex society, sometimes it's restful to go to a world where the hero has more clear-cut choices. Fantasy can lull and enfold us if we let ourselves inhabit that secret place within—that place that wants to believe.

The Centrality of Imagination

Fantasy is certainly not the only genre that stimulates the imagination. But since imagination is the key ingredient in this genre, this is a good place to look at the importance of imaginative thinking. Maxine Greene (1995), educator and philosopher, explains that imagination makes empathy possible. It allows us to make "the leap across the boundaries of our own lives and into someone else's shoes" (p. 3). It lets us put aside the familiar and make the unfamiliar real. For a moment, we can feel what it's like to live in a different place and time and see the world in a different way. As a little girl reading *Raggedy Ann Stories,* by Johnny Gruelle, and hearing what dolls talked about when out of sight of humans, I felt such empathy for my dolls that I began to make room for them in my bed at night so that they wouldn't feel neglected.

Imagination allows us to see openings through which we can move, to envision possibilities, and to explore the unknown. As a child, I was startled by the fantastical ways in which the main character of *The 21 Balloons,* by William Pène du Bois, conceived of and built hot-air balloons. One balloon had a little basket house beneath, another was a balloon merry-go-round, and another was a life raft designed to help a group of people escape from a volcanic island. This book nudged me to think about the world as I had never envisioned it before and made me aware that there were ways of seeing other than my own.

Only through imagining can one break with fixed views and see past the supposedly objective and real. To find new orders in experience, we must be able to see beyond the normal or conventional so that we can form notions of what can be or should be. Thus, imagination is at the core of learning that goes beyond the self. Imagination lets us see things that are not in our lives but could be; it lets us envision new ways of thinking and doing things. After reading *Mary Poppins,* by P. L. Travers, I wanted so much to be able to move through space as Mary did. I wondered how a mere umbrella could propel Mary upward and move her anywhere she wanted to go. I was sure there must be some device that could move humans through space the way Mary moved. I was intrigued by what I had never thought of before. Imagination took me not only beyond the boundaries of my own neighborhood and experience, but also beyond the boundaries of my own ways of thinking.

Imagination isn't a luxury but a necessity. It is needed everywhere. Changes in medicine, education, law, physics, and technology all begin with seeing things in new ways. Imagination helps us meet new challenges and devise workable solutions to problems in our society. "We have to be able to conceive of things in new ways, to think 'outside the box' and not be tied to the way things are presently. Without this capacity, little forward change would happen in our world" (Greene, 1995, p. 36). Greene reminds us that too often we view imagination as something superfluous, not realizing its essential value for all children. Imagination teaches creative thinking. It opens windows in the actual, shedding a kind of light and allowing children to see new perspectives. Imagination feeds one's capacity to feel one's way into another's vantage point. It promotes curiosity and adaptability, qualities that help us survive.

By freeing the imagination, fantasy can help children face reality with more creativity and spontaneity of thought. Stimulating and unleashing the imagination is an important part of children's education, and the use of fantasy can engage them in the very serious work of releasing the imagination.

Kinds of Fantasy

When you hear the term *fantasy,* you may think of imaginary worlds in which the forces of good fight the forces of evil or you may think of dragons and queens and castles. Yet these elements are mainly associated with high fantasy, which is only one of the many kinds of fantasy written today. The goal of this section is to give you a glimpse of the kinds of treats that exist within each of the very different categories of fantasy.

Magic in Everyday Life

Stories about magic taking place in our familiar, everyday world generally are devoid of the lofty fight for good and evil and usually include humor and zaniness. Bruce Coville's **Magic Shop** books (**Jeremy Thatcher, Dragon Hatcher; Jennifer Murdley's Toad;** and **The Skull of Truth**), which are laced with humor as well as serious undercurrents, have wide appeal to upper elementary school children and make good read-alouds. One involves a dragon, another has a talking toad, and the third features a skull that casts spells. The appearance of these animals/objects has dramatic and very humorous effects on the children who find them. Another humorous, wacky series is **Freaky Friday,** by Mary Rodgers, in which bizarre events occur, such as a child turning into his own father. Roald Dahl writes humorous, fantastic adventures, such as **Charlie and the Chocolate Factory.** Diane Duane's **Wizardry** series, including **Deep Wizardry,** will also enthrall children because its young characters acquire special powers, with fascinating and often humorous results. Also included in this category are talking animal books such as **Smart Dog,** by Vivian Vande Velde; **Bunnicula: A Rabbit-Tale of Mystery,** by Deborah Howe and James Howe; and **Dr. Dolittle: A Treasury,** by Hugh Lofting.

Books with a more serious tone that tell of unusual things happening right around us include **Tuck Everlasting,** by Natalie Babbitt; **Charlotte's Web,** by E. B. White; and **James and the Giant Peach,** by Roald Dahl. Books in which toys come to life, every child's dream, include **Raggedy Ann Stories,** by Johnny Gruelle, and **The Velveteen Rabbit,** by Margery Williams, a perennial favorite.

Some books have distinctive structures that make them hard to categorize. **Harry Potter and the Sorcerer's Stone** and the rest of J. K. Rowling's series are such books. The story begins in everyday England, but when Harry turns eleven he is escorted to a school for wizards, Hogwarts. I question whether this world filled with magic is in another dimension that Muggles (nonbelievers in magic) don't have access to or whether Muggles don't have access to this world simply because they don't know how to see it and don't believe it can exist. So the question for me in categorizing this book is whether or not it takes place in our everyday world. Another book difficult to categorize is **Skellig,** by David Almond. Although the story is set in this world, the angel-like character, Skellig, gives it a supernatural tinge as he helps the main characters, Michael and Minna, understand the power of love.

Ghost Stories

The database at *Science Fiction and Fantasy for Children: An Annotated Bibliography* has more than 400 titles. Find it at http://libnt1.lib.uoguelph.ca/SFBiblindex.htm.

Ghost stories send chills up the spine and make readers turn quickly in their chairs to confirm that they're not seeing something otherworldly from the corner of their eyes. In *Dreadful Sorry,* by Kathryn Reiss, a ghost gets intertwined with the protagonist's life until she figures out what the ghost wants her to know. Molly first discovers that something is wrong through her nightmares. Then, when she visits her father and stepmother for the summer, she is shocked to find that the old house they live in in Maine is the house in her nightmares! Mary Downing Hahn specializes in ghosts who have scores to settle. Her horror novels include *The Doll in the Garden* and *Wait Till Helen Comes.* Lois Duncan's spellbinding books, such as *Down a Dark Hall, Gallow's Hill,* and *Stranger with My Face,* also include supernatural elements.

Horror

As the sale of millions of *Goosebumps* books, by R. L. Stine, indicates, horror—sometimes with supernatural elements in it—remains popular with children. Children who read primarily for vicarious pleasure (Carlsen's stage of vicarious experience in Chapter 1) seek the deliciousness of experiencing breath-stopping fear, just as they delight in the scariest of the Disney World rides. Escaping into a horror story allows them to experience a range of intense human emotions in a safe way. Although R. L. Stine (2000) said in a presentation that he is actually "pretty squeamish," his works of horror don't indicate that. Over time, he explained, people have loved scary stories "probably as a way to deal with the scary world." He believes that part of the popularity of horror lies in children's ability to identify with the monsters. They do so because they often "feel like outsiders or different or ugly or frightened by angry feelings which they want to release and go berserk." He believes that his books provide "safe scares that end up nicely." Stine believes in giving kids what they want to read. "In my day, teachers tried to discourage kids from reading what they like and pointed them in other directions." Scary stories can be found in chapter books such as *Frankenstein Moved in on the Fourth Floor,* by Elizabeth Levy; *Blood Brothers,* by Jill Morgan; and *The Haunted House: A Collection of Original Stories,* edited by Jane Yolen and Martin H. Greenberg. Vivian Vande Velde's *Never Trust a Dead Man* and Paul Fleischman's *Graven Images* will keep readers horrified. Other masters of horror are Diane Hoh and Christopher Pike.

Time Travel

If you would like to go to another time period and see it through the eyes of the present, time travel is the type of fantasy that will take you there. Some time travel books are also called historical fantasy, because they are stories of the past told through the eyes of a person from the present. *The Root Cellar,* by Janet Lunn, takes readers back to the Revolutionary War. *Playing Beatie Bow,* by Ruth Park, takes readers to the Rocks, in Sydney, Australia, where they witness what life was like for the poor in the 19th century. Helen Hughes Vick's *Walker of Time* series takes readers back to the cliff dwellings in the 1250s, when they were the home to the Hopis.

Another type of time travel book features modern-day characters caught in long-ago times told about in legends and myths. These stories usually involve quests and the battle between good and evil. Some of the best are *A String in the Harp,* by Nancy Bond; *The Singing Stone,* by Orla Melling; *The Moon of Gomrath,* by Alan Garner; and *Many Waters,* by Madeleine L'Engle.

Some time travel books are neither historical nor based on legends. Phyllis Reynolds Naylor's *York Trilogy* deals with family members who want to know more about their family tree, which includes the legacy of Huntington's disease. Through time swirls, Dan comes in contact with people prominent in his family's past. ***Tom's Midnight Garden,*** by Philippa Pearce, is a well-loved classic in which Tom slips back in time, finding a new friend when he enters the garden at midnight. Light-hearted and humorous time travel books include Richard Peck's ***The Dreadful Future of Blossom Culp,*** in which young Blossom travels forward to our time from early in the 20th century; Susan Beth Pfeffer's ***Rewind to Yesterday,*** in which eleven-year-old twins discover that they can enter the past with the help of their VCR; and Sharon Creech's ***Pleasing the Ghost,*** in which the ghost of Dennis's uncle shows up and won't leave him alone.

High Fantasy

High fantasy brings to mind visions of dragons, swords, otherworldly places, and would-be heroes going on quests and facing overwhelming odds. These themes are certainly part of high fantasy, but it offers much more than that. Of all the kinds of fantasy, high fantasy is often the most challenging to read. Generally these stories have a serious tone. They are peopled with heroes (see Chapter 8 for Joseph Campbell's criteria for a hero), who are almost always on a quest. Since they are usually fighting evil, they often get help from forces beyond their time. Because the struggle between good and evil dominates these stories, they concern themselves with universal questions and values. Here we see such values as courage, truth, justice, goodness, and wisdom emerge in many shapes and forms as the heroes fulfill their quests. To highlight the differences among books in this category, I have divided them into stories that begin in the world we know, stories set in an imaginary world, and stories set in legendary times. Although many common elements pervade the stories in this category, the different settings give each type of high fantasy a special flavor.

CD-ROM

To find the names of additional fantasy writers, do a word search for *fantasy* under Favorite Authors.

Stories Beginning in the World We Know

In some high fantasy, the reader begins in the present world but is transported to a realm outside of time. For example, Will, in Susan Cooper's ***The Dark Is Rising*** series, lives on a farm in England. On his eleventh birthday, Will awakes to find himself in a "strange white world . . . stroked by silence" and realizes that he is in an earlier time before there were rooftops or gardens or even crumbled stone walls around his farmhouse (p. 18). Throughout the book, Will is mainly in his present-day world, but he makes forays into this other world beyond time, where he meets others like himself who are Old Ones and finds out what is expected of him. When Will is summoned, time stands still for the people in the present. Alan Garner sets ***The Owl Service*** in the world as we know it, but he weaves in Welsh legend, which puts the three main characters in touch with forces they at first don't understand.

The main characters in all these stories are on quests, moving out of the conventional safety of their own lives to undertake the journey, undergoing trials and tests, performing courageous acts, and achieving something. All complete the hero cycle. Because the stories are set in this world, they take on almost spiritual dimensions and make us wonder about what sets forces loose in our own world and how we create the energy that produces good and keeps evil at bay.

Stories Set in Another World

The heroes of some high fantasy inhabit worlds (like Narnia) that obviously are not like the one we inhabit. In these worlds, dragons may speak, witches may be a threat, or each person may have a familiar, an animal that is linked psychically to its human and can change forms to reflect the moods of the human.

Books that take place in altered worlds include Philip Pullman's ***The Golden Compass*** series. He creates a world very like 19th-century England, except that people have familiars without which they cannot live, armored bears talk, and witches fly. The struggle for good rests on the shoulders of the child Lyra, who believes herself to be an orphan. The tale takes us from the streets of London, where homeless children are disappearing, to the cold reaches of the Far North, where Lyra tries desperately to help these children. Anne McCaffrey creates a world that has little similarity to our own. In

(W)

*Tour the land of Narnia and more at **Narnia.com**. Find it at www.narnia.com/.*

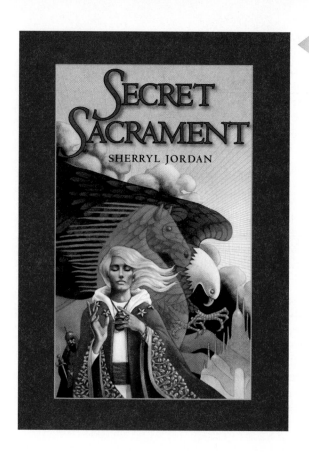

Gabriel resists family and societal pressures in order to stay with his own truth and become the person he knows he must become if he is to fulfill his destiny.

(Cover art from *Secret Sacrament* by Sherryl Jordan. Used by permission of HarperCollins Publishers.)

her dragon books about Pern, such as **Dragondrums,** codes of conduct are unlike ours, dragons have a central place, and gender roles are viewed in a different way. All her stories in this series transport us to a magical place where, every 200 years, the evil "threads" that fall from the Red Star will burn and destroy the planet unless inhabitants believe in and nurture the usefulness of the dragons. Robin McKinley sets **The Blue Sword** and **The Hero and the Crown** in a world of castles and kings and dragons.

Through creation of imaginary worlds, fantasy can take readers out of this world and enfold them in a new one where the rules are different, the stakes are high, and the adventure never seems to end. Such books give readers the sensation of floating suspended above the world, only looking down occasionally. While these books may not make readers wonder about their own world, they do make readers reflect on the major themes in the lives of all humans. Because readers are not part of the imaginary society, with its rules and regulations, they can get a close-up look at the people. The actions and motivations of people who live in imaginary worlds can be laid bare.

Stories Set in Legendary Times

Books set in legendary times, often the days of King Arthur and Merlin, usually relate to the legends of the Welsh, Scottish, Irish, or British people. T. A. Barron's **The Lost Years of Merlin** and Jane Yolen's **Hobby: The Young Merlin Trilogy** look back and re-create the life of the magician we really know so little about. Monica Furlong's **Juniper** and **Wise Child** take place in Cornwall after the time of King Arthur, but we hear about Merlin's magic.

Books set in olden times often evoke images of long-ago empires and royalty. Both of Megan Whalen Turner's books, **The Thief** and **The Queen of Attolia,** are fast-paced adventure fantasies set in the long ago, with a clever hero who understands the ways of royalty and knows how to move around kingdoms surreptitiously. **Secret Sacrament,** by Sherryl Jordan, which is also set in an empire of long ago, tells of a boy, born to be a healer, who yearns to heal the divide between people and nations.

What Is Science Fiction?

Although the natural laws are fundamental to science fiction, imagination also plays a vital part. Science fiction writer Sophie Masson (1997) writes that only imaginative literature gives real shape to the future, and this shape comes not from "fanciful descriptions of new technological marvels, but because at the very core of this type of literature is a preoccupation with the human spirit" (p. 31). Imaginative writers "seek not to prescribe, but to describe; not to answer, but to question" (p. 32). One of the most appealing aspects of science fiction is its capacity to make us think deeply and question our everyday world.

Many people do not read science fiction because they expect it to be dry and dull and mechanized. They worry that it will focus on technologies, not people; on sterile worlds, not any place they could recognize. But they are wrong. Before I opened myself up to this genre, I had to read and love Madeleine L'Engle's **A Wrinkle in Time** trilogy and then realize it was

Children enjoy science fiction because . . .

You feel like you are inside the story whether it be fighting dragons or making spells or even solving mysteries along with the characters.
—Ashley, 6th grade

It tells real things. —Patrice, 6th grade

I like to dream about what the future can be like. —Courtney, 7th grade

It makes you wonder, Is this true? Could this really exist? —Scott, 7th grade

It makes the mind dream up uncommon ideas/topics and talk about them. You never know what to expect because it is fiction. —Chris, 7th grade

I love the creativity of the author. —Allison, 7th grade

I read books that are science fiction and are about people who are pursuing their dreams and doing what they want, no matter what other people think. They are interesting and sometimes suspenseful. —Aarika, 7th grade

When action and suspense are combined together, you can't put the book down.
—Jamie, 7th grade

It is puzzling and mystifying and that makes it cool. —Liz, 8th grade

Some children are not fans because . . .

I am not into fake thoughts. —Matt, 7th grade

categorized as science fiction. The stories were gripping and the people real, and I became aware of things I had never thought about before—for example, that the shortest distance between two places is through a fold or wrinkle in time. L'Engle's books were a gentle introduction to science fiction, and from there it was easy to gradually branch outward.

Although science fiction encompasses a broad range, the stories generally include some elements of science or are set in the future in a society very different from our own. This imaginative literature is based on real scientific facts and principles so that what is described seems plausible. Settings and events are built on extensions of known technologies and scientific concepts. Unlike fantasy, science fiction deals with events that could possibly happen, given further scientific development. Children share their views of science fiction in the boxed feature Children's Voices.

*T*he Appeal of Science Fiction

Science fiction has many of the same appeals as fantasy. However, it also can appeal to its readers in some special ways.

The appeal of many science fiction stories to middle schoolers lies in the fact that characters in these stories must adjust to a changing world and become new people, which is part of the middle school experience. These students, who will be inhabiting our world in a future time, are fascinated by portraits of what it could be like. They enjoy seeing how people adapt to the new environment or world in an alternative society.

Science fiction taps into intellectual musings about questions for which we have no answers. We all wonder where we came from and what our universe is filled with—friendly others who want to be helpful, spirits that guide us, aliens ready to pounce on us, stars that

100 Favorite Children's Books contains a section on science fiction. Go to www.nypl.org/branch/kids/100/scifi.html.

may collide with us, a sun that might burn out. In *A Bone from a Dry Sea,* by Peter Dickinson, readers are taken on an archeological dig in present-day Africa but are also shown the ancient past. With chapters alternating between the point of view of a female humanoid and that of a young girl in the present, this story offers a view of how humanoids moved into awareness and grew in consciousness and intellect. The tale brings into play the theory that humans lived largely in the water for a certain period in their development. Through this story we grapple with the fascinating question of how our brain and our consciousness developed.

Science fiction helps us look at social concerns. When we read about utopias and dystopias, we are often looking at history rewritten. Lois Lowry's *The Giver* might be seen as a retelling of what happened eons ago, when people had no ability to culturally refine their black-and-white thinking. Lowry shows us a world where escaping feelings—sad or happy—is central to life. In *The Giver,* life in society was the business you went about, not a journey to discover who you were. Could we ever reach a point where we were so frightened that we would gladly turn over the decisions in our life to another in exchange for security? Because science fiction removes us from our present society, it makes it easier for us to see and discuss social problems. Science fiction often shows us what a great world could be by showing us what it is not.

CD-ROM

If science fiction appeals to you because it is *intriguing* or *engrossing,* type in these words to search Favorite Authors for authors whose writing is noted for those qualities.

Variety in Science Fiction

Even though science fiction almost always includes scientific connections and/or takes place in a future world, the variety in this genre is astounding. Science fiction deals with such topics as mental telepathy or alternative ways of communicating, mind control, genetic engineering, visitors from outer space, and social and political systems of the future. Science fiction writers involve us in questions about the kind of world we would like to live in.

Types of Science Fiction

In order to capture the flavor of science fiction, let's look at some of the types of stories often written. These include adventure stories, humor, books about other social and political structures, books that examine the possibilities in our own world, and books peopled by aliens and robots.

Adventure Stories

One way writers of science fiction move the plot forward is by having the characters engage in adventure in order to solve some kind of dilemma or mystery. In Madeleine L'Engle's *A Wind in the Door,* Charles Wallace's sister must find a way to go within his body to find the source of the evil that is making him ill. In *Heartlight,* by T. A. Barron, Kate and her grandfather discover why the sun is in danger and must act in order to save the world. *Shade's Children,* by Garth Nix, catapults four children into the role of saviors of the world. Having escaped the horror of having their brains transplanted into robots of the Overlord, they must find a way to stop the madness and evil that surrounds them, aided only by the advice of a computer voice.

Humor

Sometimes science fiction adapts the guise of humor, but the purpose remains the same— to prod us into examining our beliefs and assumptions and to broaden our thinking to include possibilities we had never considered. A master of humorous science fiction and fantasy, Daniel Pinkwater authored *Alan Mendelsohn: The Boy from Mars,* the zany story of a Martian and a junior high boy who discover a how-to book on the rudiments of mind control. When they try out these mind control skills, they successfully cause the principal to make an absurd announcement over the P.A. system. They also find a place that is a "gateway" to another aspect of the universe. Beneath Pinkwater's humor are the questions he wants to engage us in: Are there other aspects of human ability that we simply refuse to see? Could time be bent enough that a human could go to another dimension and come back? Written more than 20 years ago (and recently reissued), this book raises questions not only about human capacities but also about parallel universes. Many physicists now theorize that reality may consist of an infinite number of parallel universes. Pinkwater's light-hearted approach makes it easier and less scary to consider these questions.

Not all humorous science fiction is as weighty. Mel Gilden writes fast-paced stories, such as *The Pumpkins of Time,* which appeal to upper elementary children. Although zany and fun, Gilden's story does challenge our concept of time when the children invent a dandelion mush with which they hope to stop time.

Books About Other Social and Political Structures

Many science fiction novels take us to alternative worlds or future worlds where society is structured differently. Virginia Hamilton's *Dustland* takes place on a seemingly barren planet. Although Sonia Levitin's *The Cure* is set on this planet, both the organization of the futuristic society and the setting are unfamiliar. Lois Lowry's *The Giver* and Pamela F. Service's *Under Alien Stars* both take place sometime in the future, when societies are very different. Such novels often warn readers of dangers in our own society, such as the absence of choice.

Books That Examine the Possibilities in Our Own World

Many science fiction books are set in this world, wrapping us in the security of the known. We are almost lulled into believing that the world is the one we know, and then we realize that something is very wrong or very different.

In *Among the Hidden,* by Margaret Peterson Haddix, the society has a Population Law that allows each family only two children. Any children beyond the first two must remain hidden or be killed. The story is about what life is like for this hidden group of children, who can rarely take the chance of even going outside.

Most of William Sleator's science fiction books take place in this world, but his protagonists often meet up with elements that seem otherworldly. In *Singularity,* one twin finds a door into another world, where he can accelerate time and come back older and larger than his twin, thus gaining a measure of advantage. In *Green Futures of Tycho,* Tycho finds a shiny object while digging a garden and soon is traveling both backward and forward in time into what seem like alternative versions of reality. Sleator's *The Duplicate* has a main character who must deal with more than one version of himself. Sleator's books play with the notions of time and space and involve readers in questions about what could be possible.

Madeleine L'Engle's *A Wind in the Door* happens in the present but takes readers into the "universe" of the interior of the body. Her other two books in *The Wrinkle in Time* trilogy take readers to distant galaxies.

The well-loved *Mrs. Frisby and the Rats of NIMH,* by Robert C. O'Brien, is set in our everyday world but told from the point of view of the rats. One group, with superior intelligence gained through scientific experiments, is asked to help a normal rat family.

Books Peopled by Aliens or Robots

Stories that take place in a future world are often peopled with aliens or robots. According to O'Connor (1997), "Aliens stand in for many things. They allow the reader to experience what it's like to be a stranger in a strange land, as well as the native greeting the outsider. . . . Even at their most unusual, the aliens are us in a different contour" (p. 15). This seems to be the case in *Interstellar Pig,* by William Sleator, in which a beautiful woman and her two companions, who turn out to be aliens, rent the beach cottage next to Barney. Attracted by their spectacular appearances, Barney gets involved with them, eventually playing the game they brought with them. How could he know he was going to end up fighting for the galaxy's survival? The aliens here stand in for people who seduce us with their charm, which masks the evil lying beneath. In *Shade's Children,* by Garth Nix, robots with the

CD-ROM

Call up a list of Virginia Hamilton's work by using the CD-ROM database.

transplanted brains of fourteen-year-olds rule the world. They are directed by the Overlord, who is power hungry and will destroy and mutilate to achieve his ends.

Themes in Science Fiction

Much science fiction takes readers to new frontiers and new dimensions of experience. In *Twenty Thousand Leagues Under the Sea,* Jules Verne, one of the first science fiction writers, imagined a vessel navigating under the sea. Much of what he wrote about was realized in the 20th century. Although, at this point in society's development, many people are skeptical about new frontiers, perhaps what was written about in the 20th century will be realized in the 21st century. Several threads, or themes, appear frequently in science fiction, reflecting dreams about what this world could become.

Expanding Views of What People Can Do

Some stories encourage us to think about potential—what kinds of mental communication we're capable of, how powerful our minds could be, whether we limit people with our expectations of them, whether we could live forever or for much longer time periods, whether we could ever fly or move from place to place using only our minds. By showing humans creating, inventing, and achieving in other times and other worlds, science fiction expands our view of what humans are capable of.

In Virginia Hamilton's *Justice Cycle,* a trilogy that begins with *Justice and Her Brothers* (and was reprinted in 1998), four teenagers learn how to develop their psychic powers. They learn to mind trace (communicate telepathically), mind jump (project themselves through space by using their minds), and even use the power of their minds to vector to the surface of another planet in order to bring forth the water they sense is 70 feet beneath the surface. This story shows us that young people are very capable in important ways.

In Nancy Farmer's *The Ear, the Eye, and the Arm,* three men whose mothers were affected by plutonium have special abilities that enable them to be excellent detectives. This book makes the reader wonder whether mutations will yield extraordinary human abilities.

Confronting Ecological Issues

What are we doing to this planet? Some science fiction looks back on a nearly destroyed world and shows how the universe evolved since the time of chaos. The movie *Planet of the Apes* is one example. Monica Hughes's *The Crystal Drop* takes readers to the near future, when the most precious commodity is water! Peter Dickinson's *Eva* is set in a world where most of the forests and jungles are gone, a direct result of humankind's actions. By presenting stark images of what a future world could be like, these books encourage a close look at what we are doing physically to our planet.

Challenging Assumptions About Animals or Other Life Forms

In Peter Dickinson's book *Eva,* Eva, whose brain was implanted in the body of a chimp after a terrible car accident, makes an impassioned plea for humane treatment of the animals of the world. As a chimp who can "speak" by typing on a keyboard, she lets scientists know animals' reactions to the way they are viewed as "Other" and caged and experimented on. This book challenges current notions of how animals should be used by humans.

In this compelling story, the mental and psychic abilities of Justice and her brothers hint at what humans are really capable of.

(Cover art from JUSTICE AND HER BROTHERS by Virginia Hamilton. Cover art copyright © 1998 by Scholastic Inc. Reprinted by permission of Scholastic Inc.)

Other books put humans face to face with aliens, causing them to question their assumptions about themselves and the aliens. *The Mudhead,* by Josephine Rector Stone, and *The Golden Aquarians,* by Monica Hughes, put humans on distant planets, where they assume they have the right to do as they please. The humans discount living entities native to the planet because they view them as inferior to humans. Both stories bring the reader to the realization that alternative life forms can be compassionate, intelligent creatures and that it is the humans who are the aliens.

Challenging Ideas and Values of Society

The enormously popular *The Giver,* by Lois Lowry, paints a picture of a society seemingly without violence, where everyone has meaningful work and perfect relationships and no confrontations occur. This harmony has been achieved through a sameness that pervades the society, leaving no color, no unique dress styles, no specialness. Lowry shows us in chilling ways what this kind of society costs in terms of the human spirit and freedom. She challenges the belief that we would be happy if we were all the same. Since children seek acceptance by their peers, a book about the dangers of total sameness would be particularly provocative for them.

In Madeleine L'Engle's *A Wrinkle in Time* trilogy, the children travel to a planet where the eyeless inhabitants can "see" better than the children do. The story implies that there is more to truly seeing than the physical eye and makes readers question how much they really see.

Evaluating Fantasy and Science Fiction

Although fantasy and science fiction can be evaluated much like any other genre, there is one issue that is of special importance—how the writer gets us to suspend disbelief and enter the new world. Thus, believability in plot, characters, and setting needs to be looked at closely. Patricia Lee Gauch (1994), author and editor, says, "The building blocks of that [new] world need to be firmly set in our own world" (p. 164). In other words, the book must give us concrete details so that we can see specifically what the new world looks like. It must "burst with life at every turn—sensory life; life in the small, not merely the general; sensory life, the filaments of which attach themselves to our own experience; life arranged in a peculiarity of detail, not a generality" (p. 164). In the boxed feature Applying the Criteria: Evaluating a Fantasy, I evaluate *Harry Potter and the Sorcerer's Stone,* by J. K. Rowling, which is used frequently in upper elementary school.

Applying the Criteria *Evaluating a Fantasy*

  Plot. Science fiction and fantasy are generally heavy on plot, and this is certainly the case with the *Harry Potter* books. The intertwined plot lines offer complexity and keep the interest of the reader. We wonder how Harry will find out he is a wizard, who Nicolas Flamel is, when Voldevort will show himself, if Harry's team will win Quidditch, and why Snape wants to jinx Harry. The pace is brisk throughout the book, with enough action and foreshadowing to keep readers turning the pages. We're drawn into the plot when we read, "There was nothing about the cloudy sky outside to suggest that strange and mysterious things would soon be happening all over the country" (p. 2). The plot line is believable because the author meticulously lays the groundwork with details. The very still cat sitting on the wall outside the Dursleys' turns into a person of magic; we know right away that people in this story will have special powers. In interviews, Rowling says that she knew every detail of the world she created, down to the banking system and mail system, before she wrote a single word of the story. Another wonderful thing about this plot line is that many of the tensions of the story are dissolved and

(continued)

dealt with by the children at Hogwarts, especially Harry, Hermione, and Ron Weasley. Near the end, all three are shown as intelligent, caring people who can problem solve very efficiently and get themselves out of trouble.

2. ▶ **Characters.** Although in fantasy and science fiction the themes or plot lines sometimes are given more importance than characterization, this is not the case in ***Harry Potter.*** We get to know these characters well enough to love or hate them. Harry is easy to like. We sympathize with him for spending ten years sleeping in a closet under the stairs, suffering abuse from the Dursleys because they believed his dead parents had been very strange. His creativity and inventiveness were not appreciated, since he lived with people who saw none of his best qualities. Mrs. Dursley's total preoccupation with herself and her child and her lack of understanding and compassion make her easy to dislike. Dudley Dursley does seem to be stereotyped as an overweight, spoiled child who does nothing but whine and stuff himself with food; this characterization never changes. The Weasley family is drawn so clearly that we get to know the whole lot of them and would relish the opportunity to spend time at their home, where unexpected, interesting things seem to happen. Hagrid is easy to feel affection for because he unashamedly shows his love for Harry. Professor Dumbledore, the head of Hogwarts, is wise and caring and has a sense of what his students need; his humanity is always apparent. Although the majority of the characters are male, Hermione, a very assertive, intelligent girl, does play a large part in the story. The characters are revealed slowly through their own distinctive language, actions, and reactions, as well as what others say about them. We get to savor the development of the characters, wondering what they will reveal about themselves next.

3. ▶ **Theme.** Many high fantasy and science fiction books contain meaty themes, asking us to question ways of being and doing in our society. Fantasy readers are looking for intriguing ideas that will transform their way of thinking. Above all, they want content that is worthwhile. Although the themes in ***Harry Potter*** are not heavy, ponderous ones, nevertheless the book gives us much to think about, as Rowling satirizes many aspects of the Muggle world. Her comments on the Muggles and the way they live—unimaginative people who can't

see the wonder in the world around them—make us all look to be sure we're not worried only about the appearance of things. A major bearer of such wisdom is Dumbledore, the headmaster, who says, "It does not do to dwell on dreams and forget to live" when he encounters Harry in front of the Mirror of Erised (p. 214). Another theme that resonates with readers is that children are creative, intelligent, and capable of great things and should believe in themselves. Yet another major theme is the use of power and the importance of recognizing one's personal power.

4. ▶ **Setting.** Science fiction and fantasy require that readers suspend their disbelief and enter the story world, which often includes surreal or unusual settings. It's easy to enter the story world in ***Harry Potter*** because the story starts right in the middle of the ordinariness of the Dursley family in England. Rowling then adds fantastical details like a cat reading a map, people in long green cloaks, a cat turning into a woman, and a motorcycle falling out of the sky. Because the details are so clear and everything seems "normal," it is very easy to "see" Hogwarts in all its magic. The detailed description of Hogwarts contributes to the magical qualities of the story and makes all the events that happen there seem credible.

5. ▶ **Style—qualities of writing.** One quality that is easy to appreciate in this novel is the fascinating use of dialogue. Many characters have distinctive speech patterns and vocabulary. Hagrid says things like "Ah, go boil yer heads, both of yeh" (p. 50). Professor Dumbledore is more formal but low key, with remarks like "I shall see you soon, I expect" (p. 16). Rowling does use figurative language, as when she describes Hagrid: "He had hands the size of trash can lids, and his feet in their leather boots were like baby dolphins" (p. 14). This kind of language is limited so that it doesn't get in the way of the story. The narrator talks to us in an almost confidential manner, in a clear, strong voice, making us feel privy to the lives of the characters. The point of view is third person limited, meaning that we get inside the head of only one character—Harry—and find out how he feels and thinks about things. We know at the outset that the storyteller is on the side of Harry, because we read, "Mrs. Dursley *pretended* she didn't have a sister" (italics added, p. 2) and, speaking of their child, "*in their opinion* there was no finer boy" (italics added, p. 1).

The narrator seems to find the Dursleys to be tedious people. This third-person limited narrative voice works well to maintain suspense; if we could get into the heads of all the characters, we would know their intentions and secrets. Rowling's writing is seamless and smooth as she goes back and forth between Harry and the narrator.

6. **Emotional impact.** The friendship among Harry, Ron, and Hermione exemplifies love and caring and thus touches us. Hermione, who always does things the way they are supposed to be done and takes everything seriously, reminds us of dutiful and perfectionistic children. Hagrid's raw displays of caring also make an impact. People who can keep their center in the face of a storm are admirable, as Hagrid was when he delivered Harry's letter and explained Harry's status to the Dursleys. We root for Harry throughout the book because he touches our hearts when we watch what he goes through in living with the Dursleys.

7. **Imaginative impact.** *Harry Potter* is packed with happenings and settings that stretch the imagination. It's wonderful being in the world of Hogwarts, where food magically appears at meals, portraits talk, and there are secret passages and doors everywhere. The story stimulates the mind, setting readers to wondering and imagining. We wonder what we could do if we, too, used the power of our minds and bodies. We wonder how our world would be different if everyone saw it in terms of the magic and wonder that surround us. Because this book sparks the imagination, shows us possibilities, stretches our thinking, and makes us think in different ways, it is very appealing.

8. **Vision.** In fantasy and science fiction, the author's vision is very apparent and crucial. Rowling's vision is expansive. The world she creates is filled with humor, fun, compassion, hard work, caring families, and quirky owls, as well as people who worry over unimportant things. She pushes us to see the magic that lies beneath the surface of everyday happenings, the adventure of living, the thrill of doing the right thing. She displays foibles in people but recognizes their humanity, suggesting that they will eventually come around. She shows the intensely competitive Malfoy as a less than admirable person; Hagrid, who is rough around the edges and less educated, is revealed to be a wonderful person who cares passionately about the people and animals he loves.

Getting Started with Fantasy and Science Fiction

Of all the genres in children's literature, fantasy seems to be the one most often ignored by teachers. During a course in children's literature, it's not unusual for one student to be declaring, "I hate science fiction," while another is declaring his or her passion for it. This, of course, is a natural reflection of our varied tastes, which are shaped by our backgrounds, interests, and individual personalities. As teachers, though, we cannot let our biases influence the genres available in our classrooms. Ironically, our opinions have probably been shaped by how different genres were introduced to us. If you were taught to think that poetry has only one correct interpretation, you may be somewhat intimidated by the thought of teaching with poetry. If you were not introduced to many works of science fiction, you may assume that it is too technical, scary, or "far out."

Studying the fine works in your least favorite genres may challenge your opinions, changing your attitudes. But whether your attitudes change or not, the children in your classes will have minds of their own when it comes to favoring genres, and as a teacher you are responsible for offering children's literature in a variety of genres. Read-aloud and shared reading provide opportunities to share different genres and familiarize children with the features of each (Taberski, 2000).

Ideally this chapter has given you the information you need to help students both enjoy and benefit from fantasy and science fiction. If you have never read fantasy before, start small. One way to begin is to read short story collections, such as ***Dragons and Dreams,*** edited by Jane Yolen, Martin H. Greenberg, and Charles G. Waugh; ***Odder Than***

Ever, by Bruce Coville; *Twelve Impossible Things Before Breakfast,* by Jane Yolen; *A Knot in the Grain and Other Stories,* by Robin McKinley; *Teller of Tales,* by William J. Brooke; and *Tomorrowland: 10 Stories About the Future,* compiled by Michael Cart. If you think fantasy is just light make-believe that holds no appeal, read *Tuck Everlasting,* by Natalie Babbitt, or *The Devil's Arithmetic,* by Jane Yolen. If you're hesitant about reading science fiction, start with *The Giver,* by Lois Lowry, or *A Wrinkle in Time,* by Madeleine L'Engle, both of which will show you the depth of this genre.

Favorite Authors of Fantasy and Science Fiction

If you are a neophyte to this genre and feel unsure of how to select books even for yourself, use the list in the boxed feature Favorite Authors of Fantasy and Science Fiction as a starting point. Many readers have had wonderful experiences with these writers.

Favorite Authors of Fantasy and Science Fiction

Lloyd Alexander is a master at writing fantasy that is filled with adventure and imaginative thinking.

David Almond creates fantasies in seemingly everyday settings. His plots are engrossing, his characters are memorable, and his themes bring into focus many of the issues we struggle with in life.

T. A. Barron writes engaging and involving science fiction and fantasy stories. Plot and characters are both well developed and fascinating. Students in fourth grade and up will appreciate his well-crafted stories.

John Bellairs's compelling mystery/supernatural stories are peopled with believable characters we care about. Children from the third grade up have been reading his stories for the past 20 years.

Franny Billingsley creates fantasies that feature magical settings; strong, intriguing girls; and intricate, engrossing plot lines.

Susan Cooper, although best known for the series *The Dark Is Rising,* which older high fantasy lovers

embrace, has also written for the younger set.

Bruce Coville's fantasies and science fiction are charming, engaging, thought-provoking, and fun. His books are a hit with students in fourth grade and up.

Roald Dahl's highly imaginative thinking, well-developed characters, and compelling plots have made innumerable children Dahl fans.

Mary Downing Hahn writes haunting, fast-paced mysteries, which feature elements of the supernatural.

Brian Jacques's use of animals as characters, his nonstop action, and his well-developed plots have made the *Redwall* series a favorite with children.

Madeleine L'Engle's beautiful use of language, intriguing themes, fascinating science concepts, and well-developed characters have made her a favorite.

Robin McKinley has the ability to carry us away into new worlds because she weaves her words so carefully and writes such action-

packed, thought-provoking stories. Her work would be appreciated by avid readers in upper elementary and middle school.

Daniel Pinkwater's stories are marinated in humor. He's witty and clever, tells a good story, and always gives his readers important things to think about. Pinkwater writes for third-graders as well as middle schoolers.

Jon Scieszka's stories are outrageous, humorous, compelling, unique, and sometimes wacky and zany.

Vivian Vande Velde's tales are marked by plucky heroines, a very developed sense of humor, and a taste for the unusual.

Jane Yolen, a prolific writer who writes beautifully in many genres, is at home in fantasy, where she weaves lovely tales in the most beautiful language imaginable. Many of her books will appeal to students as young as third grade, while the ideas and writing in others of her books will please upper elementary and middle school youngsters.

Invitations

Choose several of the following activities to complete:

1. In your journal, explore the value of developing imaginative skills in children. In what areas do you feel you're imaginative? Is this a quality that has been nurtured in you and praised by others? Do you think imagination is important? Why? How has it made a difference in your life? How can books and school experiences support imaginative development?

2. As a child, you may have been read fantasies such as ***Alice in Wonderland,*** by Lewis Carroll; ***The Wind in the Willows,*** by Kenneth Grahame; ***Mary Poppins,*** by P. L. Travers; or ***The Wonderful Wizard of Oz,*** by L. Frank Baum. If you heard any of these stories as a child, how did you react to them? Did you think of them as fantasies or just as stories? Why might that have been so?

3. Read one of the ***Harry Potter*** books. Return to the questions for uncovering the beliefs beneath the writing (listed in Chapter 6), and apply them to the novel. Who's left out of the ***Harry Potter*** books? Who has power? What does the author's vision tell us about her?

4. How has your taste changed over the years in terms of what genres you read? Beginning with your earliest days in school, list the books you remember liking. Compare your list with those of others in your group and with the comments in the boxed feature Children's Voices. Can you draw any conclusions or make any generalizations about how, why, and when reading tastes change? Does it have to do with age, gender, grade, or what's happening in school? How do your findings fit with the developmental stages defined by Carlsen in Chapter 1?

To find examples in Invitations and Classroom Teaching Ideas of ways to use analytical skills in response to literature, search for such words as *generalizations, implications,* and *assumptions.*

5. Of the kinds of fantasy described in this chapter, which types appeal to you? Which types have you read? What kinds of science fiction stories have you read? Was any of this reading school-sponsored? Share your experiences with your group and discuss whether schools seem to validate this genre. What themes or strands not mentioned in this chapter have you noticed in the science fiction and fantasy? Which themes appeal to you most?

6. Evaluate a science fiction or fantasy novel. Did the criteria enumerated in this chapter work for you, or did you generate some criteria of your own? Did you notice any differences in the way you evaluated this genre? Discuss your findings with your small group.

7. Take a favorite fantasy novel and create illustrations or a sound track to accompany it. Share your creation with your group.

Classroom Teaching Ideas

1. Have students bring in a favorite stuffed toy. Talk about fantasies in which animals and toys have human characteristics. What would their toy do and say if it were suddenly animated? Have students write a story with their talking and moving stuffed toy as the central character.

2. Have students think about how stories would be different if animals could talk but people couldn't. Have them rewrite a story from a short realistic fiction picture book so that it is told by an animal present in the story. A ***Henry and Mudge*** story by Cynthia Rylant might be a good one to start with.

3. Have small groups of students collect from newspapers or the Internet stories about proposed inventions or innovations—or just brainstorm with the class about what might be possible in medicine, space travel, robotics, and so on, in the year 2100. Remind the students of what we did not have 100 years ago. Then, have groups of students collaboratively construct a setting, theme, plot, and characters that reflect these futuristic possibilities or inventions. Share the stories with the whole class. How were the groups' views of the future different? How were they similar?

4. Through class discussion, compile a list of current issues the students feel are most important. Brainstorm with the class possible inventions that might address the issues. Together, write a brief story starter in which one of the issues is clearly stated. Leave it posted in the classroom throughout the following days so that students can add sentences or paragraphs to it. After two days, go back to the story and see how the issue was handled, resolved, or made worse. Regroup to come to some conclusion or ending with the whole class.

Internet and Text Resources

1. Science Fiction and Fantasy for Children: An Annotated Bibliography provides a searchable database of 400 titles, with a detailed plot description and appropriate age and grade level for each book. Find it at

> http://libnt1.lib.uoguelph.ca/SFBib/index.htm

2. Fairy Tales with a Twist offers specific fairy tales, citing chapter books and picture books that offer variants on the tale. Go to

> www.boulder.lib.co.us/youth/booklists/booklists_fairytales.html

3. Harry Potter provides information about the author, as well as discussion guides for the books. The site also has a discussion chamber for fans and a "wizard challenge." Find it at

> www.scholastic.com/harrypotter/home.asp

4. Welcome to the Redwall Abby is the official website for the British author Brian Jacques, who writes the *Redwall* fantasies. Go to

> www.redwall.org/dave/jacques.html

5. 100 Favorite Children's Books has a section on science fiction. Find it at

> www.nypl.org/branch/kids/100/scifi.html

References

Gauch, Patricia Lee (1994). "A Quest for the Heart of Fantasy." *The New Advocate 7*, 159–167.

Greene, Maxine (1995). *Releasing the Imagination: Essays on Education, the Arts, and Social Change.* San Francisco: Jossey-Bass.

Harrison, Barbara, and Gregory Maguire, eds. (1987). *Innocence and Experience: Essays and Conversations on Children's Literature.* New York: Lothrop, Lee & Shepard.

Masson, Sophie (1997). "Times Past, Times to Come." *Bookbird 35*, 31–33.

O'Connor, Sheilah (1997). "Two Perspectives on Canadian Science Fiction." *Bookbird 35*, 12–15.

Rud, Rita (1995/1996). "How About Asking a Child for a Change? An Interview with a Ten-Year-Old *Goosebumps* fan." *Bookbird 33*, 22–24.

Stine, R. L. (2000). Presentation at the Spring National Conference of Teachers of English Convention, New York, March 16–18.

Taberski, Sharon (2000). *On Solid Ground: Strategies for Teaching Reading K–3.* Portsmouth, NH: Heinemann.

Children's Books

Alexander, Lloyd (1964). *The Book of Three (The Chronicles of Prydain)*. New York: Holt, Rinehart, and Winston.

Almond, David (1998). *Skellig*. New York: Delacorte.

Babbitt, Natalie (1975). *Tuck Everlasting*. New York: Farrar, Straus & Giroux.

Barron, T. A. (1990). *Heartlight*. New York: Philomel.

—— (1996). *The Lost Years of Merlin*. New York: Philomel.

Baum, L. Frank (1900). *The Wonderful Wizard of Oz*. New York: Hill [1899].

Bond, Nancy (1976). *A String in the Harp*. New York: Atheneum.

Brooke, William J. (1994). *Teller of Tales*. New York: HarperCollins.

Carroll, Lewis (1919). *Alice in Wonderland*. London: Oxford University.

Cart, Michael, ed. (1999). *Tomorrowland: 10 Stories About the Future*. New York: Scholastic.

Cooper, Susan (1973). *The Dark Is Rising*. Illus. Alan E. Cober. New York: Atheneum.

Coville, Bruce (1992). *Jennifer Murdley's Toad*. Illus. Gary A. Lippincott. San Diego: Harcourt Brace.

—— (1991). *Jeremy Thatcher, Dragon Hatcher*. Illus. Gary A. Lippincott. San Diego: Harcourt Brace.

—— (1999). *Odder Than Ever*. San Diego: Harcourt Brace.

—— (1997). *The Skull of Truth*. Illus. Gary A. Lippincott. San Diego: Harcourt Brace.

Creech, Sharon (1996). *Pleasing the Ghost*. Illus. Stacey Schuett. New York: Harper.

Dahl, Roald (1998). *Charlie and the Chocolate Factory*. Illus. Quentin Blake. New York: Puffin.

—— (1961). *James and the Giant Peach*. Illus. Lane Smith. New York: Knopf.

Dickinson, Peter (1993). *A Bone from a Dry Sea*. New York: Delacorte.

—— (1989). *Eva*. New York: Delacorte.

du Bois, William Pène (1947). *The 21 Balloons*. New York: Viking.

Duane, Diane (1996). *Deep Wizardry*. San Diego: Harcourt Brace.

Duncan, Lois (1974). *Down a Dark Hall*. Boston: Little, Brown.

—— (1997). *Gallow's Hill*. New York: Delacorte.

—— (1981). *Stranger with My Face*. Boston: Little, Brown.

Eager, Edward (1999). *Knight's Castle*. Illus. N. M. Bodecker. San Diego: Harcourt Brace [1956].

Farmer, Nancy (1994). *The Ear, the Eye, and the Arm*. New York: Orchard.

Fleischman, Paul (1982). *Graven Images*. Illus. Andrew Glass. New York: Harper & Row.

Furlong, Monica (1992). *Juniper*. New York: Knopf.

—— (1987). *Wise Child*. New York: Knopf.

Garner, Alan (1981). *The Moon of Gomrath*. New York: Ballantine [1967].

—— (1981). *The Owl Service*. New York: Ballantine [1967].

Gilden, Mel (1994). *The Pumpkins of Time*. New York: Browndeer.

Grahame, Kenneth (1908). *The Wind in the Willows*. New York: Scribner.

Gruelle, Johnny (1918). *Raggedy Ann Stories*. New York: Volland.

Haddix, Margaret Peterson (1998). *Among the Hidden*. Illus. Mark Ulriksen. New York: Simon & Schuster.

Hahn, Mary Downing (1989). *The Doll in the Garden*. New York: Clarion.

—— (1986). *Wait Till Helen Comes*. New York: Clarion.

Hamilton, Virginia (1980). *Dustland*. New York: Greenwillow.

—— (1978). *Justice and Her Brothers*. New York: Greenwillow.

Howe, Deborah, and James Howe (1979). *Bunnicula: A Rabbit-Tale of Mystery*. Illus. Alan Daniel. New York: Atheneum.

Hughes, Monica (1993). *The Crystal Drop*. New York: Simon & Schuster.

—— (1995). *The Golden Aquarians*. New York: Simon & Schuster.

Jones, Diana Wynne (1986). *Howl's Moving Castle*. New York: Greenwillow.

Jordan, Sherryl (1996). *Secret Sacrament*. New York: HarperCollins.

L'Engle, Madeleine (1986). *Many Waters*. New York: Farrar, Straus & Giroux.

—— (1973). *A Wind in the Door*. New York: Farrar, Straus & Giroux.

—— (1962). *A Wrinkle in Time*. New York: Farrar, Straus & Giroux.

Levitin, Sonia (1999). *The Cure*. San Diego: Silver Whistle.

Levy, Elizabeth (1979). *Frankenstein Moved in on the Fourth Floor*. Illus. Mordicai Gerstein. New York: Harper & Row.

Lewis, C. S. (1950). *The Lion, the Witch and the Wardrobe (The Chronicles of Narnia)*. Illus. Pauline Baynes. New York: Macmillan.

Lofting, Hugh (1967). *Dr. Dolittle: A Treasury*. New York: Lippincott.

Lowry, Lois (1993). *The Giver*. Boston: Houghton Mifflin.

Lunn, Janet (1983). *The Root Cellar*. New York: Scribner.

McCaffrey, Anne (1979). *Dragondrums*. New York: Atheneum.

McKinley, Robin (1982). *The Blue Sword*. New York: Greenwillow.

—— (1985). *The Hero and the Crown*. New York: Greenwillow.

—— (1994). *A Knot in the Grain and Other Stories*. New York: Greenwillow.

Melling, Orla (1996) *The Singing Stone*. Toronto: Viking Kestrel.

Milne, A. A. (1926). *The Complete Tales & Poems of Winnie-the-Pooh*. London: Methuen.

Morgan, Jill (1996). *Blood Brothers*. New York: HarperTrophy.

Naylor, Phyllis Reynolds (1981). *Faces in the Water (York Trilogy)*. New York: Atheneum.

—— (1981) *Footprints at the Window (York Trilogy)*. New York: Atheneum.

—— (1980). *Shadows on the Wall (York Trilogy)*. New York: Atheneum.

Nix, Garth (1997). *Shade's Children*. New York: HarperCollins.

Norton, Mary (1952). *The Borrowers*. Illus. Diana Stanley. London: Dent.

O'Brien, Robert C. (1971). *Mrs. Frisby and the Rats of NIMH*. New York: Atheneum.

Park, Ruth (1982). *Playing Beatie Bow*. New York: Atheneum.

Pearce, Philippa (1992). *Tom's Midnight Garden*. New York: HarperCollins.

Peck, Richard (1983). *The Dreadful Future of Blossom Culp*. New York: Delacorte.

Pfeffer, Susan Beth (1988). *Rewind to Yesterday*. Illus. Andrew Glass. New York: Delacorte.

Pinkwater, Daniel (1979). *Alan Mendelsohn: The Boy from Mars*. New York: Dutton.

Potter, Beatrix (1934). *The Tale of Peter Rabbit*. Akron, OH: Saalfield [1st American edition, Harcourt Brace, 1953].

Pullman, Philip (1996). *The Golden Compass*. New York: Knopf.

Reiss, Kathryn (1993). *Dreadful Sorry*. San Diego: Harcourt Brace.

Rodgers, Mary (1972). *Freaky Friday*. New York: HarperCollins.

Rowling, J. K. (1998). *Harry Potter and the Sorcerer's Stone*. New York: Scholastic.

Service, Pamela F. (1990). *Under Alien Stars*. New York: Atheneum.

Sleator, William (1988). *The Duplicate*. New York: Dutton.

—— (1981). *Green Futures of Tycho*. New York: Dutton.

—— (1984). *Interstellar Pig*. New York: Dutton.

—— (1985). *Singularity*. New York: Dutton.

Stone, Josephine Rector (1980). *The Mudhead*. New York: Atheneum.

Travers, P. L. (1934). *Mary Poppins*. Illus. Mary Shepard. London: Howe.

Turner, Megan Whalen (2000). *The Queen of Attolia*. New York: Greenwillow.

—— (1996). *The Thief*. New York: Greenwillow.

Vande Velde, Vivian (1999). *Never Trust a Dead Man*. San Diego: Harcourt Brace.

—— (1998). *Smart Dog*. San Diego: Harcourt Brace.

Verne, Jules (1995). *Twenty Thousand Leagues Under the Sea*. New York: Puffin [1899].

Vick, Helen Hughes (1993). *Walker of Time*. Tucson, AZ: Harbinger.

White, E. B. (1952). *Charlotte's Web*. New York: Harper.

Williams, Margery (1998). *The Velveteen Rabbit.* Philadelphia: Running [1922].

Yolen, Jane (1988). *The Devil's Arithmetic.* New York: Viking Kestrel.

—— (1996). *Hobby: The Young Merlin Trilogy.* San Diego: Harcourt Brace.

—— (1997). *Twelve Impossible Things Before Breakfast.* San Diego: Harcourt Brace.

Yolen, Jane, and Martin H. Greenberg (1995). *The Haunted House: A Collection of Original Stories.* Illus. Doron Ben-Ami. New York: HarperCollins.

Yolen, Jane, Martin H. Greenberg, and Charles G. Waugh, eds. (1986) *Dragons and Dreams.* New York: Harper & Row.

Nonfiction Books

Some people wrinkle up their noses at the mention of nonfiction, remembering flat textbook-like books. Others are happy to hear that it's an acknowledged genre in children's literature. Today's nonfiction crackles with life. The illustrations are vibrant and powerful, the language is rich and compelling, and the subjects are varied and fascinating. Nonfiction, or informational, books are some of the most exciting and stimulating books in the field of children's literature. They intrigue, fascinate, compel, engage, and occasionally shock young readers, motivating them to want to learn more. They often draw students to question information in new ways. Amy McClure (1998) explains children's reactions to the richness of nonfiction: "You can tell it's a good book when children listen spellbound as it's read aloud, when they ask questions, argue about the ideas, then rush to read it on their own. And, later, when they incorporate its language and structures into their own work responses, it's evident that the book's effect goes deep. Does this only happen with fiction? No! Well-written nonfiction which goes beyond facts to present an eloquent, informed, and well-crafted discussion of those facts can generate these same involved enthusiastic responses" (p. 39).

As very young children learn to read, they also read to learn. They are hungry for information about the world. They will happily read nonfiction to acquire information, to satisfy their curiosity, to comprehend the world more fully, to understand new concepts, to make connections to their lives and their learning, and to have fun! Kevin Spink (1996) points out that we often view reading as being informative *or* pleasurable, forgetting that it can be both. He explains that his first-graders "turn to informational books and magazines with a fervor and frequency equal to their interest in fictional stories." He is reminded of his own early preference for informational books: "My main interests then were tanks and battleships, reptiles, and anything else remotely horrifying and potentially gory." He didn't become "hooked" on books until he discovered that they "could be more than the sanitized, homogenized 'pretend' stories from our basal reader about unnaturally wholesome families or overly protective fairy godmothers" (p. 135). He continues to be frustrated with the lack of exciting "real" books for the primary grade classroom. Many children share Spink's enthusiasm for nonfiction, as the boxed feature Children's Voices indicates.

What Is Nonfiction?

Although it is difficult to pin down precisely what nonfiction is, its major purpose is to inform. Some writers of nonfiction object to defining this genre in terms of what it is not, and thus they prefer the term *informational text*. But whether it's called nonfiction or informational text, the identifying mark is that the information contained in the book must be verifiable and not deviate from what we know about the natural world. Beyond that, the variety is dizzying—true-life adventure stories, history, science, dictionaries, encyclopedias, biography, autobiography, sports stories, photographic essays, first-person narratives, interviews, and so on. *Nonfiction* is the umbrella term sheltering these vastly different kinds of writing.

The genre of nonfiction is commonly broken down into two types: narrative fiction and nonnarrative fiction. Margaret Mallett (1992) points out in *Making Facts Matter* that one way to distinguish between the two types of nonfiction is to consider the writing format. Is the book written in narrative form, with the information shared through a story format, or is it written in nonnarrative form, using an expository style that explains?

Narrative Nonfiction

CD-ROM

Create a list of Gary Paulsen's work by using the CD-ROM database.

Like informational stories, biographies, autobiographies, and diaries are often narrative nonfiction, as their primary purpose is to inform. One example of narrative nonfiction is Gary Paulsen's **Woodsong,** which describes his real-life adventure in the wild with his dogs, culminating in the running of the Iditarod. Another is **Chattanooga Sludge,** by Molly Bang, in which we learn of the toxic waste in the Chattanooga River through the story of a scientist who is trying to figure out how to make the river clean. Because so many people have erroneous ideas about nonfiction, they might not expect to find such well-written, exciting books in the nonfiction section.

Formats of Narrative Nonfiction

To see the variety of formats used in narrative informational books, let's look at five books on one topic: adoption.

1. **Picture book story.** *Adoption Is for Always,* by Linda Walvoord Girard, tells of a little girl working out her feelings about being adopted and what it means to her. Partly because the story is written as a narrative, the emotional impact is strong.

On nonfiction books . . .

I like books about puppies because I have a puppy and I want to learn how to take care of it. —Drew, 2nd grade

Gail Gibbons is my favorite author because the books are informational and they're always true. Most of them. —Andrew, 2nd grade

I like to read informational books. I read a pirate book yesterday. I liked it because the pictures looked funny and Joy Cowley wrote it. —Sarah, 2nd grade

I like to read about volcanoes! —Andy, 3rd grade

I like books that give information about animals. —Cathy, 3rd grade

I like to read about birds like hummingbirds, crows and penguins. —Ashley, 3rd grade

I like to read books about bald eagles. They are cool, awesome, and informational. —Mike, 3rd grade

I like books with cool pictures and those I can learn about the rules of skateboarding and hockey. —Eric, 4th grade

I read the encyclopedia. I liked how it told me stuff. It was cool to learn about [Charles Lindbergh]. I never knew that much about him. It was fun to read about him. —Ben, 4th grade

I wrote about Elijah McCoy. I like to read about events that happened in the past. I got the information from a book. —Joy, 4th grade

I like to read about new discoveries that take place in fields that will help us such as modern medicine. —Erin, 6th grade

I like to read about animals or the ocean or biographies of celebrities I like. —Karen, 6th grade

The only informational reading I do is the stuff they make us read in school! —Wright, 6th grade

I read Sports Illustrated because they tell me a lot of things I need to know. —Donnell, 6th grade

I like stories about horrible and unknown events to the common culture [Holocaust, Cultural Revolution, Slavery in the 19th Century]. —Kelly, 7th grade

I just find reading about places that I would normally never go interesting. —Elizabeth, 8th grade

I only like either little tidbit facts no one knew or information about different animals. I also enjoy science facts about atoms and the earth and things like that. —Katie, 7th grade

I like true stories because they can be so cruel and scary. But the scary thing is that they are true. —Jeff, 7th grade

I like some science books like on volcanoes and weather. I usually only read them for projects. —Tracey, 7th grade

You can know about the stuff that is or has happened in the world. —Nick, 7th grade

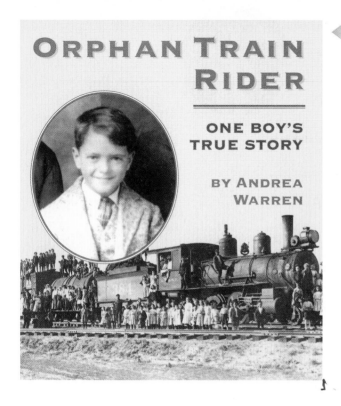

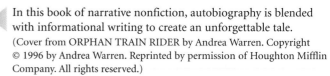

2. **Cartoon format.** *"Why Was I Adopted?,"* written by Carole Livingston and illustrated by Arthur Robins, explains adoption in a straightforward manner, using whimsical cartoonlike drawings to make a serious topic seem less scary.

3. **Photo story.** *A Forever Family,* by Roslyn Banish, tells the true-life story of eight-year-old Jennifer Jordan-Wong's adoption by a family after four years of living as a foster child with many families. The book relies on the photos as much as the short text to tell the story.

4. **Interviews.** In *How It Feels to be Adopted,* Jill Krementz, award-winning photographer and writer, shows the complexity of adoption issues by interviewing 19 adopted children and their families. The interview format allows readers to see a wide range of responses to one issue.

5. **First-person narrative.** *Orphan Train Rider: One Boy's True Story,* by Andrea Warren, uses photos, text, and first-person narrative to tell the gripping story of seven-year-old Lee, who was put on an orphan train with his three-year-old and five-year-old brothers. In alternating chapters, the author tells the history of orphan trains and the story of Lee, who was put on the train with no knowledge of what was happening. This very moving story follows him into the later years of his life.

Evaluating Narrative Nonfiction

In order to focus on elements that are particular to narrative nonfiction, let's compare two books on one topic: the 1871 Chicago fire. **The Great Fire,** by Jim Murphy, is a nonfiction book that radiates interest, from the colorful picture of the fire on the cover through the provocative last chapter. Murphy's whole presentation demonstrates his burning desire to know what really prevented the fire from being contained and whether or not blame can be placed. Because he has chosen to tell a large part of the story through the eyes of four people who were present throughout the fire, his narrative is compelling. This book, published in 1995, when technology allowed the easy printing of large-sized books filled with photos, maps, and pictures, is physically very attractive.

In *The Story of the Great Chicago Fire, 1871,* Mary Kay Phelan tells the story in an entirely different way. After shar-

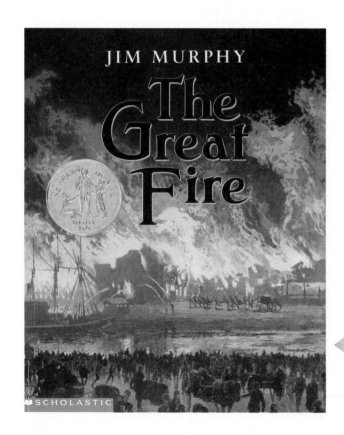

In **The Great Fire,** Jim Murphy not only provides views of the fire from several sections of the city but also examines beliefs about who was to blame.

ing one very interesting vignette about a speaker who, the night before the fire, predicted a terrible calamity, Phelan turns to explaining the history of the founding and development of Chicago. This book, published in 1971, lacks the visual appeal of Murphy's book. Like many of the older books available in most libraries, this book is likely to seem "old" to younger readers. Phelan's book does not have the same personal appeal as Murphy's book either, because she does not follow any particular eyewitness except the fire chief. Nor does she use the words of the eyewitnesses to describe what happened, although her bibliography cites at least eight eyewitness accounts.

Comparing these two books shows how important an author's choices are with respect to selection of facts and how the story is constructed or organized. Murphy uses only facts that propel the story forward, avoiding any extraneous material that will take our attention away from the fire. Phelan, an expert on the fire and the history of the city, mentions many things—including that Bret Harte's "Outcasts of Poker Flat" appeared in a Chicago newspaper that week. This kind of information appears throughout the book. While fascinating in itself, it prevents the story from moving forward as rapidly as it could. The boxed feature Applying the Criteria: Evaluating Narrative Nonfiction shows how each book stacks up with respect to the main concerns in narrative nonfiction.

Applying the Criteria *Evaluating Narrative Nonfiction*

Comparison of *The Great Fire,* by Jim Murphy, and *The Story of the Great Chicago Fire, 1871,* by Mary Kay Phelan.

1. ▶ **Organization or structure.** Organization is one of the first things readers notice in nonfiction.

   Although Murphy's *The Great Fire* is divided into chapters, the information is organized around the question of what went wrong and why the fire wasn't extinguished. This focus keeps the reader reading and wondering what else could possibly go wrong. Because the fire is shown mainly through the eyes of four eyewitnesses, readers are taken from one part of the city/fire to another and can easily follow the narrative.

   In Phelan's *The Story of the Great Chicago Fire, 1871,* the organization follows a chronological approach, beginning with a vignette, moving into the history of Chicago, and then turning to how the fire moved through buildings and businesses. The emphasis is on the destruction of the physical Chicago and not on how people responded to the fire.

2. ▶ **Author's involvement with the subject.** Does the author bring the subject to life and make it matter to the reader? Does the author sound excited about and interested in what she or he is discussing? When an author is not fully engaged with the subject, the book is less interesting and immediate.

   Murphy is very involved with his subject and wants the reader to become immersed in the Great Fire and all its complexities. He is especially persis-

tent and passionate in his last chapter, called "Myth and Reality," about who was blamed for the fire. He wants very much to set the record straight so that the "vicious personal attacks" by the newspaper on Mrs. O'Leary and the poor are shown to be false.

Phelan is also very involved in this subject, as shown by the immense amount of research she did and her scrupulous attention to detail. She explained what was happening in the city the week of the fire, from the opening of the Opera House to the appearance of a now-famous Bret Harte story in the newspaper. However, the accumulation of all these precise details overwhelms the reader; it is difficult to see why this information is included.

3. ▶ **Setting.** Although setting is certainly not an element in all nonfiction, getting the feeling that we are in the place being described is important. Setting gives the reader another layer through which to experience the text.

   Murphy brings us into the setting immediately in the first chapter, as we accompany Peg Leg Sullivan on his search for a little company, which leads to his discovery of the fire. Much of the book consists of accounts of people who were there, and the sights and sounds eyewitnesses describe keep readers right in the burning city.

   Phelan's book gives us a sense of what was happening in the city, but we get only bits and pieces of what the setting was like. Because we don't see the ravages of the fire through the eyes of an eyewitness, it is difficult to feel we are actually in the city, experiencing its burning.

(continued)

4. **Qualities of writing.** When looking at informational books, notice whether the author creates a mood conducive to wanting to explore the subject further.

The Great Fire, a Newbery Honor Book, clearly embodies the qualities of excellent writing, which entice the reader into the subject. Murphy uses details to make readers feel as if they were in Chicago. Quotations from people involved and the friendly authorial voice invite readers into the book.

Phelan's book contains much good writing, but the use of the present tense—as if the event were happening today—is distracting. Her clear writing and excellent description are marred by a distant authorial voice and an overabundance of detail.

5. **Emotional impact.** Does the information entice us, making us want to know more?

Murphy's selection of details and use of participants' own words make the fire vivid and real. We recoil when sparks from tall buildings are blown across the river, igniting buildings there. We see people fleeing in horror and stamping out sparks on their own clothing. Murphy's discussion of the fire in terms of people and the effects it had on them heightens the emotional impact.

In Phelan's book, it is difficult to feel much emotional impact because so much time is spent talking about how building owners attempted to save their goods. No single consistent eyewitness is used, so the reader has no one but the fire chief to identify with. Thus, there is little emotional pull to make the book memorable.

6. **Imaginative impact.** One aspect of imaginative impact is whether the book opens up new possibilities and new ways of thinking. When information is presented with no sense of excitement and no attempt to raise questions, readers may feel deadened by all the information and may not see new openings for their thinking.

The excitement with which information is presented in Murphy's book makes us question the established accounts of the fire. The reader may wonder whether other aspects of history suffer from such inaccuracy. *The Great Fire* encourages readers to examine other accounts of urban living to see how they have been handled by authors.

Phelan's book raises few issues or questions. Her factual approach makes it seem as if there were no questions left to be asked.

7. **Vision of the author or attitude toward the topic.** As you assess nonfiction, ask yourself whether the author makes the world seem like an amazing place by bringing up interesting-to-explore mysteries, which show how complex the world is. Or does the author plod from point A to point B without invoking a sense of wonder and mystery? Are interesting speculative questions raised? Since almost every subject is value laden, does the author bring up controversies and uncomfortable facts or just scratch the surface? Does the author make us see the world as a place of interest, filled with fascinating information? How an author feels about his or her subject comes out in many ways in his or her writing.

Murphy clearly sees the Chicago fire as an incident with many causes, as he works to piece together why it burned so long and spread so far. He is very concerned with the equitable treatment of people, as he provides evidence showing how the placing of the blame on Mrs. O'Leary and the "drunk" firefighters was unfounded. He seems passionate about uncovering attempts to capitalize on the friction between the rich and the poor in placing blame. The tone of the book indicates the author's interest in exploring the deeper equity issues that lie beneath the event itself.

Phelan's book does not provide any indication of an expansive vision of the world. She characterizes Chicago more in terms of its buildings than its people. Since she brings up none of the social issues surrounding the fire, it is hard to get a sense of her vision of the world.

8. **Authenticity.** Is the book based on solid research? How did the author learn about the subject? Murphy's acknowledgments indicate that he was in Chicago frequently to get a sense of the city he wanted to write about. He did research there, as his bibliography and sources indicate. Much of his research included eyewitness accounts. Phelan also used research extensively, as indicated by her bibliography.

Be aware that the same fact base can lead to different interpretations, viewpoints, and opinions. For instance, Phelan explains that William Lee rushed to the drugstore where the nearest alarm box had been installed and "Mr. Goll [the druggist] pulls down the lever, but for some unknown reason the signal does not register at the central fire headquarters in the courthouse" (p. 40). However, Murphy says that Druggist Goll would not give William Lee the key to the alarm box because Goll said a fire truck had already passed, and thus this first alarm signal was never sent (p. 26).

9. **Design and illustrations.** Information is made accessible through placement of illustrations and through the way the book is designed. Design elements include type size, kinds of fonts, and titles and subheads. (More elements are mentioned in the discussion of the evaluation of nonnarrative nonfiction, where they are more frequently used.)

The large size of Murphy's book, the large clear print, and the frequent maps, photos, and drawings quickly bring the reader into the story. This is not a cluttered, busy-looking book, but one whose design makes it look inviting and interesting. Because Phelan's book was published before the advent of recent technology, only a few black-and-white drawings of mediocre quality are included in the book, and they add little to its appeal.

Nonnarrative Nonfiction *expository informational*

Nonnarrative informational books for children are what people often think of as books written to explain. The text is usually expository. According to Christine Pappas (in Mallett, 1992), there are three obligatory elements. The first is the *topic presentation;* it introduces the subject. The second is the *description of attributes;* it sets out the essential features of the subject of the book. These two elements can be interspersed throughout the book or given in one block of text. The third element, called the *characteristic events,* is usually the largest element in nonnarrative informational books. The events usually include typical processes, like feeding or giving birth for animals and cycles of growth for plants. The optional features Pappas mentions are *category comparison, final summary,* and *afterword.* For instance, if the topic is squirrels, the category comparison might talk about kinds of squirrels and how they differ. The final summary usually wraps up the topic, and the afterword adds extra information at the end of the book. Margaret Mallett believes that another important optional feature is *retrieval devices,* or aids provided to help readers find information in the book. Retrieval devices include the table of contents, index, and glossary (Mallett, 1992).

Formats of Nonnarrative Nonfiction

When people think of nonnarrative nonfiction, they often oversimplify and don't realize the enormous range of formats within this seemingly narrow category. Let's look closely at three nonnarrative books and see how Pappas's and Mallett's descriptors fit these books.

The Brain: Our Nervous System, by Seymour Simon, uses expository writing but does not have subheads, a glossary, or many of the other elements readers might expect to find in nonfiction. This book depends on the stunning visuals, working in conjunction with the text to provide information. Each double-page spread is a separate unit explaining one aspect of the brain. The text on one page explains the aspect of the brain, and the facing page is filled with a photo or picture. When all these separate units are taken together, they give a complete description of the brain. Simon does present an overview of the topic, describe different aspects of the brain, and show a characteristic event (how the brain gets the message when something hot is touched). The only optional feature Simon includes is a summary.

Sickle Cell Anemia (Diseases and People), by Alvin Silverstein, Virginia Silverstein, and Laura Silverstein Nunn, is an informational book in chapter-book format. The short titled chapters each begin with a vignette or brief story about someone who has the disease. The rest of the chapter is written in an explanatory manner, with subheads and photos throughout. All three of Pappas's obligatory elements are present in this book. Of the optional elements, this book has an index, a glossary, and an afterword, which gives sources for further information. No summary or category comparison is included.

For excellent suggestions of nonnarrative nonfiction books, see *Literature in the Math and Science Classroom* at *http://enc.org/topics/across/lit.*

Flight: Fliers and Flying Machines, by David Jefferis, contains double-page spreads on single topics loosely related to an overall theme (for example, "Dreams of Flight" and "First Airliners" are connected to the topic of flight). In this book, all three obligatory elements are present. For instance, in "Helicopters," which credits Leonardo da Vinci and the Chinese for the idea, we learn what makes a helicopter so unusual—the vertical takeoff. We also learn about the parts of the helicopter that allow it to fly and to hover. Then a few uses for the helicopter are explained. This explanation falls into the category of characteristic events.

Although all three of these nonnarrative nonfiction books contain Pappas's obligatory features, they vary widely in optional features. Because new kinds of books with new formats and approaches are being written every day, the presence or absence of these elements alone cannot be used to determine whether books are of high quality. Their presence or absence can, however, be used to help readers determine what kind of book they are dealing with.

Evaluating Nonnarrative Nonfiction

Design elements are needed to make nonfiction books visually stimulating, since they are so information heavy. Thus, design and illustration have an important place in the evaluation of nonnarrative nonfiction. Design includes placement of illustrations and other nonfiction features. These include the following:

- **Fonts and special effects.** Titles, headings, boldface print, color print, italics, bullets, captions, labels, and the like signal importance in text. Different fonts, larger type, and special effects are red flags indicating "This is important. Read carefully."

- **Illustrations and photographs.** Illustrations play a prominent role in enhancing reader comprehension. Nonfiction trade books and magazines brim with colorful pictures and photographs, which kidnap young readers and carry them deeper into meaning.

- **Graphics.** Diagrams, cutaways, cross sections, overlays, distribution maps, word bubbles, tables, charts, graphs, and boxed text graphically inform nonfiction readers of important information.

- **Text organizers.** Knowing about and using an index, a preface, a table of contents, a glossary, and an appendix can save precious time.

- **Use of white space.** How much white space is evident determines how dense or open a book looks.

In the boxed feature Applying the Criteria: Evaluating Nonnarrative Nonfiction, three books mentioned earlier are compared. One is a book on a single topic, supported through illustrations and photos. One is a chapter book. The third features double-page spreads on individual topics, connected by theme to the rest of the book.

The Literary Qualities of Nonfiction

The tasks that writers of nonfiction confront are daunting: to arouse curiosity and interest in a subject as they inform their readers; to find tantalizing ways to present information; to dig deep and unearth the unusual or the little known. And above all, they must write with such clarity that complex concepts and ideas are made understandable and accessible to children.

Applying the Criteria *Evaluating Nonnarrative Nonfiction*

Comparison of *The Brain: Our Nervous System,* by Seymour Simon; *Sickle Cell Anemia (Diseases and People),* by Alvin Silverstein, Virginia Silverstein, and Laura Silverstein Nunn, and *Flight: Fliers and Flying Machines,* by David Jefferis.

1. **Organization or structure.** I first look at whether the structure is clear and inviting and makes sense.

    Simon's *The Brain* certainly measures up. Because each page of text is accompanied by a full-page photo or drawing, the structure of the book is easy to follow. Another element of the organization that I'll include here is retrieval devices, which can be a very important part of nonfiction. Simon uses none of these. There is no index or glossary, yet one doesn't seem necessary.

    Sickle Cell Anemia is organized by chapter in what seems to me to be a logical order. It starts with the background and history of the disease; goes to diagnosis, treatment, and prevention; then ends with its impact on society and what future research and gene therapy could mean for the disease. Because this book has so many technical terms, there is a glossary as well as an index.

    Flight is organized chronologically, beginning with "Dreams of Flight" and ending with "The Future." Within each two-page spread on a single topic, I could count on finding short blocks of text about the topic and large, colorful drawings with captions.

2. **Author's involvement with the subject.** Author's involvement is evidenced in each book in slightly different ways, but there's a feeling I get when I read a book where the author is really present.

    When I read *The Brain,* I can hear the author talking in quiet but excited tones. He begins by telling us, "Wiggle your toes. Scratch your nose. . . . Inside your skull is your brain. Your brain is the control center for everything you do" (unpaged). I feel as if Simon is coaching us and going along so that we won't miss learning anything as we work to understand a topic he obviously finds fascinating.

    I felt that the authors of *Sickle Cell Anemia* were very involved with their subject because they took great care in their research to find stories of people with sickle cell anemia, which they used as vignettes to open each chapter. They put a human face on this disorder and made me care about understanding it.

3. **Qualities of writing.** Some of the things I look for in the writing are whether difficult concepts are explained in ways I can understand, whether the writer involves me in his or her world, and whether factual information is woven into the book's structure.

    Seymour Simon has no trouble doing any of these because of his gift for using language. He is so clear in his writing and in his examples that I can immediately relate to what he is saying. In one part of *The Brain,* he tells us: "Because nerves don't touch one another, a message has to leap from one to the next across a tiny gap called a synapse. A synapse is about a millionth of an inch wide and is a kind of living switch" (unpaged). I can understand this direct language, in which the words seem to be so carefully chosen.

    Although the pieces of text on the double-page spreads in *Flight* are short, I found them to be very engaging. In the section on air battles, the author tells us, "As the war [WWI] rolled on, air combat became a grim business. . . . In 1917 the flying time of new combat pilots was reckoned in bare hours before they were shot down. Few pilots had parachutes: military commanders considered that their use discouraged bravery" (p. 19). Through word choices like "rolled on" and "grim" we can clearly hear the author's voice.

    One thing I noticed about these nonnarrative books is that the language is not as rich and lush as in the narrative books. If that kind of language were used, however, it might obscure the clarity of the explanations.

4. **Emotional impact.** Simon's *The Brain* had a big impact on me. His words entered my consciousness and remained there because I could so easily connect with what he explained. He made the brain seem exciting and essential to know about, and I gained new respect for its complexity. *Sickle Cell Anemia* did make an impact on me, because I can remember and empathize with the people who suffer from this disorder. While I admire the people talked about in *Flight,* I can't really say it had an emotional impact on me, perhaps because there is so much diverse information in the book.

5. **Imaginative impact.** *The Brain* definitely stimulated my mind and made me want to know more. Based on what Simon said about the cerebellum,

(continued)

the brain center for muscle movement, posture, and coordination, I started thinking about the mind-body connection.

Flight is the kind of book that makes my imagination soar, as I think about the pioneers of flight and the vision they must have had to work in aviation. It makes me want to think as far "outside the box" as I can, just as these pioneers and risk takers did, because I have so little mechanical know-how and understanding.

6. **Vision of author or attitude toward the topic.** From Simon's explanations in *The Brain,* it is obvious that he sees the world as a place filled with fascinating information. On the last page of the book, he says, "Your brain is only a small part of your whole body. It is not very big, yet it can do more jobs than the most powerful computer in the world" (unpaged). Statements like this show that Simon is in awe of his subject and respects it.

Permeating *Sickle Cell Anemia* is the authors' passion for knowing more about this disease so that people will not have to suffer. They seem to have an expansive vision of the world in which everyone works for the good of everyone else. They face controversy head on, pointing out areas of research that raise ethical questions. They made me see how much there still is to learn about this disease, which makes it seem that there are endless possibilities to explore.

Flight also demonstrates this kind of vision of the world. The overview of what has been accomplished in aviation allows us to see how far we've come and to dream about what's yet to come. Jefferis, himself a pilot, loves everything about his topic, and it shows.

7. **Authenticity.** Whenever I read a nonfiction book, I want to know whether the information is accurate. Without some knowledge about the topic, sometimes it's very hard to know whether a book is indeed accurate and without bias. Yet there are a few ways to get some information. One way is to look at the sources the author uses. Another is to look at whom the author thanks for assistance with the book.

Although Simon's *The Brain* does not list any resources, I trusted his information because I was

familiar with his attention to detail. Then I noticed on the credit page in the front of the book that he thanks a medical doctor "for her careful reading of the manuscript of the book."

Sickle Cell Anemia, a book on a very complicated topic, gives extensive chapter notes, a list of sources for further reading, and an acknowledgment thanking medical people for "their careful reading of the manuscript and their helpful comments and suggestions." The authors also thank a sickle cell patient for her insights.

David Jefferis, who could fly before he could drive and has written over 20 children's books on aeronautics, had a consultant from the Science Museum in London. So although he gives no sources, the detailed nature of his information leads me to believe that it is well researched. As you can see, although there is no one way to check an author's accuracy, there are many indicators that can be used.

8. **Design and illustrations.** *The Brain* depends on two devices to make it visually stunning. One is reverse type—white type on a black background. The other is the use of full-page color images of the brain, taken from brain scans. X-rays were changed into computer code to make these clear, colorful graphics.

Sickle Cell Anemia starts chapters almost in the middle of the page to give an uncluttered look and uses titles and subheads consistently. Boxed information appears occasionally throughout the book. Each chapter has at least two pictures or diagrams to reinforce information in the text.

Design elements become much more evident in books like *Flight,* in which the designer has done everything possible to make it look appealing because there is so much information packed into it. In *Flight,* less than one-third of the space on a page is given up to the text. The drawings are the focal point of each page, and they are placed in amazing and unusual ways. Airplanes seem to fly off the page, going beyond the normal boundaries. They are arranged from many perspectives—on one page coming toward us and on other pages flying away from us. The many smaller pictures on each page have their own captions in smaller type size.

James Cross Giblin (in Colman, 1999), writer and editor, explains what a nonfiction writer faces:

> I've written my share of fiction and in many ways found that writing nonfiction is a greater challenge; you have to absorb and present huge amounts of information in a clear, accurate, and entertaining manner. Like a writer of fiction, you must find a way to write freely and spontaneously. But at the same time . . . you always have to be on guard to make sure you're not omitting or distorting any necessary facts. (p. 221)

Penny Colman (1999), fiction and nonfiction writer, rails against the narrow view that nonfiction is not "real" literature. She explains that to write good fiction and nonfiction it is "necessary to employ many of the same literary techniques and to pay close attention to the narrative, structure, point of view, language, syntax, sequence, pace, tone, and voice" (p. 215). She believes that nonfiction is as heterogeneous a genre as fiction, encompassing good, bad, mediocre, and classic books. Just as styles and techniques differ for fiction, so do they differ for nonfiction. She adheres to the basic tenets of nonfiction writing, but uses stylistic and narrative strategies traditionally found in fiction. She calls her writing creative nonfiction and explains that it includes five elements: real life, reflection, research, reading, and writing.

Nonfiction depends on real life in that it is based on the author's or other people's experiences. The designation *nonfiction* implies that the author will not tamper with what we know about the natural world, so animals won't talk and people won't live on other galaxies. The possibility of including reflection on their subject gives authors some latitude. Lee Gutkind, cited in Colman's article, says: "A writer's feelings and responses about a subject are permitted and encouraged, as long as what they think is written to embrace the reader in a variety of ways" (p. 219). The third element, research, is the hallmark of nonfiction. Colman explains that she finds information everywhere, "including archives, attics, libraries, museums, used bookstores, historic sites, and conversation with all sorts of people, including scholars and people with firsthand experiences" (p. 220). After she immerses herself in the material, she builds a bibliography and chronology and makes notes. Part of the work is then reading other writers' books to perfect her own writing style. The last element is the actual writing. Colman tells us that writing is a "completely absorbing, complex, challenging, messy, painful, exhilarating, and emotional process. Every story I write leaves its mark on me as I engage with the material" (p. 220).

For Colman, the first writing task is to discover the structure and substructures, which are to nonfiction what plot and subplots are to fiction. "This is a very visual process for me, and as I consider various structures and substructures, I write them on pieces of paper or note cards and literally lay them side-by-side on a table or on the floor" (p. 221). For **Rosie the Riveter: Women Working on the Homefront in World War II,** her notes stretched across two rooms because she used a layered structure that incorporated five interrelated aspects of the story—information about the industrial mobilization, details about the propaganda campaign to recruit women workers, news from the battlefronts, illustrations of life on the homefront, and the collective voices and experiences of women workers. She constantly asks herself, "What's the point? Why are you compiling these facts and true stories?" Colman's comments reveal how complex the task of writing good nonfiction is and clearly indicate the attention she pays to the literary qualities embedded in her work.

A Trip Through the Dewey Decimal Classifications

The enormity of the nonfiction section of the library often causes teachers to skip over all but the sections containing science and social studies books. But nonfiction contains many surprises and is jam-packed with fascinating books. To see how useful all of the nonfiction sections can be, we'll look at each in terms of how these books could be worked into the curriculum. One of the goals of this chapter is to make sure you don't avoid any of the numbered categories simply because you can't imagine why you would want to look there.

Although the coverage of each section is by necessity brief, the intent is to encourage you to explore for yourself and see that every classification holds books that are magical, informative, or interesting.

000: Generalities

The 000 classification of the Dewey decimal system includes bibliographies, library and information science, news media, journalism, and general collections. This section has a lot more to offer than you might expect.

ETs and UFOs: Are They Real?, by Larry Kettelkamp, gives an overview of reported sightings of UFOs and encounters with aliens, as well as the agencies that monitor and investigate such claims. *Bigfoot and Other Legendary Creatures,* by Paul Robert Walker, explores myths and scientific inquiries surrounding repeated sightings of such legendary creatures as the Loch Ness monster, Bigfoot, and the Yeti. A book on just the Yeti, *Yeti: Abominable Snowman of the Himalayas,* by Elaine Landau, recounts sightings throughout history and considers the reliability of the evidence. Students could use books such as these to examine evidence or investigate differences in cultural acceptance of unproven phenomena.

The Cat's Elbow and Other Secret Languages, collected by Alvin Schwartz, presents instructions for speaking 13 secret languages, including Pig Latin. It could be used to immerse students in language issues and to explore the appeal of and reasons for secret languages. Ideas for creating math news or science news are offered in *Extra! Extra! The Who, What, Where, When, and Why of Newspapers,* by Linda Granfield, which explains the history of the newspaper and how news was gathered. *The Furry News: How to Make a Newspaper,* by Loreen Leedy, shows animals working hard at writing, editing, and printing a newspaper, with tips for students on how to make their own.

100: Philosophy and Psychology

In the children's area of the library, the 100 section is not usually a very large one. One part of the classification that is absorbing is the paranormal phenomena. Around Halloween, students might like to read about our historical fascination with ghosts. *Ghosts of the Southwest: The Phantom Gunslinger and Other Real-Life Hauntings,* by Ted Wood, describes homes, hotels, restaurants, and towns in Arizona, New Mexico, Oklahoma, and Texas and the ghosts that haunt them. Woods explains that his first lesson in ghost hunting was that ghosts can be anywhere someone died suddenly or wrongfully. He found out that some ghosts play tricks, such as turning on and off lights, fans, and radios. They also hide objects, spin silverware, and roll toilet paper in front of helpless, shocked bathroom users. This book includes great photos of the places discussed. Similarly, *Ghost in the House,* by Daniel Cohen, tells nine stories about some of the best-known haunted houses in the world, including one called the Octagon in Washington, DC. Kathleen Krull's *They Saw the Future: Oracles, Psychics, Scientists, Great Thinkers, and Pretty Good Guessers* will involve students in the predictions of those who have speculated about or claimed to see the future, from the oracles of ancient Greece to such modern figures as Edgar Cayce and Jeane Dixon. Students might investigate whether current-day psychics have had more success with predictions than their counterparts in the past.

Another part of this section focuses on psychology and contains such books as the delightful *How Are You Peeling? Foods with Moods.* Authors Saxton Freymann and Joost Elffers combed New York for expressive produce. All the photos show vegetables and fruits with twinkling or glaring black-eyed peas for eyes. Children will be amazed at how expressive a green pepper can be! The book has much to say to children of all ages about feelings and how we react to others.

CD-ROM

If you are attracted to *delightful* books, search Favorite Authors for authors who write them.

200: Religion

Although teachers might be tempted to skip the 200 classification completely, thinking there would be nothing suitable for sharing in public school classrooms, they would be wrong.

First of all, some beautiful poetry is part of this classification. In *All God's Children: A Book of Prayers,* edited by Lee Bennett Hopkins, bright, colorful pictures accompany both traditional prayers and prayers by well-known authors. Lois Duncan's "Song for Something Little" thanks God for little things: "Fuzzy mittens, butterflies/Baby colts with solemn eyes."

To help students learn about the multitude of sacred traditions, dip into such books as *This Is the Star,* by Joyce Dunbar and Gary Blythe, a beautiful book about the birth of Christ. This cumulative presentation, which uses rhyme to describe the night Christ was born, is delightful to hear. In *A Great Miracle Happened There: A Chanukah Story,* by Karla Kuskin, a mother tells her family and a young guest the story of the holiday's origin. Because the information is embedded in the story of the family's celebration, it is interesting and engaging. Unfamiliar terms are explained in understandable ways, making this an excellent choice to share with children who are not familiar with Chanukah. Norma Simon's *The Story of Hanukkah* explains the history and traditions that are part of the Jewish holiday. Softly blurred images in muted colors give the mixed-media illustrations an otherworldly quality. Other books in this classification include stories of different denominations, such as *Amish Home,* by Raymond Bial, which depicts the Amish way of life through photos and text.

300: Social Sciences

The 300 section covers such topics as political science and government, civil and political rights, slavery and emancipation, military science, social problems and services, education, commerce, communications, transportation, customs, etiquette, and folklore (discussed in Chapter 8). Just reading these categories doesn't prepare you for the magnitude of topics and the gems in this area. For instance, the gorgeous picture book *I Have a Dream,* by Martin Luther King, Jr., and Coretta Scott King, would give students a new look at King's famous speech because it is illustrated by 15 Coretta Scott King Award and Honor Book artists. The illustrations give added life to the speech and help students visualize King's words.

To begin a social studies unit on poverty or homelessness read a book such as *Lives Turned Upside Down: Homeless Children in Their Own Words and Photographs,* by Jim Hubbard. This book features what four homeless children have photographed of their lives, accompanied by Hubbard's interviews with them. The vibrancy and immediacy of this book make it memorable.

To help students understand in a concrete way the limitations of our planet's resources, read Molly Bang's *Common Ground: The Water, Earth, and Air We Share.* It tells the story of a village commons, which is supposed to be for everyone to use but is misused by a group of villagers who try to graze whole flocks of sheep on it. Eventually they leave when they are told that they can graze only one sheep per family. Bang then shows how the world is like that village, with the commons being our parks, reserves, and natural resources, such as water and air. She ends by pointing out that, unlike the villagers who could just move somewhere else, we don't have anywhere else to go. Although this book is a bit didactic, Bang articulates the interdependence of all living things in such a clear way that even very young children can understand this important concept.

The marvels of transportation can be studied through such books as Gail Gibbons's *The Great St. Lawrence Seaway.* The lovely, inviting watercolors throughout tell the history of the St. Lawrence Seaway, which opened in 1959. We learn that in 1954 Canada and the United States agreed to work together to build this 2,400-mile continuous waterway from the Atlantic Ocean to the Great Lakes.

Students will gain a new appreciation for the complexity of early ship building through David Macauley's *Ship.* The focus on details in this fascinating book brings the subject to life. The last half of the book shows in exquisite detail a boat being constructed in the 15th century. Students will be amazed to see how such complex things were built by hand without the help of machines.

Students can learn about burial practices in *The Best Book of Mummies,* by Philip Steele, a real page-turner. It tells you everything you ever wanted to know about mummies, including the background belief system, how people were mummified, what the coffins

looked like, and what was in them. Students could focus on what can be learned about a culture through looking at burial practices.

Another eye-opening book, ***Breaking Ground, Breaking Silence: The Story of New York's African Burial Ground,*** by Joyce Hansen and Gary McGowan, tells what archaeologists and anthropologists have learned by "reading" the bones and artifacts of this long-ignored burial site, opened in 1991. Students can see not only that life stories can be pieced together from remains and artifacts but also that historians can choose to ignore contributions of whole groups of people.

Ted Lewin's ***Market!*** is about the market-day practices in five different parts of the world, including Russia, Ireland, and Uganda. The lovely watercolor paintings give as much information as the words.

400: Language

The 400 section, which includes books dealing with many aspects of language, will interest children in issues of language. Ruth Heller has written a unique series on the parts of speech, using inventive imagery that will charm children as they learn the forms and functions of the parts of speech. One book in the series, ***Mine, All Mine: A Book About Pronouns,*** introduces various types of pronouns, explains how and when to use them, and provides whimsical glimpses of what our language would be without them. The text explains that pronouns take the place of nouns so that we don't have to say them over and over again. The author shows how King Cole would sound without the pronouns *his* and *he.* The bright pictures accompanying the text, as well as the clear, often zany examples, make this usually rather staid topic interesting. Heller's books would appeal to older students who need to review these concepts. Rather than bore them with the same old tedious drills, the books use humor to reinforce concepts that have been missed.

What in the World Is a Homophone?, by Leslie Presson, is a dictionary of homophones (words that sound alike but have different spellings and different meanings). It uses colorful, whimsical pictures to demonstrate the difference between words such as *shear* and *sheer.*

Taxi: A Book of City Words, by Betsy Maestro and Giulio Maestro, shows non-city people what's in a city. The reader is introduced to such typical city words as *theater, museum, office building,* and *train station* as a taxi travels in and around the city on a hectic workday. Colorful illustrations give the reader a real feel for what a big city looks like. After reading it, children can be encouraged to create their own dictionary of words for a specific place, such as a farm, a zoo, or a planetarium.

Earth Words: A Dictionary of the Environment, by Seymour Simon, introduces children to words commonly used to discuss the environment. The words are paired with vivid, delightful illustrations.

Cathi Hepworth's ***Bug Off!*** is a collection of words that contain the names of insects, accompanied by droll drawings of the insects. This book provides children with the challenge of finding even more words that contain "bugs."

Also in this category is ***Handtalk School,*** by Mary Beth Miller and George Ancona. Bright, clear photos show children using American Sign Language during a typical school day.

To introduce children to the idea of multiple languages, ***Table—Chair—Bear: A Book in Many Languages,*** by Jane Feder, presents illustrations of objects found in a child's room, labeled in Korean, French, Arabic, Vietnamese, Japanese, Portuguese, Lao, Spanish, Tagalog,

For fun with words, go to **Richard Lederer's Verbivores** at *http://pw1.netcom.com/~rlederer/.*

Cambodian, and Navajo. *First Words,* by Ivan Chermayeff and Jane Clark Chermayeff, resulted from their efforts to teach their son words in French, Spanish, German, and Italian while they were living in Europe. Each commonly used word, such as *cat,* is written in the four languages and illustrated by a photo from a museum.

To make children aware that some languages have different ways to represent letters, use *At the Beach,* by Huy Voun Lee, in which a mother amuses her son at the beach by drawing Chinese characters in the sand. Children may be surprised to see that Chinese uses pictures instead of symbols for sounds. *Alef-bet: A Hebrew Alphabet Book,* by Michelle Edwards, shows a family doing everyday activities, with labels on the activities in Hebrew. The delightful, often humorous pictures are lively enough to capture children's attention as they learn the Hebrew alphabet.

This section of the library also includes books written in Spanish and English. *A Gift for Abuelita: Celebrating the Day of the Dead,* by Nancy Luenn, shows a child dealing with the loss of her grandmother. *Gathering the Sun: An Alphabet in Spanish and English,* by Alma Flor Ada, is a collection of poems in both Spanish and English, organized around the alphabet scheme.

500: Natural Sciences and Mathematics

The 500 classification includes books about natural history, mathematics, astrology and allied sciences, physics (heat, light, sound), chemistry, earth sciences, fossils, life sciences, biology, and ecology, as well as plants and animals. To give students an unforgettable experience of what a vernal lake is and the functions it performs, read them *Disappearing Lake: Nature's Magic in Denali National Park,* by Debbie S. Miller. The stunning paintings on glossy paper bring this national park to life, as the text describes the formation of the seasonal lake and the various creatures that make their homes in and around it. In Miller's lyrical language, the book eloquently teaches that this process of going from meadow to lake to meadow contributes to the animals' food supply.

The ecosystem of the giant saguaro cactus is the subject of *Desert Giant: The World of the Saguaro Cactus,* by Barbara Bash, which documents its life cycle and the desert animals it helps support. The ecological importance of the saguaro and its contributions to the ecosystem are shown concretely. Students will learn that this cactus can grow as tall as 50 feet, weigh up to several tons, and live for 200 years! The accordion-like pleats in its skin expand in the rain, storing extra water for the long dry times. After reading this book, students will never forget that the cactus is a source of food for both animals and humans.

Aliki's *Dinosaur Bones* could be used to engage students in the fascinating study of fossils. The book discusses how scientists, studying fossil remains, provide information on how dinosaurs lived millions of years ago. Aliki takes us back about 200 years to the beginnings of modern human awareness of dinosaurs, when a woman in England found a dinosaur tooth in her garden. Aliki's delightful pictures are clear and intriguing, making the book very engaging. *Digging Up Dinosaurs,* also by Aliki, briefly introduces various types of dinosaurs whose skeletons and reconstructions are seen in museums and explains how scientists uncover, preserve, and study fossilized dinosaur bones. Students visiting a museum that houses dinosaur skeletons will look at them with new appreciation after they read about the complexity and delicacy of removing dinosaur bones from one site and reconstructing them in another.

Unusual facts about animals can be used to arouse interest in learning more about the animals. *Chickens Aren't the Only Ones,* by Ruth Heller, is an original and fascinating book on the subject of eggs and all those animals that produce them. The delightful, colorful pictures engage readers immediately, as they learn unusual facts—for example, that the duck-bill platypus is one of two mammals that lay eggs.

The delightful book *Animals Don't Wear Pajamas: A Book About Sleeping,* by Eve B. Feldman, describes human sleeping habits and rituals and then shows comparable animal ones. For instance, in connection with a picture of human children with their blankets, Feldman says, "Perhaps the strangest blanket of all is made by the parrot fish. This bubble-like covering oozes out of the fish's skin" (unpaged). Each morning, the parrot fish has to struggle out of the ooze, only to cover itself with this "blanket" again the next night.

Rattlesnake Dance: True Tales, Mysteries, and Rattlesnake Ceremonies, by Jennifer Owings Dewey, presents facts and folk beliefs about rattlesnakes, accompanied by an autobiographical account of three personal encounters with rattlesnakes. Dewey begins the book by sharing her experience of being bitten by a rattlesnake as a child and intersperses rattlesnake facts throughout the account.

Look to the North: A Wolf Pup Diary, by Jean Craighead George, is composed of brief diary entries that mark the passage of the seasons and introduce events in the lives of three wolves, as they grow from helpless pups to participants in their small pack's hunt. The format, in which each diary entry is tied to what is happening in school at that time of year, makes it easy to assimilate the information about the wolves.

They Swim the Seas, by Seymour Simon, is an excellent description of the migration of marine animals and plants through rivers, seas, and oceans. Simon always includes intriguing information:

> The oceans cover almost three-quarters of the world, yet only the smallest fraction of the water is visible. Underneath the oceans' windblown surfaces the waters go down to an average depth of sixteen thousand feet. The deepest parts of the seas stretch about seven miles below the surface. Mount Everest, the highest mountain on the land, could easily disappear below the waves in those depths. (unpaged)

Through comparisons such as these, the reader easily experiences the immensity of the ocean. The watercolor illustrations by Elsa Warnick seem magical, showing waves and beach here, a turtle or jellyfish there.

To help young readers understand math concepts, use books such as *How Much Is a Million?,* by David M. Schwartz. Through text and pictures, readers are helped to conceptualize a million, a billion, and a trillion. The examples and Steven Kellogg's zany pictures are compelling. Students will find out that counting from one to one billion would take them 95 years!

This unusual informational book weaves boxed information in with three stories about rattlesnakes (including the author's own experience of being bitten by one).

(Illustration copyright © 1997 by Jennifer Owings Dewey from *Rattlesnake Dance: True Tales, Mysteries, and Rattlesnake Ceremonies* by Jennifer Owings Dewey. Published by Boyds Mills Press, Inc. Reprinted by permission.)

600: Technology (Applied Sciences)

Included within the 600 classification are medical sciences, diseases, engineering, agriculture, hunting, fishing, conservation, home economics, family living, food and drink, child rearing, manufacturing (iron, lumber, textiles, manufacturing for specific uses), hardware, leather, fur, and buildings.

To stimulate students' interest in learning about inventors and the early part of the 20th century, use *Inventors,* by Martin W. Sandler. This beautifully designed, lively book involves the reader through its photographs, drawings, boxed quotations, and short pieces of text. Here we learn that the ferris wheel was invented in 1893, that there were many other African American inventors besides Elijah McCoy, and that high schools gave classes designed to teach young women the proper way to board trolley cars in their long skirts! The whole book is packed with interesting information.

The Wright Brothers: How They Invented the Airplane, by Russell Freedman, describes the lives of the Wright brothers and how they developed the first airplane. The text is interspersed with wonderful old photos. Although written in the narrative style, the book has several features of nonnarrative nonfiction, including an index, "About the Photographs," "Places to Visit," and "For Further Reading."

Bones: Our Skeletal System, by Seymour Simon, will leave students with clear memories of the skeletal system. This visually stunning book describes the skeletal system and outlines the many important roles the bones play in the healthy functioning of the human body. Now that scanners have made it possible to peer inside the body, we see the inside of bones and what the plates look like that make them up. Seymour's clear language adds to the impact of the book: "Your bones are like the framework of a building. Without a framework, the building would collapse." We learn that "bones grow and change just as you do. You begin life with about three hundred bones in your body. As you get older, some of those bones join together, so that by the time you are an adult you will have only about two hundred six bones" (unpaged).

To encourage students to do research on pets and to familiarize them with another format they can use to write, introduce them to *The True-or-False Book of Cats,* by Patricia Lauber, which is set up in a quiz format. A statement such as "Cats don't like to be stared at" is followed on the next page by the answer, which in this case is "true" because cats see staring as a threat. Readers also find out why it is that cats often sit in the laps of guests who don't like cats.

Spots, Feathers, and Curly Tails, by Nancy Tafuri, is another question-and-answer book for young readers. It highlights some outstanding characteristics of farm animals, such as a chicken's feathers and a cow's spots. The text is supported by illustrations.

Students in even the earliest grades will enjoy reading a true story about children creating a business. In *Once upon a company . . . A True Story,* Wendy Anderson Halperin chronologically tells the story of the Christmas wreath business her three children set up and operated to raise money for college. The lovely drawings with soft, inviting colors and the little pictures of the children's activities filling every left-hand page would be enough to make this book satisfying. But on top of that, it really does teach you how to set up a business, as it

Wendy Halperin's lovely illustrations and first-person narrative from the point of view of a child enliven the seemingly dry topic of starting a business.

Find an abundance of resources on the topic of flying at NASA's website. Go to www.nasa.gov/.

shows how the business developed over five years. This book certainly proves that *no* topic has to be written about in a less than interesting way.

To broaden students' understanding of differently abled people, use the delightful story *A Button in Her Ear*, by Ada B. Litchfield. This picture storybook tells how a little girl's hearing deficiency is detected and then corrected with the use of a hearing aid. Because the subject of deafness is dealt with in such a straightforward manner, children will find it easy to talk about and understand.

The American Family Farm: A Photo Essay, with text by Joan Anderson and photos by George Ancona, gives students a close-up look at the lives of three farm families. In this pictorial essay on the American family farm, the focus is on daily life at three different kinds of farms. The first-person narratives, along with the photos, will make students feel as if they had real contact with these three families.

700: The Arts (Fine and Decorative)

The 700 classification contains civic and landscape art, architecture, drawing and decorative arts, painting, graphic arts, photography, music, and recreational and performing arts. Sports are included in this section because they are part of the recreational arts.

Books on architecture are a good complement to a unit on any country. *A Greek Temple*, written by Fiona MacDonald and illustrated by Mark Bergin, is part of the *Inside Story* series, which includes books on structures around the world, such as an Egyptian pyramid and a medieval cathedral. This book, a series of illustrated explanations, focuses on such topics as prayer and sacrifices, festival games, temple design, and what it's like inside the Parthenon. Cut-away illustrations let readers see inside the structure of the temple.

One way to share the world of Shakespeare is to read the story of the Globe Theater, in which many of his works were performed. *William Shakespeare & the Globe*, by Aliki, tells the story of Shakespeare and the famous theater. We hear, "Comedy, tragedy, history, fairy tales—Shakespeare wrote about them all in words that dance off the tongue" (p. 11).

With Aliki's characteristic mix of delightful pictures and clear text, this book brings us close to the time when Shakespeare lived. Interesting information is put in boxes under the illustrations, and we see pictures of Elizabeth I, James I, and Ben Johnson.

Dance!, by Bill T. Jones and Susan Kuklin, introduces the basic concepts of dance through poetic text and lovely photographs. *Martha Graham: A Dancer's Life*, by Russell Freedman, is a lovely photobiography of the American dancer, teacher, and choreographer, who was born in Pittsburgh in 1895 and became a leading figure in the world of modern dance. Through his research, Freedman always seems to uncover the essence of his subjects. He tells us that Graham was an ambitious young woman who wanted to create a new kind of dance. She spent many hours at New York City's Central Park Zoo, where she would sit on a bench across from a lion in its cage and watch the animal pace back and forth, from one side of the cage to the other. "She was fascinated . . . by the purity of its movements" (p. 11). Readers learn that Graham looked upon dance as an exploration, a celebration of life, a religious calling that required absolute devotion.

CD-ROM

To see what genres Aliki writes in, use the CD-ROM database.

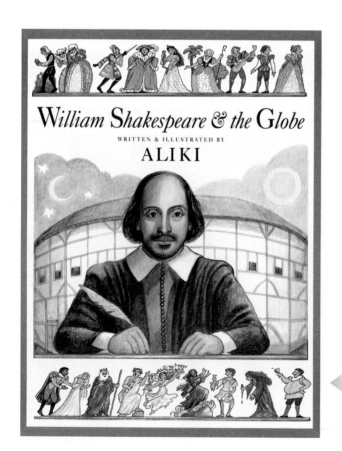

The life of Shakespeare unfolds slowly through text written in short acts and scenes and images drawn in Aliki's characteristic engaging style.

(Cover art from *William Shakespeare & the Globe* by Aliki. Cover art copyright © 1999 by Aliki. Used by permission of HarperCollins Publishers.)

A favorite category of students is books on riddles and word fun. These books are entertaining to read and to figure out and will inspire students to want to explore and think about our language. ***Bunny Riddles,*** by Katy Hall and Lisa Eisenberg, is an ***Easy-to-Read*** book with very funny riddles: "What would you get if you crossed a bunny with a giant? A tall tail!" (p. 44). Such books as ***Eight Ate: A Feast of Homonym Riddles,*** by Marvin Terban, can be used during those few minutes before the bell rings to signal the end of class. Kids love to figure out that a smelly chicken is a "foul fowl."

This section of the library includes a whole range of books on sports. ***Leagues Apart: The Men and Times of the Negro Baseball Leagues,*** by Lawrence S. Ritter, tells the story of segregation in baseball through short sketches of some of the greats who had to play in the Negro Leagues because of racial discrimination. Smokey Joe Williams played from 1905 to 1932, mainly for the Chicago American Giants, the New York Lincoln Giants, and the Homestead Grays. He had a fastball that was said to zip in at well over 90 miles an hour, about as fast as that of the legendary Walter Johnson. Williams's name is "unknown to most baseball fans because he was never permitted to wear a major league uniform" (unpaged). Students could look at the records set back then in the major leagues and see whose records would not be standing if these men had played in the major leagues.

To help students learn more about different sports and recreation opportunities, encourage them to delve into David Hautzig's ***1000 Miles in 12 Days: Pro Cyclists on Tour,*** which deals with the complex, competitive world of pro cyclists. The fabulous photos capture the excitement and fast pace of this sport. ***Night Dive,*** by Ann McGovern, describes the underwater life a twelve-year-old girl sees while scuba diving at night in the Caribbean. The first-person narrator and the photos of glowing fish, by Martin Scheiner and Jim Scheiner, make readers feel as if they were there.

Yahoo! Arts and Humanities has reading lists, reviews, and more at *http://d3.dir.dcx.yahoo.com/arts/humanities/literature/genres/children_s/.*

To find other artists noted for their use of light, search Favorite Authors for the key word *light.*

800: Literature and Rhetoric

Although most of the 800 classification is made up of fiction and shelved in a different part of the children's section, there are nonfiction books in this category that can be helpful to students. ***What's Your Story? A Young Person's Guide to Writing Fiction,*** by well-known author Marion Dane Bauer, is a beautifully written, well-explained book on writing. Bauer talks about a story plan, telling her readers that stories "take time to grow in the author's head, time to write down, and time to rework until they are ready to be read" (p. 7). She talks about choosing your best idea, choosing your point of view, and why characters are the key to good stories.

The Divide, by Michael Bedard, relates how the young Willa Cather came to appreciate the beauty of the plains of Nebraska, even though she was unhappy when her family moved there. In the afterword, Bedard tells us that people now remember Cather for her descriptive novels about this area and its people. She wrote "of the harsh beauty of that flat land, and of the women who had taught her what strength and courage meant. Her heart hid somewhere in the long grass always. It sang a new song that had never been sung before" (unpaged).

900: Geography and History

Travel, biography (discussed in Chapter 12), genealogy, the history of the ancient world, and general history of Europe, Asia, Africa, North America, South America, and other areas of the world are all contained in the 900 classification. This is a section teachers can turn to for information and stories that will enrich the teaching of social studies.

Here you can find such books as ***Angels of Mercy: The Army Nurses of World War II,*** by Betsy Kuhn, which focuses on the nurses who served on the front lines. Through their stories, often told in their own words, we see another side of the war and get a close-up view of some of the 59,000 nurses who served in the army.

Joseph Bruchac's ***Lasting Echoes: An Oral History of Native American People*** gives the histories of seven generations of American Indian people from an American Indian perspective. Bruchac skillfully weaves the testimony of more than a hundred American Indians into this compelling story. Morgan Monceaux and Ruth Katcher's beautifully illustrated ***My Heroes, My People: African Americans and Native Americans in the West*** tells the stories of

Visit The U.S. Holocaust Memorial Museum at www.ushmm.org/.

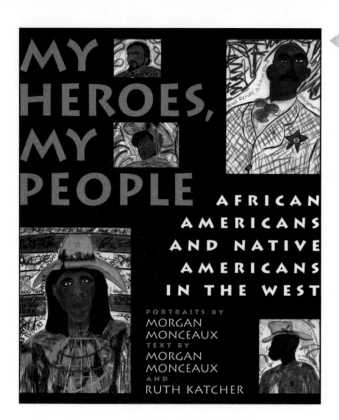

the African Americans and American Indians who were leaders in the West. Cheryl Harness's **The Amazing Impossible Erie Canal** packs fascinating facts and masterfully drawn paintings into this picture book, which gives us a real sense of what it took to make this project a reality. **Pioneers,** by Martin W. Sandler, is filled with photographs and drawings from the Library of Congress that take us into the lives of this country's pioneers. We see mining towns, frontier families, and cowboys, as well as recognition of American Indians' loss of land.

Frozen Girl, by David Getz, discusses the discovery, history, and significance of an Incan mummy found frozen in the mountains of Peru. The fascinating thing about this book is that to tell the story the author used one-on-one interviews with the men who discovered the mummy. His opening line promises a lot—"He had just wanted to get a closer look at an awakened volcano" (p. 3)—and piques readers' curiosity. The archaeologist and mountain climber Johan Reinhard told him he wanted to have a look at the erupting volcano: "The last thing I expected to find was the frozen body of a girl sacrificed five hundred years ago" (p. 5). After reading this introduction, it is almost impossible not to continue reading. The information about the journey to get the frozen mummy out of the ground and to the university was fascinating, as was the way they pieced together the story of the child's life.

As you can see, the nonfiction section holds all kinds of information and stories that you would not have expected to find. Spend time there and see what other treasures you can uncover.

Nonfiction Series Books

Many of the nonfiction books published today are part of a series. Publishers find what they consider a winning format and then publish several books on like topics, using the same format. The wonderful thing about series books is that when you find a high-quality, appealing book within a series, you can usually count on finding the same quality and appeal in the rest of the books in the series. The same is true for mediocre series books. Once you discover that the book does not have the qualities you look for in nonfiction, you can generally assume that the rest of the series suffers from the same defects. The brief sampling of series books that follows is intended to whet your appetite for more, so you won't overlook these books. Note, however, that series books are not shelved together in the library but within their library classifications.

A series used with younger readers is **In My Neighborhood,** by Kids Can Press. One of these books, **Garbage Collectors,** by Paulette Bourgeois, shows in a step-by-step manner what garbage collectors do. It is packed with fascinating facts—for example, every year each family throws out 200 bags of garbage. This thorough and thoughtful text encourages readers to think about the implications of all these piles of garbage and to discuss how they can help reduce garbage in their families.

The series *I Want to Be,* produced by Stephanie Maze, includes *I Want to Be a Firefighter,* by Catherine O'Neill Grace, which is packed with information and photographs about this occupation. There is a "Where to start" section, a "Kinds of" section, and an "In Practice" section, as well as sections on training, education, specialties, and even firefighting vocabulary. The book ends with famous firefighters, international firefighters, and other sources of information This well-designed series integrates text with frequent photos in an appealing layout. Other titles include *I Want to Be an Engineer* and *I Want to Be a Dancer,* both by Catherine O'Neill Grace.

Lerner's *People's History* is a series that includes such titles as *Buffalo Gals: Women of the Old West,* by Brandon Marie Miller, and *Farewell, John Barleycorn: Prohibition in the United States,* by Martin Hintz. *Dressed for the Occasion: What Americans Wore 1620–1970,* by Brandon Marie Miller, typifies the series because it is full of wonderful photographs and startling information. For example, Miller tells us that in colonial days most clothes were rarely washed. Only clothes made of linen, such as aprons, caps, and underclothes, were washed every six weeks or so! And bathing was considered unhealthy, so people perfumed themselves liberally to mask their smell.

Another excellent series is *The Young Person's Guide to . . . .* One book in the series, *The Young Person's Guide to the Orchestra: Benjamin Britten's Composition on CD,* narrated by Ben Kingsley and written by Anita Ganeri, contains fascinating information in a well-designed book. Each page has a photograph or drawing, boxed information, different text fonts, large colorful dropped letters to begin the text, and headings in white letters within black boxes. On the CD accompanying this book are the sounds made by each instrument. Unusual anecdotes and amazing facts make the information in the book accessible and memorable. Other books in the series include *The Young Person's Guide to Ballet* and *The Young Person's Guide to Shakespeare,* both by Anita Ganeri.

Children's Press has two series by author/illustrator Mike Venezia. One is *Getting to Know the World's Greatest Artists* and the other is *Getting to Know the World's Greatest Composers,* and both are excellent. The books have 32 pages, like most picture books. The books on artists are stuffed with photos of the artists' paintings, cartoons about the paintings, and simply written but insightful descriptions to help children understand both the painter and the paintings. The books on composers are filled with photos and cartoons and text that captures the personality and achievements of the composers.

In an article about series books, Barbara Elleman (1995) says that the *Eyewitness Books,* a series by DK Publishing that includes many science titles as well as art titles, has set a new level of quality in nonfiction by placing sharp, close-up photos on white paper. With their clear labels, eye-catching design, and crisp writing, she says that these books herald a new age in photo nonfiction. Because of the stunning use of photography and the inclusion of so many graphic devices, the series is a standard by which to measure other series of this kind. Now similar books are being produced by Children's Press, Thomson Learning, Chelsea House, Millbrook, Reader's Digest, Time Life, and National Geographic. These series tackle a multitude of subjects, have straightforward material helpful for children's school assignments, and include a generous supply of full-color illustrations and other graphics. They may take a large topic—say, "ancient civilizations"—and relegate a whole book to each civilization.

Reference Books

The main types of references used by five- to eleven-year olds are dictionaries, encyclopedias, thesauruses, and atlases. Although their purposes are the same—to provide information—the quality of these books varies widely, and it's important to pick out excellent ones for the classroom. The better dictionaries are those that stress the concept that words are fascinating and open up ideas.

On the title page of *The Dorling Kindersley Children's Illustrated Dictionary* is a picture of a child jumping for joy. This title page sets the tone for the whole book, which is cheerful and exuberant. The Editor's Introduction explains that the pictures will help draw young readers into the book. The frontmatter has a section "All About Words," which explains all the parts of speech so that children will understand the notations that appear in italics under each word in the dictionary. The color photos are beautiful, and the design makes excellent use of boxes and rectangles of irregular size. The use of different fonts and type sizes to prioritize the headings in this section of the dictionary is especially helpful. For instance, the category heading "verbs" is in a larger type size than the headings "helping verbs" and "verb tenses." The "How to Use This Dictionary" section describes a dictionary game that can be used to involve young readers in using the words. In the body of the dictionary, many entries have a sentence or a picture to contextualize the word and make it more understandable to children.

Scholastic Children's Dictionary uses lots of color throughout and has a clear, appealing introduction to the dictionary section. A dictionary entry is shown close up, with each part of the entry explained in a nearby oval. The graphics and language make this introduction inviting, encouraging children to feel confident about using the dictionary. The body of the book has two columns of text on each page, in large (probably 12-point) type. Sentences are given only when the word might not be known. Two or three pictures are usually on each double page. The layout seems very spacious and thus very appealing. An occasional word history or language note interrupts the columns, helping to keep the pages interesting looking. Some words, such as *architecture*, are highlighted and have a full page devoted to them. In this particular definition, many different buildings are shown.

Webster's New World Children's Dictionary is not as colorful as the other dictionaries. But it does have double columns; pictures every few pages; a large, readable typeface; and sentences for words that may be unfamiliar (such as *authoritative*).

The American Heritage Student Dictionary, aimed at grades 6 to 9, is very dense, with smaller type than the other dictionaries. The whole book is in black and white. Because the dictionary is aimed at an older audience, there are few sentences accompanying the entries. The guide to using the dictionary is long and quite dense; however, the body of the dictionary has two columns of text on the inside of the page and photos and drawings in the outer column. Occasional notes on the history of a word, word building strategies, or regional variation add interest.

In the boxed feature Criteria for Evaluating Dictionaries are guidelines, developed by Margaret Mallett, for choosing a classroom dictionary. The boxed feature Criteria for Evaluating Encyclopedias contains Mallett's excellent advice on choosing classroom or school encyclopedias.

Early atlases and map books for young children should have clear, colorful, and accurate illustrations and an inviting, large format. The better books use features like information

---

Criteria for Evaluating *Dictionaries*

The following criteria were adapted from Mallett (1992, p. 30).

1. The concept that words are fascinating and open up ideas is reinforced.

2. The words are contextualized through sentences or pictures when needed.

3. The definitions are not always free of controversy. On the whole, they are illuminating rather than confusing or drearier than they need to be.

4. The definitions are clear, and the amount of knowledge assumed is appropriate for the age group for which the dictionary is intended.

5. The design and layout—including placement of pictures, type size, type font, and use of white space—add to the appeal and ease of use.

Criteria for Evaluating *Encyclopedias*

The following criteria were adapted from Mallett (1992, pp. 31–33).

1. Be aware of what entries elementary children are likely to use most, and look at these entries. Make sure they provide a good, clear treatment of the topics most important at the elementary level.

2. As in most kinds of nonfiction, look for sound factual information but also ideas and speculation that will awaken curiosity and interest.

3. Make sure the indexing is adequate, directing children to appropriate parts of the volumes.

4. See whether illustrations, photographs, and drawings are included to make the reference book inviting. Color illustrations are generally more numerous in updated encyclopedias. Sometimes the illustrations vary in quality from volume to volume.

5. Check out the language. Encyclopedias specially designed for the primary years usually avoid dry, reference-book language. Stories, bits of biography, and ideas for projects all help to interest and motivate. The long dreary sentences typical of the genre are offputting.

6. Look at the whole format and how the text is integrated with the illustrations.

7. Particularly for younger children, make sure the print is large enough.

8. Look for recently prepared or updated encyclopedias that avoid a narrow ethnocentric view of the world. Mallett mentions one encyclopedia that refers to the implications of colonialism under the term *aborigines*. Rather than assuming that the land was unoccupied, the entry makes it clear that the aborigines resented settlers taking over their land (p. 32).

boxes to help children make links between what they know and the new information. For upper elementary children, the best atlases are also clear, aesthetically pleasing, up to date, and accurate, but they have more detailed information—for example, political and religious background on countries and statistics on health and population.

A Note on Blended Books

Within the genre of nonfiction are books called blended books. Usually these books are fictionalized accounts of something, and so some people call them informational fiction. But because the author creates a story around the information, often these books, although based on true information or a true event, are categorized as fiction. One such case is the wonderful ***Letting Swift River Go,*** Jane Yolen's fictionalized account of building a dam on Swift River in Massachusetts. Carol Avery (1998), who used the book with primary school students, says, "Though the book is told from the perspective of a fictional character, the information about the process of creating a reservoir is so detailed that the book qualifies as nonfiction in our classroom. *Faction* is the word the children and I often use for books such as this" (p. 218).

There is another kind of blended book that does not get high marks from Penny Colman (1999), noted nonfiction writer for children. She says, "Needless to say, I reject the trend in recent years in which some writers add fiction to their nonfiction books in order to move the story along or to make it more dramatic or to introduce facts" (p. 217). The practice of including fiction, which then flows into nonfiction and back again, is known as "edutainment." Colman states that, although this practice is not readily accepted in adult literature, "It has been widely accepted in the world of children's literature, perhaps because of the emphasis on the informational aspect of nonfiction books instead of on the assurance that nothing is made-up" (p. 217).

Colman feels that a "note explaining what is and is not made-up does not justify labeling them nonfiction. It would be more appropriate to call them informational fiction or to make up a new category" (p. 217). This critique certainly seems to apply to the wildly popular *Magic School Bus* series, which teaches children science concepts through a story with fantastical elements. The author, Joanna Cole, is always very careful to explain what is and is not true, but I know of early elementary teachers who don't use the books because their children have trouble distinguishing the fact from the fiction. Perhaps Colman's idea of creating a new category could help solve this problem.

Selecting Nonfiction Books Across the Curricula

The following wonderful list is adapted from Mallett (1992, p. 77). It summarizes the things we need to think about as we choose nonfiction for our classrooms. Books should

- Be attractive in format and layout

- Integrate illustrations with the text

- Have clear, lively writing

- Not introduce too many new words all at once

- Embed in the context any words likely to be unfamiliar

- Provide efficient, easy-to-use retrieval devices, including a glossary, table of contents, and index

- For younger readers, have a natural chronological sequence—for example, the life cycle of a creature or the life story of a person

- Not stereotype, misrepresent, or omit females or ethnic minorities

- Provide factually reliable information that represents the present state of knowledge about a topic

- Not present as neutral any information or issues that can be seen from different viewpoints

- Not just present facts but also evaluate or question information

These guidelines offer many things to think about as we go about selecting the books to introduce to the children in our classrooms.

Favorite Authors and Illustrators of Nonfiction

Often a nonfiction writer or illustrator will develop a niche and mainly produce books on that subject—whether it be geological features or animals or how to do things. Given the amount of nonfiction produced, the list in the boxed feature Favorite Authors and Illustrators of Nonfiction merely scratches the surface of excellent writers and illustrators in this genre.

Aliki's cartoon-like figures always include a diverse group of characters. Her direct, understandable explanations engross and inform readers.

George Ancona is a photographer who writes nonfiction on topics as diverse as bananas, farm families, the barrio, and carnival celebrations. His books are filled with clear, beautiful photos.

Carolyn Arnold, a writer and photographer, creates photo essays about animals and natural history. The information, clearly presented in a skillful, straightforward manner, always includes fascinating details.

Brent Ashabranner, an award-winning author, brings his nonfiction to life by selecting facts carefully, using interesting interviews, and writing clear explanations.

Susan Campbell Bartoletti is an award-winning writer of nonfiction for upper elementary and middle school children. She is an excellent researcher whose work, accompanied by poignant photos, focuses on the welfare of children in the coal fields, on the streets, and in factories.

Barbara Bash's rich, glowing watercolors and lyrical prose combine to make her books informative and memorable. She most often writes on topics related to the natural world.

Janet Bode uses interviews with young people as the basis for her nonfiction books. The honest voices of young people, telling their own stories, appeal to children, who like to learn from other children.

Joanna Cole, a prolific author best known for her science writing in the *Magic School Bus* books, writes exciting, lively, sensitive books on a wide range of topics, from adoption and childbirth to marbles, jump-rope rhymes, and sharks.

Sneed Collard, a former biologist and computer scientist, writes impassioned books about science, natural history, and the environment, packed with fascinating information.

Leonard Everett Fisher, an award-winning author, creates carefully written nonfiction books filled with interesting information and his own black-and-white drawings.

Russell Freedman, a prolific, award-winning author, writes in inviting language on subjects from animal behavior to American history.

Jean Fritz's biographies and history books are packed with interesting information and are often humorously written. She is known for her lighthearted, clever titles and her ability to pique and keep readers' interest.

Jean Craighead George, well known for her award-winning fiction, is also a prolific writer of nonfiction about wildlife and the natural world. Her respect for the animals, plants, and ecosystems she writes about comes through in her well-researched, informative books.

Gail Gibbons's colorfully and accurately drawn subjects and clean, clear use of language make her books a treat to read.

James Cross Giblin immerses himself in his subjects, giving his books a you-are-there feel. He does a masterful job of distilling information, citing highlights, and fitting all the facts together.

Linda Granfield, writer and illustrator, makes the past exciting to readers through her selection of information and her illustrations. She writes about topics such as Canada, the circus, cowboys, and newspapers.

Cheryl Harness, writer and illustrator, creates books on our country's history. Her richly colored pictures are filled with action, and her language is lively, engaging, and informative.

James Haskins has written over 100 books, including biographies and nonfiction, often about history. He focuses on the African American experience, describing racism so that children can see it and understand it.

Ruth Heller's bold, colorful pictures and spare rhyming texts delight and inform.

Jill Krementz tells stories through photographs and interviews. Her engrossing books include the series *How It Feels (to Fight for Your Life, When a Parent Dies, to Be Adopted, When Parents Divorce).*

Kathleen Krull has a genius for digging up fascinating facts about famous people and presenting them in intriguing ways.

Susan Kuklin creates stunning books on such topics as dance and social issues, filled with her clear, bright photographs and spare, poetic text.

Elaine Landau is a prolific, award-winning nonfiction writer who uses intriguing vignettes to hook her readers. She writes about a wide range of topics, from the occult to disease to tropical rain forests.

(continued)

Patricia Lauber's vividly written texts, with their carefully chosen photos, evoke as well as answer questions, mainly about science and natural phenomena.

Bianca Lavies creates photo essays with readable text and stunning photos. The photos capture the fascination and appeal of the subject, which is often in the animal or insect kingdom.

David Macauley's detailed architectural illustrations and clear explanations combine to make children want to return again and again to his books.

Betsy Maestro's simply written texts, accompanied by colorful pictures and clear diagrams, delight and inform children.

Bruce McMillan, whose big, bright color photos are the hallmark of his books, has done the research and photography for his 35-plus nonfiction books.

Milton Meltzer is a prolific, award-winning author whose work on history, biography, and social reform contains startling information, sure to interest and involve readers.

Jim Murphy, winner of a Newbery Honor award, often adopts the point of view of young people in his carefully researched, lively books.

Dorothy Hinshaw Patent, a prolific author with a Ph.D. in zoology, writes mainly about animals. The best of her books are filled with

clear, interesting information and food for thought.

Laurence Pringle writes widely respected books for young people on biological and environmental subjects. He is also a photographer, and his highly readable books have won many awards.

Seymour Simon's startlingly clear explanations, examples, and comparisons easily draw readers into his books and keep them interested. This award-winning author examines subjects thoroughly and raises as many questions as he answers.

Invitations

Choose several of the following activities to complete:

1. Find a book on palindromes, and as a group figure several out. Then list all the skills you used to get to your conclusions. What kinds of language skills did you need?

2. After reading Children's Voices, reflect on the topics you were interested in in elementary school and middle school. What ignited or quelled your interest in nonfiction? As a teacher, which of the sections of the Dewey decimal system do you envision using in your classroom? Explain your thinking to your small group.

3. From the 790 classification, pick something you'd be interested in learning to do—fly a hot-air balloon, rollerblade, golf, juggle, and so on. Then skim several books until you find one that clearly explains the subject. What makes this book the best? Generate a list of some of the characteristics of the book. Share your findings with your group.

4. Read or skim three to five books on a state, country, or animal. What differences do you find? Evaluate the books, and share your evaluations with your group.

5. Bring in nonnarrative nonfiction books and record examples of the various nonfiction elements. Which ones help you the most in understanding the material? How important are the illustrations?

6. Choose one of the books described in the section on the 500 classification, and in your small group talk about how you could envision using it with a child or a class of children. Locate a nonnarrative nonfiction book; then find a poem and a picture storybook that extend or relate to the subject of the nonfiction book. What do you learn about each genre? Share your findings with your small group.

7. Read two or three narrative nonfiction books and develop criteria that capture the qualities you find in the books. Compare your criteria with those developed by other members of your small group.

8. Look up the same word in several children's dictionaries. What differences do you notice? Look at the layouts of the books. Which do you find most helpful? Share your findings with your small group.

Classroom Teaching Ideas

1. Have students find several nonfiction books on the same topic. Ask them to compare how they are formatted. Which has the most complete information? Which is most interesting? Which is most readable? Are some more suitable for earlier readers? This activity is best accomplished in small groups, where students can bounce ideas off one another.

2. Have students select a topic that interests them and write an informational book, with illustrations, to demonstrate their knowledge of the topic. At the conclusion of this activity, students could create a display of their books and invite guests from other classrooms to come in and browse and ask questions of the "expert."

3. Have students select a volume from the encyclopedia collection. Allow them about two minutes to locate something they would like to get more information about. Allow them another two minutes to read the information, and then ask them to close the text. Allow them another two minutes to write down everything that comes to mind from their reading. Share the results with the whole class. Six-minute research is fun as well as informative.

Internet and Text Resources

1. Real World Math and Science provides Internet projects for school children, as well as information on math and science. Find it at

http://enc.org/topics/realworld

2. National Geographic has something engaging for everyone. Like the magazine, the website is full of fascinating, well-documented information. Go to

www.nationalgeographic.com/

3. The U.S. Holocaust Memorial Museum in Washington, DC has a site that memorializes the same tragic events the museum does. You can find it at

www.ushmm.org/

4. Yahoo! Arts and Humanities includes recommended reading lists, reviews, and more on children's literature. The site also includes information about specific authors. It's at

http://d3.dir.dcx.yahoo.com/arts/humanities/literature/genres/children_s

5. NASA is not to be missed at

www.nasa.gov/

6. Pitsco Resources for Educators includes lesson plans, as well as ideas and information on Math and Science. Go to

www.pitsco.com/Resources/resframe.htm

7. **Richard Lederer's Verbivores** is a great site for anyone who loves words, as it contains many language links. Find it at

http://pw1.netcom.com/~rlederer/

8. **Literature in the Math and Science Classroom** provides book lists and resources. Go to

http://enc.org/topics/across/lit

9. Cooper, C. H. (1997). *Counting Your Way Through 1-2-3 Books and Activities.* Lanham, MD: Scarecrow.

10. Duthie, Christine (1996). *True Stories: Nonfiction Literacy in the Primary Classroom.* York, ME: Stenhouse.

11. Fredericks, A. D. (1998). *Science Adventures with Children's Literature: A Thematic Approach.* Englewood, CO: Teacher Ideas.

12. Freeman, Evelyn B., and Diane Goetz Person (1992). *Using Trade Books in the Elementary Classroom.* Urbana, IL: NCTE.

13. Harvey, S. (1998). *Nonfiction Matters: Reading, Writing, and Research in Grades 3–8.* York, ME: Stenhouse.

14. Wyatt, F. R., M. Coggins, and J. H. Imber (1998). *Popular NONFICTION Authors for Children: A Biographical and Thematic Guide.* Englewood, CO: Libraries Unlimited.

References

Avery, Carol (1998). "Nonfiction Books: Naturals for the Primary Level." In R. Bamford and J. Kristo (eds.), *Making Facts Come Alive: Choosing Quality Nonfiction Literature K–8.* Norwood, MA: Christopher Gordon.

Colman, Penny (1999). "Nonfiction Is Literature, Too." *The New Advocate 12,* 215–223.

Elleman, Barbara (1995). "Toward the 21st Century—Where Are Children's Books Going?" *The New Advocate 8,* 151–165.

Mallett, Margaret (1992). *Making Facts Matter: Reading Non-Fiction 5–11.* London: Paul Chapman.

McClure, Amy (1998). "Choosing Quality Nonfiction Literature: Examining Aspects of Writing Style." In R. Bamford and J. Kristo (eds.), *Making Facts Come Alive: Choosing Quality Nonfiction Literature K–8.* Norwood, MA: Christopher Gordon.

Spink, Kevin (1996). "The Aesthetics of Informational Reading." *The New Advocate 9,* 135–149.

Children's Books

Ada, Alma Flor (1997). *Gathering the Sun: An Alphabet in Spanish and English.* Trans. Rosa Zubizarreta. Illus. Simón Silva. New York: Lothrop, Lee & Shepard.

Aliki (1988). *Digging Up Dinosaurs.* New York: Harper & Row [1981, Crowell].

—— (1990). *Dinosaur Bones.* New York: HarperTrophy [1988].

—— (1999). *William Shakespeare & the Globe.* New York: HarperCollins.

American Heritage (1998). *The American Heritage Student Dictionary.* Boston: Houghton Mifflin.

Anderson, Joan (1997). *The American Family Farm: A Photo Essay.* Illus. by George Ancona. San Diego: Harcourt Brace.

Bang, Molly (1996). *Chattanooga Sludge.* San Diego: Harcourt Brace.

—— (1997). *Common Ground: The Water, Earth, and Air We Share.* New York: Scholastic Trade.

Banish, Roslyn (1992). *A Forever Family.* New York: HarperCollins.

Bash, Barbara (1990). *Desert Giant: The World of the Saguaro Cactus.* New York: Little Brown.

Bauer, Marion Dane (1992). *What's Your Story?: A Young Person's Guide to Writing Fiction.* New York: Clarion.

Bedard, Michael (1997). *The Divide.* Illus. Emily Arnold McCully. New York: Bantam.

Bial, Raymond (1993). *Amish Home*. Boston: Houghton Mifflin.

Bourgeois, Paulette (1998). *Garbage Collectors (In My Neighborhood)*. Illus. Kim LaFave. Niagara Falls, New York: Kids Can Press.

Bruchac, Joseph (1997). *Lasting Echoes: An Oral History of Native American People*. San Diego: Harcourt Brace.

Chermayeff, Ivan, and Jane Clark Chermayeff (1990). *First Words*. New York: Abrams.

Cohen, Daniel (1993). *Ghost in the House*. Illus. John Paul Caponigro. New York: Cobblehill.

Colman, Penny (1998). *Rosie the Riveter: Women Working on the Homefront in World War II*. New York: Crown.

Dewey, Jennifer Owings (1997). *Rattlesnake Dance: True Tales, Mysteries, and Rattlesnake Ceremonies*. Honesdale, PA: Boyds Mills.

DK Publishing (1994). *The Dorling Kindersley Children's Illustrated Dictionary*. New York: Author.

Dunbar, Joyce, and Gary Blythe (1996). *This Is the Star*. San Diego: Harcourt Brace.

Edwards, Michelle (1992). *Alef-bet: A Hebrew Alphabet Book*. New York: Lothrop, Lee & Shepard.

Feder, Jane (1995). *Table—Chair—Bear: A Book in Many Languages*. New York: Ticknor & Fields.

Feldman, Eve B. (1992). *Animals Don't Wear Pajamas: A Book About Sleeping*. Illus. Mary Beth Owens. New York: Holt.

Freedman, Russell (1998). *Martha Graham: A Dancer's Life*. New York: Clarion.

—— (1994). *The Wright Brothers: How They Invented the Airplane*. New York: Holiday.

Freymann, Saxton, and Joost Elffers (1999). *How Are You Peeling? Foods with Moods*. New York: Levine.

Ganeri, Anita (1998). *The Young Person's Guide to Ballet*. San Diego: Harcourt Brace.

—— (1999). *The Young Person's Guide to Shakespeare*. San Diego: Harcourt Brace.

—— (1996). *The Young Person's Guide to the Orchestra: Benjamin Britten's Composition on CD*. San Diego: Harcourt Brace.

George, Jean Craighead (1997). *Look to the North; A Wolf Pup Diary*. New York: HarperCollins.

Getz, David (1998). *Frozen Girl*. Illus. Peter McCarthy. New York: Holt.

Gibbons, Gail (1992). *The Great St. Lawrence Seaway*. New York: Morrow.

Girard, Linda Walvoord (1991). *Adoption Is for Always*. Illus. Judith Friedman. Morton Grove, IL: Whitman.

Grace, Catherine O'Neill (1997). *I Want to Be a Dancer*. San Diego: Harcourt Brace.

—— (1997). *I Want to Be an Engineer*. San Diego: Harcourt Brace.

—— (1999). *I Want to Be a Firefighter*. San Diego: Harcourt Brace.

Granfield, Linda (1994). *Extra! Extra! The Who, What, Where, When, and Why of Newspapers*. Illus. Bill Slavin. New York: Orchard.

Hall, Katy, and Lisa Eisenberg (1997). *Bunny Riddles*. Illus. Nicole Rubel. New York: Dial.

Halperin, Wendy Anderson (1998). *Once upon a company . . . A True Story*. New York: Orchard.

Hansen, Joyce, and Gary McGowan (1998). *Breaking Ground, Breaking Silence: The Story of New York's African Burial Ground*. New York: Holt.

Harness, Cheryl (1995). *The Amazing Impossible Erie Canal*. New York: Simon & Schuster.

Hautzig, David (1995). *1000 Miles in 12 Days: Pro Cyclists on Tour*. New York: Orchard.

Heller, Ruth (1993). *Chickens Aren't the Only Ones*. New York: Price Stern Sloan.

—— (1997). *Mine, All Mine: A Book About Pronouns*. New York: Grosset & Dunlap.

Hepworth, Cathi (1998). *Bug Off!* New York: Putnam.

Hintz, Martin (1996). *Farewell, John Barleycorn: Prohibition in the United States*. Minneapolis: Lerner.

Hopkins, Lee Bennett, ed. (1998). *All God's Children: A Book of Prayers*. San Diego: Harcourt Brace.

Hubbard, Jim (1996). *Lives Turned Upside Down: Homeless Children in Their Own Words and Photographs*. New York: Simon & Schuster.

Jefferis, David (1991). *Flight: Fliers and Flying Machines*. New York: Franklin Watts.

Jones, Bill T., and Susan Kuklin (1998). *Dance!* New York: Hyperion.

Kettelkamp, Larry (1996). *ETs and UFOs: Are They Real?* New York: Morrow.

King, Martin Luther, Jr., and Coretta Scott King (1997). *I Have a Dream.* New York: Scholastic Trade.

Krementz, Jill (1993). *How It Feels to Be Adopted.* New York: Knopf.

Krull, Kathleen (1999). *They Saw the Future: Oracles, Psychics, Scientists, Great Thinkers, and Pretty Good Guessers.* Illus. Kyrsten Brooker. New York: Atheneum.

Kuhn, Betsy (1999). *Angels of Mercy: The Army Nurses of World War II.* New York: Atheneum.

Kuskin, Karla (1993). *A Great Miracle Happened There: A Chanukah Story.* New York: Perlman.

Landau, Elaine (1993). *Yeti: Abominable Snowman of the Himalayas.* Brookfield, CT: Millbrook.

Lauber, Patricia (1998). *The True-or-False Book of Cats.* Illus. Rosalyn Schanzer. New York: National Geographic Society.

Lee, Huy Voun (1994). *At the Beach.* New York: Holt.

Leedy, Loreen (1990). *The Furry News: How to Make a Newspaper.* New York: Holiday.

Lewin, Ted (1996). *Market!* New York: Lothrop, Lee & Shepard.

Litchfield, Ada B. (1976). *A Button in Her Ear.* Illus. Eleanor Mill. Morton Grove, IL: Whitman.

Livingston, Carole (1978). *"Why Was I Adopted?"* Illus. Arthur Robins. New York: Stuart.

Luenn, Nancy (1998). *A Gift for Abuelita: Celebrating the Day of the Dead.* Illus. Robert Chapman. Flagstaff, AZ: Northland.

Macauley, David (1993). *Ship.* Boston: Houghton Mifflin.

MacDonald, Fiona (1992). *A Greek Temple (Inside Story).* Illus. Mark Bergin. Broomall, PA: Bedrick.

Maestro, Betsy, and Giulio Maestro (1990). *Taxi: A Book of City Words.* New York: Clarion.

McGovern, Ann (1984). *Night Dive.* Illus. Martin Scheiner and James B. Scheiner. New York: Macmillan.

Miller, Brandon Marie (1995). *Buffalo Gals: Women of the Old West.* Minneapolis: Lerner.

—— (1999). *Dressed for the Occasion: What Americans Wore 1620–1970.* Minneapolis: Lerner.

Miller, Debbie S. (1999). *Disappearing Lake: Nature's Magic in Denali National Park.* Illus. Jon Van Zyle. New York: Walker.

Miller, Mary Beth, and George Ancona (1991). *Handtalk School.* New York: Four Winds.

Monceaux, Morgan, and Ruth Katcher (1999). *My Heroes, My People: African Americans and Native Americans in the West.* New York: France Foster.

Murphy, Jim (1995). *The Great Fire.* New York: Scholastic.

Neufeldt, Victoria, ed. (1991). *Webster's New World Children's Dictionary.* New York: Macmillan.

Paulsen, Gary (1991). *Woodsong.* New York: Puffin [1985].

Phelan, Mary Kay (1971). *The Story of the Great Chicago Fire, 1871.* New York: Crowell.

Presson, Leslie (1996). *What in the World Is a Homophone?* Illus. Jo-Ellen Bosson. Hauppauge, New York: Barrons.

Ritter, Lawrence S. (1995). *Leagues Apart: The Men and Times of the Negro Baseball Leagues.* Illus. Richard Merkin. New York: Morrow.

Sandler, Martin W. (1996). *Inventors.* New York: HarperCollins.

—— (1994). *Pioneers.* New York: HarperCollins.

Scholastic (1996). *Scholastic Children's Dictionary.* New York: Author.

Schwartz, Alvin, ed. (1988). *The Cat's Elbow and Other Secret Languages.* Illus. Margot Zemach. New York: Farrar, Straus & Giroux.

Schwartz, David M. (1993). *How Much Is a Million?* Illus. Steven Kellogg. New York: Mulberry.

Silverstein, Alvin, Virginia Silverstein, and Laura Silverstein Nunn (1997). *Sickle Cell Anemia (Diseases and People).* New York: Enslow.

Simon, Norma (1997). *The Story of Hanukkah.* Illus. Leonid Gore. New York: HarperCollins.

Simon, Seymour (1998). *Bones: Our Skeletal System.* New York: Morrow.

—— (1997). *The Brain: Our Nervous System.* New York: Morrow.

—— (1995). *Earth Words: A Dictionary of the Environment.* Illus. Mark Kaplan. New York: HarperCollins.

—— (1998). *They Swim the Seas.* Illus. Elsa Warnick. New York: Browndeer.

Steele, Philip (1998). *The Best Book of Mummies.* New York: Kingfisher.

Tafuri, Nancy (1988). *Spots, Feathers, and Curly Tails.* New York: Greenwillow.

Terban, Marvin (1982). *Eight Ate: A Feast of Homonym Riddles.* Illus. Guilio Maestro. Boston: Houghton Mifflin.

Walker, Paul Robert (1992). *Bigfoot and Other Legendary Creatures.* Illus. William Noonan. San Diego: Harcourt Brace.

Warren, Andrea (1998). *Orphan Train Rider: One Boy's True Story.* Boston: Houghton Mifflin.

Wood, Ted (1997). *Ghosts of the Southwest: The Phantom Gunslinger and Other Real-Life Hauntings.* New York: Walker.

Yolen, Jane (1995). *Letting Swift River Go.* Illus. Barbara Cooney. New York: Little, Brown.

Biography and Autobiography

"I want to give characters to readers that they won't forget. I want the characters to stand up and walk into the lives of readers and never leave," says Jacqueline Briggs Martin (2000), author of **Snowflake Bentley,** about writing biography. She believes that writing a good biography demands much more than factual knowledge. "It's our passion that gives meaning to our work," she explains. When writing **Snowflake Bentley,** she wanted to create a book with as much emotional power as factual truth.

Biographies written by authors who are passionate about their subjects can make a powerful impact, leaving the reader with unforgettable memories of the subject and her or his life. Biographies can be written as mysteries, as adventures, as romances, as coming-of-age stories, or as sports stories. Because all lives involve elements of drama, biographies can make us sit on the edge of our seats, overwhelm us with emotion, surprise and startle us, and make us laugh out loud.

The charm and the value in biographies and autobiographies—the stories of people's lives—lie in the kinds of people we meet. Christine Duthie (1998) says that these books have the "unique ability to reach into the soil of human experience and till it for the reader; these genres embrace humanness and allow the reader to gaze at the world through the eyes and experiences of another" (p. 220). For children, she says, these genres also offer valuable role models who successfully face challenges and problems. Through biography, readers can deal with human experience, issues of historical significance, and social concerns. Children have strong views on the value of biography, as the boxed feature Children's Voices shows.

Children like biographies because . . .

I like to learn about how other people do stuff—for instance, Tony Hawk and how he skateboards. —Eric, 4th grade

I enjoy reading stuff about people I like. I read biographies about artists because I like to know what's happening or what's true. —Janae, 6th grade

They tell true stories about people you like. —Angel, 6th grade

They help you relate to people and the hardships they went through. —Allison, 7th grade

When someone writes about someone else's life and it's true, it's really inspirational. —Savontae, 7th grade

They give you absolute facts. —Chris, 7th grade

They tell how things were in different time periods, and I like comparing their lives to mine. —Christi, 7th grade

It tells of a person's life, and what happened before those people "hit the spotlight." I also like to read different versions of biographies to see what others wrote about these famous people. —Matt, 7th grade

They are about the people who succeed. Like it tells me I can succeed. —Rachael, 7th grade

The only biography I've read was Roald Dahl's, and I don't think anyone could match it; it was wonderful. —Danielle, 7th grade

Others don't like biographies because . . .

They have a tendency to be boring. They have too many facts and stories on events. —Jody, 7th grade

I don't really like reading lots of stuff on everything a person has done in their life. —Casey, 7th grade

One Biographer's Journey

Jacqueline Briggs Martin (2000) first heard of **Snowflake Bentley** when she read a four-page article on him in *Cricket* magazine in 1979. Both she and her children were enthralled with the man and his work. They loved the incongruity of his life, for without a mentor he "leaped from the world of the farm into the world of science. His passion and perseverance took him out of his world." She and her children remembered him every time it snowed in Iowa; they thought about how much he would like to experience the beauty of the snowfall with them. "We carried him around with us although we couldn't see him."

By 1995, she was ready to write his biography but still needed family stories, so she set out to look for any remaining Bentleys. Although she never did find any living family members (Wilson Bentley was a bachelor and had no descendants), she did find his articles and his obituary. But she wanted more. Martin wanted to hear Wilson Bentley's voice so that she could get it right in the book. She wanted to sit in his farm kitchen and talk to him, but he had died in 1935. What she did was read other writers from the same time and place, especially Robert Frost. In Frost's poems on northern New England, she could hear the voices of New England

CD-ROM

To locate other authors who write with *passion*, search for this word under Favorite Authors.

The precise woodcuts and the snowflake design wed the illustrations to the text and highlight the nature of Wilson Bentley.
(Cover of SNOWFLAKE BENTLEY by Jacqueline Briggs Martin. Jacket art © 1998 by Mary Azarian. Reprinted by permission of Houghton Mifflin Co. All rights reserved.)

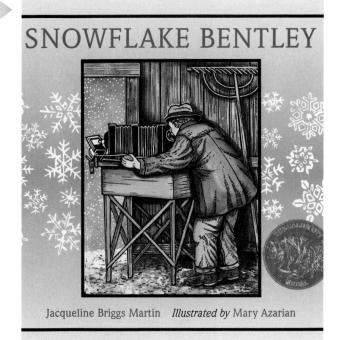

SNOWFLAKE BENTLEY

Jacqueline Briggs Martin   *Illustrated by* Mary Azarian

farmers in the dialogue. Frost helped put Martin in Bentley's neighborhood. Next, Bentley's own writings began coming to her through inter-library loan. She learned that he believed in "treasures of the snow" and felt that Vermont, which got up to 120 inches of snow each year, was one of "the favored regions of the earth." He felt so deeply about the beauty of the snow that he "couldn't afford to miss a single snowstorm." He looked at snowflakes under a microscope and photographed them so that the world wouldn't lose a single "miracle of beauty." She wanted to capture that love and that awe in the face of nature.

Martin initially thought she would make up characters such as a blacksmith, a dog, and a child to help her tell the story. But she got rid of the dog and other characters when they got in the way of "the beating heart of the story." Of course, she had too much information to fit into the 1,000-word format of a picture book, so some of the information she gathered ended up in sidebars. Martin explained how important the beginning and ending of stories are: "They carry lots of weight and have to be right." She wrote the beginning many, many different ways and knew it wasn't right. Finally, the image of the lantern came back to her, and she wrote a beginning that satisfied her. Because Martin's emphasis in her research was on finding the voice of the character, she could represent him truly and with love. Martin's care and passion for her subject make Bentley come to life for readers. This is the quality we seek in all the biographies we read.

Choices Biographers Make

Martin's experience gives us a glimpse of some of the decisions that biographers must make about what to put in and what to leave out of their stories. Milton Meltzer (1994), a prolific nonfiction writer, reminds us that biographers "must use to the full their freedom to select, to arrange, to depict. Like novelists, biographers seek to capture character in action, personality in performance" (p. 123). Thus, a biographer seeks to find patterns and order in the life he or she has studied. Sometimes this means making connections, foreshadowing, using juxtaposition, and holding back facts, all without distorting the truth. Meltzer says, "Using documentary evidence in imaginative ways without ever departing from its truth, the biographer tries to give a form to flux, to impose a design upon chronology" (p. 121). He or she creates the form into which the facts will go.

Some of the different forms biographers use can be seen by comparing three picture-book biographies about the same subject—Mark Twain. Each writer frames the life of Twain differently, emphasizing particular aspects of his life.

In *Mark Twain and the Queens of the Mississippi,* Cheryl Harness's focus is on the Mississippi River and Twain's relationship to it. The story begins with facts about the Mississippi, the people who inhabited her shores, and the beginning of the steamboat; it ends with what the Mississippi is like today. Throughout the book, Twain, who is first introduced on page 10, is shown mainly through his connection to the river. Even his most famous works are introduced through their links to the river. Harness skillfully uses the river as a central metaphor in Twain's life. In this somewhat somber picture of Twain, she leaves out much about his humor, his early writing successes, and his irrepressible nature, but she does create a strong picture of the power of the Mississippi and how it affected Mark Twain's life.

To find information on over 28,000 notable people, see the **Biographical Dictionary** at www.S9.com/biography/.

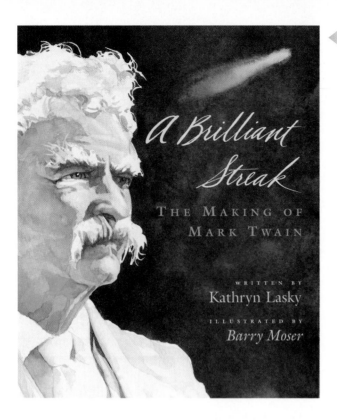

Mark Twain's determination is captured in Barry Moser's watercolors.
(Cover illustration from A BRILLIANT STREAK: THE MAKING OF MARK TWAIN by Kathryn Lasky Knight, illustrations copyright © 1998 by Barry Moser, reprinted by permission of Harcourt, Inc.)

CD-ROM

For a list of Kathryn Lasky's books, use the CD-ROM database.

In *Mark Twain? What Kind of Name Is That? A Story of Samuel Langhorne Clemens,* Robert Quackenbush uses an entirely different design, framing the story around Twain's affection for cats. We find out that Twain grew up with 19 cats! On every page, cartoons of cats provide asides—such as "Run! Here comes trouble!"—which reinforce what is said in the text. Much of the book explores what Sam was like as a child and how even his writings got him in trouble. His first 31 years are emphasized; only six pages are devoted to the entire rest of his life. On the last page, the author ties cats back into the body of the text, telling us that a cat occupied every room of the last house Twain lived in.

Kathryn Lasky's *A Brilliant Streak: The Making of Mark Twain,* illustrated by Barry Moser, begins and ends with Halley's Comet. In between, she illuminates the experiences, ideas, and actions associated with the "brilliant streak" that was Mark Twain. She shows us what made Twain tick, how he thought, what excited him, and how his imagination contributed to his brilliance. Most of the story is devoted to his boyhood and early adult years, showing how his experiences shaped him into the person he became. "He played hard, fought for every underdog, never stopped dreaming of buried treasure, learned to pilot a steamship from St. Louis to New Orleans, discovered war is stupid and politicians often more so" (p. 37). He always found the forbidden attractive and didn't worry about how others viewed him. This attitude allowed him to write with candor and humor, making fun of institutions that were "sacred cows" and considered inappropriate to mock.

Types of Biographies

Biographies are written in many different ways. Four common types of biographies are complete biographies, partial biographies, fictional biographies, and collective biographies.

Complete Biographies

Complete biographies look at the subject's whole life, focusing on the impact the person made through her or his life. *Isadora Dances,* by Rachel Isadora, is a complete biography written in the picture-book format. This brief biography of Isadora Duncan tells the story of a woman whose unique style of dance was not readily accepted by audiences at the turn of the 20th century. Duncan believed that true dance came from the soul, untouched and free. Because of Duncan and the dance school she founded, bare feet became as acceptable as shoes in dance. She never conformed to the ideas of the world in which she lived, and eventually the world came to understand her and the world changed.

Partial Biographies

Partial biographies focus on one significant event in the subject's life or one part of the subject's life. The majority of picture-book biographies are partial ones. When William Miller

(2000) writes biography, he tries to find the most important moment in the early life of the character. He thinks in terms of the inner conflicts of the character, not in terms of a beginning, a middle, and an end. "The bottom line is always the character and ending the story on a life-affirming note." In the partial biography **Richard Wright and the Library Card,** Miller focuses on how Wright managed to gain access to a library card even though black people at that time were not allowed to own a library card. He shows the impact this action had on Wright's life.

Fictional Biographies

Fictional biographies focus on a real person, but a story or context is created through which to tell the happenings. Although some fictional biographies are told from the subject's point of view, with a first-person or third-person narrator, divergent approaches may be used, such as viewing the person through the eyes of a neighbor child or a son or daughter; focusing on a significant event from the subject's life and adding characters and events that bring the subject into focus; inventing letters or diary entries by real or fictitious characters; and using art or poetry to tell the story of a creative life.

Riding Freedom, by Pam Muñoz Ryan, is a fictionalized account of the life of Charlotte Parkhurst, a woman who lived as a man so that she could do what she loved—work with horses. She also voted more than 50 years before any woman could vote in federal elections. To fill in details of early parts of Parkhurst's life about which there was no information, Ryan added characters to the story.

She's Wearing a Dead Bird on Her Head, by Kathryn Lasky, is a fictionalized account of the two women who founded the Audubon Society. This lively picture-book story of how the two women reacted to the fashion of decorating hats with whole bodies of birds has only one or two created incidents in it. The author explains in the Author's Note that, while there is no record of the two women having gone into a hat store to determine the source of the illegal feather trade, she based this created part of the story on the conventions of the times.

A very inventive fictional biography is *If a Bus Could Talk: The Story of Rosa Parks,* by Faith Ringgold. In this picture book, a bus tells of the events in Parks's life that caused her to be called the mother of the civil rights movement.

Occasionally, authors change the name of the subject of their biography when they fictionalize it. Milton Meltzer (1994) is one such author. His intended biography of Calvin Fairbank turned into the fictional *Underground Man* when he decided that his research hadn't unearthed enough evidence to do justice to the story. He simply could not make up characters, events, and dialogue that were in accord with the minimal facts. Changing the hero's name removed the barriers to invention. Although everything about the character is solidly rooted in fact, Meltzer could then "put ideas in his head, words in his mouth, and feelings in his heart that sprang from my own understanding of such a man's character and temperament" (p. 52).

Collective Biographies

Collective biographies give the reader glimpses into the lives of several subjects. Such collections are usually organized around the lives of subjects with a common ethnicity, gender, or occupation.

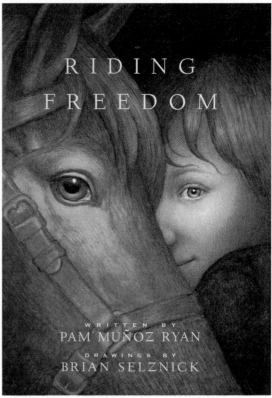

Charlotte's affinity for horses, so clearly shown on this cover, shapes the course of her life.

(From RIDING FREEDOM by Pam Muñoz Ryan. Cover art copyright © 1998 by Brian Selznick. Reprinted by permission of Scholastic Inc.)

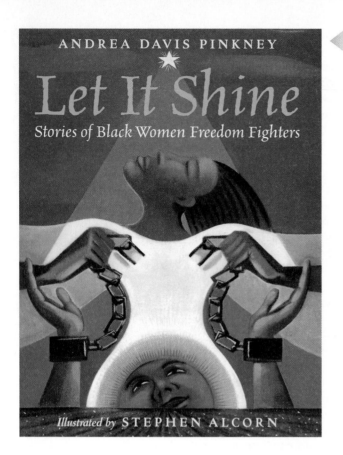

ANDREA DAVIS PINKNEY

Let It Shine

Stories of Black Women Freedom Fighters

Illustrated by STEPHEN ALCORN

Stephen Alcorn's illustration suggests the strength and joy that characterized the lives of many of these freedom fighters. (Cover illustration from LET IT SHINE: STORIES OF BLACK WOMEN FREEDOM FIGHTERS by Andrea Davis Pinkney, illustrations copyright © 2000 by Stephen Alcorn, reproduced by permission of Harcourt, Inc.)

Kathleen Krull has written several entertaining and informative collective biographies. Her *Lives of the Artists: Masterpieces, Messes (and What the Neighbors Thought)* contains fascinating tidbits about the lives and work of 16 artists. For instance, Leonardo da Vinci, a vegetarian, had to invent a water-operated alarm clock to get himself out of bed in the morning; Georgia O'Keefe killed rattlesnakes by chopping off their heads with hoes; and Andy Warhol never went out without wearing one of his 400 wigs. The caricatures by Kathryn Hewitt are priceless, and the many hints about the subjects' lives leave readers wanting to know more. In *Lives of the Musicians: Good Times, Bad Times (and What the Neighbors Thought),* we learn that the concerts of Clara Schumann, German composer and pianist, were so popular that police had to be called in to control the crowds. We also find out that Gilbert and Sullivan collaborated on their operettas by correspondence because they didn't like each other. Krull's *Lives of the Athletes: Thrills, Spills (and What the Neighbors Thought)* reveals what these 20 athletes were like as people. We learn mostly admirable but occasional quirky information about them. Babe Ruth was known for his stupendous belch. Babe Didrikson Zaharias's appearance and dress were always discussed before her considerable accomplishments in track and field or golf were. Each of these *Lives of* books is packed to the gills with information and remarkable illustrations by Kathryn Hewitt.

A quieter collection by Cynthia Rylant is called *Margaret, Frank, and Andy: Three Writers' Stories.* In her lean but lyrical language, Rylant takes us to the heart of the lives of the beloved Margaret Wise Brown, L. Frank Baum, and E. B. White. Young children who know the work of these authors will sit still to hear this lovely book read to them.

Gold Rush Women, a collection by Claire Rudolf Murphy and Jane G. Haigh, highlights the achievements of the women who participated in the Alaska gold rush. This lively book, peppered with interesting photographs, paints a much different portrait than we usually get. One interesting fact is that native women made significant contributions. *Girls Think of Everything: Stories of Ingenious Inventions by Woman,* by Catherine Thimmesh, describes what women have done in this scientific field. Collective biographies that focus on the achievements of people of color include *One More River to Cross: The Stories of Twelve Black Americans,* by Jim Haskins; *Let It Shine: Stories of Black Women Freedom Fighters,* by Andrea Davis Pinkney; and *Standing Tall: The Stories of Ten Hispanic Americans,* by Argentina Palacios. All are interesting and very readable, highlighting the events in the lives of subjects who are brought vividly to life.

Autobiographies

An autobiography is the story of a person's life written by that person. Because the whole retelling is from the subject's point of view, no people need be interviewed. But since memory is the main source of information, an autobiography can lead to a skewed view of the subject. Most writers of autobiography mention that the story is their impression of their own life; they know full well that other participants in their life might not see things the same way. Imagine how your own life story would vary, depending on whether it was

This memoir takes us into the heart of Harlem and the childhood of Walter Dean Myers, prolific writer of novels for children.
(From BAD BOY by Walter Dean Myers. Cover illustrated by Robert Andrew Parker. Used by permission of HarperCollins Publishers.)

written by you or by a jealous friend or hostile sibling. Interpretations of incidents and even events selected for inclusion would differ markedly. Thus, in an autobiography, we learn what the writer believes is important about his or her life.

Writers' autobiographies are often of interest to older children, who want to see what influences shaped the writer and ultimately the writing. Jerry Spinelli's *Knots in My Yo-Yo String: The Autobiography of a Kid* takes us into Spinelli's neighborhood, where we meet characters and places he often writes about. Walter Dean Myers's *Bad Boy: A Memoir* helps us see why Myers so clearly understands how kids can get in trouble and why so many of Myers's stories are set in New York. Other engaging autobiographies of writers include *A Girl from Yamhill: A Memoir,* by Beverly Cleary; *Homesick: My Own Story,* by Jean Fritz; *Boy: Tales of Childhood,* by Roald Dahl; *26 Fairmont Avenue,* by Tomie dePaola; *My Life in Dog Years* and *Guts: The True Story Behind the Hatchet and Brian Books,* by Gary Paulsen; *Bowman's Store: A Journey to Myself,* by Joseph Bruchac; and *The Abracadabra Kid: A Writer's Life,* by Sid Fleischman.

Life stories of entertainers are also popular. *Savion: My Life in Tap,* by Savion Glover and Bruce Weber, is the story of the young tap dancer who brought tap back to Broadway. With photographs of Savion and the story of his climb to the top of the tap world, this autobiography will command the attention of older readers.

Autobiography also includes extraordinary stories of ordinary people. *Taking Flight: My Story,* by Vicki Van Meter with Dan Gutman, is the partial autobiography of a twelve-year-old girl who flew across the Atlantic in a single-engine plane. *From Where I Sit: Making My Way with Cerebral Palsy,* by Shelley Nixon, tells of a child living with the condition. *Chinese Cinderella: The True Story of an Unwanted Daughter,* by Adeline Yen Mah, recounts her difficult early life in China. *Zlata's Diary: A Child's Life in Sarajevo,* by Zlata Filipovic, describes living in a city torn by war.

An interesting series of short autobiographies about children's writers is *Meet the Author,* published by Richard G. Owen. Each 32-page book, filled with photos of the author, describes the author's views on writing and how she or he became involved with it. Among the writers covered are Verna Aardema, Eve Bunting, Jean Fritz, Paul Goble, Karla Kuskin, Margaret Mahy, Patricia Polacco, Cynthia Rylant, and Jane Yolen. Young children could be motivated to turn to the author's work after reading one of these short books.

What Kinds of People Can Children Meet Through Biographies and Autobiographies?

Children can be brought into the center of the lives of many memorable people through biographies and autobiographies. Although they have most often been about famous people, they are beginning to be published about people who are not famous but whose lives are deemed worthy of being brought to the attention of a wider audience.

People Famous in Their Field

Just about every field imaginable is represented through biographies. Bessie Coleman, the first African American woman to earn a pilot's license (in 1921), is portrayed in *Fly, Bessie,*

Fly, by Lynn Joseph. Because of the discriminatory Jim Crow laws, Bessie had to go to Europe to get certified. This inspirational book ends with Bessie's air show over Chicago. A book aimed at older readers, ***Up in the Air: The Story of Bessie Coleman,*** by Philip S. Hart, tells more of Bessie's story. ***Flight,*** by Robert Burleigh, describes in clean, powerful language how Charles Lindbergh, another star in aviation, achieved the remarkable feat of flying nonstop and solo from New York to Paris in 1927. The book, which focuses only on the flight itself, is enhanced by the art of Mike Wimmer, whose use of light is stunning.

In sports, students can learn about the achievements of Wilma Rudolph in ***Wilma Unlimited,*** by Kathleen Krull. Overcoming crippling polio and an inability to walk, Rudolph became the first woman to win three gold medals in track at a single Olympics. The dazzling paintings by David Diaz make this book unforgettable. ***Home Run: The Story of Babe Ruth,*** by Robert Burleigh, is a poetic account of sports great Babe Ruth as he prepares to hit a home run. Mike Wimmer's illustrations are reminiscent of the work of Norman Rockwell—especially the picture of the crowd with looks of wonder and amazement on their faces. ***Satchel Paige,*** by Lesa Cline-Ransome, tells of the extraordinary pitcher who moved from the Negro Leagues in 1948 as racial barriers were crumbling. Walter Dean Myers's biography ***The Greatest: Muhammad Ali,*** about the legendary boxer, sets Ali's accomplishments in their historical and social context so that older readers can see how much Ali achieved.

Through biography, students can meet leaders in war, revolution, and social change. One of the few women ever acclaimed for military prowess is Joan of Arc. The inspirational ***Joan of Arc,*** written by Josephine Poole and illustrated by Angela Barrett, shows the peasant girl leading the French army to victory against the English. This gloriously illustrated book has rich colors and designs evocative of the 15th century. Although at the end Joan is, of course, burned, the author finishes the book in a stirring way: "But that [death] was not the end. A saint is like a star. A star and a saint shine forever" (unpaged).

Toussaint L'Ouverture: The Fight for Haiti's Freedom, by Walter Dean Myers, gives us another portrait of a courageous person. Through Jacob Lawrence's sequence of paintings, we see the uprising in Haiti and how L'Ouverture gave himself to this struggle involving both class and race. Through the story, we see the universal need to live freely and the importance of the struggle to achieve that freedom. Another person engaged in such a struggle in his own country of South Africa is Nelson Mandela. In the beautifully illustrated ***Mandela: From the Life of the South African Statesman,*** by Floyd Cooper, we learn of Mandela's early life, his introduction to apartheid when he moved to Johannesburg, and his efforts to end racist policies. This inspirational book encourages questioning as a way to the truth. One woman who fought hard—through diplomatic efforts and public speaking—for her country's right to govern itself was Princess Ka'iulani of Hawaii. Her struggle is detailed in ***Princess Ka'iulani: Hope of a Nation, Heart of a People,*** by Sharon Linnéa.

Biographies for older readers include two books on powerful women who were agents of change. In ***Ida B. Wells-Barnett: Powerhouse with a Pen,*** by Catherine A. Welch, we see this journalist take up the pen, give speeches, and help organize the NAACP to promote anti-lynching laws after her good friend was lynched. ***Mother Jones: Fierce Fighter for Worker's Rights,*** by Judith Pinkerton, gives us glimpses of the woman who, after living through the personal tragedy of losing her own husband and four children, worked ceaselessly for the downtrodden. She urged workers in such places as coal mines and textile mills to fight for their rights through labor unions.

Introducing children to literary greats through picture-book biographies can create interest in the work of the writer. In ***Coming Home: From the Life of Langston Hughes,*** Floyd Cooper's ability to write equals his ability to stun us with his gorgeous paintings. The rhyme and cadence of the language and the interaction of the words and illustrations help us to enter Langston's life and think as Langston did. The last picture in the book—of Langston looking pensively out a window in an apartment building—captures the joy, exuberance, and caring that this poet exhibited.

Another book that will whet students' appetites for work by the writer himself is ***Bard of Avon: The Story of William Shakespeare,*** by Diane Stanley and Peter Vennema. Although in picture-book format, this book aimed at older readers demonstrates Stanley's

CD-ROM

Find more books that are inspirational by searching Favorite Authors, using the word *inspirational.*

meticulous research and interest in her subject. Much has been written about Shakespeare, but because of their research Stanley and Vennema are able to highlight little-known but significant aspects of his life.

A longer biography for older readers, ***Dragonholder: The Life and Dreams (So Far) of Anne McCaffrey,*** by Todd J. McCaffrey, focuses on the family life of the woman famous in fantasy writing for her books on dragons. Another longer biography of a literary great is ***Young, Black, and Determined: A Biography of Lorraine Hansberry,*** by Patricia C. McKissack and Fredrick L. McKissack. In this book, readers learn that the playwright of ***Raisin in the Sun*** was also a hardworking activist, a brilliant essayist, and a supportive friend.

Students can be introduced to artists, entertainers, inventors, spiritual leaders, and scientists through biography. ***A Weekend with Diego Rivera,*** by Barbara Braun, is a different kind of biography. Written in the first person, the text tells of Rivera's love and respect for his country (Mexico) and its long traditions, dating back to the pre-Columbian era. This gorgeous book intersperses Rivera's paintings throughout, helping readers to learn not only about Rivera's life but also about the long tradition of art in Mexico. ***Story Painter: The Life of Jacob Lawrence,*** by John Duggleby, uses Lawrence's rich paintings to tell the story of his life. ***Vincent Van Gogh: Portrait of an Artist*** was lovingly written by Jan Greenberg and Sandra Jordan. Because both authors frequently write about art, they imbue this very engaging book with their passion for and understanding of painting. Older readers will be fascinated by ***Martha Graham: A Dancer's Life,*** by Russell Freedman; ***The Dancer Who Flew: A Memoir of Rudolf Nureyev,*** by Linda Maybarduk; ***Spellbinder: The Life of Harry Houdini,*** by Tom Lalicki; and ***Woody Guthrie: American Balladeer,*** by Janelle Yates.

The Real McCoy: The Life of an African-American Inventor, by Wendy Towle, tells of the life of the Canadian-born black inventor who studied engineering in Scotland and patented over 50 inventions, despite the obstacles he faced because of his race. When he couldn't get work as an engineer because of his race, he was hired as foreman/oilman by a railroad executive who had never heard of a college-educated black man. He eventually invented a lubricating cup that would automatically drip oil when it was needed so that trains no longer had to stop every few miles. Later, when train engineers would ask for this lubricating cup, they asked for the "real McCoy" because others had come out with an inferior product. McCoy also invented the portable ironing board, water sprinklers, and a better rubber heel.

The man who pushed the limits of photography is highlighted in ***Matthew Brady: His Life and Photographs,*** by George Sullivan. The older reader will especially enjoy seeing how Brady set up shots on Civil War battlegrounds and how rich the photo collection is. ***The Dalai Lama: A Biography of the Tibetan Spiritual and Political Leader,*** by Demi, focuses on the early years of the Dalai Lama's life. It has glorious pictures, which capture some of the mystery of his world. Although this book does not dwell on Buddhism, his words "My true religion is kindness" say volumes about the Dalai Lama and his philosophy. Another biography of a great spiritual and political leader is ***Gandhi,*** by Leonard Everett Fisher. Black-and-white paintings add to the somber, respectful tone of the book. Because of the brutal treatment of Indians by the English who ruled them, Gandhi devoted his life to helping India gain its independence from British rule. Preaching that "nonviolence is a weapon for the brave," Gandhi successfully used this technique to win great gains for India. Although his whole life is touched on, the events that cast light on his character are highlighted.

Starry Messenger, a Caldecott Honor Book by Peter Sis, is a biography of Galileo—scientist, mathematician, astronomer, philosopher, and physicist. The design of this stunning book encourages readers to wonder and want to know more about Galileo and his times. Along one side of the page is a column that contains not only the text, but also small illustrations and facts about Galileo and what it was like living at that time. The most fascinating part of this book is how and why Galileo challenged traditional beliefs. He proved that the earth was not fixed in one spot, as was widely believed, and that Aristotle was wrong about falling objects. Although a widely respected scientist and inventor, in his later years he was convicted of heresy by the Vatican. He spent the rest of his life under house arrest because he had shown that the earth was not the center of the solar system. In this memorable book, Galileo asks why he should believe "blindly and stupidly . . . and subject the freedom of my intellect to someone else who is just as liable to error as I am?" (unpaged).

Biographies: The Scientists *provides a list of hundreds of biographies of scientists at www.blupete.com/Literature/ Biographies/Science/Scients.htm.*

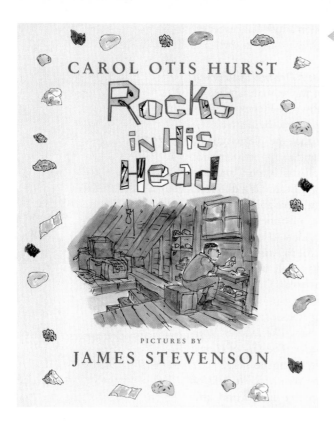

CAROL OTIS HURST

Rocks in His Head

PICTURES BY
JAMES STEVENSON

This biographical tale of the author's father encourages readers to follow their dreams and do what they love.
(From ROCKS IN HIS HEAD by Carol Otis Hurst. Cover art by James Stevenson. Used by permission of HarperCollins Publishers.)

Outstanding but Little-Known People

Through biography, children can be introduced to the achievements of people not generally well known. Carol Otis Hurst's biographical story, **Rocks in His Head,** tells of her father's lifelong passion for rock collecting. To keep the focus on his devotion to rocks, she chooses not to share his name. Instead, his ability to parlay this interest into a full-time museum job is emphasized to encourage youngsters to follow their dreams. In **Seeker of Knowledge: The Man Who Deciphered Egyptian Hieroglyphs,** by James Rumford, readers are introduced to Jean-François Champollion, whose dedication and passion caused him to devote his life to unraveling the secrets of hieroglyphs. In **Deep Blues: Bill Traylor, Self-Taught Artist,** Mary E. Lyons tells of the life and accomplishments of this 20th-century African American folk artist, who was born into slavery in 1856 and lived until he was 93. As Lyons tells his life story, she shows us Traylor's remarkable pictures, giving us a new way to think about what art is and what it means to be an artist. Aside from books on Harriet Tubman, not much is published about ex-slaves who became part of the emancipation effort. One exception is **Freedom River,** by Doreen Rappaport, the story of an ex-slave who became an active conductor on the underground railroad.

Few biographies are written about pirates, let alone female ones. But **The Pirate Queen,** by Emily Arnold McCully, is the story of the Irish Grania O'Malley, a fierce pirate and fighter who knew how to take matters into her own hands. When she wanted a sixth strategic castle, rather than fight for it, she asked the owner to marry her. He did. When she was treated brutally by the English, she went to London and approached Queen Elizabeth. She got what she wanted—a promise to give her lands back in return for defending the crown.

Kate Shelley: Bound for Legend, by Robert D. San Souci, focuses on one incident in Kate's life that illuminates her character. At 15, Kate helped avert a train disaster and became a national hero. With courage, determination, and grit, Kate battled her way to town through a savage storm to warn others that the railroad bridge was out and to get help for two men hanging onto the washed-out bridge. The pictures capture the gloom and savagery of the 1881 storm, and the subdued tones emphasize the serious story line.

Carter G. Woodson: The Man Who Put "Black" in American History, by Jim Haskins and Kathleen Benson, tells the story of a son of slaves who grew up to receive a Ph.D. from Harvard in history and devote his life to bringing the achievements of his race to the world's attention. **Stone Girl, Bone Girl: The Story of Mary Anning,** by Laurence Anholt, is about an English girl who found an ichthyosaur skeleton in 1811, when she was twelve. Important discoveries resulted from her find. Other books for older readers about little-known people include **Pick and Shovel Poet: The Journeys of Pascal D'Angelo,** by Jim Murphy, and **Heroine of the Titanic: The Real Unsinkable Molly Brown,** by Elaine Landau.

People Who Were Involved in Historical Events or Periods

Many biographies and autobiographies are written for older readers about particular eras, such as the Holocaust and the Civil War. When a time period fascinates students, they will be open to the very personal view a biography or autobiography gives. At the top of the list as far as number of biographies and autobiographies is the Holocaust. The wide array of books available allows readers to witness many different parts of the experience. **Parallel**

Find biographies of people who lived in the Old West at **New Perspectives on the West** at www.pbs.org/weta/thewest/people.

Surviving Hitler: A Boy in the Nazi Death Camps is the story of a 15-year-old boy who survives the death camps, using his people skills and his will.

(Cover art from *Surviving Hitler: A Boy in the Nazi Death Camps* by Andrea Warren. Used by permission of HarperCollins Publishers.)

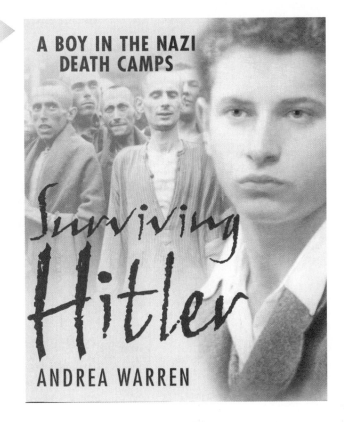

Journeys, by Eleanor H. Aver with Helen Waterford and Alfons Heck, focuses on two people, one in a concentration camp and one a member of Hitler's youth. Aver effectively contrasts their war experiences by placing their autobiographies in alternating chapters. Johanna Reiss's **The Upstairs Room** details what it was like to be in hiding during the war. *Alicia: My Story,* by Alicia Appleman-Jurman, relates the harrowing experiences of this young teen as she narrowly escaped death several times and witnessed the deaths of many of her family members. *Anna Is Still Here,* by Ida Vos, focuses on the slow process of recovery from the devastating experience of the Holocaust and the trauma of being a survivor. *Surviving Hitler: A Boy in the Nazi Death Camps,* by Andrea Warren, tells the story of a 15-year-old boy who survived three years in concentration camps. To give readers a sense of the time, Warren did extensive research, interviewed the survivor, and collected photographs.

Other titles about the Holocaust include *We Are Witnesses: Five Diaries of Teenagers Who Died in the Holocaust,* by Jacob Boas; *I Am a Star: Child of the Holocaust,* by Inge Auerbacher; *Hiding to Survive: Stories of Jewish Children Rescued from the Holocaust,* by Maxine B. Rosenberg; *Children in the Holocaust and World War II: Their Secret Diaries,* edited by Laurel Holliday; *I Have Lived a Thousand Years: Growing Up in the Holocaust,* by Livia Bitton-Jackson; *Four Perfect Pebbles: A Holocaust Story,* by Lila Perl and Marion Blumenthal Lazan; and *Upon the Head of the Goat: A Childhood in Hungary 1939–1944,* by Aranka Siegal.

Biographies from the Civil War era include those of ex-slaves, such as *I Was Born a Slave: The Story of Harriet Jacobs,* by Jennifer Fleischner; *My Family Shall Be Free! The Life of Peter Still,* by Dennis Brindell Fradin; and *Isaac Johnson: From Slave to Stonecutter,* by Hope Irvin Marston, which is based on Johnson's own book written in 1901.

Formats of Biographies

Biographies are written for students of all ages. To meet students' needs and interests, writers have formatted biographies as picture books, early readers, and chapter books.

Picture Books

Picture-book biographies depend on the illustrations and the text to bring the subject's story to life. When the blend works, we get a clear picture of the subject through both words and pictures, as in the earlier-mentioned **Coming Home: From the Life of Langston Hughes,** by Floyd Cooper.

Sadako, by Eleanor Coerr, is the story of a little girl in Hiroshima, hospitalized with the dreaded atom bomb disease, leukemia. Sadako races against time to fold 1,000 paper cranes in order to verify the legend that by doing so a sick person will become healthy. This lovely story shows what an impact one little girl had on others through the way she lived and died. Ed Young's delicate, dreamlike paintings bring the spirit of Sadako to life, touching our humanity and making us question war.

CD-ROM

To find more illustrators in Favorite Authors whose work can be described as *delicate* or *dreamlike,* use the word search feature.

Sojourner Truth's strength and ability to reach beyond her time are suggested by the cover illustration. ("Cover illustration" by R. Gregory Christie, copyright © 2000 by R. Gregory Christie, from ONLY PASSING THROUGH by Anne Rockwell, illustrated by R. Gregory Christie. Used by permission of Alfred A. Knopf Children's Books, a division of Random House, Inc.)

Anne Rockwell's *Only Passing Through: The Story of Sojourner Truth* is another biography in which the illustrations contribute to the power of the text. R. Gregory Christie's angular, dramatic pictures, which feature Truth's symbolically outsized head and hands, capture her anger, sorrow, and strength.

Early Readers

Because of the nature of early reader books, with their simple sentences, uncomplicated structure, and dependence on dialogue, biographies written in this format are mostly fictionalized. They focus on just one incident or event in the life of the subject and are often written from the point of view of someone other than the subject.

Finding Providence: The Story of Roger Williams, by Avi, is told from the point of view of Williams's young daughter. It focuses on the year 1635, in which her father, tried and found guilty of preaching dangerous ideas, flees into the wilderness rather than be sent back to England, where he would be imprisoned.

Snowshoe Thompson, by Nancy Smiler Levinson, tells the story of an immigrant who made some of the first skis in this country because he was determined to go across the mountains in winter to get the mail. Dialogue carries the weight of the story, told from the point of view of a little boy who desperately wants to hear from his father.

Chapter Books

Although on as wide a range of subjects as picture-book biographies, chapter-book biographies are generally longer. Because they are longer and because readers are older, these biographies can contain information about many more aspects of the subjects' lives. Excellent chapter-book biographies can be counted on to include the characteristics described in the boxed feature Criteria for Assessing Chapter-Book Biographies. In the boxed feature Applying the Criteria: Assessing Two Chapter-Book Biographies, these characteristics are discussed in terms of chapter books on Mary Breckinridge and Louis Braille.

Criteria for Assessing *Chapter-Book Biographies*

1. Will it appeal to both older and younger readers? Well-written biographies are sophisticated enough for the most advanced middle school readers but interesting enough to be used as read-alouds for younger readers.

2. Is the presentation interesting? Biographies written for children are often more interesting than "adult" biographies not only because of the plentiful photographs and drawings but also because of the concise, clear writing, without long, detailed "asides."

3. Are there any features that help the reader get a sense of the substance/worth of the biography and the commitment/interest of the author? These might include acknowledgments, information about the author, a foreword or afterword, photo credits, or an index.

Applying the Criteria *Assessing Two Chapter-Book Biographies*

Rosemary Wells's *Mary on Horseback: Three Mountain Stories,* illustrated by Peter McCarty, appeals to readers from early elementary through middle school. These three short stories about Mary Breckinridge, a horseback nurse in Appalachia, could be read aloud to youngsters at the earliest levels. They would find the stories appealing because two of them are told from the point of view of young children Mary helped. Older readers would become quickly involved in the fascinating subject matter and beautiful writing. The photos and gentle-looking pencil drawings that appear throughout this short book add to its appeal. The back inside flap tells us much about the author's passion for her subject. After reading Mary Breckinridge's autobiography, Rosemary Wells went to Kentucky and Wendover, Breckinridge's home, to learn more about her and the Frontier Nursing Service because she felt children should know Breckinridge's story. The acknowledgments provide evidence of Wells's thorough research efforts, while the photo credits (on the copyright page) attest to the authenticity of the photos.

Out of Darkness: The Story of Louis Braille, written by Russell Freedman and illustrated by Kate Kiesler, also appeals to a wide range of reading levels and interests. The writing is so crisp and clear that this chapter book could easily be read aloud to very young children, and the subject matter is so interesting that it would also appeal to older children. The presentation and design of the book invite the reader in. The ample space between the lines on every page evokes openness, making us feel as though we could be a part of the book. Each chapter is from four to eleven pages long and has one or more lovely pencil drawings, which add to the book's appeal. The author information on the back cover flap reminds us that Freedman wrote a biography that won the prestigious Newbery Award, as well as two other books that garnered Newbery Honor awards. In the acknowledgments, he thanks the Director of Information, American Foundation for the Blind; the Custodian of the Louis Braille Birthplace Municipal Museum; and the "hospitable people" of Coupvray (Braille's birthplace in France). Although there is no bibliography, it is apparent that Freedman did extensive research, and we can trust the authenticity of this story of the gentle but determined Braille.

Non-Series versus Series Biographies

Because publishers want to provide biographies of current celebrities and other people in whom there is popular interest, many series have been created. Unlike non-series biographies, these biographies follow a similar format from book to book.

Differences Between Series and Non-Series Biographies

Most writers of non-series biographies are intensely curious about the lives of the people they choose as their subjects. This is often the major characteristic separating a well-written biography from a mediocre biography. Series biographies can be more vulnerable to mediocrity, especially if the same person writes many books in the series without having a passion for the subject. In such books, the facts are usually accurate, but the reader isn't given a real feel for the person and sees only the outer aspects of her or his life. Although chapter-book biographies published in series have strengths of their own, often they lack information about the author and his or her interest in the subject. This is unfortunate, since such information can often help us decide whether we want to read a book.

A wide range of series biographies are published on sports and entertainment figures. Some are hurriedly published to capitalize on the current popularity of a specific celebrity, while others are carefully researched and written in lively prose. Many series sports biographies incorporate interesting information from the subject's life and illustrate why it is important. One quick way to evaluate whether a series book is worth your time is to read the first few pages of the text. If the opening commands your attention, then often the rest of the writing will be good too. If the introduction is simply a dull and plodding recitation of facts, this probably will not be a memorable book. One special strength of some series books is that they have a consultant to the series. If the consultant is a professional historian, then often the research will be scholarly and the sociopolitical context of the subjects' life will be included. However, sometimes a consultant merely writes an introduction for the whole series and her or his name does not ensure research or accuracy. Many series books are strong on graphic interest, created by the generous use of photos. Series books also tend to contain features that make it easy for students to find out more about the subject—lists of works or accomplishments of the subject, sources of further reading, and relevant websites. The wonderful thing about series biographies is that once you find one outstanding book in a series, you know that the other books will probably be of equal worth.

One thing I realized through my own reading is that if I really wanted to know about a subject, especially a celebrity, I read eagerly, without concern for writing style or research. Oftentimes the subject of a biography is enough to draw the reader into the book.

Comparison of Series and Non-Series Biographies of Eleanor Roosevelt

To see the range of quality that exists across series and non-series biographies, let's look at twelve biographies written about Eleanor Roosevelt. These biographies are from the children's section in one public library. This selection is representative of the mix of biographies often found in school libraries and public libraries, which don't contain just the newest books. After looking at the strengths and weaknesses of this group of biographies, you should be able to apply the process to similar mixes of biographies.

At the very high end of the quality spectrum is Russell Freedman's ***Eleanor Roosevelt: A Life of Discovery.*** In this beautifully written book, with glorious photographs, we learn about the interior life of Eleanor and come away feeling as if we knew the woman. Freedman turned not only to Eleanor's diaries but also to the diaries of her family and friends to give the reader a comprehensive look at this remarkable woman. This book is intended for readers who want more than just a bare-bones view of Eleanor for a report, since it encourages reflection on the qualities that contributed to Eleanor's personal achievements.

In addition to providing information about the setting, the cover illustration hints at Eleanor's loneliness as a child.

(From ELEANOR by Barbara Cooney, copyright ©1996 by Barbara Cooney. Used by permission of Viking Penguin, an imprint of Penguin Putnam Books for Young Readers, a division of Penguin Putnam Inc.)

Another non-series biography is the picture book *Eleanor,* by Barbara Cooney. While focusing on only a small part of Eleanor's life, it gives readers a sense of the person. Cooney's three years of research and her lovely writing allow readers to come away from the story knowing what Eleanor was like. This book would work well as an introduction to Eleanor Roosevelt because it gives readers a real empathy for her and a desire to know more about her. Students who have had such an introduction may then be able to read the more "facts only" biographies about her with interest because they care about her and can place the facts in an already established framework.

Several series biographies have been written for the early elementary child. David A. Adler's *A Picture Book of Eleanor Roosevelt,* part of the *Picture Book of . . .* series, contains many of the essential facts about Eleanor's life. Although it occasionally tells us how Eleanor felt, the connection with Eleanor is not strong enough to make readers care about her. *Eleanor Roosevelt: A Photo-Illustrated Biography,* by Lucile Davis, part of the *Photo-Illustrated Biography* series, is intended as a basic introduction for very young readers. Although it gives useful addresses and Internet sites for readers who want more information, what readers mainly get is a view of the roles Eleanor played. They do not come away from the book with a sense of what Eleanor was like as a person. Like the photo-illustrated biography by Davis, *Learning About Integrity from the Life of Eleanor Roosevelt,* by Nancy Ellwood, from the *Character-Building Book* series, takes a rather heavy-handed approach. In none of these books is any information given about the author's connection to or interest in the subject. In the case of all three of these books, it would be interesting to look at other books in the series and see how the format differs from book to book, if at all. Many of the headings seem as if they could fit almost any subject—"Growing Up," "Learning Integrity," "A Turning Point," and so on. This is one weakness of some series books: Instead of the subject's life shaping the framework of the book, the subject's life is made to fit into a specified format.

Eleanor Everywhere, by Monica Kulling, a chapter book that is part of the **Step into Reading** series, does not seem to be limited by the fact that it is intended for beginning readers. In this lively, engaging book of only 48 pages, the author gets to the heart of who Eleanor was. On the copyright page, the author says, "with grateful acknowledgment to Scott Rector, of the Eleanor Roosevelt National Historic Site in Hyde Park, New York, for his time and expertise in reviewing this book." This information lets us know that the author was very concerned with not misrepresenting her subject.

Eleanor Roosevelt: First Lady of the World, by Doris Faber, part of the **Women of Our Time** series, is a well-written and engaging book. In "About This Book" at the end, we learn that the author, as a reporter, actually covered many meetings that Eleanor attended and has been interested in her ever since. This book provides a good example of why a book should not be rejected by readers simply because of an early publication date. Published in 1985, it does a superior job of helping us understand Eleanor's fears and pain at being orphaned, allowing us to see her accomplishments in a new light. Faber is also a master of "showing, not telling," which seems to be lacking in some series biographies. Instead of telling us that Eleanor's mother-in-law was very proper and inflexible, Faber quotes her as saying to one of Eleanor's sons, "Don't say your hands are dirty. The proper word is soiled." That one detail shows us much about Sara Roosevelt. Although this book does not comment as much on the later accomplishments of Eleanor, it makes the reader want to know more about her.

One site devoted to achievements of women is **4000 Years of Women in Science.** *Find it at www.astr.ua.edu/4000ws/ 4000ws.html.*

The Importance of Eleanor Roosevelt, by Eileen Morey, part of the *Importance of Biography* series, focuses on Eleanor's accomplishments but does not help the reader develop empathy for her. Although this book has features that would help the reader locate more information about Eleanor, it is hard to imagine readers caring enough to pursue additional information. Nowhere in the book is reference made to any kind of connection of the author with the subject.

In *Stateswoman to the World: A Story about Eleanor Roosevelt,* by Maryann N. Weidt, part of Carolrhoda's *Creative Minds* series, readers are given a good sense of the energy Eleanor poured into causes, but any idea of what Eleanor was like as a person and what motivated her to engage in life as she did is missing. This author does seem connected to Eleanor because on the copyright page she writes: "Special thanks to . . . the Franklin D. Roosevelt Library at Hyde Park for . . . research assistance; Toni Gillman for her inspiring one-woman show; and Dr. Michael M. Piechowski for his psychological scholarship on the life of Eleanor." However, she seems to believe that she should not use narrative breaks to reflect on or evaluate the events in Eleanor's life. This results in a very factual approach, and we get no sense of how Eleanor reacted to events. In contrast, Barbara Cooney, in **Eleanor,** tells us, "Eleanor felt he [her father] was the only person in the world who really cared for her" (unpaged). In Weidt's book, the lack of such conclusions has the effect of distancing us from the subject.

Eleanor Roosevelt: Defender of Human Rights and Democracy, by David Winner, is a very dense retelling of Eleanor's life. It assumes much prior knowledge, since the introduction focuses on the Universal Declaration of Human Rights. Part of the *People Who Have Helped the World* series, the book is packed with photos, captions, quotes, and text, making the pages less than inviting. Upper elementary and middle school students would, however, find the information accurate, and the book would be a good source to use for a report. **Eleanor Roosevelt: First Lady of the 20th Century,** by Ted Gottfried, while part of a series called **Book Report Biographies,** does not share these vulnerabilities. First of all, this author has a connection to his subject, saying in his dedication that his mother gave him three things to remember: "Never mistreat a dog. Never trust a landlord. Never lose faith in Eleanor Roosevelt." Second, he is not hesitant to use narrative breaks to help readers understand how events affected Eleanor. He starts Chapter Two, "The seeds of unhappiness are sometimes planted before one is even born, in the unhappy lives of parents or grandparents. That's how it was for Eleanor Roosevelt" (p. 13). He goes on to share information about her mother's family life that appears in none of the other eleven biographies. He gives us a sense of Eleanor's insecurities and fears so that we can see how this shy child grew into the woman she did and what kinds of experiences helped her overcome her lonely early days.

Eleanor Roosevelt: Diplomat and Humanitarian, by Rachel Toor, is part of the series **American Women of Achievement,** which seeks to introduce women who have helped shape American history. Thus, it should come as no surprise that this book focuses heavily on Eleanor's human rights achievements. None of the other books explain her work in promoting passage of the anti-lynching law or her courage in standing up to Senator Joe McCarthy, who called everyone who opposed him a communist. This book clearly shows the wide-reaching effects of Eleanor's involvement. Although Toor gives us no indication of her passion for Eleanor's life, she communicates a sense of Eleanor as a person so that we can see what she had to overcome to make the kind of strides she did. Of nine chapters, only two focus on her early life, but what we learn helps us understand her. On page 25, after learning of her father's death, we read, "It seems likely that her painful youth engendered the compassion that would be her trademark in later years." Comments like these help readers to see patterns in her life. This book would be an excellent choice for upper elementary, middle school, and even high school students to read, to see what the human rights issues were in the first half of the 20th century and what Eleanor did to address them.

This overview demonstrates that high-quality biographies can be found among both series and non-series books. The purpose for which the reader is reading a biography will help determine which kind of biography is most appropriate. Even biographies that are not of high quality may be useful if children are reading or skimming them for information about particular people.

What Makes a Biography a Good One?

In the boxed feature Criteria for Evaluating Biographies, one additional criterion is added to the standard ones—author's involvement with the subject. The level of the author's interest in the life of the subject affects both the research and the writing of a biography. As I was reading the Eleanor Roosevelt biographies, I found that I wanted to rely on the author to help me make sense of her life. One thing that helped greatly was the inclusion of pivotal information about her early life that might explain her actions or feelings in later life. In Eleanor's case, two things seemed critical to me. One was whether or not the book included the incident in which the two-year-old Eleanor was thrown from the deck of a large ship into the arms of her father in a lifeboat below. This incident explained so much about her fear of water and timidity about participating in other physical activities. Also, if Eleanor's early life was not shown in enough detail, then the reader could not understand all she had to cope with in order to achieve what she did. The other important feature seemed to be whether or not the author was willing to use narrative breaks to insert reflections on events in the life of the subject so that readers could see patterns or understand the tenor of the times. In the boxed feature Applying the Criteria: Evaluating Two Biographies on page 374, the criteria for evaluating biographies are applied to two chapter-book biographies written about the same person—Maya Angelou. Both books are part of a series.

Criteria for Evaluating *Biographies*

1. **Plot or structure.** Is the book organized strictly chronologically, or are flashbacks present? What does the author do structurally to keep the reader interested? Are photos, letters, or quotations used? Are there narrative breaks? Do the events selected seem pivotal and/or important to the understanding of the subject?

2. **Character.** Does the author show the complexity of human beings, no matter how great they are? Do we learn about more than one dimension of the person? Are unhappy or unpleasant things that are part of people's lives included? Do we come to know the person and/or care about him or her?

3. **Setting.** Is the person placed in his or her historical context? This is often achieved by including photos, by putting key dates on a timeline, or by breaking away from the narrative from time to time to provide information such as "Most opportunities for training and further study were open only to men."

4. **Theme.** What themes in the subject's life does the author stress? Do the issues written about help the reader get to know the subject? Do you consider the themes selected important?

5. **Style—qualities of writing.** Does the author's voice come through loud and strong? Does the author move smoothly from one point to another, always keeping the reader involved? Is the language rich?

6. **Emotional impact.** Does the book connect us to our own humanity and that of others? Does this piece of literature make an impact? Are we moved by the beauty of the language, by the glimpses we get of the interiors of the characters, by the ideas and issues dealt with, or by the actions of the characters?

7. **Imaginative impact.** Does this book show possibilities, stretch thinking, pique curiosity, and make us think in different ways? By igniting or kindling our imagination, does this book help us jump over the boundaries of our own thinking?

8. **Authenticity.** What resources does the author use?

9. **Author's involvement with the subject.** What inspired the author to write about this subject? Did he or she seem enthusiastic about and involved with the person?

Applying the Criteria *Evaluating Two Biographies*

In the following discussion, ***Maya Angelou: Journey of the Heart,*** by Jayne Pettit, a ***Rainbow Biography,*** will be referred to as book A, and ***Maya Angelou,*** by Miles Shapiro, part of the ***Black Americans of Achievement*** series, will be referred to as book B.

1. **Plot or structure.** Book A opens with Angelou reading her poem at President Clinton's inauguration. This introduction is followed by a chronological telling of her life. The text is divided into titled chapters, and there are some photos.

After beginning with Angelou's early struggles—her wanting to be white and her longings—book B moves to her remarkable achievement of writing a poem for President Clinton's inauguration. After this first chapter, her life is explored chronologically. The text is divided into titled chapters, interspersed with photos that make clear the forms racism took at the time—for example, a picture of a railroad station with two doors, one marked "white" and one marked "colored." There are several narrative breaks in which the author reflects on events, with comments such as "The South had many ways to crush the spirit of its young black men and women" (p. 52).

2. **Character.** Angelou comes to life in book A mainly through the author's descriptions and through the excellent selection of quotes from her books. When she was reciting her inaugural poem, "She wrapped her soft, silken tones around each word, holding her listeners' attention with grace and ease" (p. 2). At the conclusion of the introductory chapter, we are told that her life "was a remarkable journey of a woman whose courage, faith, and determination had given her the strength to conquer her innermost fears in the face of overwhelming odds" (p. 3). The author lets us know throughout how Margarite (Angelou's childhood name) was reacting to the events in her life—for example, "The little boy and girl could not fight off their confusion about what was happening to them. Why had their parents decided to get a divorce and why were they sending their children so far away from home?" (p. 5).

Angelou comes to life in book B through the details the author shares, as well as the excellent selection of quotes from her books. We read, "Deeply honored but nervous by the enormity of what she was about to undertake, in the weeks leading up to the inauguration Angelou had repeatedly asked her fellow Americans to pray for her as she worked on her poem" (p. 16). That line helped me realize Angelou's humility, her longing to craft a poem that would have an effect on America, and her deep belief in prayer.

3. **Setting.** Angelou is placed in her historical context in book A, which describes the harshness of the racist society in which she was raised. We hear of the line that divided Stamps into white and black sections, of the fear Maya felt when she knew the Ku Klux Klan was out riding. The author doesn't step outside the narrative to offer readers any deeper understanding of the roots of or reasons for racism.

Like book A, book B places Angelou in her historical context, conveying the harshness of the racist society she grew up in. We even see photos of some of the horrors of the time, which give us a much fuller understanding of what it would have been like to live the life Angelou did. The author often steps outside the narrative to offer readers information and broaden their perspective on racism. For instance, the author tells us, "But for blacks in Stamps, as elsewhere in the South, the penalty for noncompliance with its racial codes could be dire. Poverty and economic dependence kept most blacks 'in their place,' but the underpinning of the entire system was violence and terror, as Maya and Bailey would soon learn" (p. 27).

4. **Theme.** Many themes are embedded in book A. We learn about the importance of family love, of acceptance, and of stamina and courage. We see that it is possible to survive a difficult childhood in a racist society and that it is not always necessary to take a straight career path.

The themes in book B are basically the same as in book A. One theme that book B emphasizes much more is the insidious, institutional racism that infected Angelou's life. This book also gives a clearer picture of how racism affected every aspect of her life because it deals so much more with the sociopolitical events of the time.

5. **Style—qualities of writing.** The good writing immediately drew me into book A. The author's voice emerges through her descriptions of Angelou and through the quotes she chooses to include. One, from a newspaper article, said that her lifetime experiences "left her with a fierce dignity and the rugged beauty of a cliff that has been battered by the wind but refuses to crumble" (p. 56).

Equally well written, book B pulses with the injustices of the time and with the triumphs of Maya Angelou. The author's voice, which is strong and sure, quickly enfolded me in the story.

6. ▶ **Emotional impact.** Book A engaged me and caused me to feel deeply for Angelou. I felt the emotional impact over and over as I read of Angelou's responses to events in her life.

In book B, the photos alone affected me emotionally, helping me see in a concrete way the horror of the times for Angelou and other blacks. I was there with Maya as a child, when she desperately wanted to be white because her race was so despised and when her grandmother humiliated her by taking her dress off to show Mrs. Flowers the intricate stitchwork she had put in it. I was there with Angelou as a teen, in her quest for male validation.

7. ▶ **Imaginative impact.** Book A immersed me in Angelou's life and raised questions. How could the white people who lived in Stamps participate in such overt discrimination? How can people be so tied in to prejudice and discrimination? Because the information was presented with such immediacy and caring, it caused me to think deeply.

My mind was swirling as I read book B. It made me wonder about how things would be different if blacks had been compensated for their years as slaves; think about how much more needs to be done in the white community to help people see how racism is still at work today; and lament how most of this history is left out of the books school children read. Because of the wealth of information,

all embedded in the context of the times, my mind and imagination seemed to explode.

8. ▶ **Authenticity.** In book A, not only are the books that Angelou wrote listed as sources, but so are five other books, interviews, and articles about Angelou. There were no apparent distortions, but I would have liked more comments on the racism of her time. For instance, we learn that her grandmother ran her own store, but we are not reminded how unusual this was at the time.

In book B, only the books Angelou wrote are listed as "Further Readings"; no others are mentioned as sources. But it is obvious that more sources were used, since James Baldwin is quoted, as are Angelou's words to students. This whole series was overseen by Nathan Irvin Huggins, one of American's leading scholars in the field of black studies, and his involvement shows in the way the history of the period is woven into the story.

9. ▶ **Author's involvement with the subject.** The author's involvement was apparent from the first page of book A in the loving way she talked about Angelou and the wonderful way she brought her to life. In the information about the author, we learn that she "was moved to write this biography when she heard Maya Angelou read her poem 'On the Pulse of the Morning' at the inauguration of President Bill Clinton" (back jacket flap).

In book B, the author's passion for his subject is evident in the loving way he shows Angelou living her life and in his dedication to helping us understand what the times were like.

Threats to Accuracy in Biographies

Accuracy can be elusive. Unless one has thoroughly studied the time period and subject, it is difficult to know whether a biography is accurate. We are told over and over again to pay attention to accuracy but given little help in figuring out how to evaluate this element. In her article "Accuracy in Biographies for Children," Judith V. Lechner (1997) reports that she has found four major kinds of inaccuracies in children's biographies: careless errors and oversimplification, inadequate data, unreliable sources, and societal expectations and taboos.

Careless Errors and Oversimplification

One biography of Rosie O'Donnell said that her mother died at age 37, just four days before Rosie's eleventh birthday; another said that her mother died at 36, just five days before Rosie's birthday. While the impact of the death is certainly more important than these minor details, the careless errors do raise the question of how such easily verifiable information could be wrong and what other information is inaccurate.

Oversimplification probably mars more children's biographies than careless errors do. For instance, in one book on Maya Angelou, the racial tenor of the times is greatly simplified, causing children to underestimate the destructive power of racism in the 1930s.

Inadequate Data

For links and information on famous deceased people, go to **Lives: The Biography Resource** *at www.amillionlives.com.*

Many times biographies are written without adequate evidence. Lechner (1997) mentions that, until recently, biographies of Pocahontas had been based on very little information, most of it from the point of view of the Jamestown settlers. In 1990, Helen Rountree's 20-year ethnohistorical study of the Powhatan Indian tribe (of which Pocahontas was a member) appeared. In *Pocahontas's People: The Powhatan Indians of Virginia Through Four Centuries,* Rountree is able to find evidence for only three of the six stories about Pocahontas that are commonly found in children's biographies. She finds no corroborating evidence for the most famous story—that Pocahontas saved John Smith. She challenges the rescue of John Smith by Pocahontas from an anthropological viewpoint, questioning whether "Powhatan welcomed and feasted a powerful guest whom his astute brother and his most trusted priests had tested and approved, and then suddenly, after 'a long consultation,' he tried to have that guest's brains clubbed out on an altar stone" (p. 232). She goes on to say that, although Pocahontas probably did see John Smith in January of 1608, it was not likely she saved his life. Lechner concludes, "Whether or not this incident occurred, the fact remains that accounts of Pocahontas's life are more legend than biography, with each generation retelling the story to suit their views about the origins of the United States and white people's relation to the Indians" (p. 233). The subjects of biographies based on inadequate data sometimes lived so long ago that few records exist. Other times, as in the case of slaves, they were not part of a population that was valued, and so few records exist about them. Biographers who have inadequate data should explain to readers the assumptions they made in cases where no data existed.

Unreliable Sources

Readers are probably most aware of unreliable sources because of all the media reports about "unauthorized" biographies of famous people. Think how different your biography would be if it were written by someone who despised you instead of someone who admired you. The two biographers would seek out different kinds of people to interview and use information that validated their viewpoint.

In children's books, this kind of unauthorized writing is not usually a problem. But when primary sources have been less than forthright in their accounts of a person's doings, the resulting biography will not be accurate. One case pointed out by Lechner is biographies of John Audubon, whose granddaughter heavily edited his journals. Several biographers used this source extensively, perhaps not realizing that Maria, in sanitizing the journals, removed aspects of Audubon's life that he and his heirs wished to hide. Readers are not usually going to be aware of these kinds of research issues. We have to hope that biographers have read enough scholarly works about their subjects to know whether there appears to have been any tampering with so-called primary sources.

Societal Expectations and Taboos

Since biographies and their authors tend to reflect the mores and values of their times, societal expectations and taboos are probably the biggest reason for inaccuracy in children's biographies. Even 25 years ago, biographies were usually quite bland because no mention was made of any qualities that would make the subject seem less than perfect. Fortunately for children, that has changed, and we now have such colorful biographies as those by Kathleen Krull.

The inaccuracy goes even deeper when biographies distort portrayals of whole groups of people so that the subject looks heroic. Milton Meltzer (1994), author of a biography of Christopher Columbus, tells us that the version of Columbus's life most often portrayed in children's literature is not consistent with documents left by Columbus and his men. As these documents make clear, "The idea that the Indians might have a right to determine their own way of life and to govern themselves never occurred to Columbus. His mission was to bring them under the authority of God and Spain, peacefully if he could, by the sword if necessary" (p. 159). Documents also reveal that the only relationship Columbus could imagine was that of master and slave, and that the Indians' lands were viewed as prizes to be seized and exploited. Meltzer urges, "Surely it is time for young people, as well as ourselves, to see the man in all his dimensions" (p. 163).

Meltzer goes on to explain that often inaccuracies in the portrayals of historical characters reflect the way the culture wishes to view them. By imbuing the people who made history with only positive characteristics, a culture shapes its stories to support positive views of its history. Meltzer (1998) points out that most biographies do not mention that Thomas Jefferson used young black children to make nails, working them twelve hours a day, six days a week. When they ran away out of boredom, he had them hunted down relentlessly and then had them flogged in front of the other slaves (p. 99). Meltzer also notes that earlier biographies of Theodore Roosevelt never brought up his racism, although TR was known to have called Indians "treacherous, vengeful, and fiendishly cruel savages" (p. 101). *Bully for You, Teddy Roosevelt!* is a biography of TR by Jean Fritz, published in 1991. Although based on excellent research, it never mentions his racism and even says that he "gave first place to his good friend, an old Indian-fighter, Leonard Wood" (p. 67), without commenting on this description.

Biographies are particularly likely to gloss over aspects of a subject's life that our society is uncomfortable dealing with, such as homosexuality. Omitting the fact that a famous person is gay or lesbian withholds information on the contributions that gay men and lesbians have made to our society and thus perpetuates inaccurate stereotypes. A few biographies today do deal openly with the homosexuality of the subject, such as **James Baldwin: Voice from Harlem,** by Ted Gottfried.

Favorite Authors and Illustrators of Biographies

A well-written biography is engaging, demonstrates the care and passion of the writer for the subject, and is based on research that uncovers the voice of the character. Many authors of biographies are fine writers of fiction and nonfiction who do not limit themselves to biography. Since many writers of excellent biographies work primarily in other genres, the list in the boxed feature Favorite Authors and Illustrators of Biographies is short.

Favorite Authors *and* Illustrators *of* Biographies

Robert Burleigh writes picture-book biographies that focus on a single incident in the life of his subjects. His poetic language and sure sense of detail bring his subjects roaring to life.

Demi, both an author and an illustrator of picture-book biographies, uses beautiful language and exquisite illustrations to capture the spirit of her subjects.

Russell Freedman, a masterful biographer and winner of the Newbery Medal for his biography of Lincoln, is known for his impeccable research and engaging, powerful writing.

Jean Fritz writes fast-paced biographies that are laced with humor. With her engaging writing, she delivers on her clever titles, which involve young readers.

Cheryl Harness writes biographies packed with information. Since she is also an artist, what she can't get in

(continued)

the text, she gets into the drawings. Reading her books is an adventure.

Kathleen Krull focuses on collective biographies. In the few pages she has to write about each character, readers are given memorable information based on meticulous research. Her light touch and engaging writing make her books favorites with students.

Kathryn Lasky's picture-book biographies demonstrate her ability to connect to her subjects and to frame the stories in such a way that readers view the subjects in new ways.

Patricia McKissack's prose sparkles with the energy and passion that characterize her subjects.

Milton Meltzer frequently writes about the lives of reformers and change agents. Clear, clean prose, love of research, and the desire to capture the essence of his subject in honest ways are the marks of his work.

Carolyn Meyer writes relatively long biographies based on research and interest in her subjects. She is mindful of accuracy in re-creating scenes.

Andrea Davis Pinkney writes lively, engrossing picture-book biographies, which demonstrate her love of language and willingness to play with it.

Diane Stanley, both a writer and an illustrator, is a careful researcher who gives her readers views of subjects never unearthed before. Her biographies are picture books but are intended for older readers.

Mike Venezia writes about the lives of artists. He involves young readers with cartoons and photographs and short snippets of the artists' lives.

Invitations

Choose several of the following activities to complete:

1. After reading several picture-book biographies, respond to them in terms of the characteristics you most admire in the subjects and the characteristics you would most like to have.

2. Write the story of a childhood incident you remember clearly that was also witnessed by someone else—a sibling, parent, coach, or friend. Then ask that person to write up the same incident. What differences do you notice? What implications do these differences have for accuracy in biographies and autobiographies?

3. Bring to class a picture-book biography. Share this biography with the rest of your group, and then as a group talk about what each subject would have to say to the subjects of the other books. What questions would they have? What actions of the others would they admire? What actions would they disagree with? Could they have been friends?

4. Read two or more biographies on one subject. Compare them in terms of the form the author uses to present the subject. Which did you prefer and why? Share your findings with your group.

5. In either the library or the bookstore, find a series book that is not mentioned in the chapter. Summarize the qualities present in the book and evaluate it. Is this a series you could see yourself using in a classroom? Explain your reactions to your small group.

6. After reading a biography, select several poems that the subject would like. Share the poems with your small group, explaining what appeal the poems would have to the subject of your biography. Do the same thing with a picture book or an informational book.

7. Do you remember reading biographies when you were in school? Compare your attitudes to those of the children in Children's Voices.

Classroom Teaching Ideas

1. Have students read a biography of someone they are interested in. Ask them to keep secret the identity of the person they read about. Decide on a day when everyone will come dressed as the person he or she read about. Allow students to ask questions of one another to discover each person's identity.

2. Many famous people have known each other—Thomas Jefferson and Alexander Hamilton, Ralph Waldo Emerson and Henry David Thoreau, as well as contemporary friends Oprah Winfrey and Maya Angelou, to name a few. Have students read biographies in pairs, with an eye for how friendships or rivalries are reported, and compare them. Have them report their findings to the class.

3. Select biographies of several people from the same time period who were not acquainted (for example, a slave and a Civil War general), and have students compare the events in their lives.

4. After reading several picture-book biographies or autobiographies together to see what kinds of events are presented in them, have students write and illustrate their own autobiography.

5. Have each student select someone within the class to write her or his biography. As a class, formulate a list of the kinds of information to be included. Remember to leave room for including something unique to the individual. When the biography is written, allow the student who is the focus of the work to review it for accuracy and inclusion of appropriate material. The subject may wish to illustrate it, or the author may illustrate it.

6. Ask students to think about writing a biography of someone in their family who is no longer living. Talk about how students would have to interview relatives, neighbors, or others who knew this person to get the information they would need.

7. Have students compare several biographies of the same person. How are they different? How are they similar? Do you get a clearer or more personal picture from one than from another? Which one is most interesting?

Internet and Text Resources

1. Biographies: The Scientists is a great source for hundreds of biographies of scientists. There is a brief description of their work, along with links to more sites that continue the study. Find it at

www.blupete.com/Literature/Biographies/Science/Scients.htm

2. Biographical Dictionary contains information on more than 28,000 notable men and women. Find it at

www.s9.com/biography/

3. Lives, the Biography Resource provides links and information only on famous people who have died. Go to

http://amillionlives.com

4. New Perspectives on the West is packed with biographies of the men and women who lived in the Old West. Find it at

www.pbs.org/weta/thewest/people

5. 4000 Years of Women in Science provides biographies of female scientists. Go to

www.astr.ua.edu/4000ws/4000ws.html

References

Daniels, Harvey (2002). *Literature Circles: Voice and Choice in Book Clubs and Reading Groups.* Portland, ME: Stenhouse.

Duthie, Christine (1998). "It's Just Plain Real! Introducing Children to Biography and Autobiography." *The New Advocate 11,* 219–227.

Lechner, Judith V. (1997). "Accuracy in Biographies for Children." *The New Advocate 10,* 229–242.

Martin, Jacqueline Briggs (2000). "When History Comes to Life: The Importance of Listening to the Past in Writing the Historical Caldecott Picture Book." IRA Annual Convention, Indianapolis, IN, April 30–May 5, 2000.

Meltzer, Milton (1998). "If the Fish Stinks." *The New Advocate 11,* 97–105.

—— (1994). *Nonfiction for the Classroom.* New York: Teachers College Press.

Miller, William (2000). "Journeys and Quests: Themes That Bring Literature to Life for Young Adults." IRA Annual Convention, Indianapolis, IN, April 30–May 5, 2000.

Rountree, Helen (1990). *Pocahontas's People: The Powhatan Indians of Virginia Through Four Centuries.* Norman: University of Oklahoma.

Children's Books

Adler, David A. (1991). *A Picture Book of Eleanor Roosevelt.* Illus. Robert Casilla. New York: Holiday.

Anholt, Laurence (1999). *Stone Girl, Bone Girl: The Story of Mary Anning.* Illus. Sheila Moxley. New York: Orchard.

Appleman-Jurman, Alicia (1998). *Alicia: My Story.* New York: Bantam.

Auerbacher, Inge (1993). *I Am a Star: Child of the Holocaust.* Illus. Israel Bernbaum. New York: Puffin.

Avi (1997). *Finding Providence: The Story of Roger Williams.* Illus. James Watling. New York: HarperTrophy.

Ayer, Eleanor H., with Helen Waterford and Alfons Heck (2000). *Parallel Journeys.* New York: Aladdin.

Bitton-Jackson, Livia (1997). *I Have Lived a Thousand Years: Growing Up in the Holocaust.* New York: Simon & Schuster.

Boas, Jacob (1995). *We Are Witnesses: Five Diaries of Teenagers Who Died in the Holocaust.* New York: Holt.

Braun, Barbara (1994). *A Weekend with Diego Rivera.* New York: Rizzoli.

Bruchac, Joseph (2001). *Bowman's Store: A Journey to Myself.* New York: Lee & Low.

Burleigh, Robert (1991). *Flight.* Illus. Mike Wimmer. New York: Putnam & Grosset.

—— (1998). *Home Run.* Illus. Mike Wimmer. San Diego: Harcourt Brace.

Cleary, Beverly (1988). *A Girl from Yamhill: A Memoir.* New York: Morrow.

Cline-Ransome, Lesa (2000). *Satchel Paige.* Illus. James E. Ransome. New York: Simon & Schuster.

Coerr, Eleanor (1993). *Sadako.* Illus. Ed Young. New York: Putnam.

Cooney, Barbara (1996). *Eleanor.* New York: Viking.

Cooper, Floyd (1994). *Coming Home: From the Life of Langston Hughes.* New York: Philomel.

—— (1996). *Mandela: From the Life of the South African Statesman.* New York: Philomel.

Dahl, Roald (1984). *Boy: Tales of Childhood.* New York: Farrar, Straus & Giroux.

Davis, Lucile (1998). *Eleanor Roosevelt: A Photo-Illustrated Biography.* Mankato, MN: Bridgestone.

Demi (1998). *The Dalai Lama.* New York: Holt.

dePaola, Tomie (1999). *26 Fairmont Avenue.* New York: Putnam.

Duggleby, John (1998). *Story Painter: The Life of Jacob Lawrence.* San Francisco: Chronicle.

Ellwood, Nancy (1999). *Learning About Integrity from the Life of Eleanor Roosevelt (Character Building).* New York: Rosen.

Faber, Doris (1985). *Eleanor Roosevelt: First Lady of the World (Women of Our Time).* Illus. Donna Ruff. New York: Viking Kestral.

Filipovic, Zlata (1994). *Zlata's Diary: A Child's Life in Sarajevo.* New York: Scholastic.

Fisher, Leonard Everett (1995). *Gandhi.* New York: Atheneum.

Fleischman, Sid (1999). *The Abracadabra Kid: A Writer's Life.* New York: Greenwillow.

Fleischner, Jennifer (1997). *I Was Born a Slave: The Story of Harriet Jacobs.* Illus. Melanie Reim. Brookfield, CT: Millbrook.

Fradin, Dennis Brindell (2001). *My Family Shall Be Free! The Life of Peter Still.* New York: HarperCollins.

Freedman, Russell (1993). *Eleanor Roosevelt: A Life of Discovery.* New York: Clarion.

—— (1998). *Martha Graham: A Dancer's Life.* New York: Clarion.

—— (1997). *Out of Darkness: The Story of Louis Braille.* Illus. Kate Kiesler. New York: Clarion.

Fritz, Jean (1991). *Bully for You, Teddy Roosevelt!* Illus. Mike Wimmer. New York: Putnam.

—— (1987). *Homesick: My Own Story.* Illus. Margot Tomes. Santa Barbara, CA: Cornerstone.

Glover, Savion, and Bruce Weber (2000). *Savion: My Life in Tap.* New York: Morrow.

Gottfried, Ted (1997). *Eleanor Roosevelt: First Lady of the 20th Century (Book Report Biography).* New York: Watts.

—— (1997). *James Baldwin: Voice from Harlem.* New York: Watts.

Greenberg, Jan, and Sandra Jordan (2001). *Vincent Van Gogh: Portrait of an Artist.* New York: Delacorte.

Harness, Cheryl (1998). *Mark Twain and the Queens of the Mississippi.* New York: Simon & Schuster.

Hart, Philip S. (1996). *Up in the Air: The Story of Bessie Coleman.* Minneapolis: Carolrhoda.

Haskins, Jim, and Kathleen Benson (2000). *Carter G. Woodson: The Man Who Put "Black" in American History.* Illus. Melanie Reim. Brookfield, CT: Millbrook.

—— (1992). *One More River to Cross: The Stories of Twelve Black Americans.* New York: Scholastic.

Holliday, Laurel, ed. (1996). *Children in the Holocaust and World War II: Their Secret Diaries.* New York: Washington Square.

Hurst, Carol Otis (2001). *Rocks in His Head.* Illus. James Stevenson. New York: Greenwillow.

Isadora, Rachel (1998). *Isadora Dances.* New York: Viking.

Joseph, Lynn (1998). *Fly, Bessie, Fly.* Illus. Yvonne Buchanan. New York: Simon & Schuster.

Krull, Kathleen (1995). *Lives of Artists: Masterpieces, Messes (and What the Neighbors Thought).* Illus. Kathryn Hewitt. San Diego: Harcourt Brace.

—— (1995). *Lives of the Athletes: Thrills, Spills (and What the Neighbors Thought).* Illus. Kathryn Hewitt. San Diego: Harcourt Brace.

—— (1993). *Lives of the Musicians: Good Times, Bad Times (and What the Neighbors Thought).* Illus. Kathryn Hewitt. San Diego: Harcourt Brace.

—— (1996). *Wilma Unlimited: How Wilma Rudolph Became the World's Fastest Woman.* Illus. David Diaz. San Diego: Harcourt Brace.

Kulling, Monica (1999). *Eleanor Everywhere: The Life of Eleanor Roosevelt.* Illus. Cliff Spohn. New York: Random.

Lalicki, Tom (2000). *Spellbinder: The Life of Harry Houdini.* New York: Holiday.

Landau, Elaine (2001). *Heroine of the Titanic: The Real Unsinkable Molly Brown.* New York: Clarion.

Lasky, Kathryn (1998). *A Brilliant Streak: The Making of Mark Twain.* Illus. Barry Moser. San Diego: Harcourt Brace.

—— (1995). *She's Wearing a Dead Bird on Her Head!* Illus. David Catrow. New York: Hyperion.

Levinson, Nancy Smiler (1992). *Snowshoe Thompson.* Illus. Joan Sandin. New York: HarperTrophy.

Linnéa, Sharon (1999). *Princess Ka'iulani: Hope of a Nation, Heart of a People.* Grand Rapids, MI: Eerdman.

Lyons, Mary E. (1994). *Deep Blues: Bill Traylor, Self-Taught Artist.* New York: Scribner.

Mah, Adeline Yen (1999). *Chinese Cinderella: The True Story of an Unwanted Daughter.* New York: Delacorte.

Marston, Hope Irvin (1995). *Isaac Johnson: From Slave to Stonecutter.* New York: Dutton.

Martin, Jacqueline Briggs (1998). *Snowflake Bentley.* Illus. Mary Azarian. Boston: Houghton Mifflin.

Maybarduk, Linda (1999). *The Dancer Who Flew: A Memoir of Rudolf Nureyev.* New York: Ballantine.

McCaffrey, Todd J. (1999). *Dragonholder: The Life and Dreams (So Far) of Anne McCaffrey.* New York: Ballantine.

McCully, Emily Arnold (1995). *The Pirate Queen.* New York: Putnam.

McKissack, Patricia C., and Fredrick L. McKissack (1998). *Young, Black, and Determined: A Biography of Lorraine Hansberry.* New York: Holiday.

Meltzer, Milton (1990). *Underground Man.* San Diego: Harcourt Brace.

Miller, William (1997). *Richard Wright and the Library Card.* Illus. R. Gregory Christie. New York: Lee & Low.

Morey, Eileen (1998). *The Importance of Eleanor Roosevelt.* San Diego: Lucent.

Murphy, Claire Rudolf, and Jane G. Haigh (1997). *Gold Rush Women.* Seattle: Alaska Northwest.

Murphy, Jim (2000). *Pick and Shovel Poet: The Journeys of Pascal D'Angelo.* New York: Clarion.

Myers, Walter Dean (2001). *Bad Boy: A Memoir.* New York: HarperCollins.

—— (2001). *The Greatest: Muhammed Ali.* New York: Scholastic.

—— (1996). *Toussaint L'Ouverture: The Fight for Haiti's Freedom.* Illus. Jacob Lawrence. New York: Simon & Schuster.

Nixon, Shelley (1999). *From Where I Sit: Making My Way with Cerebral Palsy.* New York: Scholastic.

Palacios, Argentina (1994). *Standing Tall: The Stories of Ten Hispanic Americans.* New York: Scholastic.

Paulsen, Gary (2001). *Guts: The True Stories Behind Hatchet and the Brian Books.* New York: Delacorte.

—— (1999). *My Life in Dog Years.* New York: Yearling.

Perl, Lila, and Marion Blumenthal Lazan (1996). *Four Perfect Pebbles: A Holocaust Story.* New York: Greenwillow.

Pettit, Jayne (1996). *Maya Angelou: Journey of the Heart.* New York: Lodestar.

Pinkerton, Judith (1996). *Mother Jones: Fierce Fighter for Worker's Rights.* Minneapolis: Lerner.

Pinkney, Andrea Davis (2000). *Let It Shine: Stories of Black Women Freedom Fighters.* Illus. Stephen Alcorn. San Diego: Harcourt.

Poole, Josephine (1998). *Joan of Arc.* Illus. Angela Barrett. New York: Knopf.

Quackenbush, Robert (1984). *Mark Twain? What Kind of Name Is That? A Story of Samuel Langhorne Clemens.* Englewood Cliffs, NJ: Prentice-Hall.

Rappaport, Doreen (2000). *Freedom River.* Illus. Bryan Collier. New York: Jump at the Sun.

Reiss, Johanna (1973). *The Upstairs Room.* Boston: G. K. Hall.

Ringgold, Faith (1999). *If a Bus Could Talk: The Story of Rosa Parks.* New York: Simon & Schuster.

Rockwell, Anne (2000). *Only Passing Through: The Story of Sojourner Truth.* Illus. R. Gregory Christie. New York: Knopf.

Rosenberg, Maxine B. (1998). *Hiding to Survive: Stories of Jewish Children Rescued from the Holocaust.* Boston: Houghton Mifflin.

Rumford, James (2000). *Seeker of Knowledge: The Man Who Deciphered Egyptian Hieroglyphs.* Boston: Houghton Mifflin.

Ryan, Pam Muñoz (1998). *Riding Freedom.* Illus. Brian Selznick. New York: Scholastic.

Rylant, Cynthia (1996). *Margaret, Frank, and Andy: Three Writers' Stories.* San Diego: Harcourt Brace.

San Souci, Robert D. (1995). *Kate Shelley: Bound for Legend.* Illus. Max Ginsburg. New York: Dial.

Shapiro, Miles (1994). *Maya Angelou.* Bromall, PA: Chelsea.

Siegal, Aranka (1999). *Upon the Head of the Goat: A Childhood in Hungary 1939–1944.* New York: Econo-Clad [1981, Farrar, Straus & Giroux].

Sis, Peter (1996). *Starry Messenger.* New York: Farrar, Straus & Giroux.

Spinelli, Jerry (1998). *Knots in My Yo-Yo String: The Autobiography of a Kid.* New York: Knopf.

Stanley, Diane, and Peter Vennema (1992). *Bard of Avon: The Story of William Shakespeare.* Illus. Diane Stanley. New York: Morrow.

Sullivan, George (1994). *Matthew Brady: His Life and Photographs.* New York: Cobblehill.

Thimmesh, Catherine (2000). *Girls Think of Everything: Stories of Ingenious Inventions by Women.* Illus. Melissa Sweet. Boston: Houghton Mifflin.

Toor, Rachel (1989). *Eleanor Roosevelt: Diplomat and Humanitarian (American Women of Achievement).* New York: Chelsea.

Towle, Wendy (1993). *The Real McCoy: The Life of an African-American Inventor.* Illus. Wil Clay. New York: Scholastic.

Van Meter, Vicki, with Dan Gutman (1995). *Taking Flight: My Story.* New York: Viking.

Vos, Ida (1993). *Anna Is Still Here.* Boston: Houghton Mifflin.

Warren, Andrea (2001). *Surviving Hitler: A Boy in the Nazi Death Camps.* New York: HarperCollins.

Weidt, Maryann N. (1991). *Stateswoman to the World: A Story about Eleanor Roosevelt.* Illus. Lydia M. Anderson. Minneapolis: Carolrhoda.

Welch, Catherine A. (1997) *Ida B. Wells-Barnett: Powerhouse with a Pen.* Minneapolis: Carolrhoda.

Wells, Rosemary (1998). *Mary on Horseback: Three Mountain Stories.* Illus. Peter McCarty. New York: Dial.

Winner, David (1991). *Defender of Human Rights and Democracy: Eleanor Roosevelt.* Milwaukee: Gareth Stevens.

Yates, Janelle (1995). *Woody Guthrie: American Balladeer.* Staten Island, NY: Ward Hill.

Wrapping It Up

Now that you've finished the text and immersed yourself in children's books, I hope you've discovered authors, illustrators, and poets whose works you love and want to share with your future students and with your classmates. One way of pulling together the information you've studied is to try one of these ending invitations, which invite you to integrate and apply your reading of the text, your exploration of children's books, and your classroom experiences.

Ending Invitations

Choose one or more of the following:

1. **Book fair.** After choosing an age level, design a thematic unit around a focus book. Develop ten or more lesson plans for this unit, using response activities and language activities. Be sure to include cross-curricular lessons incorporating social studies, science, math, geography, art, and music. Put these lessons in a notebook, and include it with the display you create for your unit. In this display, use books, artifacts from the focus book, and any other aesthetically pleasing and attention-getting props, including art or display boards, to advertise your thematic unit. Plan to share your project with your classmates during a Library Fair Night. Remember that your job is not only to create a sound literature unit but also to entice visitors to your Fair Booth. (Hint: Food is always a great incentive.)

2. **Genre presentation.** Form groups and select one genre for your group to "teach" and promote to the class. Become an expert in the genre by reading widely. Through book talks, your group should discuss appeals of the genre, criteria for evaluating the genre, and key authors and books. As a group, write a script based on a book in the genre and perform it using the readers theater approach.

3. **Exchange of book documentation.** Keep records of all the trade books you read (a trade book is any book that is not a textbook), and file them in a notebook or on index cards. Include teaching information—genre, publishing data, summary, ideas for teaching the book, and any other information you might find useful. Share your collection with your small group and ask them for responses.

4. **Literary luminary.** Share a powerful scene from a favorite book with your classmates. Read the scene aloud—or, better yet, dress up as the main character and talk about the scene in persona.

5. **Multicultural night.** Break into small groups and select a multicultural group on which your group will become expert. Explore the literature of this group by reading across the genres. Create an exhibit with food, music, art, and information celebrating the cultural group you represent. Talk about a favorite book.

6. **Literature circle.** Create literature circles around a variety of chapter books for older elementary and young adult readers. Harvey Daniels (2002) has designed clear descriptions of eight roles through which a student might contribute to a literature circle. Over a period of two or three class meetings have students read, respond within their role, and share and discuss a book. This activity ends with each group making a presentation to the class. The presentations will vary considerably depending on the text and the creative impulses of the students. Some students may choose readers theater, while others choose full drama with costumes and food. Some may include the class in an activity, while others will present to the class. Each circle has so much autonomy that the presentations will be varied, interesting, and always fun!

7. **"Selling" a ground-breaking book.** John Newbery and Amos Comenius (from Chapter 6) are considered ground-breakers in the field of children's literature. Can you think of any authors or illustrators of books you read as a child whom you would consider ground-breakers? As you read this semester, what books did you find that did something no one else had done before? Bring in one or two books that you think qualify the author or illustrator as a ground-breaker. Then "sell" your book to the class, explaining the features that you thought were most impressive. After nominations are heard from the whole class, categories can be devised and a vote taken to produce winners.

8. **Data analysis.** Return to the reading annotations you've kept this semester and analyze the books, presenting an overview of your findings. Investigate one or more of the following issues: gender representation, age representation, ethnic representation, and representation of all kinds of diversity, including characters with handicapping conditions. Draw some conclusions and discuss the implications of your study.

Award Winners Since 1980

Newbery Awards

2002 *A Single Shard*, by Linda Sue Park. Clarion/Houghton Mifflin.

Honor: *Everything on a Waffle*, by Polly Horvath. Farrar, Straus & Giroux.

Carver: A Life in Poems, by Marilyn Nelson. Front Street.

2001 *A Year Down Yonder*, by Richard Peck. Dial.

Honor: *Because of Winn-Dixie*, by Kate DiCamillo. Candlewick.

Hope Was Here, by Joan Bauer. Putnam.

Joey Pigza Loses Control, by Jack Gantos. Farrar, Straus & Giroux.

The Wanderer, by Sharon Creech. HarperCollins.

2000 *Bud, Not Buddy*, by Christopher Paul Curtis. Delacorte.

Honor: *Getting Near to Baby*, by Audrey Coloumbis. Putnam.

Our Only May Amelia, by Jennifer L. Holm. HarperCollins.

26 Fairmont Avenue, by Tomie dePaola. Putnam.

1999 *Holes*, by Louis Sachar. Farrar Straus & Giroux.

Honor: *A Long Way from Chicago*, by Richard Peck. Dial.

1998 *Out of the Dust*, by Karen Hesse. Scholastic.

Honor: *Ella Enchanted*, by Gail Carson Levine. HarperCollins.

Lily's Crossing, by Patricia Reilly Giff. Delacorte.

Wringer, by Jerry Spinelli. HarperCollins.

1997 *The View from Saturday*, by E. L. Konigsburg. Atheneum.

Honor: *A Girl Named Disaster*, by Nancy Farmer. Orchard.

Moorchild, by Eloise McGraw. Simon & Schuster.

The Thief, by Megan Whalen Turner. Greenwillow.

Belle Prater's Boy, by Ruth White. Farrar, Straus & Giroux.

1996 *The Midwife's Apprentice*, by Karen Cushman. Clarion.

Honor: *What Jamie Saw*, by Carolyn Coman. Front Street.

The Watsons Go to Birmingham—1963, by Christopher Paul Curtis. Delacorte.

Yolonda's Genius, by Carol Fenner. Simon & Schuster.

The Great Fire, by Jim Murphy. Scholastic.

1995 *Walk Two Moons*, by Sharon Creech. HarperCollins.

Honor: *Catherine, Called Birdy*, by Karen Cushman. Clarion.

The Ear, the Eye, and the Arm, by Nancy Farmer. Jackson/Orchard.

1994 *The Giver*, by Lois Lowry. Houghton Mifflin.

Honor: *Crazy Lady!* by Jane Leslie Conly. HarperCollins.

Eleanor Roosevelt: A Life of Discovery, by Russell Freedman. Clarion.

Dragon's Gate, by Laurence Yep. HarperCollins.

1993 *Missing May*, by Cynthia Rylant. Jackson/Orchard.

Honor: *What Hearts*, by Bruce Brooks. HarperCollins.

The Dark-Thirty: Southern Tales of the Supernatural, by Patricia C. McKissack. Knopf.

Somewhere in the Darkness, by Walter Dean Myers. Scholastic.

1992 *Shiloh*, by Phyllis Reynolds Naylor. Atheneum.

Honor: *Nothing But the Truth: A Documentary Novel*, by Avi. Jackson/Orchard.

The Wright Brothers: How They Invented the Airplane, by Russell Freedman. Holiday.

1991 *Maniac Magee*, by Jerry Spinelli. Little, Brown.

Honor: *The True Confessions of Charlotte Doyle*, by Avi. Jackson/Orchard.

1990 *Number the Stars*, by Lois Lowry. Houghton Mifflin.

Honor: *Afternoon of the Elves*, by Janet Taylor Lisle. Jackson/Orchard.

The Winter Room, by Gary Paulsen. Jackson/Orchard.

Shabanu, Daughter of the Wind, by Suzanne Fisher Staples. Knopf.

1989 *Joyful Noise: Poems for Two Voices*, by Paul Fleischman. Illus. Eric Beddows. Zolotow/Harper.

Honor: *In the Beginning: Creation Stories from Around the World*, by Virginia Hamilton. Illus. Barry Moser. Harcourt.

Scorpions, by Walter Dean Myers. Harper.

1988 *Lincoln: A Photobiography*, by Russell Freedman. Clarion.

Honor: *After the Rain*, by Norma Fox Mazer. Morrow.

Hatchet, by Gary Paulsen. Bradbury.

1987 *The Whipping Boy*, by Sid Fleischman. Illus. Peter Sis. Greenwillow.

Honor: *On My Honor*, by Marion Dane Bauer. Clarion.

Volcano: The Eruption and Healing of Mount St. Helens, by Patricia Lauber. Bradbury.

A Fine White Dust, by Cynthia Rylant. Bradbury.

1986 *Sarah, Plain and Tall*, by Patricia C. MacLachlan. Zolotow/Harper.

Honor: *Commodore Perry in the Land of the Shogun*, by Rhoda Blumberg. Lothrop, Lee & Shepard.

Dogsong, by Gary Paulsen. Bradbury.

1985 *The Hero and the Crown*, by Robin McKinley. Greenwillow.

Honor: *The Moves Make the Man*, by Bruce Brooks. Harper.

One-Eyed Cat, by Paula Fox. Bradbury.

Like Jake and Me, by Mavis Jukes. Illus. Lloyd Bloom. Knopf.

1984 *Dear Mr. Henshaw*, by Beverly Cleary. Illus. Paul O. Zelinsky. Morrow.

Honor: *The Wish Giver: Three Tales of Coven Tree*, by Bill Brittain. Illus. Andrew Glass. Harper.

Sugaring Time, by Kathryn Lasky. Illus. Christopher G. Knight. Macmillan.

The Sign of the Beaver, by Elizabeth George Speare. Houghton Mifflin.

A Solitary Blue, by Cynthia Voigt. Atheneum.

1983 *Dicey's Song*, by Cynthia Voigt. Atheneum.

Honor: *Graven Images*, by Paul Fleischman. Illus. Andrew Glass. Harper.

Homesick: My Own Story, by Jean Fritz. Illus. Margot Tomes. Putnam.

Sweet Whispers, Brother Rush, by Virginia Hamilton. Philomel.

The Blue Sword, by Robin McKinley. Greenwillow.

Doctor De Soto, by William Steig. Farrar, Straus & Giroux.

1982 *A Visit to William Blake's Inn: Poems for Innocent and Experienced Travelers*, by Nancy Willard. Illus. Alice Provensen and Martin Provensen. Harcourt.

Honor: *Ramona Quimby, Age 8*, by Beverly Cleary. Illus. Alan Tiegreen. Morrow.

Upon the Head of the Goat: A Childhood in Hungary 1939–1944, by Aranka Siegal. Farrar, Straus & Giroux.

1981 *Jacob Have I Loved*, by Katherine Paterson. Crowell.

Honor: *The Fledgling*, by Jane Langton. Illus. Erik Blegvad. Harper.

A Ring of Endless Light, by Madeleine L'Engle. Farrar, Straus & Giroux.

1980 *A Gathering of Days: A New England Girl's Journal, 1830–1832*, by Joan W. Blos. Scribner.

Honor: *The Road from Home: The Story of an Armenian Girl*, by David Kheridan. Greenwillow.

(For a complete list, go to www.ala.org/alsc/newbery.html.)

Caldecott Awards

The winner of the award is the illustrator, whose name appears in boldface.

2002 *The Three Pigs*, by **David Wiesner.** Clarion/Houghton Mifflin.

Honor: *The Dinosaurs of Waterhouse Hawkins*, by Barbara Kerley. Illus. **Brian Selznick.** Scholastic.

Martin's Big Words: The Life of Dr. Martin Luther King, Jr., by Doreen Rappaport. Illus. **Bryan Collier.** Jump at the Sun/Hyperion.

The Stray Dog, by **Marc Simont.** HarperCollins.

2001 *So You Want to Be President*, by Judith St. George. Illus. **David Small.** Philomel.

Honor: *Casey at Bat*, by Ernest Lawrence Thayer. Illus. **Christopher Bing.** Handprint.

Click, Clack, Moo: Cows That Type. by Doreen Cronin. Illus. **Betsy Lewin.** Simon & Schuster.

Olivia, by **Ian Falconer.** Atheneum.

2000 *Joseph Had a Little Overcoat*, by **Simms Taback.** Viking.

Honor: *A Child's Calendar*, by John Updike. Illus. **Trina Schart Hyman.** Holiday.

Sector 7, by **David Wiesner.** Clarion.

When Sophie Gets Angry—Really, Really Angry, by **Molly Bang.** Scholastic.

The Ugly Duckling, by Hans Christian Andersen, adapted by **Jerry Pinkney.** Morrow.

1999 *Snowflake Bentley*, by Jacqueline Briggs Martin. Illus. **Mary Azarian.** Houghton Mifflin.

Honor: *Duke Ellington*, by Andrea Davis Pinkney. Illus. **Brian Pinkney.** Hyperion.

No David!, by **David Shannon.** Blue Sky/Scholastic.

Snow, by **Uri Shulevitz.** Farrar, Straus & Giroux.

Tibet: Through the Red Box, by **Peter Sis.** Foster/Farrar, Straus & Giroux.

1998 *Rapunzel*, by **Paul O. Zelinsky.** Dutton.

Honor: *The Gardener*, by Sarah Stewart. Illus. **David Small.** Farrar, Straus & Giroux.

Harlem, by Walter Dean Myers. Illus. **Christopher Myers.** Scholastic.

There Was an Old Lady Who Swallowed a Fly, by **Simms Taback.** Viking.

1997 *Golem*, by **David Wisniewski.** Clarion.

Honor: *Hush! A Thai Lullaby*, by Minfong Ho. Illus. **Holly Meade.** Kroupa/Orchard.

The Graphic Alphabet, by **David Pelletier.** Ed. Neal Porter. Orchard.

The Paperboy, by **Dav Pilkey.** Jackson/Orchard.

Starry Messenger, by **Peter Sis.** Foster/Farrar, Straus & Giroux.

1996 *Officer Buckle and Gloria*, by **Peggy Rathmann.** Putnam.

Honor: *Alphabet City*, by **Stephen T. Johnson.** Viking.

Zin! Zin! Zin! A Violin, by Lloyd Moss. Illus. **Marjorie Priceman.** Simon & Schuster.

The Faithful Friend, by Robert D. San Souci. Illus. **Brian Pinkney.** Simon & Schuster.

Tops & Bottoms, adapted by **Janet Stevens.** Harcourt.

1995 *Smoky Night,* by Eve Bunting. Illus. **David Diaz.** Harcourt.

Honor: *Swamp Angel,* by Anne Isaacs. Illus. **Paul O. Zelinsky.** Dutton.

John Henry, by Julius Lester. Illus. **Jerry Pinkney.** Dial.

Time Flies, by **Eric Rohmann.** Crown.

1994 *Grandfather's Journey,* by **Allen Say.** Houghton Mifflin.

Honor: *Peppe the Lamplighter,* by Elisa Bartone. Illus. **Ted Lewin.** Lothrop, Lee & Shepard.

In the Small, Small Pond, by **Denise Fleming.** Holt.

Owen, by **Kevin Henkes.** Greenwillow.

Raven: A Trickster Tale from the Pacific Northwest, by **Gerald McDermott.** Harcourt.

Yo! Yes?, by **Chris Raschka.** Orchard.

1993 *Mirette on the High Wire,* by **Emily Arnold McCully.** Putnam.

Honor: *The Stinky Cheese Man & Other Fairly Stupid Tales,* by Jon Scieszka. Illus. **Lane Smith.** Viking.

Working Cotton, by Sherley Anne Williams. Illus. **Carole Byard.** Harcourt.

Seven Blind Mice, by **Ed Young.** Philomel.

1992 *Tuesday,* by **David Wiesner.** Clarion.

Honor: *Tar Beach,* by **Faith Ringgold.** Crown.

1991 *Black and White,* by **David Macauley.** Houghton Mifflin.

Honor: *Puss in Boots,* by **Fred Marcellina.** di Capua/Farrar, Straus & Giroux.

More More More Said the Baby, by **Vera B. Williams.** Greenwillow.

1990 *Lon Po Po: A Red-Riding Hood Story from China,* by **Ed Young.** Philomel.

Honor: *Color Zoo,* by **Lois Ehlert.** Lippincott.

Hershel and the Hanukkah Goblins, by Eric Kimmel. Illus. **Trina Schart Hyman.** Holiday.

Bill Peet: An Autobiography, by **Bill Peet.** Houghton Mifflin.

The Talking Eggs, by Robert D. San Souci. Illus. **Jerry Pinkney.** Dial.

1989 *Song and Dance Man,* by Karen Ackerman. Illus. **Stephen Gammell.** Knopf.

Honor: *Mirandy and Brother Wind,* by Patricia C. McKissack. Illus. **Jerry Pinkney.** Knopf.

Goldilocks and the Three Bears, by **James Marshall.** Dial.

The Boy of the Three-Year Nap, by Diane Snyder. Illus. **Allen Say.** Houghton Mifflin.

Free Fall, by **David Wiesner.** Lothrop, Lee & Shepard.

1988 *Owl Moon,* by Jane Yolen. Illus. **John Schoenherr.** Philomel.

Honor: *Mufaro's Beautiful Daughters: An African Tale,* by **John Steptoe.** Lothrop, Lee & Shepard.

1987 *Hey, Al,* by Arthur Yorinks. Illus. **Richard Egielski.** Farrar, Straus & Giroux.

Honor: *The Village of Round and Square Houses,* by **Ann Grifalconi.** Little, Brown.

Alphabatics, by **Suse MacDonald.** Bradbury.

Rumpelstiltskin, by **Paul O. Zelinsky.** Dutton.

1986 *The Polar Express,* by **Chris Van Allsburg.** Houghton Mifflin.

Honor: *The Relatives Came,* by Cynthia Rylant. Illus. **Stephen Gammell.** Bradbury.

King Bidgood's in the Bathtub, by Audrey Wood. Illus. **Don Wood.** Harcourt.

1985 *Saint George and the Dragon,* retold by Margaret Hodges. Illus. **Trina Schart Hyman.** Little, Brown.

Honor: *Hansel and Gretel,* retold by Rika Lesser. Illus. **Paul O. Zelinsky.** Dodd.

The Story of Jumping Mouse: A Native American Legend, retold by **John Steptoe.** Lothrop, Lee & Shepard.

Have You Seen My Duckling?, by **Nancy Tafuri.** Greenwillow.

1984 *The Glorious Flight: Across the Channel with Louis Bleriot,* by **Alice Provensen** and **Martin Provensen.** Viking.

Honor: *Ten, Nine, Eight,* by **Molly Bang.** Greenwillow.

Little Red Riding Hood, retold by **Trina Schart Hyman.** Holiday.

1983 *Shadow,* by Blaise Cendrars. Trans. **Marcia Brown.** Scribner.

Honor: *When I Was Young in the Mountains,* by Cynthia Rylant. Illus. **Diane Goode.** Dutton.

A Chair for My Mother, by **Vera B. Williams.** Greenwillow.

1982 *Jumanji,* by **Chris Van Allsburg.** Houghton Mifflin.

Honor: *Where the Buffaloes Begin,* by Olaf Baker. Illus. **Stephen Gammell.** Warne.

On Market Street, by Arnold Lobel. Illus. **Anita Lobel.** Greenwillow.

Outside Over There, by **Maurice Sendak.** Harper.

A Visit to William Blake's Inn: Poems for Innocent and Experienced Travelers, by Nancy Willard. Illus. **Alice Provensen** and **Martin Provensen.** Harcourt.

1981 *Fables,* by **Arnold Lobel.** Harper.

Honor: *The Grey Lady and the Strawberry Snatcher,* by **Molly Bang.** Four Winds.

Truck, by **Donald Crews.** Greenwillow.

Mice Twice, by **Joseph Low.** McElderry/Atheneum.

The Bremen-Town Musicians, retold by **Ilse Plume.** Doubleday.

1980 *Ox-Cart Man,* by Donald Hall. Illus. **Barbara Cooney.** Viking.

Honor: *Ben's Trumpet,* by **Rachel Isadora.** Greenwillow.

The Treasure, by **Uri Shulevitz.** Farrar, Straus & Giroux.

The Garden of Abdul Gasazi, by **Chris Van Allsburg.** Houghton Mifflin.

(For a complete list, go to www.ala.org/alsc/caldecott.html.)

Aesop Prizes

The Aesop Prize is awarded by the Children's Folklore Section of the American Folklore Society.

2001 *Fiesta Femenina: Celebrating Women in Mexican Folktales.* Retold by Mary-Joan Gerson. Illus. Maya Christina Gonzalez. Barefoot.

2000 *The Day the Rabbi Disappeared: Jewish Holiday Tales of Magic,* by Howard Schwartz. Illus. Monique Passicot. Viking.

1999 *King Solomon and His Magic Ring,* by Elie Wiesel. Illus. Mark Podal. Greenwillow.

1998 *Echoes of the Elders: The Stories and Paintings of Chief Lelooska,* by Chief Lelooska. DK Publishing.

1997 *The Hired Hand: An African-American Folktale,* by Robert D. San Souci. Illus. Jerry Pinkney. Dial.

Earth Tales from Around the World, by Michael J. Caduto. Illus. Adelaide Murphy Tyrol. Fulcrum.

1996 *Next Year in Jerusalem,* retold by Howard Schwartz. Illus. Neil Waldman. Viking.

Nursery Tales Around the World, retold by Judy Sierra. Illus. Stefano Vitale. Clarion.

1995 *Fair Is Fair: World Folktales of Justice,* by Sharon Creeden. August.

(For a complete list, go to http://afsnet.org/sections/children/aesop.htm.)

Jane Addams Children's Book Awards

2001

Longer Book: *Esperaza Rising,* by Pam Muñoz Ryan. Scholastic.

Honor: *The Color of My Words,* by Lynn Joseph. HarperCollins.

Darkness Over Denmark: The Danish Resistance and the Rescue of the Jews, by Ellen Levine. Holiday.

Walking to the Bus-Rider Blues, by Harriet Gillem Robinet. Atheneum.

2000

Longer Book: *Through My Eyes,* by Ruby Bridges. Scholastic.

Honor: *The Birchbark House,* by Louise Erdrich. Hyperion.

Kids on Strike!, by Susan Campbell Bartoletti. Houghton Mifflin.

Picture Book: *Molly Bannaky,* by Alice McGill. Illus. Chris K. Soentpiet. Houghton Mifflin.

Honor: *A Band of Angels: A Story Inspired by the Jubilee Singers,* by Deborah Hopkinson. Illus. Raúl Colón. Schwartz/Atheneum.

When Sophie Gets Angry—Really, Really Angry, by Molly Bang. Blue Sky/Scholastic.

1999

Longer Book: *Bat 6,* by Virginia Euwer Wolff. Scholastic.

Honor: *The Heart of a Chief,* by Joseph Bruchac. Dial.

No More Strangers Now, by Tim McKee. Illus. Anne Blackshaw. Kroupa /DK Ink.

Restless Spirit: The Life and Work of Dorothea Lange, by Elizabeth Partridge. Viking.

Picture Book: *Marianthe's Story: Painted Words/Spoken Memories,* by Aliki. Greenwillow.

Honor: *Hey, Little Ant,* by Phillip Hoose and Hannah Hoose. Illus. Debbie Tilley. Tricycle.

i see the rhythm, by Toyomi Igus. Illus. Michele Wood. Children's Book Press.

This Land Is Your Land, by Woody Guthrie. Illus. Kathy Jakobsen. Little, Brown.

1998

Longer Book: *Habibi,* by Naomi Shihab Nye. Simon & Schuster.

Honor: *The Circuit: Stories from the Life of a Migrant Child,* by Francisco Jimenez. University of New Mexico Press.

Seedfolks, by Paul Fleischman. HarperCollins.

Picture Book: *Seven Brave Women,* by Betsy Hearne. Illus. Bethanne Andersen. Greenwillow.

Honor: *Celebrating Families,* by Rosmarie Hausherr. Scholastic.

Passage to Freedom: The Sugihara Story, by Ken Mochizuki. Illus. Dom Lee. Lee & Low.

1997

Longer Book: *Growing Up in Coal County,* by Susan Campbell Bartoletti. Houghton Mifflin.

Honor: *Behind the Bedroom Wall,* by Laura E. Williams. Milkweed.

Second Daughter: The Story of a Slave Girl, by Mildred Pitts Walter. Scholastic.

Picture Book: *Wilma Unlimited,* by Kathleen Krull. Illus. David Diaz. Harcourt Brace.

Honor: *The Day Gogo Went to Vote,* by Elinor Batezat Sisulu. Illus. Sharon Wilson. Little, Brown.

1996

Longer Book: *The Well,* by Mildred D. Taylor. Dial.

Honor: *From the Notebooks of Melanin Sun,* by Jacqueline Woodson. Blue Sky/Scholastic.

On the Wings of Peace: Writers and Illustrators Speak Out for Peace in Memory of Hiroshima and Nagasaki, edited by Sheila Hamanaka. Clarion.

The Watsons Go to Birmingham—1963, by Christopher Paul Curtis. Delacorte.

Picture Book: No award given

Special Commendation: *The Middle Passage,* by Tom Feelings. Dial.

1995

Longer Book: *Kids at Work: Lewis Hine and the Crusade Against Child Labor,* by Russell Freedman. Clarion.

Honor: *Cezanne Pinto,* by Mary Stolz. Knopf.

I Hadn't Meant to Tell You This, by Jacqueline Woodson. Delacorte.

Picture Book: *Sitti's Secrets,* by Naomi Shihab Nye. Illus. Nancy Carpenter. Four Winds.

Honor: *Bein' with You This Way,* by W. Nikola-Lisa. Illus. Michael Bryant. Lee & Low.

1994

Longer Book: *Freedom's Children: Young Civil Rights Activists Tell Their Stories,* by Ellen Levine. Putnam.

Honor: *Eleanor Roosevelt: A Life of Discovery,* by Russell Freedman. Clarion.

Picture Book: *This Land Is My Land,* by George Littlechild. Children's Book Press.

Honor: *Soul Looks Back in Wonder,* by Tom Feelings. Dial.

1993

Longer Book: *A Taste of Salt: A Story of Modern Haiti,* by Frances Temple. Orchard.

Honor: *Letters from a Slave Girl: The Story of Harriet Jacobs,* by Mary E. Lyons. Scribner.

Picture Book: *Aunt Harriet's Underground Railroad in the Sky,* by Faith Ringgold. Crown.

Honor: *Mrs. Katz and Tush,* by Patricia Polacco. Bantam.

1992 *Journey of the Sparrows,* by Fran Leeper Buss with Daisy Cubias. Lodestar.

Honor: *Now Is Your Time! The African-American Struggle for Freedom,* by Walter Dean Myers. HarperCollins.

1991 *The Big Book for Peace,* edited by Ann Durell and Marilyn Sachs. Dutton.

Honor: *The Journey: Japanese-Americans, Racism and Renewal,* by Sheila Hamanaka. Jackson/Orchard.

The Middle of Somewhere: A Story of South Africa, by Sheila Gordon. Orchard.

1990 *A Long Hard Journey: The Story of the Pullman Porter,* by Patricia C. McKissack and Fredrick L. McKissack. Walker.

Honor: *Number the Stars,* by Lois Lowry. Houghton Mifflin.

Shades of Gray, by Carolyn Reeder. Macmillan.

The Wednesday Surprise, by Eve Bunting. Clarion.

1989 (tie): *Anthony Burns: The Defeat and Triumph of a Fugitive Slave,* by Virginia Hamilton. Knopf.

Looking Out, by Victoria Boutis. Four Winds.

Honor: *December Stillness,* by Mary Downing Hahn. Clarion.

The Most Beautiful Place in the World, by Ann Cameron. Knopf.

Rescue: The Story of How Gentiles Saved Jews in the Holocaust, by Milton Meltzer. Harper & Row.

1988 *Waiting for the Rain: A Novel of South Africa,* by Sheila Gordon. Orchard/Watts.

Honor: *Nicolas, Where Have You Been?,* by Leo Lionni. Knopf.

Trouble at the Mines, by Doreen Rappaport. Crowell.

1987 *Nobody Wants a Nuclear War,* by Judith Vigna. Whitman.

Honor: *All in a Day,* by Mitsumasa Anno. Philomel.

Children of the Maya: A Guatemalan Indian Odyssey, by Brent Ashabranner. Illus. Paul Conklin. Dodd, Mead.

1986 *Ain't Gonna Study War No More: The Story of America's Peace Seekers,* by Milton Meltzer. Harper & Row.

Honor: *Journey to the Soviet Union,* by Samantha Smith. Little, Brown.

1985 *The Short Life of Sophie Scholl,* by Hermann Vinke. Trans. Hedvig Pachter. Harper & Row.

Honor: *The Island on Bird Street,* by Uri Orlev. Trans. Hillel Halkin. Houghton, Mifflin.

Music, Music for Everyone, by Vera B. Williams. Greenwillow.

1984 *Rain of Fire,* by Marion Dane Bauer. Clarion/Houghton Mifflin.

1983 *Hiroshima No Pika,* by Toshi Maruki. Lothrop, Lee & Shepard.

Honor: *The Bomb,* by Sidney Lenz. Lodestar/Dutton.

If I Had a Paka: Poems in Eleven Languages, by Charlotte Pomerantz. Greenwillow.

West Coast Honor: People at the Edge of the World: The Ohlone of Central California, by Betty Morrow. Bacon.

Special Recognition: *All the Colors of the Race,* by Arnold Adoff. Lothrop, Lee & Shepard.

Children as Teachers of Peace, by Our Children. Celestial.

1982 *A Spirit to Ride the Whirlwind,* by Athena V. Lord. Macmillan.

Honor: *Let the Circle Be Unbroken,* by Mildred D. Taylor. Dial.

Lupita Mañana, by Patricia Beatty. Morrow.

1981 *First Woman in Congress: Jeannette Rankin,* by Florence Meiman White. Julian Messner.

Honor: *Chase Me, Catch Nobody!,* by Erik Haugaard. Houghton Mifflin.

Doing Time: A Look at Crime and Prisons, by Phyllis Clark and Robert Lehrman. Hastings.

We Are Mesquakie, We Are One, by Hadley Irwin. Feminist Press.

1980 *The Road from Home: The Story of an Armenian Girl,* by David Kheridian. Greenwillow.

West Coast Honor: *Woman from Hiroshima,* by Toshio Mori. Isthmus.

Special Recognition: *Natural History,* by M. B. Goffstein. Farrar, Straus & Giroux.

(For a complete list, go to www.soemadison.wisc.edu/ccbc/ public/jaddams.htm.)

Coretta Scott King Author Awards

2002 *The Land,* by Mildred D. Taylor. Penguin Putnam.

Honor: *Money Hungry,* by Sharon G. Flake. Jump at the Sun/Hyperion.

Carver: A Life in Poems, by Marilyn Nelson. Front Street.

2001 *Miracle's Boys,* by Jacqueline Woodson. Putnam.

Honor: *Let It Shine! Stories of Black Women Freedom Fighters,* by Andrea Davis Pinkney. Illus. Stephen Alcorn. Harcourt.

2000 *Bud, Not Buddy,* by Christopher Paul Curtis. Delacorte.

Honor: *Francie,* by Karen English. Farrar, Straus & Giroux.

Black Hands, White Sails: The Story of African American Whalers, by Patricia C. McKissack and Fredrick L. McKissack. Scholastic.

1999 *Heaven,* by Angela Johnson. Simon & Schuster.

Honor: *Jazmin's Notebook,* by Nikki Grimes. Dial.

Breaking Ground, Breaking Silence: The Story of New York's African Burial Ground, by Joyce Hansen and Gary McGowan. Holt.

The Other Side: Shorter Poems, by Angela Johnson. Orchard.

1998 *Forged by Fire,* by Sharon Draper. Atheneum.

Honor: *I Thought My Soul Would Rise and Fly: The Diary of Patsy, a Freed Girl,* by Joyce Hansen. Scholastic.

Bayard Rustin: Behind the Scenes of the Civil Rights Movement, by James Haskins. Hyperion.

1997 *Slam!,* by Walter Dean Myers. Scholastic.

Honor: *Rebels against Slavery: American Slave Revolts,* by Patricia C. McKissack and Fredrick L. McKissack. Scholastic.

1996 *Her Stories: African American Folktales, Fairy Tales and True Tales,* by Virginia Hamilton. Illus. Leo Dillon and Diane Dillon. Scholastic.

Honor: *The Watsons Go to Birmingham—1963,* by Christopher Paul Curtis. Delacorte.

Like Sisters on the Home Front, by Rita Williams-Garcia. Dutton.

From the Notebooks of Melanin Sun, by Jacqueline Woodson. Scholastic.

1995 *Christmas in the Big House, Christmas in the Quarters,* by Patricia C. McKissack and Fredrick L. McKissack. Illus. John Thompson. Scholastic.

Honor: *The Captive,* by Joyce Hansen. Scholastic.

Black Diamond: The Story of the Negro Baseball Leagues, by Patricia C. McKissack and Fredrick L. McKissack. Scholastic.

I Hadn't Meant to Tell You This, by Jacqueline Woodson. Delacorte.

1994 *Toning the Sweep,* by Angela Johnson. Orchard.

Honor: *Malcolm X: By Any Means Necessary,* by Walter Dean Myers. Scholastic.

Brown Honey in Broomwheat Tea, by Joyce Carol Thomas. Illus. Floyd Cooper. HarperCollins.

1993 *The Dark-Thirty: Southern Tales of the Supernatural,* by Patricia C. McKissack. Illus. Brian Pinkney. Knopf.

Honor: *Sojourner Truth: Ain't I a Woman?,* by Patricia C. McKissack and Fredrick L. McKissack. Scholastic.

Somewhere in the Darkness, by Walter Dean Myers. Scholastic.

Mississippi Challenge, by Mildred Pitts Walter. Bradbury.

1992 *Now Is Your Time! The African American Struggle for Freedom,* by Walter Dean Myers. HarperCollins.

Honor: *Night on Neighborhood Street,* by Eloise Greenfield. Illus. Jan Spivey Gilchrist. Dial.

1991 *The Road to Memphis,* by Mildred D. Taylor. Dial.

Honor: *Black Dance in America: A History Through Its People,* by James Haskins. Crowell.

When I Am Old with You, by Angela Johnson. Illus. David Soman. Orchard.

1990 *A Long Hard Journey: The Story of the Pullman Strike,* by Patricia C. McKissack and Fredrick L. McKissack. Walker.

Honor: *Nathaniel Talking,* by Eloise Greenfield. Illus. Jan Spivey Gilchrist. Black Butterfly.

The Bells of Christmas, by Virginia Hamilton. Illus. Lambert Davis. Harcourt.

Martin Luther King, Jr., and the Freedom Movement, by Lillie Patterson. Facts on File.

1989 *Fallen Angels,* by Walter Dean Myers. Scholastic.

Honor: *A Thief in the Village and Other Stories,* by James Berry. Orchard.

Anthony Burns: The Defeat and Triumph of a Fugitive Slave, by Virginia Hamilton. Knopf.

1988 *The Friendship,* by Mildred D. Taylor. Illus. Max Ginsburg. Dial.

Honor: *An Enchanted Hair Tale,* by Alexis De Veaux. Illus. Cheryl Hanna. Harper.

The Tales of Uncle Remus: The Adventures of Brer Rabbit, by Julius Lester. Illus. Jerry Pinkney. Dial.

1987 *Justin and the Best Biscuits in the World,* by Mildred Pitts Walter. Lothrop, Lee & Shepard.

Honor: *Lion and the Ostrich Chicks and Other African Folk Tales,* by Ashley Bryan. Atheneum.

Which Way Freedom?, by Joyce Hansen. Walker.

1986 *The People Could Fly: American Black Folktales,* by Virginia Hamilton. Illus. Leo Dillon and Diane Dillon. Knopf.

Honor: *Junius Over Far,* by Virginia Hamilton. Harper.

Trouble's Child, by Mildred Pitts Walter. Lothrop.

1985 *Motown and Didi,* by Walter Dean Myers. Viking.

Honor: *Circle of Gold,* by Candy Dawson Boyd. Apple/Scholastic.

A Little Love, by Virginia Hamilton. Philomel.

1984 *Everett Anderson's Goodbye,* by Lucille Clifton. Illus. Ann Grifalconi. Holt.

Special Citation: *The Words of Martin Luther King, Jr.,* compiled by Coretta Scott King. Newmarket.

Honor: *The Magical Adventures of Pretty Pearl,* by Virginia Hamilton. HarperCollins.

Lena Horne, by James Haskins. Coward-McCann.

Bright Shadow, by Joyce Carol Thomas. Avon.

Because We Are, by Mildred Pitts Walter. Lothrop, Lee & Shepard.

1983 *Sweet Whispers, Brother Rush,* by Virginia Hamilton. Philomel.

Honor: *This Strange New Feeling,* by Julius Lester. Dial.

1982 *Let the Circle Be Unbroken,* by Mildred D. Taylor. Dial.

Honor: *Rainbow Jordan,* by Alice Childress. Putnam/Coward.

Lou in the Limelight, by Kristin Hunter. Scribner.

Mary: An Autobiography, by Mary E. Mebane. Viking.

1981 *This Life,* by Sidney Poitier. Knopf.

Honor: *Don't Explain: A Song of Billie Holiday,* by Alexis De Veaux. Harper.

1980 *The Young Landlords,* by Walter Dean Myers. Viking.

Honor: *Movin' Up: Pop Gordy Tells His Story,* by Berry Gordy, Sr. Harper.

Childtimes: A Three-Generation Memoir, by Eloise Greenfield and Lessie Jones Little. Harper.

Andrew Young: Young Man with a Mission, by James Haskins. Lothrop, Lee & Shepard.

James Van DerZee: The Picture Takin' Man, by James Haskins. Dodd.

Let the Lion Eat the Straw, by Ellease Southerland. Scribner.

Coretta Scott King Illustrator Awards

The illustrator's name appears in boldface.

2002 *Goin' Someplace Special,* by Patricia McKissack. Illus. **Jerry Pinkney.** Atheneum.

Honor: *Martin's Big Words,* by Doreen Rappaport. Illus. **Bryan Collier.** Jump at the Sun/Hyperion.

2001 *Uptown,* by **Bryan Collier.** Holt.

Honor: *Freedom River,* by **Bryan Collier.** Hyperion.

Only Passing Through: The Story of Sojourner Truth, by Anne Rockwell. Illus. **R. Gregory Christie.** Random.

Virgie Goes to School with Us Boys, by Elizabeth Fitzgerald Howard. Illus. **E. B. Lewis.** Simon & Schuster.

2000 *In the Time of the Drums,* by Kim L. Siegelson. Illus. **Brian Pinkney.** Jump at the Sun/Hyperion.

Honor: *My Rows and Piles of Coins,* by Tololwa M. Mollel. Illus. **E. B. Lewis.** Clarion.

Black Cat, by **Christopher Myers.** Scholastic.

1999 *i see the rhythm,* by Toyomi Igus. Illus. **Michele Wood.** Children's Book Press.

Honor: *I Have Heard of a Land,* by Joyce Carol Thomas. Illus. **Floyd Cooper.** HarperCollins.

The Bat Boy and His Violin, by Gavin Curtis. Illus. **E. B. Lewis.** Simon & Schuster.

Duke Ellington: The Piano Prince and His Orchestra, by Andrea Davis Pinkney. Illus. **Brian Pinkney.** Hyperion.

1998 *In Daddy's Arms, I AM TALL: African Americans Celebrating Fathers,* by **Javaka Steptoe.** Lee & Low.

Honor: *Ashley Bryan's ABC of African American Poetry,* by **Ashley Bryan.** Atheneum.

The Hunterman and the Crocodile: A West African Folktale, by **Baba Wague Diakite.** Scholastic.

Harlem, by Walter Dean Myers. Illus. **Christopher Myers.** Scholastic.

1997 *Minty: A Story of Young Harriet Tubman,* by Alan Schroeder. Illus. **Jerry Pinkney.** Dial.

Honor: *The Palm of My Heart: Poetry by African American Children,* edited by Davida Adedjouma. Illus. **R. Gregory Christie.** Lee & Low.

Running the Road to ABC, by Denizé Lauture. Illus. **Reynold Ruffins.** Simon & Schuster.

Neeny Coming, Neeny Going, by Karen English. Illus. **Synthia Saint James.** Bridgewater.

1996 *The Middle Passage: White Ships Black Cargo,* by **Tom Feelings.** Dial.

Honor: *Her Stories: African American Folktales, Fairy Tales and True Tales,* by Virginia Hamilton. Illus. **Leo Dillon** and **Diane Dillon.** Scholastic.

The Faithful Friend, by Robert San Souci. Illus. **Brian Pinkney.** Simon & Schuster.

1995 *The Creation,* by James Weldon Johnson. Illus. **James E. Ransome.** Holiday.

Honor: *Meet Danitra Brown,* by Nikki Grimes. Illus. **Floyd Cooper.** Lothrop, Lee & Shepard.

The Singing Man, by Angela Shelf Medearis. Illus. **Terea Shaffer.** Holiday.

1994 *Soul Looks Back in Wonder,* by **Tom Feelings.** Dial.

Honor: *Brown Honey in Broomwheat Tea,* by Joyce Carol Thomas. Illus. **Floyd Cooper.** HarperCollins.

Uncle Jed's Barbershop, by Margaree King Mitchell. Illus. **James E. Ransome.** Simon & Schuster.

1993 *The Origin of Life on Earth: An African Creation Myth,* by David Anderson. Illus. **Kathleen Atkins Wilson.** Sights.

Honor: *Working Cotton,* by Sherley Anne Williams. Illus. **Carole Byard.** Harcourt.

Little Eight John, by Jan Wahl. Illus. **Wil Clay.** Lodestar.

Sukey and the Mermaid, by Robert San Souci. Illus. **Brian Pinkney.** Four Winds.

1992 *Tar Beach,* by **Faith Ringgold.** Crown.

Honor: *All Night, All Day: A Child's First Book of African-American Spirituals,* by **Ashley Bryan.** Atheneum.

Night on Neighborhood Street, by Eloise Greenfield. Illus. **Jan Spivey Gilchrist.** Dial.

1991 *Aida,* adapted by Leontyne Price. Illus. **Leo Dillon** and **Diane Dillon.** Harcourt.

1990 *Nathaniel Talking,* by Eloise Greenfield. Illus. **Jan Spivey Gilchrist.** Black Butterfly.

Honor: *The Talking Eggs,* retold by Robert D. San Souci. Illus. **Jerry Pinkney.** Dial.

1989 *Mirandy and Brother Wind,* by Patricia C. McKissack. Illus. **Jerry Pinkney.** Knopf.

Honor: *Storm in the Night,* by Mary Stolz. Illus. **Pat Cummings.** HarperCollins.

Under the Sunday Tree, by Eloise Greenfield. Illus. **Amos Ferguson.** Harper.

1988 *Mufaro's Beautiful Daughters: An African Tale,* by **John Steptoe.** Lothrop, Lee & Shepard.

Honor: *What a Morning! The Christmas Story in Black Spirituals,* compiled by John Langstaff. Illus. **Ashley Bryan.** McElderry/Macmillan.

The Invisible Hunters: A Legend from the Miskito Indians of Nicaragua, edited by Harriet Rohmer, Octavio Chow, and Morris Vidaure. Illus. **Joe Sam.** Children's Book Press.

1987 *Half a Moon and One Whole Star,* by Crescent Dragonwagon. Illus. **Jerry Pinkney.** Macmillan.

Honor: *Lion and the Ostrich Chicks and Other African Folk Tales,* by **Ashley Bryan.** Atheneum.

C.L.O.U.D.S., by **Pat Cummings.** Lothrop, Lee & Shepard.

1986 *The Patchwork Quilt,* by Valerie Flournoy. Illus. **Jerry Pinkney.** Dial.

Honor: *The People Could Fly: American Black Folktales,* by Virginia Hamilton. Illus. **Leo Dillon** and **Diane Dillon.** Knopf.

1985 No award given.

1984 *Ma Mama Needs Me,* by Mildred Pitts Walter. Illus. **Pat Cummings.** Lothrop, Lee & Shepard.

1983 *Black Child,* by **Peter Magubane.** Knopf.

Honor: *I'm Going to Sing: Black American Spirituals,* by **Ashley Bryan.** Atheneum.

Just Us Women, by Jeannette Caines. Illus. **Pat Cummings.** HarperCollins.

All the Colors of the Race, by Arnold Adoff. Illus. **John Steptoe.** Lothrop, Lee & Shepard.

1982 *Mama Crocodile: An Uncle Arnadou Tale from Senegal,* adapted by Rosa Guy. Trans. Birago Diop. Illus. **John Steptoe.** Delacorte.

Honor: *Daydreamers,* by Eloise Greenfield. Illus. **Tom Feelings.** Dial.

1981 *Beat the Story Down, Pum-Pum,* by **Ashley Bryan.** Atheneum.

Honor: *Grandma's Joy,* by Eloise Greenfield. Illus. **Carole Byard.** Philomel.

Count on Your Fingers African Style, by Claudia Zaslavsky. Illus. **Jerry Pinkney.** Crowell.

1980 *Cornrows,* by Camille Yarbrough. Illus. **Carole Byard.** Coward-McCann.

(For a complete list, go to www.ala.org/srrt/csking/winners.html.)

Michael L. Printz Awards

2002 *A Step from Heaven,* by An Na. Front Street.

Honor: *The Ropemaker,* by Peter Dickinson. Delacorte.

Heart to Heart: New Poems Inspired by Twentieth-Century American Arts, by Jan Greenberg. Abrams.

Freewill, by Chris Lynch. HarperCollins.

True Believer, by Virginia Euwer Wolff. Atheneum.

2001 *Kit's Wilderness,* by David Almond. Delacorte.

Honor: *Many Stones,* by Carolyn Coman. Front Street.

The Body of Christopher Creed, by Carol Plum-Ucci. Harcourt.

Angus, Thongs, and Full-Frontal Snogging, by Louise Rennison. HarperCollins.

Stuck in Neutral, by Terry Trueman. HarperCollins.

2000 *Monster,* by Walter Dean Myers. Scholastic.

Honor: *Skellig,* by David Almond. Delacorte.

Speak, by Laurie Halse Anderson. Farrar, Straus & Giroux.

Hard Love, by Ellen Wittinger. Simon & Schuster.

(For a complete list, go to www.ala.org/yalsa/printz/index.html.)

Boston Globe–Horn Book Awards

2002

Fiction and Poetry Book: *Lord of the Deep,* by Graham Salisbury. Delacorte.

Honor: *Saffy's Angel,* by Hilary McKay. McElderry.

Amber Was Brave, Essie Was Smart, by Vera B. Williams. Greenwillow.

Nonfiction Book: *This Land Was Made for You and Me: The Life and Songs of Woody Guthrie,* by Elizabeth Partridge. Viking.

Honor: *Handel, Who Knew What He Liked,* by M. T. Anderson. Illus. Kevin Hawkes. Candlewick.

Woody Guthrie: Poet of the People, by Bonnie Christensen. Knopf.

Picture Book: *"Let's Get a Pup!" Said Kate,* by Bob Graham. Candlewick.

Honor: *I Stink!,* by Kate McMullan. Illus. Jim McMullan. Cotler/Harper.

Little Rat Sets Sail, by Monika Bang-Campbell. Illus. Molly Bang. Harcourt.

2001

Fiction and Poetry Book: *Carver: A Life in Poems,* by Marilyn Nelson. Front Street.

Honor: *Everything on a Waffle,* by Polly Horvath. Farrar, Straus & Giroux.

Troy, by Adèle Geras. Harcourt.

Nonfiction Book: *The Longitude Prize,* by Joan Dash. Illus. Dusan Petricic. Foster/Farrar, Straus & Giroux.

Honor: *Rocks in His Head,* by Carol Otis Hurst. Illus. James Stevenson. Greenwillow.

Uncommon Traveler: Mary Kingsley in Africa, by Don Brown. Houghton Mifflin.

Picture Book: *Cold Feet,* by Cynthia DeFelice. Illus. Robert Andrew Parker. DK Ink.

Honor: *Five Creatures,* by Emily Jenkins. Illus. Tomek Bogacki. Foster/Farrar, Straus & Giroux.

The Stray Dog, retold by Marc Simont. HarperCollins.

2000

Fiction and Poetry Book: *The Folk Keeper,* by Franny Billingsley. Atheneum.

Honor: *King of Shadows,* by Susan Cooper. McElderry.

145th Street: Short Stories, by Walter Dean Myers. Delacorte.

Nonfiction Book: *Sir Walter Ralegh and the Quest for El Dorado,* by Marc Aronson. Clarion.

Honor: *Osceola: Memories of a Sharecropper's Daughter,* edited by Alan Govenar. Illus. Shane W. Evans. Jump at the Sun/Hyperion.

Sitting Bull and His World, by Albert Marrin. Dutton.

Picture Book: *Henry Hikes to Fitchburg,* by D. B. Johnson. Houghton Mifflin.

Honor: *Buttons,* by Brock Cole. Farrar, Straus & Giroux.

a day, a dog, by Gabrielle Vincent. Front Street.

1999

Fiction and Poetry Book: *Holes,* by Louis Sachar. Foster/Farrar, Straus & Giroux.

Honor: *The Trolls,* by Polly Horvath. Farrar, Straus & Giroux.

Monster, by Walter Dean Myers. Illus. Christopher Myers. HarperCollins.

Nonfiction Book: *The Top of the World: Climbing Mount Everest,* by Steve Jenkins. Houghton Mifflin.

Honor: *Shipwreck at the Bottom of the World: The Extraordinary True Story of Shackleton and the Endurance,* by Jennifer Armstrong. Crown.

William Shakespeare & the Globe, by Aliki. HarperCollins.

Picture Book: *Red-Eyed Tree Frog,* by Joy Cowley. Illus. Nic Bishop. Scholastic.

Honor: *Dance!,* written by Bill T. Jones and Susan Kuklin. Hyperion.

The Owl and the Pussycat, by Edward Lear. Illus. James Marshall. diCapua/HarperCollins.

Special Citation: *Tibet: Through the Red Box,* by Peter Sis. Foster/Farrar, Straus & Giroux.

1998

Fiction and Poetry Book: *The Circuit: Stories of the Life of a Migrant Child,* by Francisco Jimenez. University of New Mexico Press.

Honor: *While No One Was Watching,* by Jane Leslie Conly. Holt.

My Louisiana Sky, by Kimberly Willis Holt. Holt.

Nonfiction Book: *Leon's Story,* by Leon Walter Tillage. Illus. Susan L. Roth. Farrar, Straus & Giroux.

Honor: *Martha Graham: A Dancer's Life,* by Russell Freedman. Clarion.

Chuck Close, Up Close, by Jan Greenberg and Sandra Jordan. DK Ink.

Picture Book: *And If the Moon Could Talk,* by Kate Banks. Illus. Georg Hallensleben. Foster/Farrar, Straus & Giroux.

Honor: *Seven Brave Women,* by Betsy Hearne. Illus. Bethanne Andersen. Greenwillow.

Popcorn: Poems by James Stevenson. Greenwillow.

1997

Fiction and Poetry Book: *The Friends,* by Kazumi Yumoto. Trans. Cathy Hirano. Farrar, Straus & Giroux.

Honor: *Lily's Crossing,* by Patricia Reilly Giff. Delacorte.

Harlem, by Walter Dean Myers. Illus. Christopher Myers. Scholastic.

Nonfiction Book: *A Drop of Water: A Book of Science and Wonder,* by Walter Wick. Scholastic.

Honor: *Lou Gehrig: The Luckiest Man,* by David A. Adler. Illus. Terry Widener. Gulliver/Harcourt.

Leonardo da Vinci, by Diane Stanley. Morrow.

Picture Book: *The Adventures of Sparrowboy,* by Brian Pinkney. Simon & Schuster.

Honor: *Home on the Bayou: A Cowboy's Story,* by G. Brian Karas. Simon & Schuster.

Potato: A Tale from the Great Depression, by Kate Lied. Illus. Lisa Campbell Ernst. National Geographic.

1996

Fiction and Poetry Book: *Poppy,* by Avi. Illus. Brian Floca. Jackson/Orchard.

Honor: *The Moorchild,* by Eloise McGraw. McElderry.

Belle Prater's Boy, by Ruth White. Farrar, Straus & Giroux.

Nonfiction Book: *Orphan Train Rider: One Boy's True Story,* by Andrea Warren. Houghton Mifflin.

Honor: *The Boy Who Lived with the Bears: And Other Iroquois Stories,* by Joseph Bruchac. Illus. Murv Jacob. Harper.

Haystack, by Bonnie and Arthur Geisert. Illus. Arthur Geisert. Houghton Mifflin.

Picture Book: *In the Rain with Baby Duck,* by Amy Hest. Illus. Jill Barton. Candlewick.

Honor: *Fanny's Dream,* by Caralyn Buehner. Illus. Mark Buehner. Dial.

Home, Lovely, by Lynne Rae Perkins. Greenwillow.

1995

Fiction and Poetry Book: *Some of the Kinder Planets,* by Tim Wynne-Jones. Kroupa/Orchard.

Honor: *Jericho,* by Janet Hickman. Greenwillow.

Earthshine, by Theresa Nelson. Jackson/Orchard.

Nonfiction Book: *Abigail Adams: Witness to a Revolution,* by Natalie S. Bober. Atheneum.

Honor: *It's Perfectly Normal: Changing Bodies, Growing Up, Sex, and Sexual Health,* by Robie H. Harris. Illus. Michael Emberley. Candlewick.

The Great Fire, by Jim Murphy. Scholastic.

Picture Book: *John Henry,* retold by Julius Lester. Illus. Jerry Pinkney. Dial.

Honor: *Swamp Angel,* by Anne Isaacs. Illus. Paul O. Zelinsky. Dutton.

1994

Fiction and Poetry Book: *Scooter,* by Vera B. Williams. Greenwillow.

Honor: *Flour Babies,* by Anne Fine. Little, Brown.

Western Wind, by Paula Fox. Orchard.

Nonfiction Book: *Eleanor Roosevelt: A Life of Discovery,* by Russell Freedman. Clarion.

Honor: *Unconditional Surrender: U. S. Grant and the Civil War,* by Albert Marrin. Atheneum.

A Tree Place and Other Poems, by Constance Levy. Illus. Robert Sabuda. McElderry.

Picture Book: *Grandfather's Journey,* by Allen Say. Houghton Mifflin.

Honor: *Owen,* by Kevin Henkes. Greenwillow.

A Small Tall Tale from the Far Far North, by Peter Sis. Knopf.

1993

Fiction and Poetry Book: *Ajeemah and His Son,* by James Berry. Harper.

Honor: *The Giver,* by Lois Lowry. Houghton Mifflin.

Nonfiction Book: *Sojourner Truth: Ain't I a Woman?,* by Patricia C. McKissack and Fredrick L. McKissack. Scholastic.

Honor: *Lives of the Musicians: Good Times, Bad Times (And What the Neighbors Thought)*, by Kathleen Krull. Illus. Kathryn Hewitt. Harcourt.

Picture Book: *The Fortune Tellers*, by Lloyd Alexander. Illus. Trina Schart Hyman. Dutton.

Honor: *Komodo!*, by Peter Sis. Greenwillow.

Raven: A Trickster Tale from the Pacific Northwest, by Gerald McDermott. Harcourt.

1992

Fiction and Poetry Book: *Missing May*, by Cynthia Rylant. Jackson/Orchard.

Honor: *Nothing But the Truth*, by Avi. Jackson/Orchard.

Somewhere in the Darkness, by Walter Dean Myers. Scholastic.

Nonfiction Book: *Talking with Artists*, edited by Pat Cummings. Bradbury.

Honor: *Red Leaf, Yellow Leaf*, by Lois Ehlert. Harcourt.

The Handmade Alphabet, by Laura Rankin. Dial.

Picture Book: *Seven Blind Mice*, by Ed Young. Philomel.

Honor: *In the Tall, Tall Grass*, by Denise Fleming. Holt

1991

Fiction and Poetry Book: *The True Confessions of Charlotte Doyle*, by Avi. Orchard.

Honor: *Paradise Cafe and Other Stories*, by Martha Brooks. Joy Street.

Judy Scuppernong, by Brenda Seabrooke. Cobblehill.

Nonfiction Book: *Appalachia: The Voices of Sleeping Birds*, by Cynthia Rylant. Illus. Barry Moser. Harcourt.

Honor: *The Wright Brothers: How They Invented the Airplane*, by Russell Freedman. Holiday.

Good Queen Bess: The Story of Elizabeth I of England, by Diane Stanley and Peter Vennema. Illus. Diane Stanley. Four Winds.

Picture Book: *The Tale of the Mandarin Ducks*, by Katherine Paterson. Illus. Leo Dillon and Diane Dillon. Lodestar.

Honor: *Aardvarks, Disembark!*, by Ann Jonas. Greenwillow.

Sophie and Lou, by Petra Mathers. Harper.

1990

Fiction and Poetry Book: *Maniac Magee*, by Jerry Spinelli. Little, Brown.

Honor: *Saturnalia*, by Paul Fleischman. Harper.

Stonewords, by Pam Conrad. Harper.

Nonfiction Book: *The Great Little Madison*, by Jean Fritz. Putnam.

Honor: *Insect Metamorphosis: From Egg to Adult*, by Ron Goor and Nancy Goor. Atheneum.

Picture Book: *Lon Po Po: A Red-Riding Hood Story from China*, trans. Ed Young. Illus. Ed Young. Philomel.

Honor: *Chicka Chicka Boom Boom*, by Bill Martin, Jr., and John Archambault. Illus. Lois Ehlert. Simon & Schuster.

Special Citation: *Valentine and Orson*, by Nancy Ekholm Burkert. Farrar, Straus & Giroux.

1989

Fiction and Poetry Book: *The Village by the Sea*, by Paula Fox. Orchard.

Honor: *Eva*, by Peter Dickinson. Delacorte.

Gideon Ahoy!, by William Mayne. Delacorte.

Nonfiction Book: *The Way Things Work*, by David Macaulay. Houghton Mifflin.

Honor: *The Rainbow People*, by Laurence Yep. Harper.

Round Buildings, Square Buildings, & Buildings That Wiggle Like a Fish, by Philip M. Isaacson. Knopf.

Picture Book: *Shy Charles*, by Rosemary Wells. Dial.

Honor: *Island Boy*, by Barbara Cooney. Viking.

The Nativity. Illus. Julie Vivas. Gulliver/Harcourt.

1988

Fiction and Poetry Book: *The Friendship*, by Mildred D. Taylor. Illus. Max Ginsburg. Dial.

Honor: *Granny Was a Buffer Girl*, by Berlie Doherty. Orchard.

Joyful Noise: Poems for Two Voices, by Paul Fleischman. Illus. Eric Beddows. Harper/Zolotow.

Memory, by Margaret Mahy. McElderry.

Nonfiction Book: *Anthony Burns: The Defeat and Triumph of a Fugitive Slave*, by Virginia Hamilton. Knopf.

Honor: *African Journey*, by John Chiasson. Bradbury.

Little by Little: A Writer's Education, by Jean Little. Viking.

Picture Book: *The Boy of the Three-Year Nap*, by Dianne Snyder. Illus. Allen Say. Houghton Mifflin.

Honor: *Where the Forest Meets the Sea*, by Jeannie Baker. Greenwillow.

Stringbean's Trip to the Shining Sea, by Vera B. Williams. Illus. Jennifer Williams and Vera B. Williams. Greenwillow.

1987

Fiction and Poetry Book: *Rabble Starkey*, by Lois Lowry. Houghton Mifflin.

Honor: *Georgia Music*, by Helen V. Griffith. Illus. James Stevenson. Greenwillow.

Isaac Campion, by Janni Howker. Greenwillow.

Nonfiction Book: *The Pilgrims of Plimoth*, by Marcia Sewall. Atheneum.

Honor: *Being Born*, by Sheila Kitzinger. Illus. Lennart Nilsson. Grosset and Dunlap.

The Magic Schoolbus at the Waterworks, by Joanna Cole. Illus. Bruce Degen. Scholastic.

Steamboat in a Cornfield, by John Hartford. Crown.

Picture Book: *Mufaro's Beautiful Daughters*, by John Steptoe. Lothrop, Lee & Shepard.

Honor: *In Coal Country*, by Judith Hendershot. Illus. Thomas B. Allen. Knopf.

Cherries and Cherry Pits, by Vera B. Williams. Greenwillow.

Old Henry, by Joan W. Blos. Illus. Stephen Gammell. Morrow.

1986

Fiction and Poetry Book: *In Summer Light*, by Zibby Oneal. Viking.

Honor: *Prairie Songs,* by Pam Conrad. Harper.

Howl's Moving Castle, by Diana Wynne Jones. Greenwillow.

Nonfiction Book: *Auks, Rocks, and the Odd Dinosaur: Inside Stories from the Smithsonian's Museum of Natural History,* by Peggy Thomson. Crowell.

Honor: *Dark Harvest: Migrant Farmworkers in America,* by Brent Ashabranner. Illus. James. C. Giblin. Crowell.

The Truth about Santa Claus, by James C. Giblin. Crowell.

Picture Book: *The Paper Crane,* by Molly Bang. Greenwillow.

Honor: *Gorilla,* by Anthony Browne. Knopf.

The Trek, by Ann Jonas. Greenwillow.

The Polar Express, by Chris Van Allsburg. Houghton Mifflin.

1985

Fiction and Poetry Book: *The Moves Make the Man,* by Bruce Brooks. Harper.

Honor: *Babe: The Gallant Pig,* by Dick King-Smith. Illus. Mary Rayner. Crown.

The Changeover: A Supernatural Romance, by Margaret Mahy. Atheneum/McElderry.

Nonfiction Book: *Commodore Perry in the Land of the Shogun,* by Rhoda Blumberg. Lothrop, Lee & Shepard.

Honor: *Boy,* by Roald Dahl. Farrar, Straus & Giroux.

1812: The War Nobody Won, by Albert Marrin. Atheneum.

Picture Book: *Mama Don't Allow,* by Thatcher Hurd. Harper.

Honor: *Like Jake and Me,* by Mavis Jukes. Illus. Lloyd Bloom. Knopf.

How Much Is a Million?, by David M. Schwartz. Illus. Steven Kellogg. Lothrop, Lee & Shepard.

Special Citation: *1,2,3,* by Tana Hoban. Greenwillow.

1984

Fiction and Poetry Book: *A Little Fear,* by Patricia Wrightson. Atheneum/McElderry.

Honor: *Archer's Goon,* by Diana Wynne Jones. Greenwillow.

Unclaimed Treasures, by Patricia MacLachlan. Harper.

A Solitary Blue, by Cynthia Voigt. Atheneum.

Nonfiction Book: *The Double Life of Pocahontas,* by Jean Fritz. Illus. Ed Young. Putnam.

Honor: *Queen Eleanor: Independent Spirit of the Medieval World: A Biography of Eleanor of Aquitaine,* by Polly Schoyer Brooks. Lippincott.

Children of the Wild West, by Russell Freedman. Clarion.

The Tipi: A Center of Native American Life, by David Vue and Charlotte Vue. Knopf.

Picture Book: *Jonah and the Great Fish,* by Warwick Hutton. Atheneum/McElderry.

Honor: *Dawn,* by Molly Bang. Morrow.

The Guinea Pig ABC, by Kate Duke. Dutton.

The Rose in My Garden, by Arnold Lobel. Illus. Anita Lobel. Greenwillow.

1983

Fiction and Poetry Book: *Sweet Whispers, Brother Rush,* by Virginia Hamilton. Philomel.

Honor: *Homesick: My Own Story,* by Jean Fritz. Illus. Margot Tomes. Putnam.

The Road to Camlann, by Rosemary Sutcliff. Dutton.

Dicey's Song, by Cynthia Voigt. Atheneum.

Nonfiction Book: *Behind Barbed Wire: The Imprisonment of Japanese Americans During World War II,* by Daniel S. Davis. Dutton.

Honor: *Hiroshima No Pika,* by Toshi Maruki. Lothrop, Lee & Shepard.

The Jewish Americans: A History in Their Own Words: 1650–1950, by Milton Meltzer. Crowell.

Picture Book: *A Chair for My Mother,* by Vera B. Williams. Greenwillow.

Honor: *Friends,* by Helme Heine. Atheneum/McElderry.

Yeh-Shen: A Cinderella Story from China, by Ai-Ling Louie. Illus. Ed Young. Philomel.

Doctor De Soto, by William Steig. Farrar, Straus & Giroux.

1982

Fiction and Poetry Book: *Playing Beatie Bow,* by Ruth Park. Atheneum.

Honor: *The Voyage Begun,* by Nancy Bond. Atheneum.

Ask Me No Questions, by Ann Schlee. Holt.

The Scarecrows, by Robert Westall. Greenwillow.

Nonfiction Book: *Upon the Head of the Goat: A Childhood in Hungary 1939–1944,* by Aranka Siegel. Farrar, Straus & Giroux.

Honor: *Lobo of the Tasaday,* by John Nance. Pantheon.

Dinosaurs of North America, by Helen Roney Sattler. Illus. Anthony Rao. Lothrop, Lee & Shepard.

Picture Book: *A Visit to William Blake's Inn: Poems for Innocent and Experienced Travelers,* by Nancy Willard. Illus. Alice Provensen and Martin Provensen. Harcourt.

Honor: *The Friendly Beasts: An Old Christmas Carol,* by Tomie dePaola. Putnam.

1981

Fiction and Poetry Book: *The Leaving,* by Lynn Hall. Scribner.

Honor: *Ida Early Comes Over the Mountain,* by Robert Burch. Viking.

Flight of the Sparrow, by Julia Cunningham. Pantheon.

Footsteps, by Leon Garfield. Delacorte.

Nonfiction Book: *The Weaver's Gift,* by Kathryn Lasky. Illus. Christopher G. Knight. Warne.

Honor: *You Can't Be Timid with a Trumpet: Notes from the Orchestra,* by Betty English. Lothrop, Lee & Shepard.

The Hospital Book, by James Howe. Illus. Mal Warshaw. Crown.

Junk Food, Fast Food, Health Food: What America Eats and Why, by Lila Perl. Clarion.

Picture Book: *Outside Over There,* by Maurice Sendak. Harper.

Honor: *Where the Buffaloes Begin,* by Olaf Baker. Illus. Stephen Gammell. Warne.

On Market Street, by Arnold Lobel. Illus. Anita Lobel. Greenwillow.

Jumanji, by Chris Van Allsburg. Houghton Mifflin.

1980

Fiction and Poetry Book: *Conrad's War*, by Andrew Davies. Crown.

Honor: *The Night Swimmers*, by Betsy Byars. Delacorte.

Me and My Million, by Clive King. Crowell.

The Alfred Summer, by Jan Slepian. Macmillan.

Nonfiction Book: *Building: The Fight Against Gravity*, by Mario Salvadori. Illus. Saralinda Hooker and Christopher Ragus. Atheneum/McElderry.

Honor: *Childtimes: A Three-Generation Memoir*, by Eloise Greenfield. Illus. Jerry Pinkney. Crowell.

Stonewall, by Jean Fritz. Illus. Stephen Gammell. Putnam.

How the Forest Grew, by William Jaspersohn. Illus. Chuck Eckart. Greenwillow.

Picture Book: *The Garden of Abdul Gasazi*, by Chris Van Allsburg. Houghton Mifflin.

Honor: *The Gray Lady and the Strawberry Snatcher*, by Molly Bang. Greenwillow.

Why the Tides Ebb and Flow, by John Chase Bowden. Illus. Marc Brown. Houghton Mifflin.

Special Citation: *Graham Oakley's Magical Changes*, by Graham Oakley. Atheneum.

(For a complete list, go to www.hbook.com/bghb.shtml.)

Mildred L. Batchelder Awards

2002 Cricket Books/Carus Publishing for *How I Became an American*, by Karin Gündish. Trans. James Skofield.

Honor: Viking Press for *A Book of Coupons*, by Susie Morgenstern. Illus. Serge Bloch. Trans. Gill Rosner.

2001 Scholastic/Arthur A. Levine for *Samir and Yonatan*, by Daniella Carmi. Trans. Yael Lotan.

Honor: Godine for *Ultimate Game*, by Christian Lehmann. Trans. William Rodarmor.

2000 Walker and Company for *The Baboon King*, by Anton Quintans. Translated from Dutch by John Nieuwenhuizen.

Honor: R & S Books for *Vendela in Venice*, by Christina Björk. Illus. Inga-Karin Eriksson. Translated from Swedish by Patricia Crampton.

Farrar, Straus & Giroux for *Collector of Moments*, by Quint Buchholz. Translated from German by Peter F. Neumeyer.

Front Street for *Asphalt Angels*, by Ineke Holtwijk. Translated from Dutch by Wanda Boeke.

1999 Dial for *Thanks to My Mother*, by Schoschana Rabinovici. Translated from German by James Skofield.

Honor: Viking for *Secret Letters from 0 to 10*, by Susie Morgenstern. Translated from French by Gill Rosner.

1998 Henry Holt for *The Robber and Me*, by Josef Holub. Ed. Mark Aronson. Translated from German by Elizabeth D. Crawford.

Honor: Scholastic Press for *Hostage to War: A True Story*, by Tatjana Wassiljewa. Translated from German by Anna Trenter.

Viking Publishing for *Nero Corleone: A Cat's Story*, by Elke Heidenrich. Translated from German by Doris Orgel.

1997 Farrar, Straus & Giroux for *The Friends*, by Kazumi Yumoto. Translated from Japanese by Cathy Hirano.

1996 Houghton Mifflin for *The Lady with the Hat*, by Uri Orlev. Translated from Hebrew by Hillel Halkin.

Honor: Henry Holt for *Damned Strong Love: The True Story of Willi G. and Stephan K.*, by Lutz Van Sijk. Translated from German by Elizabeth D. Crawford.

Walker and Co. for *Star of Fear, Star of Hope*, by Jo Hoestlandt. Translated from French by Mark Ploizzotti.

1995 Dutton for *The Boys from St. Petri*, by Bjarne Reuter. Translated from Danish by Anthea Bell.

Honor: Lothrop, Lee & Shepard, for *Sister Shako and Kolo the Goat: Memories of My Childhood in Turkey*, by Vedat Dalokay. Translated from Turkish by Guner Ener.

1994 Farrar, Straus & Giroux for *The Apprentice*, by Pilar Molina Llorente. Translated from Spanish by Robin Longshaw.

Honor: Farrar, Straus & Giroux for *The Princess in the Kitchen Garden*, by Annemie Heymans and Margriet Heymans. Translated from Dutch by Johanna H. Prins and Johanna W. Prins.

Viking for *Anne Frank Beyond the Diary: A Photographic Remembrance*, by Ruud van der Rol and Rian Verhoeven, in association with the Anne Frank House. Translated from Dutch by Tony Langham and Plym Peters.

1993 No award given.

1992 Houghton Mifflin for *The Man from the Other Side*, by Uri Orlev. Translated from Hebrew by Hillel Halkin.

1991 E. P. Dutton for *A Hand Full of Stars*, by Rafik Schami. Translated from German by Rika Lesser.

1990 E. P. Dutton for *Buster's World*, by Bjarne Reuter. Translated from Danish by Anthea Bell.

1989 Lothrop, Lee & Shepard for *Crutches*, by Peter Hartling. Translated from German by Elizabeth D. Crawford.

1988 McElderry Books for *If You Didn't Have Me*, by Ulf Nilsson. Translated from Swedish by Lone Thygesen Clecher and George Blecher.

1987 Lothrop, Lee & Shepard for *No Hero for the Kaiser*, by Rudolph Frank. Translated from German by Patricia Crampton.

1986 Creative Education for *Rose Blanche*, by Christophe Gallaz and Robert Innocenti. Translated from Italian by Martha Coventry and Richard Craglia.

1985 Houghton Mifflin for *The Island on Bird Street*, by Uri Orlev. Translated from Hebrew by Hillel Halkin.

1984 Viking Press for *Ronia, the Robber's Daughter*, by Astrid Lindgren. Translated from Swedish by Patricia Crampton.

1983 Lothrop, Lee & Shepard for *Hiroshima No Pika*, by Toshi Maruki. Translated from Japanese through Kurita-Bando Literacy Agency.

1982 Bradbury Press for *The Battle Horse*, by Harry Kullman. Translated from Swedish by George Blecher and Lone Thygesen Blecher.

1981 William Morrow & Co. for *The Winter When Time Was Frozen*, by Els Pelgrom. Translated from Dutch by Maryka Rudnik and Raphael Rudnik.

1980 E. P. Dutton for *The Sound of the Dragon's Feet*, by Aliki Zei. Translated from Greek by Edward Fenton.

(For a complete list, go to www.ala.org/alsc/batch.html.)

NCTE Poetry Award for Excellence

2000 X. J. Kennedy

1997 Eloise Greenfield

1994 Barbara Juster Esbensen

1991 Valerie Worth

1988 Arnold Adoff

1985 Lilian Moore

1982 John Ciardi

1981 Eve Merriam

1980 Myra Cohn Livingston

1979 Karla Kuskin

1978 Aileen Fisher

1977 David McCord

(For more information, go to www.ncte.org/elem.poetry/.)

Pura Belpré Award

Where the winner of the award is the illustrator, the illustrator's name appears in boldface.

2002

Narrative: *Esperanza Rising*, by Pam Muñoz Ryan. Scholastic.

Honor: *Breaking Through*, by Francisco Jiménez, Houghton Mifflin.

Illustration: *Chato and the Party Animals*, by Gary Soto. Illus. **Susan Guevara.** Putnam.

Honor: *Juan Bobo Goes to Work*, by Marisa Montes. Illus. **Joe Cepeda.** HarperCollins.

2000

Narrative: *Under the Royal Palms: A Childhood in Cuba*, by Alma Flor Ada. Atheneum.

Honor: *From the Bellybutton of the Moon and Other Summer Poems/Del ombligo de la luna y otros poemas de verano*, by Francisco X. Alarcon. Illus. Maya Christina Gonzalez. Children's Book Press.

Laughing Out Loud, I Fly: Poems in English and Spanish by Juan Felipe Herrera Illus. Karen Barbour. HarperCollins.

Illustration: *Magic Windows*, by **Carmen Lomas Garza.** Children's Book Press.

Honor: *Barrio: Jose's Neighborhood*, by **George Ancona.** Harcourt Brace.

The Secret Stars, by Joseph Slate. Illus. **Felipe Davalos.** Marshall Cavendish.

Mama and Papa Have a Store, by **Amelia Lau Carling.** Dial.

1998

Narrative: *Parrot in the Oven: Mi vida*, by Victor Martinez. Cotler/HarperCollins.

Honor: *Laughing Tomatoes and Other Spring Poems/Jitomates Risuenos y otros poemas de primavera*, by Francisco X. Alarcon. Illus. Maya Christina Gonzalez. Children's Book Press.

Spirits of the High Mesa, by Floyd Martinez. Arte Publico.

Illustration: *Snapshots from the Wedding*, by Gary Soto. Illus. **Stephanie Garcia.** Putnam.

Honor: *In My Family/En mi familia*, by **Carmen Lomas Garza.** Children's Book Press.

The Golden Flower: A Taino Myth from Puerto Rico, by Nina Jaffe. Illus. **Enrique O. Sanchez.** Simon & Schuster.

Gathering the Sun: An Alphabet in Spanish and English, by Alma Flor Ada. English translation by Rosa Zubizarreta. Illus. **Simon Silva.** Lothrop, Lee & Shepard.

1996

Narrative: *An Island Like You: Stories of the Barrio*, by Judith Ortiz Cofer. Kroupa/Orchard.

Honor: *The Bossy Gallito/El gallo de bodas: A Traditional Cuban Folktale*, by Lucia Gonzalez. Illus. Lulu Delacre. Scholastic.

Baseball in April, and Other Stories, by Gary Soto. Harcourt.

Illustration: *Chato's Kitchen*, by Gary Soto. Illus. **Susan Guevara.** Putnam.

Honor: *Pablo Remembers: The Fiesta of the Day of the Dead*, by **George Ancona.** Lothrop, Lee & Shepard.

The Bossy Gallito/El gallo de bodas: A Traditional Cuban Folktale, by Lucia Gonzalez. Illus. **Lulu Delacre.** Scholastic.

Family Pictures/Cuadros de familia, Spanish text by Rosa Zubizarreta. Illus. **Carmen Lomas Garza.** Children's Book Press.

(For a complete list, go to www.ala.org/alsc.belpre.html.)

Edgar Allen Poe Awards for Best Juvenile Mystery

2002 *Dangling*, by Lillian Eige. Simon & Schuster/Atheneum.

Nominated: *Ghost Soldier*, by Elaine Marie Alphin. Holt.

Ghost Sitter, by Peni R. Griffin. Penguin-Putnam/Dutton.

Following Fake Man, by Barbara Ware Holmes. Random/Knopf.

Bug Muldoon, by Paul Shipton. Penguin-Putnam/Viking.

2001 *Dovey Coe*, by Frances O'Roark Dowell. Atheneum.

Nominated: *Trouble at Fort La Pointe*, by Kathleen Ernst. American Girl.

Sammey Keyes and the Curse of Mustache Mary, by Wendelin Van Draanen. Knopf.

Walking to the Bus-Rider Blues, by Harriette Gillem Robinet. Atheneum.

Ghosts in the Gallery, by Barbara Brooks Wallace. Atheneum.

2000 *The Night Flyers,* by Elizabeth McDavid Jones. Pleasant.

Nominated: *Howie Bowles, Secret Agent,* by Kate Banks. Illus. Isaac Millman. Farrar, Straus & Giroux.

Shadow Horse, by Alison Hart. Random.

Dolphin Luck, by Hilary McKay. McElderry/Simon & Schuster.

Green Thumb, by Rob Thomas. Simon & Schuster.

1999 *Sammy Keyes and the Hotel Thief,* by Wendelin Van Draanen. Knopf.

Nominated: *The Kidnappers,* by Willo Davis Roberts. Atheneum.

Alice Rose & Sam, by Kathryn Lasky. Hyperion.

The Wreckers, by Iain Lawrence. Delacorte.

Holes, by Louis Sacher. Farrar, Straus & Giroux.

1998 *Sparrows in the Scullery,* by Barbara Brooks Wallace. Atheneum.

Nominated: *Turn the Cup Around,* by Barbara Mariconda. Delacorte.

Christie and Company Down East, by Katharine Hall Page. Avon.

Secrets at Hidden Valley, by Willo Davis Roberts. Atheneum.

Wolf Stalker, by Gloria Skurzynski and Alane Ferguson. National Geographic.

1997 *The Clearing,* by Dorothy Reynolds Miller. Yearling.

No other nominees.

1996 *Looking for Jamie Bridger,* by Nancy Springer. Dial.

Nominated: *The 13th Floor,* by Sid Fleischman. Greenwillow.

Running Out of Time, by Margaret Peterson Haddix. Simon & Schuster.

Marvelous Marvin and the Pioneer Ghost, by Bonnie Pryor. Morrow.

The Bones in the Cliff, by James Stevenson. Greenwillow.

1995 *The Absolutely True Story . . . How I Visited Yellowstone Park with the Terrible Rubes,* by Willo Davis Roberts. Atheneum.

Nominated: *Harvey's Mystifying Racoon Mix Up,* by Eth Clifford. Houghton Mifflin.

Hester Bidgood, Investigatrix of Evil Deeds, by E. W. Hildick. Macmillan.

Trouble Will Find You, by Joan M. Lexau. Houghton Mifflin.

Caught, by Willo Davis Roberts. Atheneum.

1994 *The Twin in the Tavern,* by Barbara Brooks Wallace. Atheneum.

Nominated: *Tangled Webb,* by Eloise McGraw. McElderry.

The Face in the Bessledorf Funeral Parlor, by Phyllis Reynolds Naylor. Atheneum.

Spider Kane and the Mystery at Jumbo Nightcrawler's, by Mary Pope Osborne. Knopf.

Sam the Cat, Detective, by Linda Stewart. Scholastic.

1993 *Coffin on a Case,* by Eve Bunting. HarperCollins.

Nominated: *Fish and Bones,* by Ray Prather. Harcourt Brace.

The Widow's Broom, by Chris Van Allsburg. Houghton Mifflin.

Susannah and the Purple Mongoose, by Patricia Elmore. Dutton.

The Treasure Bird, by Peni R. Griffin. McElderry.

1992 *Wanted . . . Mud Blossom,* by Betsy Byars. HarperCollins.

Nominated: *Mystery on October Road,* by Alison Cragin Herzig and Jane Lawrence Mali. Viking.

Double Trouble Squared, by Kathryn Lasky. Harcourt Brace.

Witch Weed, by Phyllis Reynolds Naylor. Delacorte.

Finding Buck McHenry, by Alfred Slote. HarperCollins.

1991 *Stonewords,* by Pam Conrad. Harper & Row.

Nominated: *The Midnight Horse,* by Sid Fleischman. Greenwillow.

The Tormentors, by Lynn Hall. Harcourt Brace.

To Grandmother's House We Go, by Willo Davis Roberts. Atheneum.

Cave Ghost, by Barbara Steiner. Harcourt Brace.

1990 No award given.

1989 *Megan's Island,* by Willo David Roberts. Atheneum.

Nominated: *Following the Mystery Man,* by Mary Downing Hahn. Clarion.

Is Anybody There?, by Eve Bunting. Lippincott.

Something Upstairs, by Avi. Orchard.

The Lamp from the Warlock's Tomb, by John Bellairs. Dial.

1988 *Lucy Forever and Miss Rosetree, Shrinks,* by Susan Shreve. Holt.

Nominated: *Bury the Dead,* by Peter Carter. Farrar, Straus & Giroux.

The House on the Hill, by Eileen Dunlop. Holiday.

The Twisted Window, by Lois Duncan. Delacorte.

Through the Hidden Door, by Rosemary Wells. Dial.

1987 *The Other Side of Dark,* by Joan Lowery Nixon. Delacorte.

Nominated: *Floating Illusions,* by Chelsea Quinn Yarbo. Harper & Row.

The Secret Life of Dilly McBean, by Dorothy Haas. Bradbury.

The Skeleton Man, by Jay Bennett. Franklin Watts.

The Bodies in the Bessledorf Hotel, by Phyllis Reynolds Naylor. Atheneum.

1986 *The Sandman's Eyes,* by Patricia Windsor. Delacorte.

Nominated: *Locked in Time,* by Lois Duncan. Little, Brown.

On the Edge, by Gillian Cross. Holiday.

Playing Murder, by Sandra Scoppettone. Harper & Row.

Screaming High, by David Line. Little, Brown.

1985 *Night Cry,* by Phyllis Reynolds Naylor. Atheneum.

Nominated: *Chameleon the Spy and the Case of the Vanishing Jewels,* by Diane R. Massie. Harper & Row.

The Ghosts of Now, by Joan Lowery Nixon. Delacorte.

The Island on Bird Street, by Uri Orlev. Houghton Mifflin.

The Third Eye, by Lois Duncan. Little, Brown.

1984 *The Callender Papers,* by Cynthia Voigt. Atheneum.

Nominated: *The Dollhouse Murders,* by Betty Ren Wright. Holiday.

The Griffin Legacy, by Jan O'Donnell Klaveness. Macmillan.

Shadrach's Crossing, by Avi. Pantheon.

The Maze Stone, by Eileen Dunlop. Coward-McCann.

1983 *The Murder of Hound Dog Bates,* by Robbie Branscum. Viking.

Nominated: *Cadbury's Coffin,* by Glendon Swarthout and Kathryn Swarthout. Doubleday.

The Case of the Cop Catchers, by Terrance Dicks. Lodestar/Dutton.

Clone Catcher, by Alfred Slote. Lippincott.

Kept in the Dark, by Nina Bawden. Lothrop, Lee & Shepard.

1982 *Taking Terri Mueller,* by Norma Fox Mazer. Avon.

Nominated: *Detective Mole and the Halloween Mystery,* by Robert Quackenbush. Lothrop, Lee & Shepard.

Detour to Danger, by Eva-Lis Wuorio. Delacorte.

Hoops, by Walter Dean Myers. Delacorte.

Village of the Vampire Cat, by Lensey Namioka. Delacorte.

1981 *The Séance,* by Joan Lowery Nixon. Harcourt Brace.

Nominated: *When No One Was Looking,* by Rosemary Wells. Dial.

We Dare Not Go A-Hunting, by Charlotte MacLeod. Atheneum.

More Minden Curses, by Willo Davis Roberts. Atheneum.

The Doggone Mystery, by Mary Blount Christian. Atheneum.

1980 *The Kidnapping of Christina Lattimore,* by Joan Lowery Nixon. Harcourt Brace.

Nominated: *Mystery Cottage in Left Field,* by Remus F. Caroselli. Putnam.

The Whispered Horse, by Lynn Hall. Follett.

Chameleon Was a Spy, by Diane Redfield Massie. Crowell.

Mystery of the Eagle's Claw, by Frances Wosmek. Westminister.

(For updates, go to www.mysterywriters.org/awards/ edgars_02_nominees.html.)

Américas Awards for Children's and Young Adult Literature

2001 *A Movie in My Pillow,* by Jorge Argueta. Illus. Elizabeth Gomez. Children's Book Press.

Breaking Through, by Francisco Jiménez. Houghton Mifflin.

2000 *The Composition,* by Antonia Skarmeta. Illus. Alfonso Ruano. Greenwood.

The Color of My Words, by Lynn Joseph. HarperCollins.

1999 *Crashboomlove,* by Juan Felipe Herrera. University of New Mexico Press.

1998 *Barrio: Jose's Neighborhood,* by George Ancona. Harcourt Brace.

Mama and Papa Have a Store, by Amelia Lau Carling. Dial.

1997 *The Circuit,* by Francisco Jiménez. University of New Mexico Press.

The Face at the Window, by Regina Hanson. Illus. Linda Saport. Clarion.

1996 *In My Family/En mi familia,* by Carmen Lomas Garza. Children's Book Press.

Parrot in the Oven, by Victor Martinez. HarperCollins.

1995 *Tonight, by Sea,* by Frances Temple. Orchard.

1994 *The Mermaid's Twin Sister,* by Lynn Joseph. Clarion.

1993 *Vejigante Masquerader,* by Lulu Delacre. Scholastic.

(For a complete list, go to www.uwm.edu/Dept/CLACS/ outreach_americas.html.)

Scott O'Dell Historical Fiction Awards

2002 *The Land,* by Mildred D. Taylor. Penguin Putnam.

2001 *The Art of Keeping Cool,* by Janet Taylor Lisle. Atheneum.

2000 *Two Suns in the Sky,* by Miriam Bat-Ami. Front Street/Cricket.

1999 *Forty Acres and Maybe a Mule,* by Harriette Gillem Robinet. Atheneum.

1998 *Out of the Dust,* by Karen Hesse. Scholastic.

1997 *Jip: His Story,* by Katherine Paterson. Puffin.

1996 *The Bomb,* by Theodore Taylor. Harcourt Brace.

1995 *Under the Blood Red Sun,* by Graham Salisbury. Delacorte.

1994 *Bull Run,* by Paul Fleischman. HarperCollins.

1993 *Morning Girl,* by Michael Dorris. Hyperion.

1992 *Stepping on the Cracks,* by Mary Downing Hahn. Clarion.

1991 *A Time of Troubles,* by Pieter Van Raven. Scribner.

1990 *Shades of Gray,* by Carolyn Reeder. Simon & Schuster.

1989 *The Honorable Prison,* by Lyll Becerra de Jenkins. Puffin.

1988 *Charley Skedaddle,* by Patricia Beatty. Morrow.

1987 *Streams to the River, River to the Sea,* by Scott O'Dell. Houghton Mifflin.

1986 *Sarah, Plain and Tall,* by Patricia C. MacLachlan. Harper & Row.

1985 *The Fighting Ground,* by Avi. HarperCollins.

1984 *The Sign of the Beaver,* by Elizabeth George Speare. Houghton Mifflin.

(For updates, go to www.scottodell.com/sosoaward.html.)

Orbis Pictus Award for Outstanding Nonfiction for Children

2002 *Black Potatoes: The Story of the Great Irish Famine, 1845–1850,* by Susan Campbell Bartoletti. Houghton Mifflin.

Honor: *The Cod's Tale,* by Mark Kurlansky. Illus. S. D. Schindler. Penguin Putnam.

The Dinosaurs of Waterhouse Hawkins: An Illuminating History of Mr. Waterhouse Hawkins, Artist and Lecturer, by Barbara Kerley. Illus. Brian Selznick. Scholastic.

Martin's Big Words: The Life of Dr. Martin Luther King, Jr., by Doreen Rappaport. Illus. Bryan Collier. Hyperion.

2001 *Hurry Freedom: African Americans in Gold Rush California,* by Jerry Stanley. Crown.

Honor: *The Amazing Life of Benjamin Franklin,* by James Cross Giblin. Illus. Michael Dooling. Scholastic.

America's Champion Swimmer: Gertrude Ederle, by David A. Adler. Illus. Terry Widener. Gulliver.

Michelangelo, by Diane Stanley. HarperCollins.

Osceola: Memories of a Sharecropper's Daughter, by Alan B. Govenar. Illus. Shane W. Evans. Jump at the Sun.

Wild and Swampy, by Jim Arnosky. HarperCollins.

2000 *Through My Eyes,* by Ruby Bridges and Margo Lundell. Scholastic.

Honor: *At Her Majesty's Request: An African Princess in Victorian England,* by Walter Dean Myers. Scholastic.

Piano Virtuoso, by Susanna Reich. Clarion.

Mapping the World, by Sylvia A. Johnson. Atheneum.

Snake Scientist, by Sy Montgomery. Illus. Nic Bishop. Houghton Mifflin.

The Top of the World: Climbing Mount Everest, by Steve Jenkins. Houghton Mifflin.

1999 *Story of Shackleton and the Endurance,* by Jennifer Armstrong. Crown.

Honor: *Black Whiteness: Admiral Byrd Alone in the Antarctic,* by Robert Burleigh. Illus. Walter Lyon Krudop. Atheneum.

Fossil Feud: The Rivalry of the First American Dinosaur Hunters, by Thom Holmes. Messner.

Hottest, Coldest, Highest, Deepest, by Steve Jenkins. Houghton Mifflin.

No Pretty Pictures: A Child of War, by Anita Lobel. Greenwillow.

1998 *An Extraordinary Life: The Story of a Monarch Butterfly,* by Laurence Pringle. Illus. Bob Marstall. Orchard.

Honor: *A Drop of Water: A Book of Science and Wonder,* by Walter Wick. Scholastic.

A Tree is Growing, by Arthur Dorros. Illustrated by S. D. Schindler. Scholastic.

Charles A. Lindbergh: A Human Hero, by James Cross Giblin. Clarion.

Kennedy Assassinated! The World Mourns: A Reporter's Story, by Wilborn Hampton. Candlewick.

Digger: The Tragic Fate of the California Indians from the Missions to the Gold Rush, by Jerry Stanley. Crown.

1997 *Leonardo da Vinci,* by Diane Stanley. Morrow.

Honor: *Full Steam Ahead: The Race to Build a Transcontinental Railroad,* by Rhonda Blumberg. National Geographic.

The Life and Death of Crazy Horse, by Russell Freedman. Holiday.

One World, Many Religions: The Ways We Worship, by Mary Pope Osborne. Knopf.

1996 *The Great Fire,* by Jim Murphy. Scholastic.

Honor: *Dolphin Man: Exploring the World of Dolphins,* by Laurence Pringle. Illus. Randall S. Wells. Atheneum.

Rosie the Riveter: Women Working on the Home Front in World War II, by Penny Colman. Crown.

1995 *Safari Beneath the Sea: The Wonder World of the North Pacific Coast,* by Diane Seanson. Sierra.

Honor: *Wildlife Rescue: The Work of Dr. Kathleen Ramsay,* by Jennifer Owings Dewey. Boyds Mills.

Kids at Work: Lewis Hine and the Crusade against Child Labor, by Russell Freedman. Clarion.

Christmas in the Big House, Christmas in the Quarters, by Patricia C. McKissack and Fredrick L. McKissack. Scholastic.

1994 *Across America on an Emigrant Train,* by Jim Murphy. Clarion.

Honor: *To the Top of the World: Adventures with Arctic Wolves,* by Jim Brandenburg. Walker.

Making Sense: Animal Perception and Communication, by Bruce Brooks. Farrar, Straus & Giroux.

1993 *Children of the Dust Bowl: The True Story of the School at Weedpatch Camp,* by Jerry Stanley. Crown.

Honor: *Talking to Artists,* by Pat Cummings. Bradbury.

Come Back, Salmon, by Molly Cone. Sierra.

1992 *Flight: The Journey of Charles Lindbergh,* by Robert Burleigh. Philomel.

Honor: *Now Is Your Time! The African-American Struggle for Freedom,* by Walter Dean Myers. HarperCollins.

Prairie Vision: The Life and Times of Solomon Butcher, by Pam Conrad. HarperCollins.

1991 *Franklin Delano Roosevelt,* by Russell Freedman. Clarion.

Honor: *Seeing Earth from Space,* by Patricia Lauber. Orchard.

Arctic Memories, by Normee Ekoomiak. Holt.

1990 *The Great Little Madison,* by Jean Fritz. Putnam.

Honor: *The Great American Gold Rush,* by Rhoda Blumberg. Bradbury.

The News about Dinosaurs, by Patricia Lauber. Bradbury.

(For a complete list go to www.ncte.org/elem/orbispictus/.)

Kate Greenaway Medals

2000 Lauren Child, *I Will Not Ever Never Eat a Tomato*. Orchard.

1999 Helen Oxenbury, *Alice's Adventures in Wonderland*. (text by Lewis Carroll). Walker.

1998 Helen Cooper, *Pumpkin Soup*. Doubleday.

1997 P. J. Lynch, *When Jessie Came Across the Sea* (text by Amy Hest). Walker.

1996 Helen Cooper, *The Baby Who Wouldn't Go to Bed*. Doubleday.

1995 P. J. Lynch, *The Christmas Miracle of Jonathan Toomey*. Walker.

1994 Gregory Rogers, *Way Home* (text by Libby Hathorn). Andersen Press.

1993 Alan Lee, *Black Ships before Troy*. Frances Lincoln.

1992 Anthony Browne, *Zoo*. Julia MacRae.

1991 Janet Ahlberg, *The Jolly Christmas Postman* (text by Allan Ahlberg). Heinemann.

1990 Gary Blythe, *The Whales' Song* (text by Dyan Sheldon). Hutchinson.

1989 Michael Foreman, *War Boy: A Country Childhood*. Pavilion.

1988 Barbara Firth, *Can't You Sleep, Little Bear?* (text by Martin Waddell). Walker.

1987 Adrienne Kennaway, *Crafty Chameleon* (text by Mwenye Hadithi). Hudder & Stoughton.

1986 Fiona French, *Snow White in New York*. Oxford University Press.

1985 Juan Wijngaard, *Sir Gawain and the Loathly Lady* (text by Selina Hastings). Walker.

1984 Errol LeCain, *Hiawatha's Childhood*. Faber.

1983 Anthony Browne, *Gorilla*. Julia MacRae.

1982 Michael Foreman. *Long Neck and Thunder Foot* (text by Helen Piers); and *Sleeping Beauty and other Favorite Fairy Tales* (selected by Angela Carter). Kestral and Gollancz.

1981 Charles Keeping, *The Highwayman*. Oxford University Press.

1980 Quentin Blake, *Mr. Magnolia*. Cape.

(For a complete list, go to www.carnegiegreenaway.org.uk/green.html.)

Carnegie Medals

2000 Beverly Naidoo, *The Other Side of Truth*. Puffin.

1999 Aidan Chambers, *Postcards from No Man's Land*. Bodley Head.

1998 David Almond, *Skellig*. Hodder.

1997 Tim Bowler, *Riverboy*. Oxford University Press.

1996 Melvin Burgess, *Junk*. Andersen.

1995 Phillip Pullman, *His Dark Materials: Northern Lights* (published in the United States as *The Golden Compass*). Scholastic.

1994 Theresa Breslin, *Whispers in the Graveyard*. Methuen.

1993 Robert Swindells, *Stone Cold*. Hamish Hamilton.

1992 Anne Fine, *Flour Babies*. Hamish Hamilton.

1991 Berlie Doherty, *Dear Nobody*. Hamish Hamilton.

1990 Gillian Cross, *Wolf*. Oxford University Press.

1989 Anne Fine, *Goggle-eyes*. Hamish Hamilton.

1988 Geraldine McCaughrean, *A Pack of Lies*. Oxford University Press.

1987 Susan Price, *The Ghost Drum*. Faber & Faber.

1986 Berlie Doherty, *Granny was a Buffer Girl*. Methuen.

1985 Kevin Crossley-Holland, *Storm*. Hinemann.

1984 Margaret Mahy, *The Changeover*. Dent.

1983 Jan Mark, *Handles*. Kestral.

1982 Margaret Mahy, *The Haunting*. Dent.

1981 Robert Westall, *The Scarecrows*. Chatto and Windus.

1980 Peter Dickinson, *City of Gold*. Gollancz.

(For a complete list, go to www.carnegiegreenaway.org.uk/carnegie/list.html.)

Text Credits

p. 31, From THE POLAR EXPRESS by Chris Van Allsburg. Copyright © 1985 by Chris Van Allsburg. Reprinted by permission of Houghton Mifflin Company. All rights reserved; From THE WHALES' SONG by Dyan Sheldon, copyright © 1992 by Dyan Sheldon. Used by permission of Dial Books for Young Readers, an imprint of Penguin Putnam Books for Young Readers, a division of Penguin Putnam Inc.; p. 52, From *The Lotus Seed* by Sherry Garland. Reprinted by permission of Harcourt, Inc.; p. 59, From "How to Choose Great Books for the Classroom," by Katherine Paterson, *NEA Today,* May, 2001. Reprinted by permission of the National Education Association; p. 62, From "Supporting Critical Conversations in Classrooms," speech by Jerome Harste to Michigan Council of Teachers of English, October 9, 1998. Used by permission of Jerome Harste; p. 73, From *Alison's Zinnia* by Anita Lobel. Reprinted by permission of HarperCollins Publishers Inc.; From *Aster Aardvark's Alphabet Adventure,* by Steven Kellogg. Reprinted by permission of HarperCollins Publishers Inc.; From QUENTIN BLAKE'S ABC by Quentin Blake. Reprinted by permission of Random House Children's Books, a division of Random House, Inc.; p. 74, From *The Ocean Alphabet* by Jerry Pallotta. Copyright © 1986 by Jerry Pallotta. All rights reserved. Used with permission by Charlesbridge Publishing, Inc.; From A IS FOR AFRICA by Ifeoma Onyefulu, copyright © 1993 by Ifeoma Onyefulu. Used by permission of Cobblehill Books, an affiliate of Dutton Children's Books, an imprint of Penguin Putnam Books for Young Readers, a division of Penguin Putnam Inc.; From THE ABC BUNNY by Wanda Gag, copyright 1933 by Wanda Gag, renewed © 1961 by Robert Janssen. Used by permission of Coward-McCann, an imprint of Penguin Putnam Books for Young Readers, a division of Penguin Putnam Inc.; From *The ABC Mystery,* by Doug Cushman. Reprinted by permission of HarperCollins Publishers Inc.; p. 78, From *Hello! Good-bye!* by Aliki. Reprinted by permission of HarperCollins Publishers Inc.; p. 84, From *Silly Tilly's Valentine* by Lillian Hoban. Reprinted by permission of HarperCollins Publishers Inc.; From *The Fat Cat Sat on the Mat* by Nurit Karlin. Reprinted by permission of HarperCollins Publishers Inc.; From *Wizard and Wart at Sea* by Janice Lee Smith. Reprinted by permission of HarperCollins Publishers Inc.; From *Sid and Sam* by Nola Buck. Reprinted by permission of HarperCollins Publishers Inc.; From *The Great Snake Escape* by Molly Coxe. Reprinted by permission of HarperCollins Publishers Inc.; p. 189, From *Wizard and Wart at Sea* by Janice Lee Smith. Reprinted by permission of HarperCollins Publishers Inc.; From *Toby, Where Are You?* by William Steig. Reprinted by permission of HarperCollins Publishers Inc.; From *Noel the First,* by Kate McMullan. Reprinted by permission of HarperCollins Publishers Inc.; p. 204, From TAR BEACH by Faith Ringgold. Reprinted by permission of Crown Children's Books, a division of Random House, Inc.; p. 205, *Heroes* text copyright © 1995 by Ken Mochizuki. Permission arranged with LEE & LOW BOOKS Inc., New York, NY 10016; p. 233, From UNDER THE CHERRY BLOSSOM TREE by Allen Say. Copyright © 1997 by Allen Say. Reprinted by permission of Houghton Mifflin Company. All rights reserved; p. 236, From JOSEPH HAD A LITTLE OVER-COAT by Simms Taback, copyright © 1999 by Simms Taback. Used by permission of Viking Penguin, an imprint of Penguin Putnam Books for Young Readers, a division of Penguin Putnam Inc. All rights reserved; From BIT BY BIT by Steve Sanfield, copyright © 1995 by Steve Sanfield, text. Used by permission of Philomel Books, an imprint of Penguin Putnam Books for Young Readers, a division of Penguin Putnam Inc. All rights reserved; p. 244, From *Mike Fink* by Steven Kellogg. Reprinted by permission of HarperCollins Publishers Inc.; p. 245, From SWAMP ANGEL by Anne Isaacs, copyright © 1994 by Anne Isaacs. Used by permission of Dutton, a division of Penguin Putnam Inc.; From *The Bunyans* by Audrey Wood. Reprinted by permission of Scholastic Inc.; From *Sally Ann Thunder Ann Whirlwind Crockett* by Steven Kellogg. Reprinted by permission of HarperCollins Publishers Inc.; From *Keelboat Annie* by Janet P. Johnson. Copyright © 1998 by Troll Communications L.L.C. Published by and reprinted with permission of Troll Communications, L.L.C.; From JOHN HENRY by Julius Lester, copyright © 1994 by Julius Lester. Used by permission of Dial Books for Young Readers, an imprint of Penguin Putnam Books for Young Readers, a division of Penguin Putnam Inc.; From *Paul Bunyan: A Tall Tale* by Steven Kellogg. Reprinted by permission of HarperCollins Publishers Inc.; p. 246, From SEVEN BLIND MICE by Ed Young, copyright © 1992 by Ed Young. Used by permission of Philomel Books, an imprint of Penguin Putnam Books for Young Readers, a division of Penguin Putnam Inc.; p. 337, From "Song for Something Little" by Lois Duncan, in *All God's Children,* compiled by Lee Bennett Hopkins. Reprinted by permission of Harcourt, Inc.; p. 341, From *Bones— Our Skeletal System* by Seymour Simon. Reprinted by permission of HarperCollins Publishers Inc.; p. 342, From *William Shakespeare & the Globe* by Aliki. Reprinted by permission of HarperCollins Publishers Inc.; p. 360, From *A Brilliant Streak: The Making of Mark Twain* by Kathryn Lasky. Reprinted by permission of Harcourt, Inc.; p. 364, From JOAN OF ARC by Josephine Poole. Reprinted by permission of Alfred A. Knopf Children's Books, a division of Random House, Inc.; p. 365, Excerpt from STARRY MESSENGER by Peter Sis. Copyright © 1996 by Peter Sis. Reprinted by permission of Farrar, Straus and Giroux, LLC.; p. 372, From ELEANOR by Barbara Cooney, copyright © 1996 by Barbara Cooney. Used by permission of Viking Penguin, an imprint of Penguin Putnam Books for Young Readers, a division of Penguin Putnam Inc.

Name and Title Index
for Children's Books

Buck, Nola, 84, 85
Bud, Not Buddy (Curtis), 4, 131, 201
Buddy (Joyce), 95
Buffalo Gals: Women of the Old West (Miller), 345
Bug Off! (Hepworth), 338, 339
Bull Run (Fleischman), 287
Bully for You, Teddy Roosevelt! (Fritz), 377
Bunnicula: A Rabbit-Tale of Mystery (Howe), 18, 307
Bunny Riddles (Hall), 343
Bunting, Eve, 22, 50, 51, 53, 63, 85, 96, 134, 201, 264, 268, 280, 282, 363
Bunyans, The (Wood), 244
Burleigh, Robert, 41, 92, 162, 364, 377
Burningham, John, 72, 96, 100
Burton, Virginia Lee, 5
Bus Ride, The (Miller), 63
Button in Her Ear, A (Litchfield), 342
Buz (Egielski), 39, 51, 52
Byard, Carole, 44, 46, 206, 209
Byars, Betsy, 22, 85, 86, 100, 263, 265, 290

C

Cactus Poem (Asch), 162
Calders, Pere, 216, 218
Call Down the Moon: Poems of Music (Livingston), 159
Call It Courage (Sperry), 214
Calmenson, Stephanie, 231
Campbell, Eric, 261
Cannon, Janell, 22, 47, 87, 96
Canto Familiar (Soto), 147, 162, 206
Canyons (Paulsen), 261
Captive, The (Hansen), 279
Capucilli, Alyssa Satin, 263
Carle, Eric, 67, 80, 96, 102, 127, 205
Carlsen, Lori M., 206
Carr, Jan, 160
Carroll, Lewis, 301, 319
Cart, Michael, 318
Carter G. Woodson: The Man Who Put "Black" in American History (Haskins), 366
Case of the Lion Dance, The (Yep), 207, 265
Catalanotto, Peter, 22, 49, 80, 91, 96
Catherine, Called Birdy (Cushman), 286
Catrow, David, 282
Cats Are Cats (Larrick), 151
Cat's Elbow and Other Secret Languages, The (Schwartz), 336
Cay, The (Taylor), 180
Celebration Song: A Poem (Berry), 161
Cha, Dia, 22, 89
Chair for My Mother, A (Williams), 49, 191, 192
Chameleon Wore Chartreuse, The: A Chet Gecko Mystery (Hale), 265
Changes, Changes (Hutchins), 79
Chanticleer and the Fox (Chaucer), 67
Charbonneau, Eileen, 207

Charley Skedaddle (Beatty), 281, 286
Charlotte's Web (White), 5, 128, 301, 307
Chato's Kitchen (Soto), 203
Chattanooga Sludge (Bang), 326
Chaucer, Geoffrey, 67
Chermayeff, Ivan, 339
Chermayeff, Jane Clark, 339
Cherries and Cherry Pits (Williams), 91
Cherry, Lynn, 85, 89
Chester's Way (Henkes), 90
Ch'I-Lin Purse, The: A Collection of Ancient Chinese Stories (Fang), 207
Chicka Chicka Boom Boom (Martin and Archambault), 100
Chicken Doesn't Skate, The (Korman), 265
Chicken Soup with Rice: A Book of Months (Sendak), 101
Chickens Aren't the Only Ones (Heller), 340
Child Bride (Russell), 278
Child of the Owl (Yep), 263
Children in the Holocaust and World War II: Their Secret Diaries (Holliday), 367
Children of the Longhouse (Bruchac), 207
Child's Garden of Verse, A (Stevenson), 155
Chin-Lee, Cynthia, 74
Chinese Cinderella: The True Story of an Unwanted Daughter (Mah), 363
Chocolate, Debbi, 79
Choi, Sook Nyul, 210
Choi, Yangsook, 210, 283
Choosing Up Sides (Ritter), 266
Christie, R. Gregory, 96, 368
Christmas in the Big House, Christmas in the Quarters (McKissack), 281
Christopher, Matt, 266
Chronicles of Prydain, The (Alexander), 301
Chrysanthemum (Henkes), 87, 101, 135
Ciardi, John, 154, 161, 164
Circle of Thanks, The: Native American Poems and Songs of Thanksgiving (Bruchac), 162
Circuit, The: Stories from the Life of a Migrant Child (Jimenez), 63
City Dog (Kuskin), 157
Clambake: A Wampanoag Tradition (Peters), 206
Clark, Emma Chichester, 77
Classroom at the End of the Hall, The (Evans), 266
Clay Marble, The (Ho), 22
Cleary, Beverly, 122, 263, 265, 290, 363
Clement, Rod, 90, 96, 101
Clements, Andrew, 266
Clever Katya: A Fairy Tale from Old Russia (Hoffman), 101, 242, 250
Climo, Shirley, 249, 253
Cline-Ransome, Lesa, 364
Coerr, Eleanor, 367
Cohen, Daniel, 336
Cole, Babette, 51, 95, 96, 175, 176, 265
Cole, Brock, 264

Cole, Joanna, 23, 85, 231, 232, 348, 349
Cole, Norma, 75
Coleman, Evelyn, 63
Coles, Robert, 137
Collard, Sneed B., III, 22, 349
Collected Poems of William Carlos Williams, The (Williams), 152
Collier, Bryan, 96
Collier, Christopher, 286, 292
Collier, James Lincoln, 286, 292
Collington, Peter, 81
Collodi, Carlo, 120, 135
Colman, Penny, 335
Colón, Raúl, 49, 50, 63, 269
Coman, Carolyn, 264, 268, 290
Come Away from the Water, Shirley (Burningham), 100
Comenius, John Amos, 190
Coming Home: From the Life of Langston Hughes (Cooper), 364, 367
Common Ground: The Water, Earth, and Air We Share (Bang), 89, 337
Complete Tales & Poems of Winnie-the-Pooh, The (Milne), 5, 301
Confetti: Poems for Children (Mora), 151
Conford, Ellen, 265
Conly, Jane Leslie, 21, 264
Cooke, Trish, 43, 53, 87
Cool Salsa: Bilingual Poems on Growing Up Latino in the United States (Carlsen), 206
Coolies (Yin), 277, 278
Cooney, Barbara, 67, 96, 371, 372
Cooper, Deborah, 63
Cooper, Floyd, 49, 96, 206, 209, 283, 364, 367
Cooper, Susan, 301, 309, 318
"Could Be Worse!" (Stevenson), 40
Couloumbis, Audrey, 271, 272
Count! (Fleming), 75
Count Silvernose: A Story from Italy (Kimmel), 242, 250
Cousins (Hamilton), 207
Coville, Bruce, 21, 189, 268, 290, 305, 307, 317, 318
Coxe, Molly, 85
Craft, M. Charlotte, 247, 248
Crayon Counting Book, The (Ryan and Pallotta), 75
Crazy Lady! (Conly), 21, 264
Creativity (Steptoe), 63
Creech, Sharon, 264, 309
Cresswell, Helen, 265
Crews, Donald, 80
Crystal Drop, The (Hughes), 314
Cullinan, Bernice E., 160
cummings, e. e., 158
Cummings, Pat, 127, 128
Cumpian, Carlos, 157
Cupid and Psyche (Craft), 247, 248
Cure, The (Levitin), 313

Hobby: The Young Merlin Trilogy (Yolen), 310
Hoberman, Mary Ann, 150, 161, 164
Hoestlandt, Jo, 217
Hoffman, Mary, 21, 101, 242, 250, 251
Hoh, Diane, 308
Holbrook, Sara, 148, 161, 164
Holes in Your Nose, The (Yagyu), 219
Holliday, Laurel, 367
Holt, Kimberly Willis, 268
Holzwarth, Werner, 216
Hom, Nancy, 2
Home: A Collaboration of Thirty Distinguished Authors and Illustrators of Children's Books to Aid the Homeless (Rosen), 161
Home: A Journey Through America (Locker), 159
Home Place (Dragonwagon), 100, 149, 158
Home Run (Burleigh), 364
Home to Medicine Mountain (Santiago), 202
Homecoming (Voigt), 263
Homesick: My Own Story (Fritz), 363
Honoring Our Ancestors: Stories and Pictures by Fourteen Artists (Rohmer), 22
Hooks, William H., 282
Hoops (Burleigh), 41, 92, 162
Hope, Laura Lee, 174
Hopkins, Lee Bennett, 150, 157, 159, 160, 162, 164, 337
Hopkinson, Deborah, 282
Horton, Joan, 161
House of Dies Drear, The (Hamilton), 207
Houston, Gloria, 21, 89, 277, 278, 286
How Are You Peeling? Foods with Moods (Freymann and Elffers), 336
How It Feels to Be Adopted (Krementz), 328
How Much Is a Million? (Schwartz), 340
How Now, Brown Cow? (Shertle), 162
How Tía Lola Came to Visit Stay (Alvarez), 204
How to Make an Earthquake (Krauss), 190
Howard, Elizabeth Fitzgerald, 95, 206, 282
Howard, Ellen, 282
Howe, Deborah, 18, 307
Howe, James, 18, 307
Howl's Moving Castle (Jones), 304
Huang, Benrie, 210
Hubbard, Jim, 337
Hubbell, Patricia, 161
Hudson, Wade, 206
Hughes, Langston, 164
Hughes, Monica, 314, 315
Hughes, Shirley, 97, 217
Hunter, Anne, 91
Hunter, Sara Hoagland, 283
Hurd, Thacker, 91
Hurry, Hurry, Mary Dear (Bodecker), 161
Hurst, Carol Otis, 366

Hutchins, Pat, 79

I

I Am a Star: Child of the Holocaust (Auerbacher), 367
I Am Phoenix: Poems for Two Voices (Fleischman), 156, 161
I Am the Mummy Heb-Nefert (Bunting), 282
I Believe in Water: Twelve Brushes with Religion (Singer), 21
I Hadn't Meant to Tell You This (Woodson), 21, 264
I Have a Dream (King), 337
I Have Heard of a Land (Thomas), 162
I Have Lived a Thousand Years: Growing Up in the Holocaust (Bitton-Jackson), 367
I Heard a Scream in the Street: Poetry by Young People in the City (Larrick), 156
I Like You, If You Like Me: Poems of Friendship (Livingston), 161
I Never Said I Wasn't Difficult (Holbrook), 148, 161
I Saw Esau: The Schoolchild's Pocket Book (Opie), 229
i see the rhythm (Igus), 92, 94
I Want to Be a Dancer (Grace), 345
I Want to Be a Firefighter (Grace), 345
I Want to Be an Engineer (Grace), 345
I Was a Rat! (Pullman), 240
I Was Born a Slave: The Story of Harriet Jacobs (Fleischner), 367
I Went Walking (Williams), 100
Iceman (Lynch), 267
Ida B. Wells-Barnett: Powerhouse with a Pen (Welch), 364
If a Bus Could Talk: The Story of Rosa Parks (Ringgold), 282, 361
If I Forget, You Remember (Williams), 268
If I Had a Pig (Inkpen), 84
If I Were in Charge of the World and Other Worries: Poems for Children and Their Parents (Viorst), 161
If You Come Softly (Woodson), 264
If You Give a Mouse a Cookie (Numeroff), 85
If You Give a Pig a Pancake (Numeroff), 90, 91, 100
Igus, Toyomi, 92, 94
I'll Take You to Mrs. Cole (Gray), 216
I'm José and I'm Okay (Holzwarth), 216
Importance of Eleanor Roosevelt, The (Morey), 372
In-Between Days, The (Bunting), 268
In Daddy's Arms I AM TALL: African Americans Celebrating Fathers (Steptoe), 49, 161
In the Beginning: Creation Stories from Around the World (Hamilton), 246
In the Swim: Poems and Paintings (Florian), 162
In the Time of Drums (Siegelson), 282

In the Time of the Wolves (Charbonneau), 207
Inch by Inch (Lionni), 100
Indian in the Cupboard, The (Banks), 174, 177, 184, 185, 191
Indio (Garland), 279
Ingpen, Robert R., 238
Ininatig's Gift of Sugar: Traditional Native Sugarmaking (Wittstock), 206
Inkpen, Mick, 84
Inner City Mother Goose, The (Merriam), 156
Innocenti, Roberto, 219
Insectlopedia: Poems and Paintings (Florian), 150, 151
Interstellar Pig (Sleator), 313
Inventors (Sandler), 341
Invisible Princess, The (Ringgold), 200, 206
Ira Sleeps Over (Waber), 88
Is Somewhere Always Far Away? Poems about Places (Jacobs), 161
Is Your Mama a Llama? (Guarino), 100
Isaac Johnson: From Slave to Stonecutter (Marston), 367
Isaacs, Anne, 244
Isadora, Rachel, 360
Isadora Dances (Isadora), 360
Island of the Blue Dolphins (O'Dell), 269
Isn't My Name Magical? Sister and Brother Poems (Berry), 161
It Doesn't Have to Be This Way: A Barrio Story (Rodríguez), 203, 206
It's Showtime: Poetry from the Page to the Stage (Wolf), 162
Izuki, Steven, 157

J

Jacket I Wear in the Snow, The (Neitzel), 85
Jackson Makes His Move (Glass), 127
Jacob Have I Loved (Paterson), 111
Jacobs, Leland B., 161
Jacobson, Rick, 282
Jacques, Brian, 318
James, Will, 214
James and the Giant Peach (Dahl), 307
James Baldwin: Voice from Harlem (Gottfried), 377
Jar of Dreams, A (Uchida), 207
Jar of Tiny Stars, A: Poems by NCTE Award-Winning Poets (Cullinan), 160
Jefferis, David, 332, 333, 334
Jeffers, Susan, 158
Jennifer Murdley's Toad (Coville), 305, 307
Jeremy Thatcher, Dragon Hatcher (Coville), 307
Jiang, Ji Li, 131
Jimenez, Francisco, 63
Jingle Dancer (Smith), 206
Joan of Arc (Poole), 364
Joey Pigza Loses Control (Gantos), 263
John Burningham's ABC (Burningham), 72

Mochizuki, Ken, 47, 52, 60, 63, 101, 128, 204, 206, 210, 211, 212, 282, 283

Mohr, Nicholasa, 201, 211

Moja Means One-Swahili Counting Book (Feelings), 76

Momma, Where Are You From? (Bradby), 206

Monceaux, Morgan, 22, 343

Monster (Myers), 191, 269

Montgomery, Lucy Maud, 190

Moon of Gomrath, The (Garner), 308

Moore, Eva, 160

Moosetache (Palatini), 265

Mora, Pat, 23, 63, 151, 164, 211

More More More Said the Baby (Williams), 43, 87, 206

More Than Anything Else (Bradby), 282

Morey, Eileen, 372

Morgan, Jill, 308

Morning Girl (Dorris), 22, 202, 207, 287

Moser, Barry, 97, 237, 268, 360

Moses Supposes His Toeses are Roses and Seven Other Silly Old Rhymes (Patz), 230

Moss, Jeff, 160

Moss, Marissa, 283

Mother Earth, Father Sky: Poems of Our Planet (Yolen), 162

Mother Jones: Fierce Fighter for Worker's Rights (Pinkerton), 364

Motown and Didi (Myers), 266

Mountain Valor (Houston), 21, 277, 286

Mouse Paint (Walsh), 127

Mouse Tales (Lobel), 83

Movable Mother Goose, The (Sabuda), 191

Mudhead, The (Stone), 315

Mullins, Patricia, 76

Murphy, Claire Rudolf, 362

Murphy, Jim, 328, 329, 330, 331, 349, 366

Musgrove, Margaret, 201

Music, Music for Everyone (Williams), 191

Mutén, Burleigh, 237

My Brother, My Sister, and I (Watkins), 276

My Brother Sam is Dead (Collier), 292

My Family Shall Be Free! The Life of Peter Still (Fradin), 367

My Grandfather's House (Coville), 268

My Great-Aunt Arizona (Houston), 89

My Heroes, My People: African American and Native Americans in the West (Monceaux and Katcher), 22, 343

My Home Is Over Jordan (Wilson), 63

My House Has Stars (McDonald), 128

My Land Sings: Stories from the Rio Grande (Anaya), 207

My Life in Dog Years (Paulsen), 363

My Little Sister Ate One Hare (Grossman), 77, 100

My Man Blue (Grimes), 151

My Mexico~México Mio (Johnston), 161

My Name Is Jorge: On Both Sides of the River (Medina), 206

My Name Is SEEPEETZA (Sterling), 202, 207

My Own Song and Other Poems to Groove To (Strickland), 159

My Place (Wheatley and Rawlins), 217

My Very First Mother Goose (Opie), 229

My Visit to the Aquarium (Aliki), 206

Myers, Christopher, 47, 48, 145, 270

Myers, Walter Dean, 22, 92, 158, 161, 191, 201, 207, 209, 261, 269, 284, 291, 363, 364

Mysteries of Harris Burdock, The (Van Allsburg), 95

Mysterious Tales of Japan (Martin), 233

Mythical Birds & Beasts from Many Lands (Mayo), 250

N

Namioka, Lensey, 207, 210, 268, 269, 279, 291

Napoli, Donna Jo, 240, 253

Napping House, The (Wood), 90, 100

National Museum of the American Indian, 151, 156, 206

Navajo: Visions and Voices Across the Mesa (Begay), 160

Naylor, Phyllis Reynolds, 263, 291, 308

Necessary Roughness (Lee), 264

Neitzel, Shirley, 85

Nettie's Trip South (Turner), 282

Never Trust a Dead Man (Vande Velde), 308

New England Primer, The, 193

Newbery, John, 190

Newsome, Effie Lee, 144

Nhuong, Huynh Quang, 22

Nielsen, Cliff, 268

Night Dive (McGovern), 343

Night Garden: Poems from the World of Dreams (Wong), 157

Nightmares—Poems to Trouble Your Sleep (Prelutsky), 134

Nikola-Lisa, W., 162

Nim and the War Effort (Lee), 283

Nina Bonita (Machado), 216, 217

Nine for California (Levitin), 282

19 Varieties of Gazelle: Poems of the Middle East (Nye), 206

Nix, Garth, 312, 313

Nixon, Shelley, 363

Nocturne (Yolen), 91

Noel the First (McMullan), 189

Nolan, Dennis, 283

Nomura, Takaaki, 89, 175, 216

North by Night: A Story of the Underground Railroad (Ayres), 278, 284

Norton, Mary, 301

Nory Ryan's Song (Giff), 128

Not One Damsel in Distress: World Folktales for Strong Girls (Yolen), 237

Nothing But the Truth (Avi), 269

Nothing Here But Trees (Van Leeuwen), 282

Now Is Your Time: The African-American Struggle for Freedom (Myers), 207

Now One Foot, Now the Other (dePaola), 137

Number the Stars (Lowry), 128, 129, 131, 285

Numeroff, Laura, 85, 90, 91, 100

Nunn, Laura Silverstein, 331, 333

Nursery Rhymes from Mother Goose: Told in Signed English (Bornstein), 230

Nursery Treasury, The: A Collection of Baby Games, Rhymes, and Lullabies (Emerson), 230

Nye, Naomi Shihab, 21, 89, 100, 156, 160, 162, 206, 264, 268

O

O'Brien, Robert C., 313

Ocean Alphabet Book, The (Pallotta), 74

Odder Than Ever (Coville), 317

O'Dell, Scott, 269, 279

Of Colors and Things (Hoban), 77

Okutoro, Lydia Omolola, 156

Old Elm Speaks: Tree Poems (George), 162

Old Mother Hubbard: A Nursery Rhyme (Johnson), 230

Old People, Frogs, and Albert (Wilson), 63

Old Turtle (Wood), 88, 101

On the Day You Were Born (Frasier), 89

On the Wing: Bird Poems and Paintings (Florian), 162

Once on This Island (Whelan), 279

Once upon a company . . . A True Story (Halperin), 341

Once Upon Ice: And Other Frozen Poems (Yolen), 162

One at a Time (McCord), 147, 149, 154

One-Eyed Giant, The: And Other Monsters from Greek Myths (Rockwell), 250

One Horse Waiting for Me (Mullins), 76

One Moose, Twenty Mice (Beaton), 75

One More Border: The True Story of One Family's Escape from War-Torn Europe (Kaplan), 63

One More River to Cross: The Stories of Twelve Black Americans (Haskins), 362

1,000 Miles in 12 Days: Pro Cyclists on Tour (Hautzig), 343

1,000 Years Ago on Planet Earth (Collard), 22

O'Neill, Mary, 152

Only Passing Through: The Story of Sojourner Truth (Rockwell), 368

Onyefulu, Ifeoma, 74

Oodgeroo, 176

Opie, Iona, 229

Weiss, George David, 134, 206

Welch, Catherine A., 364

Welcome With Love (Overend), 219

Wells, Rosemary, 98, 229, 369

Wersba, Barbara, 265

Westervelt, Linda, 74

Westing Game, The (Raskin), 265

Whales' Song, The (Sheldon), 30, 31, 32, 33, 34, 35, 133

What a Wonderful World (Weiss and Thiele), 134, 206

What in the World? (Merriam), 150

What in the World Is a Homophone? (Presson), 338

What Jamie Saw (Coman), 264

What's the Most Beautiful Thing You Know About Horses? (Van Camp), 92

What's Your Story? A Young Person's Guide to Writing Fiction (Bauer), 343

Wheatley, Nadia, 217

Whelan, Gloria, 279

When She Hollers (Voigt), 264

When the Beginning Began: Stories about God, the Creatures, and Us (Lester), 248

When the Chenoo Howls: Native American Tales of Terror (Bruchac), 207

When the Rain Sings: Poems by Young Native Americans (National Museum of the American Indians), 151, 156, 206

When You're Not Looking . . . A Storytime Counting Book (Kneen), 77

When Zachary Beaver Came to Town (Holt), 268

Where is Grandpa? (Barron), 90, 268

Where the Broken Heart Still Beats (Meyer), 281, 285

Where the Red Fern Grows (Rawls), 263

Where the Sidewalk Ends (Silverstein), 143, 161

Where the Wild Things Are (Sendak), 5, 60, 88, 190

Whirligig (Fleischman), 63

Whistle Me Home (Wersba), 266

White, E. B., 5, 18, 128, 301, 307

White, Mary Michaels, 160

White, Ruth, 21, 263, 268

White Socks Only (Coleman), 63

White Wash (Shange), 63

Who Killed Mr. Chippendale? A Mystery in Poems (Glenn), 269

Who Said Red? (Serfozo), 77

Who Sank the Boat? (Allen), 137

Why Lapin's Ears Are Long: And Other Tales from the Louisiana Bayou (Doucet), 238

Why Mosquitoes Buzz in People's Ears: A West African Tale (Aardema), 201

"Why Was I Adopted?" (Livingston), 328

Wiesner, David, 50, 80, 98, 101

Wildsmith, Brian, 36, 37, 72, 77, 217

Wiley and the Hairy Man (Sierra), 101

Will Goes to the Post Office (Landstrom), 216

Will's Mammoth (Martin), 82, 127

Willard, Nancy, 160, 163

Willey, Margaret, 266, 267

William Shakespeare & the Globe (Aliki), 342

Williams, Carol Ann, 234, 251

Williams, Carol Lynch, 268

Williams, Garth, 5

Williams, Margery, 307

Williams, Sherley Anne, 45, 46, 206

Williams, Sue, 100

Williams, Vera B., 43, 49, 87, 91, 98, 191, 192, 206

Williams, William Carlos, 152

Wilma Unlimited: How Wilma Rudolph Became the World's Fastest Woman (Krull), 364

Wilson, Gina, 158, 159

Wilson, Nancy Hope, 63

Wimmer, Mike, 49, 98, 364

Wind in the Door, A (L'Engle), 312, 313

Wind in the Willows, The (Grahame), 5, 301, 319

Window (Baker), 81, 89, 95, 101

Window, The (Dorris), 207

Winner, David, 372

Winni Allfours (Cole), 96

Winslow, Vicki, 63

Winter, Jeanette, 137

Winter Rescue (Valgardson), 218

Wise Child (Furlong), 310

Wisniewski, David, 4, 22, 92, 265

With Every Drop of Blood: A Novel of the Civil War (Collier), 286

Wittstock, Laura Waterman, 206

Wizard and Wart at Sea (Smith), 84, 189, 265

Wolf, Allan, 162

Wolff, Virginia Euwer, 22, 63, 269, 280, 291

Wolfson, Margaret Olivia, 248

Women of Hope: African Americans Who Made a Difference (Hansen), 63

Wonderful Wizard of Oz, The (Baum), 301, 319

Wonders: The Best Children's Poems of Effie Lee Newsome (Bishop), 144

Wong, Janet S., 23, 151, 157, 164, 206, 210

Wood, Audrey, 91, 100, 244

Wood, Don, 90

Wood, Douglas, 88, 101

Wood, Michele, 92, 93

Wood, Ted, 336

Woodson, Jacqueline, 21, 44, 45, 98, 115, 116, 117, 133, 209, 212, 264, 269, 291

Woodsong (Paulsen), 326

Woody Guthrie: American Balladeer (Yates), 365

Words of Wisdom: A Treasury of African-American Poetry and Art (Rochelle), 160

Words with Wrinkled Knees: Animal Poems (Esbensen), 162

Working Cotton (Williams), 45, 46, 206

World from My Window, The (Samton), 127

World of Daughter Maguire, The (Wyeth), 263

~~*Worst*~~ *Best School Year Ever, The* (Robinson), 18

Wreck of the Zephyr, The (Van Allsburg), 91

Wrestling with Honor (Klass), 267

Wright Brothers, The: How They Invented the Airplane (Freedman), 341

Wringer (Spinelli), 63, 118, 263, 267, 268

Wrinkle in Time, A (L'Engle), 4, 179, 310, 313, 315, 318

Wyeth, Sharon Dennis, 49, 50, 88, 125, 206, 209, 263, 269

Y

Yagyu, Genichiro, 219

Yang the Second and Her Secret Admirers (Namioka), 207

Yang the Third and Her Impossible Family (Namioka), 207, 269

Yard Sale (Stevenson), 86, 87

Yates, Janelle, 365

Year Down Yonder, A (Peck), 21

Yee, Paul, 210

Yep, Laurence, 22, 199, 200, 201, 206, 207, 210, 263, 265, 280, 284, 291

Yeti: Abominable Snowman of the Himalayas (Laudau), 336

Yin, 277, 278

Yolen, Jane, 21, 87, 91, 98, 148, 151, 162, 164, 189, 206, 217, 237, 246, 249, 253, 281, 282, 287, 308, 310, 317, 318, 347, 363

Yolonda's Genius (Fenner), 201, 269

York Trilogy (Naylor), 308

You Be Good & I'll Be Night: Jump-on-the-Bed Poems (Merriam), 161

You Read to Me, I'll Read to You (Ciardi), 154, 161

Young, Black, and Determined: A Biography of Lorraine Hansberry (McKissack), 365

Young, Ed, 41, 49, 98, 201, 210, 240, 246, 367

Young Person's Guide to Ballet, The (Ganeri), 345

Young Person's Guide to Shakespeare, The (Ganeri), 345

Young Person's Guide to the Orchestra, The: Benjamin Britten's Composition on CD (Ganeri), 345

Your Move (Bunting), 63

Yummy! Eating Through a Day (Hopkins), 159

Yumoto, Kazumi, 218

Z

General Index

A

ABC books
  characteristics of, 79
  purposes of, 72–75
  structure in, 74
Accessibility, 12, 14
  in chapter books, 18–19
  conceptual information and, 16
  controlled vocabulary and, 84
  in early reader books, 14–18
Accommodation, 12
Accuracy
  in biographies, 375–377
  in folk tales, 229, 251
  in traditional literature, 251, 252
Acrylic paint, effects created by, 46
Adventure stories
  in realistic fiction, 261
  in science fiction, 312
Aesop Prize, 58, 388
Aesthetic experience in reading, 20
African Americans. *See also* Multicultural
    literature
  as authors and illustrators, 209
  in biographies, 363, 364, 365, 366, 367,
    374, 375
  early books about, 191–192, 201–202
  in folk tales, 237, 238
  oral traditions of, 187
  positive portrayals of, 200–201
  stereotypes of, 174, 180, 191
Afterwords. *See* Author's notes
Albers, Peggy, 56
Alexander, Lloyd, 302
Aliens, in science fiction, 313–314
Alliteration
  in early reader books, 84
  in poetry, 143, 145
Alvarez, Julia, 270
American Indians. *See also* Multicultural
    literature
  as authors and illustrators, 209–210
  criteria for evaluating bias toward, 182

in folk tales, 234
oral traditions of, 187
as protagonists, 203
stereotypes of, 174, 177, 179, 180, 186,
  191, 203, 214
Américas Award for Children's and Young
  Adult Literature, 58, 399
Angelou, Maya, 374–375
Animals
  in early reader books, 85, 87
  in fables, 244
  in fantasy, 302
  in realistic fiction, 261, 263
  in science fiction, 314
Anthologists of children's poetry, 164
Appearance of book, and accessibility,
  18
Art
  emotional impact of, 51–54
  modeling response to, 127
  in poetry books, 157
  as reflection of a book, 38–40
  as response to literature, 123–128
Artistic quality, 6
Artists. *See also* Illustrators
  biographies of, 364
  media and materials used by, 40–48
  styles of, 48–51
Arts, fine and decorative, 342–343
Asia, in historical fiction, 279
Asian Americans, as authors and illustrators, 210. *See also* Multicultural
  literature
Assimilation, 12
Assumptions, readers', 172–175
Audience, in book selection, 60
Authenticity
  author's responsibility for, 212
  in biography, 22, 373, 375
  in early reader books, 17
  in ethnic representations, 214
  in historical fiction, 22, 286–287
  in nonfiction, 22, 330, 334

Authors
  authenticity and, 212
  of biographies, 377–378
  of color, 209–211
  of fantasy, 318
  of historical fiction, 290–291
  intentionality of, 4
  of nonfiction, 348–350
  of picture books, 96–98
  of poetry, 164
  of realistic fiction, 290–291
  of science fiction, 318
  selection of facts and, 329
  subjects and, 358–359
  of traditional tales, 253
  world view of, 172, 175, 181, 191, 228,
    287
Author's notes
  in biography, 361
  in historical fiction, 284, 287
  in nonfiction, 334
  in tall tales, 242
  in traditional literature, 228, 233, 234
Autobiographies, 362–363
Avanti, Susan, 52
Avery, Carol, 9, 76, 231, 347
Award-winning books. *See also* Book
  awards; *specific awards*
  criteria for evaluating, 57
  stereotypes in, 56, 124, 175, 186, 187,
    191, 214
Ayres, Katherine, 284

B

Babbitt, Natalie, 305
Balance, in book selection, 62
Balick, Dana, 119, 123
Basals, 15, 17
Batchelder, Mildred L., 215, 396–397
Bauer, Marion Dane, 193, 343
Beatty, Patricia, 286
Beauty, appreciating, in picture story-
  books, 91

Hubbard, Ruth Shagoury, 123, 124, 125, 126, 129
Humor, 83, 86
  in early reader books, 83
  in realistic fiction, 264
  in science fiction, 312
  in tall tales, 245
Hunt, Peter, 189

I

Illness, in realistic fiction, 268
Illustrations. *See also* Illustrators
  accuracy in, 251, 283
  bias in, 182
  in early reader books, 83, 85
  evaluating, 51–54, 331, 332
  expressionism in, 49
  in folk tales, 235
  paintings as, 42
  racism/sexism in, 180
  realism in, 49
  as reflection of a book, 38–40
  relevance of, 17
  shapes in, 39
  stereotypes in, 180, 182
  surrealism in, 50
Illustrators. *See also* Artists
  of biographies, 377–378
  of color, 209–211
  of nonfiction, 348–350
  of picture books, 96–98
  of traditional tales, 253
Imagery in poetry, 144–145
Imagination, 81
  fantasy and, 302, 306–307, 309–310
  importance of, 306–307
  picture storybooks and, 90
Imaginative impact, 34–35
  of biography, 373, 375
  of fantasy, 317
  of nonfiction, 330, 333
  of realistic fiction, 272, 274
  of traditional literature, 252
Immigration, in realistic fiction, 269
Implied messages in children's literature, 172
Inclusion, 124
  of different family structures, 193
  of different kinds of characters, 186, 191
  ethnic, need for, 201
  of topics, 189, 193
Inferences, room to make, 16, 19
Informational fiction, 347
Informational text, 326. *See also* Nonfiction
Inner conflicts, in realistic fiction, 268
Intentionality of authors, 4
International figures, in biography, 364, 365, 366, 367
International literature, 200, 215–219
  awards for, 58, 59

benefits of, 214–215
countries represented in, 217–218
selection of, for publication, 219
translation of, 215, 218, 219
Internet resources, 24, 65, 102, 138, 166, 195–196, 220–221, 255–256, 293, 320, 352, 379
Interview format in narrative nonfiction, 328
Involvement of author with subject, 358–359
  in evaluating biographies, 373, 375
  in evaluating nonfiction, 329, 333

J

Jane Addams Children's Book Awards, 58, 388–389
Japanese folk tales, 233–234
Jordan, Sandra, 38, 39
Journals, in historical fiction, 278

K

Karr, Kathleen, 274
Kate Greenaway Medal, 59, 401
Keene, Ellin Oliver, 115, 116, 117, 118
Kennedy, Dorothy, 142, 152
Kennedy, X. J., 142, 152
Kinesthetic learning, 132–134
King, Coretta Scott. *See* Coretta Scott King Awards
Kirkpatrick, Katherine, 284
Kismaric, C., 15
Klein, Melanie, 304
Koch, Kenneth, 152
Kohl, Herbert, 8, 33, 35, 120, 121, 135, 172, 186, 287
Korman, Gordon, 260
Kozel, Jonathan, 71

L

Langer, Judith, 112–113, 116, 117, 123
Language
  accessibility and, 16, 19
  in the Dewey decimal system, 338–339
  historical, 189
  in historical fiction, 286, 288, 289
  importance of, 16
  playing with, 72, 150
  in poetry, 147, 150
  stereotypes and, 182, 183, 185
  in tall tales, 245
Larrick, Nancy, 200
Latinos. *See also* Multicultural literature
  as authors and illustrators, 210–211
  as characters, 22, 200, 202
Leaders, as biographical subjects, 364
Learning, kinesthetic, 133–134
Lechner, Judith V., 375, 376
Lee, Philip, 211
Legends, 228, 238–239

Lessons in traditional literature, 228, 241
Letters, in historical fiction, 278
Levine, Gail Carson, 284
Lewis, E. B., 283
Limericks, 148
Line breaks in poetry, 146
Lines in illustrations, 38
Literacy-rich environment, 231
Literary appreciation, stages of, 20, 308
Literary elements, 175
Literary greats, in biographies, 364
Literary merit, 5. *See also* Literary qualities
Literary qualities
  accessibility and, 16–17, 19
  of multicultural literature, 199, 201, 213
  of nonfiction, 332, 335
Literature
  children's. *See* Children's literature
  in the Dewey decimal system, 343
Literature-based reading programs, 17
Loaded words, 182, 183, 185, 214
Lorde, Audre, 177
Loss/death, in realistic fiction, 268
Lowry, Lois, 285
Lyric poems, 148

M

MacLeod, Anne Scott, 187, 286, 287
Magic in everyday life, in fantasy, 302, 307–308
Maguire, Gregory, 153
Mallett, Margaret, 326, 331, 346, 347, 348
Marketing, 4
  mass, 23
  trends in, 23
Martin, Jacqueline Briggs, 357, 358, 359
Martin, Rafe, 233
Masson, Sophie, 310
Mathematics, 339–340
McClure, Amy, 325
McCormick, Kathleen, 7–8, 118, 174, 175, 177
McDermott, Gerald, 246
McGillis, Roderick, 270
Meaning
  accessibility and, 14–15
  making, and response, 110
Media, mixed, 47
Meltzer, Milton, 277, 359, 361, 376, 377
Memoirs, in historical fiction, 276
Merriam, Eve, 143
Messages
  in fairy tales, 240
  in folk tales, 235
  in myths, 248
Mexican Americans. *See* Latinos
Meyer, Caroline, 285
Michael L. Printz Award, 58, 392
Middle Ages, in historical fiction, 279
Mildred L. Batchelder Award, 58, 396–397
Miller, Ken, 218

Semantic cueing system, 17
Sensory details in poetry, 146
Series books, 22
    appeals of, 270
    in biographies, 370–373
    in historical fiction, 283–284
    in nonfiction, 344–345
    in realistic fiction, 270
Setting, 34, 213
    comparing, in two folk tales, 236
    in evaluating biographies, 373, 374
    in evaluating fantasy, 316
    in evaluating of historical fiction,
        287–289
    in evaluating narrative nonfiction, 329
    in evaluating realistic fiction, 272, 273,
        274
    in evaluating traditional literature, 251,
        252
Sexism, 173, 174, 175, 176, 177–178, 179,
    187. See also Gender stereotypes
    author's world view and, 181
    copyright date and, 181
    criteria for evaluating books for,
        180–182
    in illustrations, 180
    plot and, 181
    power and, 177
Shapes in illustrations, 39
Short stories, multicultural, 207
Singer, Jerome L., 304
Sipe, Lawrence, 285
Slapin, Beverly, 180, 182, 184, 185
Social/cultural significance, authentic, 17
Social issues, 21–23, 193
    in biographies, 376–377
    in poetry, 156
    in realistic fiction, 264
    in science fiction, 312, 313
Social sciences, 337
Societal constructs, in children's literature,
    175–176
Societal values in children's literature, 172,
    175
Sociocultural background, 7
Socioeconomic awareness in children's lit-
    erature, 177, 178, 184, 186, 187, 191
Sociopolitical, factors
    in book selection, 57, 213–214
    influencing children's literature, 21, 312,
        313
Soter, Anna, 124
Sound devices in poetry, 145
Sounds of poetry, 143–144
Sources, unreliable, 376
Spanish, books published in, 203–204
Speare, Elizabeth George, 285
Spink, Kevin, 325
Spiritual elements. See also Religion
    in fantasy, 309
    in folk tales, 232, 233, 234

Spiritual leaders, in biographies, 365
Sports
    biographies and, 364
    realistic fiction and, 266–267
Stan, Susan, 218, 219
Stereotypes, 177, 179, 213, 216
    avoidance of, 251
    in award-winning books, 56, 124, 175,
        186, 187, 191, 214
    behavioral definition of, 178
    in biographies, 377
    of characters, 191
    confronting, 186, 187
    of the elderly, 175
    examples of, 175, 184, 204
    gender. See Gender stereotypes; Sexism
    in illustrations, 180, 182
    language and, 182, 183, 185
    of people of color, 172, 174, 177, 180,
        191
    of women, 172
Stewig, John, 271
Stine, R. L., 270, 308
Street rhymes, 230–231
Structure
    in ABC books, 74
    in chapter books, 18, 86
    in counting books, 77
    creating, in biographies, 359–360
    evaluating, in nonfiction, 329, 333, 335
Subconscious, and fantasy, 305
Subjectivity in the award selection process,
    55–56
Success, definitions of
    for middle and upper class, 18
    for minorities, 180, 182
Surrealism in illustrations, 50
Survival as theme
    in historical fiction, 279–280
    in realistic fiction, 268–269
Sutcliff, Rosemary, 286
Swearingen, R. A., 214
Syntactic cueing system, 17

T

Taberski, Sharon, 9, 76
Taboos, in biographies, 376–377
Talbert, Marc, 285
Talk, 120–123
    in book clubs, 122
    as critical to thought, 61
    eliciting, 121
    importance of, with multicultural litera-
        ture, 212
    about racism, 204
    as response to literature, 120–123
Tall tales, 228, 242–245
    author's notes in, 242
    characteristics of, 245

cultural values revealed in, 244
    heroes in, 245
Tax laws, and publishing, 23
Taxel, Joel, 187
Teacher's role
    in bringing poetry alive, 143
    in creating social awareness, 174, 177,
        179, 180, 185, 187
    in examining stereotypes, 204, 214
    in using multicultural literature, 212
Teaching ideas. See Classroom teaching
    ideas
Technology, 341
    book appearance and, 193
    impact of, 23
    nonfiction and, 190, 328
Tempera, effects created by, 43
Text organizers, and nonnarrative nonfic-
    tion, 332
Text-to-self connections, 115–116
Text-to-text connections, 115–116
Text-to-world connections, 115–116
Texture in illustrations, 39
Themes, 34, 83, 86, 92
    in biography, 213, 373
    in chapter books, 86
    comparing, in two folk tales, 236
    in early reader books, 83
    in fantasy, 316
    in historical fiction, 278–280, 288, 289
    in picture storybooks, 92
    in poetry, 151, 161–162
    in realistic fiction, 267–269, 272, 273
    in science fiction, 314–315
    in traditional literature, 252
Third-person narrative
    in biography, 361
    in historical fiction, 281
    in realistic fiction, 267
Three sharings in talk about books, 121
Time travel
    in fantasy, 302, 308–309
    in historical fiction, 281
Tokenism, 180
Tomlinson, Carl, 219
Tongue twisters, 230
Topics
    appeal of, 18
    avoided, 189, 219
    in history, 189
Tourist approach to literature, 213
Traditional literature, 6, 228. See also
    specific types of stories
    author's notes in, 228, 233, 234
    awards for, 58
    cultural beliefs in, 229
    evaluating, 251, 252
    kinds of, 207, 229, 232, 236, 238, 239,
        242, 244
Translated books, 215, 218
Transmediation, 119

Trends in children's literature
as influenced by marketing and technology, 23
as influenced by sociopolitical factors, 21–23
Trickster tales, 228, 237
Truth
in fantasy, 305
in myths, 247
in traditional literature, 228

U

Unconscious delight in reading, 20
Universal issues, 227
Universal messages in myths, 248

V

Valsner, Jaan, 61
Values, 5, 59, 175, 190
in award-winning books, 56
in biographies, 376
in fantasy, 309
in folk literature, 232, 234, 235, 236, 240, 241
in science fiction, 315
in tall tales, 244
van der Veer, Rene, 61
Vicarious experience in reading, 20
through fantasy, 305, 308
Victorian England, in historical fiction, 279
Vision of author
in evaluating fantasy, 317
in evaluating nonfiction, 330, 333

in evaluating realistic fiction, 272, 274
in evaluating traditional literature, 252
Visual, the
accuracy of, in traditional literature, 251, 252
learning and, 74–75
in nonnarrative nonfiction, 332
responding to, in picture books, 36–38
Visual expression, 125
Vocabulary, controlling, 15
Vygotsky, Lev, 61, 123, 154

W

Walsh, Jill Paton, 286
Walter, Mildred Pitts, 285
Watercolor, effects created by, 43–45
Websites for children's literature, 24, 65, 102, 138, 166, 195–196, 220–221, 255–256, 293, 320, 352, 379
Webster, Renee, 122
Werlin, Nancy, 265
White space, use of
in nonnarrative nonfiction, 332
in poetry, 146
Whitin, Phyllis, 123
Whole language experience, 231
Wilhelm, Jeff, 131
Williams, Carol Ann, 234
Wolf, Dennie Palmer, 119, 120, 123
Women
as characters. *See* Female characters
as publishers, 175
stereotypes of, 172

Wonder, in fantasy, 301
Wordless books, 79–82
characteristics of, 82
purposes of, 79–82
World view, 172
of authors of historical fiction, 287
of authors of traditional literature, 228
expanding, 202
factors affecting, 173
in folk tales, 233
reading and, 174
recognizing our own, 173, 176
World War II, in historical fiction, 280
Writing
of biography, 358–359
expository, 326, 331
of historical fiction, 284–287
of nonfiction, 335
outside one's culture, 229
as response to literature, 128–129
styles of, 34, 213, 236, 252, 272, 273, 316, 330, 333, 373, 374
Writing workshop, 9

Y

Yolen, Jane, 208

Z

Ziegler, Alan, 152
Zimmerman, Susan, 115, 116, 117, 118
Zone of proximal development, 15, 61, 154